The Octagon of Arsinoë IV in Ephesos

A Ptolemaic Queen's tomb at the transition
from a Hellenistic to a Roman Imperial city

This book is dedicated to Hilke Thür

without whose contribution the Octagon would still be considered

as just another curious monument of Ephesos.

Ernst Rudolf, Peter Scherrer

The Octagon of Arsinoë IV in Ephesos

A Ptolemaic Queen's tomb at the transition from a Hellenistic to a Roman Imperial city

Nünnerich-Asmus
Verlag & Media

Plan 1: Topograph-
ical overview of
Ephesos (for the
Embolos see plan 3)

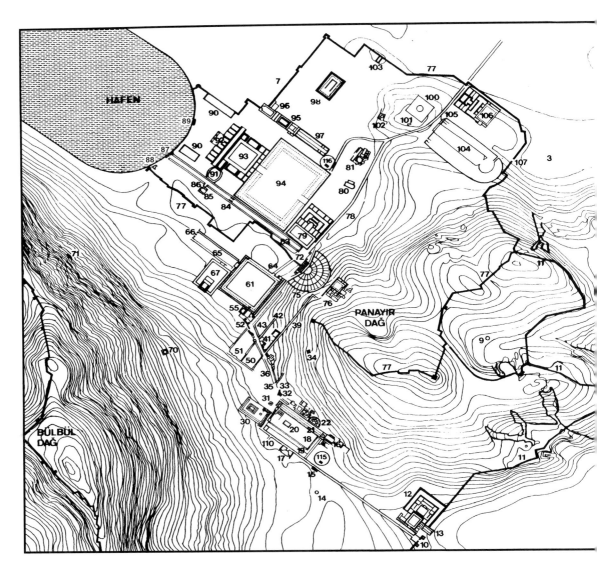

1 Artemision
2 So-called Tribune near the
Artemision
3 Koressos Harbour
4 Rock shrine
(Meter-Cybele shrine)
5 Byzantine aqueduct
6 Defensive wall
(Koressos)
7 Stoa of Damianus
8 Seven Sleepers cemetery
9 Armenian place of worship
10 Magnesian Gate
11 Hellenistic city wall
12 East Gymnasium
13 Basilica in the East Gymnasium
14 St. Luke's Grave (so-called)
15 Street well / fountain
16 Baths on the State Agora
17 Fountain
18 So-called State Agora
19 Doric Gatehouse and South
Colonnade of State Agora
20 Temple on the State Agora

21 Basilike Stoa
22 Odeion / Bouleuterion
23 Temenos with Double
Monument
24 Prytaneion
25 Banqueting House by the
Prytaneion
26 Kathodos of Prytaneion
with Enbasis
27 Chalcidicum
28 Pollio Monument and Fountain of Domitian
29 Hydrekdocheion of Laecanius Bassus
30 Temple of the Emperors
(Temple of Domitian)
31 Niche Monument
32 Memmius Monument
33 Hydreion
34 Round Monument on the
Panayırdağ
35 Hercules Gate
36 Curetes Street (Embolos)
37 Trajan's Gatehouse
38 Nymphaeum Traiani

39 Bath Street
40 Temple of Hadrian
(Embolos)
41 Varius Baths / Baths of
Scholasticia
42 Academy Street
43 Latrine and "House of
Pleasure"
44 Alytarchs' Stoa
45 Hellenistic Well
46 Hexagon / Nymphaeum
47 Octagon
48 Hypelaios Nymphaeum /
Androclos Heroon
49 Hadrian's Gate
50 Terrace House 1
51 Terrace House 2
52 Foundations of an altar
53 Hellenistic Peristyle House
54 So-called Tube or Culvert
Gate
55 Celsus Library
56 South Gate of the Agora
57 Grave of Dionysios Rhetor
58 Brick vault (Embolos)

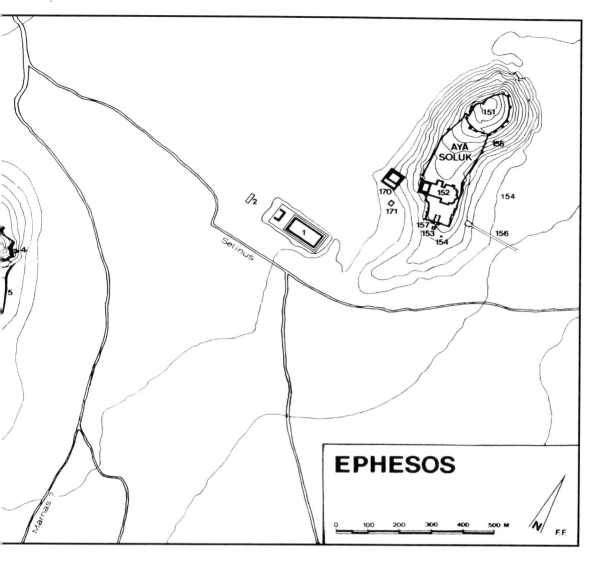

EPHESOS

0 100 200 300 400 500 M

N F.F.

Printed with the generous support of the Office of the Provincial Government of Styria, Department of Science and Research, and the University of Graz, Dept. of Classics.

376 pages with 123 illustrations
Cover Image: Architectural sample of the Octagon in the Kunsthistorisches Museum, Vienna.

Bibliographic Information of the German National Library
The German National Library lists this publication in the German National Bibliography; detailed bibliographic data are available on the Internet at http://dnb.dnb.de.

© 2024 by Nünnerich-Asmus Verlag & Media, Oppenheim am Rhein
ISBN 978-3-96176-250-7

Translation: In parts by Sarah Homan-Cormack
Editors: Annette Nünnerich-Asmus, Tina Sieber
Cover Design: hjwiehr, Oppenheim
Layout: Bild1Druck GmbH, Dirk Gerecke, Berlin
Print: bookSolutions Vertriebs GmbH, Göttingen

Printed in Germany by Nünnerich-Asmus Verlag & Media
You can find more titles from our publishing programme at: www.na-verlag.de.

Table of Content

Arsinoë(s) in Ephesos – the historical background   74

The architectural development of Hellenistic Ephesos and the expansion of the city under Augustus   92

The protector of Ephesos – Artemis and her sacred Triodos   110

The Embolos – a walk of fame   127

The Triodos, the Octagon and the Embolos: Conclusions 201

In search of the skull from the Octagon 214

Concluding remarks 252

Prologue

In September 1982, the authors (E.R., P. S.) were two students of archaeology and still lean enough to fit through the uncovered narrow opening into the burial chamber of an octagonally shaped mausoleum in the centre of Ephesos. The vault contained a sarcophagus, its skeleton had been revealed during a scientific investigation authorised by Josef Keil in 1929 as being the one of an unidentified young female individual. The experience left a deep impression on them, and decades later the two, one meanwhile a forensic medical expert, and the other with half a life's experience in the excavations of Ephesos, decided to return to those days.

In 1990, Hilke Thür had published her fascinating proposal that this Octagon was the sepulchre of Arsinoë IV, the youngest daughter of the Macedonian-Egyptian Pharaoh Ptolemaios XII and sister of the famous Kleopatra VII. Yet, too many questions had remained unanswered, and in particular: is the age at death of the young female individual compatible with Arsinoë's biographical data as reported by ancient sources? Does the tomb indeed refer to the famous Pharos Tower of Alexandria? Why was her tomb only erected a couple of years after her death, why as a temple-like structure, and why at this location in the middle of the city? And would it be possible to find her skull, which was removed from Ephesos in 1929 and probably last seen around 1952?

Thus began a long journey, an enterprise with many stops, hours in libraries and archives, letters and phone calls to other researchers and curators in museums, archives, academies, and universities. And step by step, we were not only able to develop plausible arguments regarding specific issues of the grave, but we were also lucky enough to discover the whereabouts of the lost skull from the Octagon, finally completing our endeavour.

We would like to express our gratitude to the many friends, colleagues, and professionals who generously helped us in our research (see acknowledgements). Among them, we highlight some: Hilke Thür, who read our manuscript, made many suggestions for improvement, and who altruistically shared all her knowledge with us; Sarah Homan-Cormack, who translated large sections of the text and not only improved our English, but also some factual content; Markus Hafner, who carefully screened the Greek and Latin citations; and most of all Gabriele Scherrer who eagerly discussed with us the many diverse and complex aspects of our passion. Ultimately, we hope that our book will be as enjoyable for readers as its writing was for us.

Finally, we would like to provide an important note. After lengthy discussions, we decided to break with a long tradition in English scientific literature by spelling all ancient Greek and Roman proper names in their original form (e.g., Livius instead of Livy or Plinius instead of Pliny), thus showing respect for their personality and keeping them embedded in their historical environment. Similarly, we have avoided the sometimes euphemistic and ameliorating translations of antique source texts, and kept them as close as possible to the original. Therefore, we ask readers to view the language of sometimes blunt violence, sexism, and vulgarity within its proper historical context.

Introduction

With the enlightened support of the Ottoman Sublime Porte, the 'Imperial and Royal Austrian Archaeological Institute' began the research of Levantine Ephesos on the "Asian mead by the waters of Kaystrios" (Hom. Il. II 461) in the late 19th c. Thanks to the efforts of several generations of researchers, the ruins of the Greco-Roman-Byzantine metropolis have developed into an impressive site since then, whose monuments once formed the stage for many a historical episode.

For a long time, it has been suspected that one such documented event is illustrated by a temple-like memorial in the centre of Ephesos dating back to the early Augustan time. Since the discovery of its remains in 1904, the "peculiarity" of the structure has been repeatedly emphasised. Apart from being a mausoleum at a prominent location *intra muros*, it belongs to the few early buildings of octagonal shape, which led to its designation as the 'Octagon'. A young female was interred within the grave, adding to the idiosyncrasy of the monument. However, no obvious evidence was found to indicate to whom such an outstanding edifice might have been dedicated.

Nevertheless, the Austrian excavators considered it worthwhile to attempt an identification of the mausoleum's owner, who died at the end of the Roman Civil Wars, coinciding with the decline of the Lagid rule over Egypt. It was only when Josef Weninger comprehensibly described the juvenile developmental state of the Octagon's skull in 1953 that a possibility emerged. In 1990, Hilke Thür linked the gravesite to Arsinoë IV, short-lived anti-Queen to her elder sister Kleopatra VII during Caesar's 'Alexandrian War', who was blasphemously killed on the territory of the sacred Ephesian Artemision. However, Thür's proposal was met with reasonable doubts and has remained a controversial issue ever since.

Despite the exceptionalism of the Octagon, no publication exists which addresses its several aspects, nor has a detailed presentation of the postcranial skeleton been undertaken. Nonetheless, much research has been devoted to the monument and the remains of its owner in recent decades. Accordingly, the proposed connection of the sepulchre to Arsinoë IV can now be approached in a more differentiated way.

Starting with a reassessment of the ancient sources referring to Arsinoë IV, we compare the biographical reports with the results of several anthropological examinations of the Octagon's skeleton. Afterwards, we address certain issues of the tomb's date, shape, and ornamentation. Since the mausoleum was never a monument in isolation, we expand our investigation to include the Hellenistic and Augustan topography of the city, the importance of the Embolos street with its numerous nymphaea, honorary buildings and intramural tombs, and the significance of the Triodos with the Amazons' altar of Artemis and the 'Library of Celsus'. The resulting observations lead us to the importance of Ptolemaic Queens named Arsinoë, after one of whom Ephesos was briefly named 'Arsinoeia', making the name meaningful for the city.

Finally, the unique possibility presented itself to secure DNA from a supposed Lagid family member. However, all efforts so far have failed to obtain valid samples from the postcranial skeleton. Accordingly, we began investigating the whereabouts of the Octagon's skull which had been taken to Europe by the excavators, and which had been considered lost for decades. A thorough search into its past ultimately revealed its location, thus making it available for further investigations. These have been initiated while this book goes into print, and one may think that the results will be published in the near future.

We hope that our considerations and analyses not only shed new light on the life and afterlife of Queen Arsinoë IV, but also on religious, political and social processes in antiquity and their expression in the historical development of urban space.

Fig. 1: Marble portrait of Ptolemaios XII Auletes   Fig. 2: Marble portrait of Kleopatra VII

The Alexandrian Queen Arsinoë IV

The 12th Ptolemaios of Egypt, "called the new Dionysus"[1] (ca. 110–51 BC; "died of disease"; fig. 1),[2] had five children, three daughters[3] and two sons (tab. 1):[4]

➢ Berenike IV (ca. 77–55 BC, killed on the order of her father at the age of 22 years),[5]
➢ Kleopatra VII (69–30 BC, died by suicide at the age of 39 years; fig. 2),[6] and
➢ Arsinoë IV;
➢ Ptolemaios XIII (61–47 BC, "disappeared on the Nile" at the end of the 'Alexandrian War' at the age of 14 years),[7] and
➢ Ptolemaios XIV (59–44 BC,[8] poisoned on the order of Kleopatra VII at the age of 15 years).[9]

Ptolemaios XII was married to Kleopatra Tryphaina.[10] According to Strabon, Berenike IV was the only legitimate female child of Ptolemaios XII.[11] Such a statement implies that Kleopatra Tryphaina was not the mother of Kleopatra VII and of Arsinoë IV.[12] In line with that, a stele at the British Museum mentions "the wives" of Ptolemaios XII.[13] Since the stele, furthermore, indicates his "children" in its plural, the monument should date after the birth of Kleopatra VII at the earliest.[14] However, another document dating to 69 BC addresses "the Queen" in its singular form next to Ptolemaios XII and "the children".[15] In 53/52 BC with Ptolemaios XII still alive, his children except Berenike IV having already been killed by then,[16] are again mentioned in an inscription.[17] Eusebius of Caesarea (3rd/4th c. AD) states that "when the new Dionysus [= Ptolemaios XII] died [in 51 BC], he left four children, two Ptolemaios, Kleopatra and Arsinoë".[18]

Ancient sources provide the chronological ages of Kleopatra VII, Ptolemaios XIII, and of Ptolemaios XIV at certain historical events (tab. 1). Accordingly, Kleopatra VII was forty years of age minus one in 30 BC (i.e. born in 69 BC),[19] Ptolemaios XIII thirteen years of age in 48 BC (i.e. born in 61 BC),[20] and Ptolemaios XIV fifteen years of age in 44 BC (i.e. born in 59 BC).[21] Arsinoë's "year of birth remains unclear".[22] Strabon calls the two sons of Ptolemaios XII "infants"[23] in 58 BC being then three and two years of age, respectively. Appianos addresses Kleopatra VII as a "child" in 56/55 BC being then 13/14 years of age,[24] a term, he also used to classify "the sovereigns" of Alexandria when reporting the incidents regarding the murder of Cn. Pompeius Magnus in 48 BC.[25] Since Kleopatra VII was already 21 years old at that time, this reference should characterise Ptolemaios XIII, Ptolemaios XIV, and Arsinoë IV. Accordingly, ancient sources repeatedly describe Ptolemaios XIII as *puer* or as "child" in 48 BC.[26]

*Arsinoë IV was a historical figure during the fading
Ptolemaic dynasty which is why she is mentioned
in ancient sources.*

All five children of Ptolemaios XII figured as Queen or King in Alexandria during the last years of the declining Lagid rule over Egypt, some for a longer, some for a shorter time. In particular, Arsinoë IV played the role of an actual and potential counter-Queen to Kleopatra VII within the sixth decade of the 1st c. BC. For this reason, a set of ancient texts mainly report three episodes from her life, which took place in Alexandria, Rome, and finally Ephesos (tab. 1):

  ➢ Her short-lived reign as Queen of Alexandria in 48 BC;
  ➢ Her exposure at Caesar's Egyptian triumph in 46 BC, and
  ➢ Her murder in 41 BC within the precinct of the Ephesian Artemision.

Along with that, certain biographical details of Arsinoë IV are passed down within various ancient sources.[27]

1. The youngest daughter of Pharaoh Ptolemaios XII

After the death of Ptolemaios XII in 51 BC, Kleopatra VII and Ptolemaios XIII, his oldest (surviving) daughter and his oldest son,[28] were declared co-regents of Egypt in accordance with his testament.[29] Already in 49/48 BC, the interest group using the 12/13-year-old Ptolemaios XIII[30] as figurehead expressed for the first time its aversion against Kleopatra VII[31] and sent her together with Arsinoë IV into exile.[32] After the Battle of Pharsalos in 48 BC, some Δαίμον[33] led Cn. Pompeius Magnus to the Egyptian shores precisely where Ptolemaios XIII had drawn up his army against that of Kleopatra VII. The famous counsel took place where the three tutors behind the sovereign Ptolemaios XIII, Pothinos, Achillas, and Theodotos,[34] decided to treacherously end the life of the Roman commander.[35]

Shortly thereafter,[36] C. Iulius Caesar arrived in Alexandria in pursuit of Cn. Pompeius Magnus and was captured by the sight of Kleopatra VII,[37] who was then "in full bloom".[38] He reinstated her[39] and Ptolemaios XIII as co-regents,[40] thereby upholding the legacy of Ptolemaios XII.[41] At the same time, C. Iulius Caesar went to great lengths in order to stabilise Ptolemaic Egypt. Probably with the intention of removing Arsinoë IV and Ptolemaios XIV from the Alexandrian court, he granted them Cyprus.[42] This decision returned the island to Ptolemaic rule, which had already been annexed by Rome in 58 BC.[43]

Various ancient sources address Arsinoë IV as *filia minor Ptolomaei regis*,[44] i.e. the younger daughter of Ptolemaios XII, in comparison to Kleopatra VII, and as such the youngest daughter of Ptolemaios XII.[45] Accordingly, J. P. Mahaffy (1899) calls Arsinoë IV "a girl hardly grown up",[46] A. E. P. Brome Weigall (1914) "little princess",[47] P. Green "barely adolescent",[48] H. J. Gehrke (2005) "a very young princess",[49] C. Schäfer (2006) "young girl"[50] and J. Tyldesley (2008) "teenager".[51]

Arsinoë IV was the youngest daughter of Ptolemaios XII.

According to ancient sources, Arsinoë IV was the youngest daughter of Ptolemaios XII and a rival to her siblings for the Lagid throne of Egypt.

2. A girl-Queen in the 'Alexandrian War'

Caesar's intervention did not calm the situation for long.[52] Cassius Dio provides the cause that started the 'Alexandrian War'.[53] According to him, the Alexandrians considered it "a shame to be ruled by a woman",[54] because they suspected that C. Iulius Caesar would eventually hand over the kingdom to Kleopatra VII alone.[55] Yet, the Alexandrians' discontent lacked "a representative from the Ptolemaic dynasty",[56] since C. Iulius Caesar had kept all *proles Lagea*[57] isolated in the palace.[58] As logic as this caution appears, C. Iulius Caesar seems to have suffered from an incomplete understanding of the complex internal Ptolemaic dissent by reducing it to the one between Kleopatra VII and the interest group behind Ptolemaios XIII.[59] There is no other explanation for the fact that Caesar recognised the danger posed by Ptolemy XIII and had him closely guarded in the Alexandrian palace,[60] whereas Arsinoë IV escaped his attention.[61] It was the eunuch Ganymedes, the tutor of Arsinoë IV, who took advantage of this mistake to strengthen his position in the conflict.[62] Ganymedes secretly removed Arsinoë IV from the Alexandrian palace and brought her to the Egyptians, where she was declared Queen,[63] thus occupying the vacant throne.[64]

With this background, Ganymedes was able to put Achillas, a partisan of Ptolemaios XIII and a "man of unique audacity"[65] to death.[66] Accordingly, pseudo-Caesar states that Ganymedes was the true power behind the throne;[67] he "exercised his reign in the name of Arsinoe" IV.[68] "Arsinoe [was] acting through the eunuch Ganymedes",[69] but in fact there was a "cruel autocracy of Ganymedes",[70] to whom "the kingdom was entrusted".[71] Like Ptolemaios XIII, Arsinoë IV was rather a Lagid figurehead in 48 BC.[72]

Regarding Arsinoë's stage of life at that time, Appianos addresses the offspring of Ptolemaios XII in general as "children" in 48 BC and most likely also Arsinoë IV.[73] Confirming that, pseudo-Caesar handed down a most important statement by saying that Arsinoë IV was a *puella* in 48 BC.[74] Such information is validated by a scholiast on Lucanus referring to Titus Livius.[75] Considering Arsinoë IV as a *puella* in 48 BC explains why she was under tutelage.[76] Similarly, the *puer*[77] Ptolemaios XIII was under a tutorship which took care of his affairs due to his minor age and lack of education.[78] Strabon says that Ptolemaios XIII was "quite young" when he assumed the throne in 48 BC,[79] at that time being thirteen years of age.[80] Accordingly, Arsinoë IV and her brother Ptolemaios XIII occupied similar roles as *puella*-Queen and *puer*-King in 48 BC,[81] both guarded by tutors. Supposedly, tutelage for girls ended at the age of twelve, while boys were considered to need guardianship until the age of fourteen years.[82] Since Ptolemaios XIII's age in 48 BC falls within the appropriate age limit, Arsinoë IV should have been below the respective threshold as well.[83] Therefore, the reports of Appianos, pseudo-Caesar, and of T. Livius should indicate a *terminus postquem* of 60 BC for the birth of Arsinoë IV.

Ancient sources suggest that Arsinoë IV was the youngest child of Ptolemaios XII when figuring as puella-Queen under guardianship in 48 BC.

According to ancient sources, Arsinoë IV was a child and, in particular, a *puella* under the care of a *nutricius* in 48 BC. This record indicates that she was likely younger than twelve years, which would place her birth date after 60 BC. A female born before that would not have been under guardianship in 48 BC and it would be unlikely for her to be referred to as a *puella* at that time. In conclusion, Arsinoë IV was not only the youngest daughter of Ptolemaios XII, but also his *youngest child* altogether. It is not known where Arsinoë IV took up residence after the conclusion of the 'Alexandrian War', i.e. between 47 and 46 BC.[84] However, pseudo-Caesar reports that C. Iulius Caesar once again determined her to leave the kingdom.[85]

3. On a processional litter

Considering Arsinoë's age and status as a girl-Queen in 48 BC may well explain the second documented episode of her life, which occurred about eighteen months later. In 46 BC, C. Iulius Caesar staged a triumph in Rome, a part of which was dedicated to his Alexandrian success.[86] In order to entertain the crowd, he presented Arsinoë IV "in chains"[87] exposed on a processional litter (*ferculum*)[88] and probably beside a *tropaion*.[89] Cassius Dio reports the reaction of the populace to the spectacle. Accordingly, the sight of Arsinoë IV in submission did not provoke any feelings of victory over a worthy enemy, as Vercingetorix had done at the same occasion.[90] Quite in keeping with her being a child,[91] the sight of Arsinoë IV caused "great wailing"[92] reminding the Roman citizens of their own "misfortunes".[93] Cassius Dio's use of the term γυνή to refer to Arsinoë IV in both 48 BC[94] and 46 BC[95] does not contradict this reasoning. Apart from the fact that the author wrote from a distance of about 250 years to the events, this term is a general equivalent of 'female'.[96]

Just as in 48 BC, C. Iulius Caesar did not remove Arsinoë IV from his strategy after the *pompa*[97] as might have been expected. Refraining from killing her, he released Arsinoë IV, which was clearly in opposition to Kleopatra VII.[98] An interesting statement of Cassius Dio might explain Caesar's intentions. According to him, Arsinoë IV was set free "because of her siblings",[99] whereby Ptolemaios XIII was already dead by then (tab. 1). As neither Kleopatra VII nor Ptolemaios XIV would have had any interest in seeing Arsinoë IV alive, the only logical explanation behind Dio's report may be found in the triumvir's distrust regarding the unstable Lagid conditions. Accordingly, Dio's statement may be read as Caesar's perspective on Arsinoë IV as a potential option to counterbalance her siblings.[100]

It is not known where Arsinoë IV went after the *pompa triumphalis*. As she was under the protection of C. Iulius Caesar, there was no reason for her to seek shelter at that time. It is possible that she returned to Cyprus, where Serapion was Ptolemaic strategos, at least in 43 BC.[101] He seems to have been well disliked by Kleopatra VII, which may have made him a potential ally for Arsinoë IV.[102]

Quite in keeping with her young age, the sight of Arsinoë IV primarily caused pity at Caesar's pompa triumphalis of 46 BC.

When perceiving Arsinoë IV as a guarded *puella*-Queen of less than twelve years in 48 BC, she was a scared weeping child "in chains" about a year and a half later. The sight of her caused spontaneous pity in the huge crowd of onlookers during Caesar's Alexandrian triumph of 46 BC. However, this did not end Arsinoë's career as a figurehead. Probably due to his realistic assessment of Lagid Egypt, C. Iulius Caesar kept his options open and supposedly retained Arsinoë IV as a potential counterweight or alternative to her siblings.[103]

4. The victories of a Pharian woman

Although belonging to the same "sacred gender of women"[104] according to Poseidippos (3rd c. BC), Arsinoë IV is mainly depicted by the ancient sources as a girl under guardianship and as a helpless and pitied victim finally seeking shelter, whereas Kleopatra VII represents the sheer opposite to that. Not only her intellectual qualities are emphasised,[105] but also her beauty (fig. 2).[106] Accordingly, she was a threat to males when adorned like Hera in Homer's Iliad,[107] in order to provoke the "desire to lie by her side and embrace her body in love".[108] Yet, underneath such disguise lurked a ruthless *fatale monstrum*,[109] an epithet reminiscent of the *vilia animalia* by which Statius addressed Egyptian crocodiles.[110] Indeed, Octavian had denarii minted after the 'Ptolemaic War', the reverse of which shows a crocodile in connection with the inscription *Aegypto Capta*.[111] Propertius even goes so far as to address her as *meretrix regina*.[112]

Flavius Josephus mentions Kleopatra's πλεονεξίᾳ[113] (greed) and παρανομία[114] (acting against custom and law).[115] In this regard, she had a Roman counterpart in Fulvia,[116] the wife of Marcus Antonius since 46/45 BC[117] who was addressed with a similar array of pejoratives in Augustan propaganda[118] such as greed,[119] jealousy,[120] and cruelty.[121] Instead of adhering to the woman's duties such as "spinning and housekeeping",[122] Fulvia sometimes "would gird herself with a sword".[123] She wished to "rule the ruler and command the commander".[124] Accordingly, Kleopatra VII was "indebted to Fulvia [later on] for teaching Antonius to endure a woman's sway, since she took him over quite tamed, and educated to obey women".[125]

In 48 BC, father-loving[126] Kleopatra VII had successfully involved the fifty-two-year-old C. Iulius Caesar in the Ptolemaic conflict between herself and Ptolemaios XIII,[127] which had finally made her sole Lagid Pharaoh at the age of twenty-one years.[128] Lucanus calls her amorous victory over C. Iulius Caesar *Pharios triumphos*.[129] With his death, however, Kleopatra VII had unexpectedly lost her protective support,[130] so that she undoubtedly had to fear another round of dynastic quarrels with her two remaining siblings.

In 44 BC, Marcus Antonius seems to have continued Caesar's logic. According to Strabon, he handed Cyprus over to Kleopatra VII and her sister Arsinoë IV.[131] Either, Arsinoë IV already resided on the island then, or she was "set up as a fresh and less accessible dynastic foil to Cleopatra"[132] thus hovering in Cyprus as a risk to her elder sister. Kleopatra VII probably feared being killed and, thus, exchanged at the side of Ptolemaios XIV by Arsinoë IV.[133] Accordingly, it appears quite logical that Kleopatra VII poisoned her brother right away, "because she knew that he was to be King".[134] Yet, Arsinoë IV seems to have been out of reach,[135] a volatile situation Kleopatra VII had to address sooner or later. An opportunity arose not long afterwards.

After the Battle of Philippi in 42 BC, Marcus Antonius was the leading force in the Eastern Mediterranean.[136] He faced "three serious options with respect to Egypt's disposition: to continue to recognise Cleopatra whatever the vagaries of her behaviour since 44 [BC]; to replace her with Arsinoe notwithstanding the latter's flirtation with the Republicans; or to bring the country under the direct rule of Rome".[137] in 42/41 BC,[138] Marcus Antonius summoned[139] Kleopatra VII to Tarsos.[140] According to Octavian, *futuit Glaphyran Antonius* at that time,[141] a fair ἑταίρα[142] from Cappadocia.[143] Such a circumstance may additionally explain why Kleopatra VII aspired to make such a pompous appearance in Tarsos as described by Plutarchos.[144] However, Kleopatra VII knew how to impress Romans after her affairs with the Cn. Pompeius Magnus the younger[145] and with C. Iulius Caesar.[146] She appeared in Tarsos as Aphrodite to Dionysos.[147]

It was said that Marcus Antonius "had already fallen in love with her [Kleopatra VII] long ago when she was still a child"[148] in 56/55 BC and while "he was serving as master of cavalry under Aulus Gabinius in Alexandria".[149] In 42/41 BC, he was to meet her again, but now "at the very age [of twenty-seven years] when the beauty of women shines forth in all its fullness, and with the spirit in all its vigour" (fig. 2).[150] Quite understandably, he "became her captive as if he were a young man,[151] although being beyond forty years",[152] he "fell for her upon sight".[153] As a result, the hierarchy became reversed. "Whatever Cleopatra ordered was done" by Marcus Antonius.[154] "He no longer cared about his honour; he made himself the slave of the Egyptian woman and was concerned only with his love for her".[155]

Furthermore, Marcus Antonius "gave himself the name of the new Dionysos"[156] thus taking over the epitheton of Kleopatra's father.[157] In 41 BC,[158] the year of Arsinoë's murder, he was exuberantly welcomed by the Ephesian citizens as Dionysos, "source of joy and benefactor";[159] but he was considered by most as Dionysos, "carnivore and savage".[160] In Alexandria, he gave orders to be addressed as Pater Liber (Dionysos) whom he even impersonated carrying a *thyrsos*.[161]

Naturally, Kleopatra's permission to "serve under her yoke",[162] or in Antonius' own vulgar words: to "spike" her,[163] came with conditions. She requested from Marcus Antonius the extradition of Serapion, the Ptolemaic strategos of Cyprus,[164] of the Artemisian *Megabyzos* (High Priest) as well as the deaths of an impostor pretending to be Ptolemaios XIII and of Arsinoë IV,[165] the last of her sibling rivals to the Egyptian throne.[166] "Corrupted by love",[167] i.e. "dominated by his passion for Kleopatra and her magic",[168] Marcus Antonius indulged her in all of these demands, with only the High Priest being released after the Ephesians had begged for his life to Kleopatra VII herself.[169]

Apart from this tendentious presentation,[170] Marcus Antonius' decision to choose Kleopatra VII had doubtlessly quite factual reasons.[171] By disposing of Arsinoë IV, Marcus Antonius effectively ended a decade of rivalry for the throne amongst the Ptolemies and secured the Egyptian resources[172] for his own ambitions.[173] Also his preference for Kleopatra VII over Arsinoë IV may have been, after all, dictated by logical reasoning. Throughout her reign, Kleopatra VII faced opposition in Alexandria,[174] while Arsinoë IV was favoured there.[175] Therefore, Marcus Antonius may have perceived Kleopatra VII in her weak position as much more dependent on him than Arsinoë IV.[176] However, "by having Arsinoë IV executed, he deprived himself of the possibility of ever being able to use her as a counter-queen".[177] In other words, Kleopatra's victory over Marcus Antonius is evident in the fact that she successfully reduced his options. Unlike C. Iulius Caesar, Antonius was not able enough to prevent such a defeat.

In 42/41 BC, Marcus Antonius' decision at Tarsos to prefer Kleopatra VII sealed the fate of Arsinoë IV. Such a historical event is a *terminus post quem* for her death.[178]

5. The end of a counter-Queen

5.1 A former Queen as a supplicant

The final documented episode of Arsinoë's life takes place in Ephesos. It is stated that she was a supplicant[179] to the Ephesian Artemis.[180] The choice of exile appears significant. Arsinoë IV was probably still a παρθένος at that time,[181] i.e. an unmarried female,[182] so that it makes sense that she sought protection of Artemis, the goddess known for her everlasting virginity.[183] Indeed, the epigram of a certain Damagetes refers to an "Arsinoë, the Ptolemaian virgin"[184] who devoted a lock "cutting it from her lovely tresses" at a temple of Artemis, a ritual known within the context of supplication.[185] As fitting as it may be, it is not clear which Ptolemaic Arsinoë is addressed within the text nor at which temple the dedication took place. Yet, there seems to be no other Πτολεμαῖς παρθένος Ἀρσινόη who sought protection within an Artemision according to our knowledge.[186]

Having been kept alive by C. Iulius Caesar, Arsinoë IV was an ongoing threat to her elder sister Kleopatra VII (fig. 2).[187] Such an assumption is supported by the record that Arsinoë IV was welcomed as Queen by the *Megabyzos*[188] of the Ephesian Artemision after 46 BC,[189] a reverence that he almost had to pay for with his life later on. P. J. Bicknell tries to explain the "undiplomatically hospitable Megabyzos"[190] who may have taken "her imminent restoration to Alexandria for granted and accorded appropriate hospitality".[191]

5.2 An obscure murder on Artemisian ground

Three ancient authors report Arsinoë's killing in the precincts of the Ephesian Artemision. Flavius Josephus says that "she [Kleopatra VII] urged Marcus Antonius to murder her sister Arsinoë [although] she was a supplicant within the Artemision of Ephesos"[192]. Cassius Dio renders a flawed account of the tragedy.[193] Appianos confuses the Artemision of Ephesos with the Artemis Leukophryene temple in Magnesia and the Temple of Apollon at Didyma near Miletos.[194] Apart from such disinterest in the location, the uncertainty might have derived from Strabon who mentions these three temples together in a text passage.[195] However, Appianos somewhat corrected himself by concurrently saying that "the priest of Artemis at Ephesos, whom they called the Megabyzus [...] had once received Arsinoe as queen".[196]

After having been defeated by Kleopatra VII, Marcus Antonius no longer respected the fact that his predecessor "within"[197] Kleopatra VII, C. Iulius Caesar, had spared Arsinoë's life twice,[198] i.e. after the 'Alexandrian War'[199] as well as after his *pompa* in 46 BC.[200] According to Appianos, Marcus Antonius sent assassins into the Artemision in order to kill Arsinoë IV.[201] In other words, she fell victim to an obscure attack within the holy precinct. Interestingly, a guard was set up within the Artemisian sanctuary shortly after that, i.e. in 39/38 BC "in the 10th year of Caesar's victory" at Pharsalos over Pompeius.[202]

Flavius Josephus and Appianos frame Arsinoë's murder in a particular way. Reporting the actual incident with only a few words, the ancient authors embed the assassination into a general character attack on Kleopatra VII and Marcus Antonius. Their topics are the sexual dependence of Marcus Antonius and the outright vile character of Kleopatra VII.[203] Appianos states that Kleopatra VII ignored "human and divine laws".[204] In keeping with that, Flavius Josephus says that no *asylum* in the whole world was respected by Kleopatra VII,[205] directly relating such a statement to the murder of Arsinoë IV. In his second text, Flavius Josephus even emphasised the blasphemy by saying that Arsinoë IV was killed *in templo*.[206]

According to ancient sources, Arsinoë IV was accepted as supplicant in the Ephesian Artemision and subsequently killed by assassins although under divine protection.

At some point after 46 BC, Arsinoë IV likely felt threatened by her sister Kleopatra VII, and sought refuge in the Ephesian Artemision. Indeed, the High Priest there welcomed her as a Queen and accepted her supplication. In 41 BC, Kleopatra VII made use of her newly acquired Roman resource, Marcus Antonius, and instigated him to assassinate Arsinoë IV on the grounds of the Artemision, so that the fate of an actual and potential counter-Queen concluded here. With this act, Kleopatra VII had finally eliminated the last of her siblings, leaving no opponents to the Lagid throne.[207]

6. Arsinoë IV – born in Ephesos?

Having been a child and, in particular, a *puella*-Queen under guardianship, we concluded that Arsinoë IV was below the age of twelve completed years in 48 BC and thus born after 60 BC.[208] Yet, such reasoning is contradicted by the long-standing and often repeated idea, whereby Arsinoë IV was born between 68 and 65 BC, which would have made her 24–27 years of age at her death in 41 BC.[209] Although not often mentioned as its source,[210] such an age estimation derives from Max Leberecht Strack[211] who wrote in 1897:

> *Arsinoe escapes from Caesar's royal castle soon after the first battle of the Alexandrian War in mid-September 48, becomes queen of the land army and knows how to play such role to the full, Dio XLII 39 [...]. According to this, her birth is not after 65. Her elder sister Kleopatra was born in 69, ergo her birth falls between 68 and 65.*[212]

As can be seen, Strack's sole argument concerns Arsinoë's suspected ability "to play the role of a queen" in 48 BC.[213] Strack seems to have assumed an age of about twenty years for somebody capable of performing such a duty.[214] At this point, it is worth considering that Ptolemaios XIII became co-regent with Kleopatra VII in 51 BC at the age of ten years, sent her into exile in 49 BC at the age of twelve years, opposed her in front of C. Iulius Caesar in 48 BC at the age of thirteen years,[215] and drowned in 47 BC at the age of fourteen years. Ptolemaios XIV became co-regent at the side of Kleopatra VII in 47 BC at the age of twelve years, and was poisoned by her in 44 BC at the age of fifteen years (tab. 1).[216]

However, the main flaw in Strack's argument is found in his incomplete referral to ancient sources. In essence, several age-related pieces of information regarding Arsinoë IV are gained from such literature.[217] Accordingly, she was

- ➢ the younger daughter of Ptolemaios XII in comparison to Kleopatra VII,[218] which reveals nothing more than that she was born after her elder sister;[219]
- ➢ A "child" in 48 BC,[220] and, in particular,
- ➢ A *puella*[221] in need of a *nutricius* in 48 BC,[222] a statement that should indicate an age of less than twelve years at that time.

Strack referred to the first record only.[223] If he had recognised the other reports too, he would undoubtedly have changed his estimation, since he states regarding Ptolemaios XIII:

> *Ptolemaios [XIII], according to Appian, bell. civ. II 84, was about 13 years old in the year 48, i.e. born around 61. The report is essentially confirmed by Caesar (bell. civ. III 103), who calls him "puer" and by the fact that he still has guardians.*[224]

Yet there may be another reason why Strack considered Arsinoë IV as a female adult. For the one, Cassius Dio had addressed her as γυνή in 48 BC[225] as well as in 46 BC.[226] In addition, W. Duncan (1833)[227] as well as W. S. Bohn and W. A. McDevitte (1872)[228] had proposed translations of "Caesar's commentaries on the Gallic and Civic Wars" in the 19th c., wherein the crucial terminus *puella* had been rendered (and thus seemingly understood) as "woman".[229] After that, Arsinoë IV was not characterised as *puella*, neither by Walter Judeich (1885),[230] John Pentland Mahaffy (1899),[231] and Auguste Bouché-Leclercq (1904),[232] nor by Ulrich Wilcken (1895),[233] Felix Stähelin (1921),[234] and Hans Volkmann (1927).[235] Judeich only names Arsinoë's *nutricius* Ganymedes,[236] and Bouché-Leclercq simply reiterates Strack's age estimation.[237] In line with ancient sources, Wilcken addresses Arsinoë IV as "youngest daughter of Ptolemaios XII",[238] Stähelin as "Kleopatra's youngest sister",[239] and Volkmann again as "youngest daughter"[240] of Ptolemaios XII.[241]

A slight variation of Strack's assessment is provided by Edwyn Robert Bevan with a likewise dubious reasoning. He speaks of Ptolemaios XIV and Arsinoë IV as the "the two younger children of Ptolemy Auletes" (sic!) adding a somewhat strange calculation:

> [Kleopatra's] younger sister Arsinoe, a girl then of about fifteen [...]. She escaped from the palace with the eunuch under whose care she had been brought up, Ganymedes, and took up her position as the representative of the royal house, with the army of Achillas (late autumn? 48 BC).[242]

With that, Bevan suggests a birth year of 63 BC for Arsinoë IV, i.e. *before* her brothers Ptolemaios XIII and Ptolemaios XIV.[243] Concomitantly, he calls Ptolemaios XIII a "boy king"[244] and Ptolemaios XIV a "boy-husband [of] about twelve" years.[245]

Strack's estimation of Arsinoë's birth time seems to have been questioned only once in the past. In 1964, Heinz Heinen[246] commented on Strack, pointed out its weakness and added the sources regarding Arsinoë's state of youth in 48 BC:

> M. L. Strack [...] states that Arsinoe, when she became queen of the army, 'knew how to play this role completely [...]. Accordingly, her birth cannot be dated after 65 [BC]'. However, the actual leadership of the army and the war was taken over by Ganymedes, the nutricius of Arsinoe [...]. Even if the year 65 [BC] is not entirely improbable as a lower limit, a later year of birth would by no means be excluded, especially when one thinks of the similar role of Ptolemy XIII, born in 61 [BC].[247]

According to our knowledge, Heinen's contribution was not adopted afterwards.[248] Instead, Strack's flawed reckoning prevailed and it is still repeated as of today.[249] However, ancient sources rather suggest that Arsinoë IV was born *after* her brother Ptolemaios XIV (born 59 BC)[250] and within the fifth decade of the 1st c. BC[251] making her the *youngest child* of Ptolemaios XII altogether. According to this assessment, she was a maximum of 17 years when she was assassinated in Ephesos in 41 BC having been born in 58 BC at the earliest. Such reasoning inevitably draws the attention to a specific life-episode of her father Ptolemaios XII.

In 58 BC, Ptolemaios XII was forced to flee from Alexandria.[252] After taking residence in Rome, he went to Ephesos in 57 BC where "he stayed near to the Goddess".[253]

He should remain there until 55 BC.[254] Quite in line with Strabon's indirect report whereby Ptolemaios' wife was not the mother of Arsinoë IV,[255] Kleopatra Tryphaina remained in Alexandria[256] where she died in 57 BC.[257] Setting Arsinoë's birth date after that of Ptolemaios XIV in 59 BC, it is a reasonable assumption that she was born between 57 and 55 BC,[258] during which time Ptolemaios XII resided in the Ephesian Artemision, as she could not have been born after that time. In such event, Arsinoë IV was

> - 0/2 years in 55 BC when she returned with her father Ptolemaios XII to Alexandria;[259]
> - 4/6 years in 51 BC when her father "died of disease";[260]
> - 6/8 years in 49 BC when she went into exile together with her elder sister Kleopatra VII;[261]
> - 7/9 years in 48 BC when she figured as *puella*-βασιλίς of Alexandria;[262]
> - 8/10 years in 47 BC at the end of the 'Alexandrian War';
> - 9/11 years in 46 BC at Caesar's Alexandrian triumph in Rome;[263]
> - 11/13 years in 44 BC, when Marcus Antonius supposedly handed Cyprus over to her and Kleopatra VII;[264]
> - 13/15 years in 42 BC, when Marcus Antonius became the leading force in the Eastern Mediterranean after the Battle of Philippi[265] and
> - 14/16 years in 41 BC when she was murdered in Ephesos.[266]

As the youngest child of Ptolemaios XII, it is a
reasonable assumption that Arsinoë IV was born during
the stay of her father in the Ephesian Artemision
from 57 until 55 BC.

Following these arguments, we reiterate that Arsinoë IV was rather born in the fifth decade of the 1st c. BC during the exile of her father Ptolemaios XII in the Ephesian Artemision. For this reason, she was called Arsinoë,[267] a name reminiscent of Lagid Ephesos; because of that, she had a special relationship to the city and its divine protector Artemis, a place to which she therefore returned when in desperate need.

7. Conclusions

Due to its immense resources,[268] Lagid Egypt was an important factor during the final convulsions of the Roman Civil Wars in the 1st c. BC.[269] Such a circumstance concurred with the quarrels for the throne between the members of the ending Ptolemaic dynasty, i.e., between the hostile siblings of Ptolemaios XII, one of whom was Arsinoë IV.

Decade 1st c. BC	Year BC	Events
4th	69	Birth of Kleopatra VII
	61	Birth of Ptolemaios XIII
5th	59	Birth of Ptolemaios XIV
	58	Ptolemaios XII is forced into exile
	57–55	Ptolemaios XII resides within the Ephesian Artemision and finally returns to Alexandria (suspected birth time of Arsinoë IV)
	56/55	M. Antonius meets Kleopatra VII for the first time in Alexandria, when "she was still a child"
	51	Death of Ptolemaios XII. Co-regency of Kleopatra VII and Ptolemaios XIII
6th	49	Ptolemaios XIII sends Kleopatra VII and Arsinoë IV into Syrian exile
	48	Battle of Pharsalos. Death of Cn. Pompeius Magnus. C. Iulius Caesar reinstates Kleopatra VII and Ptolemaios XIII in Alexandria and grants Cyprus to Arsinoë IV and Ptolemaios XIV. 'Alexandrian War' with *puella*-Queen Arsinoë IV and *puer*-King Ptolemaios XIII both being under guardianship
	47	Death of Ptolemaios XIII and end of the 'Alexandrian War'. Co-regency of Kleopatra VII and Ptolemaios XIV
	46	Triumphal procession in Rome with Arsinoë IV "in chains" on a *ferculum*
	44	Death of C. Iulius Caesar. Death of Ptolemaios XIV poisoned on the order of Kleopatra VII; Arsinoë IV perhaps in Cyprus
	42	Battle of Philippi
	42/41	Meeting of Kleopatra and Marcus Antonius in Tarsos. After that, murder of Arsinoë IV in Ephesos
7th/8th	31	Battle of Actium
	30	End of the 'Ptolemaic War'. Suicides of Kleopatra VII and Marcus Antonius
	<30	Erection of the Octagon as Arsinoë's grave

Tab. 1: Timetable of the fading Lagid rule over Egypt

Ancient sources emphasise that Arsinoë IV was the youngest of the three daughters of Ptolemaios XII. Moreover, it is stated that Arsinoë IV was a child and, in particular, a *puella* in need of a *nutricius* in 48 BC, not yet having reached an age of twelve completed years. Considering that Ptolemaios XIV was born in 59 BC, such a report sets Arsinoë's birth time after his, making her not only the youngest daughter, but also the youngest child of Ptolemaios XII altogether.

Since Ptolemaios XII resided within the Ephesian Artemision from 57 till 55 BC, it is a reasonable assumption that Arsinoë IV was born during that time. Supposedly because of that, the meaningful name was given to her, as Lagid Ephesos under

Lysimachos had briefly been called 'Arsinoeia' in the 3rd c. BC.[270] Because of that, she had a special relationship to Ephesos and its protective goddess.

Despite her young age, Arsinoë IV did play a role during the last years of the declining Ptolemaic rule over Egypt, which is why she is repeatedly mentioned in the ancient sources. As a Lagid offspring, she figured as the actual and potential counter-Queen to Kleopatra VII in the sixth decade of the 1st c. BC, illustrating the dynastic quarrels amongst the Ptolemaic "sibling-lovers".[271]

The 'Alexandrian War' of 48/47 BC finds Arsinoë IV as *puella*-Queen against her elder sister Kleopatra VII for a short time. Probably because of her young age, she was pitied at Caesar's Alexandrian triumph in 46 BC. After that, Arsinoë IV still remained a potential threat to Kleopatra VII, and, in particular, after Caesar's death in 44 BC. Having lost her Roman protector, Kleopatra VII had to fear becoming replaced at the side of Ptolemaios XIV by Arsinoë IV.[272] Confronting such a danger, Kleopatra VII ordered her minor brother Ptolemaios XIV to be poisoned at the age of fifteen years. Arsinoë IV would have understood the significance of this and returned, perhaps via Cyprus, as a supplicant to her supposed birth place, the Artemision of Ephesos, in order to seek shelter.

Arsinoë IV was born as a Ptolemaic princess and killed as a παρϑένος, supposedly both on the holy ground of the Ephesian Artemision.

After the decision of Philippi in 42 BC, there was a reasonable chance that Marcus Antonius contemplated Arsinoë IV as his Lagid figurehead. Yet in the eyes of a 43-year-old Roman commander, 28-year-old Kleopatra VII prevailed. This victory finally ended the career of an actual and potential counter-Queen. On the instigation of Kleopatra VII, Marcus Antonius sent assassins to the Ephesian Artemision that killed the Ptolemaic princess. In other words, Marcus Antonius not only committed ἱεροσύλία (sacrilege) by impiously murdering Arsinoë IV on holy ground; he also went so far as to kill a παρϑένος who had supposedly been born under divine eyes within the Artemision.

8. Epilogue

With the murder of Arsinoë IV in 41 BC, Kleopatra VII "had put to death all her kindred, till no one near her in blood remained alive".[273] After that, Kleopatra VII was, again by Roman grace, the last and now uncontested Ptolemaic Pharaoh of Egypt for the remaining fourth decade of her life. After the Battle of Actium, her final efforts to change sides again failed.[274] Upon encountering her, Octavian wisely avoided her looks,[275] so that he would not be allured under her "yoke".[276] Unlike C. Iulius

Caesar in 48 BC and Marcus Antonius in 42 BC, he removed the "incestuous"[277] Ptolemaic dynasty and its obvious problems from his strategy,[278] a goal that also encompassed his killing of Caesarion, the son of Kleopatra VII and C. Iulius Caesar.[279]

Interestingly, Octavian intended a fate for Kleopatra VII similar to that of Arsinoë IV some seventeen years earlier.[280] He wanted to keep her alive,[281] so that "she would enhance the radiance of his triumph" in Rome.[282] Just as C. Iulius Caesar had staged a *pompa* in 46 BC, Octavian[283] also planned to present a Lagid Pharaoh as a trophy in 29 BC.[284] However, Kleopatra VII suspected Octavian's intention.[285] Quite in keeping with that, a statement of Kleopatra VII is passed down according to which she said: "I will not be paraded".[286] She preferred death to such a humiliation,[287] a "heroic" act[288] that finally commanded respect from the Romans. Accordingly, she was no "ordinary woman"[289] and of "lofty spirit".[290]

And so, it came to pass that during Octavian's triumph[291] only a dramatised image[292] of Kleopatra VII was presented to the *turba*.[293] As the children Arsinoë IV of Alexandria and Iuba II of Numidia[294] were displayed in Caesar's triumph, Kleopatra's twins with Marcus Antonius, Kleopatra Selene and Alexandros Helios, then about eleven years of age,[295] had to accompany the painting of Kleopatra VII.[296]

When looking back from the 4th c. AD, Eusebius of Caesarea summarised:

> *Ptolemaios, called the new Dionysos, whose reign lasted for 29 years. His daughter Kleopatra was the last of the Lagid lineage.[297] Her reign lasted for 22 years […]. At that time, C. Iulius Caesar conquered Egypt for the Romans. After Caesar Octavius who is Augustus, had killed Kleopatra, he put an end to the Ptolemaic empire which had ruled for 295 years.[298]*

Tab. 2: The research history of the Octagon covers 120 years and is mainly connected to R. Heberdey, W. Wilberg, J. Keil, J. Weninger, and H. Thür

Year	Comment
1904	The Octagon is recognised on the western 'Curetes Street' (figs. 3f.) and addressed as a "monument of victory". Some of its architectural elements are transported to Vienna, Austria (fig. on jacket).
1915	1st edition of Keil's Ephesos guide summarizing the results of the 1st research period of the OeAI in Ephesos until its termination in 1913.
1926	The 2nd research period of the OeAI commences as the result of the fund-raising efforts of G. A. Deißmann (fig. 79a).
1929	J. Keil investigates the Octagon's pedestal (figs. 3f.) and detects the burial chamber (figs. 7–10a) thus identifying the monument as "heroon". He removes the skull from the sarcophagus and transports it to the University of Greifswald.
1930	J. Keil publishes the excavation report of the Ephesian 1929–campaign and the 2nd edition of his Ephesos guide, wherein he refers to the assessment of Greifswald regarding the Octagon's skull. Accordingly, the mausoleum was dedicated to a young female individual.
1953	J. Weninger publishes the Octagon's skull (fig. 85) confirming that a young female individual was interred in the tomb. After that, the bone vanishes.
1955	J. Keil publishes the 3rd edition of his Ephesos guide that include the results of the 2nd research period of the OeAI until its termination in 1935. The 3rd Ephesian research period of the OeAI commences (fig. 5).
1978	The Ephesos Museum opens its doors in Vienna, Austria, with an architectural probe of the Octagon on display (fig. on jacket).
1982	Keil's opening of the Octagon's vault is accessed for the 2nd time by the authors (E. R., P. S.) who encounter the site just as Keil had left it in 1929 (figs. 7–10a).
1990	H. Thür publishes her proposal, whereby the Octagon is the mausoleum of the Ptolemaic Queen Arsinoë IV.
1993	The postcranial skeleton of the Octagon is examined for the first time by E. Reuer and S. Fabrizii-Reuer; the results remain unpublished.
2009	Kanz et al. publish a conference poster regarding a 2nd examination of the Octagon's postcranial skeleton.

An octagonal mausoleum in Ephesos

About a millennium ago, a catastrophic earthquake caused the collapse of a Hellenistic mausoleum in the centre of the already abandoned Greco-Roman metropolis of Ephesos, situated on the western Mediterranean coast of Asia Minor (plan 2). Over time, layers of earth gradually covered the remnants of this testament to antique architecture. Centuries later, Austrian researchers recognised the building as it was left after the moment of its destruction. Since no inscriptions were found indicating to whom the tomb was dedicated, it was simply named 'Octagon' because of its distinctive shape. What followed was an intermittent occupation with the monument, which unexpectedly culminated in the proposal that it might be the sepulchre of the Ptolemaic Queen Arsinoë IV of Alexandria, younger sister of Kleopatra VII and her rival for the Macedonian-Egyptian throne. However, no consensus has been reached regarding this interpretation, leaving one of the most intriguing issues of Ephesian archaeology unresolved.

1. Excavation history

1.1 A "monument of victory" in 1904

In 1904,[1] the Austrian Archaeological Institute[2] (OeAI) carried out one of the excavation campaigns of its first Ephesian research period[3] (tab. 2)[4] mainly taking place at what was called "budrumia" by the local Turkish people.[5] At the southeast corner of this area,[6] the efforts addressed the "street to the east of the [Celsus] Library"[7] (fig. 66; plans 1 and 3).[8] At its southern curb and next to the "fountain" (figs. 3f., 47–50; plans 1, 3–4),[9] an edifice was recognised on 03.10.1904,[10] which was called 'Octagon' henceforth,[11] and which Rudolf Heberdey[12] described as follows (figs. 3f.):[13]

> *On a high square base, inaccessible from below, [resides] a temple–like building without an interior, except that [...] the cella is designed as an octagon surrounded by a peristasis of eight Ionic columns arranged according to the corners of the octagon. The entablature shows various peculiarities; an octagonal stepped pyramid is secured to be the roof, the upper end of which was formed by a colossal sphere.[16] One would like to think of it as being surmounted by a figure of Nike and see in the whole a magnificent monument of victory.[17]*

Fig. 3: The excavation site of the Octagon from the north with the core masonry of the socle containing the not yet recognised burial vault. Note the fragments of the collapsed building on the Curetes Street, and the screens of the 'fountain' at the right side of the pedestal[14]

Fig. 4: The excavation site of the Octagon from the south presenting the polygonal layout of the krepis and the pseudo–cella distinctly. Note that an Attic base with a column fragment of the octastyle peristasis was found in situ[15]

One might ask why Heberdey addressed the Octagon as "a magnificent monument of victory [...] being surmounted by a figure of Nike".[18] In this regard, it is worth noting that he mentioned the discovery of a Nike torso at the site in the Ephesian excavation diary (EED).[19] Furthermore, Heberdey stated that the wreckage of architecture was found "in such a position as they can only have fallen through the collapse of the immediately nearby building".[20] In other words, the archaeologists encountered the Octagon as resulting from its breakdown towards the north and the east (figs. 3f.), i.e. towards the downhill side of Mount Preon (Bülbüldağ, plan 2f.), probably due to a severe earthquake in the mediaeval period.[21] Based on its many discovered fragments,[22] Wilhelm Wilberg[23] was able to produce constructional drawings of the monument (fig. 12).[24] Referring to the so-called Parthian reliefs that had been found the previous year,[25] Heberdey finally excluded "the combination with the reliefs found in front of the [Celsus] library, which certainly originated from a similar construction".[26]

Maybe because of the perception of the Octagon as an unusual edifice, some of its architectural elements (fig. on jacket) were transported to Vienna, Austria,[27] together with the famous Parthian reliefs[28] under the explicit permission of "His Majesty, the Eminent Sultan Abdul Hamid II, the Protector and Promoter of the Austrian research in Ephesos".[29] Remarkably, also two torch holders shaped as Egyptianesque "columns with 2 leaf calyxes" of about 1.5 m height (fig. 35)[30] that had been found at the site of the Octagon and the adjoining "fountain"[31] (figs. 47–50; plans 1, 3–4), were taken along (tab. 2).

In 1904, the remains of the collapsed Octagon were recognised, which was initially interpreted as a "magnificent monument of victory".

The monument is only briefly mentioned in the following years.[32] Josef Keil (fig. 79)[33] stated in his first–edition guide to Ephesos from 1915[34] "no inscription provides information about the purpose and the time of origin of the building".[35] However, Keil said later on that he had disagreed with Heberdey's and Wilberg's assumption of its being a "monument of victory",[36] instead interpreting the Octagon as a "heroon",[37] i.e. as the tomb of an outstanding personality.[38] Only twenty–five years after the discovery of the building, he was able to prove his suspicion regarding the monument's funeral character.[39]

1.2 A "heroon" in 1929

For the research campaign of 1929,[40] the OeAI had set itself the task to complete "objects excavated before the War" (= WW I).[41] Under this premise, Keil returned to the Octagon on 01.10.1929 (tab. 2). Upon inspecting the core of its "high square

Fig. 5: a) An early view of the Octagon towards the west (probably from the 1950s) with some of the orthostat slabs reapplied to the masonry of the pedestal facing the Curetes Street; b) The Curetes Street from the west showing the appearance of the 'fountain' and the Octagon, when F. Miltner re–started the Ephesian excavations in 1954. Note that the Octagon's architectural fragments of fig. 3 had remained on the pavement

AN OCTAGONAL MAUSOLEUM IN EPHESOS

base" from above (figs. 3f.), he detected a vault structure, removed one of its stones,[42] and entered the burial chamber.[43] Keil described what he encountered (fig. 6):

> Squeezing through the gap thus created, we entered a chamber quite carefully constructed of rough marble blocks and vaulted with a man-high barrel roof of such blocks, whose heavy air, completely saturated with moisture, at first made breathing difficult. Near the north–east wall, which had two niches for placing lamps and grave goods, stood a carefully crafted but completely unadorned marble sarcophagus.[44]

As can be seen, Keil not only mentions the sarcophagus (figs. 6f.), but also two niches at the northern wall of the chamber (figs. 8f.), which seem to have been empty at his visit.[45] Furthermore, Keil recognised the door at the southern wall of the room blocked by a stone slab (fig. 10a), which he rightly attributed to the "corridor leading into the chamber from the south side as part of the building plan".[46] Keil hoped to find "a clue to the dating" of the Octagon inside the dromos.[47] Yet, he did not open the door inside the burial chamber at first.[48] Instead, he searched for an outer entrance at the southern side of the monument (fig. 10b).[49] On 09.10.1929, he found the outer end of the dromos, which appeared closed by a marble slab.[50]

With the opening of its burial chamber in 1929,
the Octagon was readily understood as a "heroon", i.e. as the tomb
of an outstanding personality.

1.3 Tomb raiders and water

Within his writings from 1929/30, two details dominate Keil's description of the Octagon's sarcophagus: it appeared somewhat disturbed, and it was full of water. Regarding the first notion, Keil said:

> A [...] marble sarcophagus, the lid of which had been pushed aside after removal of the bracing and rested askew on the chest [...]. The bones, which in some places had been brought out of their natural position, and amongst which there was not the slightest grave good.[51]

Keil opined, "grave robbers had once penetrated the chamber, burst open the sarcophagus and had searched for valuable grave goods".[52] Since there was no other entrance into the grave chamber, Keil concomitantly stated

> "the grave robbers, however, had not come through the vaulted ceiling as we had done, but through the passageway provided in the building plan leading from the south side into the chamber, which was closed at the

Fig. 6: A modern view from the southern dromos into the burial vault of the Octagon containing the sarcophagus with the reapplied lid that shows the light cone coming through Keil's opening of the vault. The clamp–beds are clearly cut and do not present any signs of a violent removal, as if such a closure was never implemented

Fig. 7: View into the western end of the sarcophagus after having been emptied of water and mud (photo taken in 1982). Note how tightly the sarcophagus fits into the chamber as well as the evaporation lines visible inside the container, which indicate its repeated flooding

inner end by a rough marble slab and at the outer end by a beautifully decorated heavy marble slab".[53]

In other words, Keil found both the inner and the outer end of the dromos blocked by marble slabs,[54] and still presumed that grave robbers had come "through the passageway".[55] However, it is highly unlikely that tomb raiders would have put both marble slabs of the dromos back into their original place after having searched the chamber. In this regard, it is worth noting that the clamp–beddings of the sarcophagus appear remarkably unharmed and without a patina, so that such irons may never have been applied (fig. 6). Accordingly, no safeguard prevented the lid from shifting out of its position during the several and severe earthquakes over the centuries,[56] one of which finally caused the collapse of the mausoleum.[57] In other words, the disturbances of the sarcophagus described by Keil may well be the result of repeated seismic activities. The fact that no grave goods were found within the chamber does not prove the presence of tomb raiders, since such a possibility is not unknown as Keil himself had recognised.[58]

The second curiosity that had puzzled Keil, may have contributed to the disturbed appearance of the sarcophagus' contents:

Surprisingly, the box was filled with water up to about 0.1 m below the edge.[59]

Apart from Keil's reasoning,[60] this aspect is of no surprise. The Octagon is located at the lower Embolos[61] where the surface waters converge flowing from the southern slope of Mount Pion (the southern part of today's double peaked Panayırdağ; fig. 90) and the northern slope of Mount Preon (Bülbüldağ, plan 3). If one has ever experienced, as the present authors have,[62] the force of the huge amount of rain discharging into the area (fig. 37) flanked by the large altar (fig. 44; plan 4),[63] the Library of Celsus (figs. 37, 66; plans 1 and 3)[64] and the South Gate of the Lower Agora (figs. 41–43; plans 1 and 3),[65] it is easily understandable that the Octagon's burial chamber (fig. 6) has been repeatedly flooded in the past.[66] Accordingly, also the authors (E.R., P.S.) found the vault's air "saturated with moisture"[67] and the sarcophagus full of water in 1982, although Keil had emptied it in 1929.[68] Nevertheless, whereas the water regularly found its way out of the chamber through the floor, it remained within the chest. On the one hand, this fact explains why "the sarcophagus is covered by a massive crust of sinter" (fig. 6),[69] and, furthermore, why "the bones [within the sarcophagus] had been brought out of their natural position in some places".[70]

In conclusion, we would like to suggest that the disturbed aspect of the Octagon's sarcophagus as described by Keil in 1929 was not caused by tomb raiders. Rather, it was the result of severe earthquakes that firstly shifted the lid of the sarcophagus slightly out of place, which subsequently allowed its likewise repeated flooding. In other words, Keil largely encountered the Octagon's *antrum*[71] in 1929 as it was left after the funeral ceremony around two millennia before.[72]

Apart from the impact of earthquake and water, J. Keil probably encountered the Octogon's burial chamber as it was left after the funeral ceremony around two millennia before.

In summary, Keil dealt with the grave structure of the Octagon from 01.10.–12.10.1929:

> ➢ On 01.10.1929, he removed some of the core masonry of the Octagon's socle from above (figs. 3f.) and opened an access through the vault into the burial chamber;[73]
> ➢ On 02.10.1929, he entered the vault, saw the sarcophagus with the skeleton inside (figs. 6f.), the empty two niches at the northern wall (figs. 8f.), and the closed door to the dromos at the southern wall (fig. 10a);[74]
> ➢ On 08.10.1929, he started the search for the outer entrance into the dromos at the southern side of the monument (fig. 10b);[75]
> ➢ On 09.10.1929, he detected the closed outer door (fig. 10b);[76]
> ➢ On 10.10.1929, he opened the outer door and described the dromos (fig. 10a);[77]
> ➢ On 12.10.1929, he closed the outer door of the dromos and "filled up everything again".[78]

During these two weeks, Keil removed the skull from the Octagon's sarcophagus and, finally, transported it to Greifswald, Germany.[79] It has to be assumed that also the mandible was taken along.[80]

1.4 A Ptolemaic grave?

After Keil had announced, "the riddle [of the construction][81] is solved, the octagon is a heroon",[82] and the "Octagon is done",[83] the mausoleum was removed from the agenda of the OeAI.[84] The "mysterious"[85] mausoleum would have undoubtedly remained in this state of slumber, if Hilke Thür[86] had not linked it to Arsinoë IV of Alexandria in 1990.[87] In her most recent publication on the Octagon,[88] Thür lists altogether six arguments in order to support her suggestion:[89]

> ➢ The location of the tomb "reserved only for those of royal lineage who have provided special services to the city";
> ➢ The form of the sepulchre resembling "the dynastic tombs known as the Mausoleum of Halicarnassos or Belevi";
> ➢ The "dating of the structure [to] the second half of the 1st c. BC";

- The anthropological examinations of the skeleton concluding on a young woman of 17.5 years at the time of death;[90]
- The "decorative elements [of the Octagon] that clearly demonstrate a connection to Egypt[91] (such as griffins,[92] palm–leaf–style columns resembling torch–bearers,[93] and the pyramid–shaped roof[94])";
- "The octagonal shape of the structure, which emphasises the central section of the world–famous Pharos lighthouse in Alexandria [likely intending] to signify the origin of the person buried within".[95]

However, Thür's association of the "heroon" with such a member of the Ptolemaic dynasty[96] remained a controversial issue,[97] sometimes repeated or accepted[98] and sometimes doubted.[99]

> Since ancient sources suggest that Arsinoë IV died in her adolescence, the first and foremost question arises as to whether the developmental state of the Octagon's skeleton is indeed compatible with This record.

2. The skeletal remains of the Octagon

2.1 The skull

On 03.10.1929, Keil wrote in the Ephesian excavation diary (EED):

> *We found* [...] *the relatively well–preserved skeleton of the deceased, apparently of a not quite adult man, lying on earth and small stones on the floor* [of the sarcophagus]. *The position of the skeleton was disturbed, the head was upside down.*[100]

Accordingly, Keil initially considered the Octagon as the tomb of a distinguished[101] "not quite adult man".[102] Probably in order to investigate such an individual further, he removed the skull from the vault[103] and took it to the University of Greifswald, Germany.[104] Already in 1930, he provided the undocumented "impression [of the] Greifswald colleagues" who, no doubt to his surprise, concluded that the skull belonged to a female individual that had "died at the young age of about 20 years".[105] In other words, it was known since then that the Octagon is the grave of a young female individual. Still, no investigation into Ephesian history regarding such a person is documented for decades.

The bone resurfaced only once after that. In 1953, the "calvaria", i.e. the skull without the mandible,[106] was published in detail by the Austrian anthropologist Josef

Weninger (fig. 77).[107] In his article,[108] he adopted three remarkable details of Keil's understanding regarding the Octagon:

> ➤ The labelling of the monument as "heroon";[109]
> ➤ The dating of the tomb to "early Roman times",[110] which Weninger interestingly translated as the "time around the birth of Christ",[111] and perhaps also
> ➤ The assumption of an Egyptian background of the grave's owner.[112]

Weninger confirmed the female sex of the Octagon's individual and specified the age estimation of the Greifswald experts, this time, however, based on a reasonable documentation (tab. 2). In particular, Weninger referred to the incomplete root mineralisation of the upper second molars,[113] and the "wide open synchondrosis sphenooccipitalis",[114] both findings that prove the young age at death of the Octagon's owner. Weninger concluded: "Hence, the individual died in adolescence (Juvenis). The exact physical age can be given as about 16–17 years".[115] Furthermore, he pointed to the "undisturbed development of the skull".[116]

---

*In 1929, Keil removed the skull from the Octagon's burial chamber.
It was not published until 1953.*

After Weninger's publication, the skull is not mentioned any more, and, as time went by, it was finally considered "lost".[117] In 1972, W. Alzinger seems to have referred to Greifswald and Weninger when saying that the Octagon's sarcophagus harboured "the skeleton of a ca. 18–20–year–old girl".[118] In 2009, Weninger's documentation was utilised to manufacture a 3D–model of the Octagon's skull for a dramatised TV–feature.[119] Based on that, the idea was proposed that Arsinoë IV (and Kleopatra VII) was partly of black African origin, a suggestion that was broadly discussed in the social media.[120] However, the proposal was never substantiated by means of a publication, so that it does not merit further attention.

2.2 The postcranial skeleton

Thirty excavation reports after 1929 do not document any further visit of the Octagon's burial structure,[121] i.e. Keil's covering of the socle and at the southern side of the monument remained untouched. Also, a work group from the Kunsthistorisches Museum that visited Ephesos in the late 1970s in preparation for the Ephesos Museum, Vienna,[122] did not enter the burial chamber of the Octagon.[123] Only in 1982, i.e. 53 years after Keil's initial visit,[124] an adjacent excavation at the northern slope of Mount Preon (Terrace House 2) finally reached the lower Curetes Street and, thus, the Octagon (fig. 23; plan 3).[125] The debris on top of the Octagon's pedestal was removed[126] permitting access to Keil's opening into the vault again.[127] Upon entering the burial chamber for only the second time altogether,[128] the present authors (E.R., P.S.), at

Fig. 8: Skeletal remains within the western niche of the burial chamber's northern wall as left by the workers of Keil in 1929 (photo taken in 1982)

Fig. 9: Skeletal remains within the eastern niche of the burial chamber's northern wall as left by the workers of Keil in 1929 (photo taken in 1982)

2. THE SKELETAL REMAINS OF THE OCTAGON   41

this time still students, encountered the site just as J. Keil had left it,[129] providing an interesting insight into the early times of Ephesian archaeology (figs. 7–10a).[130]

The lid of the sarcophagus now stood upright against the chest (fig. 7), which was completely filled with water as it had been in 1929.[131] The inner door lay on the ground of the dromos (fig. 10a), and the outer one was closed shut, both again as Keil had left it in 1929.[132] Finally, the rubble with which Keil had filled up the southern space of the Octagon was removed and the outer door was re-opened (fig. 10b).[133] In other words, this backfilling "down to the profile of the wall"[134] was not the primary one any more.[135]

As Keil had done in 1929, we emptied the chest of the water and removed the mud from the bottom into the sun outside in order to dry and sift it. Whereas Keil had found the skeleton of the Octagon's individual inside the sarcophagus in its largely original setting,[136] we could not retrieve skeletal remains from the chest any

Fig. 10: a) The entrance to the burial chamber as seen from the dromos with the inner door on the floor (photo taken in 1982). The left corner of the relieving triangle above the lintel bears the accumulation of bones as left by the workers of Keil in 1929. Note the Λ–placed slabs forming the ceiling of the dromos[142] and the stud holes at the lintel for the two pins, which originally held the door in place; b) Modern photograph of the southern side of the Octagon with the outer door of the dromos

more.[137] Instead, we saw bones distributed into the two niches of the chamber's northern wall (figs. 8f.), and others above the lintel at the inner end of the dromos (fig. 10a). Obviously, the workers of Keil had removed the bones from the sarcophagus into the two niches of the grave chamber,[138] before searching the mud of the chest for grave goods as we did.[139] Some worker may have returned the findings from this procedure into the tomb, this time, however, already through the open dromos and then only into the space above the lintel. Such a scenario may explain why some bones remained in the grave chamber, whereas others ended up at the inner end of the dromos.[140]

Our visit of the Octagon's burial chamber of 1982 remained undocumented; neither the EED nor the excavation report of that year mentions it.[141] However, this episode did not alter how Keil had left the burial, apart from the re–opening of the outer door of the dromos (fig. 10b).[143] In particular, we did not touch the skeletal remains. For that reason, Thür found that the bones had remained within the chamber's two niches (figs. 8f.) when re-entering the tomb in 1993.[144] For the first time, an investigation of the postcranial bones was assigned to E. Reuer[145] and S. Fabrizii–Reuer (tab. 2).[146] The anthropologists concluded an age of "15 to 16 years" of a female individual at the time of death,[147] thus confirming the result of J. Weninger from 1953 (tab. 3).[148] Furthermore, E. Reuer and S. Fabrizii–Reuer did not detect any trauma to the bones.[149] Although announced,[150] their analysis was never published.[151] However, the anthropologists discovered a remaining tooth within the sarcophagus,[152] with which H. Thür intended to screen the collections of the University of Greifswald where she supposed the Octagon's skull to be.[153]

In 1995, "a very precise and detailed three–dimensional survey of the octagon was carried out, which included a stone–by–stone survey of the burial chamber".[154] In 2005, B. Thuswaldner started a project aiming at the virtual "stone–by–stone reconstruction of the Octagon".[155] She still saw the bones within the dromos (fig. 10a).[156] Accordingly, it has to be assumed that only the postcranial bones from the two niches of the burial chamber had been removed and investigated by E. Reuer and S. Reuer-Fabrizii.

In 2007, a second anthropological examination of the postcranial skeleton by Kanz et al. took place, now including the material of the dromos,[157] whereby X–ray images of some long bones were performed.[158] The mandible remained missing.[159] The results of this investigation were not published beyond a conference poster (tab. 2),[160] wherein the developmental state of crucial osseous age indicators, including the medial clavicle,[161] the proximal humerus,[162] the distal radius,[163] and others were hardly specified in detail.[164] Nevertheless, the images of the bones presented by Kanz et al.[165] show, amongst other things, unfused epiphyses at the distal femur[166] and the proximal tibia[167] equalling a stage two of maturation according to the acknowledged classification.[168]

It is, however, impossible to apply age–related statistical parameters of contemporary studies regarding the developmental state of certain osseous age markers to a skeleton from more than 2,000 years ago. The only conclusion that can be drawn from the images of the skeleton that were provided by Kanz et al. concerns the unfinished osseous differentiation of the Octagon's individual at the time of death.[169] In keeping with that, Kanz et al. repeated the age estimation of Reuer, Fabrizii–Reuer,[170] and of Weninger:[171] "Assessing all the results together an age between 15 to 17 seems to be the most reliable" (tab. 3).[172]

Kanz et al. added that "the whole skeleton appeared to belong to a slim and fragile individual [of] 154 cm (+/- 3 cm)"[173] body height quite in line with the remark of Cassius Dio that the crowds pitied Arsinoë IV, when she was exposed at Caesar's victory parade in 46 BC.[174] "Stress markers, like 'Harris' lines[175] were absent and no signs for heavy workload or pre– or perimortal traumas were found",[176] the latter as before.[177] Yet, traces of a killing by means of swords or knives leading to cuts on the bones are not to be expected, if the skeleton belonged to Arsinoë IV. One would like to think that even the assassins sent by Marcus Antonius[178] wanted to avoid bloodshed on holy ground, so that Arsinoë IV was presumably garrotted to death by means of a ligature.[179] Such an assumption, however, can only be proven by a possibly broken hyoid bone,[180] to which diagnosis an in-depth investigation of the Octagon's skeleton would be necessary.

Tab. 3: Examinations of the Octagon's skeleton

Year	Researchers	Age at death	Source/comment
1929/30	G. Just(?)[181]	Ca. 20 years	Keil 1930a, 45
1953	J. Weninger	16 – 17 years	Weninger 1953, 161
1995	E. Reuer, S. Fabrizii–Reuer	15 – 16 years	Thür 1995b, 92 n. 364
2004	K. Grossschmidt, F. Kanz[182]	–	DNA–sample taken from „a tarsal bone"[183]
2006	K. Grossschmidt, F. Kanz	–	DNA–sample taken from the left femur[184]
2009	Kanz et al.	15 – 17 years	Kanz et al. 2009
2010	M. Schultz, J. Nováček	–	New examinations[185]
2014	?	–	Samples taken for DNA and isotope analyses[186]
2016	?	–	Examination for age and gender[187]

Kanz et al. stated that "the diaphysis of the preserved long bones showed no signs of disproportion; therefore, an undisturbed growth of the individual can be assumed, [and that] signs of illnesses on the bones were absent".[188] In the end, Kanz et al. concluded:

The investigations could not disprove the theory on the origin of the remains being Arsinoe IV. But also, no identification could be definitively proven.[189]

Tab. 3 lists various attempts to gain information from the Octagon's skeleton since the very detection of the grave chamber in 1929, efforts that increased after Thür's proposal.[190] Apart from the impossibility of providing the mentioned exact chronological age statements,[191] altogether three independent anthropological examinations correspondingly concluded that the Octagon's female owner died in her adolescence, i.e. within her 2nd decade of life.[192] Based on these findings, the Octagon was neither erected for an elderly public official, a priest or a city's male benefactor,[193] nor was it built as "monarchic representation"[194] or as a self–display[195] of an otherwise prominent male personality. Instead, it was dedicated to a female individual of unfinished dental and skeletal differentiation, whose skull demonstrated "a calm, undisturbed development",[196] as the post cranium showed "undisturbed growth", and the absence of "signs of illnesses".[197]

According to anthropological examinations, an adolescent female individual of "undisturbed" osseous development was buried within the Octagon.

In conclusion, the developmental state of the Octagon's skeleton does not "contradict",[198] but conforms well with the biographical details of Arsinoë IV as mentioned by ancient sources. Represented by a *nutricius*, she was highly probably below twelve years of age in 48 BC, and below nineteen years in 41 BC at the time of her death. Such a conspicuous coincidence is the first strong argument that the Octagon represents her mausoleum.

SINCE THE DEVELOPMENTAL STATE OF THE OCTAGON'S SKELETON CORRESPONDS WELL WITH THE BIOGRAPHICAL DETAILS OF ARSINOË IV AS REPORTED BY ANCIENT SOURCES, THE QUESTION ARISES WHETHER THE ERECTION DATE OF THE BUILDING COMES CLOSE TO ARSINOË'S DEATH IN 41 BC.

3. The date of the Octagon's construction

The dating of the Octagon has been addressed repeatedly in the past.[199] Amongst the first contributions is that of W. Wilberg who dated the mausoleum around 50 BC.[200] In his first–edition guide to Ephesos from 1915, J. Keil placed the monument in the 1st c. BC.[201] Such was the chronological perspective, before the Octagon's burial chamber was opened.

3.1 One author, one year, two datings

Fifteen years later, J. Keil published the second edition of the Ephesos guide[202] as well as the excavation report of the 1929 campaign (tab. 2).[203] Although both texts were printed in the same year of 1930, a remarkable disparity is found regarding his dating of the Octagon. Whereas Keil remained vague in the excavation report ("between the first c. BC and the first c. AD"),[204] he attributed the Octagon to a specific historical period in the Ephesos guide ("into early Roman times"),[205] a surprising change, for which he ought to have had a reason. In this regard, one might contemplate a passage from his excavation report:

> *Only if it should prove possible in some way to identify the person buried in the heroon, it will also be possible to determine the time. Such a determination of the owner is not quite as hopeless as it might appear at first sight. For if, on the one hand, it must have been a very distinguished person who was buried all alone in the stately heroon, the head skeleton shows that this person died at the young age of about 20 years. And should the impression gained by my colleagues in Greifswald during the examination of the skull be confirmed, another clue would be gained; for we would then have to reckon with a young woman as the owner of the heroon.*[206]

Obviously, Keil saw a possibility to identify the individual to whom the mausoleum was dedicated. As it seems, the recognition of its young female owner led him to a reconsideration of his chronological approach. Although Keil never communicated whom he had in mind,[207] it is a reasonable assumption that he reflected on Arsinoë IV as a female candidate for the Octagon, since he undoubtedly knew[208] that she was killed in Ephesos in about "early Roman times".[209] One might argue that Keil even forwarded such an idea to J. Weninger later on, since the latter, somewhat erratically, placed the Octagon's skull next to "Greek–Egyptian mummy portraits [...] and mummy heads from Thebes" in his article from 1953. In so doing, he addressed the notion as far as possible from his perspective.[210] However, Keil never communicated such a suspicion, instead calling the mausoleum's owner "apparently a girl or a young woman" from 1930 onwards.[211]

3.2 Pre–Augustan and Augustan

In 1974, W. Alzinger[212] dated the Octagon from its architectural features "most likely at the beginning of the Augustan period, and hardly much earlier",[213] an opinion that was also shared by H. Thür in 1989 ("from Augustan times").[214] Only one year later, in 1990, Thür described the Ephesian mausoleum as the grave of Arsinoë IV. Because of Arsinoë's death after the meeting in Tarsos in 42/41 BC,[215] she assumed that the mausoleum was erected either straightaway in 41 BC[216] or within the "third quarter of the first c. BC",[217] and, accordingly, at the behest of Marcus Antonius and Kleopatra VII.[218] In other words, Arsinoë's death year and Marcus Antonius and Kleopatra VII as the contracting authorities assumed by her for the Octagon are inextricably linked in Thür's argumentation. Hence, it became a problem for her[219] when subsequent excavations at the southern side of the Octagon (fig. 10b) confirmed Keil's and Alzinger's assessment[220] and placed the building rather into the fourth quarter of the 1st c. BC[221] and hence *after* the suicides of Marcus Antonius and *ultimae Cleopatrae Alexandrinorum reginae*.[222] Accordingly, there is a time gap between Arsinoë's death and the erection of the Octagon as her supposed tomb,[223] a fact that requires an explanation,[224] if the monument represents her mausoleum.

3.3 The time gap

Indeed, it is hardly conceivable that Kleopatra VII and Marcus Antonius would have instigated the building of a monument in 41 BC reminding people of their hideous deed.[225] Likewise, the Ephesians would not have seen a reason at the time to draw attention to Antonius' blasphemy by means of a memorial within the city centre.[226] At that point, one might consider that Ephesos held an important position as the base of his Parthian strategy in the seventh decade of the 1st c. BC.[227] In other words, if the Octagon refers to Arsinoë's sacrilegious murder, it should not date before Kleopatra VII and Marcus Antonius vanished into political irrelevance in 30 BC.[228]

Following this reasoning, there has to be a difference in time between Arsinoë's murder and the erection of the Octagon as her supposed tomb. A memorial to the circumstances of her death would have appeared utterly inappropriate between 41 and 30 BC; an unspectacular primary burial of Arsinoë's body would most likely have been favoured. Accordingly, a mausoleum for her should only date after the 'Ptolemaic War' as suggested by W. Huß,[229] C. Bennett,[230] and G. Plattner.[231] Retaining Thür's hypothesis, Plattner assumes, therefore, Augustus himself as the contracting authority of the Octagon[232] and proposes that Arsinoë's body was relocated from an initial setting into the later tomb.[233]

Regarding the dating of the Octagon, no further clarification was gained from recent examinations of its marbles. Samples were taken from different parts of the structure that could be assigned to three quarry–sites near Ephesos[234] partly related to the Artemision.[235] Obviously, the stone was selected due to the different qualities deemed necessary for the architecture of the superstructure ("white marble of high quality [...] medium–grained"),[236] the vault and the sarcophagus ("coarse–grained and very massive").[237] In particular, the marble of the "simple sarcophagus"[238] probably comes from the quarry of Tavşan tepe ("Ab–u Hayat quarry")[239] that was exploited in "the late Hellenistic or early Augustan period".[240] Considering the fact that the sarcophagus fits tightly into the burial chamber (fig. 7) and must, therefore, have been moved into place during the construction of the room, i.e. in the early building phase of the monument, both should date contemporaneously.[241]

Accordingly, the entire Octagon's marble is of local origin, and the stone of the sarcophagus comes from a site that was exploited in "the late Hellenistic or early Augustan period". The recognition that the quarries partly lead into the sphere of the Artemision, underpins Huß' suggestion, whereby the *Megabyzos*, the High Priest of the Artemision, may have commissioned the Octagon.[242]

There is a time gap between Arsinoë's death in 41 BC and the erection of the Octagon after the 'Ptolemaic War'.

In conclusion, the construction date of the Octagon closely aligns with the time of Arsinoë's death, although there is a time gap between 41 BC and the period when the mausoleum was built after the 'Ptolemaic War'. This delay does not contradict Thür's hypothesis[243] but only challenges her assumption about the contracting authority.[244] Instead, the shift appears quite comprehensible if not even inevitable. Considering her scandalous murder, a tomb for Arsinoë IV was only possible after Kleopatra VII and Marcus Antonius ended their lives in 30 BC, resulting in a changed political situation. One might think that the body of Arsinoë IV was secondarily relocated from an initial interment into the Octagon. Such reasoning is indeed strongly supported by Keil´s precise surveillance that the skeleton was stored in the coffer "on soil and small stones" (see above). While soil may have easily been swept into the sarcophagus by repeated floodings, stones cannot be explained by those. Accordingly, the corpse was moved into the sarcophagus inside an already (partly) cankered – and thus with soil and stones polluted – wooden coffin that completely disintegrated over time.

IF THE SACRILEGIOUS KILLING OF ARSINOË IV FORMS THE ACTUAL BACKGROUND FOR THE DELAYED ERECTION OF THE OCTAGON, SUCH A BLASPHEMY SHOULD HAVE BEEN HIGHLIGHTED BY THE ANCIENT SOURCES.

4. Arsinoë's assassination within the Artemisian *asylum*

Both Flavius Josephus and Appianos do not simply report Arsinoë's murder. Rather, the ancient authors accentuate that Arsinoë IV was put to death by Kleopatra VII and Marcus Antonius, *although* she was considered a supplicant[245] within the Artemision[246] and therefore under divine protection.[247] Cassius Dio mentions the sacrilegious killing of Kleopatra's "siblings" as the consequence of Antonius' moral depravity caused by her.[248] In other words, the violation of Artemisian divine territory[249] is emphasised, equalling an act of temple desecration (ἱεροσύλία)[250] doubtless causing 'maculation'[251] that demanded compensation, if not a "punishment deserved".[252] Moreover, the sacrilege was not committed at just any sanctuary, but within the boundaries of the foremost *asylum* altogether.[253]

4.1 The Artemisian *asylum* – a delicate issue

The purity of the Artemisian precinct (Temenos)[254] was a sensitive issue for Ephesos. Since time immemorial, the shrine had been not only a preferred focus of pilgrimage;[255] it also stored money deposits,[256] which were protected by the inviolability of the holy grounds. Consequently, the implications of the mere possibility of ἱεροσυλία within the Artemision must have seemed catastrophic to Ephesos, all the more as such a sacrilege committed by the Ephesians themselves during the 'Mithridatic War' ('Ephesian Vespers')[257] some decades earlier was surely not forgotten at that time.[258] Probably, the "asylia [of the Artemision] was abolished as a result of the killing of Roman partisans who took refuge there in 88 BC"[259] or at least the *asylum* was "restricted".[260] Nevertheless, it must have been reinstated before 44 BC according to an inscription from Sardes which refers to the Ephesian Artemision as the prime example of a sacred *asylum*.[261] In other words, Arsinoë IV sought divine protection in the Artemision around the time when the *asylum* was reinstated.

Considering such a *terminus ante quem* of 44 BC, it is worth noting that C. Iulius Caesar protected the funds of the Artemision.[262] He was praised in Ephesos as the "saviour of human life",[263] and a statue was erected for him.[264] The 'Pharsalian Era', a new calendar starting with 48 BC, was introduced in Ephesos as a reminder of his victory over Pompeius.[265] In line with such tributes, C. Iulius Caesar or the *proconsul* P. Servilius Isauricus in his name, who was venerated as a god in Ephesos even in the 2nd c. AD, may have re-established the Artemisian *asylum* between 48 and 44 BC, and in so doing renewing one of the basic Ephesian foundations.[266] The desecration of the territory of the Artemision by Marcus Antonius occurred shortly after that, once again endangering the reputation of the sanctuary. It can be assumed that Marcus Antonius was aware of the effect of his deeds.[267] In this light, his activities regarding the Artemision might be considered as compensations. He enlarged the territory of the Artemisian *asylum*,[268] and he donated a generous sacrifice to the city's goddess.[269]

Ancient sources emphasise the sacrilegious character of Arsinoë's murder equalling an act of temple desecration.

In summary, ancient sources highlight the blasphemous character of Arsinoë's murder, which desecrated the territory of the Artemision in a manner reminiscent of the 'Ephesian Vespers'. Such ἱεροσυλία constituted a significant threat to the economic well–being of Ephesos, since its prosperity relied in large part on this aspect of the shrine.[270] Accordingly, Ephesos and the Artemision should have had the utmost interest to restore the reputation of the sanctuary. After the suicides of Kleopatra VII and Marcus Antonius, the erection of a memorial intended as the mausoleum for Arsinoë IV might have seemed appropriate to pay tribute to Artemis and as a manner of demonstrating that one of Ephesos' most important traits, namely the inviolability of Artemisian grounds, was functional again. In accordance with that, Huß agrees with Thür's allocation, but suggests that it was the *Megabyzos* of the Artemision who commissioned the Octagon.[271] However, the erection of a monument addressing ἱεροσυλία on Artemisian grounds was decidedly a delicate task that demanded caution and care. Perhaps because of that, a *direct* reference to Arsinoë IV was avoided on the Octagon. It should be assumed, however, that any Ephesian citizen would have known about the circumstances leading to the erection of the memorial at the time.[272]

> IF THEN THE OCTAGON SUPPOSEDLY BEARS A RELATIONSHIP TO THE ARTEMISION, THE VERY SITE OF ITS ERECTION SHOULD REFLECT THAT.

5. The site of the Octagon

Because of its location, Keil considered the Octagon as "a heroon [...] in a privileged place".[273] Later on, it was recognised that the Ephesian mausoleum represents just one of a number of heroa at this specific site of the city (figs. 49, 64),[274] a fact that highlights the significance the place would have carried.[275]

5.1 The "Triodos"

The Octagon was built at the "Triodos" ("Threeway"; figs. 27, 36f.; plan 4)[276] where the street from the Ephesian theatre turns into the one leading to the 'Upper Agora' and further on to the city gate on the road to Magnesia (plan 1). A third route, the processional road arriving from the Ortygian sanctuary,[277] the mythical birth grove of Apollon and Artemis,[278] discharges into the junction.[279] The importance of the Triodos for the Artemis cult (ἱερὸς τόπος) has been outlined.[280] D. Knibbe[281] relates the large altar (fig. 44; plan 4) adjoining the 'Library of Celsus' (fig. 66; plans 1 and 3) to Artemis,[282] a monument that was never investigated completely.[283] Quite remarkable in this context is the fact that a classicising Amazon relief of Sciarra type (figs. 45, 71)[284] was found together with some architectural elements "of similar workmanship" not far away, i.e. next to the Ephesian theatre (plan 1).[285] According to W. Wilberg, this set of worked pieces ought to have belonged to a monument in the vicinity.[286] Likewise, Knibbe attributes an inscription with an oracle of Apollon that was found nearby to the Artemis altar (fig. 44; plan 4).[287] Further references to Artemis are found at the Triodos (figs. 27, 36f.). The Gate of Mazaios and Mithridates (= Agora South Gate; figs. 41–43; plans 1 and 3) displays images of Artemis (fig. 43),[288] while depictions of the Amazonian mythology were applied to the frieze zone of the so–called Temple of Hadrian (figs. 69f., 72; plans 1 and 3) diagonally opposite the Octagon.[289] Furthermore, a base with a worn relief of Artemis was found close by.[290]

Hence, the Octagon was not erected at just any "prominent" place.[291] A place of outstanding importance for the Artemis cult was chosen, one that was supposedly dominated by a large intraurban Artemis altar (fig. 44; plan 4).[292]

The location chosen for the Octagon demonstrates a meaningful connection to the Artemis cult.

In summary, the very site of the Octagon's erection indicates its strong relationship to the Artemision. Accordingly, the outstanding importance of the Octagon's young female occupant for the Artemision can be deduced. The circumstances of Arsinoë's nefarious killing fit well into such a setting, as well as Huß' suggestion regarding the Artemision as the contracting authority of the Octagon.

> SINCE THE OCTAGON RELATES TO THE ARTEMIS CULT BECAUSE OF ITS LOCATION, THE LAYOUT OF THE BUILDING MIGHT REFER TO SUCH A CONTEXT TOO.

6. The shape of the Octagon

6.1 Octagonality

The striking characteristic of the Ephesian mausoleum is found in its strict adherence to an octagonal, i.e. to a geometrical principle (figs. 11a, 12). A square pedestal supports

> ➤ An octagonal *krepis* with
> ➤ An octastyle *peristasis*, whereby the columns are *"arranged according to the corners"*[293] of
> ➤ An octagonal pseudo-*cella* with
> ➤ An octagonal entablature, and
> ➤ An octagonal stepped pyramidal roof presenting eight isosceles roof areas.[294]

Octagonal architecture is scarce at the time of the Ephesian tomb's erection and the recognition that the Octagon stands at the beginning of an eminent architectural tradition where this geometry is applied,[295] is of little help in tracing its origins.[296] Yet, the Ephesian mausoleum is by no means a polygon without earlier and contemporary parallels.[297]

The oldest known octagonal monument from Greek antiquity[298] is mentioned in various ancient and medieval sources and appears to have been a tomb in Catania.[299] According to Suetonius (1st/2nd c. AD), Iulius Pollux (2nd c. AD),[300] and others,[301] the renowned lyricist Stesichoros of Himera (ca. 640/630–555 BC)[302] was buried in a sepulchre described as having "eight pillars, eight steps and eight corners",[303] hence the phrase 'πάντα ὀκτώ' (everything in eights,[304] eightfold in every respect,[305] or everything eight).[306] Probably because of this famous tomb, 'Stesichoros' was proclaimed, when the number of dice eyes in the astragal game amounted to eight.[307] In other words, "the structure of the Catanese tomb apparently gave birth to a motto".[308]

W. Alzinger[309] relates the Ephesian Octagon to the 'Tower of the Winds' at Athens, which represents the earliest example of a preserved antique octagonal edifice.[310] In order to explain its eight–fold structure, Vitruvius connects the latter to the eight winds, thus putting it into a meteorological context.[311] Probably because of this *horologium*[312] and the middle tier of the Pharos Tower,[313] H. Thiersch[314] calls the building type of the 'octagon' "a Hellenistic layout"[315] and a concept of "Alexandrian tradition".[316] He discusses the 'Tower of Abusir' located in a cemetery outside of Taposiris Magna.[317] Thiersch states that the monument might have been erected secondarily over a grave due to differences concerning technicality and orientation between the building and its *hypogeum*.[318] Von Hesberg refers to an octagon in Pola.[319] Another octagonal comparison is the (Augustan?) Tour Magne in Nîmes of undecided purpose, which supposedly also had a relationship to Egypt.[320] The Arsinoeion of Samothrake received an octagonal roof in "early imperial times".[321]

Finally, a highly interesting funeral monument that should date about contemporarily to the Ephesian mausoleum,[322] has been found in the north-eastern French département of Haut-Marne.[323] In Faverolles near Langres, a mausoleum or a cenotaph[324] was detected consisting of three building levels of Corinthian order once rising to a height of about 24 m.[325] A square pedestal (width 7.7m at the bottom and with a dedication)[326] supported an octagonal middle part, and an octastyle canopy with a centre column and a polygonal pyramidal roof that remarkably culminates in a large Corinthian top capital (fig. 11b),[327] a finial that it shares with the *horologium* at Athens.[328] The "oak wreaths" at the basis of the third-level *tholos* are reminiscent of the analogous garland frieze at the Ephesian Memmius Monument (fig. 19c).[329]

Fig. 11: a) The model of the "temple–like" Octagon in the Ephesos Museum, Vienna (KHM); b) The reconstruction of the funeral monument at Faverolles with an octagonal middle tier, an octastyle tholos, and a curved octagonal roof structure

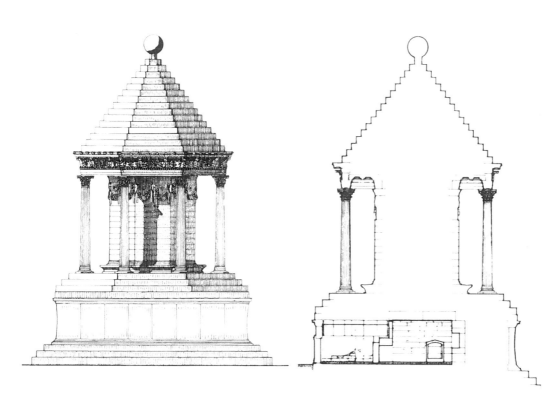

Fig. 12: Wilberg's drawings of the Octagon from 1904: a) a reconstructed elevation. Note the fifteen steps of Wilberg's roof;[334] b) a cross section along a north/south vertical plane that was amended by M. Theuer,[335] who inserted the burial chamber in 1929. Note the two doors at the inner and the outer end of the dromos

6.2 A 'temple–mausoleum'

When Austrian researchers discovered the remnants of the collapsed Octagon in 1904 (figs. 3f.), its burial character was not recognised.[330] Instead, R. Heberdey described the monument quite rightly as "a temple-like building without an interior" (figs. 11a, 12),[331] i.e. without an inner *sanctum*. Still, a false door maintains the illusion of a *cella*.[332] Only upon the detection of the grave chamber within the pedestal in 1929 did the meaning of the building become clear (figs. 6f., 12b).[333] Somewhat puzzled, J. Keil described the tomb as a "peculiar edifice [...] not easily classified".[336] Von Hesberg lists the Octagon under "special forms".[337] S. Cormack describes it as an "intramural memorial building with burial",[338] and Anevlavi et al. simply as a "grave of honour".[339] I. Kader shows her "surprise":

> *In view of the octagon's location, however, one is completely surprised by the burial chamber in its base, which contained a sarcophagus [...]. At first glance, the octagon's function as a funerary building is not apparent, for its construction [...] rather belongs to the realm of conventional monument architecture [...]. There seems to be an insurmountable conflict between the form chosen for its structure and its actual function. The question therefore arises as to what prompted the builder to present the tomb construction in such a way that it no longer appeared as a tomb in the context of the memorial buildings on the Curetes Street.*[340]

Accordingly, the Octagon is, in fact, a grave, but it appears as a monument from the religious sphere (figs. on jacket, 11a, 12) although with the "peculiarity" of an octagonal feature with hardly any comparable funeral examples from its time.[341] In order to relate the tomb to Arsinoë IV, Thür emphasised, amongst other notions,[342] precisely the unusual polygonal aspect, considering it a "citation" of the middle tier of the Alexandrian Pharos Tower (fig. 13):[343]

> *Of the building forms [...] the octagonal form can be associated with Egypt or rather Alexandria [...]. My suggestion to see Arsinoe IV in the tomb of the octagon would find important support if one interpreted the octagonal structure of the heroon as a quotation of the characteristic octagonal central part of the Pharos [...]. The octagonal shape, new for a tomb, symbolised the emblem of Alexandria and thus inevitably established the connection with the Ptolemaic princess [...]. On the tomb in Ephesos, therefore, the use of the octagonal form is to be interpreted as a symbol for the origin and person of the tomb's owner.*[344]

In other words, Thür suggested that the Octagon's contracting authority (Kleopatra VII and Marcus Antonius according to her)[345] intended a pars pro toto reference to the Alexandrian Pharos (fig. 13), which would have announced the Egyptian background of the tomb's owner and which would also have been understood as such by a contemporary onlooker. Accordingly, the questions arise

➢ whether the Alexandrian Pharos Tower would have been taken as an Egyptian or Alexandrian symbol at the time of the Octagon's erection, and

➢ whether an association between the two monuments was indeed likely for a contemporary bystander.

> ONE OF THÜR'S ARGUMENTS TO CONNECT THE OCTAGON TO ARSINOË IV CONCERNS A POSTULATED TYPOLOGICAL RELATIONSHIP BETWEEN THE EPHESIAN MAUSOLEUM AND THE MIDDLE SECTION OF THE ALEXANDRIAN PHAROS TOWER.

6.3 The Alexandrian lighthouse

Located on the island of Pharos,[346] the Alexandrian lighthouse was a well-known monument of fame in its era (fig. 13), although not yet integrated into the early lists of the "Seven Wonders of the World".[347] It was used as a model and generic name for a lighthouse in general. Claudius built an *altissimam turrem in exemplum Alexandrini Phari*[348] at the *Portus Romae*,[349] while Juvenal names the *Tyrrhenamque pharon*.[350] Also, Valerius Flaccus addresses the Tyrrhenean lighthouse as *Pharos*.[351] Suetonius calls the lighthouse of Capri *turris phari*.[352] Referring to the Pharos, Plinius states that the Romans built "similar fires" in Ostia (= *Portus Romae*) and Ravenna.[353]

Furthermore, ancient authors quite often make use of the attribute *Pharius*[354] and Φάριος[355] taking it metonymously for (Macedonian) Egypt and Alexandria.[356] Martialis speaks of the *Phariis armis*,[357] the *Phariae coniugis arma*,[358] the *Pharios Memphiticus hortos,*[359] and the *Pharia Memphiticus urbe*.[360] Remarkably, he names the *nutricius* of Ptolemaios XIII the *Pharius* [...] Pothinos, i.e. the Egyptian or Alexandrian Pothinos.[361] Statius mentions the *Phariis agris*[362] and Lucanus the *Phariae harenae*.[363] The latter calls the Nile *Pharias aspidas*[364] and its flood the *Phariae undae*.[365] Iuvenalis states that the Senatorian wife Eppia "ran off with the gladiators to Pharos", i.e. to Egypt or Alexandria.[366] Ausonius addresses the Alexandrian Arsinoeion as *Pharium templum*,[367] and he mentions the *Memphitica Pharos*.[368] A connection to Ephesos is *Isis Pharia*[369] who was – at least according to the romance of Apuleius – also worshipped in the temple of Ephesos.[370] Concerning her cult, Apuleius mentions the *phariaticum sistrum*[371] and Statius the *Phariae iuuencae*.[372] The list could be extended; it includes amongst others Ovidius, Valerius Flaccus, Tertullianus, and Claudianus later on.

Most importantly, the Ptolemies were similarly addressed. Carmen de bello Actiaco indicates *Phariis* [...] *regnis*,[373] Lucanus names the *Pharios reges*,[374] the *regna*

Phari,[375] and *Phario tyranno.*[376] He calls Kleopatra VII *Pharii proles clarissima Lagi.*[377] Kleopatra VII says: "I am not the first woman to rule the cities of the Nile; for Pharos knows how to bear a Queen without distinction because of gender."[378]

Finally, it is worth noting that Arsinoë IV was placed next to an allegory of the Nile and an effigy of "the Pharos similarly burning flames"[379] at Caesar's triumph of 46 BC in order to demonstrate the Alexandrian background of the *pompa.*[380] In light of the statements above and considering the strategic importance of the Pharos Tower and of the Nile during the 'Alexandrian War',[381] such a presentation appears quite self-explanatory.

Within ancient sources, the Pharos Tower is used in order to illustrate an Alexandrian or Lagid–Egyptian background.

In conclusion, the Alexandrian Pharos Tower was indeed used to characterise an Egyptian or Alexandrian background within ancient sources.

IF THE PHAROS TOWER WAS TAKEN METONYMOUSLY FOR EGYPT AND ALEXANDRIA, THE QUESTION ARISES WHETHER THE EPHESIAN OCTAGON IS INDEED REMINISCENT OF IT.

6.4 The Octagon – a 'Pharian' edifice?

From the very beginning, Thür's logic whereby "the octagonal shape [...] symbolised the emblem of Alexandria and thus inevitably established the connection with the Ptolemaic princess" suffered from an obvious problem.[383] The Ephesian mausoleum is by no means reminiscent of the *luminis mons*;[384] no one would have drawn such an association merely from the appearance of the monument. Sostratos[385] placed a huge polygon of about 30 m in height on top of a likewise gigantic pedestal of about 60 m, which in turn carried a circular canopy (fig. 13).[386] In contrast to that, a viewer in antiquity who observed the Ephesian Octagon probably saw nothing more than the usual sequence of a socle, a *monopteros*[387] with a polygonal *cella*–like core, the whole crowned by a stepped roof structure (figs. cover, 11a, 12).[388] The fact that Arsinoë IV was presented next to a burning effigy of the Pharos tower at Caesar's *pompa* in 46 BC,[389] hardly substantiates the connection of an octagonal mausoleum in Ephesos to Arsinoë IV.[390]

Accordingly, only a few authors support Thür in her reasoning.[391] Mostly, Thür's assumption has been met with disagreement.[392] C. Berns states, "one will hardly be able to assign such a precise meaning to the octagonal form".[393] I. Kader denies a meaning of the octagonal shape altogether[394] and rejects Thür's proposal with the interesting argument that the layout of the Octagon "speaks against a monar-

chic owner",[395] i.e. against a monarchic principal authority. W. Huß considers Thür's connection of the grave to the Pharos octagon as "less likely".[396] R. Fleischer sees no sense in the "citation" of a functional building at a mausoleum.[397] Anevlavi et al. call Thür's comparison of the Octagon to the Pharos "not completely convincing",[398] and M. Spanu "estremamente fragile".[399] H. Schörner even says, "the desire to see a Ptolemaic princess in the dead woman seems to have been at the root of this thought".[400]

Fig. 13: a) The Ephesian mausoleum (figs. 11a, 12) by no means recalls the *mons luminis* of Alexandria; b) The view into a vault of the Qāitbāy citadel[382] from the 15th c. AD built on the site of the Pharos and echoing its threefold geometry

The Octagon does not reflect the Alexandrian Pharos Tower,
at least not directly.

Still, the fact remains that the Ephesian mausoleum is one of only a few early edifices displaying an octagonal principle, a feature that, therefore, ought to have been selected with a certain intention.[401] Consequently, another reason has to be explored in order to explain the unusual layout. In this regard, the centrally planned, octagonal building with its multiple axes of symmetry suggests that a geometrical rationale was applied to the ground plan.

THÜR'S CONNECTION OF THE OCTAGON TO THE ALEXANDRIAN PHAROS WAS MET WITH DOUBTS SO THAT ANOTHER REASON FOR THE TOMB'S EXCEPTIONAL LAYOUT HAS TO BE SOUGHT.

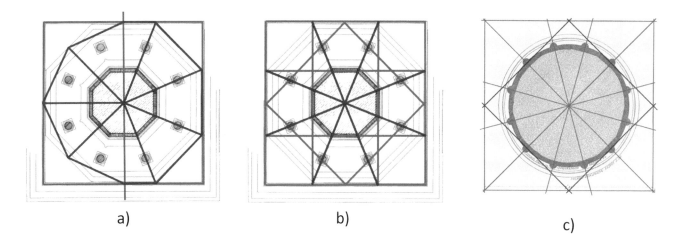

a)   b)   c)

Fig. 14: a) The two main ways of inscribing a regular octagon into a reference square, from which the Octagons architect chose the version on the right side; b) The flights and points of the Octagon as resulting from the differentiation of a reference square into a certain geometrical pattern; c) The ground plan of the Round Monument on the Panayırdağ is based on the incircle radius of r^2 concentrically inscribed into the reference square (fig. 16a)

6.5 Geometry provides a lot of support to the architect

It has been generally accepted that ancient Greek architects utilised geometrical concepts to lay out the ground plan of buildings.[402] With regard to the Roman era, M. Tullius Cicero (1st c. BC) says: "Among them [i.e. the Greeks], geometry was held in the highest honour, and, therefore, no one was more distinguished among mathematicians. But we have limited the use of this art to the measurement and calculation of practical matters".[403] Sextus Iulius Frontinus (1st c. AD) even calls the "celebrated works of the Greeks pointless".[404] M. Vitruvius Pollio who wrote his "Ten Books on Architecture" at about the time when the Octagon was built, repeatedly refers to Greek architects[405] and highlights the value of geometry in architecture.[406] An architect should be, therefore, "versed in geometry".[407] In addition, Vitruvius emphasises the importance of *eurythmia*[408] and *symmetria*[409] in architecture, both terms that address the need of proportionality with regard to the relationship of the parts to the whole.

However, one should bear in mind that the main means available for constructing a plan at the time were the beam compass and the straight edge,[410] so that the Octagon's ground plan should be considered as the result of 'practical geometry', and hardly any understanding of the analytical geometry involved would be required.[411] Accordingly, the square[412] and the circle[413] should form the basis of the construction plan. Vitruvius states that the proposal for a building was presented to the contracting authority by means of ground (*ichno–graphia*)[414] and elevation drawings (*ortho–graphia*).[415] Accordingly, an understanding of the Octagon's rationale may commence from there.

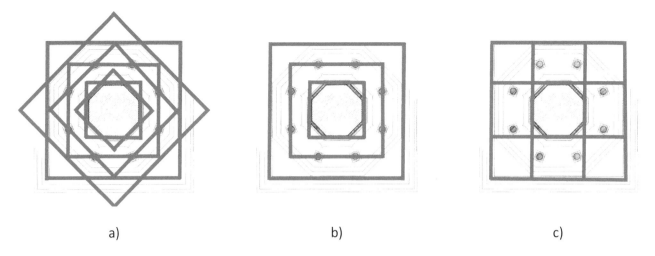

Fig. 15: The flights and points of the Octagon's drawing plan at the intersections of various geometric patterns all related to each other. a) Three concentric interlocking pairs of squares, whereby the inner couple deviates from the 'ad quadratum' sequence; b) Three concentric squares with side parallelism forming the basis of three inscribed octagons (the outer Q_1 with $s_o = 1$, the middle Q_2 with $s_m = r$, the inner Q_3 with $s_i = \sqrt{2}-1$; c) The $\sqrt{2}$–grid with nine proportionally related areas: $x = (\sqrt{2}-1)^2/2$ at the edges, $\sqrt{2}x = (\sqrt{2}-1)^2/\sqrt{2}$ at the sides and $2x = (\sqrt{2}-1)^2$ in the centre, i.e. $x : \sqrt{2}x : \sqrt{2}\sqrt{2}x$ (all values in a unit square)

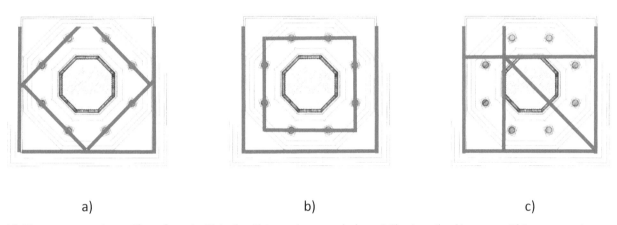

Fig. 16: Three geometric motifs as found within the Octagon's ground plan. a) The inscribed 'square within a square', whereby the inner one is tilted by 45° ($A = r^2 = s^2/2$); b) The inscribed 'square within a square' with side parallelism ($A = r^2 = s^2/2$) having its vertices at the midpoints of the four smaller squares at the corners (fig. 15c); c) The 'square within a square', whereby r^2 is located at a corner of the reference square and the smaller square at the opposite, the latter with the side length $= (\sqrt{2}-1)/\sqrt{2}$ and the diagonal $= s_8$. The accentuated diagonal of $r^2 = s$ (all values in a unit square)

6.6 *Ichnographia* and *Orthographia*

The starting point of the Octagon's ground plan is a reference square of about 9 by 9 m (approximately 30 by 30 feet).[416] Fig. 14a shows the two main ways of inscribing a regular octagon into a square.[417] As can be seen, the difference concerns the four main axes of the polygon. On the left scheme of fig. 14a, those run along the diagonals and the medians of the reference square, so that the octagon's sides are tilted in relation to the sides of the reference square. The Octagon's architect, however, chose the scheme presented in fig. 14a on the right side,[418] which partly presents side parallelism.[419]

From each of the four vertices[420] of the reference square, the radius[421] of its circuit (r)[422] is measured to both adjoining sides (s) denoting eight points[423] altogether (figs. 14b, 18b). These eight points also occur if the reference square is concentrically tilted by 45° (figs. 15a, 18b) resulting in the motif of the paired interlocking squares. By connecting each of these points to its counterpart diagonally across, the four main axes[424] of a regular octagon occur (fig. 14b). In a subsequent step, these eight points are connected to their opposite counterparts, providing the edges of the octagonal pseudo–*cella* at the intersections with the octagonal axes (fig. 14b). Logically, the centre square is also delineated when inscribing r^2 from opposite edges of the reference square (fig. 16c).[425] Outlining finally r^2 tilted by 45° into the reference square (fig. 16a), the sides of such a square provide the locations of the columns, again at the intersections with the axes of the octagon (fig. 14b).[426] As a result, the Octagon's ground plan is characterised by three pairs of interlocked squares[427] resulting in three inscribed octagons that are all based on the ratio r/s of the corresponding three squares,[428] whereby the inner couple deviates from an *ad quadratum* sequence (fig. 15a).[429] However, no geometrical ideal can be expected from the finally realised Octagon. For one thing, it is not based on a completely symmetrical square.[430] In addition, the building consists of individually manufactured pieces of stone from multiple hands, obviously leaving room for slight aberrations.[431]

In summary, the ground plan of the Octagon is easily drawn with few steps.[432] It is based on a certain geometrical pattern (fig. 14b) that served as the construction guide for everything that was outlined within, and, thus, determined all crucial points and flights,[433] i.e. the octagonal krepis, the octastyle peristasis and the solid octagonal pseudo–cella (fig. 14b).[434] If seen from the perspective of this 'practical geometry', the chronologically closely related Round Monument on the Panayırdağ (fig. 60; plan 1),[435] was constructed from a similar geometrical design (fig. 14c),[436] a possibility that might also be found at the Ephesian Memmius Monument at the upper end of the Curetes Street (figs. 19c, 58f.; plans 1 and 3).[437] Accordingly, it comes as no surprise that the coffered ceilings of all three monuments address some of the applied geometrical motifs.[438] However, the motif of fig. 16c is already seen on an Aeginetan stater from the 5th/4th c. BC.[439] In addition, there is an incision on a stone slab that was found in the Galerian complex of Thessaloniki.[440] The image shows a sequence of interlocked paired squares inscribed into an outer square overlaid by a dense pattern of centrifugal rays and concentric circles (fig. 18a),[441] whereby the inner geometry embodies an exact replica of the Octagon's ground plan (fig. 15a). Since a 4th c. octagon was detected at the finding site of the slab, attempts were made to relate the incision to it.[442]

6.7 Euklidean geometry

Without much effort, some basic Euklidean geometry[443] is found within the rationale of the Octagon's floor plan. First of all, the Pythagorean Theorem[444] describes the relationship of the parameter of a square, i.e., of the diagonal (d), the side length (s), and the radius of the circuit (r = d/2). From the corresponding isosceles right triangles[445] of a square result $2s^2 = d^2$ or $\sqrt{2}s = d$, $2r^2 = s^2$ or $\sqrt{2}r = s$, and $2(s/2)^2 = r^2$ or $\sqrt{2}(s/2) = r$.[446] In other words, $d/s = s/r = r/(s/2) = \sqrt{2}$.[447] Accordingly, the main parameters of a square (d, s, r) are related to each other by the incommensurable,[448] i.e. irrational[449] number $\sqrt{2}$ ($\approx 7/5$) that can be drawn,[450] but not ultimately calculated.[451]

If the side length (s) and the circuit's radius (r) of a reference square are related by $\sqrt{2}$ (s/r = $\sqrt{2}$), then the measuring of r into s from both ends of the latter results in the same proportion of the three subsequent segments, i.e. $2\Delta_{s-r}/s\text{-}2\Delta_{s-r} = s\text{-}2\Delta_{s-r}/\Delta_{s-r} = \sqrt{2}$, whereby the middle segment equals the side length of the regular octagon ($s\text{-}2\Delta_{s-r} = s_8$) inscribed into the reference square (figs. 14b, 15c, 18b). From the relationship $s_8/\Delta_{s-r} = \sqrt{2}$ it follows furthermore that the diagonal of the smaller squares (with a side length of Δ_{s-r}) in the corners of the reference square (figs. 14b, 15c) equals s_8 thus completing a regular octagon (fig. 18b). As stated above, the corresponding differentiation of a square's side into two times Δ_{s-r} with $s\text{--}2\Delta_{s-r}$ ($= s_8$) in between also results from concentrically tilting the reference square by 45°.[452] From the perspective of 'practical geometry', this value s_8 is easily gained from Δ_{d-s} ($= \sqrt{2}\text{-}1$ in a unit square with s = 1). In other words, the length of s_8 is the result of a simple geometrical construction and not of some algebraic abstraction.

Another consequence of the Pythagorean Theorem is Plato's 'doubling the square'.[453] If the diagonal of a square is taken as the side length of a second one, the area of the former is found doubled in the latter ($d^2 = 2s^2$), i.e. s of the former is found as r of the latter. Also, this motif is found in the Octagon's ground plan, since s_8 equals the side length of the centre square of the Octagon's ground plan encompassing the pseudo–*cella* as well as the diagonal of the small squares at the edges of the reference square (figs. 14b, 15c).[454]

6.8 A 'sublime proportion'

Vitruvius states that width and height of a monument should be in *eurythmia*,[455] whereby the width clearly represents the output variable and the height the dependent one. In this regard, B. Thuswaldner suggested that the Octagon's width (w $\approx$ 9 m)[456] and height (h $\approx$ 14.3 m)[457] are related by the 'Golden' ratio φ ($= (\sqrt{5}+1)/2 \approx 8/5$ in a unit square), i.e. $h/w = \varphi/1$.[458] Furthermore, she states that the "proportio divina,[459] i.e. the golden cut, [is] already first mentioned" in Eukl. elem. II 11,[460] which is, however, not the case verbatim, but still conceptually (fig. 17a).

Thuswaldner uses here the terms 'Divine'[461] and 'Golden'[462] proportion, both metaphors that were coined long after Eukleides. As can be seen from the two oldest preserved manuscripts of his Στοιχεῖα ('Elements')[463] from the 9th c. AD, the Vatican-Euclid[464] and the Byzantine Oxford-Euclid,[465] Eukleides actually called the ratio ἄκρος καὶ μέσος λόγος (AKML).[466] In his 6th book, he defines the term AKML as the relationship of the two segments of a straight line,[467] when it is cut medially in a certain way.[468] In other words, Eukleides describes the geometrical construction of the sectional point inside a straight line (a+b), so that the ensuing segments (a and b with a>b) are related by the quotients (a+b)/a = a/b.[469] He designates this very proportion (λόγος)[470] with the attributes ἄκρος and μέσος, whereby the latter seems quite self-explanatory.[471] The term ἄκρος, on the other hand, appears much more interesting and its understanding has caused problems.[472]

R. Fitzpatrick (2008) translates AKML as "extreme and mean ratio",[473] J. F. Lorenz (1781) as "continuos proportion",[474] I. L. Heiberg (1884),[475] P. Warius (1763),[476] T. Tacquet (1762),[477] J. Ozanam (1699),[478] C. Clavius (1627),[479] J. Kepler (1619),[480] S. Gracilis (1558),[481] J. Scheubelius (1550),[482] and I. Hervagium (1546)[483] as *extrema et media ratio*, and F. Feltrio (1599) as "l'estrema & meza proportione".[484] Interestingly, I. P. Dou (1618),[485] and W. Holtzman (1562)[486] understood AKML simply as "proportional section". Finally, E. Ratdolt (1482),[487] and L. Pacioli (1509) interpret the term as *proportionem habentem medium duoque extrema*.[488] Only the latter addresses Eukleides' ratio as "Divina Proportione"[489] thus attributing an aesthetic quality to ἄκρος λόγος for the first time.

6.9 Inner section and outer extension

Thuswaldner repeats that the construction of the 'Golden' cut appears "fairly complicated",[490] and illustrates this statement with a non-Eukleidean drawing depicting the *inner* section of a straight line according to AKML.[491] Yet, the architect of the Octagon had to *extend* the baseline of the monument towards its height, so that the question arises, whether there is a not-"complicated" Eukleidean geometrical approach to that.

Indeed, Eukleides uses the term AKML not only for the segments of an interiorly cut straight line.[492] He also describes expressis verbis the geometrical procedure to extend a given straight line, so that the initial and the elongated lines are again related by AKML.[493] Since such construction, furthermore, provides the inner section according to Eukl. elem. VI ὅρος β΄ (fig. 17a: AB/AH = AH/BH), the corresponding ratios are (a+b)/a = a/b = (2a+b)/(a+b) (with a = AH, and b = BH; fig. 17a). In other words, the Octagon's architect applied an Eukleidean geometrical construction in order to relate the monument's height to its width (fig. 17b) quite in line with the

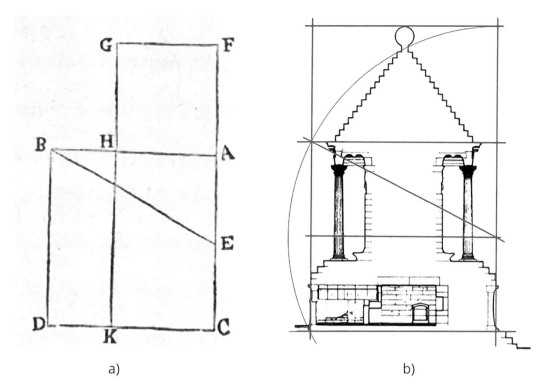

a)

b)

Fig. 17: a) Eukl. elem. II 11[497] illustrates the extension of a straight line AC (with AE = CE), so that the elongated result CF is parted at A (with BE = EF = √5/2, and AE ≠ AF) according to ἄκρος καὶ μέσος λόγος (FC/AC = AC/AF);[498]
b) The section of the Octagon along a north/south vertical plane overlaid by the geometry of Eukl. elem. II 11. Since the extension factor of the baseline accounts for (√5+1)/2, the Octagon's elevation is outlined according to h/w = φ/1 (all values in a unit square with s = 1)

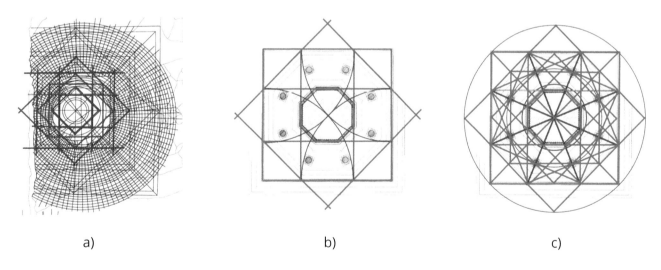

a)

b)

c)

Fig. 18: a) A stone slab from the Galerian complex of Thessaloniki with an elaborate cutaway presenting the Octagon's geometrical scheme amidst a dense pattern of concentric circles and centrifugally radiating beam rays; b) The 'Sacred Cut' r/s according to Brunés forms the rationale of the Octagon's ground plan and indicates s_8 at the sides of the reference square; c) The layout as chosen for the Octagon's ground plan represents a pattern of proportionality that can be differentiated virtually indefinitely idea of 'practical geometry' as seen at the Octagon's ground plan, whereby ἄκρος καὶ μέσος λόγος appears to fulfil Vitruvius' postulate of *eurhythmia*.

One might ponder whether Eukleides himself coined the term *in comparison* to less favourable proportions, since ἄκρος λόγος may also be translated as 'sublime proportion'.[494] Certainly, other geometrical procedures to elongate a straight line based on a value as resulting from a reference square are conceivable. E.g., a baseline (s) may be extended by s/2 to 1.5,[495] by √2-1 to ≈1.4, or by √2+1/2 to ≈1.9.[496] However, such attempts either lead to a stout or to an overstretched appearance of the corresponding rectangles in comparison to the 'Golden' rectangle with b/a = φ/1 (≈1.6). In other words, ἄκρος λόγος provides the most satisfying extension of a baseline to a height from an aesthetic point of view.

The Octagon's architect applied Euclidean concepts in order
to lay out the monument's ground plan and height.

In conclusion, both the Octagon's ground (fig. 14b) and elevation plan (fig. 17b) are the result of 'practical geometry' utilising Eukleidean concepts. No abstract calculations are required; everything is easily crafted on plan with nothing more than a straight edge and a beam compass.[499] Quite in line with Vitruvius' statement,[500] one might surmise that width and height, flights, areas, and the dimensions of the worked pieces relate to each other within a certain proportional system,[501] which has its root in drawings.

> THE OCTAGON'S GROUND PLAN FOLLOWS A CERTAIN GEOMETRICAL SCHEME LEADING TO THE QUESTION, WHETHER THERE IS AN UNDERLYING MEANING INHERENT IN IT.

6.10 The 'Sacred Cut'

Yet it is not the building geometry as such that represents the remarkable aspect of the Octagon.[502] Rather, the question arises *why* its architect pursued this unusual layout and so strictly adhered to it when laying out the ground plan. In this regard, the Danish architect T. Brunés contributed an important observation. He found the quotient r/s rooted in a set of ancient monuments within the sphere of holy precincts, and therefore termed it the 'Sacred Cut' (fig. 18b).[503] Accordingly, the 'sacred' proportion r/s belongs to a religious context; the corresponding differentiation of a reference square forms a regular octagon (fig. 14b). Such a proportion and its consequences seem to illustrate Plato's idea that "God always geometrises",[504] considering the possibility that the described geometry can be differentiated towards the interior and the exterior virtually indefinitely (fig. 18c). The question arises whether there is any evidence in the ancient sources indicating a religious meaning of octagonality at the time of the Octagon's construction.

IF A SACRED OCTAGONALITY IS MANIFESTED IN THE TEMPLE–LIKE CHARACTER OF THE EPHESIAN MAUSOLEUM, THE QUESTION ARISES WHETHER THERE IS WRITTEN EVIDENCE THAT MAY UNDERPIN SUCH REASONING.

6.11 All is eight (πάντα ὀκτώ)

Plato delivers his cosmological view in Politeia. He describes "eight spindle whorls[505] [with] eight singing sirens [symphoniously producing] one harmony from all eight [ἐκ πασῶν δὲ ὀκτὼ]", i.e. the sound of the universe.[506] Theon of Smyrna (2nd c. AD) states that in such a vision, Plato followed Pythagoras.[507] Accordingly, the oldest known perception of ὀκτώ as being the "absolute principle" (λόγος τέλειος)[508] probably stems from the Pythagoreans.[509] Yet it is not a "perfect number" (τέλειος ἀριθμός) according to the understanding of Eukleides.[510] Also, the Pythagorean relationship between cosmos and the eightfold partition within music is referred to by Theon.[511] In this regard, it is interesting to note that Vitruvius repeatedly demands from an architect knowledge of music.[512] Against this background, it seems more than likely that the already mentioned tomb of Stesichoros was inspired by Pythagorean thoughts as well.[513]

The cosmological understanding of Eratosthenes, bibliothecary of the Alexandrian Library (3rd c. BC),[514] is mentioned in the *theologumena arithmeticae*: "The eighth sphere encompasses the whole – hence the saying "All is eight" [πάντα ὀκτώ]. In eight spheres they revolve in a circle around the ninth, earth, says Eratosthenes".[515] Such a statement is repeated by Theon of Smyrna.[516] Similarly, M. Tullius Cicero describes eight spheres revolving around the earth.[517] Perhaps against such a backdrop, the *Sidus Iulium*,[518] the symbol of Caesar's divinisation, is mainly depicted with eight beams. Within the *theologumena arithmeticae*,[519] epitheta concerning the ογδοάς are found: παναρμόνια (all–encompassing harmony), ἔδρασμα *(foundation)* and, most importantly within our context, μητέρα (mother).

Herodotos says that a change was made from the eight Gods to the twelve in Egypt.[520] Zenobios (2nd c. AD) refers to the adage: "All is eight. Evander said that there are eight gods that hold all things: Fire, Water, Earth, Heaven, Moon, Sun, Mithras, and Night".[521] Addressing such a notion, Theon mentions: "Some say that there are eight main Gods within the universe, as it can be found within the Orphic oaths".[522]

From an astronomical point of view, Censorinus (3rd c. AD) describes the *oktaeteris*, the "great year" of the Greeks (*annus magnus*), that was supposedly invented by Eudoxos of Knidos (4th c. BC).[523] It encompasses the period of eight full cycles of the year. Censorinus states the importance of this interval by saying that "many cults celebrate their highest festivals according to this period, and also in Delphi, the Pythian games were held after every eighth year".[524] According to Censorinus, the *oktaeteris* was also called the *enneaeteris*, since the "initial year always returns in the ninth year".[525] In this regard, it is worth noting that Homeros names Minos ἐννέωρος βασίλευε, i.e., the King of every ninth year, thus emphasizing an eight–year cycle.[526]

Michael Apostolios (15th c. AD) states: "Some say [...] that Aletes on the basis of an oracle for the foundation of Corinth divided the citizens into eight tribes and the city into eight parts, always using the eight [...] Others indicate that there are eight races in Olympia: stadium race, double race, dolichoic race, oplitic race, wrestling, pankration and the rest, hence the saying 'Everything is eight [πάντα ὀκτώ]'" (see also Zenobios above).[527] Further reference of the πάντ' ὀκτώ is found at Obbink and Gonis.[528]

Finally, Agrippa of Nettesheim (15th/16th c. AD) states: "The number eight is called by the Pythagoreans the number of justice and fullness, and this because it can be divided first among all into equal even numbers, namely into four; also, in the repeated division (twice two) the same relation takes place. Because of this equality of division, it received the name of righteousness".[529] Against this backdrop, J. J. Bachofen says:

> *The universality of the πάντα ὀκτώ persists and proclaims the truth of the word, that everything on earth occurs only in connection, nothing appears and becomes comprehensible in isolation.*[530]

In summary, the number ὀκτώ indeed carried a symbolic meaning when the Ephesian Octagon was built, representing a universal completeness and a cosmological harmony. Accordingly, the penchant of the Octagon for such geometry presumably relates to a religious context, and thus suggests the Artemision as the contracting authority.[531] One might speculate that "a small octagonal temple"[532] may have been a condition for the tomb, since Vitruvius states "the dipteros is octastyle [such as] the ionic one of Diana at Ephesos, built by Ktesiphon".[533] Plinius says that the diameter of the columns at the Ephesian dipteros was determined as being ⅛ of their height.[534]

The octagonal order of the Ephesian mausoleum indicates
a relationship to the sacred sphere and was supposedly intentional
on the part of those who commissioned it.

In conclusion, the octagonal layout of the Ephesian mausoleum suggests a religious symbolism that accords well with its 'Artemisian' location and the "temple–like" character of the monument. This evidence makes sense, if the Artemision was responsible for the erection of the memorial.[535] Because of that, the Octagon was designed "in such a way that it no longer appeared as a tomb",[536] but as a building from a religious context. Such a reasoning finally bridges the "insurmountable conflict between the form chosen for [the Octagon's] structure and its actual function".[537]

IF THE OCTAGON IS RELATED BY ITS TEMPLE–LIKE APPEARANCE, ARTEMISIAN LOCATION AND SACRED GEOMETRY TO THE ARTEMISION, THE DECOR OF THE BUILDING MIGHT ALSO CONTAIN A REFERENCE TO THAT.

7. The fascia of Artemis

Although the Ephesian Octagon seems to avoid any *obvious* reference to its owner[538] and the circumstances of its erection, there is still one striking detail to be seen between the festoon's convexities undulating around its pseudo–*cella* (figs. on jacket, 11a, 12). The frieze combines two well–known motifs. One manifests as skeletonised bovine heads (*bucrania*)[539] supporting garlands bound by broad *taeniae*[540] descending between the festoons (figs. 19a-b).[541] The other motif, however, presents *bucrania* ornamented with astragal–like cords (στέμματα)[542] terminating in tassels (θύσανοι).[543] The motif is depicted at the Rotunda of Samothrake[544] and at the Athena Nikephoros sanctuary in Pergamon[545]. Interestingly, a chronologically close parallel for the association of *bucrania*, garlands and στέμματα is seen in the circular frieze which was found at the upper end of the Ephesian Curetes Street (figs. 19c).[546] Due to the proximity of its find–spot, U. Outschar associated the frieze with the already mentioned Memmius Monument (figs. 19c, 58f.; plans 1 and 3).[547]

7.1 Astragal–shaped cords

Dedicating στέμματα to the Gods was part of the ἱκέσια (supplication) ritual.[548] Accordingly, those symbols of supplication on the Octagon may have referred to Artemis *hikesia*. On the other hand, G. Seiterle prefers to narrow down its use to the animal offerings that were performed on Artemisian grounds.[549] Nevertheless, the meaning of such woollen threads within a sacral context is far from specific. As R. Fleischer and R. Grüßinger pointed out, στέμματα have to be understood in a broader sense: "On the objects to which they are attached, they denote the state of consecration";[550] "They mark that which is consecrated to the gods and indicate religious inviolability".[551] In other words, στέμματα illustrate individuals consecrating themselves and objects having been consecrated to the Sacred, both being thus removed from worldly affairs and placed under a god's protection. Hence, the symbol is also encountered in connection with other deities and other sacred places.[552] Conforming with this reasoning, Grüßinger points out that στέμματα are almost exclusively found in a "cultic" context,[553] and E. Papagianni does not present a single bucranion/festoon sarcophagus which integrated such cords in its decorative programme.[554]

Apart from this general appreciation, any onlooker passing by the Octagon in antiquity would have made a more specific association, since στέμματα with tassels were one of the key attributes of the Ephesian Artemis, dangling from the extended hands of her cult images (fig. 73).[555] The meaning of the sacred chaplets would have been connected to her kindness in providing shelter for the persecuted and the wounded, for example, the prototypical Amazons in that sense (figs. 45, 71, 73).[556] The Alexandrian lexicographer Hesychios names the Artemisian στέμματα explicitly as κληῖδες,[557] a wording containing a relation to κλείς.[558]

7.2 Keys

Homeros describes the location where Achilles drove his spear into Hektor's body as the "opening where the κληῖδες [i.e. the collar bones] part neck and shoulders".[559] In addition, he denotes the ancient Greek hook key of large sigmoid shape as κλείς[560] that acquired its form from pushing back a door latch through a hole from the outside.[564] From such an image is probably derived the name of the rowing benches of Greek ships as κληῖδες,[565] since the oars were turned through the ship's wall like a key in its hole.[566] Also, the bent moving stick of the Roman hoop game[567] was named clavis trochi.[568] Accordingly, the terminus κλείς does not refer to an attribute, a tool, a function or a bone. It predominantly denotes a shape of curved or sigmoid outline. In its plural form κληῖδες, it appears to be a factual description of the woollen threads, which were wound around sacred items dedicated to the Ephesian Artemis.

In summary, the στέμματα with tassels hermeneutically characterise objects and individuals consecrated to and protected by a god, thus relating to a sacral context in its broadest sense. Within the context of an Ephesian monument, however, the woolen threads are reminiscent of the Artemisian κληῖδες, a symbol whose meaning would have been obvious to any onlooker in antiquity due to its relationship to the Ephesian *asylum* linking the monument, therefore, to the Artemision. One would like to think that also Arsinoë IV received and carried the cords as the sign of her accepted plea for shelter. Having been a prominent supplicant, κληῖδες were,

a)

b)

c)

Fig. 19: Garland frieze of the Ephesian Octagon (a-b) compared to the one of the Memmius Monument (c).
a-b) The στέμματα are wound around the base of the bucranion's horns,[561] descend behind the garlands on top of (a; photo taken in 1982) or next to (b; photo taken in 1986)[562] the broad taeniae between the festoons, and end in tassels;
c) In comparison, the astragal–shaped cords at a circular festoon relief supposedly from the Memmius monument (photos taken in 2023)[563]

therefore, added to the ornamentation of her tomb. Yet Arsinoë's *hikesia* had failed, so that the κλῆῖδες on the mausoleum rather seem to demand respect for the goddess; otherwise severe punishment must be feared, as was suffered by Kleopatra VII and Marcus Antonius.

In conclusion, a particular detail of the Octagon's ornamentation, in combination with the building's location, the "temple–like character", and its sacred layout may indeed confirm the Artemision as the contracting authority of the monument.[569] Considering the adolescent female individual who was buried inside,[570] the sacrilegious killing of Arsinoë IV appears to provide the historical context, explaining why the Octagon was built.

7.3 A weapon relief

The suggested religious context of the Octagon would be somewhat disturbed, if one follows V. M. Strocka.[571] Due to its place of discovery close to the Octagon, he suggested the affiliation of a weapon relief to its *cella*-like core just above the bench, thus bestowing a somewhat curious appearance to the building.[572] Strocka based his proposal on information he had received from the Austrian architect F. Hueber:[573]

> *When I asked you, dear Friedmund* [Hueber]*, for more details* [...] *you willingly provided information* [...]*. "The plate* [...] *is cut diagonally backwards at its right end* [i.e., the right side] *so that it represents the right end of one side of an octagonal prism"* [...]*.*[574] *If the plate "represents the right end of one side of an octagonal prism", the Octagon immediately comes to one's mind (and to yours* [i.e. Hueber's] *probably too when you wrote this), which is indeed located directly to the east of the so–called heroon* [= the 'fountain'] *at the Lower Embolos.*[575]

As can be seen, already Hueber seems to have implied a certain context of the weapon relief with his few words. B. Thuswaldner repeated the idea in 2015,[576] although she recognised that its find-spot, in secondary use as paving at the lower Embolos, contradicts such a connection.[577] However, the decisive argument that speaks against Strocka's suggestion comes from W. Prochaska: the marble of the weapon relief is not consistent with the marble of the superstructure of the Octagon, which shows a remarkable consistency with regard to the lithic source.[578]

REVIEWING FINALLY THE EVIDENCE PRESENTED, THE OBVIOUS QUESTION ARISES AS TO WHY A CONNECTION BETWEEN THE OCTAGON AND ARSINOË IV WAS NOT MADE EARLIER?

8. Not an Ephesian hero, but a Greco–Egyptian heroine

Based on the arguments presented here, one might think that the attribution of the Octagon to Arsinoë IV ought to have been possible long before Thür's article,[579] and, in particular, since the understanding of the Ephesian mausoleum and its owner derived from statements of J. Keil and J. Weninger. Accordingly, it was

- ➤ A mausoleum of "early Roman imperial times"[580]
- ➤ Built in the "peculiar"[581] shape of a Hellenistic–Egyptian geometrical layout[582]
- ➤ For "a very distinguished personality"[583]
- ➤ Of female sex[584]
- ➤ With a possible Greco–Egyptian background[585]
- ➤ Having died as "apparently a girl or a young woman",[586] i.e. in her adolescence,[587] and
- ➤ Having received "the honour of being buried in a privileged place within the city walls" (plans 3f.).[588]

This quite specific appreciation of the Ephesian Octagon and its similarly unusual owner can hardly be understood as anything other than a description of the heroine[589] Arsinoë IV and her tomb. No such conclusion, however, was reached.[590] It seems as if Strack's long-standing miscalculation[591] whereby Arsinoë IV was born shortly after her elder sister Kleopatra VII, could not be aligned with the youth of the Octagon's owner at death; this may have inhibited the recognition of Arsinoë's mausoleum, as obvious as such connection was, in particular after Weninger's article.[592]

The reasoning of J. Keil and J. Weninger regarding the Octagon and its occupant suggested its being Arsinoë's gravesite since 1953.

In summary, all arguments which might have led to the recognition of the Octagon as Arsinoë's mausoleum were available since 1953. Nevertheless, it would take almost four decades until Hilke Thür revisited the issue and presented her proposal.[593]

9. Conclusions

The research history of the octagonal temple tomb in the centre of Ephesos (plans 3f.) spans 120 years (tab. 2). It can be divided into two chapters, separated by Hilke Thür's suggestion, made in 1990, that the monument might be identified as the mausoleum of the Ptolemaic Queen Arsinoë IV, younger sister of Kleopatra VII and her rival for the Macedonian-Egytian throne. Prior to that, the Octagon was considered to be simply a curious building in Greco–Roman Ephesos. With the "exciting publication by H. Thür",[594] however, the sepulchre became a monument which attracted scrutiny. As a result, the research output regarding some of its features increased.[595] The architecture of the Octagon was repeatedly assessed, the post-cranial skeleton frequently examined, and the topographical context discussed. Nonetheless, Thür's proposal continued to be a subject of controversy. However, a number of seemingly insurmountable inconsistencies regarding explicit notions of the Octagon did not arise from a straightforward approach to the monument, but rather from certain assumptions that could not be attuned with the idea of a tomb for Arsinoë IV and its dating. These include M.L. Strack's incorrect estimation of her birth date[596] as well as Kleopatra VII and Marcus Antonius as the supposed contractees of the tomb.[597]

Inferences from archaeological findings are mostly based on a limited amount of evidence, so that any ensuing interpretations are typically evaluated based on the consistency of the argumentation put forth. Unambiguity is difficult to achieve and not required. If there is sufficient plausibility, the resulting conclusion is not a "triumph of conjecture over certainty",[598] but simply a possible or probable perspective. There can never be any "certainty" that Arsinoë IV was actually buried within the Octagon, unless an unequivocal inscription comes to light[599] or the DNA of its skeletal remains can be related to another member of the Lagid family.

After reviewing certain issues of the Octagon, we believe that Thür's hypothesis represents the most logical explanation for the mausoleum's peculiar features; everything speaks in favour of her suggestion and nothing against it. In other words, there is no evidence for "alternative scenarios for the dedication of the Octagon" as of now.[600] Perhaps the strongest arguments in support of the theory are the osseous and dental developmental state of the grave's female owner at the time of her death, coinciding with the biographical details of Arsinoë IV as handed down by ancient sources, combined with the dating of the tomb somewhat after Arsinoë's murder.[601] Our only minor disagreement with Thür's proposal pertains to Kleopatra VII and Marcus Antonius as the assumed contracting authorities of the Octagon. Instead, the Artemisian site of the sepulchre (plans 3f.)[602] together with its "temple-like" appearance, the acknowledgement of its sacred geometry, the astragal–like cords which are reminiscent of the identical attribute of Artemis, and some of the lithic sources suggest that the Ephesian Artemision played a significant role in the erection of the building, a proposition that, furthermore, may explain its delayed erection.

The Octagon probably represents the only known
Ptolemaic gravesite and has, therefore,
preserved the skeleton of a Lagid family member.

In conclusion, we suggest that Ephesos has preserved the only known Ptolemaic gravesite including the only available skeleton of a Lagid family member.[603] It was built as a memorial to honour the importance of the Ephesian *asylum* by addressing the sacrilegiously murdered Arsinoë IV, a specific incidence within a complex historical context that was only known from ancient sources until Hilke Thür published her remarkable theory.[604]

Arsinoë(s) in Ephesos –
the historical background

The name Arsinoë had a great tradition in the Lagid dynasty during the 4th and 3rd centuries BC. However, after a break of nearly two centuries, it was only Ptolemaios XII who revived the name for his youngest daughter.

The first known Arsinoë, wife of the Macedonian aristocrat Lagos, was a distant relative and thus a member of the Macedonian royal family, the Argeads. Her son Ptolemaios served as a general for Alexander the Great and later became the King of Egypt and Alexandria. Some ancient and modern historians support the now much-doubted story that Arsinoë became pregnant by King Philippos II who was assassinated in 336 BC.[1]

For a better understanding of the attitude of Ptolemaios XII
on the name Arsinoë, we have to survey its history.

There was also another Macedonian lineage in which Arsinoë was a common name. Lysimachos, a colleague of Ptolemaios I as a general and later a diadoch, and his ally against the powerful diadoch Seleukos I Nikator, named his younger daughter Arsinoë as well, possibly after his own mother or that of his first wife Nicaea. Around 285 BC, she was married to Ptolemaios II to strengthen the bonds of friendship between the Lagid dynasty and Lysimachos, the King of Thrace, who also controlled the lands along the eastern shores of the Aegean. Thus, she became Arsinoë I, Queen of Egypt, and mother of Ptolemaios III and at least two more children, Lysimachos (the younger) and Berenice. Some time after her father's death in 281 BC (no later than 274 BC) and the arrival of his widow, Ptolemaios II's sister Arsinoë (II) in Alexandria in 279 BC, Arsinoë I was accused of conspiracy and subsequently banished to Coptos, while Ptolemaios II married his sister Arsinoë II. From then on, the couple was known as the φιλάδελφοι, the "loving siblings".[2]

1. Lysimachos and Arsinoë (II ?) as city founders of Ephesos

Lysimachos, the former bodyguard of Alexander the Great who ascended to the position of King of Thrace at the end of the 4th c. BC and therefore was one of the, albeit rather ephemeral, Diadochi, conquered Ephesos for a short period in 302/301 and remained in the city from 294 until his death at the Battle of Koroupedion. He probably planned his new capital city here with a favourable harbour.[3] To this end, he relocated the city from the plain near the Artemision to the bay at the foot of the mountains of Preon (today, Bülbüldağ) – also known in the tradition as Lepre Akte – and Mount Pion (the southern part of today's double peaked Panayırdağ; fig. 90);[4] he also increased the population by means of forced colonisation from Kolophon, Teos, and Lebedos. The most important sources of our knowledge regarding the relocation of Ephesos by King Lysimachos, in addition to a few contemporary inscriptions, consist of textual passages primarily from the Roman imperial Era by Strabon and Pausanias, that is, compiled at a great remove of nearly 300 or more than 400 years, even if they are informed by older sources. These texts convey important basic information and should therefore be quoted verbatim.

Strabon reports the fact that Lysimachos named the city after his wife Arsinoë – Can this be true?

Strab. XIV 1, 21:

> Τὴν δὲ πόλιν ᾤκουν μὲν Κᾶρές τε καὶ Λέλεγες, ἐκβαλὼν δ᾽ ὁ Ἄνδροκλος τοὺς πλείστους ᾤκισεν ἐκ τῶν συνελθόντων αὐτῶι περὶ τὸ Ἀθήναιον καὶ τὴν Ὑπέλαιον, προσπεριλαβὼν καὶ τῆς περὶ τὸν Κορησσὸν παρωρείας. μέχρι μὲν δὴ τῶν κατὰ Κροῖσον οὕτως ᾠκεῖτο, ὕστερον δ᾽ ἀπὸ τῆς παρωρείου καταβάντες περὶ τὸ νῦν ἱερὸν ᾤκησαν μέχρι Ἀλεξάνδρου. Λυσίμαχος δὲ τὴν νῦν πόλιν τειχίσας, ἀηδῶς τῶν ἀνθρώπων μεθισταμένων, τηρήσας καταρράκτην ὄμβρον συνήργησε καὶ αὐτὸς καὶ τοὺς ῥινούχους ἐνέφραξεν ὥστε κατακλύσαι τὴν πόλιν· οἱ δὲ μετέστησαν ἄσμενοι. ἐκάλεσε δ᾽ Ἀρσινόην ἀπὸ τῆς γυναικὸς τὴν πόλιν, ἐπεκράτησε μέντοι τὸ ἀρχαῖον ὄνομα. ἦν δὲ γερουσία καταγραφομένη, τούτοις δὲ συνῄεσαν οἱ ἐπίκλητοι καλούμενοι καὶ διώικουν πάντα.

> "The city of Ephesos was inhabited both by Karians and by Leleges, but Androklos drove them out and settled the most of those who had come with him round the Athenaion and the Hypelaios, though he also included a part of the country situated on the slopes of Mt. Koressos. Now Ephesos was thus inhabited until the time of Kroisos, but later the people came down from the mountainside and abode round the present temple until the time of Alexander. Lysimachos built a wall round the present city, but the people were not agreeably disposed to change their abodes to it; and therefore, he waited for a downpour of rain and himself took advantage of it and blocked the sewers so as to inundate the city; and the inhabitants were then glad to make the change. He named the city after his wife Arsinoê; the old name, however, prevailed. There was a senate, which was conscripted; and with

these were associated the epikletoi, as they were called, who administered all the affairs of the city." (transl. Jones 1929)

Paus. I 9, 7:

διέβη δὲ καὶ ναυσὶν ἐπὶ τὴν Ἀσίαν καὶ τὴν ἀρχὴν τὴν Ἀντιγόνου συγκαθεῖλε. συνῴκισε δὲ καὶ Ἐφεσίων ἄχρι θαλάσσης τὴν νῦν πόλιν, ἐπαγαγόμενος ἐς αὐτὴν Λεβεδίους τε οἰκήτορας καὶ Κολοφωνίους, τὰς δὲ ἐκείνων ἀνελὼν πόλεις ...

"He [sc. Lysimachos] also crossed with a fleet to Asia and helped to overthrow the empire of Antigonos. He founded also the modern city of Ephesos as far as the coast, bringing to it as settlers people of Lebedos and Kolophon, after destroying their cities [...]". (transl. Jones 1918)

Paus. VII 3, 4f.:

Κολοφωνίοις δὲ ὅπως μὲν τὴν πόλιν συνέπεσεν ἐρημωθῆναι, προεδήλωσέ μοι τοῦ λόγου τὰ ἐς Λυσίμαχον· ἐμαχέσαντο δὲ Λυσιμάχῳ καὶ Μακεδόσι Κολοφώνιοι τῶν ἀνοικισθέντων ἐς Ἔφεσον μόνοι, τοῖς δὲ ἀποθανοῦσιν ἐν τῇ μάχῃ Κολοφωνίων τε αὐτῶν καὶ Σμυρναίων ἐστὶν ὁ τάφος ἰόντι ἐς Κλάρον ἐν ἀριστερᾷ τῆς ὁδοῦ.

"How it befell that Kolophon was laid waste I have already related in my account of Lysimachos. Of those who were transported to Ephesos only the people of Kolophon fought against Lysimachos and the Macedonians. The grave of those Colophonians and Smyrnaeans who fell in the battle is on the left of the road as you go to Klaros." (transl. Jones 1933)

The actual influence of Lysimachos (fig. 20) on the construction of the new city was dependent on the time and the financial means available. After the Battle of Ipsos and the death of Antigonos Monophthalmos, Ephesos reluctantly fell to Lysimachos as part of his spoils.[5] His authorised military governor (στρατηγός) at the takeover of the city in 302/301 BC was a certain Prepelaos; one of his first actions was to exempt the Artemision from all taxes and duties. The Ephesians presented one of his officers, presumably the city commander named Euphronios, with citizenship due to his merit during these proceedings.[6] In this manner, Lysimachos and his general Prepelaos proved themselves to be benefactors of the sanctuary, although not to the same extent as Alexander the Great had previously been; the latter had even relinquished to the Artemision all the civic tributes of Ephesos.[7]

Until 294 BC, control over Ephesos, however, apparently repeatedly reverted to Demetrios Poliorketes, the son of Antigonos who had fallen at Ipsos.[8] Only after he had been expelled and Lysimachos' rule in Ionia had been secured, attested by, amongst other things, an inscription honouring his strategist Hippostratos by the Ionian League in 289/288,[9] could the expansion of the city be undertaken in earnest.

Until now, the earliest possible time for this event has been assumed to be the year 294 BC,[10] in which the Lysimachean general Lykos probably wrested the city from the commander Ainetos who served Demetrios.[11] The rapidly changing political situation is particularly evident in a variety of coin series dating to after ca. 305/301/295 and before 288 BC – many issues cannot be more precisely dated on their own terms. Newly appearing motifs include, for example,

Fig. 20: Portrait of a Hellenistic ruler, found in Ephesos below the early Byzantine pavement of the Embolos Street and supposedly an image of King Lysimachos

a female head and a head of Alexander on the obverse. Subsequently, probably after 295/294 BC, Arsinoë is celebrated as the new patroness of the city and the abbreviations of the new city name, AP or APΣI (for Arsinoeia), appear instead of the previously customary EΦE.[12]

Admittedly, Pausanias' report regarding the city foundation evokes the impression that the people of Kolophon and Lebedos had been forcibly brought by Lysimachos to Ephesos immediately after the Battle of Ipsos in 302 and the destruction of their cities, in order to increase the citizenry. In fact, already in 300 the new citizen Nikagoras, a factionist of Demetrios, was assigned to the chiliastys (sub-group of 1,000 citizens) of the Lebedioi (in the phyle Ephesioi); from the period of Lysimachos we already hear of the phyle of the Teians as well, while the Smyrnaians, equally assigned by Lysimachos to a chiliastys, have until now only been documented in imperial-period inscriptions and without a known affiliation to a phyle.[13] Nevertheless D. Knibbe, who like all other scholars until now proceeded from a new building of Ephesos after 294 BC, reached the opposite conclusion from the Nikagoras inscription, namely, that these groups of one thousand, as a sub-unit of a phyle, ought not to be associated with the measures carried out by Lysimachos, "regardless of how convincing this assumption might appear at first".[14] It may well be, however, that from the very beginning the relocation of the city to the sea coast was a concern of the king, since in the wake of the Battle of Ipsos and after the expansion of his kingdom from the northern Aegean to south-western Asia Minor at least as far as Miletos, a secure and well-developed harbour in the newly acquired regions was viewed as particularly important.

A further argument for an early dating for the relocation of the city is offered by the awarding of citizenship to Athenis of Kyzikos, who "regarding the building of the city wall had provided service to the city".[15] The decree is found on a marble ashlar block from the Artemision, found rebuilt into the Church of St Mary, immediately below a citizenship decree for the otherwise unknown Sostratos, a commander under Demetrios; due to the royal title mentioned, this is to be dated after 306 BC but in any event before 295 BC.[16] This signifies that, at least immediately after the final departure of Demetrios from Ephesos in 295 BC, the construction of the city wall was already well advanced. Theoretically, there is nothing to prevent the assumption that a new construction of the city by Lysimachos, already started in 302/301 BC, could also have been continued under Demetrios Poliorketes, who could have perceived the advantages of the new location of the city just as well as his rival had done. In actuality, after the death of Lysimachos the Ephesians even tore down parts of the new city walls in order to acclaim Seleukos I Nikator as liberator, perhaps in the (nonetheless futile) hope that they would be allowed to return to or stay in their old residences near the Artemision.[17]

The new royal city, as attested by inscriptions and coins from the foundation period,[18] bore the name Arsinoë or Arsinoeia (πόλις Ἀρσινοέων), from the name of the second wife of Lysimachos, according to Strabon. During the Battle of Koroupedion, which was fatal for Lysimachos, Arsinoë stayed in the new capital city of Ephesos, and as soon as the news of his defeat was announced, she fled in disguise by ship to Kassandreia in Macedonia, a city which belonged to her. A slave who, in her place, had been dressed up as the Queen was slain by the advancing troops of Seleukos I.[19] Apparently, the venerable city name of Ephesos was immediately readopted. Another consequence was that the sparse and also later (preserved) literary tradition regarding the events under Lysimachos was characterised by a decidedly hostile stance towards the king. The alleged blocking of the drains, the tearing down of the city walls, or a purported partial withdrawal of the people from Kolophon[20] to the 16 km distant city of Notion, the "New Kolophon on the Sea", can probably be viewed as part of this negative propaganda.

Approximately at the same time as Ephesos, Old Smyrna (today's İzmir) was also relocated next to the sea and received the name Eurydike from Lysimachos' daughter, sister, or mother.[21] In this regard, the supposition first voiced by S. Burstein that the new name of Ephesos ought to refer to a daughter of Lysimachos named Arsinoë and not to his second wife of the same name, who first played a greater role in his court only in the 280s,[22] seems worthy of consideration, in spite of the contrary tradition handed down by Strabon. Independent of the actual historicity, the evidence of Strabon, who according to his own statements gained his information at the site[23] and was therefore a reliable witness, leaves no doubt that apparently at least in the early Roman imperial period Arsinoë II – as she was listed by historians as Queen in Alexandria and Egypt – was viewed as the 'godmother' of the city. This version may have been circulated shortly after 280 BC, when the Ptolemies with their new Queen asserted claims to Asia Minor and Ephesos, or even much later, when Ptolemaios IV Philopator (221–204 BC) and his wife Arsinoë III (Queen since 220 BC) became rulers of Ephesos. We will return to this point below.

A significant document from the foundation period, only fragmentarily preserved and apparently containing regulations regarding ownership in the course of the city relocation, provides important evidence for the city planning with the dative designation δυτ[ικῆι ἀ]γορᾶι, that is, the western market of the polis of the Arsinoeians (πόλις Ἀρσινοέων).[24] J. Keil had already surmised that this agora was near the harbour,[25] where such a space was also laid out and which probably must have still been preserved in the Roman period. Unfortunately, hardly any excavations have taken place in the harbour plain up until now. The large, flat plain is disturbed by absolutely no visible ruins or unevennesses and is located between the so-called Medusa Gate (at the end of the avenue leading to the west from the Tetragonos Agora; see plan 1 no. 66) and the harbour. It provides the perfect location for the western market (fig. 21). From the considerations above, Lysimachos – and intermediately Demetrios Poliorketes – had at least 13, and probably even 20 years at his disposal for the new foundation of the city until his death in 281 BC. Strabon's report that the Ephesians refused to leave the old city near the Artemision indeed provides no explanation for this behaviour, yet it does show that the construction of the new city was energetically pursued. It is in any event likely that the alleged subterfuge of the king, namely, the blocking of the drains after a heavy rainfall,

Fig. 21: The Hellenistic-Roman city with the assumed location of the west agora (blue W)

may be dismissed as a later legend.[26] The temporary existence of the lagoon of Selinousia, located between the Artemision and the former harbour Koressos (on the north slope of today's Panayırdağ; see plan 2) in the Hellenistic period[27], sheds light on the situation. The old city and, with it, the sanctuary were threatened with flooding in the (later) 4th c. due to the increase in groundwater following the rise in sea level and riverine alluvion, and the harbour had become unusable.[28] As the report of Pausanias clearly emphasizes, the city had to be relocated to a slightly raised location from the lagoon to the sea, that is, to an open harbour, in order to secure its economic security for the long term; this is a situation that modern Venice knows only too well.

2. The Ptolemaic Queens Arsinoë II and Arsinoë III in Ephesos

According to current scholarly opinion, the history of the political affiliation of Ephesos after the death of Lysimachos is characterised by frequent and often sudden alterations.[29] The widow Arsinoë at first fled to her half-brother Ptolemaios Keraunos, who had just been made King of Thrace and Macedonia, and married him. In spite of promises to the contrary, he caused her two youngest sons with Lysimachos to be killed, while the oldest fell in battle, leaving no direct heir of Lysimachos alive. Keraunos forced Arsinoë into exile to the sanctuary at Samothrake, which she had previously generously sponsored. After his death on the battlefield against the Celts in 279 BC, she returned to Alexandria and there married, probably between 276 and 274 BC, her significantly younger full brother Ptolemaios II; this marriage apparently remained childless. After 272 BC, the two of them allowed themselves to be venerated in their kingdom as "Sibling Deities" (θεοὶ φιλάδελφοι).[30] With Arsinoë II as Queen, the Ptolemies had a far better claim to their rights on the former kingdom of Lysimachos.[31] In 274/273 BC, the sibling couple waged the first Syrian War against Antiochos I Soter, the son of Seleukos I who had been murdered by Ptolemaios Keraunos.

With Arsinoë II as Queen, the Ptolemies had a far better claim
to their rights on the former kingdom of Lysimachos;
did it really work?

Scholars frequently refer to two fragments of inscriptions, found in the so-called Terrace House 2 at Ephesos, for the successful expansion of rule by Ptolemaios II and Arsinoë II over much of the Aegean region and, in any event, over Ephesos.[32] A. Meadows first raised objections in 2013, declaring that Ptolemaios IV Philopator (221–204 BC) and his (sister)-wife Arsinoë III were the addressees.[33] His argument is multi-layered.

On the one hand, he categorically disputes a Ptolemaic rulership over Ephesos before 246 BC, while on the other hand double-dedications like these ones first begin in Egypt itself under Ptolemaios III and Berenike II, and therefore in his opinion an earlier dedication in a peripheral region would hardly be conceivable. Nevertheless, E. Fassa, after examining Meadows' theory, returned to the earlier dating of ca. 270 BC.[34] Thus far, two (approximately) identical so-called double-dedications were always accepted, attesting to the ruler cult for a King Ptolemaios and a Queen Arsinoë in connection with

Fig. 22: Photo montage of the inscription fragments for the Ptolemaic ruling couple Ptolemaios IV and Arsinoë III from Terrace House 2, Residential Unit 7

Sarapis and Isis. In 2014, L. Bricault first published the cognition that the fragments belonged to one and the same inscription.[35] Since these inscription fragments are not only important for the history of Ephesos but also contain remarkable information for the topography of the city, they will be investigated here in a detailed fashion (fig. 22), including their precise find-spots that have been poorly presented in the literature up to now.

Fragment 1 (height of letters 2.2 cm):[36]

> [Βασιλεῖ Πτ]ολεμαίω[ι]
> [καὶ βασιλί]σσηι Ἀρσι-
> [νόηι καὶ Σ]αράπιδι καὶ
> [Εἴσιδι ------------------]

Fragment 2 (height of letter from 2 cm declining to 1.5 cm):[37]

> βασιλεῖ Πτ[ολεμαίωι]
> καὶ βασιλί[σσηι Ἀρσι]-
> [ν]όηι καὶ Σ[αράπιδι καὶ]
> Εἴσιδ[ι ὁ δεῖνα —]
> 5   καὶ οἱ ἡγε[μόνες καὶ]
> οἱ στρατι[ῶται οἱ τε-]
> [τ]αγμένοι [ἐπὶ τῆι]
> [ἄκ]ραι τ[ὸ]ν [βωμόν]
> [ἀ]νέθηκαν [ἐπὶ ταῖς]
> 10 συντελου[μέναις]
> αὐτοῖς θυ[σίαις].

Meadow's proposals for Fragment 2 brought great progress. On the one hand, he diagnosed the corresponding hyphenations of both fragments, while on the other hand he recognised the notation Εἴσιδ[ι - - -] for Isis in line 4; furthermore, he was the first to emend the inscription into an overall meaningful text. In addition, he pointed to the phrourarchs (commanders) as the responsible persons in such "double-dedications" and referred to other, important parallels in the usual inscriptions of this type.[38] Subsequently, Bricault recognised the apparent cohesiveness of both fragments, whose broken borders very clearly directly fit together without any missing pieces based on the photographs of the squeezes (fig. 22) and texts.[39] The size of the letters and the writing style have long been recognised as very similar; the fact that they were discovered in the same building is also significant.[40]

The precise find-spot of the inscription fragments inside Terrace House 2 was, however, unfortunately not documented in the earlier epigraphic reports. Nevertheless, for both fragments approximate allocations can be made from the sketch books and preliminary excavation reports (fig. 23). According to the excavation report, the smaller fragment was found in 1977 in Residential Unit 7 in the region of Rooms R32 to R 37.[41] The find-spot of the larger fragment consisting of two matching pieces is located in the peristyle area of Residential Unit 7, to the north of R38 and R38a,[42] whereby the find-spot must be in the courtyard (Rooms R38b) or nearby, that is, in the immediate vicinity of the smaller Fragment 1. Both fragments apparently originate from the Late Antique fill covering the residential houses after their destruction in the 3rd c. AD (very likely by an earthquake in or around 263).

Directly below Terrace House 2, approximately 25 m distant from the find-spot of the inscription,[43] a fountain house is located on the Embolos or Curetes Street, as it is called today (fig. 23; plan 3 no. 12); according to the stratigraphic context and the lion's head waterspouts its construction is most likely to be dated to the advanced 3rd c. BC, in any event at the latest in the mid-2nd c. BC. This information will be reviewed in greater detail in the topographical section.[44] Here we limit ourselves to stating that a dedication elsewhere exists which is parallel in content. It was made at Itane on Crete by the phrourarch, descending originally from Rome, Lucius C(ai) f(ilius), to Ptolemaios IV Philopater and Arsinoë III;[45] the dedication records his construction of a surge tank (ὕδρευμα) and a nymphaeum. The fountain house at Ephesos is located not only in the immediate vicinity of the secondary find-spot of the inscription fragments, but it also fits perfectly chronologically. Until now, it is the only known structure at Ephesos dating to this period. The garrison (lines 7f: [τ] αγμένοι [ἐπὶ τῆι] / [ἄκ]ραι) stationed on the acropolis on the arid Tracheia (north peak of the Panayırdağ, cf. plan 2; fig. 90) had a corresponding need for secure access to water. Such a nymphaeum could also optimally represent royal power – as clearly occurred in monarchic self-presentation after the period of Alexander

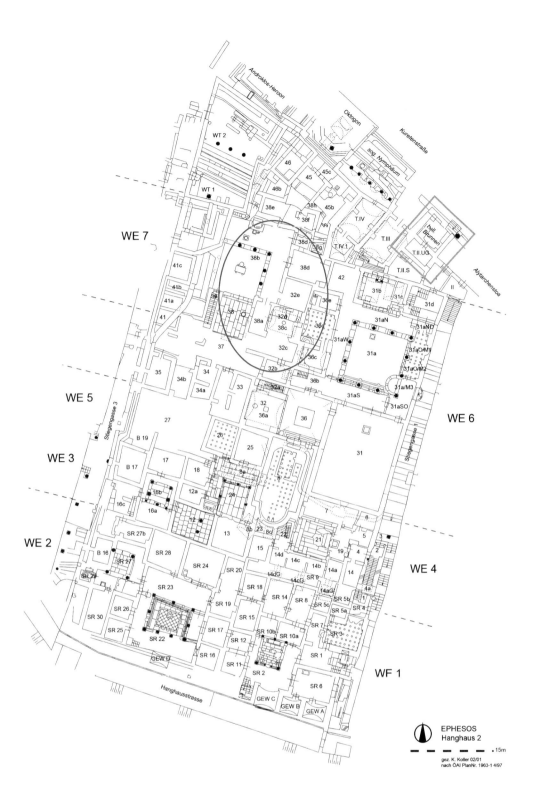

Fig. 23: Plan of Terrace House 2 and adjacent buildings on the so-called Curetes Street with the Hellenistic fountain (green square) and with the approximate find spots (inside area marked by the red oval) of the inscription fragments honouring Ptolemaios IV and Arsinoë III

the Great. As will be demonstrated, the fountain house indeed lay within the city walls, yet it was also on the border of or outside the actually inhabited city area at that time; in other words, perfect for the needs of the occupying troops. For these reasons, and also due to the better restoration of the known lengths of the lines with two additional letters, here the text in line 8 will be restored with 'the fountain house' (τὸ Ν[υμφαῖον]) as the object of the donation, instead of 'the altar' (τ[ὸ]ν [βωμόν]) proposed by Meadows.[46]

Consequently, the following combined reading of the two fragments (fig. 22), with new proposals for restorations, is presented:

βασιλεῖ Πτολεμαίωι	To King Ptolemaios
καὶ βασιλίσσηι Ἀρσι-	and Queen Arsi-
[ν]όηι καὶ Σαράπιδι καὶ	noë and to Sarapis and
Εἴσιδ[ι ὁ δεῖνα (as phrourarch)]	Isis [name of a phrourcharch]
5 καὶ οἱ ἡγε[μόνες καὶ]	and the troop commanders and
οἱ στρατι[ῶται οἱ τε-]	the officers,
[τ]αγμένοι [ἐπὶ τῆι]	who constitute the battalion on the
[ἄκ]ραι τὸ] Ν[υμφαῖον]	heights (= acropolis), have
[ἀ]νέθηκαν [ἐπὶ ταῖς]	dedicated the nymphaeum,
10 συντελου[μέναις]	whereby sacrifices are
αὐτοῖς θυ[σίαις]	carried out in their honour.

The Lagidai were first able to gain a foothold in the northern Aegean, and therefore in Ephesos, in 246 BC under Ptolemaios III.

If, as the majority of scholars assume, Ptolemaios II Philadelphos and Arsinoë II as the ruling couple were addressed here,[47] then the dedication must have been made between the successful Syrian War of 274/273 BC and the death of Arsinoë II in about 270/268 BC.[48] In many interpretations of the kingdom of the Diadochi as well as the urban history of Ephesos, it is accordingly assumed[49] that Ephesos at that time was briefly Ptolemaic, yet then quickly fell back under Seleucid control, and then after 258 BC became Ptolemaic again. Ptolemaios II Philadelphos apparently then appointed his illegitimate son Ptolemaios Physkos as governor; the son nevertheless renounced his father and formed an alliance with the tyrant of Miletos, Timarchos, in order to stabilise his rule. After approximately 10 years, he was overthrown by Antiochos II Theos and – in violation of the right of *asylum* – was slain by Thracian soldiers in the Artemision. Shortly after the death of Antiochos II in 246 BC, Ephesos became Ptolemaic again and remained so until 196 BC, when Antiochos III the Great systematically conquered the foreign possessions of the Ptolemies in Asia Minor.[50]

In contrast, however, the firm opinion is repeatedly held[51] that the Lagidai were first able to gain a foothold in the northern Aegean, and therefore in Ephesos, in 246 BC under Ptolemaios III.[52] For this reason these double-dedications, apparently first created under Ptolemaios III and Berenike II, to a Ptolemaios and an Arsinoë at Ephesos in any case could only mean Ptolemaios IV and Arsinoë III between 220–204 BC.[53] So, a legend of Arsinoë II as ´godmother´ of the city Arsinoeia/Ephesos might well have been installed already shortly after 276, or later after 246 BC, when Ptolemaic control became reality.

Soon afterwards in 188 BC, the Romans first massively intervened in Asia Minor with the Peace of Apameia, and the Attalids of Pergamon obtained supremacy over all of western Asia Minor, including Lycia. The Ephesians nevertheless are likely to have felt more comfortable under the Ptolemies, with their distant residential city of Alexandria, than under the Seleucids and above all the Attalids, who now emerged as new masters for 50 years.[54] Amongst other evidence for this is the fact that after 188 BC agonistic contests were instituted for the Attalid Eumenes II (contests for youths and pedagogues are primarily attested), yet a similar, older contest with the name of Epinikia Ptolemaia continued to be celebrated.[55] With a degree of probability the Ephesians possessed a certain autonomy within the Pergamene dominion – perhaps at the urging of the Romans – and probably counted at least after the mid–2nd c. BC as a "free" city. Rome must have immediately confirmed this status after it assumed dominion in Asia Minor after the death and subsequent testament of Attalos III in 133 BC.[56] The construction of the theatre on the west slope of Mount Pion (south area of the Panayırdağ, see plan 1 no. 75; fig. 90) could also have promoted this autonomy some time after 188 BC, most likely around the (early) second quarter of the 2nd c. BC.[57] This was probably at the initiative of Eumenes II: the peoples' assemblies also took place here, and therefore a power that was at that time hardly actually legislative could be suggested.

In this historical context, we turn to an over life-size female portrait head (height of head, 33 cm; total height 52 cm). The head, dating to the 3rd c. BC and which certainly wore a now-lost diadem (fig. 24), was originally set into a statue wearing a mantle and was made of Ephesian marble. According to its find-spot in the debris of the theatre of Ephesos, the head was apparently still displayed there in Late Antiquity or the early Byzantine period. With good argumentation, M. Laubenberger has assigned the portrait to Arsinoë III, although Arsinoë II or Berenike II "cannot be completely ruled out."[58] Why and when this portrait came into the theatre needs to be discussed. Before Rome took over Asia Minor, it is unlikely that such a demonstrable harking back to Ptolemaic rule occurred in a building of Attalid times. For such an action one thinks at the earliest of the time when Marcus Antonius and Kleopatra VII stayed in Ephesos, yet precisely at that time the name of Arsinoë would not have been a symbol of diplomatic sensitivity. Perhaps the head was moved into the theatre during its somewhat obscure renovation under Augustus or, preferably, first during its expansion under Domitian and Trajan.[59] The portrait was perhaps originally set up at the already discussed Ptolemaic nymphaeum on the Embolos; this structure, based on excavation evidence, was redesigned roughly during the Hadrianic period (fig. 49) and this would have been a good opportunity to bring the Queen´s portrait to the theatre. In any event, the obvious assimilation to portraits of divinities[60] is definitely an additional indication that this head could originally belong together with the double-dedication discussed above.

3. Observations on the political and administrative structural reform of Arsinoeia/Ephesos and its consequences in the Roman imperial period

Did Lysimachos, with Arsinoeia, plan only a relocation of Ephesos to a more favourable area? Or did he actually want to create a city subservient to him alone, one which was now approximately 2 km beyond and therefore clearly apart from the Artemision and independent from the influence of the sanctuary's priesthood? An answer in favour of the latter was formulated already 30 years ago: [61] "The Hellenistic King Lysimachos [...] followed the example of other successors of Alexander [...], founding his own city, one that would no longer be under the domination of the mighty goddess and her powerful hierarchy of priests." From this perspective the actions of Prepelaos[62], namely, to have the civic taxes paid no longer to the Artemision but instead to the king are even more understandable; at the same time, the early dating of the (planning of a) city relocation to 301 BC is self-evident.

King Lysimachos founded his own city, one that would no longer be under the domination of the mighty goddess.

A further fact points to a degree of 'political' independence of the city of Arsinoeia from the Artemision: the citizenship decrees under Lysimachos were no longer countersigned by the highest administrative organ of the Artemision, the Essen (ἐσσήν), but by the gerousia (γερουσία or συνέδριον τῶν γερόντων or συνέδριον τῶν πρεσβυτέρων), revalorised or more likely newly created under Lysimachos, or by the new commissioners, the epikletoi (ἐπίκλητοι), installed by Lysimachos and obviously disestablished immediately after his death.[63] On the other hand, the apparently continued custom of registering the citizenship decrees in the Artemision speaks against a complete exclusion of the goddess from civic cult events.[64] One can most likely imagine a planned parallel existence and co-existence between Arsinoeia and the Artemision, similar to the relationship between Miletos and the sanctuary of Apollon at Didyma. In order to achieve such a reduction of the sanctuary only to the area of the sacred legitimation in politics, a certain spatial distance between the city and its inhabitants, and the temple precinct, was surely necessary. At Ephesos, however, this co-existence was not permanent due to the death of the king on the battlefield.

Of the administrative civic organisations created or strongly promoted by Lysimachos, the gerousia at least endured, although there is no evidence regarding its significance in the following Hellenistic period.[65] The geographer Strabon, however,[66] mentions that during his time, the Augustan period, a gymnasium was located in the harbour plain (fig. 25) in the region of the abandoned village of Smyrna, to the

Fig. 24: Portrait of a Ptolemaic Queen, presumably Arsinoë III; found in the theatre of Ephesos

west of the Tetragonos Agora (plan 1 no. 61; fig. 27). This gymnasium can only have been that of the gerousia, because the gymnasium of the boys (παῖδες) should be located in the area of the later so-called State Agora (plan 1 no. 18; plan 5).[67] Numerous inscriptions, re-used during the general restoration of the Tetragonos Agora under Theodosius I in the late 4th c. AD and referring to the gerousia, confirm Strabon's approximate localisation.[68] Amongst these is an early imperial architrave recording the construction of a building by Aphrodisios Kleandrou, grammateus (head secretary) and gymnasiarch of the gerousia.[69] A number of orthostat blocks

Fig. 25: Area of the harbour plain in Ephesos showing the possible localisation of the gymnasium of the gerousia (blue G)

from a wall of the gerousia building, reused as drain cover slabs in front of the west stoa of the agora, are of particular importance. These slabs preserve letters which confirm privileges for the organisation by C. Iulius Caesar as well as Octavian, and their repeated confirmation in the Julio-Claudian period by Agrippa, Germanicus, and even the *proconsul Asiae* P. Petronius in 31/32 AD among others.[70] These privileges confirm that the association rose to a certain importance, at least in the cultic and sacral-legal area, which it maintained up until the 3rd c. AD. The gerousia therefore appears to have played a role in particular in the cult, created by Lysimachos (?), of Artemis Soteira in Ortygia, the birthplace of Artemis Ephesia which unfortunately has still not been archaeologically identified.[71] In addition to the prytaneis and the collegium of Curetes, the gerousia was involved in the related bestowals of citizenship and the admission of young citizens as full members of the polis. The gerousia was still appropriately honoured as an important corporation in the high imperial period, in the foundations of C. Vibius Salutaris in 104/105 AD, and by a certain Nikomedes under Emperor Commodus (180–192 AD).[72] The public role of the gerousia in the life of the city, and its clear, constant invocation of King Lysimachos in inscriptions during the Roman imperial period indicate that it was not at all forbidden, at the latest after Octavians's victory in Actium to refer back to Lysimachos as founder of the city.

A firm piece of evidence for this harking back to Lysimachos is the endowment by the Roman knight C. Vibius Salutaris in 104/105 AD, mentioned above; its charter was chiselled into the theatre of Ephesos.[73] In addition to various other provisions on the occasion of the great procession on 6th Thargelion (the month corresponds to today's May), the birthday of Artemis, the role of the ephebes – that is, the future young citizens – is emphasised. The ephebes were responsible for taking over groups of statues, brought from the Artemision, at the city gate and carrying them into the theatre; amongst these statues, not only Artemis (dominating with 9 statues) and the emperors Augustus and Trajan, but also the mythical founder Androklos and Lysimachos are accentuated.[74] Via analogy with the seating order in the theatre based on social groups (the phylai, and additionally the members of the city council, the ephebes, and the gerousia), these statues were displayed almost as 'ushers', in accordance with the division of the citizenry into the six phylai at the time. The fundamental division of the citizens into five phylai and their sub-divisions, the chiliasties, also occurred under Lysimachos; the sixth phyle, named *Sebaste* (Σεβαστή) after Augustus, was added probably during the reign of Claudius.

Each group, the six phylai as well as the council (βουλή), the gerousia and the ephebes were – apart from a statue of Artemis – denoted by another one which served as the hero of the phyle or marker of the group. The phyle of the Ephesioi, which gave its name to the city, was denoted by the Emperor Trajan and his wife Plotina as well as by the people of the Ephesians (δῆμος Ἐφεσίων), while the phyle of the Karenaioi, as Greek immigrants, was represented by their mythical leader Androklos, the phyle of the Teoi newly created by Lysimachos was represented by an image of him, and the youngest phyle, *Sebaste*, was represented by an image of Augustus. The remaining two phylai were represented by local figures: the mountain of Pion (for the Bembinaioi) into which the theatre was built (fig. 90), and the shepherd Euangelos (for the Euonymoi), who was credited with having discovered the marble quarry for the construction of the temple of Artemis (and many other buildings). The Ephesian society was juxtaposed with that of Rome by means of additional pairs of statues: the boule was confronted with the *senatus*, the ephebes with the knights (*ordo equester*), and the gerousia with the *populus Romanus*.[75]

The re-equipping of the theatre in the Trajanic period became tangible with the endowment of Salutaris; in this context a portrait of Arsinoë (II) as wife of Lysimachos would be urgently expected. Under the circumstances, such a portrait could be taken away from the Ptolemaic nymphaeum on the Curetes Street; the fountain apparently required an alteration or a renovation and was scaled down in the early 2nd c. AD.[76] The only small flaw – that this portrait originally most likely depicted Arsinoë III – was probably not noticed by anybody in the early 2nd c. AD due to the fundamental similarity of the portraits.

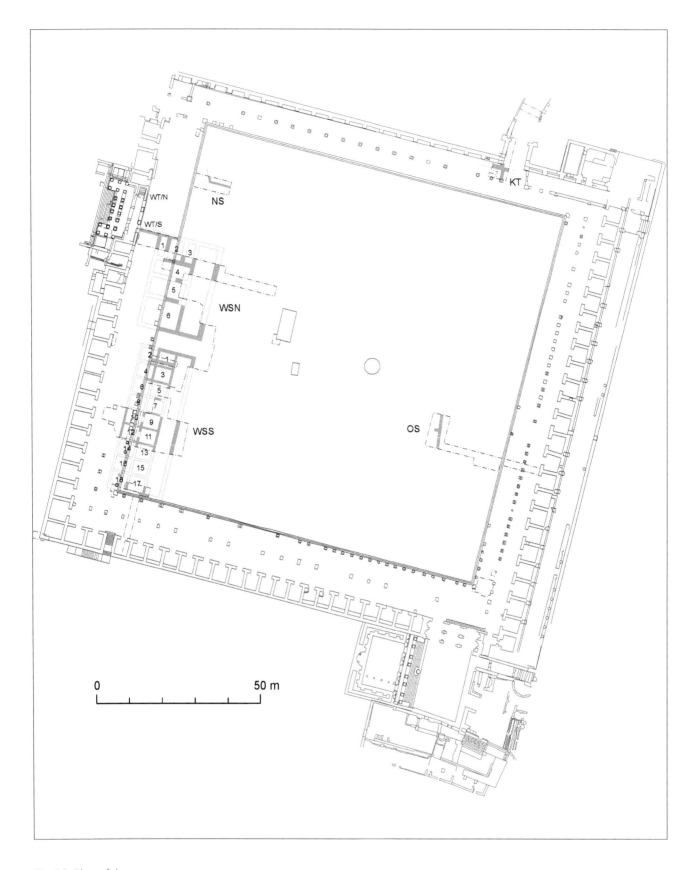

WT/N

NS

WT/S

1 2 3
4
5
WSN
6

2 1
4
3
5
7
10
12 9
11 WSS
14
13
16
15
18 17

OS

KT

0   50 m

Fig. 26: Plan of the
excavated Helle-
nistic remains of
the Tetragonos
Agora and of the
Koressian Gate

4. Historical Conclusions

The name of Arsinoë again became important in Ephesos, at least indirectly, with this new orientation of civic history in favour of Lysimachos, at the latest in the era of Octavian/Augustus if not immediately after Rome's takeover of the kingdom of the Attalids after 133 BC. In the struggle for power between Marcus Antonius and Kleopatra VII, on the one hand, and Octavian on the other, Arsinoë IV played a role as a possible alternative to Kleopatra. Her flight to Ephesos and and the protection granted in the Artemision by the *Megabyzos*, whom Kleopatra probably also added to her death list for that reason,[77] were therefore no coincidence. Her name, identical with Arsinoë II,[78] the wife of the city's new founder Lysimachos, and with Arsinoë III, the sister-wife of Ptolemaios IV Philopater and publicly remembered in Ephesos with cultic honours and portraits, possessed a particular calibre precisely in Ephesos. As the name had already not been in use in the Lagid family for more than 150 years, its comeback may have had a certain background: the birth of the youngest daughter of Ptolemaios XII in – as we argued above[79] – Ephesos, where this name had such an illustrious history.

Did Arsinoë IV play a role in Roman politics as a possible alternative to her sister Kleopatra VII?

Since Caesar had repeatedly spared her,[80] Arsinoë automatically became his client; a status she would also hold with his adoptive son and heir, Octavian. The city of Ephesos, and above all the Artemision certainly also had a strong client relationship to Caesar; after all, he had protected the sanctuary from depredations, in addition to his other benefactions to the city.[81] Given this general political background, Arsinoë IV's quest for the *asylum* of Artemis Ephesia was logical and predetermined. At the same time, the name as well as the person of Arsinoë constituted a direct reference both to the city founder Lysimachos and to Caius Iulius Caesar,[82] honoured as god and saviour (σωτήρ) of Ephesos, as well as to Augustus, the *restaurator* and κτίστης (founder) of the city,[83] who had also already created a solid financial basis for the Artemision in 30/29 via his *procurator* Publius Vedius Pollio.[84]

The architectural development of Hellenistic Ephesos and the expansion of the city under Augustus

The research on a Greco-Roman metropolis such as Ephesos is determined by its sheer magnitude with regard to its area and historic periods. Accordingly, even 125 years of Ephesian excavations have only provided a limited view onto it, all the more so since the archaeological efforts have mainly concerned the urban districts dominated by Roman imperial and Late Antique architecture. In contrast, the harbour plain and the western slope of the large urban hill, originally named Lepre Akte, later Πρεών (today Bülbüldağ) bordering the coast remain almost completely unexplored.[1] In what follows, an attempt will nevertheless be made to represent the entire topography of Hellenistic Ephesos, at least in broad outline, as this should lead to important insights – also with regard to the choice of the building site for the Octagon, the central feature of this book, and its location within the urban fabric.

For a better comprehension of the particular situation of the urban development of Ephesos, and consequently the archaeological investigation of the city, a few brief observations may be presented that will also allow an understanding of why precisely here the philosopher Herakleitos is believed to have said, "We step and do not step into the same rivers," which was later abbreviated to the famous πάντα ῥεῖ (everything flows).[2]

1. Preliminary remarks on the location of the city at the coast, and its harbours

Ephesos is located in the estuarine bay of the Kaystros (today, Küçük Menderes) that, alongside other smaller rivers, tends to meander and forms lagoons that gradually silt up, slowly displacing the sea coast further and further to the west. In addition, for approximately 60,000 years the water level of the Mediterranean has been rising in irregular episodes, particularly strongly apparently in the 1st millennium BC.[3]

"We step and do not step into the same rivers."
(Herakleitos)

As a consequence, the riparian strips favourable for a settlement, and the associated harbour basins and therefore the urban settlement sites, altered every few centuries.[4] The rebuilding of the late Classical Temple of Artemis after the fire of 356 BC, supposedly on the night of the birth of Alexander the Great, was constructed at a level exactly 2.76 m higher than its predecessor building of the 7th/6th c. BC.[5] In other words, the alluvial material from the rivers, continually flowing more slowly due to the constantly decreasing incline, increasingly determined the geography of the settlement area; for this reason Ephesos today lies 7 km away from the coast. Our knowledge regarding the approximate course of the coastline in the area of the Hellenistic city is therefore only based on geological drilling and a few open-area excavations, and must mostly be calculated via interpolation.[6] Thus, for example, the site at which the western gateway of the Commercial Market (plan 2; fig. 26) was erected in the 3rd c. BC was still located directly at the coastline in the 6th/5th c. BC (fig. 27). Precisely in the harbour plain, much building land in the former marine region was gained by large-scale dumping of earth, from the time of Lysimachos up until the Early Byzantine period; especially – perhaps excluding a couple of islands – the entire region on both sides of the main connecting street from the harbour to the theatre, known around 400 AD as the Arkadiane after Emperor Arcadius (plan 1 no. 83 and no. 87). Before the later 1st c. AD, no extensive development could arise here, yet after the 7th c. AD the centre of the city lay in this area.

Consequently, it is still not clear even today where the main harbour(s) of the Lysimachean city precisely locates; the harbour basin still easily recognisable today (plan 1; fig. 34) was bordered by heavy quay walls only in the Trajanic-Hadrianic period, designed to protect against further silting up.[7] This harbour, or one which already had roughly the same location, at least with regard to its southern landing along the western part of Mt. Preon (Bülbüldağ) at the far west of the city must go back no less than to the very early Roman imperial period. In support of this assumption is the fact that, in the Neronian period between 54 and 59 AD as Agrippina is mentioned along with her son, as one of numerous building measures following the devastating earthquake of 23 AD with contributions by rich citizens and the fishermen's guild, a fishery customs house at this harbour had to be rebuilt under the responsibility of a Roman citizen named L. Fabricius Vitalis.[8] Therefore the original building as well as the harbour must have already existed beforehand, at least in the early Julio-Claudian period. But we might trace its existence even further back into earlier times.

The fishery customs house appears to have been connected with a Samothrakion, according to the identification of the dedication of Vitalis. Whether this dates back, however, to the foundation phase under Lysimachos and Arsinoë, who were closely connected with the sanctuary of Samothrake,[9] remains speculative at the moment.

Fig. 27: Sketch of the situation of the street crossing (Triodos) with graves and the settlement Smyrna at the coastline in Archaic and Classical times

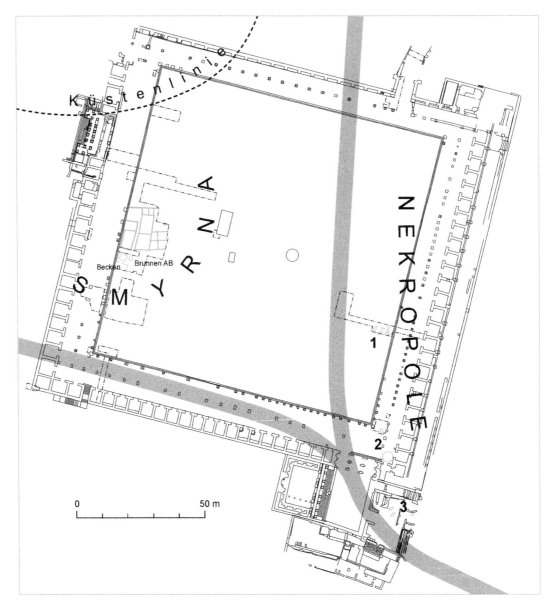

It is important that this customs house in the harbour area was still in use in Hadrianic times, when a certain Cominia Iunia dedicated a statue of and an altar for Isis.[10] This provides clear evidence that, besides Artemis Ephesia as the main dedicatee in both known inscriptions,[11] also Isis and the gods of Samothrake played an important role for those involved in the fish business over the course of time. Even if Isis may have come into the fishermen's focus only under Hadrian, the veneration of the goddess in harbours is typical for cities under Ptolemaic rulership and may have evolved in Ephesos already in the later 3rd c. BC, according to other inscriptions dedicated to Isis and Serapis.[12] Thus both the customs house and the harbour in its principal location may well date back to the very early phase (3rd c. BC) of Hellenistic Ephesos. Therefore, this customs house very likely already served as one of the locations for the financing of Hellenistic rulers[13] or the temple of Artemis Ephesia. Especially the revenues of fishery, withdrawn by the Attalid Kings and later the Roman *publicani* from the Artemision, were the subject of long quarrels between the Ephesians and Pergamon as well as Rome throughout the 2nd c. BC.[14]

According to literary sources and inscriptions, a sanctuary to Aphrodite must also have existed at the coast or near the harbour, at the latest since the 2nd c. BC; its precise location and appearance are, however, not known.[15] Recently S. Ladstätter has advocated the theory, with very interesting considerations, that this cult could have been secondary in the Roman harbour, and that in the 3rd/2nd c. BC a temple of Aphrodite might have existed on the most exterior cape of Tracheia, projecting far into the sea and to the north (outside) of the Lysimachean city.[16] At this location traces of the foundations of the so-called Crevice Temple (prostyle of 14.7 × 22.2 m; plan 1 no. 103; fig. 29 no. 1) of the early Hellenistic period have been discovered, which probably – similarly to the temple at Cape Sounion – served ships as a point of orientation and the city as a hallmark feature. According to the finds, in this sanctuary at the latest after the mid-3rd c. BC a female divinity was apparently worshipped; her name is disputed in the scholarship.[17] Ladstätter sees the possibility of an identification of the sanctuary with a cult of Arsinoë II, during her lifetime, as Aphrodite, via analogy with Cape Zephyrion near Alexandria.[18] But, as argued above, if the harbour was already located in its known place of the Trajanic or early Hadrianic era, the assumption of a relocation of the sanctuary of Aphrodite seems an unnecessary complication, and we ought to search for another goddess as the dedicatee of the Crevice Temple.

Most likely, another harbour is meant, when Strabon records a dam project carried out by Attalos II in the 2nd c. BC. It failed and, as an artificial lagoon wall, caused an even more rapid silting up of the harbour as had previously been the case.[19] It can be assumed that – as research in the 19th c. had already supposed[20] – this (second) original harbour of the early Hellenistic period was situated deeper in the bay, approximately in the area of the Arkadiane (plan 1, roughly between no. 84 and no. 87) and the Xystoi (so-called Halls of Verulanus; plan 1 no. 94) or further to the north somewhere along the peninsula with the Crevice Temple. Recent research is looking for this harbour in the region of the Hadrianic Olympieion (plan 1 no. 98) to the north of the former bay.[21] As we shall discuss later, the Hellenistic Ephesian writer Kreophylos, in the excerpt of Athenaios, ought to have designated this harbour as "sacred harbour" (ἱερὸς λιμήν).[22]

This harbour probably served the war fleet that participated in 191 BC in the Roman-Syrian war, a harbour that according to Livius had a capacity of 100 triremes.[23] The obviously isolated fortification on the so-called Acropolis Hill (plan 1 no. 102), apparently erected in the early 2nd c. BC,[24] would have been an appropriate protection of this large harbour. With this exposed location outside the city, the military harbour would have been removed from any access or seizure by the citizens of Ephesos, and would have been solely under the control of the garrison of the respective ruler. The natural silting and eventual vanishing of this harbour in the course of the 2nd c. BC did not cause problems as the new masters of Republican Rome no longer needed a large war harbour. So it did not matter that the whole area between the Hellenistic city wall south of the later Arkadiane street and the Tracheian peninsula successively was silted and subsequently became building land at the latest between Augustus and Hadrian.

The conclusion is that the centre of the city, that according to the words of Pausanias had to be relocated by Lysimachos "as far as the sea"[25] because the old harbours at Koressos (plan 1 no. 3: plan 2) and near the Artemision were no longer functional and the rising groundwater flooded the houses, is to be sought in the level area of dry land between the Tetragonos Agora up to the west until the southern side of the harbour basin of the high imperial period, still recognisable today, as well as the adjacent slopes of Mt. Preon.

2. Public buildings: agoras, theatre, gymnasia

As already mentioned above, up until the death of Lysimachos in 281 BC, not only the broadly extended city walls were already functioning; in addition, a public plaza described in an inscription as the *western agora* (δυτικὴ ἀγορά)[26] was at such a state of completion that public decrees could be inscribed on the walls of the administrative buildings that were already in use as well.[27] This agora was accordingly the "Free Agora" (ἐλευθέρα ἀγορά)[28] already posited by Aristotle; this space should primarily serve the political and cultic purposes of the polis as well as gatherings and exchanges of opinion of its citizens, not hampered by the noise and dirt associated with the trading of goods. Based on its name, its location can be assumed at the west of the harbour plain; a space that has never been investigated but which is topographically appropriate tentatively marked with "W" in fig. 21.

In rough outlines, the essential areas and the chronology of the second plaza claimed by Aristotle, the Commercial Agora, with dimensions of ca. 95 × 125 m, are known. Its construction began, according to the stratigraphic data, most likely at first in about 270/260 BC;[29] in a total of at least four large-scale building phases, it developed from an open space with at least one free-standing hall in the west into a plaza closed on all sides and framed by stoas (fig. 26). In the west, that is, in the direction of the harbour, a gate (directly under the West Gate of the later Roman agora) can be assumed; the remaining sides are too inadequately studied for such insights. Since the early 3rd c. BC a gravelled road, archaeologically investigated, led here from the West Gate down to the former seabed; this road must have been laid out as one of the central axes (plateia; plan 1 no. 65; fig. 29 no. 15, today called West Street) of the new city, running through the harbour plain. It probably connected the West Agora with the Commercial Agora.

During the Augustan period, the Hellenistic Commercial Agora (fig. 26) was built over by a significantly larger (154 m in the square) market place (fig. 33), in the west at a level up to 6 m higher; at least after this time, it was designated as the *Tetragonos Agora* (τετράγωνος ἀγορά). While construction was still taking place, this site was destroyed by a serious earthquake (almost certainly in 23 AD), and was only opened under Emperor Claudius with a partially altered building plan. The final completion, however, occurred under Emperor Nero; during his reign, the dedication of a two-aisled law basilica took place, identified epigraphically as an *auditorium* (today called Neronian Hall; figs. 33b. 34. 36. 37) in the area of the upper storey of the east side, along the Marble Street.[30]

"The agora for merchandise must be different from the free agora,
and in another place." (Aristoteles, pol. 1331 b1)

An additional public building of grand scale is the theatre on the west slope of Mt. Pion (southern part of the Panayırdağ; fig. 90). According to the most recent research, the theatre goes back to a core building of the (mid?) 2nd c. BC, that is, it could not have belonged to the original structures of the Hellenistic city, at least not at this location.[31] During the Augustan era, alterations took place, while in the Domitianic-Trajanic period the stage façade was built anew and the koilon was reconstructed in grand style with a third diazoma.[32] The date of the completion can be very well argued with the endowment inscription, engraved in the stage wall, of the equestrian C. Vibius Salutaris from the year 104/105 AD, since with this endowment amongst other regulations the awarding of seats for the most important civic groups (gerousia, ephebes, phylai etc.) is regulated.[33]

The so-called State Agora (also modernly called the 'Upper Agora'; plan 1 no. 18; plan 5), located in the saddle between the two city hills Mt. Pion and Mt. Preon (fig. 90), has been viewed for a long time as the political centre of the city already in the Hellenistic period.[34] Recently, however, studies have shown that here, after the early 2nd c. BC under Ptolemaic and Attalid rule, a gymnasium (plan 5, red parts no. 1–4) with a xystos, a training raceway in the length of a stadium (ca. 180 m) (plan 5 no. 1), and perhaps also a stadium was laid out.[35] In the early Augustan period, the imperial cult found its first home here, especially in the so-called Rhodian peristyle (plan 5 no. 7).[36] The worship of the imperial house, increasingly expressed in large buildings such as the Basilike Stoa (completed 11 AD; plan 5 no. 5) and the erection of a temple (plan 5 no. 15) at the site shortly thereafter, forced the practice of sport out of this area completely in the course of the early 1st c. AD.[37] At first under Domitian, however, the new building of a stadium – already fairly advanced at the latest under Nero – was completed in the furthest northern extent of the expanded civic area (plan 1 no. 104).[38]

Probably already under Augustus or Tiberius, the prytaneion of the city (plan 5 no. 6) was relocated to the area of the former sport site; the prytaneion nevertheless had to be renewed from the ground up after the earthquake of 23 AD.[39] It is the subject of a long debate, whether there was an earlier (Hellenistic) prytaneion in another place in the city or if the prytanis, as the eponymous "high-priest", had his office in the Artemision.[40] As the prytanis and the collegium of the Curetes, headed by him, were deeply involved in the process of transforming ephebes to full citizens, the location in the immediate vicinity of the Gymnasium of the Paides/Ephebes under Augustus seems a well-considered political act to supervise the youth and train the boys in Roman thought and imperial cult, as happened in Rome itself and most other cities by the *iuventus* organisation. But only with a new bouleuterion (plan 5 no. 8)[41] – erected behind the Basilike Stoa and next to the prytaneion and the imperial cult area of the early Augustan period (the Rhodian peristyle) – in the time around 100 AD the modern designation of the area as a 'State Agora' seems justified.

On the city plan of the Roman imperial period, this State Agora lies apparently very centrally, but seen from the harbour, the actual nerve centre of the city, the area is rather remote.[42] Thus, the already frequently cited demand of Aristotle, to situate the gymnasium of the ephebes – at Ephesos, according to the inscription it was the youths (*paides*) and the new citizens (*neoi*) who trained here[43] – at the borders of the city so that the noise and exuberance of the youths would not disturb civic life, is well satisfied with the location of this gymnasium beneath the later State Agora, if one considers the probable extent of the city and the course of the city walls in the Hellenistic period.

3. City walls and gates

Scholars have generally assumed that the entire known course of the city walls, mostly 2.90 m wide and originally ca. 6.50 m high, was already planned and substantially completed under Lysimachos (plan 1 no. 11, and plan 2; fig. 29).[44] In recent years, however, it has become apparent – above all due to the discovery of a city gate of the 3rd c. BC in the area of the Roman Tetragonos Agora (see fig. 26, site KT) and based on new studies at the Magnesian Gate in the east of the city – that an extensive urban expansion under Augustus, and consequently also a partial relocation of the city walls, has to be reckoned with. In order to be able realistically to assess the extent of the Lysimachean city foundation, a new analysis of the existing building stock (fig. 29 no. 14) is therefore required.

The defensive installations, beginning in the west far in front of the (today still recognisable) harbour basin with a fortress in the form of a four-chambered tower (tower 1; side length ca. 14.50–14.60 m) run from the sea up to the Astyages Hill to another tower of the same form (tower 3), which has been known since the 17th c.

as St. Paul's Prison (plan 2; fig. 29 no. 17).[45] Then the city wall runs further to the west to the Hermaion Hill that projected (at that time) like a cape into the sea; first after this, the wall turns to the south and the east.

In 1912, J. Keil could already prove that the large tower 1 at the coast could not have functioned as a gate.[46] It can therefore be presumed that the gate was located further to the east, perhaps at the western end of the harbour installation. The main source for the assumption of this coastal defence, which in itself seems logical anyway, is an inscription earlier fixed on tower 3, the so-called St. Paul's Prison: "From the leasehold we exclude a path to the sea of twenty feet, in that we cut off from the land twenty feet towards the wall on the property of Kleitophon …".[47] With the course of the road between the coast and the wall, an optimal forefield defence was created, since assailants could be attacked from the wall on their unprotected sword-carrying side. As up to now no trace of this wall along the shore could be detected, a complete removal in Roman imperial times can be taken into consideration.

While for many other Greek cities it is a long standing knowledge
that Roman Emperors generously widened not only their extension,
but also their enclosures, in Ephesos such a possibility
has never been discussed.

At the same time, the course of the wall in this section indicates that the entire, gentle coastal section of Mt. Preon (Bülbüldağ), including its foothills that were, as already said, designated in antiquity as Lepre Akte, was envisaged as a main settlement area of the city.

From the Hermaion, the wall climbs up to Mt. Preon, runs along its ridge to the east, with another large free-standing commando tower at the peak, and then follows the hill back down to the plain (fig. 28). In this section, the wall possesses 46 single-chamber towers (side length between ca. 8 and 10.5 m; wall width between 1.6 and 2.5 m), and in addition 19 posterns and 23 stairs to guards' walkways are attested on the Bülbüldağ. The entire course of the wall is therefore characterised by a zig-zagging of the wall route, representative of Hellenistic defensive walls (so-called sawtooth section), designed on the one hand for a better view of the exterior side, and on the other hand, because the wall course always sprung to the inside at the staircase platforms, to provide the defenders hurrying there with direct access to the battlements.

At the south-eastern end of the Bülbüldağ, at the lowest tower in the course of the descent of the wall from the hill, the style of the wall course abruptly changes (the section described in the following is marked with a red line in plan 2). At first, it

Fig. 28: Well-pre-
served part of the
Lysimachean city
wall on Mount
Preon (Bülbüldağ)
with postern gate

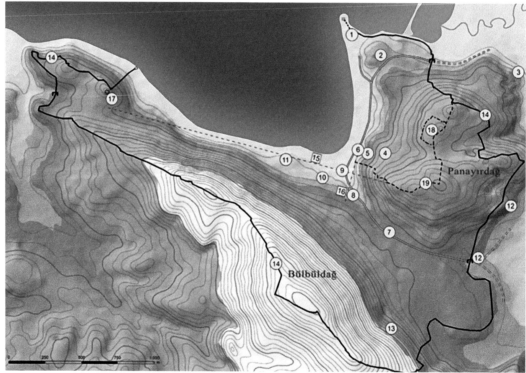

Fig. 29: Mapping
of Hellenistic
building remains
in Ephesos (after
Ladstädter 2016).

1: So-called Crevice Temple	5: So-called Heroon	11: Küçük Tepe	17: Tower (so-called St. Paul´s Prison)
2: So-called Ionian Acropolis	6: Great Theatre	12: Necropolis	18: Akra (military base)
3: Sanctuary of Meter	7: Upper Agora	13: Aqueduct	19: Byzantine city wall, probably partly on Hellenistic founda- tions
4: Complex above the Theatre	8: Terrace Houses	14: City Wall	
	9: Lower Agora	15: East-West Street	
	10: So-called Serapeion	16: North-South Street	

THE ARCHITECTURAL DEVELOPMENT OF HELLENISTIC EPHESOS

runs for a short distance along the contour line towards the city, then it proceeds straight into the valley, where it constitutes a wide loop towards the outside. At the opposite end of the loop, at the foot of Mt. Pion, the most well-known city gate of Ephesos, the Magnesian Gate (Μαγνητικὴ πύλη) locates;[48] from this point onwards, the wall continues again for a good 100 m straight on to the beginning of the steep slope of the Panayırdağ. We shall return to this section later on and discuss its possible date as belonging to the Augustan enlargement of the city.

Subsequently, the course of the wall can only be recognised in patches, mostly by the lines of the outer faces of the wall with a width between them of 2.90 m, or at the most by individual rows of stones. The course of the wall with its only short and straight or slightly curved sections, sharp corners between the towers, and sawtooth section, as also typical for the wall remains on Mt. Preon, is nevertheless comprehensible.[49] The wall also encloses the southern and eastern side of Mt. Pion and then ascends the slope up until just below the peak, to the north, where it finally peters out high up above the theatre and just inside the Byzantine city wall, at least in its latest phase.[50]

The scant remains of two circular fortifications, of fundamentally similar building technique as the city wall, are evident on the outside of the city wall on the Tracheia (northern part of the Panayırdağ) (plan 2; fig. 29 no. 18, 90).[51] The upper circle at the peak probably constituted the *akra,* epigraphically attested by the Ptolemaian phrourarch of Ptolemaios (IV), that is, the fortified heights in which the garrison commanded by him lay (compare also fig. 29 no. 18).[52] The lower, larger circle most probably served as a reserve room for the occasional stationing of larger troop units and animals, or as a site of refuge for the rural population in case of war.[53]

After the Peace of Apameia in in 188 BC, the Pergamene representative probably erected a residence for himself (plan 1 no. 76; fig. 29 no. 4) in a large, peristyle house[54] directly above the theatre (which was apparently constructed at roughly the same time or slightly earlier), and thereby under the protection of the *akra*[55]; this location was both easily accessible as well as secure, and had a prestigious effect in the distance. The view of the tiers of the Hellenistic large-scale buildings, beginning with the theatre at the foot of the cliff, past the governor's palace (called basileia by the excavators), and up to the *akra*, must have been most impressive to incoming ships. Perhaps for this reason, Plinius the Elder wrote in the mid–1st c. AD that Ephesos "rises up Mount Pion" (*attollitur monte Pione*).[56]

The next secure indication for the course of the Hellenistic city wall in the north, running down from Mt. Pion to the coast, was provided by a surprise discovery in 1997 underneath the North Gate of the imperial-period Tetragonos Agora. Here, another city gate, probably the Koressian Gate (Κορησσικὴ πύλη), could be localised (figs. 26. 30. 31).[57] The date of the gate, to the early 3rd c. BC, is stratigraphi-

Fig. 30: View of the western inner corner of the presumed Koressian Gate beneath the North Gate of the Agora

cally at any rate secure. Based on the nevertheless scant remains, excavated in a narrow sondage in the Late Antique gateway, the gate was a frontal gate with forecourt open at the front and possibly a small compound lying behind the outer gate.[58] A country road, whose name was probably *Plateia in Koressos*, led through the gate into the city.[59] In contrast to the long-distance connection to Magnesia through the eastern main gate, here only a local hinterland was accessible, namely, the earlier Koressos harbour (plan 2) and the settlement lying nearby; according to epigraphic evidence, this settlement was located, at least still in the Roman imperial period, outside the fortified city.[60]

From the Koressian Gate the city wall (light green lines in plan 2) ran, on the one hand, towards the west, most probably in a fairly straight, but zig-zagging line as far as the coast at that time and/or to the eastern border of the harbour bay. The western part of this wall, the course of which reveals the typically Hellenistic sawtooth section, was integrated into the new city wall apparently in the Byzantine period (probably in the early 7th c. AD), or the Byzantine wall was built on its foundations (plan 1 no. 77; plan 2).[61] An excavation of the foundations or a building investigation, which might bring certainty, has unfortunately never taken place.

In the other direction, the city wall ran from the eastern side of the Koressian Gate in a straight line to the north (figs. 31 and 32a+b; plan 2 light green line), and indeed precisely at the western side border of the Marble Street (as is its modern name), on whose eastern side the theatre lay.[62] This street, roughly parallel to the old country road, must have existed already in the Hellenistic age and took over the role of the old main road (*plateia in Koressos*) in the early Roman imperial period, after the expansion of the Tetragonos Agora to the east as wide as an entire block.[63] This then served as a new main approach road from the north, that is, from the Artemision across the slowly silting up lagoon Selinousia; it also ensured that an adequate traffic axis was preserved for the new stadium, planned at the northern border of the city, as well as for the enlarged theatre and the audience connected with its performances. Consequently, the only possibility for the necessary widening of the street was the removal of the city wall down to the paving level of this new main artery.

The further extent of the city wall to the north cannot be argued based on finds at the moment. Since, however, as described above, it is again recognisable some-

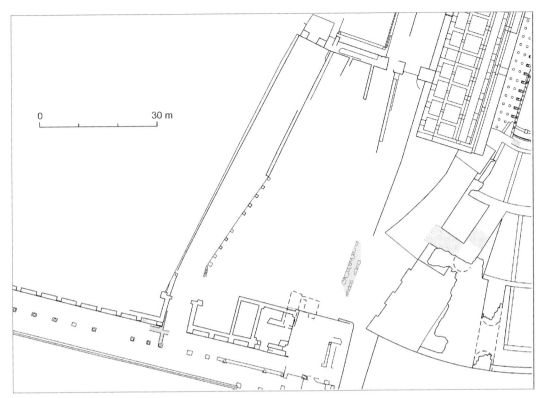

Fig. 31: Sketch plan of the excavated parts of the city gate and the city wall between the Tetragonos Agora and the Theatre

Fig. 32: The course of the Hellenistic city wall along the western side of the Marble Street opposite the southern analemma walls of the theatre; a) view to the south towards the northern end of the Neronian Hall; b) view to the west from the theatre

what to the north of the peak area of Mt. Pion (fig. 90), just to the north of the Hellenistic theatre, it must have curved to the east or south-east somewhat north of the theatre, and then climbed up the cliff slope.[64]

According to current knowledge, therefore, both the Harbour Gate in the west as well as the Koressian Gate lay in verified positions, with the coast close by on one side of the forefield, and with a section of the city wall accompanying the approach road on the other side. This situation corresponded to the strategic standards of the time: geographically close by, an exceptional parallel for this topographical condition is found at the main gate (East Gate) of Priene, dating approximately 30 to max. 50 years earlier.[65]

This circumstance, however, was in no way applicable at the known Magnesian Gate at the eastern end of the city. As already noted above, it was located frontally in a straight stretch of wall and was prestigiously visible from far away in the plain. The projecting course of the wall, after a few metres in a loop to the east and leading diagonally from the gate, could no longer guarantee a real defence of the forefield (plan 1 no. 10; fig. 29 near no. 12). Due to this, the dating of the Magnesian Gate, and therefore that of the entire segmental arch of the city wall, reaching far into the plain and creating large, intra-urban spaces for development, in the lightly falling away plain between Mts. Pion and Preon (fig. 90) where archaeological or architectural-historical investigations have never taken place – with the exception of the area of the Magnesian Gate itself – must be questioned for several reasons.

City gates in the Roman imperial times were not necessarily easily defensive, but presented the dignitas and urbanitas of cities in the pax Romana.

The Magnesian Gate, until today only partially excavated due to the modern asphalt road, was already discovered by J. T. Wood in 1869 and was for a long time self-evidently viewed as early Hellenistic in origin, even if the existing structural elements were dated rather to the period around 100 BC, above all due to a few weapon reliefs.[66] Doubt was first cast on this early construction date when an alteration to the northern corner tower in the forecourt could be stratigraphically ascribed with certainty to the early imperial period (probably after the earthquake of 23 AD).[67] Furthermore, a building seam was recognised between this tower – the southern one was in any case completely newly built in Late Antiquity – and the wall of the gate courtyard running to the north of this on the city side; in terms of building technology, this wall and accordingly the whole gate must be more recent than the northern tower.[68] More recent excavations in the region of the threshold wall of the frontal double gate indeed revealed a foundation wall below, which is older in comparison to the existing building elements of the gate and which was attributed to the early Hellenistic city wall, but no reliable evidence for a pre-imperial date was discovered.[69] For this reason, the city wall and the frontal gate in this location appear to date, in their oldest existing building stock, most likely to the period of and after Augustus. Consequently, one of the typical, ostentatious, (early) imperial Asia Minor court gates was erected here, designed not for defence but for prestige.[70] Based on the most recent investigations, archaeologists have meanwhile been able to similarly date the typologically close gate installations at Side and Perge which were previously assigned to the high Hellenistic period. These were also first erected in or more likely after the Augustan period,[71] whereas in Ephesos the body of the building was so badly damaged by the earthquake of 23 AD (?), that extensive parts of it had to be built anew. At this site and in this form, all these gates contradicted everything that we know about (early) Hellenistic fortifications. Their location and construction made them extremely exposed and therefore correspondingly endangered, but the gates now could be seen from far away as a signature of the city.[72]

As a consequence, we should assume that the Magnesian Gate of the Lysimachean period must be located significantly further to the west, on a higher spot; in this case, the city walls ought to have run from both sides, in the form of a funnel, towards the gate which would have then been well-protected. The innermost point at which the gate can originally have been built lies just to the east of the State Agora (= Hellenistic Gymnasium of the Neoi), where today the approach road to the ancient ruins bends in a 90 degree curve to the south and ascends the Bülbüldağ (plan 1 no. 115). Localising the early Hellenistic gate at this area, or slightly below, would ideally correspond with the locations on the Bülbüldağ and Panayırdağ regarding the course of the contour lines (plan 2, light green line). In those locations, the known city wall notably diverges from its typical course of very short, straight stretches with many projections and recesses, instead constituting an extremely direct or extended, curved track in which absolutely no sawtooth sections are evident.[73] If this were the case, the Gymnasium of the Neoi and the stadium, assumed to be in this typically peripheral location near the city wall – compare again the neighbouring city of Priene with many close parallels to the site at Ephesos[74] – and the absence of Hellenistic architectural evidence in the entire region to the east (cf. fig. 29) would be easily explained.

4. Conclusions regarding the extent of the Hellenistic city and the Augustan urban expansion

In addition to the residents of the old city of Ephesos and the population of the village of Smyrna that was destroyed in the course of the refounding, Lysimachos also settled people from Lebedos, Kolophon, and Teos in his new foundation of Arsinoeia. Yet even this considerable increase in population of the new city, compared to old Ephesos, could probably fill only a part of the new urban area, broadly surrounded by city walls.[75] The part of the city that lay at a higher elevation and further inland was enclosed by the walls probably mainly for strategic reasons and as a reserve for the expansion and growth of the city, or as an open area for the intake of the rural population and animals in the case of hostilities.[76]

The picture of the city in the early Hellenistic period that has been obtained so far from excavation, surveys, and combined analyses reveals an elongated city plan along the lower slopes on the north side of Mt. Preon and on the relatively narrow, flat, coastal land in front of it; the southern part of Mt. Pion was equally included

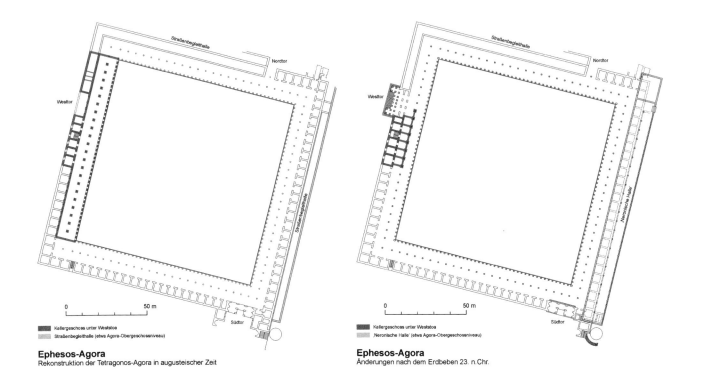

Ephesos-Agora
Rekonstruktion der Tetragonos-Agora in augusteischer Zeit

Ephesos-Agora
Änderungen nach dem Erdbeben 23. n.Chr.

Fig. 33: Plan of the Tetragonos Agora; a) Augustan construction; b) alterations after the earthquake of 23 AD with smaller basement in the west and newly added Auditorium (Neronian Hall)

in the protected area. Most of the public installations such as the agoras and the gymnasium of the gerousia lay in the harbour plain.

The majority of the residential buildings must have spread along here and on the gentle slopes of the Bülbüldağ up until the Marble Street. Until now, however, excavation has only identified definitively Hellenistic residential development at a few locations, for example small sections of late Hellenistic houses and commercial buildings in the courtyard of the so-called Serapeion (plan 1 no. 67; fig. 29 no. 10).[77] Along the Marble Street, houses must have stood at least on the western side, before the Augustan expansion of the Tetragonos Agora (fig. 26 and 33a) and the Neronian Hall (fig. 33b) finally occupied this area up to the street.[78] The non-existent development of the eastern urban area applied already to the larger part of the Embolos quarter with the Curetes Street. Immediately after its commencement at the intersection with the Marble Street, beneath the two Terrace Houses (plan 1 no. 50 and no. 51), that is, in the slope area directly south of the Octagon, no dense Hellenistic urban development before the middle of the 1st c. BC could be identified; individual terrace walls and wells indicate a loose settlement pattern (fig. 29 no. 8).[79]

From the current state of research it emerges that large areas in the east of the urban area remained (widely) undeveloped up until the early Roman imperial period, and probably the street system was not even completely developed.[80] For this reason, in spite of a certainly well-planned Hellenistic street grid, the naturally sloping rut which bore the descriptive name Embolos (ἔμβολος = wedge)[81] between the two hills of the city, served as an irregular traffic route, probably characterised by curves. Only after the Augustan period was this broadway-like course of the nowadays known as Curetes Street more precisely defined by increasing development on both sides (plans 1–3; fig. 90);[82] the street therefore was developed into a prestigious main artery in order to facilitate travel from the harbour plain in dignified fashion to the new imperial cult centre on the saddle (State Agora) and the newly built quarter around it, and vice versa. The first paving of the route, formerly only gravelled, occurred at the earliest under Nero, yet first demonstrably under Domitian.[83] The terms Embolos and Embolitai (for the inhabitants of this city quarter) are only attested, up until now, in imperial inscriptions after the late 1st c. AD, and not for the Hellenistic period, for which we know of no street names in Ephesos.[84] Whether this naming refers to the natural formation of the "incision" or whether it is simply a designation for a main road, occasionally used in other cities as well, must remain open at the moment.[85]

The layout and structure of Hellenistic Ephesos
will not be satisfyingly explainable as long as the harbour plain
is not the subject of intensive archaeological investigation.

The garrisons of the non-resident rulers in the Hellenistic period were located on the dominant heights of the Tracheia (*akra*) and its north-western ridges (harbour fortification after the 2nd c. BC?), and were at a considerable distance from the civil urban area with its more or less autonomous polis administration.

At the earliest at the transition from the 3rd to the 2nd c. BC, at the eastern border of the city (in the region of the later State Agora) an additional area, one which was considerably further east and at a higher elevation, was extensively developed within the city walls; the laying out of the Gymnasium of the Neoi, to which a xystos (practice running track) and perhaps a stadium were associated (plan 5), is evidence of this development. The next constructions, probably almost contemporary or immediately afterwards, were the theatre and the residence (basilcia) on the western slope of Mt. Pion (fig. 90). The installations at the harbour and the sea are blatantly obvious, while the Embolos (Curetes Street), as the intramural section of the road leading to Magnesia and Priene, ran through broadly undeveloped terrain, with the exception of fountain houses (plan 3 nos. 9 and 12) in its lowest area.

The generous Augustan civic expansion came up with a new urban area that projected far into the plain in the east, from the land side, denoted from the outside by the splendid gate with forecourt on the Magnesian Road; this expansion probably additionally included a new quarter along the Tracheia and a new Koressian Gate, not yet located, in the north of the city in the land newly won from the sea. Precisely in these new urban quarters – on the one side from the region of the expanded Tetragonos Agora to the north and north-west, and on the other side from the former gymnasium (that was now developed into a cult centre for Augustus and the imperial family) to the east – a system of development characterised by square blocks of buildings, in contrast to the elongated rectangular street pattern of the Hellenistic period, appears to have been measured out.[86]

If the two city gates on the landward side were relocated to the outside under Augustus, then the parts of the city walls that belonged to them can only have been erected at that time at the earliest. The stretches of the Hellenistic city wall that were removed, above all around the theatre and on the adjacent slopes of Mt. Pion, were reused for their construction (plan 2, red lines).[87] In this manner, not only did the construction of the new wall traces save significant costs, but they also ensured a very similar appearance to those of approximately 300 years earlier.

The new walls, however, as partly recognisable at the line along the heights in the northern part of Panayırdağ and down to the stadium[88], were no longer constructed in the Hellenistic emplekton technique, but with *opus caementicium*, meaning that the joints between the ashlar blocks of the outer faces and the entire core were mortared, a technique that is not demonstrable in the city in the period before Augustus.

As it appears, the akra on the peak of the Tracheia was completely razed for the new building, perhaps also due to the prestigious symbol of a "free city" that this action expressed. The new construction probably began at the connecting wall of the actual city wall at the height of the Pion, ran first over the peak of the Tracheia, and then down towards the stadium, at that time newly planned (cf. plan 2). Where exactly the Augustan wall met the early Byzantine city wall (violet lines in plan 2), cannot be definitely decided without extensive investigations in the area around the stadium. Following an inscription that in the high imperial period still names a civic *quarter of the Koressites* in front of the city between the stadium (plan 1 no. 104) and the city gate,[89] in any event allows the conclusion that the Augustan wall ran more or less along the southern side the stadium,[90] then curved to the south along the contour line of the mountain, finally climbing down the slope to reach the old *plateia in Koressos*[91] in the direction of the theatre. Most likely, after the early imperial period,[92] the Koressian Gate is to be located slightly to the north of the so-called theatre gymnasium (plan 1 no. 79); here the street leaves its natural course in the terrain and continues its course (almost) in a straight line, in the grid of the urban street system (e.g. at the location in plan 1, where the entry for no. 78 is placed).[93] The dashed red line in plan 2 is only intended to give a rough idea of a possible course.

In the north as well as in the east of the city, therefore, under Augustus and in the early Roman imperial period, the urban area was substantially expanded by means of new city gates and the erection of, in part, new wall sections as well as the demolition of troubling older stretches of city wall; due to these measures, a generous Roman metropolis, one which was capable of development, was created in contrast to the confined Hellenistic proportions with the centre in the harbour plain. In this new city, the former Gymnasium of the Neoi from this time on was located at the centre of the urban (*prytaneion*) and imperial cult; furthermore, its location between the city hills meant that it also occupied the 'highest' position. As a consequence, under Domitian after 84 AD the first provincial imperial cult temple (neocorate temple) also was located here on an artificial terrace, and in a further direct consequence around 100 AD, with the new bouleuterion the most important building for the urban government was also set up (plan 5).

Fig. 34: Aerial photo of the Ephesian harbour plain; in the foreground the Marble Street, the Tetragonos Agora and the Triodos area with the Library of Celsus and the Amazon Altar (at the very left lower corner; only stairs to a platform remain); behind the agora are the ruins of the so-called Serapeion (middle left), in the background lies the (Roman) harbour, still flooded with water, and the Late Antique channel leading to the sea (uppermost part of the photo); to the left of the harbour are the lower gentle slopes of Mount Preon (Bülbüldağ) and the isolated Astyagos Hill with so-called St. Paul's Prison

The protector of Ephesos –
Artemis and her sacred Triodos

The main street network of Ephesos is well known for the Roman imperial period. To facilitate orientation, a short introductory overview will be provided, even if one or the other points of argument regarding the precise course and date of certain streets will first be addressed in the course of the discussion.

Even if a city was newly planned, the layout with a persistent regular grid system was challenged by the topography, different needs of citizens and rulers, and the historical development.

Fig. 35: Candelabrum (2nd c. AD?), lighting the Embolos street in front of the Hypelaios Fountain (in its last Late Antique usage)

At the border of the plain between Mts. Pion and Preon, more or less at the foot of the slope of Mt. Pion, the modern road leading to the Upper Entrance to the ruins (plan 1 no. 115) runs through the Magnesian Gate (plan 1 no. 10)[1] up to the State Agora; in so doing, within the ancient city area, this road follows almost exactly the old route of the *plateia*, named today the South Street. From Late Antiquity we know its designation as the street of the *hippoi* (horses' street), and we also know that this main thoroughfare, just like the Arkadiane (plan 1 no. 88) which connected the Roman harbour with the theatre, was artificially lit up at night.[2] Since two large candelabras were set up directly in front of the so-called Heroon of Androklos (plan 3 no. 9) in the Late Antique paving of the Curetes Street (fig. 35),[3] one can reasonably assume that the entire street system from the Magnesian Gate in the east to the harbour – that is, the South Street

as far as the first neocorate temple (so-called Temple of Domitian; plan 1 no. 30), then the so-called Alley of Domitian, the Curetes Street at the Embolos (plan 1 near no. 36), the Marble Street along the Agora (plan 1 no. 61; fig. 36) as far as the theatre (plan 1 no. 75), and then the Arkadiane as far as the harbour – was not only continuously illuminated, but also constituted the main axes of Ephesos in the Roman imperial period up until the early 7th c. AD.

Additional significant streets were the connection from the former harbour settlement of Koressos near the stadium, leading through the Koressian Gate to the theatre (plan 1 no. 78), its continuation to the south as far as the Embolos constituting the Marble Street in the Roman period (figs. 36 and 37); and the physically unknown street that led, in a continuation of the Curetes Street south of the Tetragonos Agora, past the harbour and further to the city gate to Pygela. In addition, parallel to this in the north, a wide boulevard (the West Street; plan 1 no. 65) ran from the Tetragonos Agora as far as the Medusa Gate (plan 1 nos. 61. 65. 66); this, as proved by excavation results,[4] dates back to the Hellenistic foundation phase and probably connected the two agoras with each other. Moreover, as shown above,[5] in the Hellenistic period the entrance to the city through the Koressian Gate lay a city block to the west at that time below the later Agora North Gate (plan 1 no. 64; fig. 26 marked KT; fig. 33), at the eastern border of the Hellenistic commercial agora. Between the city gate and the agora another street leading to the harbour area in the west must have served for heavy transport and other commercial traffic.

A main reason for irregularities, especially of the course of main routes from the gates to the centre, was their function as processional streets with certain fixed spots, where important cult activities or political acts had their place.

Given these conditions, the South Gate – paid for by the freedmen Mazaios and Mithridates – of the expanded Augustan Tetragonos Agora (plan 3 no. 2; figs. 33. 37. 41) lay fairly precisely at the original intersection, known as the Triodos, of the three old long distance roads that were in part used as streets of tombs in the Archaic–Classical periods (plan 2; fig. 27).[6] Since the time of Lysimachos these func-

Fig. 36: View of the Triodos, the Marble Street with the adjacent Neronian Hall and the Tetragonos Agora (seen from the south) as found in the excavations around 1904

Fig. 37: View today of the Triodos, the Marble Street with the adjacent Neronian Hall and the Tetragonos Agora (seen from the south-east) after the excavations and reconstruction works in the later 20th c.

tioned as main axes of the city, and the city gates that were set up on them were named – as is still often common today – after the directions in which they led from Ephesos. Here, the roads that led to Koressos, Magnesia, and Pygela (Kuşadası) all met. Dieter Knibbe connected this last-mentioned road above all with the as yet undiscovered site of Ortygia, the mythical birthplace of Ephesian Artemis, and attempted to introduce the term "Ortygia Street" into the literature. Unfortunately, we know neither the exact location of the city gate, compellingly assumed to be in the west, nor its ancient name, so that the actual name of the street and of the gate remains obscure.[7] According to Strabon, this Ortygia with its temple installations and eating houses nevertheless lay on the mountain of Solmissos, in such a manner that it could be seen from the boat journey between Pygela and Ephesos; Pausanias mentioned the location at the river Kenchrios.[8] At Ortygia, after a great procession the Ephesians celebrated the annually recurring festival of the birth of their goddess, and the college of the Curetes carried out sacred rituals, probably during the bestowal of citizenship on the ephebes.[9] The site has not yet been found today, but recently, without convincing arguments, it has been localised in the valley which is known today as Arvalya.[10]

The Triodos, until Augustan times directly in front of the South Gate (figs. 36f.) was laid out in its ultimate form in the second decade of the 2nd c. AD and the space was completely redesigned when the Library of Celsus (fig. 66; plan 1 no. 55),[11] and further to the west the so-called Serapeion (fig. 34; plan 1 no. 67),[12] were erected over the old coast road towards Pygela that up to this time ran immediately to the south of the agora. Now, with the so-called Hadrian's Gate (probably erected already under Trajan in 114/115 AD; plan 4; fig. 49),[13] a new intersection was marked at the end of the Marble Street and, to the south of the South Gate, an almost enclosed

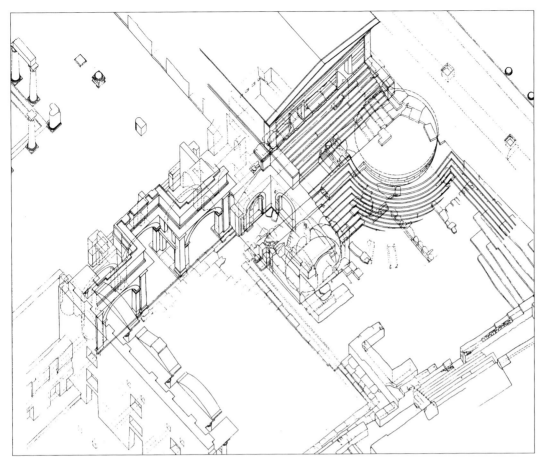

Fig. 38: Trigonometric representation of the area in front of the South Gate of the Agora with the vestibule to the entrances of the three tombs of Mithridates, Dionysios Rhetor, and Flavius Hypsikles. In the east the staircase from the plaza up to the auditorium adjoins, surrounding the circular monument for the *Aqua Iulia*, built at the demand of and paid for by Augustus

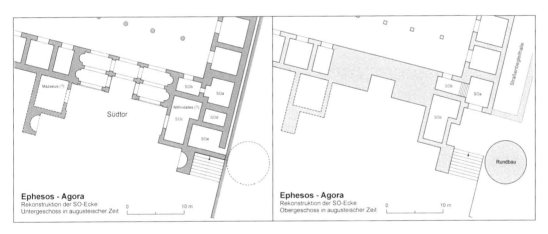

Fig. 39: Reconstruction of the plan of the south-east corner of the Augustan Tetragonos Agora; a) ground floor; b) upper storey

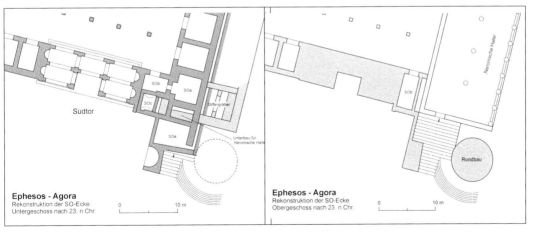

Fig. 40: Plan of the south-east corner of the Tetragonos Agora after the earthquake of 23 AD; a) ground floor; b) upper storey

plaza was created (plan 3). The road towards Pygela now ran to the south of Hadrian's Gate, while at the lower end of the Curetes Street a cohesive architectural backdrop arose at its south side, down to the library below.

The designation 'Triodos' until now has only appeared in one inscription of the Augustan–Tiberian period, that was carved on a marble ashlar block from a wall, reused in Late Antiquity as a staircase block. The steps led from the Marble Street down to the plaza in front of the South Gate. The text, a large part of which is preserved, is as follows:[14]

[Ἡρακλείδης Ἀπολ]λωνίου Πασσαλᾶς προενοήθη
[τοῦ μὴ β]λάπτεσθαι τὴν ἀγορὰν ἐκ τῶν καταφερομένων
[εἰς αὐτὴ]ν ῥείθρων κατασκευάσας ἐγδοχῖα καὶ τὸ δυσπαρόδευτον
[τὸ ἐπὶ τῆς] Τριόδου, στρῶμα ἀνελόμενος, διωρθώσατο ἐκ τῶν ἰδίων
[παρασχό]μενος τὸ εἰς αὐτὰ δαπάνημα

"Herakleides] Passalas, son of [Apol]lonios, took precautions that the torrents flowing down did not damage the agora, in that he laid out collectors, and eliminated the circumstance that one could not walk on the Triodos, in that he raised the paving; he paid for the necessary expenses from his own means."

With the reference to "Triodos", the inscription naturally does not designate the South Gate itself, as Dieter Knibbe and Gerhard Langmann assumed, but instead the small "plaza" in front of it.[15] This was inundated with water that subsequently flooded the agora. The installation of large collecting pools beneath the passages of the South Gate necessitated the raising of the pavement level in the passages, whereby holes for water drainage were mortised into the kerbstones (fig. 38). From here, at first two drains ran into the agora court; these united after a couple of metres, creating a main drainage canal running diagonally to the north-west across the agora. From the level of its vaulted upper surface it conforms more to the Tiberian-Claudian rebuilding of the agora than to the Augustan original plan, which lies one ashlar level deeper.[16] The original building planning for the South Gate (fig. 39) and the Augustan agora probably did not take into consideration periodic flooding for the reason that the quantity of water was originally channelled into the coastal road running directly to the south of the agora and could be diverted away. Probably, it was precisely the South Gate with its wings (fig. 39), projecting far forwards, that contributed to the fact that the water could not (completely) flow away into that street, but instead was redirected towards the gate and into the agora.

The South Gate itself, therefore, was not the Triodos, but instead constituted its northern demarcation. To this conclusion fits the fact that the original building, with its two structural wings, formed a funnel to the south; the honorary tombs of the two founders, Mazaios, freedman of Augustus, and Mithridates, freedman of Augustus' friend and field marshal Marcus Vipsanius Agrippa, were envisaged here.[17] These side wings widen out from the gate with the same sequence of architraves and archivolts or conches that also decorate the gate itself; they projected even more to the outside so that the gate virtually invited the two streets in front of it (the Embolos from the east and the coast road from the west) to turn into it. In precisely this manner, the typical three-passage situation arose (fig. 39); with a frontal gate building in a straight line, in contrast, a commonplace T–formed street intersection would have arisen, by which the gate would have completely swallowed up the character of the Triodos. This ingenious solution, unique in antiquity, that with the eastern front building obstructed the difficult slope situation in optimal fashion, only existed, however, for about a quarter of a century due to the earthquake of 23 AD.

As in most other cases of human actions, alterations in city centres,
often caused by changing natural conditions, social demands or political will,
always bring up new difficulties and insufficient situations,
which make further action necessary.

With the necessary rebuilding of the agora in the Tiberian-Claudian period, and the replanning in the eastern area with the Neronian Hall (auditorium), the flight of steps existing east of the South Gate was also rebuilt and was decisively lengthened and raised for the entrance to the Neronian Hall (compare figs. 39f.). In the cavity beneath these stairs – in addition to the assumed grave of Mithridates in the winged building and another one in the substructure of the Neronian Hall –, numerous additional honorary graves for worthy builders and famous rhetors and sophists were laid out in the course of the next 100 years (plan 3 and fig. 64). One of these so honoured was Titus Claudius Flavianus Dionysius Rhetor,[18] a favourite of Hadrian's; in spite of further rebuilding phases, his sarcophagus could be discovered (almost) in situ (fig. 74). Beneath it, steps were inserted,[19] on the building stones of which the Triodos inscription was discovered in 1989. We will return to these tombs extensively later on. Briefly it is important to point out that Dionysios, as Philostratos in his "Lives of the Sophists" notes, was buried in the most prestigious place of all of Ephesos:[20]

> Ἀνδρῶν μὲν οὖν ἐπιφανῶν πᾶσα γῆ τάφος, Διονυσίῳ δὲ σῆμα ἐν τῇ ἐπιφανεστάτῃ Ἐφέσῳ· τέθαπται γὰρ ἐν τῇ ἀγορᾷ κατὰ τὸ κυριώτατον τῆς Ἐφέσου, ἐν ᾗ κατεβίω, παιδεύσας τὸν πρῶτον βίον ἐν Λέσβῳ.

> "Famous men have the whole earth as their memorial [after Thuc. II 43, 3], yet the tomb monument of Dionysios is located in esteemed Ephesos, for he is buried in the agora, in the most important place in Ephesos, where his life ended, after he had taught in his earlier life on Lesbos."

This literary passage has been construed in many different ways: the phrase was formerly translated as "in the agora, the most noble place in the city", and by Helmut Engelmann more precisely as "in the most important area of the agora".[21] If, however, we compare the actual situation of the tomb, the passage can also be viewed as a very precise indication of the actual circumstances, suggesting two independent realities. In matter of fact, the tomb of Dionysios in the projecting east wing of the South Gate belonged structurally to the agora, where graves of heroes were traditionally located. At the same time, however, the entrance to the 'Triodos plaza' was found in front of the agora, and it was this, not the agora, that was indicated with the expression τὸ κυριώτατον. One would like at all events to consider that τὸ κυριώτατον was not only meant topographically,[22] but also hinted at Artemis Ephesia, the "highest mistress of the Ephesians". Such a Sophist, knowledgeable as he was in the topology and history of the city, could certainly be credited with such a double meaning. A partly preserved honorary inscription of a priestess of Artemis also indicates this, saying: ὁ ἱερὸς τόπος Ἐμβολει/τῶν τῶν παρὰ τῇ κυρίᾳ / ἡμῶν θεᾷ Ἀρτέμιδι ("The sacred locality of the people living in the Embolos, near our Lady, the goddess Artemis").[23] With this reference, in the first half of the 3rd c. AD (publication under Gordian III, 242/43) Philostratos attests that the old Triodos plaza was still the most noble site in Ephesos,[24] although long before his time – and practically since the beginning of the construction of the Augustan agora – the actual intersection was transferred to the south-east and then formed by the Marble Street, the Curetes Street/Embolos, and the coastal road to the west behind Hadrian´s Gate, which probably already since 114/115 AD marked the (new) Triodos (plans 3 and 4).

Fig. 41: South Gate of the Tetragonos Agora, view from the south with the protruding wings in the original state

This assessment of the "Triodos plaza" also did not alter in Late Antiquity: a mid–4th c. inscription continues to celebrate the Embolos again as "the most beautiful (spot) in the city", obviously after the earthquake damages of the Gallienic period had been repaired in this section.[25]

In spite of the necessary relocations of all of the streets that once ran together there – due to the expansion of the Tetragonos Agora, then the building of the so-called Serapeion (begun probably under Domitian), and the Library of Celsus (Tra-Janic) –, an entire series of very diverse monuments to Artemis in this area accords with the resilience of the Triodos as a 'place of meaning' at this traditional location, a resilience that was grounded in cult practices.

At first place in this series is the relief of Hekate Triformis in the middle of the western wall of the South Gate – that is, on the western side of the western passage –, a relief already frequently referenced in this connection (fig. 42a). In a related inscription chiselled in to the south-east conch (fig. 42b), Hekate threatens individuals who answer the call of nature in this area, in a very similar fashion to other gate constructions at Ephesos.[26]

The relief of Hekate in the west wall was accompanied on both sides by reliefs of Artemis Ephesia.[27] These today are strongly covered with calcareous deposits and, in addition, were almost completely scratched away, probably in Late Antiquity; in essence, only the extended arms of the goddess with her woollen bands (κληῖδες) are recognisable (fig. 43a+b). In addition, very primitive reliefs of Artemis Ephesia (fig. 43c) and of torch-bearing Hekate are found on the east side of the gate. M. Weißl assumes that the reliefs were created at different times and by various originators, yet the three reliefs in the west, approximately the same size and quality, appear to constitute a unity. It is in any event clear that here, as also frequently and precisely on gate buildings elsewhere in Ionia, Hekate appears as a specific hypostasis of Artemis.[28]

"And not a few of them that practised curious arts brought also their books together, and burned them in the sight of all."
(Acts 19, 19; after the expelling of the evil spirit by St. Paul in Ephesos)

This specific, intimate connection between the two goddesses (or their designations) as distinct aspects with great effect is even more obvious in an oracular pronouncement preserved for the most part, that was set up in the area of the Triodos:[29]

EIL[....]Ạ.Ḥ.[- -]ΩΙΔΑΠ[- - -]....ΗΣ[- - -]
[Ἄρ]τεμιν εὐφαρέτρειαν ἐμῆς γενεῆς γεγαυῖαν·
[π]άσης γὰρ πόλιος προκαθηγέτις ἐστὶ γενέθλης
μαῖα καὶ αὐξήτειρα βροτῶν καρπῶν τε δότειρα·
5   ἧς μορφὴν Ἐφέσοιο κομίσσατε χρυσοφάεννον,
κάτθετε δ' ἐν νηῷ πολυγηθέες· ἥ κεν ἀλύξει
πήματα καὶ λοίμοιο βροτοφθόρα φάρμα[κ]α λύσει
λαμπάσι πυρσοφόροις νυχία φλογὶ μάγματα κηροῦ
τηΐξασα, μάγου κακοτήϊα σύμβολα τέχνης·
10   αὐτὰρ ἐπὴν τελέσητε θεῇ προστάγματ' ἐμεῖο
ὕμνοις ἰοχέαιραν ἀπρόσμαχον ἰθυβέλειαν
καὶ θυσίαις ἄζεσθε κλυτὴν ἐπιωπέα κούρην,
ἔν τε χοροῖς ἔν τ' εἰλαπίναις κοῦραί θ' ἅμα παισὶν
παρθένον ἀλμήεσσαν ὑπὲρ χθόνα Μαίονος Ἕρμου
15   πάντη κυδαίνοντες ἀναστέφε<τ>' εὐρέα μύρτα
κεκλόμενοι γαίης Ἐφεσηΐδος Ἄρτεμιν ἁγνήν
εἰς αἰὲν ὅππως ὕμμι πέλοι ἄχραντος ἀρωγός·
δέ τε μὴ τελέοιτε, πυρὸς τότε τείσετε ποινάς.
χρηματισθεὶς ὑπὸ τοῦ Ἀπόλλωνος

"[---] Artemis with beautiful quiver, from my lineage. Leader of every city, she is foster mother and patroness of the race of men, giver of fruits. Take her image, gleaming in gold, and joyfully display it in a temple, she who will dispel pains and dissipate the plague of poisonous spells that corrupt mankind, when she with her fire-bearing torches causes moulded figures of wax, the terrible images of the art of magic, to melt away by nocturnal firelight.

When you fulfil my commands for the goddess, then honour her, she who slings arrows, invincible, far-reaching, much lauded, sharp-eyed Kore, with hymns and sacrifices, and with roundelays and festive banquets the maidens and youths in the brackish land of the Maionian Hermos should praise the virgin goddess and decorate themselves with myrtle wreaths and call to sacred Artemis of the Ephesian land, so that she will be a pure helper for all time. If however you do not fulfil my commands, you will pay the punishment of fire (fever). Commanded by Apollon."

The inscription therefore relates that the inhabitants of the city of Koloe in the upper Hermos valley, in the salty hinterland (today Mermere Gölü) of Sardes,[30] received the dictum from Apollon to bring the golden image of his divine sister, Ephesian Artemis, into their home city as deliverance from a plague, and to celebrate particular rituals on behalf of the goddess. If his will should not be obeyed, additional deaths (by fever) would follow. The positive magical aspect (white magic) of Artemis emerges in particularly striking fashion here, when the oracle speaks of wax figures which should be burned by her torches at night to heal the plague. These magic figures were elsewhere dedicated to Hekate in the course of harmful magical acts (black magic), in order to cause evil to other people or groups, similar to modern voodoo practices. Here, therefore, Artemis is doubly responsible, just like her brother who is plague-bringer and healer; she alone decides if black or white magic gains the upper hand, if sickness or health comes to pass. In this regard, the placement of the inscription at the Triodos instead of in the Artemision is certainly no coincidence, but is connected to the powers that were active there. This conjunction of divine powers into a single, great, almighty, protective goddess fits particularly well to the later 2nd and 3rd c. AD, as does the connection discovered by D. Knibbe with the so-called Antonine Plague. This plague is proposed by Knibbe as a consequence of the Parthian War after 165 AD,[31] even though this must remain speculative and a closer dating, as well as identifying the type of plague, are not possible.

In this context of salvation and healing at the Triodos, an inscription set up on a column drum (H. 0.95 m, Dm. 0.49 m) fits very well;[32] it was found on the road leading to the coast from Hadrian's Gate, near the Library of Celsus. Helmut Engelmann dates it to the 1st c. AD based on the style of the letters.[33] The inscription names one C. Iulius Atticus, priest of Artemis Soteira (saviour) of the imperial house. That this (Artemis) Soteira even had her own temple at Ephesos is clear from the endowment document of a certain Nikomedes on behalf of the gerousia, from the time of the sole rule of Commodus; the document celebrates the (new?) erection of the cult image and temple of Soteira.[34] It is conceivable that this temple was located at Ortygia, and in the opinion of certain scholars it could hark back to King Lysimachos and, thereby, to the period of the new city foundation in the early 3rd c. BC;[35] very likely, it was he who gave Artemis Soteira an important function in the process of making the ephebes new full citizens, as already the Homeric Hymn to Aphrodite claims, where Artemis is set in opposition to Aphrodite with the following characteristic:[36]

οὐδέ ποτ᾿ Ἀρτέμιδα χρυσηλάκατον κελαδεινήν
δάμναται ἐν φιλότητι φιλομμειδὴς Ἀφροδίτη·
καὶ γὰρ τῆι ἅδε τόξα καὶ οὔρεσι θῆρας ἐναίρειν
φόρμιγγές τε χοροί τε διαπρύσιοί τ᾿ ὀλολυγαί
  τε σκιόεντα δικαίων τε πτόλις ἀνδρῶν.

"Nor does smile-loving Aphrodite ever overpower Artemis
of the gold arrow-shafts and loud cries with love;
for she is interested in bows and in killing wild animals in the mountains,
and in lyres, dances, shrill hosannahs,
shady sacred groves, and the city of just men."

Thereby, in any event, the connection of the cult site of the Triodos, as Knibbe had already established – nevertheless without referring to the relevant inscriptions in his argument – to the Artemis processions on her birthday, and the mysteries celebrated in Ortygia connected to the intake of young citizens, as well as to the imperial cult, is again made clear.[37] That Artemis is supplied with the epithet "Soteira (saviour) of the imperial house" precisely at the Triodos finds a good parallel in Megiste in Lycia, where she is honoured together with Apollon Pylaios in a high Hellenistic inscription on a gateway.[38] At Ephesos, the topographical site was by no means randomly chosen, since at this intersection all of the participants in the procession leading to Ortygia on the occasion of the bestowal of citizenship on the ephebes all met up. These participants probably came down the Curetes Street, with the Curetes and other cult officials, from the Gymnasium of the Neoi in the area of the later State Agora, where after the Augustan period the prytaneion also lay. The gerousiasts processed there from their official house or gymnasium over the Tetragonos Agora or the street running past it at the south, while the members of the priesthood came from the Artemision via the Koressian Gate to the theatre, where additional citizens probably also assembled, and then the procession proceeded over the Marble Street to the Triodos.

Small clay jugs bearing stamped impressions with representations of Artemis Ephesia have recently been claimed by Friedrich Krinzinger as additional pieces of evidence for a cult practice in the area of the Triodos already in the Hellenistic period.[39] The impressions not only include the image of the city goddess, with a particular similarity to gold coins (staters) of the late 2nd c. BC, but they also include the epithets NO-MO and ΔH-MO. For this reason Verena Gassner, in spite of the varying sizes of the total of 9 vessels discovered, inferred their possible usage as measuring vessels or oil vessels issued by the state, as these are occasionally present, with inscriptions such as δημόσιον, in other Greek cities and sport sites such as Athens and Olympia.[40] Such a usage would actually be supported by their find-spot in the neighbourhood of the commercial agora. Of particular interest for their meaning is the fact that the close dating to the late 2nd c. BC of these certainly late Hellenistic wares is based not only on their vessel form and the metallic, gleaming slip, but also on the fact that the only find-spot for these vessels, the drainage between the rear wall of the agora's east colonnade and the terrace wall lying behind it, was at that time still dated to the 2nd c. BC. The newer excavations in the agora have clearly indicated, however, – also for the supporting wall around a terracing set up in the Augustan period for the expanded rebuilding of the agora in the slope that was explicitly dug out for this,[41] – that considerably later material, up to the period around 20/10 BC, could also have been deposited in the infill of the drainage with old rubble. Given the current state of research, it is better to refrain from conjectures regarding a cultic usage – similar to the Attic choes. They certainly cannot, unfortunately, be used to support an argument for Hellenistic ritual practices at the Triodos.

The next piece of evidence to be examined here is a partially preserved inscription from the Tetragonos Agora, already dealt with by Knibbe in this connection, from the 3rd c. AD. The inscription, shortly mentioned above, refers to a priestess of Artemis who was particularly exemplary in her duties, the daughter of a certain M. Aurelius Hierocles Apollinaris, who served the city as council member, agoronomos, and strategos, and who obtained the title Philosebastos (friend of the emperor).[42] The donor of the honorary statue for this Aurelia was an entity or group that designated themselves as "the embolites (who) (live) with our mistress, the goddess Artemis", marking the site as her "sacred locality". Knibbe extracted the only possible

Fig. 44: The platform for the Altar of Artemis opposite the South Gate with Late Antique alterations, and the partially re-erected Gate of Hadrian in the background

conclusion from this, that in the area of the Embolos, the city quarter between the Tetragonos Agora and the State Agora, an important cult site (altar) dedicated to Artemis Ephesia must have stood.[43]

Within a few years after excavation, the meagre remains of the altar gave rise to various dating proposals and attempts at interpretation.

Consequently, Knibbe furthermore assumed that the large courtyard altar (plan 3 no. 5; plan 4; fig. 37: left lower corner; fig. 44) which was completely removed in Late Antiquity and replaced by a colonnaded hall, and whose excavator Werner Jobst preferred to identify with the so-called Parthian Monument from the 2nd c. AD,[44] must have been the long-presumed altar of Artemis inside the civic area.[45] Since the excavations at the altar could not be carried out at a single place in the undisturbed foundation layers due to the dense, subsequent constructions and the Late Antique usage of the vault set into the slope and carrying the altar platform, Jobst supported his theory with two fundamental arguments.[46] On the one hand, he viewed the altar as later in terms of relative stratigraphy than the so-called Hadrian's Gate adjacent to the east; Friedmund Hueber correctly raised objections to this.[47] In fact, no clear argument can be won here; one would rather see the gate as set at the corner of the altar than the other way round. On the other hand, Jobst excavated a denarius of Iulia Domna from the stepped substructure at the edge of the preserved steps of the 7.2 m wide staircase leading down from the altar to the Triodos plaza. Jobst argued, completely justifiably, that the staircase, from a technical viewpoint, must be slightly later than the altar, and therefore presumed a building date in the second half of the 2nd c. AD. Yet, since the altar was obviously frequently altered, and even converted into a colonnade in Late Antiquity or the early Byzantine period, the staircase could also have been adjusted at some point – in particular after the earthquake damage of the 3rd c. AD – or even built then for the first time. A definitive chronological close relationship between the altar building and a (last) construction of the staircase cannot, therefore, be compellingly assumed. Jobst's hypothesis that the monumental structure opposite the South Gate of the agora should be the chronologically latest in a long series of known antique courtyard altars[48] cannot, furthermore, be persuasively proven. In contrast, Hueber proposed a construction already in the Julio-Claudian period, based on structural and technical details;[49] one of these is the fact that the substructure of the altar contains branches of the canalisation system that subsequently led to the Tetragonos Agora, suggesting a contemporary planning.

Hilke Thür, in a work in a Festschrift which unfortunately has not had much impact in the scholarly literature, has assigned a series of long-known architectural elements from a courtyard altar to this particular altar structure. These elements were

found as early as 1900 in front of the north wing of the analemma of the theatre, laid down in the Late Antique street paving of the Marble Street.[50] They consist of a number of orthostat blocks with wooden fence motif, architraves with a length of 1.55 m which must have covered Ionic capitals of 0.46 m diameter, sima blocks with Ionic cyma and astragals, as well as a relief at the inner corner with the wounded Amazon of the Sciarra type (fig. 45). According to Thür, the Amazon relief and four additional similar pieces ought to be placed in the altar courtyard in the niches of the inner wall arrangement of the south side. The fence motif, however, should be placed on the altar socle, thereby creating a border for the sacred zone.[51]

All of these architectural elements, together with additional ones with meander friezes built into the late antique scaenae of the theatre and the Isabey Mosque,[52] were invoked for the original late Classical courtyard altar of the Artemision by Anton Bammer, since 1967, and later vehemently by Ulrike Muss in a series of articles.[53] Other scholars have always judged the architectural elements as dating to the Hellenistic up to the Antonine period.[54] Precisely the wooden fence motif has frequently been seen as a reference to the Ara Pacis as well as other Augustan courtyard altars, primarily at the legislative assembly sites of the western provinces such as Tarraco and Lugdunum.[55]

Independently of the fact established by Thür's entire reconstruction, that at least the building elements found in front of the theatre fit perfectly to the ground plan of the altar on the Triodos, there are additional arguments to be made here. Thür gives the required column diameter as 0.46 m; assuming a slight entasis, the col-

Fig. 46: Inscription of Demeas, found near the altar and the Gate of Hadrian

umn drums found at the altar with the early imperial Artemis Soteira inscription and a greatest diameter of 0.49 m would ideally fit.[56] Furthermore, in the Late Antique paving of the Marble Street additional building elements from the area of the Triodos were laid down, for example the tomb plaque of Mithridates and, above all, the wall block with the oracular pronouncement of Apollon; in other words, a large-scale clearing away and tidying up occurred here, with the goal of achieving a comprehensive new plastering of the Marble Street before the new (Christian) configuration could begin.

Based on results so far, one can also probably assign additional inscriptions from the immediate surroundings of the Artemis altar. Such a piece of evidence was found secondarily built into a wall in the so-called Stepped Lane 3, leading from Hadrian's Gate to the south at the west side of Terrace House 2 (see plan 3); here it was reported in the late 2nd c. AD that children offered up their jewellery to Artemis – a common procedure on the occasion of being declared adults.[57] A fine, late indication for the courtyard altar being dedicated to Artemis is the inscription found directly to the east of the building, near Hadrian's Gate, and erected by the Christian Demeas. He prided himself on having obliterated the image of the demon Artemis and having replaced it with the cross, the victorious, immortal symbol of Christ (fig. 46);[58] the text reminds one of the pictures of the tumbling down of the statues of the communist heroes in some Central European countries in the late 20th c.:

> [† δαίμ]ονος Ἀρ/τέμιδος καθελὼν / ἀπατήλιον εἶδος / Δημέας ἀτρεκίης /⁵ ἄνθετο σῆμα τόδε, / εἰδώλων ἐλατῆρα / θεὸν σταυρόν τε / γερέρων, νικοφό/ρον Χριστοῦ σύν/¹⁰βολον ἀθάνατο †

> "After Demeas had dragged down the treacherous goddess, the demon Artemis, he dedicated this sign to the obvious truth in that he set up God, the ejector of graven images, and the cross, the victory-bringing symbol of immortal Christ."[59]

Based on purely architectonic considerations, in her reconstruction Thür presented an articulation of the inner wall of the altar's south side, in which five niches would each contain a relief depicting a wounded Amazon (fig. 45).[60] In this manner the (Augustan) reliefs would constitute a complete citation of the five free-standing Amazons created in the context of a sculptural competition in the 5th c. BC by Polykleitos, Pheidias, Kresilas, Kydon, and Phradmon (fig. 71).[61] We may assume that the five[62] wounded Amazons from the artists' contest were not unnamed, but were individually named due to their significance in the foundation myth.[63] A good indication for this is found in the immediate neighbourhood of the altar itself, at the Library of Celsus. In the upper storey of the façade an inscription appeared that refers to a dignitary named Stephanos, otherwise hard to identify, but to be dated into the mid-6th c. AD, saying that Ptelee has decorated him, as he has decorated Ptelee with golden works.[64]

The wounded Amazons as the first who were seeking asylum in the temple of Artemis, were so popular in the city that even the statue of the demos of the Ephesians appeared in the shape of an Amazon (fig. 73).

Until now, the Amazon name Ptelee (or Ptelea) was viewed simply as a metaphorical designation for all of Ephesos. It is more probable, however, that Stephanos arranged for the restoration of the plaza and possibly, thereby, also for the construction of the portico on the former altar platform. This specific renovation of the space that was central in the Ephesian consciousness, the Triodos, led to his being honoured. In this way, even in the Christian period a reference in this location to the (already demolished and re-dedicated) Amazon altar glints through.

Kallimachos' 3rd c. BC hymn to Artemis already names the Amazon Queen Hippo as female builder of the sanctuary, with a wooden cult image.[65] Hyginus names Otrere, a Queen of the Amazons and consort of the war god,[66] whereas lastly the Byzantine Etymologicum Magnum speaks of an eponymous Amazon Ephesos.[67] Plinius the Elder also claims that the Amazons were the founders, and states that the city has many names:[68]

> *in ora* [...] *Ephesus, Amazonum opus, multis antea expetita nominibus, Alopes, cum pugnatum apud Troiam est, mox Ortygiae, Amorges, Zmyrna, cognomine Tracheia, et Haimonion et Ptelea.*

> "Along the coast: [...] Ephesos, a work of the Amazons. This city has often changed its name. At the time of the Trojan War it was called Alopes, then Ortygia, Amorges, Smyrna with the epithet Tracheia, Haimonion, and Ptelea."

Most of the names certainly have to do with Ephesian districts, while others perhaps also do; at the same time, however, these are also names of Amazons, with the exception of Tracheia and Haimonion.[69] Strabon had already made a connection between Ephesian districts with the Amazon *Smyrna* and another one by the name of Sisyrbe.[70]

Σμύρνα δ᾽ ἦν Ἀμαζὼν ἡ κατασχοῦσα τὴν Ἔφεσον, ἀφ᾽ ἧς τοὔνομα καὶ τοῖς ἀνθρώποις καὶ τῇ πόλει, ὡς καὶ ἀπὸ Σισύρβης Σισυρβῖται τινὲς τῶν Ἐφεσίων ἐλέγοντο· καὶ τόπος δέ τις τῆς Ἐφέσου Σμύρνα ἐκαλεῖτο, ὡς δηλοῖ Ἱππῶναξ "ᾤκει δ᾽ ὄπισθε τῆς πόλιος ἐνὶ Σμύρνῃ μεταξὺ Τρηχείης τε καὶ Λεπρῆς ἀκτῆς".

"Smyrna was the Amazon who had taken possession of Ephesos, the people as well as the city were named after her, in the way that some of the Ephesians were also named Sisyrbites after Sisyrbe; and there was a specific district in Ephesos that was called Smyrna, as Hipponax shows: 'he lives behind the city in Smyrna between Tracheia and Lepre Akte.'"

Therefore – like Smyrna at the coastline to the west of the later Tetragonos Agora (fig. 27) –, *Ptelea* in the inscription on the Library of Celsus could also refer to a very specific district, namely, the one at the Triodos. In any case, the five Amazons named by Plinius (Alopes, Ortygia, Amorges, Smyrna, Ptelea) would correlate remarkably well with the above-mentioned contest between the five sculptors in the 5th c. BC, providing a further, positive indication for the validity of the reconstruction of the altar building at the Triodos.

The Amazons on the altar of the Artemision are reminiscent of the mythical early period of Ephesos; they were twice defeated by a son of Zeus and also by a mortal, namely Herakles and Dionysos, and later by Theseus, and on each occasion they found protection in the sanctuary of Artemis which they had founded.[71] These wounded Amazons are the archetype for the Hiketides who made use of the *asylum* of the Artemision.[72] In the city centre of Hellenistic-Roman Ephesos, reference is made to them twice, at close quarters: at the Augustan altar at the Triodos, and on the frieze of the pronaos of the so-called Temple of Hadrian (plan 3; figs. 69f.),[73] which perhaps was originally dedicated to the expected Parthian victory of Trajan.[74]

In this way, the will of the Roman emperors to respect and, if need be, to enforce the *asylum* of Artemis is expressed; yet at the same time, Ephesos' claims to regional leadership, as one of the oldest cities of Asia Minor and home of one of the most famous sanctuaries, are also underscored. From such claims, a direct line of considerations – from both the mythological-historical-cultural side as well as the economic side – should have led to the choice of the location for the Octagon, as already demonstrated above.[75]

The Embolos – a walk of fame

"... it is likely that those who commissioned further buildings to stand in this
space paid close attention to what was already there, and what it said.
In the metropolis of Ephesos, the desires and decisions of initial builders would
be received by a wide audience of varied elites, who furthered and modified
that reception with their own dedications." (Burrell 2009)

---

1. The Hellenistic fountain buildings and honorific monuments on the lower Embolos

The locating of water for (new) settlements is originally the role of the divinity and of the leader of the people chosen by it. Thus, Moses became apparent as the true prophet of Yahweh when he struck his staff on a rock from which a spring emerged. In a similar fashion, Mithras legitimised himself as a god when he shot an arrow at the rock face, causing water to gush out. For the Greeks, it was frequently the oracle that connected the location of the new foundation of a polis, with the discovery of a source of water.

1.1 The Hypelaios fountain: a re-assessment of the written sources

---

A fish, a boar, olives, and fresh water – food, water and wilderness with nearly
no enemies – the ideal place for a new city.

The Greek colonists coming to the Ephesian bay were told by the oracle of Apollon in Delphi to found their city in the place where a fish and a boar gave a sign, as Athenaios reports, citing the local Ephesian historian Kreophylos:[1]

> Κρεώφυλος δ᾽ ἐν τοῖς Ἐφεσίων Ὥροις (FGrH 417 F 1) · οἱ τὴν Ἔφεσον, φησί, κτίζοντες καὶ πολλὰ ταλαιπωρηθέντες ἀπορίᾳ τόπου τὸ τελευταῖον πέμψαντες εἰς θεοῦ ἠρώτων ὅπου τὸ πόλισμα θῶνται. ὁ δὲ αὐτοῖς ἔχρησεν (Delphic Oracle L54 Fontenrose) ἐνταῦθα οἰκίζειν πόλιν, ᾗτινι ἂν ἰχθὺς δείξῃ καὶ ὗς ἄγριος ὑφηγήσηται. λέγεται οὖν, ὅπου νῦν ἡ κρήνη ἐστὶν ⌐ἡ⌐ Ὑπέλαιος καλουμένη καὶ ὁ ἱερὸς λιμήν, ἁλιέας ἀριστοποιεῖσθαι, καὶ τῶν ἰχθύων τινὰ ἀποθορόντα σὺν ἀνθρακιᾷ εἰσπεσεῖν εἰς φορυτὸν καὶ

ἀφθῆναι ὑπ᾽ αὐτοῦ λόχμην ἐν ᾗ ἔτυχε σῦς ἄγριος ὤν· ὃς ὑπὸ τοῦ πυρὸς θορυβηθεὶς ἐπέδραμε τοῦ ὄρους ἐπὶ πολύ, ὃ δὴ καλεῖται Τρηχεῖα, καὶ πίπτει ἀκοντισθεὶς ὅπου νῦν ἐστιν ὁ τῆς Ἀθηνᾶς ναός. καὶ διαβάντες οἱ Ἐφέσιοι ἐκ τῆς νήσου ἔτεα εἴκοσιν οἰκήσαντες τὸ δεύτερον κτίζουσι Τρηχεῖαν καὶ τὰ ἐπὶ Κορησσόν, καὶ ἱερὸν Ἀρτέμιδος ἐπὶ τῇ ἀγορῇ ἱδρύσαντο Ἀπόλλωνός τε τοῦ Πυθίου ἐπὶ τῷ λιμένι.

"And Kreophylos, in his Annals of the Ephesians, says — 'Those who colonised Ephesos, being much perplexed for want of a place where they could settle, sent at last to the oracle, and asked where they should build themselves a city; and he told them to build a city in that place which a fish should show them, and to which a wild boar should guide them. Accordingly, it is said that some fishermen were breakfasting at the spot where now the fountain called Hypelaios is, and the harbour which is called the sacred harbour; and that one of the fish leaped up with a burning cinder sticking to him, and fell on some of the refuse; and that by this means a thicket was set on fire, in which there happened to be a wild boar; and he, being disturbed by the fire, ran for some distance up the mountain which is called the Tracheia (Rough Mountain), and at last was transfixed by javelins, and fell where the temple of Athena now stands. And the Ephesians, having crossed over from the island, occupied that for twenty-one years, and in the twenty-second year they founded Trachea and the towns around Koressos, and erected a temple to Artemis in the market-place, and one to the Pythian Apollo overlooking the harbour´."

Although Athenaios writes at a late date, under the Severan emperors at the transition from the 2nd to the 3rd c. AD, according to his information he nevertheless repeats the (precise) words of an otherwise unknown Ephesian local historian of the 4th/3rd c. BC named Kreophylos.[2]

The story begins with fishermen breakfasting on grilled fish at the water source. The fact that the water source where they encamped was called Hypelaios – that is, an additional indication of olive trees connected with it – made the region perfect for a settlement: a good source of fresh water, abundance of fish in the sea, uncultivated yet fertile land marked by the boar sacred to Artemis, and very few enemies.

The identification of this source of water, Hypelaios, which was so important for the history of the city, has nevertheless not yet been possible. According to the text of the story, it must have been situated, on the one hand, in the vicinity of the ἱερὸς λιμήν, that means the *sacred harbour* or better the harbour under the protection of a god(dess), and on the other hand near the Tracheia. Scholars have frequently discussed this 'sacred harbour', and it is generally viewed as a harbour near the Artemision (plan 1 no. 1) due to its closer definition as 'sacred'.[3] But 'sacred' can hardly refer here to the Artemision as the harbour's locality, when we take Kreophylos (or Athenaios) at his word, because the boar would then have had to travel first around the broad bight to the Koressos harbour (plan 1 no. 3; compare plan 2) and then further along the long strip of land with the Crevice Temple (plan 1 no. 103). Kreophylos, however, does not mention the Artemision at all, and furthermore a connection between Hypelaios and the Artemision is not made anywhere else. The Koressos harbour at the north coast of the Tracheia (plan 2) also can be discounted, since the boar ran in its vicinity; that is, the Koressos harbour has to be differentiated from the *sacred harbour*. Therefore, the latter can actually only lie in the large bay to the west of the Roman theatre or the Hellenistic-Roman Tetragonos Agora, at that place where Lysimachos most likely installed his harbour.[4] Theoretically, one could assume that the new sacred harbour replaced the old Koressos harbour, which had formerly connected the old city with the Artemision as especially the story in Herodotos tells us; during the siege of King Kroisos, the tyrant Pindaros interconnected the city with the temple by a rope seven stadia in length.[5] Parallel to that, in other Greek cities a gate leading to an extramural sanctuary was sometimes called "sacred" (ἱερὰ πύλη).[6] But in our case the adjective "sacred" most likely indicates a military harbour.[7] In Greek poleis, not infrequently organisations, installations or buildings that were particularly important for the survival of the city in war were referred to as "sacred"; one thinks, for example, of the "sacred throng" (ἱερὸς λόχος) of the Thebans.

The formulation "there, where the source, which is also called Hypelaios, and the sacred harbour are now located" is also unusual. This sounds as if there was not only a new harbour, but also a newly instituted tapping of a spring, before the eyes of the narrator. For only a "new" nymphaeum can be intended; the water source itself could indeed not be relocated. Since the lifetime of Kreophylos is completely unknown and can only very roughly be assigned to the 4th/3rd c. BC, it cannot be determined by independent sources whether he was writing before or after the new foundation by Lysimachos. But the novelty of the harbour and the tapping of the spring absolutely allow us to place the composition of the text at the earliest in the 3rd c. BC, more or less immediately after Ephesos had received its new location; in fact, this would have been an ideal occasion for a new history of the city.

Independently from these rather vague considerations, everything in the story itself speaks for the fact that the water spring should be sought at the edge of the harbour plain between Bülbüldağ and Panayırdağ. From this point, the boar ran along the coast in a northerly direction along the Tracheia and up the slopes around Koressos, and was killed near an equally unidentified, later temple of Athena.

Strabon, however, apparently provides an antithesis in his text on Kreophylos. Regarding the already above mentioned location of a settlement, Smyrna, that belonged to Ephesos, he writes:[8]

> καὶ τόπος δέ τις τῆς Ἐφέσου Σμύρνα ἐκαλεῖτο, ὡς δηλοῖ Ἱππῶναξ "ᾤκει δ᾽ ὄπισθε τῆς πόλιος ἐνὶ Σμύρνῃ | μεταξὺ Τρηχείης τε καὶ Λεπρῆς ἀκτῆς." ἐκαλεῖτο γὰρ Λεπρὴ μὲν ἀκτὴ ὁ πρηὼν ὁ ὑπερκείμενος τῆς νῦν πόλεως, ἔχων μέρος τοῦ τείχους αὐτῆς· τὰ γοῦν ὄπισθεν τοῦ πρηῶνος κτήματα ἔτι νυνὶ λέγεται ἐν τῇ Ὀπισθολεπρίᾳ· τραχεῖα δ᾽ ἐκαλεῖτο ἡ περὶ τὸν Κορησσὸν Παρώρειος. ἡ δὲ πόλις ἦν τὸ παλαιὸν περὶ τὸ Ἀθήναιον τὸ νῦν ἔξω τῆς πόλεως ὂν κατὰ τὴν καλουμένην Ὑπέλαιον, ὥστε ἡ Σμύρνα ἦν κατὰ τὸ νῦν γυμνάσιον ὄπισθεν μὲν τῆς τότε πόλεως, μεταξὺ δὲ Τρηχείης τε καὶ Λεπρῆς ἀκτῆς.

> "Also a certain place belonging to Ephesos was called Smyrna, as Hipponax plainly indicates: 'He lived behind the city in Smyrna between Tracheia and Lepra Acte;' for the name Lepra Acte was given to Mt. Preon, which lies above the present city and has on it a part of the city's wall. At any rate, the possessions behind Mt. Preon are still now referred to as in the "opistholeprian" territory, and the country alongside the Koressos was called "Tracheia". The city was in ancient times round the Athenaeum, which is now outside the city near the Hypelaeus, as it is called; so that Smyrna was near the present gymnasium, behind the old city, but between Tracheia and Lepra Acte." (transl. based on Jones 1929)

If we follow this – partly restored – text[9] and the translation by Jones, Strabon located the Hypelaios in the immediate vicinity of the temple of Athena. The position of this sanctuary is unknown to us, but nobody doubts its location somewhere in or close to the early Archaic city, as Kreophylos also stated. Following that, the Hypelaios should also be located in "the country alongside the [harbour] Koressos". But this location of the Hypelaios by Strabon may be influenced by a text slightly earlier in his book, where he already names the Athenaion and Hypelaios in a row:[10]

> "The city of Ephesos was inhabited both by Karians and by Leleges, but Androklos drove them out and settled the most of those who had come with him round the Athenaeum and the Hypelaios, though he also included a part of the country situated on the slopes of Mt. [note: better today "above (the harbour)"][11] Koressos." (transl. Jones 1929)

Here, Strabon only says that there were three different places where Androklos and his people settled: round the Athenaion, near the Hypelaios and on the slopes above the Koressos harbour. The text does not say anything about the distances between the three landmarks. His later thought about a close neighbourhood of Athenaion and Hypelaios seems meaningless, because it would contradict the entire series of events according to the oracle: the boar would then have run only a couple of metres or in a circle, but not straight along the entire Tracheia. We have more certainty in Strabon's localisation of Smyrna. This Archaic village was discovered during excavations in the 1990s under the western part of the Tetragonos Agora[12] and a number of houses were closely investigated (plan 2; fig. 27).[13] How far to the west the development extended is still unknown, but Strabon's statement – κατὰ τὸ νῦν γυμνάσιον – could have referred to the Gymnasium of the Gerontes, slightly to the west of the agora and deduced from many pieces of evidence (fig. 25).[14] The somewhat abrupt jump to Smyrna in Strabon's later text (XIV 1.4) would be better explicable, if the Hypelaios could be linked to that village instead of to the Athenaion.

Regarding Strabon's two text passages, we may now infer an additional meaning than has been considered up until now, and assume that Androklos did not settle all his men in one site, but instead some lived near the Athenaion and others near the Hypelaios (meaning: in Smyrna), and a third part in Koressos. Strabon therefore does not speak about only one location, but gives a list of settlements for the early period of Ephesos. This is the more likely as the entire slopes of the double hill of the Panayırdağ, both Mt. Pion in the south as well as the Tracheia in the north (fig. 90), can be excluded as the site of springs due to the karst appearance of the mountain.[15] This geological fact caused, as already discussed, problems to the Hellenistic garrisons on the akra,[16] and will further be relevant for the ensuing topographical discussion.

On the other hand, the slope of the Bülbüldağ which levels off in the area of the lower Embolos, directly below and in front of Terrace House 2 (plan 1 no. 51; plan 3 no. 13; fig. 23) proves to be particularly remarkable for the water supply of the city, with both natural springs and water from man-made wells.[17] In the 3rd and 2nd c. BC, this area lay outside the densely developed inner city zone, but immediately above the Triodos junction,[18] at which three important land routes converged. In addition to providing water to the urban quarter around the (Tetragonos) agora, the public fountains established here in the Hellenistic period also had the function of providing a first point of welcome for washing and refreshment for travellers entering the city from the country route, that is, through the Magnesian Gate. In this way, the site constituted very good preconditions to serve as the 'visiting card' for the city, where Ephesos could present its history and significance to any newcomers.

1.2 The identification of the city spring Hypelaios (so-called Heroon of Androklos)

An especially elaborately designed fountain house (plan 3 no. 9) lies at the lowest end of the Curetes Street, on its south side bordering the water-bearing slope of Mt.

Preon (fig. 90). The structure, which lies between Hadrian's Gate and the Octagon, was never completely buried by rubble and was therefore always partially visible (fig. 47). Ernst Curtius already identified the construction as a "city spring" in the 19th c.[19] The early Austrian excavators just called it "fountain" and in modern scholarship it is often described as a "heroon"; the barrier plaques decorated with Christian symbols in front of the water basin,[20] dating to a Late Antique rebuilding, also led to it being termed a "Byzantine fountain".[21] In the only extensive publication of the structure to date, H. Thür proposed the designation "Monument of Androklos" due to the relief decoration in the upper storey (fig. 48).[22]

The difficulties in interpreting archaeological monuments:
a fountain or a heroon?

The U–form structure, originally more than 13 m in height (plan 4; fig. 49),[23] encompasses a surface of 10.35 × 5.80 m at its base, and is still preserved to a height of 4 m. The foundation and core in the lower storey consist of unjoined, often sec-

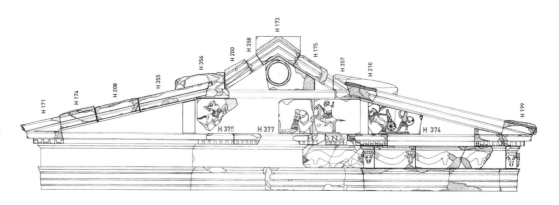

Fig. 48: Hypelaios fountain, frieze with scenes from the foundation myth and the life of Androklos (partial reconstruction by H. Thür)

ondarily employed bolstered ashlar blocks and other limestone blocks, while the interstices are filled with stone flakes, earth, and ceramics. The three-stepped sub-structure is lacking on the north side towards the street, because the water basin joins the structure or the structure forms its rear wall. The basin also occupies the recessed middle section, which in this area was not covered with marble revetment, yet the core was carefully smoothed. It is obvious that the floor surface of the basin and the socle of the barrier construction belonged to the original structure; the building therefore was planned from the beginning as a nymphaeum.[24] For this reason, the search for parallels for the building type of a 'heroon', or the idea that something completely new was created here in the context of sepulchral and me-morial architecture, is superfluous.[25]

The lower storey had a blind Doric architecture, while the upper storey was of the Ionic order with two free-standing columns on each of the projecting wings. The re-lief frieze extended over the entire length of the structure, both over the architraves of the two projecting wings as well as in the recessed central gable. A total of seven, partly fragmented blocks of the frieze were discovered in the area of the so-called Heroon; these can easily be inserted into the reconstruction of the building (fig. 48).[26]

Thür's comprehensive stylistic classification of the architectural decoration, in par-ticular the Doric metopes with phialai and rosettes, the Ionic capitals, and the gar-land frieze, resulted in a construction date from the middle to the second half of the 2nd c BC, while for the stylistic classification of the battle frieze she stated that "a dating in the 2nd c. is probable".[27] This dating has been broadly confirmed in recent works.[28] The evaluation of the pottery would fit – appropriately for the style of the frieze – to a construction date around 120/110 BC.[29]

Thür interpreted the scenes represented as the story of the myth of the city founder Androklos, often reported in ancient literature, and pointed to the close parallels to its representation in the frieze (block A) of the pronaos of the so-called Temple of Hadrian diagonally opposite on the other side of the street (plan 3 no. 15; fig. 69).[30] Below the central gable, Androklos as a rider in the type of Alexander hunts the boar (compare fig. 70A), while at the right, wounded, he fights against a horseman for his life. The single combat around a fallen warrior (in the left side gable), as a representa-tion of the death of Androklos on the battlefield during an auxiliary expedition in support of Priene, also accords well with the myth; but one has to add that this spe-cific pisode is only recorded by Pausanias and not mentioned in older sources.

Furthermore, a chariot in the gable part at right, ascending to the middle, is also interpreted as a war chariot, yet it could also signify an apotheosis.[31] Further to the right a heavily-armed figure is still preserved, whereas the rest is missing.

In the central area, therefore, the most important scenes were located: the founda-tion of Ephesos and the death of the hero in battle at Priene. The latter scene is also represented in abbreviated fashion at the so-called Temple of Hadrian (fig. 70A). According to the evidence of the Temple of Hadrian, the water spring Hypelaios and the fleeing boar would be expected at the heroon, probably exactly in the middle, as well.[32] To the right and left, then, additional battles would have been depicted, including probably the fight for the body of Androklos.

In order to shed more light on the myth surrounding Androklos and the founding of Ephesos, represented in the images on the frieze of the nymphaeum and repeated approximately a quarter of a millennium later at the so-called Temple of Hadrian, and above all its significance in the late Hellenistic and Roman imperial periods,[33] a number of important pieces of textual evidence should be presented, beginning with Pausanias:[34]

[VII 2.8] Λέλεγες δὲ τοῦ Καρικοῦ μοῖρα καὶ Λυδῶν τὸ πολὺ οἱ νεμόμενοι τὴν χώραν ἦσαν: ᾤκουν δὲ καὶ περὶ τὸ ἱερὸν ἄλλοι τε ἱκεσίας ἕνεκα καὶ γυναῖκες τοῦ Ἀμαζόνων γένους. Ἄνδροκλος δὲ ὁ Κόδρου--οὗτος γὰρ δὴ ἀπεδέδεικτο Ἰώνων τῶν ἐς Ἔφεσον πλευσάντων βασιλεύς--Λέλεγας μὲν καὶ Λυδοὺς τὴν ἄνω πόλιν ἔχοντας ἐξέβαλεν ἐκ τῆς χώρας: τοῖς δὲ περὶ τὸ ἱερὸν οἰκοῦσι δεῖμα ἦν οὐδέν, ἀλλὰ Ἴωσιν ὅρκους δόντες καὶ ἀνὰ μέρος παρ' αὐτῶν λαβόντες ἐκτὸς ἦσαν πολέμου. ἀφείλετο δὲ καὶ Σάμον Ἄνδροκλος Σαμίους, καὶ ἔσχον Ἐφέσιοι χρόνον τινὰ Σάμον καὶ τὰς προσεχεῖς νήσους:

[VII 2.9] Σαμίων δὲ ἤδη κατεληλυθότων ἐπὶ τὰ οἰκεῖα Πριηνεῦσιν ἤμυνεν ἐπὶ τοὺς Κᾶρας ὁ Ἄνδροκλος, καὶ νικῶντος τοῦ Ἑλληνικοῦ ἔπεσεν ἐν τῇ μάχῃ. Ἐφέσιοι δὲ ἀνελόμενοι τοῦ Ἀνδρόκλου τὸν νεκρὸν ἔθαψαν τῆς σφετέρας ἔνθα δείκνυται καὶ ἐς ἐμὲ ἔτι τὸ μνῆμα κατὰ τὴν ὁδὸν τὴν ἐκ τοῦ ἱεροῦ παρὰ τὸ Ὀλυμπιεῖον καὶ ἐπὶ πύλας τὰς Μαγνήτιδας: ἐπίθημα δὲ τῷ μνήματι ἀνήρ ἐστιν ὡπλισμένος.

[VII 2.8] "The inhabitants of the land were partly Leleges, a branch of the Karians, but the greater number were Lydians. In addition, there were others who dwelt around the sanctuary for the sake of its protection, and these included some women of the race of the Amazons. But Androklos the son of Kodros (for he it was who was appointed King of the Ionians who sailed against Ephesos) expelled from the land the Leleges and Lydians who occupied the upper city. Those, however, who dwelt around the sanctuary had nothing to fear; they exchanged oaths of friendship with the Ionians and escaped warfare. Androklos also took Samos from the Samians, and for a time the Ephesians held Samos and the adjacent islands.

[VII 2.9] But after that the Samians had returned to their own land, Androklos helped the people of Priene against the Karians. The Greek army was victorious, but Androklos was killed in the battle. The Ephesians carried off his body and buried it in their own land, at the spot where his tomb is pointed out at the present day, on the road leading from the sanctuary in the direction leading to the Olympieion[35] and to the Magnesian gate. On the tomb is a statue of an armed man." (transl. based on Jones 1933)

Numerous texts of Strabon have already been cited above, but this passage is particularly important:[36]

ταύτης δέ φησι Φερεκύδης Μίλητον μὲν καὶ Μυοῦντα καὶ τὰ περὶ Μυκάλην καὶ Ἔφεσον Κᾶρας ἔχειν πρότερον, τὴν δ᾽ ἑξῆς παραλίαν μέχρι Φωκαίας καὶ Χίον καὶ Σάμον, ἧς Ἀγκαῖος ἦρχε, Λέλεγας· ἐκβληθῆναι δ᾽ ἀμφοτέρους ὑπὸ τῶν Ἰώνων καὶ εἰς τὰ λοιπὰ μέρη τῆς Καρίας ἐκπεσεῖν. ἄρξαι δέ φησιν Ἄνδροκλον τῆς τῶν Ἰώνων ἀποικίας, ὕστερον τῆς Αἰολικῆς, υἱὸν γνήσιον Κόδρου τοῦ Ἀθηνῶν βασιλέως, γενέσθαι δὲ τοῦτον Ἐφέσου κτίστην. διόπερ τὸ βασίλειον τῶν Ἰώνων ἐκεῖ συστῆναί φασι, καὶ ἔτι νῦν οἱ ἐκ τοῦ γένους ὀνομάζονται βασιλεῖς ἔχοντές τινας τιμάς, προεδρίαν τε ἐν ἀγῶσι καὶ πορφύραν ἐπίσημον τοῦ βασιλικοῦ γένους, σκίπωνα ἀντὶ σκήπτρου, καὶ τὰ ἱερὰ τῆς Ἐλευσινίας Δήμητρος.

"Pherecydes says concerning this seaboard that Miletos and Myous and the parts round Mykale and Ephesos were in earlier times occupied by Karians, and that the coast next thereafter, as far as Phokaia and Chios and Samos, which were ruled by Ankaios, was occupied by Leleges, but that both were driven out by the Ionians and took refuge in the remaining parts of Karia. He says that Androklos, legitimate son of Kodros, the King of Athens, was the leader of the Ionian colonization, which was later than the Aeolian, and that he became the founder of Ephesos; and for this reason, it is said, the royal seat of the Ionians was established there. And still now the descendants of his family are called kings; and they have certain honours, I mean the privilege of front seats at the games and of wearing purple robes as insignia of royal descent, and staff instead of sceptre, and of the superintendence of the sacrifices in honour of the Eleusinian Demeter." (transl. Jones 1929)

Fig. 49: Preliminary reconstruction (by H. Thür) of the sequence of buildings on the Embolos in front of Terrace House 2 (right to left): a) Hellenistic and Augustan monuments: Hypelaios Fountain, Octagon, Hexagon, Ptolemaic Fountain; b) from the 2nd c. AD onwards: Hadrian's Gate, Hypelaios Fountain, Octagon, Late Roman fountain house built on former Hexagon, Ptolemaic Nymphaeum altered in the 2nd c. AD

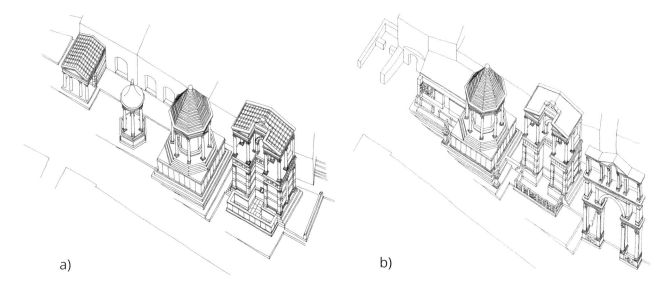

a)   b)

No ancient text relates the myth compellingly and completely. Whereas Kreophylos via Athenaios explains the events concerning the foundation oracle leaving Androklos out completely, Strabon twice alludes to a connection of the spring Hypelaios with Androklos, yet does not mention the oracle. Strabon and Pausanias are in agreement that Androklos forced out the Leleges (Strabon also says the Karians), whereby the earlier authors up until Strabon do not mention a city for these. A favourable starting point for the Greeks, with a somewhat sparse, autochthonous population consisting primarily of farmers or shepherds, arises indirectly from the oracle pronouncement, according to which the boar still dominated the land. When Pausanias suddenly creates a contrast between those who live in the "upper city" and others who have their homes around the Artemision, then this is a typical construction of the Second Sophistic;[37] the Androklos myth is here connected to the Artemision, and at the same time the historicity of a right of *asylum*, that was already respected by Androklos, is transferred into the mythical prehistory. In this way, Pausanias also vaguely introduces the Amazons as a further parallel topos of the other foundation myths in Ephesos, in which the goddess grants protection to the Amazons as founders of Ephesos or of the sanctuary of Artemis, against Dionysos, Herakles, or Theseus and even tries to correct the mythological/historical tradition:[38]

> οὐ μὴν πάντα γε τὰ ἐς τὴν θεὸν ἐπύθετο ἐμοὶ δοκεῖν Πίνδαρος, ὃς Ἀμαζόνας τὸ ἱερὸν ἔφη τοῦτο ἱδρύσασθαι στρατευομένας ἐπὶ Ἀθήνας τε καὶ Θησέα. αἱ δὲ ἀπὸ Θερμώδοντος γυναῖκες ἔθυσαν μὲν καὶ τότε τῇ Ἐφεσίᾳ θεῷ, ἅτε ἐπιστάμεναι [τε] ἐκ παλαιοῦ τὸ ἱερόν, καὶ ἡνίκα Ἡρακλέα ἔφυγον, αἱ δὲ καὶ Διόνυσον τὰ ἔτι ἀρχαιότερα, ἱκέτιδες ἐνταῦθα ἐλθοῦσαι: οὐ μὴν ὑπὸ Ἀμαζόνων γε ἱδρύθη, Κόρησος δὲ αὐτόχθων καὶ Ἔφεσος – Καΰστρου δὲ τοῦ ποταμοῦ τὸν Ἔφεσον παῖδα εἶναι νομίζουσιν –, οὗτοι τὸ ἱερόν εἰσιν οἱ ἱδρυσάμενοι, καὶ ἀπὸ τοῦ Ἐφέσου τὸ ὄνομά ἐστι τῇ πόλει.

> "Pindaros, however, it seems to me, did not learn everything about the goddess, for he says that this sanctuary was founded by the Amazons during their campaign against Athens and Theseus. It is a fact that the women from the Thermodon, as they knew the sanctuary from of old, sacrificed to the Ephesian goddess both on this occasion and when they had fled from Herakles; some of them earlier still, when they had fled from Dionysos, having come to the sanctuary as suppliants. However, it was not by the Amazons that the sanctuary was founded, but by Kore(s)sos, an aboriginal, and Ephesos, who is thought to have been a son of the river Kaystros, and from Ephesos the city received its name." (transl. by Jones 1933)

The demise of Androklos in battle against the Karians while supporting Priene is equally only reflected in Pausanias. He also appends to this a localisation of the tomb of Androklos in the form of a tumulus with a statue of a warrior at its apex.

This burial mound was apparently still visible during his time, on the route from the Artemision, past the silted-up bay at the Koressos settlement, and on to the Olympieion (plan 1 no. 98).[39]

Thür interpreted the heroon-nymphaeum that she investigated as a further tomb-like cenotaph for Androklos, as she well noticed that the form of the building itself and also the position nevertheless prohibit a connection with the tomb of Androklos as described by Pausanias.[40]

Any future discovery of the central relief from the spring, which may be assumed based on the parallel of the so-called Temple of Hadrian, would be decisive for the definitive interpretation of the structure. In any event, in the frieze-gable area the story of Androklos is illustrated, and in this the spring takes up a crucial role as the point of departure for the action of the city foundation. Thür questioned the motive for the erection in the later 2nd c. BC and arrived at a thoroughly plausible result. The myth of the city foundation in connection with the son of the Athenian King, as attested by Pherekydes (cited by Strabon) for the classical period,[41] is a conglomerate of differing stories with different backgrounds and intentions. Its highlighting would provide the citizens of Ephesos, as descendants of an Attic prince in the newly-created Roman province – or one which was finally brought to order around 120 BC after the uprising of Aristonikos and other unfortunate events – with a particular status and, above all, the desired *libertas* (autonomy) for their polis.[42]

Furthermore, Thür assembled numerous inscriptions, mostly from the immediate vicinity of the nymphaeum, which have in common a meeting point of the paraphylakes (officers of the civic police) called an "Androkloneion" and the cult of the ktistes Androklos. As would seem natural, the nymphaeum with the Androklos frieze will have contributed to the name. The premises of the office were probably the small trapezoidal plaza (8 × 3–3.80 m) surrounded by benches, and seats of the steps of the substructure of the nymphaeum, directly to the west of the nymphaeum (figs. 49f.). Here, wine was imbibed and "Androklos' Day" was celebrated, on which the gymnasia of the city also received donations of oil.[43] In its original form the plaza was most probably laid out in the Augustan period.[44]

Even if the existence and building history of this fountain house is secure for about 700 years, it still seems to reach further back lasting for more than a millenium.

Research up until now has explained the new construction of the spring house in the later 2nd c. BC and its later significance even in the Roman imperial period, but not, however, the construction – already emphasised by Kreophylos – of an original structure in the 4th or 3rd c. BC. The reuse of a number of ashlar blocks in the foundation and the core of the 2nd c. BC nymphaeum confirms that such an earlier structure existed. Before we turn to this issue, a few additional Hellenistic finds and pieces of evidence from close proximity should be presented, since these contribute important arguments to the formation of the thesis for an earlier Hypelaios-nymphaeum.

The siting of a spring house on the Curetes Street, just above the Triodos intersection, at the border of or just outside the densely developed region of the newly founded city, was in any case ideally situated: it offered in greeting a swig of water from the mountain source, combined with a history lesson, to those coming from Magnesia or from the Artemision who were already within the city yet nevertheless at the edge of its centre.

1.3 Nymphaea of the Ptolemies and Attalids

The nymphaeum on the south side of the Curetes Street below Terrace House 2, already mentioned above in the historical chapter, is the oldest, elaborate fountain building known to date on the Embolos (plan 3 no. 12; plan 4; figs. 23. 49 and 51), indeed in the Hellenistic city at all. The fountain house has been dated to the 3rd c. BC on account of its structural details and above all due to the execution of its lions' head waterspouts.[45] Stratigraphically, only one small complex of finds is relevant, which in any event indicates a construction date before the middle of the 2nd c. BC.[46] We are dealing here with a building that was certainly roofed, with 4.20 m long walls on three sides; on each wall three locations for the withdrawal of water with lion heads as waterspouts were originally set up. The floor, of cut limestone plaques, extended ca. 2.75 m to the north towards the street in an open area, creating a forecourt. During a renovation in the 2nd c. AD (approximately during the Hadrianic era) the lions' heads were removed, and the fountain house was redesigned and made smaller. After excavation one of the lions´ heads, found in the debris, was relocated to its original place (fig. 51).

Water as benefit for the occupied city or self-representation of foreign rulers?

The proposals for the dating of the nymphaeum fit very well with the inscription found only ca. 20–25 m away in Terrace House 2 (figs. 22 and 23), with a double dedication to Ptolemaios IV and his sister-wife Arsinoë III (see fig. 24) as well as Isis and Serapis, most probably set up in the penultimate decade of the 3rd c. BC, very likely in the years 220–216 BC due to the absence of the title 'Theoi Philopatores', which was in use from 215 onwards.[47] The probable connection in content between the nymphaeum and the inscription has already been treated in the historical section.[48] The proximity of the secondary find spots and the fragmentation into four pieces – three of which were recovered during excavations – that almost certainly first occurred there, speaks equally for an original erection close by, that is, at the fountain house on the Curetes Street.

This would accord well with the geological-topographical and socio-political situation. The practically waterless limestone rocks of the Panayırdağ certainly presented significant problems for the water supply to the garrison on the peak of the Tracheia (fig. 90).[49] It was therefore obvious that a natural water source at the city border, as easy to reach as possible and where the garrison could safely satisfy their water requirements without having

Fig. 51: Hellenistic fountain house on the Embolos, view through the Late Antique walls to the relocated lion's head water-spout

to affect the densely developed settlement areas, needed to be developed. At the same time, this choice of site fulfilled the usual claims for prestige by the rulers, and that of the Lagidai as new civic masters was made publicly visible.

Thus, it is no surprise that the new masters of Ephesos after the Peace of Apameia (188 BC), the Pergamene Attalids, built a similar nymphaeum for their purposes as well. The late Hellenistic fountain house (plan 1 no. 72; fig. 52), even if significantly smaller (3.82 × 1.45 m) than the one in the Embolos, with two Ionic columns at the front, erected in front of the north analemma of the theatre, provides a good parallel. This must have been in some degree chronologically and functionally connected with the construction of the theatre and the residence of the Attalid governor erected above it (plan 1, buildings nos. 75 and 76; fig. 9 nos. 4–6);[50] at the same time, however, it would have served the sovereign prestige of the Pergamene Kings.[51] In the late 1st c. AD it was attached to the new Marnas water conduit and was extended towards the front with a second row of columns.[52] Whether a spring flowed out here at the foot of the Panayırdağ in the Hellenistic period must remain open, yet it is not very likely. It is more probable that a short water conduit existed here from the south, from the area of the lower Embolos along the Marble Street. This must have been destroyed at the latest during the Domitianic rebuilding of the theatre, and the small nymphaeum was expanded in depth by about 2 m and linked up to the new water supply leading from the State Agora to the Harbour Gymnasium complex.

Fig. 52: Hellenistic Nymphaeum near the Theatre, with porch of the Domitianic period

1.4 A statue of Lysimachos and the Hypelaios Spring

The connection between the ruler cult and water at the time of the Diadochoi goes directly back to the example of Alexander the Great. Vitruvius relates an impressive story demonstrating that the water supply for a new foundation is one of the main duties of the ktistes. He describes the plan, nevertheless rejected by Alexander, by the architect Deinokrates of Rhodos to found a city on Mt. Athos and to carve into the flank of the mountain a huge statue of Alexander, with a city in one hand and a jug from which a river flows in the other hand. At Ephesos, the Androklos myth and the Hypelaios Spring mentioned in the foundation oracle provided an additional, powerful connecting factor that allowed – as will be shown – the neos ktistes Lysimachos as well as the subsequent Hellenistic dynasties, and even the Roman emperors, to link up not only with the Alexander succession but also with a local tradition.

A Hellenistic portrait head with ruler's fillet (fig. 20), found in 1967 during clean-up operations at the Curetes Street opposite Terrace House 2 and in the small lane branching from here to the north and leading to the western entrance to the Baths of Scholasticia (plan 3 no. 14), is of great importance for the overall interpretation of the group of monuments on the lower Curetes Street. The portrait lay below the Late Antique street paving, apparently at the junction of the two streets, with its face oriented upwards. In a meticulous study its discoverer, Erol Atalay, identified the portrait as Lysimachos.[53] This identification was occasionally questioned in the scholarship, without, however, a constructive counter-proposal being made. Repeatedly, and also recently, Atalay's dating of the head (290/280 BC) has been substantially confirmed.[54] Since an identification with another of the Diadochoi of this period – for Ephesos in the early 3rd c. BC only Demetrios Poliorketes, Seleukos I Nikator, or Ptolemaios II come into question – is not possible due to the well-known physiognomies of these other rulers, this leaves only Lysimachos as the person depicted. This raises the question of where an over life-size statue of Lysimachos[55] could originally have been displayed, and how it was integrated into the subsequent Hellenistic epoch and Roman imperial period, until in Christian Late Antiquity[56] a relatively 'reverential' depositing under the street paving occurred.

How can the portrait of a supposedly hated ruler survive for 1000 years?

The detailed description above of the role of Lysimachos in Ephesos as a ktistes[57] certainly explains the respectful display of the statue during the period of Roman rule over the city; indeed, after the end of the Roman Republic the gerousia which he had founded emerged in particular as a protagonist.[58] This history, however, does not explain the statue's fate in the ca. 150 years previously, from the death of the king in 281 BC until the bequest of the last of the Attalids in 133 BC. The find-spot in the lower Curetes Street in the immediate vicinity of the Hellenistic nymphaea suggests an original display in this area. Precisely if the statue of Lysimachos was set up earlier in this region with reference to a spring or a nymphaeum, a direct later connection through the ruling couple Ptolemaios IV and Arsinoë III and their veneration at a fountain house in the immediate proximity would be even more logical.

It follows that the ideal location for the erection of the statue in the environs of its find-spot should be sought in the area of the spring, which was viewed as Hypelaios at least in the later 2nd c. and early 1st c. BC. But Kreophylos reported already in the 4th/3rd c. BC that during his time it was newly conceived. The development of the spring – as argued above – could therefore easily have occurred under Lysimachos. When, in the early period of the Roman province, the city celebrated its regained freedom under the Romans, and at the same time set about positioning itself against Pergamon as the first and greatest central city of Asia (ἡ πρώτη καὶ μεγίστη μητρόπολις τῆς Ἀσίας), the Androklos nymphaeum was created in the building form known today. A secondary displaying of Lysimachos, who at this time was politically inoffensive for Rome and who emphasised the autonomy of Ephesos in the Hellenistic period – in contrast to others of the Diadochoi – would be an almost ingenious scenario, for example in the central space within the U-form ground plan of the fountain building for the Hypelaios Spring.

It is precisely against this backdrop of a contemporary veneration of Androklos and Lysimachos as founders of the city that the attachment of weapon reliefs on the nymphaeum, first proposed by V. M. Strocka, and according to H. Thür as balustrade reliefs in the upper storey, would be an exceedingly rational ornamentation.[59] These reliefs are today relatively far away, built into a mosque in Selçuk, yet since parts of the Neronian Hall (figs. 37 and 40b) were also built in here, an allocation to the nymphaeum is absolutely conceivable. In any case this allocation can be well-argued both on stylistic grounds and based on the measurements. The blocks in question are 0.90 m tall, and are decorated with round and oval shields, swords, spears, and battering rams from ships.[60] Weapon reliefs during the Hellenistic period appeared on funerary buildings as a symbol of the virility of the deceased, yet also frequently on public buildings with functions of civic prestige, such as city gates and municipal buildings.[61] On the Hypelaios Spring, they could have constituted a reference to well-fortified Ephesos and its militant founding heroes.[62]

During the Christianisation of the fountain in the 5th or 6th c. AD, there was ultimately no longer any place for the royal heros ktistes.[63] The head of the statue was not, however, broken off and burned down into lime, but was carefully removed and reverently buried. A very similar occurrence befell, with great probability, a great architectural patron of the Roman period, Tiberius Claudius Aristion (d. ca. 120 AD), whose tomb building was located in the environs of the heroon. His portrait head was laid in his sarcophagus, and this was secondarily buried in the 'festival plaza' of the paraphylakes (fig. 50) at the west side of the heroon.[64] Aristion also received the honour of being described in many inscriptions, probably set up in front of his tomb building on the Curetes Street,[65] as "beautifier" of the city. The edict of the *proconsul Asiae* for the protection of the water conduit erected by him identified Aristion posthumously as most bright figure (ἀνὴρ διασημότατος) of his highly famous native city, in a similar fashion as Perikles, according to Thoukydides, is said to have spoken at the tomb of those who fell (τὸν τάφον ἐπισημότατον) in the first year of the Peloponnesian War.[66]

Let us return to Lysimachos. It would have almost been a culpable failure, had he not used the water source, rather fortuitously located in the centre of his new city Arsinoeia, for propagandistic purposes. If one addresses his life history, then distinct parallels emerge with the story of Androklos, some of which can also be assessed, for a bellicose aristocratic society, as inherent in the system. In particular, the killing of a boar virtually belonged to the duties of the Macedonian aristocracy as a symbol of virility; before they had done this, they were not allowed to recline at the table with other men, but instead they had to sit like women.[67] Seleukos I Nikator is said to have killed a boar on the occasion of the founding of Laodikeia, and to have dragged it with his own hands around the borders of the new city.[68] The heroic hunter in the vestments of Alexander, as Androklos is often depicted in Ephesos,[69] appears for the first time on the sarcophagus of Alexander´s client King Abdalonymos in Sidon.[70] The pictorial language of the Androklos myth was therefore formed at precisely the time in which Lysimachos, who saw himself as a worthy descendant of Alexander the Great, developed his own royal propaganda.[71] The fact that Lysimachos, like Androklos, would die on the battlefield, could be utilised in the 2nd c. BC as an additional allusion. The appearance of the original, highly probably Lysimachean monument at the Hypelaios we will not be able to discover. The Androklos myth ought to have already been applied there, with the neos ktistes standing on a step with the mythical founder. The above life-size statue of Lysimachos was probably taken over from the first building and integrated into the new monument, or erected in its immediate environment.

1.5 The site of the Octagon as part of the Hellenistic nymphaeum terrace

The Octagon has been allocated to a site between the city spring Hypelaios, connected with Lysimachos (and therefore with Arsinoë II), and a nymphaeum, erected most probably in honour of Ptolemaios IV Philopator and his sister-wife Arsinoë III. In this manner, the tomb monument of Arsinoë IV was linked topographically with significant architectural monuments of her ancestors (plan 4; fig. 49). As the last child born of her dynasty, one that was connected to Ephesos for roughly 300 years in a variety of respects, yet also as the bearer of the short-lived name of the city, her death brought an epoch to an end.

Attempting to make amends to an unfortunate princess
changes the face of a city

Apart from that, in constructing this monument the city and the Artemision removed a heavy debt to her, as in spite of the heroic intervention of the *Megabyzos* they had not been able to protect the suppliant princess from a death ordered by her own sister.

The Hellenistic monuments of the 3rd c. BC at the lower Embolos, the extrapolated yet not demonstrable Hypelaios nymphaeum of Lysimachos and the Ptolemaic nymphaeum, emphasise the connection between the actual rulers and the water supply of the city. This situation altered when, in the late 2nd c. BC, the Hypelaios spring was erected in a new, monumental form; in addition to the original founder Androklos, also probably Lysimachos was represented here, but not as a living ruler anymore but as a younger yet equally historical ktistes. In this way, the cult of heroes stepped into the foreground at this fountain instead of the veneration of living rulers. Nevertheless, physically burying here a descendant of the former city rulers, who were honoured at this location, was still difficult. The decisive inducement was rather not the achievements of the deceased, but far rather the atonement of the city and of the Artemis sanctuary on her behalf.[72] At Ephesos, this concession for an intramural burial and ultimately also the burial site chosen are crucially connected with the Artemis altar at the Triodos.

The knowledge that the old rural roads, which converged here until the relocation of the city under Lysimachos, were used as streets of tombs almost certainly played a role as well. Until now, dense burial layouts have been found from the 7th/6th c. until the late 4th c. BC in the region of the State Agora, on the slopes alongside the entire Curetes Street as far as the South Gate of the agora, and further along the street towards Koressos inside the (later) agora (plan 2; fig. 27); some of the burial pits discovered during excavations were cleared out; the burials had been detected and removed apparently during Augustan and later building works.[73] For us today, an indissoluble dichotomy arises between the simultaneous removal[74] and the new laying out of graves. Ultimately, we cannot determine whether these older burial sites played a role in the decision to bury Arsinoë IV at the lower Embolos.[75] Rulers, founders and other outstanding persons had frequently been honoured with intramural graves in Greek cities since the 7th c. BC, but the number of identifiable graves, even if increasing in Hellenistic times, was relatively small.[76] It is no accident that in some cases of such extraordinary honours, which were in opposition to the normal customs, a city planning an intramural tomb asked the oracle in Delphi for a religious authorisation; a well-known example for this practice is conveyed by Plutarch for Sikyon in 213 BC for the strategos Aratos after his death on the battleground.[77] In Ephesos, the highest authority in sacred affairs was the Artemision, whose priesthood decided about the permissibility of proposals like this. Probably because of that, the uncommon choice for the place along a street – much earlier already used as a burial ground –, close to the altar of Artemis at the Triodos and in between other Lagid monuments was made; city authorities otherwise normally chose the agora, a gymnasium, or the courtyard of the bouleuterion for honorary tombs.[78] The fact that this area, even if inside the city walls, was a nearly empty ground in Augustan times might also have been factor for the location at the Embolos; no dwellings would be in close proximity to the new tomb.

What we can say without doubt is that Arsinoë IV had an exceptionally strong connection to Ephesian Artemis.[79] She was almost certainly born (57/56 BC) in Ephesos, very likely in the *asylum*, during the time her father Ptolemaios XII took up residence or better a safe haven in the town. With this, she must have held a status of almost being a citizen of Ephesos. She was killed by her half-sister's and Marcus Antonius' henchmen while still a *parthenos* and a suppliant to virgin Artemis. Thus, the minimum the city of Ephesos and the temple wardens of Artemis could do was to honour her as a Queen and a heroic person, at least after her death.

The status of Arsinoë IV as a client of C. Iulius Caesar and subsequently Octavian must have been beneficial for this intent. Especially Roman laws may also have played a decisive role for her intramural burial. In Rome only two groups of persons had the right to be buried inside the borders of the *urbs*: imperators after their triumph and the Vestal virgins, as Servius states:[80] *lege cavit, ne quis in urbe sepeliretur … imperatores et virgines Vestae quia legibus non tenentur, in civitate habent sepulchra ….* ("… obeyed the law that nobody should be buried inside the town … imperators and Vestal virgins, because the laws were not valid for them, have their tombs in the city …"). Even if Arsinoë IV was not a priestess of Artemis (which we cannot exclude), the parallels are obvious, as she had cut her curls as a virgin in seeking protection.[81]

Has the octagon served as the initial spark for a boom in grave constructions?

In any event, at Ephesos (almost) immediately after the decision to install the Octagon, or at least contemporary with its planning and construction, a boom in intramural honorific structures and burial sites took place. Many of these, notably, were directly connected with nymphaea or were at least adjacent to them.[82] Whether this "fashion" in fact relates back to the close proximity of the Octagon to the Hypelaios

Spring is in no way demonstrable, but might provide an explanation. Coincidentally, the Hellenistic tradition of erecting nymphaea in honour of living rulers was continued. In order to prove this proposition – and thereby to deduce a compelling explanation for the Octagon – the Augustan building programme, to which the Octagon belongs, in the core region of Ephesos has to be reviewed more closely.

2. Honorific structures for Augustus in the region of the Embolos

Right at the beginning of his rule, Augustus coequally joined the ranks of the illustrious group of ktisteis of Ephesos with his reorganisations and new constructions. These included the reorganisation of the Artemision by P. Vedius Pollio and other representatives, as well as the generous expansion of the intramural space via the erection of the new city walls and gates in the east (Magnesian Gate) and north (Koressian Gate); the new construction of the Tetragonos Agora, probably extensively financed by resident Italians in Ephesos;[83] the probable transferral of the prytaneion to the State Agora (plan 5 no. 6); a renovation or expansion of the theatre which, however, cannot be clearly comprehended; and the construction of two long-distance aqueducts, to mention only the most significant undertakings. In gratitude for these works, the emperor received a cult area named *Augusteum* in the Artemision[84] and an additional cult space in the region of the Gymnasium of the Neoi in the so-called Rhodian Peristyle (plan 5 no. 7). Generous expansions in this area also included the stadium-length Basilike Stoa (dedicated in 11 AD; plan 5 no. 5), which served as a gallery of the Julio-Claudian family and the late Augustan or immediately post-Augustan temple on the central plaza (plan 5 no. 15) of the State Agora, which was almost certainly erected for the imperial cult.[85] Aside from the South Gate of the Tetragonos Agora (4/3 BC), dedicated to Augustus and Agrippa as the patrons of the freedmen who erected it, the overwhelming importance of Augustus for Ephesos found clear expression in at least two additional honorific monuments, both of extraordinary form, on the lower Embolos.

Pax Augusta: the omnipresence of the monarch in an exploding city.

2.1 The *Aqua Iulia* and the round water feature at the south-east corner of the Tetragonos Agora

After the systematic excavations in the agora, it is now decisively clear that the circular building with water fountain function, earlier viewed as Hellenistic in date (plan 3 no. 4; figs. 33. 36. 37. 53. 54) stands directly on the terrace wall of the agora's

Fig. 53: Augustan Circular Monument at the southeast corner of the Tetragonos Agora, supposedly the terminal station of the *Aqua Iulia*; behind the Circular Monument, the south side of the Neronian Hall with the former entrance to the tomb chamber (modern walling with small stones and covering with a concrete slab)

east wall, extended over the agora front to the south for this purpose. It was thus erected at the same time as the staircase to the upper storey of the agora.[86] Hence, an approximately contemporary or slightly later date of origin, in comparison to the adjacent South Gate (4/3 BC) of the agora, is confirmed.[87] The six-columned monopteros, projecting from the structural alignment of the agora into the Marble Street, must have had a particular significance as a corner structure of the agora, and at the same time for the new Augustan city quarter extending to the west and the north.[88] In situ, only three rows of rustic ashlar masonry from the substructure are preserved (Dm. 7.50 m). The corresponding architectural elements were set up on the foundations as an architectural sample in the 1990s (fig. 53), but were regrettably removed again and brought to a depot in the agora. The columns and capitals of the Corinthian order are drilled through, while the cone-shaped roof displays strongly sintered recesses in which the water was channelled to the roof peak, whence it flowed down in cascades and sprays (fig. 54).[89]

A fragment of a marble statue base for Augustus, as sponsor of the *Aqua Iulia,* was found in Late Antique debris very close to the building. Until now, this is the only secure evidence for this oldest demonstrable Ephesian long-distance aqueduct.[90] According to the text of the inscription, the conduit was financed by the emperor himself, while an unknown *proconsul Asiae* was apparently personally responsible for the construction:[91] *[Imp. Cae]s Aug[u]stu[s] / divi f. / aquam Iuliam / adduxit / [c]ivitati Ephesiae [- - - - -] procos.* The inscription belongs at all events to the years between 27 BC and 4 AD at the latest.

The rare, and until now hard to understand expression *adduxit*[92] ("he led to") instead of the more common *induxit* ("he led in", namely, into the city) now finally finds a

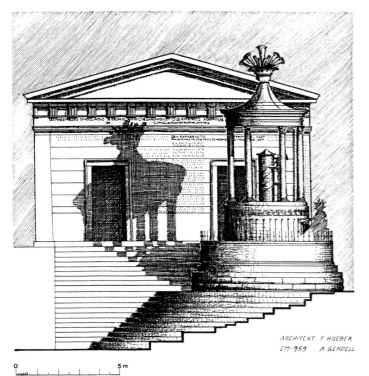

Fig. 54: Reconstruction of the Augustan Circular Monument at the south-east corner of the Tetragonos Agora. In the centre, instead of the pillar, an inscribed base for a statue of Augustus should be reconstructed

satisfactory explanation with the connection to the water feature. *Adduxit* refers to the water feature as one of the buildings supplied by this water supply system.[93] An above life-size statue of Augustus as constructor of the aqueduct, in a colonnaded building surrounded with water flowing down from the roof must have been a splendid sight. The erection at the (from now on actually new) Triodos junction provided the image of the emperor not only with optimal visibility from all sides, but also a particular character as benefactor both of the city and of the Artemision.

In this manner, Augustus certainly vastly surpassed the earlier benefactors with their nymphaea obliquely opposite on the other side of the street of the lower Embolos. From Augustus, the city had received not only a tapping of a spring, but indeed two long-distance aqueducts of a probable length of 8 and 6 km.[94] The direct connection of an image of the emperor with an aqueduct that was inaugurated and, at least substantially, financed by him also shows that the Hellenistic rulers' gesture as benefactors of water was adopted by the Roman emperors as early as the Augustan period – and not under Domitian, as has been assumed until now.[95] Furthermore, this occurred by no means coincidentally at Ephesos, and within the city, at precisely this location.

2.2 The Hexagon: a monument of Augustus and his grandchildren?

Augustus himself, however, was also present on the Hellenistic royal terrace. The foundations of an almost completely demolished monument of the Augustan period have been discovered, below and in the floor of a Late Antique structure interpreted as a nymphaeum, between the Octagon and the Ptolemaic nymphaeum (plan 3 no. 11; plan 4; fig. 49).[96] In ground plan, the structure is a hexagonal monopteros on a three- (in the eastern part) to four-stepped (in the western part) substructure (fig. 55). The side lengths of the six-sided figure were recorded by H. Thür as 2.55 m, yet this must designate the shorter, interior lengths, since the total length over the longer diagonal amounts to 5.60 at the exterior, and the total depth over the parallel walls amounts to 4.80 m.[97] In fact, the published plan shows an exterior side length of approximately 2.80 m. According to H. Thür, the socle level consists of marble, with a core of mortared rubble faced by marble orthostats. At the corners, large limestone blocks serve as foundations for the columns. Very probably, two Ionic corner capitals (stored at the lower Embolos) and a dentilated block (belonging to a circular building with ca. 4 m diameter), which must have been produced in the Augustan period, can be assigned to the architecture of the super-structure. The finds suggest the hypothetical reconstruction of a monopteros with a total height of approximately 9–10 m (fig. 49a).[98]

Are we allowed to assemble the scattered remains of marbles
into a meaningful monument?

Inherently, it is naturally ambitious to suggest a closer dating or even an interpretation and attribution from these modest material remains. Nevertheless, an additional Augustan monument for the centre of Ephesos has been known for a long time from parts of a marble statue basis, with reliefs and inscriptions for Augustus and his three grandsons (figs. 56f.).[99] Two plaques (0.76 × 1.46 m each) with rich decoration – ovolo, palmettes and astragal – and parts of an inscription were discovered built into the early Byzantine steps to the head building at the northern end of the Neronian Hall. The two plaques together form the covering of a square base on which the four statues easily could have been disposed without shortage of space. F. Eichler additionally ascribed three blocks with divine figures, from the latest paving of the Marble Street, to the socle (figs. 56f.).[100] These were found near

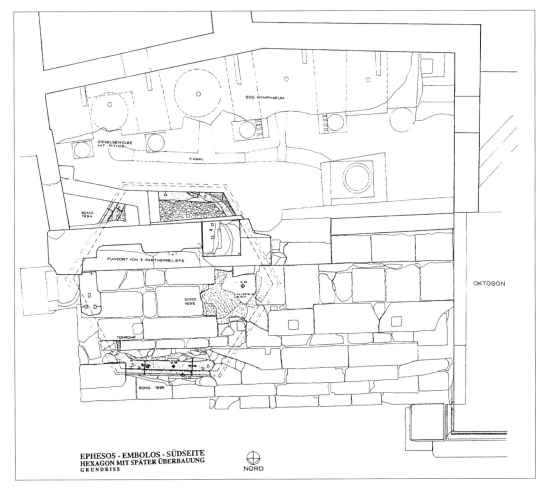

Fig. 55: Hexagon, parts of the substructure with steps

Fig. 56: Monument for Augustus and his three grandsons: parts of marble statue base, with reliefs and inscriptions

the theatre, very close to the covering plaques, and were transferred here probably at the same time as the architectural elements of the Amazon altar discussed above. Therefore, they could easily have been brought here for their final usage from a monument lying close by on the Embolos. Eichler recognised the same archaistic tendencies in the relief figures as characterise the architectural elements of the Amazon altar as well. Although their content excludes a direct affiliation to that altar, the same building programme or the same workshop could be behind both groups of fragments.

Fig. 57: Monument for Augustus and his three grandsons: blocks with divine figures

Eichler was able to suggest a probable total representation, with 12 (Olympian) gods on three sides of the base. Athena, Ares and Poseidon are preserved on one side, and most likely Aphrodite, opening her mantle, appears as a corner figure on another one.[101] The rear side of the base shows three nymphs and Pan in a grotto. On one block, the end of the inscription that begins on the covering plaque is still extant. Although the name of the consecrator is not preserved, nevertheless the genitive form τῶν τέκνων (children) makes clear that a family, instead of an individual, was named as the patron.[102]

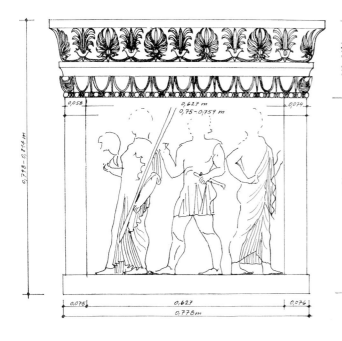

According to the partially preserved dedication inscription to Augustus and his three grandsons Gaius, Lucius, and Agrippa, the monument belongs to the period between 12

and 2 BC; a date of around 5 BC is most probable based on parallels of this group from other cities and on the architectural decoration.[103] Its original position has not yet been found.

With the current state of research, the connection between the monument for Augustus and his grandsons with the Hexagon can only be hypothetical. There was certainly sufficient space in the monopteros (diameter around 4 m), and a magnificent view of the statuary group was guaranteed from all sides from the street due to the wide space between the columns and the delicate architecture. The contrast, however, between the dynastic self-representation of Augustus surrounded by his grandsons in an open circle of columns, and the neighbouring Octagon as a symbol of the extinct family of the Lagidai, with its closed central chamber, could hardly be more sharply drawn. In addition, moreover, this immediate proximity was also a symbol of the exceptional qualities of Augustus as a ruler: ultimately, he brought an end to the period of (civil) wars, to lawless violence, to uncontrolled murder even in the protection of great sanctuaries – his dominion had surely restored all rights and capabilities of the Artemision. All of these accomplishments allowed Arsinoë IV at least a worthy tomb monument.

The question therefore arises if the Octagon, perhaps first completed around the turn of the eras,[104] and the Hexagon were planned contemporaneously, and were consciously conceived as a pair of unusual polygonal buildings.[105] This would be most likely to have happened during the months-long stay of Octavian in Ephesos during the winter of 30/29 BC. At that time, however, Octavian had no grandchildren; his only daughter Iulia was ten years old. Therefore, for such an early date for a plan,[106] the original concept must have involved Iulia in the foreground;[107] she represented a promise for the future ruling generations of Rome in contrast to Arsinoë IV, who was murdered as a virgin and the last-born child of her dynasty. Until the realisation of the planned building, and once the grandchildren had actually appeared, the statuary display could have been accordingly adjusted; around 5 BC Iulia herself was already compulsorily married to Tiberius and was no longer a dynastic figurehead for Augustus.[108]

If we wish to pursue the idea of this furnishing further, the symbolism goes far beyond a mere comparison between the dying-off dynasty of the Lagidai and that of the family of the Roman princeps. As noted earlier, Arsinoë IV probably did not seek protection coincidentally, since, like Ephesos and the Artemision, she belonged to the clientele of Caesar and therefore, after his death, to that of Octavian. It might be entirely possible that Caesar, and above all Octavian, played with the idea of keeping Arsinoë IV in the background as a potential rival Queen to her sister Kleopatra VII. After the suicide of Kleopatra on 10 August 30 BC and the disposal shortly afterwards of her son and co-regent Ptolemaios (XV) Kaisar (*Ptolemaeus Caesar*),[109] born on 23 June 47 BC, the dynasty was officially extinct.[110] In this way, after the autumn of 30 BC, Octavian could justly claim that all of the dynasties of the Diadochoi, and therefore all of the ruling houses viewed as descendants of Alexander the Great, had died out. He, as *princeps senatus* of Rome, could accede to the line of succession of Alexander as the sole legitimate claimant. During his visit to the tomb of Alexander, when asked if he also wanted to see the tombs of the Lagidai, according to Suetonius he reacted indignantly: *...regem se voluisse ait videre, non mortuos* ("I came to see a King, not corpses!").[111]

According to accepted scholarly opinion, the Corinthian order established itself for the planning of imperial monuments very rapidly in the ruling circles in Rome, and was transferred from here into the provinces as the standard.[112] The circular building with water feature at the agora, discussed above, therefore constitutes one of the earliest examples. Nevertheless, the Hexagon on the Hellenistic "Royal Terrace", if the conjecture of the allocation of corresponding capitals by H. Thür is correct, appears to have been erected in the Ionic order. We therefore have a first indication that the Artemision, and the intention of the Ephesians to commend their patron goddess in particular to Rome, is also reflected in the architecture of the Hexagon.[113] The fact that the monument, if the attribution of the base for Augustus and his grandsons is correct, was actually not planned at court or by Romans resident in Ephesos, but instead by an Ephesian of Greek origin, also emerges from the dedication on the base, which is only in Greek and is not very conspicuous.[114]

It should have been no coincidence that two seemingly contemporary and neighbouring honorific buildings for Augustus, the Hexagon and the round building with water feature diagonally opposite at the agora, each possessed six columns (plan 3 nos. 4 and 11; plan 4). The ground plan of the Hexagon has an even more striking effect in contrast to the round monopteros at the agora: this ground plan appears architecturally for the first time. Subsequently, hexagonal buildings were also seldom constructed. Indeed, Vitruvius already mentioned the motif for designs for floors,[115] but as a free-standing structure the form is apparently first encountered again in the Trajanic harbour basin, well known from numismatic images, at Ostia.[116] The central, hexagonal water basin in the middle of the Oceanus mosaic of the luxurious villa in Bad Kreuznach seems to be an allusion to this Trajanic construction. In the provincial mosaic, all around, harbour landscapes, island landscapes and other landscapes are represented with human actors. Perhaps the *negotiator* from Kreuznach traded goods through the harbour of Ostia, which therefore represented the source of his wealth. According to the preserved inscription with consular year, the mosaic was created in 234 AD.[117]

An independent hexagon is first encountered again in the (late) Severan Temple of Iuppiter at Baalbek; here, perhaps astrological considerations regarding the weekday planets were decisive for the choice of the form.[118] From this point, circumstantial evidence could perhaps lead back to the Augustan Hexagon at Ephesos, if we wish to recognise here a symbol of the new Golden Age (*aurea aetas*) and the reign of Saturn renewed by Octavian/Augustus, as is obviously expressed in the somewhat later Gemma Augustea. Saturn is the ruler of the sixth day of the week, and played an important role in the horoscope of Augustus.[119] One could also think in more general terms of a numerical symbolism, in which the number six is linked with emerging and vanishing, increasing and decreasing, qualitative and local alterations,[120] which would reinforce the dynastic representation assumed here. If one of these backgrounds was decisive for the choice of the building form at Ephesos, we would nonetheless – in spite of the randomness of the literary tradition – probably find additional literary evidence as well as architectonic parallels.

The so-called Honeycomb Conjecture, probably published in 36 BC, by M. Terentius Varro appears extremely significant for the choice of form; Varro states that the hexagonal honeycomb exhibits the optimal form regarding stability and maximization of surface area:[121]

> *Non in favo sex angulis cella, totidem quot habet ipsa pedes? Quod geometrae hexagonon fieri in orbi rutundo ostendunt, ut plurimum loci includatur.*

> *"Does not the chamber in the comb have six angles, the same number as the bee has feet? The geometricians prove that this hexagon inscribed in a circular figure encloses the greatest amount of space."*

This assumption long occupied the mathematicians, and above all the geometry that was responsible for architectural issues in antiquity; but it could only definitively be verified in 1999 by the mathematician T. C. Hales.[122] Although Varro named his work *de rebus rusticis* (On Agriculture), in actuality in this work he records (fictive) conversations, mainly against the background of agriculture and carried out by members of the élite in a villa.[123] Since Varro composed his numerous additional works on Roman antiquities and the Latin language after the end of the civil war against Pompeius (magnus), whom he supported, at the instruction of Caesar and later of Augustus,[124] he was much read at court and his works in fact reflected actual problems.

When Octavian spent the winter of 30/29 in Ephesos, we may assume that many issues concerning the future building programme were discussed at that time, and that appropriate honorific buildings associated with him were planned. This ambitious programme included, above all, the construction of the new city walls and thereby entire urban quarters, with the agora and the cult centre at the State Agora as well as the aqueducts, and also the reform of the Artemision. At this date, Varro's publication was approximately five years in the past. Furthermore, the honeycomb problem was of eminent significance for Ephesos, since bees in addition to the stag were the outstanding symbolic animals of Artemis Ephesia. For a long time, the bee represented the heraldic animal of Ephesos on the civic coinage.[125] A cultic society of young girls in the service of the temple was named αἱ μέλισσαι τῆς θεοῦ (honeybees of the goddess).[126] These became even more significant when the *Megabyzos*, who had still represented the Artemision in 41 BC, no longer appears after the Augustan reform of the Artemision.[127] From this point on, the administration of the sanctuary was carried out primarily by other civic officials, the Neopoiai or Neopoioi (temple wardens), who are already known since the Lysimachean reforms in 302/301 BC. They were elected for a period of time – two Neopoioi per phyle, that is, in the Hellenistic period ten, and after the mid–1st c. AD, 12.[128] A hypothesis posited long ago by S. Karwiese[129] points in this direction; he connected the Latin loanword *apis* (bee) together with Apaša and Ephesos or Ephesia, and thereby gave the goddess the name "Queen of the bees", as indeed high priestly officials of Artemis Ephesia in the Hellenistic-Roman era were titled as ἐσσῆν(ες) – Pausanias explains the word as "King of the bees" and mentions a function as *hestiatoris* (host for banquets).[130]

Delian Apollon and Artemis Ephesia: the divine twins meet again.

In fact, the hexagon pattern, interpreted as a honeycomb, already appears as a decorative element on ashlar blocks and large wall areas on numerous late Archaic buildings in the sanctuaries of Leto (temple, ca. 540 BC) and of Apollon (so-called hexagonal building or oikos of the Delians, ca. 520 BC) on Delos and subsequently on additional Cycladic islands. This pattern was viewed by G. Gruben as a significant element in the cult of the Delian triad of Leto, Apollon, and Artemis.[131] During the Augustan period, many Roman merchants who had formerly resided on Delos now lived permanently or for the medium term at Ephesos.[132] It is not inconceivable that these merchants could very well have taken over this symbol and employed it for the unusual ground plan of the Hexagon. The particular connection of a hexagon to Augustus was probably due to his generally known closeness to Apollon, but also to a much lesser visible connection to the god's sister Artemis. The oldest Temple of Apollon and Latona in Rome, dedicated in 431 BC, had its dedication festival on 23rd September, that is, on precisely the birthday of Augustus, just as did the new Temple of Apollon *in circo* (so-called Temple of Apollo Sosianus).[133] From this background, it seems noteworthy that the temple for Apollo on the Palatine Hill was vowed by Octavian on the occasion of the battle at Naulochos (36 BC), even if not only Apollo but much more Artemis was responsible for the final victory there.[134] With this, Octavian was also linked with Artemis and it is no surprise that the group of cult statues in the Palatine temple (finished in 28 BC), as in Delos and Klaros, consisted of Leto and the twins Apollo and Artemis, as Propertius states in his elegies.[135]

By means of its hexagonal ground plan and its Ionic order in its superstructure, an honorific building that made reference to the arcane power of the city goddess – and one which was located directly next to the Octagon that was equally constructed in the interest of the Artemision – would in any event be a masterpiece in the context of the formation of an ensemble. It seems logical that it was almost compulsory for the city to build the Corinthian circular building at the agora, in order to honour the accomplishments of the *princeps* on behalf of the city. At the same time the Artemision might have caused the construction of the hexagonal honorific monument for the new world leader and his dynasty, who should rule under the grace of the city goddess.

Furthermore, the hexagonal plan referred not only to Artemis and therefore also to her brother Apollon, but probably additionally to Augustus himself. With convincing arguments, R. J. King ascribed the birthplace of Octavian in the centre of Rome, *ad capita bubula*,[136] mentioned by Suetonius, to an arithmetic expression of the land surveyors (*agrimensores*). The expression is first handed down in the mid- to late 1st c. AD by Columella.[137] "Ox head" apparently refers to a piece of land whose lozenge-shaped form arose from two equilateral triangles mirrored at their base. Three such figures constitute a hexagon or, conversely, the surface area of a hexagon could easily be calculated from it, in that this would be partitioned into six equilateral triangles or three *capita bubula*.[138] Knowledge eludes us, unfortunately, whether the birth site of Octavian actually lay on a hexagonal piece of land. The knowledge of the name – independently of the number of *capita bubulorum* – and of the possible creation of a hexagon from three such geometric figures, could also constitute a sufficiently comprehensible allusion. If, however, Augustus was now represented and venerated in this Hexagon with, of all things, his three grandsons, then the formation of the ground plan can also be viewed as a sign of the beneficial influence of the "goddess of the bees", Artemis, which extended to the fertility of Italy in the human as well as the agricultural sector, as well as to the continuance of the Julian imperial house.

The fact that such reflections of the Ephesians, which may have appeared arrogant to an outsider, were perceived completely differently in the city of Artemis is revealed by many similar examples in the subsequent course of history. Already under Tiberius in 17 AD, during the bid for a site to be awarded for an imperial temple for the province (neocorate temple) that was ultimately granted to the rival city Smyrna (today's İzmir) the Ephesians staked everything on the omnipotence of Artemis, as Tacitus reports:[139]

> *Primi omnium Ephesii adiere, memorantes non, ut vulgus crederet, Dianam atque Apollinem Delo genitos: esse apud se Cenchreum amnem, lucum Ortygiam, ubi Latonam partu gravidam et oleae, quae tum etiam maneat, adnisam edidisse ea numina, deorumque monitu sacratum nemus, atque ipsum illic Apollinem post interfectos Cyclopas Iovis iram vitavisse. Mox Liberum patrem, bello victorem, supplicibus Amazonum quae aram insiderant ignovisse. auctam hinc*

concessu Herculis, cum Lydia poteretur, caerimoniam templo neque Persarum dicione deminutum ius; post Macedonas, dein nos servavisse.

"First of all came the people of Ephesos. They declared that Diana and Apollo were not born at Delos, as was the vulgar belief. They had in their own country a river Cenchrius, a grove Ortygia, where Latona, as she leaned in the pangs of labour on an olive still standing, gave birth to those two deities, whereupon the grove at the divine intimation was consecrated. There Apollo himself, after the slaughter of the Cyclops, shunned the wrath of Iuppiter; there too father Bacchus, when victorious in war, pardoned the suppliant Amazons who had gathered round the shrine. Subsequently by the permission of Hercules, when he was subduing Lydia, the grandeur of the temple's ceremonial was augmented, and during the Persian rule its privileges were not curtailed. They had afterwards been maintained by the Macedonians, then by ourselves."

In a very similar fashion, a temple was also planned for Emperor Trajan at Ephesos, intended not only to embed him in the history of the city but also to unite him in the cult image with Artemis. The site of the small temple (the so-called Temple of Hadrian, plan 3, no. 15) on the Curetes Street was hardly chosen randomly, but instead, together with the neighbouring Nymphaeum Traiani, continued the series of imperial monuments along that central avenue.[140] In a similar fashion, Trajan was depicted as the protégé of Zeus Philios in the neocorate temple at Pergamon.[141]

3. Private funerary monuments of the Augustan and Julio-Claudian period on the Embolos

3.1 The Monument of Memmius

At the uppermost point of the Embolos a two-storeyed Roman funerary tower monument[142], typical for the late Republic and early imperial period, rose up to a height of approximately 23 m (plan 1 no. 32; plan 3 no. 21). The structure was positioned diagonally to the street intersection in order to ensure visibility also from the so-called Domitian Lane laid out to the south (fig. 58). Whereas the three visible sides appear richly decorated and articulated (fig. 59), the rear side, turned towards the cliff slope of the Panayırdağ, was not readily accessible and visible; therefore, it was constructed as a relatively simple wall.[143]

A four-stepped crepidoma (H. 0.90 m) rises above a foundation socle (H. 1.62 m; ground plan 8.7 × 8.7 m) with a shell of rusticated ashlars and *opus caementicium* core.[144] Above this is a socle zone with orthostats (H. 2.64 m; ground plan ca. 6.60 × 6.60 m), supporting the ground floor storey (H. 5.23 m) with a strongly recessed

niche on each side, and façade arches supported by caryatids. At the rear of each niche is a false door.

The building, which was dedicated to *C(aio) Memmio, C(ai) f(ilio) Sullae Felicis n(epoti) ex pequnia (sic!) [...]*, cannot be definitively linked to a specific person despite the information in the Latin inscription,[145] since all evidence relating to an official career (*cursus honorum*) is missing. A number of scholars consider the most likely candidate to be the suffect consul of the year 34 BC. They assume that this individual, shortly after the consulate, was active as *proconsul Asiae* in Ephesos and died here while in office.[146] If this is true, then Memmius was active as *proconsul* of Asia at roughly the same time as Octavian's sojourn in Ephesos (winter 30/29 BC), and when Vedius Pollio carried out his mission as commissioner for the installation of the imperial cult and the revitalisation of the Artemision. At that time, the extensive Augustan urban expansion and building programme must have been developed, and the *proconsul* would have played a decisive role in a similar fashion as, for example, the dedication about 25 years later of the statue of Augustus in the water feature at the agora by an unknown provincial governor shows.[147] If the identification with the consular figure, however, does not pertain, then an unknown family member with the same name, who had interests in Ephesos, must be postulated. Nevertheless, Memmii are hardly demonstrable in Ephesos as private individuals in business,[148] and definitely not at all as representatives of the state in Ephesos.

In the upper storey of the structure (H. 3.76 m) a peristasis of Corinthian order surrounds the core, which is veneered with above life-sized male relief figures. On each of the three visible sides, as far as the preserved reliefs allow this to be judged, a togate figure was flanked at each side by an accompanying figure wearing the exomis or tunic, and in part with military weapon (sword). The three *togati* are interpreted as the people named in the tomb inscription – the deceased C. Memmius, his father of the same name, and his grandfather L. Cornelius Sulla.[149] The figures in Greek clothing have long been assumed to be in a servile function, but one may also imagine the deceased and his ancestors surrounded by allegorical figures – e.g. virtues or civic personifications.[150] A close parallel is found at the tomb of the freedman and favourite of Octavian/Augustus, C. Iulius Zoilos, in Aphrodisias.[151]

A monument for an unknown – what was the importance of Sulla´s grandson?

The uppermost termination of the structure consists of a bucrania-garland frieze above a four-stepped roof edge, followed by a pyramid decorated with scales, and with pinecone finial (total height of roof: 7.50 m). The bucrania-garland frieze shows a rare feature, which is otherwise documented in sepulchral architecture only in the Octagon at the lower end of Curetes Street: it is ornamented with astragal–like cords (στέμματα) terminating in tassels (fig. 19c).[152]

Fig. 59: Monument of Memmius (reconstruction by U. Outschar)

Until now, most scholars have dated the structure to the (early) Augustan period, on the one hand due to the inscription, and on the other hand due to the classification of the architectural decoration, whereby the numerous similarities with the Octagon are emphasised.[153] In fact, the employment of mortar in the core of the socle makes a date earlier than about 30 BC not possible.[154] Nevertheless, the empty fields in the cassettes of the ceiling[155] could be an indication that the Memmius Monument was completed before the Octagon and the so-called Round Monument on the Panayırdağ,[156] with their rich rosettes and flowers in the cassette fields. If this is the case, then the Memmius Monument would be the oldest tomb monument on the Embolos and its completion would be placed around 10 BC, at the latest in any event in the final decade of the 1st c. BC.

The discussion regarding whether the structure represents a honorific monument, a cenotaph, or an actual tomb has recently leaned heavily towards the last suggestion, particularly since many elements such as the false doors in the lower storey and the benches on the steps of the base – compare the same elements, for example, at the Octagon – are indicative of sepulchral furnishing.[157] The location of an urn for the cremated deceased can be postulated in the walled core towards the rear wall (or below the foundations).

Since the inscription names the honoured (deceased) in the dative case, it can be surmised that the construction was carried out by a third party; if the deceased had built it himself, the nominative case for his name would be expected. Not only for this reason, the frequently proposed emendation at the end of the inscription to *pequnia [sua...]* is rather unlikely.[158] The tomb was probably financed with public funds of the city (*pecunia publica*) and, since it stood on public ground, required in any event the permission of the city administration, as is documented for the somewhat later tomb of Sextilius Pollio nearby.[159] Thus, it might well be that at the end of the inscription there appeared a magistrate of Ephesos as the responsible person; then the inscription, which starts right at the corner, would also better match to the available space.[160]

The togate figures in the upper storey and the inscription which is only written in Latin, however, – apart from the form of the tomb and several architectural details – intentionally supply a "Roman" accent,[161] which is reinforced by the simple reference to the father and to Sulla Felix as maternal grandfather. It could therefore be likely that the numerous Italians, who at that time were leading the civic administration in Ephesos, consciously wished to express a sign of Roman power,[162] yet perhaps also wanted to make a statement of reconciliation with the past, as Sulla had once deprived the city of its freedom during the Mithridatic Wars due to the "Ephesian Vespers" (88 BC).[163]

In early- or mid-Augustan times, the burial of a Roman citizen *intra muros* of a Greek city was anything but normal. An early case was M. Castricius, who had lived and died in Smyrna (shortly) before 59 BC as a merchant and must have won highest merits on behalf of the city.[164] The next known cases – aside from Memmius in Ephesos and Zoilos in Aphrodisias – are the late Augustan tombs of C. Iulius Artemidoros in Knidos,[165] L. Vaccius in Kyme[166] (both located in gymnasia), and Mazaios and Mithridates in Ephesos (in the immediate environment of the Agora South Gate sponsored by themselves).[167] Thus, we can observe a considerable increase during the Augustan era. However, around 30/20 BC Caius Memmius must have held a specific significance for Ephesos beyond mere euergetism to warrant such remarkable tomb at an outstanding location. The idea that the Ephesians allured him as their patron and advocate in Rome, assuming a role entirely opposite to that of his grandfather for the city, could provide one plausible explanation thereby.

Cremation versus inhumation – how to identify
Roman tombs in a Greek city?

The location of the structure at the upper end of the Embolos supports, as already mentioned above, a claim to rule from a Roman perspective,[168] not only over the city but also within the civic administration in Ephesos. For those walking up the street, the entire valley section was dominated by the eye-catching, almost 23 m tall building.[169] In this manner, the Embolos, from its beginning near the South Gate of the agora and the Circular Water Monument with its statue of Augustus up to its upper termination, was characterised as a splendid, "Roman" boulevard. The former dictator Sulla, as a general, had saved the markets and income of the Roman merchants in Asia Minor and particularly in Ephesos. Through the honouring of his grandson, also he indirectly received a magnificent monument, via the knights and rich freedmen who had become leading Ephesian citizens in the time of peace under Octavian/Augustus. In the empire under Augustus, however, Sulla was not allowed to come to the fore too directly; for this reason, all of the people named refrained from mentioning their offices, for to do so might have aroused the displeasure of the current ruler.

Finally, the testimony of the monument itself draws the attention to yet another possible background. The astragal–like cords (στέμματα) on the bucrania-garland frieze (fig. 19c) on its top,[170] connect it with the Octagon (figs. 19a+b) in quite a striking manner.[171] One may suspect that the reasons for implementing this meaningful element into both monuments were identical or closely connected. During the Mithridatic War as well as in the 30 years of Roman Civil Wars from Caesar´s struggle against Pompeius until Octavian´s final victory in the battle of Actium (31 BC), amongst the thousands of victims who were Roman and Italian citizens, there were also numerous individuals who had fled, seeking *asylum*, into the sanctuary of Artemis and who were nevertheless killed.[172] Probably, C. Memmius was one of those who had suffered such fate. In this way, the Octagon of the Hellenistic Queen Arsinoë IV and the tomb of Roman senatorial C. Memmius could have served as memorials to the victims from both the Greek/Ephesian and Latin/Roman segments of the population, symbolizing unity within the now peaceful and reconciled Empire.

3.2 The Round Monument on the Panayırdağ

On the south slope of the Panayırdağ, high above the upper, eastern end of the Curetes Street (fig. 90), a monument with a square socle faced with rusticated ashlar blocks and a cylindrical, two-storeyed construction above it (Dm. 6.04 m) (plan 1 no. 34; fig. 60) rises up.[173] Above a base torus with Lesbian cymation, the lower storey displays an architecture of engaged Doric columns; in the upper storey, twelve Ionic free-standing columns surround an enclosed building core with a ring of projecting consoles. The precise reconstruction of the configuration (see for a preliminary sketch of the ground plan fig. 14c) and the question of the structure's function have caused difficulties even until now. The frieze blocks of the upper storey in any event are bonded into the enclosed core structure and constitute the basis for a cassette ceiling in the narrow pteron. The cassettes are filled with diverse motifs, with four diagonal heart leaves on a stem with central flower, an omphalos bowl, a disc, or a flower inscribed in a lozenge or free-standing in the middle. George Niemann reconstructed the roofing in the form of a stepped cone with finial.

Even at present, the precise appearance, dating, and significance of the building have not been adequately explained. Immediately after the initiation of the Austrian excavations, G. Niemann and R. Heberdey interpreted the circular structure as a new rebuilding of a tropaion, dating to the mid-1st c. BC, erected to commemorate the naval victory of the Ephesian fleet against Aristonikos at Kyme in 132 BC.[174] On the other hand, J. Keil proposed the identification of the structure as an honorific monument for P. Servilius Isauricus, the *proconsul Asiae* of 46–44 BC, who was accorded divine honours even in the 2nd c. AD at Ephesos on account of his services to the city during the implementation of the reforms of Caesar.[175]

A mysterious circular monument keeps archaeologists busy.

In his extensive study of Augustan architecture in Ephesos, Wilhelm Alzinger stated:[176] "The frieze surface, obliquely slanting backwards, connects the circular monument on the Panayırdağ with the Octagon." In addition, he pointed to the fact that the frieze and the architrave are of equal height at both buildings, an idiosyncrasy that he saw as still belonging to the late Hellenistic tradition. Due to the poured wall work (*opus caementicium*) in the core, however, Alzinger was unwilling to recognise too great a chronological distance to the Augustan period, and decided upon a dating before the Octagon, which at that time was viewed as early Augustan (40–20 BC); he therefore agreed with the early Austrian excavators on a date of ca. 50 BC.[177]

Fig. 60: Round Monument on the Panayırdağ (reconstruction by G. Niemann)

Nevertheless, Armin von Gerkan had already pointed out that *opus caementicium* first appears in Asia Minor under Augustus, and therefore an earlier date is out of the question;[178] the latest excavations at Ephesos continually confirm this insight anew. Even in Augustan times, mortar was rather more a lime paste than a hardening binding material, and its usage was by no means self-evident. Even if the Octagon in opposition to the Round Monument on the Panayırdağ is viewed as more advanced from the perspective of its structural technique, this is not necessarily a relative and certainly not an absolute dating criterion; a number of building workshops were able to demonstrate significant architectonic innovations of varying degrees of progressiveness simultaneously at a single period of time. In any case, with the moving of the date of the Octagon into the late, or end of the 1st c. BC, a dating for the Round Monument on the Panayırdağ in the last third or even quarter of the 1st c. BC can be presumed to be most likely.[179] The rich variety of filling motifs in the cassette slabs of the roof of the pteron in the upper storey can also be seen as an additional indication for this; the motifs in the preserved rosettes at the Octagon are distinctly more simple, whereas at the Memmius Monument, in turn, they are absent; at this last building the cassette backgrounds are still smooth and undecorated, which speaks for a date at the earlier Augustan period.[180] An even appreciably later date, the Flavian period as a pronounced phase of experimentation in the development of Roman architecture, was proposed by Anton Bammer on the basis of certain details of the architectonic decoration, above all the Ionic capitals covered with tendrils and acanthus leaves;[181] until now, however, nobody seems to have followed this later dating.[182]

The question of whether the Round Monument on the Panayırdağ represents an honorific or commemorative monument, or a tomb, has often been raised but never decided.[183] The closed-in structural core behind the ring of columns, again similar to the Octagon, speaks rather for a tomb building; for an honorific monument one would preferably like to imagine an open monopteros with a statue in the interior, as, for example, at the almost contemporary Circular Monument with water feature at the south-east corner of the Tetragonos Agora (figs. 53 and 54) or the Hexagon (fig. 49a).[184] If the structure was for a Roman individual, one would at least think of an urn burial for this chronological period; yet a burial here can hardly be demonstrated anymore. For the overall style of a two-storeyed circular structure surrounded by columns as a tomb, a close contemporary parallel is found at Aix-de-Provence (Roman *colonia Aquae Sextiae*) with the so-called Tour d'Horloge.[185]

3.3 The Cupola Tomb (so-called Circular Building) on the Bülbüldağ

Based on current knowledge, the area of honorific monuments and tombs on the Embolos is bordered at the southwest by a tomb building that is likely situated at a street junction on the north slope of the Bülbüldağ (plan 1 no. 70). The building contains a chamber with a cupola (ext. Dm. 9.70 m, clear height without cupola ca. 4.80 m); within the interior room the base slabs of four sarcophagi were found in situ (fig. 61).[186] The round socle made of mortared rubble clad in marble had a socle profile, a Lesbian cymation above a torus, and a crowning sima; the roof took the form of a cupola with marble covering (Dm. 6.3 m, height of the base cylinder 2.72 m).[187] Franz Miltner proposed a date for the structure to the late Augustan period or immediately thereafter, based on the employment of the typical white mortar and the wall profiles, as well as the presence of oil lamps and other small artefacts.[188]

The run of local elites for intramural burial sites seemingly started within only a few years.

In spite of its poor state of preservation, the Cupola Tomb is in many regards significant for the overall interpretation of the funerary area along the Embolos. On the one hand, it provides evidence due to its location, for the extension of this area in the early 1st c. AD and serves as a strong indication that in this time there was no regular dwelling zone planned in this area; on the other hand, due to the sarcophagi preserved and the exterior marble revetment, for the diversity of those buried here. In addition to the monuments of the Italians and Romans, whose urns were buried in multi-storey and architectonically elaborate structures, the building on the Bülbüldağ provides evidence that the class of local dignitaries of Greek origin, such as for example the family of the Passalas often encountered in the Augustan pe-

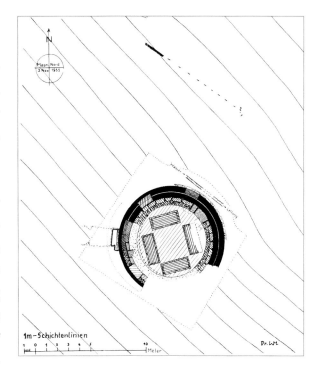

Fig. 61: Cupola Tomb on the Bülbüldağ, ground plan and section

riod, could also find a place with traditional sarcophagus burials in this honorific area in the early 1st c. AD. With the cupola of the tomb building, this class of population visibly integrated itself into the Roman world[189] without giving up their Greek identity (for example, inhumation burial).[190] Even if it is not currently possible to associate the tomb with a specific family by name, the prominent role of the Passalas in the Augustan period within the Greek population of Ephesos must nevertheless be referenced. Naturally, imperial freedmen such as the "prytanis for life" C. Iulius Nicephorus, or an Ephesian notable family recently vested with Roman citizenship, would also be suitable candidates.[191] One will not, however, be able to reckon with many more than five families as possible owners.

3.4 The Heroon of Pollio, the *Aqua Throessitica* and the public fountains along the Domitian Lane

In the late Augustan and Tiberian periods, one of the most important building contractors and wealthiest inhabitants of Ephesos was the Italian immigrant C. Sextilius Pollio who – in part together with his wife Ofillia Bassa and his step-son and later adoptive son C. Ofillius Proclus – constructed a series of monumental buildings.[192] As *epimeletes* (building commissioner), between 4 and 14 AD Sextilius Pollio oversaw for Emperor Augustus the construction of the 6 km long *Aqua Throessitica* and paid for the large, well-preserved aqueduct bridge in today's Dervend valley from his own funds.[193] This aqueduct most probably ran to the area around the State Agora and supplied water to the new imperial cult centre and the bath-gymnasium adjacent to the east (plan 1 no. 16; plan 5 no. 9),[194] and also to the entire city quarter that grew up here after the Augustan period.

Fig. 62: View from the Flavian emperors' temple terrace to the buildings along the western side of the so-called State Agora. In the foreground the Domitian Lane ending at the protruding west- ern chalcidicum of the Basilike Stoa, finished under Emperor Nero; to the right follow the tomb of Sextilius Pollio and the Flavian Apsidal Fountain. In the background the steps of the Basilike Stoa, and behind, the Prytaneion and an open courtyard (so-called Rhodian Peristyle) with an altar for the cult of Augustus and Artemis or otherwise C. Iulius Caesar, as well as the western part of the Bouleute- rion are recogni- sable

Sextilius Pollio must have lived long into the reign of Tiberius, since he is named in the third position in the so-called Great Donor List with a sum of 2,500 denarii; after the earthquake of 23 AD this list provides evidence of the reconstruction measures in the Artemision and the city, perhaps also in particular the financing of a monu- ment for Emperor Tiberius in thanks for his exceptional aid in the rebuilding of the city.[195]

Along the entire north façade of the State Agora the family financed a 160 m long, three-aisled *basilike stoa* (royal hall); the building inscription securely dates its com- pletion to the year 11 AD (plan 1 no. 21; plan 5 no. 5; fig. 62).[196] In its eastern head rooms (*chalcidicum*), statues of seated Augustus and his wife Livia (and likely Tiberus as co-regent) were located. If its west chalcidicum, with a building inscription hon- ouring Emperor Nero, was either first added after the earthquake of 23 AD or only renewed remains open. In any case, very close to it to the south, and adjacent to the western border wall of the State Agora, at the level of the Domitian Lane running past here (fig. 62), C. Ofillius Proclus built for his step-father an honorific funerary monument decorated with the statues of his parents, on "land provided by the city" after 23 AD (plan 5 no. 16).[197] The city itself also erected an honorific statue of Sextil- ius Pollio at that site, as attested by the inscribed statue base found in the Domitian Lane.[198] Of the building itself, essentially only the pedestal of more than 6 m height (surface area 8 × 6.5 m) is preserved. The honorific structure for Pollio was probably never completely finished.[199] The wall technique is identical with that of the *basilike stoa*: a mortared rubble core was faced with pseudo-isodomic marble plaques.

According to H. Thür, a fountain belonged to the tomb building already in its first phase (fig. 63); the collecting basin was preserved on the west side, oriented to- wards the Domitian Lane.[200] The water probably flowed out of the round arcuated niche (H. 3.20 m, W. 1.80 m) lying above the socle and in which the statue of Sextilius Pollio ought to have been set up, into the 1.20 m tall basin projecting from the socle.

Almost nothing is preserved of the superstructure of the tomb monument, probably a monopteral construction housing statues of Pollio and his family,[201] because in the Domitianic period a sumptuous fountain house was constructed, with Domitian in the guise of Zeus in a central aedicula facing the State Agora and the river gods Marnas and Klaseas flanking him in aediculae.[202]

Due to this rebuilding and the generally poor state of preservation of the structure, a decisive question remains open, namely, whether the Pollio monument was first erected after the earthquake of 23 AD as a tomb, or whether it originally served as the head structure of the ca. 20 years' older *Aqua Throessitica* and was only secondarily redesigned into a tomb. A causal dedication as the terminal building of an aqueduct would correlate well chronologically with the architectural correspondences recognised by W. Alzinger with the buildings that he denoted as "Augustan Architectural Group A" (e.g. the Memmius Monument and the South Gate of the Agora),[203] and would also explain the connection between fountain and tomb. On the other hand, the *Aqua Throessitica* was certainly clearly completed before Sextilius Pollio's death, and a subsequent re-engineering of a public fountain must have brought with it certain difficulties.

Fig. 63: Supposed original layout of the tomb of Sextilius Pollio with a fountain supplied by the *Aqua Throessitica* (reconstruction by H. Thür)

Water for the Ephesians – a great benefactor and his posthumous ruler´s attitudes.

Directly to the south of the tomb monument, however, lay another fountain building, the so-called Apsidal Fountain (plan 5 no. 15; fig. 62). The modern name refers to the large niche spanned by a ca. 6.20 m wide façade arch, which opened up here onto the Domitian Lane, already expanded into a plaza-like area at the upper end of the Embolos.[204] Based on the preserved architectural decoration the fountain can be dated to the Domitianic period,[205] but – given the current status of research – we cannot definitively exclude the possibility of an older phase. To be sure, the *Aqua Throessitica* must have served as the original water supply of the Pollio monument, as there was no other one in this area in Augustan times, but during the reign of Domitian both of the new fountains – the one on the roof of the Pollio monument (Domitian's Fountain) and the Apsidal Fountain south of it – were connected to the new Marnas aqueduct.[206] A probable solution might be that the *Aqua Throessitica* was damaged in this area by the earthquake of 23 AD and terminated somewhat earlier to the east after that date. Thus, the original fountain house could have been altered to Pollio's tomb and the new Marnas aqueduct of 92 AD might have used the existing installations for new fountains. Under these premises the urgent need for, and at the same time the water supply of another fountain house, the Hydrekdocheion of the *proconsul Asiae* (78/79 AD) Gaius Laecanius Bassus at the corner of the so-called South Street (*Hippoi*) and Domitian Lane (plan 5 no. 18) would find an explanation. If the public fountain house later used as the tomb of Pollio and another one adjacent to the Memmius Monument, the Hydreion (plan 3 no. 20), no longer had any water supply after 23 AD, the water from the *Aqua Throessitica* could have been redirected to the Hydrekdocheion.[207]

How did Odysseus come to blind Polyphem in Ephesos?

Let us return to the Apsidal Fountain: in the recess of the apse, in addition to the torso of an Aphrodite Euploia,[208] numerous fragments of a large figural group were discovered, representing the adventures of Odysseus with Polyphemos. At least in or after the Domitianic era, the statues were set up on a semicircular wall bench (width in the middle 1.30 m, at the sides decreasing to 0.70 m); in the centre appeared Polyphemos and Odysseus proffering wine. Following a series of extensive publications by B. Andreae, who surmised an original display in the gable of a Dionysos temple in honour of Marcus Antonius, the chronological classification of this group has been connected with that individual's procession into Ephesos as Neos Dionysos at the beginning of the year 41 BC.[209] The temple in the central axis of the State Agora (plan 5 no. 15) that Andreae had drawn upon for such a Dionysos cult has, however, in the meantime been dated significantly later; due to this central axis being shifted by the construction of the *basilike stoa* (11 AD), it cannot have been constructed before this time, so it therefore belongs at the earliest to the last years of the reign of Augustus.[210] Independently of this fact, the entire thesis of Andreae, not only the attempted display in the gable of a temple, has been strongly criticised;[211] the dating and chronological unity of the group should also be questioned. Apparently, secondarily used statues of various time periods – and perhaps also figures which were created for this display – were set up here together anew; most recently, D. Maschek assumed the origin of many of the used figures in the course of the 2nd and 1st c. BC, used secondarily in the well.[212] The golden age of the Polyphemos episode in grottoes flowing with water and dark cave-like spaces, for example the Tiberian Sperlonga and the Claudian Baiae as well as the furnishing of the *Domus Aurea* of Emperor Nero, however, lies in the Julio-Claudian epoch[213] and would correlate well chronologically with the activities of Pollio. Just as a suggestion, it is therefore proposed here not to exclude a chronological and thematic connection of the so-called Apsidal Fountain – including an original display with at least parts of the Polyphemos group – with the *Aqua Throessitica* and Sextilius Pollio as an earlier phase; instead, future research on the structure should focus on a possible function as a nymphaeum at the termination of this aqueduct in the reign of Tiberius.[214] If one considers the previously mentioned torso of an Aphrodite from a presumably Rhodian workshop (first half of the 1st c. BC), the statuary display could have been purchased *in toto* either in the late Augustan – Tiberian period by Sextilius Pollio or in the Flavian era for the Apsidal Fountain, and brought to Ephesos. Such a scenario would make the long intermediate storage at an unknown place envisioned by Andreae unnecessary. In any case, this structure would not be the only nymphaeum in the Ephesian civic revitalisation programme that was reminted and newly designed for Domitian on the occasion of the neocorate in Ephesos, as the grammateus of the Demos (a function like a modern mayor) Tigellius Lupus decreed in the year 94/95 to repair and adorn older or ruined buildings, "so that their ugly appearance does not tarnish the prestige of the new imperial buildings and thus the city".[215]

Viewed from the perspective of its contents, however, the grotto with Odysseus and Polyphemos would much better match the preferences of Tiberius than Domitian. As a final consideration, we would like to introduce the possibility that the Apsidal fountain could have also been the substitution of the nymphaeum nearby, originally built by Pollio as head building of the aqueduct, which was later altered to his tomb by his stepson. This new fountain might have additionally served as a honorary monument to Tiberius, a present of the citizens of Ephesos for his extraordinary help in the desperate situation after the catastrophe. This aid is mentioned in the so-called Great Ephesian Donors List, which lists Sextilius Pollio and his family among the main sponsors for an up-to-now unknown monument for the emperor;[216] such a nymphaeum honoring the ruler would very well match to the local tradition, demonstrated at the Embolos.

Another fountain directly in front of the Memmius Monument (plan 1 no. 33; plan 3 no. 20; fig. 58) also needs to be mentioned here again; this very likely was fed by the *Aqua Throessitica* too. Its original Augustan design is hardly recognizable as it was refurnished in the Severan age, when it was now referred to as a *Hydreion*.[217] That Sulla and his family were perceived here (hidden) in the attitude of a Hellenistic ruling dynasty has already been surmised from another circumstance above. With this fountain, the creation of an ensemble that continued the tradition of Hellenistic heroic fountains like the Hypelaios at the lower Embolos might have been intended.[218] The prolongation is the connection of the tomb of Pollio with the water supply financed by him. To conclude, we might therefore state that the *Aqua Throessitica* with its fountains and their conscious connection with the tombs of Memmius as well as of Pollio – and the more, if also Tiberius was honoured with the Polyphem-Odysseus grotto – was certainly a programmatic issue. On the one hand, it may have served as a mirror of the *Aqua Iulia* and its waterspout house at the Triodos honouring the Emperor Augustus. In this manner, related to the prestigious water supply, the Embolos was marked at both ends with fountain buildings fed by the two Roman long-distance aqueducts. On the other hand, it shows how early the heroic scenery, long reserved for Hellenistic rulers and Roman Senators (like Memmius), and subsequently for the first Roman emperors, could be used in a diminished way for civil citizens and local sponsors in the sense of a "private apotheosis"[219] as the cases of Sextilius Pollio in Ephesos and C. Iulius Zoilos in Aphrodisias clearly show.

3.5 The benefactors' graves during the construction of the Roman Tetragonos Agora

During the course of the construction of the Augustan Tetragonos Agora and its immediate reconstruction after the earthquake of 23 AD, a number of graves of benefactors, involved in the building processes, appear to have been laid out. These are architecturally directly connected with the structures they financed, and designate the Triodos and the lower Embolos as a burial site already from the Augustan until the Neronian period.

3.5.1 Mazaios and Mithridates

The systematic investigation of the building substance of the South Gate of the Augustan Tetragonos Agora and its reconstruction has clearly confirmed that the gate first came into being with the entire new building of the agora, and that it is integrated into it. The gate, completed in 4/3 BC, possessed wings projecting to the south;[220] the eastern wing supported the slope and optically closed off the substructure of the water feature, erected at a higher level, of the *Aqua Iulia* and the steps to the agora's upper storey (fig. 39a+b, room SOc; fig. 75), whereas the western wing probably disguised the eastern end of the street colonnade along the agora's exterior side, which we can assume existed here almost with certainty.[221] A door opening was located practically directly adjacent to the gate. The chambers lying behind it – of which only the eastern one (room SOc in fig. 39a; see also fig. 38) is secure in the archaeological record, while the western one in contrast, because of the erection of the Celsus Library, can only be extrapolated based on symmetrical grounds,[222] – ought to have served as the tomb chambers of the two benefactors of the South Gate, Mazaios, *Augusti libertus*, and Mithridates, *Agrippae libertus*, or at least must have been intended as such.[223] At the west wall of the eastern chamber, which projects backwards south of the chamber to the east, that is, oriented to the passageway area between the gate's wings, a niche (so-called exedra) is still found today (fig. 75); here, the statue of one of the two benefactors was probably displayed. According to the evidence of the building inscription, this was most likely Mithridates, who caused the eastern half of the gate to be constructed, while Mazaios was responsible for the western part. The two donors appear to have worked with separate accounts, perhaps even with different building workshops, a conclusion that arises from the building seam discovered during the reconstruction and which does not fit optimally with the altitude of the structure. The western side carried the building inscription of Mazaios and the eastern that of Mithridates.[224]

In Augustan times, outstanding Roman imperial freedmen
took over the role of local aristocrats in Asia Minor.

In fact, the bilingual funerary inscription of *Mithradates* (sic!) *Agrippae libertus* was found reused in the Late Antique – early Byzantine paving of the Marble Street, together with many other architectural elements from the region of the Triodos and the lower Embolos that have already been in part extensively discussed here.[225] This suggests that his tomb chamber in the (probable) eastern wing of the South Gate more or less survived the earthquake of 23 AD and fulfilled its original function until Late Antiquity. Nevertheless, the new construction of the agora required a partial demolition of the projecting wing structures and a reduction in size of the chamber SOc in the area directly east of the South Gate, that is, probably the area where the sarcophagus of Mithridates was set up. (cf. fig. 40a).

3. PRIVATE FUNERARY MONUMENTS   169

3.5.2 The benefactors' tombs beneath the Neronian Hall

There were hardly any limits to the fantasies of the donors to set up graves in the most diverse types of buildings.

In addition, it is necessary here to address an architectural element that has until recently been misunderstood and therefore not sufficiently appreciated, due to the poor state of preservation of the so-called Neronian Hall – probably the epigraphically attested *auditorium*.[226] During his investigations, Stefan Karwiese discovered a tomb chamber, compartmentalised many times, built into the southeast corner below the level of the Hall.[227] According to his preliminary report, the feature (fig. 40a and 64) was excavated in 1984 and subsequently built over with a concrete surface in the course of the attempt of Friedmund Hueber at that time to partially reconstruct the Hall. From the door opening (still visible in the reconstruction today as an interruption of the Hall's floor construction, see fig. 53) at the eastern edge of the substructure of the south wall of the Hall, access was provided to an antechamber with a width of 2.5 m. Along its west side three funerary niches were set up in a row, the central one taking up the greatest space. The room was plastered and painted, and the walls graduated for klinai for the dead. According to the stratigraphic evidence, the tomb chamber was without doubt filled in during the late 4th or early 5th c. AD, when the Neronian Hall was extensively reconstructed. There are hardly any secure finds for the construction of the tomb chamber and its period of usage. Karwiese surmised that its construction was connected with the earthquake of 262 AD, and that its usage came to an end in the late 3rd or early 4th c. AD. This dating may indeed be valid for a post-construction later usage of the tomb chamber. Its original planning in the architectural concept of the Neronian Hall, however, is very clear according to the archaeological evidence: euthynteria blocks belonging to the original building substance and the foundation lying beneath them terminate at precisely this entrance and constitute a corner (fig. 53). With a certain degree of probability, we may assume the original function of the installation as a grave house for the benefactor family named in the building inscription, which is unfortunately only preserved in fragments.[228] Regrettably, we do not know the name of the constructor, but only that of his wife who is mentioned as co-benefactor, Claudia Metrodora. Not completely coincidentally, a certain Tib. Claudius Metrodorus, probably the father or brother of this lady, equally made a donation of three columns and a paving of Phocaian marble for the new fishery customs house at the harbour between 54 and 59 AD. In so doing, he contributed the third-largest amount within the long list of individuals recorded on the building according to their contribution.[229] We therefore know the affiliation of the building contractor(s) of the Neronian Hall to the Ephesian elite, and with the honorific tomb dedicated to them, in addition to the very probably Tiberian Pollio Monument, we can add yet another link to the chronological chain of benefactors' tombs at the Embolos dating to the early second half of the 1st c. AD.

4. The embellishment of the Embolos from Domitian to Hadrian

It is hardly an accident that apparently in Ephesos – and furthermore precisely in the area of the Embolos – after Augustus (and Tiberius?), other Roman emperors from the late 1st c. AD onwards embraced the image of water-providing rulers.[230] With Domitian's claim to absolute power, and the construction of the neocorate temple of the Emperors (officially indicated as ναὸς τῶν Σεβαστῶν)[231] which was so important for Ephesos – Tib. Claudius Aristion is recorded as the first *archiereus* (arch-priest) for 88/89 AD –, under this emperor (cf. plan 1 no. 30) the mood was right for a resumption of the long tradition of a relationship between ruler and water supply.

After Ephesos had lost the contest against Smyrna to be the seat of the official imperial temple of the province of Asia under Tiberius, perhaps due to the earthquake destruction of 23 AD, and after an additional temple was awarded to Miletos under Caligula, the assignation of the status as *neokoros* for Ephesos was of existential significance in the rivalry amongst the cities.[232] The structure which is generally designated as the Temple of Domitian in the scholarship[233] (plan 1 no. 30) brought the city the long-desired title ὁ νεωκόρος δῆμος ὁ Ἐφεσίων (the temple-nurturing people of Ephesos) and ἡ νεωκόρος Ἐφεσίων πόλις (the temple-nurturing city-state of the Ephesians), and with it an equal ranking with the other metropoleis of the province of Asia. Ultimately, however, it was not a question of prestige, but also of the organisation of great festivals with international competitions of both sporting and musical-rhetorical nature, and the reception of envoys from other cities who poured large amounts of money into the coffers. To house the Corinthian temple at the south-west of the State Agora, a terrace was created[234] with a typically Roman U-form *cryptoporticus* – the only one known so far in the Greek east; an altar decorated with weapon reliefs also stood on this terrace.[235] The three-storeyed terrace façade displayed captive barbarians as entablature supports in the middle storey, glorifying Domitian's German victory (triumph in 84 AD) and his victorious nature in general (fig. 65).

A new construction programme aimed at the emperors
finally adorns the Embolos
as fully developed main street.

Fig. 65: Façade of the Flavian Temple of the Divine Emperors with figures of subdued barbarians (reconstructed section)

The fact that a large-scale building programme was instituted immediately after the awarding of the neocorate temple, a programme which included the expansion of the theatre (completed 104/105 AD), a new aqueduct from the Marnas valley, and a gymnasium at the harbour (completed in 92/93 AD), is hardly a coincidence. In addition, the incumbent grammateus of the people, M. Tigellius Lupus, called for the embellishment and renovation of the entire inner city area so that the new, prominent structure for the imperial cult would not be depreciated by an unworthy surrounding environment.[236] Furthermore, the first street paving of the Embolos occurred at exactly this time.[237] The final relocation of the Triodos junction one city block to the south-east (fig. 37), already discussed above, and the construction of a three-storeyed splendid gate in honour of Trajan (cf. plan 3 no. 6; plan 4; figs. 44 and 49b) next to the Artemis altar in ca. 114/115 AD,[238] belonged to the building programmes of Domitian and Trajan that were in many ways overlapping – compare, for example, the great theatre. The relocation of the Triodos obliquely across the old street was necessary at the latest after 113 AD with the construction of the Library of Celsus (cf. plan 3 no. 3); it could, however, already have been required during the reign of Domitian with the large-scale terracing work for the so-called Serapeion (plan 1 no. 67).[239]

The construction of the elaborate Marnas aqueduct (opened 92/93 AD) and the associated extraction fountains in the area of the State Agora, on three sides of the new imperial temple, as well as in front of the theatre, with the magnificent endpoint, namely the imperial gymnasium (Sebaston Gymnasium? see plan 1 no. 93) at the harbour, placed the water supply of Ephesos on new foundations. The same situation repeated itself almost exactly a quarter of a century later under Trajan, with the aqueduct of Aristion and his two elaborated nymphaea on the South Street shortly after the Magnesian Gate (plan 1 no. 15) and in the middle of the Embolos (plan 3 no. 18), and the intraurban Baths of Vales Varius (plan 3 no. 14) at the lower Embolos. It is probable that an additional neocorate temple was planned for Trajan (perhaps the temple precinct generally termed the so-called Serapeion to the west of the Tetragonos Agora, plan 1 no. 67), yet Pergamon was instead given this award. In a manner of speaking, the Ephesians erected the model for the imperial temple likewise on the Embolos, within the new bathing establishment (plan 3 no. 15).

Tib. Claudius Aristion, three-time asiarch (chair and senior priest of the state council), grammateus, prytanis, and gymnasiarch of Ephesos, held a key position in both building programmes.[240] In the first case, he contributed extensively to the construction of the imperial temple and, with a building consortium, financed the Harbour Gymnasium; in the second case he was involved with the construction of an aqueduct and two nymphaea (the so-called Street Fountain on the plateia near the Magnesian Gate,[241] and the Nymphaeum Traiani) as well as the completion of the Library of Celsus; he also probably contributed to the construction of the Serapeion.[242] In a letter, Plinius the Younger described him, not without good reason, as *princeps Ephesiorum*.[243]

At this juncture, we must note that, after a supposition by M. Wörrle, the lady Varilla, frequently named in building inscriptions as daughter of P. Quintilius Vales Varius (builder of the baths on the Embolos and the so-called Temple of Hadrian), can quite safely be identified as Quintilia Varilla, wife and widow of Ti. Iulius Celsus Polemaeanus.[244] In turn, Iulia Lydia Laterane, the spouse of Aristion and who appears only late in the inscriptions, could have been a daughter or rather granddaughter of Celsus.[245] Therefore, probably not coincidentally, a number of buildings were begun or completed at the same time (under the grammateus Tib. Claudius Lucceianus in 114/115 – perhaps a further relative of Aristion). A comprehensive building concept is evident here, with individuals related by blood or marriage, a concept that in concert and with intent redesigned a central region of the city.[246] With this in mind, it goes without saying that the aqueduct of Aristion had to be constructed as a priority for the water supply for the Baths of Varius.[247] Furthermore, Aristion did not complete the library of his (grand?)father in law shortly before his own death (ca. 118/119 AD) out of pure altruism but out of familial duty.

4.1 The Marnas aqueduct and the Fountain of Domitian

In 92 AD, an extremely elaborate aqueduct, fed by a number of springs and known as the ὕδωρ Δομιτιανόν (aqueduct of Domitian) or Μαρναντιανὸν ὕδωρ (Marnas aqueduct) to Ephesos was inaugurated.[248] It ran through almost the entire city, with water extraction locations from the State Agora down to the Harbour Gymnasium which opened contemporaneously and which at that time was probably entitled as the Gymnasium of Emperor Domitian.[249] The main purpose of the Marnas aqueduct was certainly to supply the rapidly expanding city quarter around the State Agora with water, as this supply was no longer adequately guaranteed by the old *Aqua Throessitica*.

The Fountain of Domitian, as discussed already earlier, lay at the upper end of the Curetes Street on the western edge of the State Agora (fig. 90), built partly on top of the tomb of Sextilius Pollio (plan 5 no. 16). The location provided an ideal visual connection to the recently inaugurated imperial temple of the province of Asia. The sculptural decoration of the fountain displayed the emperor in the guise of Zeus between the two river gods Marnas and Klaseas.[250] Based on the imperial titles, names of governors, and local magistrates mentioned in the inscriptions from the building and the statues, the fountain was inaugurated between the 15th and the 23rd September 92 AD by the *proconsul Asiae* P. Calvisius Ruso.[251] As was pointed out recently, the whole programme, but especially the adornment of the fountain with Domitian´s portrait for the statue of Zeus/Iuppiter, is a perfect mixture between autocratic rule, Roman Imperialism and the adornment of a provincial capital by its governor.[252]

A second fountain, the so-called Apsidal Fountain was erected or newly designed directly to the south, joining on to the Pollio Monument at the Domitian Lane.[253] The placement and layout of this fountain as a grotto, where water debouched thunderously into the sunlight of the small plaza at the very end of the narrow and dark Domitian Lane between the Temple of the Emperors and the State Agora, has received rave compliments by modern scholars.[254] From here, the main entrance to the new imperial temple ensued via a large staircase with many wings, to a three-storeyed façade with captive barbarians as atlas figures in the middle storey (fig. 65).

Together with the main distributor of the aqueduct on the so-called South Street (plan 1 no. 17), not far from the main entrance to the State Agora an ensemble of public water stations was also created here. From many sides, this ensemble focused the view of all persons collecting water towards the Temple of Domitian, thereby once again emphasising the ruler as a benefactor of water in Ephesos and taking up the Hellenistic–Augustan tradition.[255]

On the route to the harbour, the Marnas aqueduct, as already mentioned above, also now supplied the late Hellenistic fountain house (fig. 52) in front of the theatre, which was at that time currently being expanded. At this occasion the fountain house was also substantially increased in size. During this work an inscription ἐκ τοῦ Μάρναντος ("from the Marnas")[256] was chiselled into one of the new columns of the front row, announcing the connection to the new water channel. At the latest with this renovation, the remembrance of the original builders, probably the Attalid Kings, was erased and the fountain additionally associated directly with the ruling Emperor Domitian.

4.2 The Library of Celsus

For Tiberius Iulius Celsus Polemaeanus, the former *proconsul Asiae* (period of office probably 105/106 or 106/107 AD), his son and heir the consul Tib. Iulius Aquila (*consul suffectus* 110)[257] caused a tomb building in the form of a public library[258] to be erected after ca. 113 directly next to the South Gate of the Tetragonos Agora, across the former main road along the south side of the agora (plan 1 no. 55; plan 3 no. 3). Since Aquila also died during the period of construction, the library was completed by Tib. Claudius Aristion, related to the family by marriage, as epimeletes (building patron).[259] As Aristion also died in around 118/120, the ultimate completion of the building, termed in an inscription as τὴν Κελσι/[αν]ὴν βιβλιοθήκην, can be assumed to have occurred during the first years of the reign of Hadrian.[260]

The 2nd Sophistic: global players choose Ephesos
as adopted home town.

Celsus was originally from Sardes, attained the position of *consul suffectus* for the year 92 AD under Domitian in Rome, and subsequently held the position (ca. 93–95) as minister of buildings for the city of Rome (*curator aedium sacrarum et operum locorumque publicorum*). In the course of his career, he was active in the eastern Roman provinces many times as special commissioner and governor, and as the highpoint of his *curriculum vitae* received the proconsulate for the province of Asia.[261] During his time in Rome, he developed good connections to the workshops and leading architects there, and from here he probably took the idea with him to have his own tomb building designed in the form of a library in his adoptive home city, Ephesos. To what extent this was part of a larger programme, for example in connection with the contemporary establishment of a Mouseion – an educational facility for doctors and pedagogues as well as rhetors that appears in inscriptions from Ephesos at precisely this time –,[262] cannot be ascertained at the moment. In any event, the construction of this building over the former main road to the harbour and to Pygela was only possible because this road had to be shifted to the south, due to the construction of a large temple precinct (the so-called Serapeion) further to the west. The beginning of this road, at the end of the Marble Street directly next to the presumed Triodos Altar, was marked by a three-storeyed gate in 113/114 AD.[263] Meanwhile, the so-called Serapeion has also been recognised as a library with strong associations in its overall layout to the Library of Hadrian at Athens and the Red Hall at Pergamon; to what extent it is identical with the Mouseion just mentioned has to remain an open question for now.[264]

The Library of Celsus (plan 3 no. 3; fig. 66), a magnificent building with two-storeyed, three-doored façade and seemingly baroque columnar architecture, was reconstructed between 1970–78 and functions today as a well-known official symbol not only for Ephesos but also for Turkish tourism in general (figs. 34. 36. 37. 64. 66).[265] The ornamented façade, strongly influenced by the Forum Traiani and the Basilica Ulpia in Rome, is full of references to the official powers of Celsus (for example, the *fasces* of a lictor), yet also with references (erotes and sacrificing Victories embedded in vine tendrils) to death and the afterlife.[266] The four statues representing his virtues in the lower storey as well as his own statue, supplemented by one of his son Aquila,[267] in the upper storey must have been particularly impressive. The statues of virtues that are visible today, of which one (*Ennoia*) was devoted in Late Antiquity to a certain Philippos,[268] were set up here after an earthquake (262 AD); the originals are all lost. The series of qualities, arrayed from left to right as *sophia* (wisdom), *arete* (integrity), *ennoia* (wealth of ideas), and *episteme* (knowledge), not only represents Celsus as a correct Roman office holder and successful military commander, but also follows the ideals of culture and virtue of the Second Sophistic; in the frame of this spiritual movement the library served as the symbol of the 'heroisation of culture'.[269]

Fig. 66: View of the Library of Celsus after the anastylosis of 1978

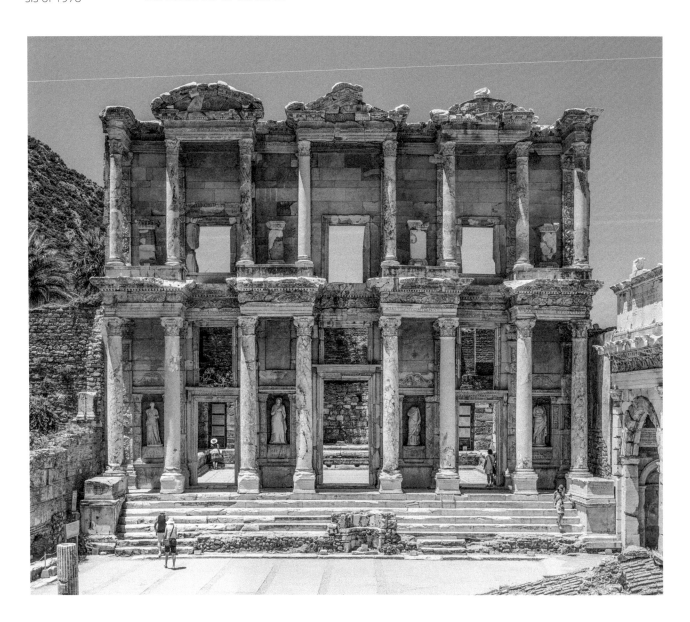

In front of the library, two equestrian statues of Celsus were displayed at the sides of the building. The façade and its statue bases were extensively inscribed in both Latin and Greek, and for this reason we are extremely well-informed about Celsus as well as about the building and its construction.[270] Amongst these is an inscription referring to an endowment that was intended to secure the operation of the library and the purchase of new books over a period of decades.[271]

A flight of steps with nine stairs running across almost the entire width of the façade leads to the entrances into the reading hall, an inner space surrounded by columns with a clearance of 16.72 × 10.92 m (figs. 64 and 66). The steps serve to increase the height of the structure, causing it to dominate already from afar the view for those coming down the Embolos. This increased elevation also was useful for the location of the tomb chamber of Celsus beneath the ground of the central apse (Dm. 4.38 m) of the interior room. The interior space on both sides of the apse was divided into three-storeyed galleries. The manner of access to these is still unclear today; it is probable that there was a two-winged staircase on the exterior wall at the rear which has not been studied yet, in a similar fashion as at the Serapeion.[272]

The grave chamber in the basement can only be accessed via a maintenance passage, only 0.90 m wide, from the north side of the library. The mighty sarcophagus with thick garlands supported by Nikai and Erotes as exterior decoration[273] and the inner lead sarcophagus are therefore well-preserved; the skeleton was found in place without any grave goods except the bronze buttons of a mantle.[274] In the apse located above the tomb chamber we can assume that there most likely stood a colossal statue of the deceased himself, of a divinity associated with libraries, or of the emperor.[275] In contrast to the Roman Trajan, the Greek Celsus was not cremated, but his body reposed in the basement in the manner of Alexander the Great, of whom Cicero had said that his (conserved) body (σῶμα) was the base for everything, like the corpus of books in the surrounding library. Thus, his grave (σῆμα) symbolised the world, just as the letters in the books in Alexandria expressed the complete knowledge of mankind.[276]

4.3 The aqueduct with the Nymphaeum Traiani and the honorific tomb of Aristion

About 25 years after the Marnas aqueduct, a new, 210 stadia (ca. 38 km) long aqueduct running from the Tire valley via Belevi to Ephesos was constructed by the powerful Ephesian building contractor and holder of many offices, Tiberius Claudius Aristion.[277] The aqueduct, which perhaps was already completed in 113 AD[278] supplied water to the bathing complex (… ἐν τῷ Οὐαρίῳ Βαλανείῳ, … "in the Varius Baths", today mostly known as the Baths of Scholasticia) on the lower Embolos built at the same time by P. Quintilius Vales Varius and his family. The public latrines (*paidiskeion*) associated with it had to be housed in the adjacent building block to the west due to reasons of space (plan 1 no. 41; plan 3 no. 14).[279] Their dating is secured by, amongst other things, the so-called Temple of Hadrian (plan 3 no. 15) which was dedicated in 117/118 AD and was built into the baths on the street side.[280]

Tiberius Claudius Aristion, first of the Ephesians, beautifier of his hometown: the exception who did not want to make a Roman career.

Somewhat to the east, almost in the middle of the Curetes Street, Aristion together with his wife Iulia Lydia Laterane erected the Nymphaeum Traiani (plan 3 no. 18; figs. 67 and 68) as the monumental terminus of the aqueduct.[281] A colossal statue of Trajan with a globe near his feet stood here in the centre precisely above the water outlet, surrounded by a magnificent statuary programme integrated into the two-storeyed and two-winged façade and including mythical figures as well as the benefactor and his family.[282]

Fig. 67: The Nymphaeum Traiani at the Embolos

It seems that Aristion himself, celebrated as "beautifier of the homeland with many and great works"[283] on account of his numerous buildings in Ephesos, received his honorific tomb directly adjacent to the nymphaeum. Only a few indications and architectural elements, including a gable with a round shield, can be adduced today

for its probable location at the east of the nymphaeum.[284] His presumed sarcophagus – with a portrait placed into it secondarily during a Late Antique transfer of the remains – was nevertheless transferred in the 5th c. AD to the small site known as the Androkloneion, to the west of the Hypelaios Spring.

4.4 The so-called Temple of Hadrian on the Embolos – a temple planned for Trajan

Here, nearly at the conclusion of our tour, the so-called Temple of Hadrian (plan 3 no. 15; fig. 69) must be extensively discussed as a particularly significant structure for the architectural embellishment of the Embolos.[285] As will be shown, its collective representation of all of the important Ephesian foundation myths (Amazons, Androklos) with a strong reference to contemporary events – that is, the official programme of Trajan – fulfilled a typical commission for the (early) Second Sophistic, with this nexus of local and imperial history.

The temple fulfilled a typical commission in the age
of the (early) Second Sophistic,
with this nexus of local and imperial history.

The building inscription of the small temple pertains to Artemis Ephesia, Hadrian, and the neocoros (temple-warding) Demos of Ephesos. As can probably be assumed for the entire bathing complex, the inscription also originally named P. Quintilius Vales Varius, his wife whose name has unfortunately not been handed down, and his daughter Varilla as the sole financers of the structure, from the foundations up, including the entire architectural decoration (κόσμος) and the cult image (ἄγαλμα). The temple was vowed during the period of office of the grammateus of the people, Tib. Claudius Lucceianus (23 Sept. 114 – 22 Sept. 115) and dedicated during the office of the grammateus and asiarch P. Vedius Antoninus as well as the *proconsul Asiae* Servaius Innocens, that is, between 23 September 117 and the end of June 118.[286]

The temple building (ναός) with transverse cella (7.5 m wide, 5 m deep) and a pronaos with two columns in antis of the Corinthian order with Syrian gable has recently been published in monographic form by U. Quatember. Since its discovery by F. Miltner, the figural frieze consisting of four beams has

Fig. 68: Reconstruction of the Nymphaeum Traiani (by H. Pellionis 1962/63)

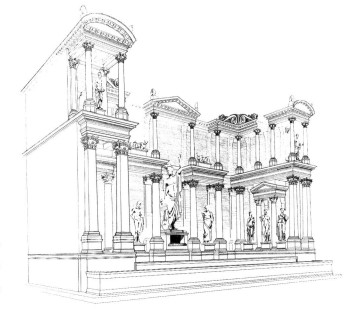

been viewed as secondary and belonging to Late Antiquity. Quatember's study, however, has now proven with complete certainty from a technological viewpoint that the frieze is to be counted amongst the original inventory of the early 2nd c. AD.[287] The following remarks pertain above all to this frieze and its figural programme;[288] subsequently an attempt will be made to understand in broad terms the content of the agalma, that is, the cult image or the cult image group mentioned in the building inscription and which is now completely lost. In this manner we can attempt at least rudimentarily to understand this meticulous iconographic programme as a homage on the part of the city of Ephesos to Emperor Trajan.

4.4.1 The frieze in the pronaos

At first the individual frieze blocks (fig. 70) should be introduced in greater detail; in what follows, we will emphasize only what is essential and what has until now been otherwise interpreted. We embark immediately on a combination of simple description and analysis (figural identification).[289]

In its clockwise-running narrative, the frieze begins on a block which is only partially preserved, Block A, which led from the corner column at the west to the front of the cella. Precisely the deeply carved contour lines around nearly all of the figures here led R. Fleischer and B. Brenk to a late dating. Fleischer, as F. Miltner had done earlier, thought of the Theodosian period,[290] whereas Brenk concluded a date in the first Tetrarchy and drew a comparison with the Arch of Galerius in Thessalonica and

Fig. 70: The
original frieze
(blocks A–D) of the
so-called Temple
of Hadrian in the
Selçuk Museum

1   2   3   4   5

1   2   3   4   5   6   7   8 9 10   11

1   2   3   4 5 6 7   8   9   10

1   2   3   4   5   6   7 8 9 10 11 12 13

4. THE EMBELLISHMENT OF THE EMBOLOS   181

other monuments from the period around 300 AD.[291] These chronological proposals were not based purely on art historical arguments, however, but arose from the entire situation of the building, since in around 300 AD a statue of a Tetrarch was set up in front of each column in front of the temple; of these, at an even later date, the image of Maximian was replaced by one honouring the father of Theodosius I.[292]

In fact, such contour lines – if by far not in this abundance – can be found on similar monuments of roughly the same date and size even in Rome and in an imperial context (cf. for example the triumphal frieze on the Arch of Titus, the small frieze on the Arch at Benevento, or the reliefs of the representations of the provinces at the Hadrianeum). In particular, somewhat flat background figures or at least their arms, legs and attributes which are close to the background, are outlined in this way. The solution, however, is based far rather in the fact that the frieze block at Ephesos was apparently not completely worked, and much more of the background remains than was originally conceived,[293] so that the contour lines are presented much more starkly than they were intended. This impression is strengthened when one observes the male figure A1 positioned at the broken edge at the far right of the block; he is carved out much more clearly and – with the exception of his mantle at the side of his neighbouring figure A2 – without contour lines, however with fine undercutting out from the background in comparison to the other figures. For the neighbouring female figure A2, this carving away of the background only occurred on the side of the male figure just discussed, and here also only at the mid-section; at her raised right elbow and along the right lower leg and foot, more stone material still remains. Furthermore, the more one looks to the right, the deeper are the contour lines around the subsequent figures, and the flatter are the figures. As was so often the case in the Roman imperial period, the block simply remained unfinished with regard to the relief ground. This may indeed well be related to the rededication from Trajan to his successor Hadrian, as Wörrle already stated. If the programme was meant for Trajan, after the unexpected change in rule and the associated paradigm change in imperial policy, one would probably not have wanted to invest too much more effort.

The incompleteness of this block (preserved length 169 cm, height 61 cm) – about 45 cm must be missing compared to the block on the opposite narrow side of the pronaos[294] – makes a total interpretation of the scenes represented difficult, yet the essential features seem clear. Optically, a rider A4 is prominent in the right part of the block; his mount rears up completely in the style of the Trajanic iconography in the manner of Alexander, with a now lost, long lance held in both hands, billowing mantle and loose hair (without a helmet?). In this iconography, normally a fallen enemy warrior is about to be trampled to the ground in front. This equestrian feat of levade or the very similar pesade is dramatically staged on the so-called Trajanic Battle Frieze on the Arch of Constantine,[295] as well as appearing on Roman imperial coinage where it is a particularly favoured motif of Trajan.[296] Here, however, the fallen warrior A5, supporting himself on the ground with his sword arm and protecting himself with his raised shield, turns away from the rider towards the right, apparently towards an opponent who is not represented but whose presence is obligatory. The rider A4 and the fallen warrior, therefore, do not belong to the same scene. In fact, in the upper right corner a boar apparently seems to be running away from the rider. An additional group is formed by the warrior A3 further to the left, and the already mentioned, frontally represented young woman A2; the female figure is reclining on a rock or is, rather, half-standing and leaning against it. She is represented in the gesture of defence, with raised right arm and hand hovering above her head; in addition, she holds an amphora, lightly tipping downwards, in her left hand. On the one hand, the gesture of her right arm depicts her as the type of the famous Ephesian wounded Amazon Sciarra (comp. figs. 45. 71),[297] while on the other hand the amphora characterises her as a nymph associated with a spring. Her upper body is naked, with a mantle covering only her hips and upper thighs; the corner of the mantle is wrapped around her lower left arm. A helmeted warrior A3 stands to the right of the female figure A2, with his back towards the rear of the rider. This figure, who is turned towards the female, wears a cuirass with pteryges and straps, greaves on his preserved lower right leg, and carries a probably hexagonal shield in his left hand. In his broken-off right hand, according to the extended hand of the nymph, a weapon, most likely a sword, can perhaps be added with which he threatens the Amazon/nymph. The standing man A1 wearing a himation and already mentioned here above, constitutes the left end of the preserved block. His head is badly damaged so that it is not clear if he is turning to the woman at his right; it seems rather as if he is looking in the other direction, due to the position of his right foot which points to the left. The descriptions of the figure until now assume that his left hand holds the wad or the tip of the mantle;[298] due to a small circular form above the hand, however, we would like to recognise a scroll in his hand. The right arm is badly damaged just below the shoulder; there appears, however, to have been a thick, staff-like object leaning against his upper arm or – more likely – his lower arm was raised (in a gesture of address?). In this figure, we might then recognise a mantle figure of the classical type[299] who can be viewed as a symbol for the citizen and/or official participating in discussions at the agora,[300] or who could be characterised in general as a philosopher or rhetor on account of the possible scroll.

Scholars until now are unanimous in their interpretation that Block A displays the mythical foundation of Ephesos by Androklos, a presumed son of the Athenian King Kodros. For this reason the foundation myth already discussed here above, a myth that was already traced back by Athenaios to Kreophylos and which was extensively reported by Strabon as well as Pausanias,[301] should once again be briefly revisited.

According to the myth, Androklos, the leader of the Greek colonists and the son of the Athenian King, received an oracle in Delphi relating that a fish and a boar would show him a favourable site for a city foundation. The new arrivals, camped at the harbour near the water spring Hypelaios, were grilling fish; the sparks set shrubbery on fire, a boar came charging out of the undergrowth, and after a long chase along Mt. Tracheia was speared by Androklos. Subsequently the Greeks set up a settlement at Koressos and its environs, forced out the indigenous Karians and Lelegians, yet lived in peace with the part of the population, including Amazons, already settled at the Artemision. Later on there was (probably) a short-term occupation of Samos and afterwards additional battles, during which Androklos came to the aid of the threatened city of Priene. In this battle, which was otherwise victorious for the Greeks, Androklos lost his life and was buried at Ephesos in a funerary monument crowned by his statue.

The reliefs show the merging of different, originally independent founding myths and use the scenes for allusions to the present.

Against this background, let us make an attempt to identify the figures on Block A, reserving the discussion of the first preserved figure at the left (A1) until the end.

The subsequent scene to the right appears clear: Androklos[302] takes possession of the region around the spring of Hypelaios.[303] The fact that the spring nymph is patterned almost exactly on the type of the Amazon Sciarra (fig. 71) – with the exception of her clothing and amphora – which surprisingly nobody seems to have recognised, strengthens the local colour and makes a reference to Blocks B and C on the long side of the pronaos with additional Amazon battles.[304] Consequently, there could also be a reference here to Androklos' respecting of the *asylum* zone at the Artemision with the spring nymph represented in the type of the wounded Amazon.[305] If one does not wish to restore a sword in the missing arm of the warrior, but rather prefers to see an outstretched hand, then a gesture of aid or appeasement could have been intended.

Androklos appears once again as a skilful and victorious rider in battle and – if the boar in fact belongs to the scene – as a hunter in fulfilment of the oracle. Actually, however, the ancient texts never relate that Androklos hunts the boar on horseback and such a scene would be unlikely: all of the known Greek mythical boar hunts take place on foot, if only due to the impassable wooded terrain. Only after the beginning of the Hellenistic period[306] and above all during the Roman imperial period, the boar hunt on horseback was taken over from the Orient and became a fixed type for the heroic ruler; one thinks for example of the Hadrianic tondi on the Arch of Constantine.[307] Here at least an anachronism exists,[308] to which we must return. The boar alone sufficed as a reference to the foundation myth, as is clearly seen on Ephesian coin images and potentially other monuments as well;[309] a sya-gros-monument, that is, a boar monument on the Arkadiane, only attested epigraphically, can also be mentioned.[310] The fact that this depiction of a rider refers back to a conscious assimilation of Androklos, as ktistes, to Alexander is attractive, as the Ephesian local hero was represented like Alexander in other cases as well. [311] The relief depiction in the gable of the late Hellenistic Hypelaios nymphaeum,[312] located almost opposite on the southern side of the street, probably served as a direct model, whereby in turn inferences can be drawn for the missing elements of this representation from the Trajanic temple.[313]

One may equally recognise Androklos in the fallen figure of the warrior A5, who raises his shield in protection, indicating the final battle of the founding hero against the Karians.[314] As is known, he fell in battle near Priene, and the warrior who has fallen to the ground and who attempts to cover himself with his shield is an allusion to his imminent death. A triumphing opponent on the relief would have only robbed him of his dignity.[315]

The standing figure in himation (A1) was interpreted by N. Saporiti as Zeus[316] and by R. Fleischer as a personification of Koressos,[317] the site at which the Greek new arrivals settled and erected temples to Athena, Artemis, and Apollon. If one follows the view that the figure holds a book scroll, these interpretations would be invalid. The figure in turn could far rather be Androklos, who has just received the oracle, or who proclaims laws as oikistes, or who carries out similar activities connected with the city founding. In the east frieze of the Parthenon, an identification as magistrates of the city or heroes of the phylai has gained currency for typologically very similar figures wearing a mantle. A similar interpretation in the Ephesian frieze would in any event constitute a coincidence for the documented role of Androklos as a figurehead of the phyle of the Karenaioi in the endowment of Vibius Salutaris, precisely ten years before the vowing of the temple.[318] Making recourse to the high Classical period would, in addition, exactly correspond to the intentions of the Second Sophistic. Accordingly, in the lost part of Block A, an assembly of the Ephesian heroes of the different phylai or a legislative act could have been depicted, in which Ephesos documented its relationship to Athenian or pan-Hellenic Hellenism.

In conclusion we can state that Block A narrated the history of the founding of Koressos (as a synonym or as *pars pro toto* for Ephesos) in continuous narrative, and that Androklos was depicted here more than once in a variety of scenes that paraphrase the foundation myth. The importance of the spring nymph as a central figure and as the site personification of Ephesos is emphasised by her disposition

Fig. 71: So-called Amazon Sciarra, Roman copy of a bronze original of Kresilas ca. 440/430 BC, in Berlin

in the middle of the frieze block; around her, the various scenes with Androklos, the protagonist of the mythical foundation play out. Through his genealogical connection to Athens, Androklos embodied the claims of Ephesos to a high ranking in the world of the Greek poleis. In this manner may be understood the scene with Androklos (?) with a scroll (?), unfortunately partially lost, yet probably related to the cultural ideal of paideia and the emergent Second Sophistic.

In the Second Sophistic it was of enormous importance for Greek cities to emphasise their old age and close ties to Athens.

To cite the words of the author Philostratos, writing approximately 125 years after the construction of the temple, in his biography of the 1st c. figure Apollonios of Tyana: [319]

> τὴν δὲ Ἔφεσον τίς ἀφαιρήσεται τὸ{υ} σώζεσθαι βεβλημένην μὲν τὰς ἀρχὰς τοῦ γένους ἐκ τῆς καθαρωτάτης Ἀτθίδος, ἐπιδεδωκυῖαν δὲ παρὰ πάσας, ὁπόσαι Ἰωνικαί τε καὶ Λύδιοι, προβεβληκυῖαν δὲ ἐπὶ τὴν θάλατταν διὰ τὸ ὑπερήκειν τῆς γῆς, ἐφ' ἧς ᾠκίσθη, μεστὴν δὲ φροντισμάτων οὖσαν φιλοσόφων τε καὶ ῥητορικῶν, ὑφ' ὧν ἡ πόλις οὐχ ἵππῳ, μυριάσι δὲ ἀνθρώπων ἰσχύει, σοφίαν ἐπαινοῦσα;

> "Who would forbid Ephesos to be saved, a city that from the beginning of its lineage was of the purest Attic origin, that has become larger than all, and that pushed as many Ionian and Lydian cities that there are into the sea because it outgrew the land upon which it was founded, and that is filled with the sophisticated speeches of the philosophers and rhetors, thanks to which the city is strong, and not due to its cavalry, but due to the ten thousand people by whom it [the city] promotes wisdom?"

The figures of Block B from left to right can be briefly described as follows: B1 is a calm male figure wearing a chiton/tunic and standing with one leg bent and one weight-bearing leg. In his left hand he holds an oval shield; he rests his right hand on its exterior. Like his neighbour B2, he looks calmly – that is, as a non-participating or perhaps chronologically distanced spectator – at the figures who carry out actions further to the right. The male figure B2 is completely naked, apart perhaps from an Attic helmet (?) – Fleischer thought rather of a wreath[320] – and his musculature is strongly emphasised. His upper body leans slightly forwards, with his right lower arm resting in relaxed fashion on his own back. The figure leans on its lance with its left shoulder, while the heavily damaged lower left arm hangs slackly on the lance. A winged female figure appears next, who can be identified without further ado as Nike/Victoria in a floor-length peplos. In a well-known scheme, she accompanies a general carrying out a sacrifice, and holds a palm branch in her left hand. It is likely that she crowned the general B4 standing in front of her with her lost, although in any event raised, right hand. Figure B4 wears a robe with many folds and a mantle, and is in the act of completing a sacrifice at an altar standing in front of him. Behind the altar can be seen a small figure, B5, most probably a sacrificial servant with an incense box.[321] The following figure B6 is again a fully naked male who, like B2 but in mirror-inverted pose, leans in relaxed fashion on his lance which rests against his right inner elbow. He is the only figure on this block, with the exception of the sacrificial servant, who stands almost frontally; his weight-bearing leg is turned towards the altar, while his relaxed leg and his head turn slightly to the other side as if he could not quite decide which activity he should observe. In comparison to his pendant figure B2, he has an equally well-trained physique, yet is clearly slimmer and is therefore perhaps intended to be younger. He also rests his free hand on his back or his rear. After this figure, we easily recognise a vigorous Herakles (B7) with lion's pelt and club; his right lower arm and hand are missing. To his right, four Amazons clad in chlamys are represented rapidly running away from Herakles (B8–B11); two of these carry a pelta shield (B8 and probably also B11), otherwise they are without weapons. The Amazon at the front (B11) has fallen or has sunken down on one knee; we will revisit this issue due to the similarity to the scene on Block C.

With the Amazons fleeing from Herakles, the relief block alludes to an additional, well recorded foundation myth of Ephesos involving the Amazons, as has been recognised all along.[322] The further interpretation of the scenes on Block B has, however, triggered a fierce discussion in the scholarship regarding its meaning.[323] The interpretation of the altar scene has caused particular controversy. Already N. Saporiti recognised here – with additional iconographic arguments supported by B. Brenk – a Roman emperor crowned by Nike while carrying out a sacrifice.[324] R. Fleischer, in contrast, was not at all willing to accept the validity of this interpretation, an infringement in the action of a Greek, mythological story.[325] We can, however, illustrate that the two naked heroes with lances framing the sacrificial scene observe the scene as if from a great (chronological) distance, which has not been seen in this light before. Therefore, we may indeed reckon with a rupture in time apparent on Block B, or a view into the contemporary era of the temple building.

The powerful hero B2 has been identified by Saporiti as *Bonus Eventus*, which in the later scholarship was justifiably rejected.[326] In the two heroes B2 and B6 Fleischer recognised Bellerophon and Achilles, and in the sacrificing figure B4 originally Theseus, and later Androklos; he then proposed that the figure B6 was Theseus.[327] In this manner, all of the other essential fighters against the Amazons in Greek mythology would be assembled here. Modifying Fleischer's proposals, I would like here to recognise the slim youthful figure B6 as Achilles, with B2 as Theseus. Then the only remaining figure without a name is B1. Since the figure is a warrior obviously clothed in Greek rather than Roman fashion, and not a naked hero, it should then represent a historical personality, perhaps even the city founder Androklos himself.

As a result, the Greek heroes Theseus (B2), Achilles (B6), and Herakles (B7) – and if this proposal is accepted, also the Ephesian local hero Androklos (B1) – would look on favourably from a "historical distance" as the Roman emperor, with the usual sacrifice before the campaign – compare the corresponding scenes on Trajan's Column in Rome – prepares himself to permanently expel the Amazons (Persians/Parthians) from Asia and the neighbouring regions.

The campaign of Trajan against Persia was seen by contemporaries as the ultimate conquest of the greatest Greek trauma of all time: the final overcoming of the Persian menace, which had its forerunners in the Amazon battles of Dionysos and the heroes Herakles and Theseus and in the successful campaign of Alexander the Great.

The essential features of the rather poorly preserved Block C – in terms of the surface of the reliefs – can be summarised with R. Fleischer:[328] Block C with its representation constitutes a pendant to Block B: At the left, three Amazons with pelta shields are fleeing (C2–4). A fourth one at the door to the cella (C1) has, like B11, already suppliantly fallen onto one knee seeking *asylum*. In. the middle part stands lurking Dionysos (C6) with his thyrsos in the right hand, surrounded by two satyrs (C5 and C7); behind the legs of Dionysos and in front of the satyr C5 the only preserved rear part of a jumping panther is to be recognised. Further to the right side follow an additional satyr (C8) throwing a spear and another one riding on an elephant (C9). The final figure of a dancing maenad (C10) already celebrates the victory of Dionysos. The whole Dionysian thiasos is obviously depicted as if returning from its victory over the Indians. Fleischer has compiled the sources for the Indian procession of Dionysos in exemplary fashion and emphasises the fact that this myth emerged only in the post-Alexander era.[329] The Amazons from Block C flee from Dionysos in even more panic-stricken fashion than those on Block B flee from Herakles, yet essentially it is a mirror-inverted representation. Following Tacitus[330] the Ephesians already employed the two variants of the Amazon battles or expulsions when they unsuccessfully promoted their claim for the neocorate temple in front of Emperor Tiberius.

To Fleischer's overview can only be noted that at that time he assumed a Late Antique secondary usage of the frieze blocks at the temple, and therefore held the view that at the ends of both blocks B and C, oriented towards the temple, something must have been chiselled off – possibly the altar or the cult statue of Artemis Ephesia, to which the fleeing Amazons had turned. In their position, length and programme, however, both blocks were conceived for the building and are complete;[331] it would also be surprising, if such a closely mirrored pendant representation had existed at another building, and that these could have been similarly shortened and reused in such a way. We must therefore assume that the two Amazon groups are fleeing, so to speak, into the interior of the cella to the cult image or to a cult group mentioned in the building inscription as the agalma erected there; in this manner, they invited the observer and visitor, following this line of sight, to look through this door or to enter it. The foremost Amazon, already sunken onto one knee in sight of this agalma, refers to the *hikesia*, the expected protection in the *asylum*. We will return to this idea further below.

The example of the Tycheion in Alexandria: Twelve gods – and a divine man?

Block D shows a total of 13 standing figures (and a dog), whose interpretation is in part very simple yet in part almost impossible.[332] For simplification of argument, we will begin by making a few fundamental observations on the identification of the individual figures. Following Fleischer, the armed female figure D1 is certainly Roma due to the lack of an aegis, while at the other end the figure D13 is without doubt Athena. These two symbolic figures of the Greek and Roman world frame, as it were, the "assembly of gods" appearing between them. Attention needs to be drawn here to the fact that, for Block D, the same direction of reading from right to left is valid as for the neighbouring relief Block C: the narrative is therefore oriented towards and proceeds towards the cella door, creating a mirror image to Block B; such a scheme was also present in the East frieze of the Parthenon. In this manner Athena, at the front at the street side, is to be seen as the starting point, and Roma almost as the consummation of the world represented. This interpretation is strengthened by the fact that only Athena is depicted in profile looking towards the figures who follow; she looks as it were on or into her own future, as the heroes Androklos and Theseus (?) looked towards the sacrificing emperor on Block B. All of the other figures, in contrast, are presented frontally towards the viewers, as if these viewers were walking through a gallery of statues in a large stoa and ultimately arrived at Roma, or allegorically as if they had travelled from Athens to Rome. Therefore, for the first time a content-related explanation emerges for the frontality of those represented in the frieze block, a frontality which is actually unusual for the (early) 2nd c. AD and which previously formed a substantial argument for the (later) stylistic dating of the frieze.[333]

This succession of divinities in completely non-canonical fashion nevertheless consists of a total of 13 figures and not, as is usual, a pantheon of twelve gods. Furthermore, we will see that this is only a selection of the otherwise common Olympian divinities, who are supplemented by figures who are important for the connection shown here. In addition, the entire representation is actually apportioned to two partial blocks, carved with a diagonal joint between them; the southern block – which R. Fleischer was able to prove – was employed as a replacement during the completion of the frieze[334] and displays a substantially denser sequence of figures than on the adjacent block. Apparently, the pictorial programme was quickly and efficiently altered in order to include an additional figure, which in turn explains the non-canonical number of 13 figures. In our opinion, the deceased and divinized Trajan has been incorporated into the assembly of twelve gods and heroes which, in the original building concept, was intended to represent the Greco-Roman cosmos from the imperial-Ephesian perspective. The conceptual prototype for this can probably be found in the Tychaion in Alexandria, where the deceased Alexander was represented in the circle of the twelve Olympian gods.[335] We are therefore dealing with the reliefs of statues who do not interact with each other but only with the viewer,[336] for whom they symbolise the world (or its evolution).

Let us now discuss the individual figures in turn. Next to Athena D13 stands a young man D12, clothed in a cuirass and chlamys/paludamentum as well as boots; Fleischer identified him as most likely Ares/Mars, explaining his lack of weapons as due to lack of space.[337] If, however, we view the "cosmos" in the sense of what was said above – and we are dealing with the part of the relief that was produced anew immediately after Hadrian's accession to power – then Mars has put down his weapons, including his helmet, which suits perfectly the new programme of government. The identification as Mars is also supported by the following figure D11, a matronly, demure Aphrodite in long dress (a peplos or rather a stola and a long tunic?)[338] and mantle, holding a mirror in front of her breast.[339] After her follows a figure of Hekate (D10), with some kind of mural crown, who as Fleischer astutely observed formed a pendant to Selene with crescent moon (D2), both of whom appear "to have been taken up as hypostases of Artemis".[340] Next to Hekate, Fleischer proposes that the male figure D9, dressed in chiton and diagonal mantle as well as boots, is Hermes/Mercurius, while Fleischer identifies his neighbour D8, a wreathed youth with a mantle slung around the hips, as Dionysos.[341] His right hand hangs loosely down to the mantle fold, while in his slightly extended left hand he holds an unrecognisable, somewhat rounded object. Fleischer, however, connected that attribute to the neighbouring figure of Hermes D9, and thought of a *marsupium* (purse), the distinctive mark of the Roman Mercurius. Nevertheless, the left upper arm with the mantle fold of figure D8 is depicted as slightly in front of the left arm of figure D9 in the relief, and therefore the lower arm represented should rather belong to figure D8 than to D9. The next figure (D7) is the naked Herakles with a club which he swings above his head. The diagonal seam in the relief block runs through his body, so that the right third of his body, both feet, his right leg as well as parts of his right arm from the original part of the block are now missing. A naked youth D6 takes up almost precisely the middle of frieze block D; he supports himself on a now lost lance. His right, extended lower arm is broken off, so it cannot be determined whether an attribute once existed. Behind him and partially hidden by his legs stands a lean hunting dog, who looks up alertly towards his master.[342]

Fleischer recognised a naiskos above the head of the hunting hero, and thought of Androklos as ktistes in connection with images of Artemis Ephesia.

On the temple itself an unnoticed yet apt parallel exists for this detail, namely, the bust, generally identified as Tyche, with a naiskos on its head, located on the front of the Syrian gable of the pronaos (fig. 72).[343] The bust is depicted with a chlamys and obviously naked breast, and therefore an Ephesian Amazon as city founder is intended and not Tyche, who is always chastely fully clothed. This Amazon therefore constitutes, as in the foundation myths,[344] the pendant to Androklos. Fleischer's interpretation of the figure as the foundation hero Androklos remains convincing, based on both the pictorial type which appears frequently at Ephesos[345] as well as the context of the frieze. Further to the left Artemis D5 appears in a long, flared peplos, followed

Fig. 72: Bust with naiskos on its head, on the Syrian gable of the pronaos of the so-called Temple of Hadrian

by her naked brother Apollon, represented as the Lykaios type.[346] Fleischer left the interpretation of the following, heavily damaged male figure D3 open. The figure of Selene D2, identified by the crescent moon on her head,[347] appears to the left, and finally the already mentioned Roma D1 concludes the assembly. Fleischer indeed postulated that D3 might be Helios due to the vicinity to Selene, but rejected this proposal due to the lack of a radiate crown. Since so much of this figure's head is missing, however, in my opinion there may well have once been a radiate crown, possibly applied as forward-projecting metal bars; Helios should therefore be considered again for figure D3. This reading would also be supported by the other divine pairs who are related to each other: Apollon – Artemis, Aphrodite – Ares, and finally Athena – Roma.

For the contextual interpretation of the row of statues, we must return once again to the centre of the pictorial field and observe the addition of a new part of the block from Herakles towards the right. As R. Fleischer already recognised, this reworking of the entire block must go back to the aim of including one (or at the most two) more additional figure(s) than were originally intended.[348] The excavator of the Temple of Hadrian, F. Miltner, in turn thought – on the basis of his dating to the late 4th c. – that the two shod figures D9 and D12 were humans. Due to the hairstyle of D9 Miltner proposed Theodosius I, and for D12 his son Arcadius.[349] If we now assume a dating in the early Hadrianic period as secure, then figure D9 with its distinctive hairstyle can only be intended as Trajan, as far as this is permissible as an argument at all, given such a small-scale figure.[350] In this case the similarity in the clothing and the overall figure to Ares/Mars (D12) would in no way be accidental: Trajan would be depicted as a general 'in plain clothes' on the frieze. The additional figure in the frieze would therefore be figure D9, formerly identified as Hermes/Mercurius, who in fact nevertheless should be the deceased and divinized emperor. Thereby, *divus Traianus* appears in a row with the fighters against the Amazons, Herakles and Dionysos, who in Blocks B and C are the main protagonists. Together with Androklos, he frames the two heroes, just as on Block B his act of sacrifice is framed by Greek heroes. On Block A, the rider Androklos permits strong associations with Alexander the Great and with Trajan as (anticipated) *victor* over the Persians.[351] On Block D, the new *divus* appears in the circle of the gods, as Alexander had done in the Tycheion, yet here nonetheless in a particular selection of divinities which on the one hand forms an Ephesian-Roman axis, and on the other focuses on combatants against the Persians (victors over the Amazons). We have already discussed the divine pairs who appear on Block D. Since Trajan was added to the relief and in this new version apparently is related to Androklos, only Meter-Hekate remains as it were alone. She thus constituted part of an original pair with Androklos. Both individuals play a particular role in Ephesian Koressos, the one as the founder of the settlement, the other as the goddess who was specifically venerated there. Hekate was also worshipped at the Triodos junction directly below the temple, while Androklos played a significant role at the Hypelaios Spring and might have been honoured in the adjacent Androkloneion.[352] They framed the pair of Amazon conquerors Herakles and Dionysos, who appear on this frieze as mythical ancestors and role models of Trajan. In this manner, the exceptional importance of Ephesos in the emperor's recently initiated Parthian campaign would have been emphasised during the vowing of the small temple in 114/115.

Now the chronological multivalence of the individual frieze parts can be explained. The rider on Block A is Androklos, who at the same time refers both to Alexander and to Trajan. Block B is located in the late Trajanic present, which in turn is explained through the mythical history of the city. Block C can be read from the past, the conquest of India by Bacchus/Dionysos and Alexander, and to the next task awaiting Trajan after the defeat of the Parthians. This all remained an ambitious dream, yet Block D at least could represent the *apotheosis* of Trajan, in turn based on the model of the great Macedonian Alexander. Likewise, the logic of the Second Sophistic, the perfection of the Greek (Athenian) world in and through Rome – in Block A only allusively comprehensible – is shown here.

The fact that Trajan's Parthian campaign, just as the Persian war of Alexander the Great, finds its mythical parallel on Block B with the imperial sacrifice and the expulsion of the Amazons, does not need further discussion. On Block C, the expulsion of the Amazons by Dionysos with the help of an elephant reflects Alexander's Indian journey, which first arose as a mythical story after this event.[353] Ultimately, this allusion to Alexander may also be understood on a third level as an allegory of an Indian campaign, perhaps at least envisaged, by Trajan at the time of the building of the temple, according to Cassius Dio.[354] Consequently, with this temple Ephesos prepared itself for the triumphal return of the emperor from the east.[355] The framing of the frieze and the decoration of the architrave soffits with laurel garlands also specifically allude to this theme of victory.

Briefly summarised, the fundamental concept of the frieze was probably somewhat as follows: as, in the myth, Herakles and Dionysos expel the Amazons, so did the founder of Ephesos, Androklos in distant memory, proceed against the local forces. Like the divine heroes, however, he did not kill the Amazons; beaten and defeated, they were able to flee to *asylum* and the protection of Artemis, the great goddess of Ephesos. Afterwards they were able to recover and then became part of Ephesos; indeed they were viewed as founders of additional settlement areas, namely Smyrna and Ptelea.[356] Likewise, it was to be expected that now, after a successful Parthian campaign, Trajan would incorporate the defeated lands as provinces into the civilized world.[357] That which was begun by the Greeks (Athena), would now be completed in the immediate future by Roma, and the divinities that were particularly important for Ephesos and the seasoned combatants against the Amazons would thereby lend their support. The unexpected death of Trajan – and probably likewise the unexpected military defeat previously – nevertheless required adaptions to this programme. How much was actually altered is beyond our knowledge. Block D was certainly supplemented with the deceased emperor. Whether Block A also received alterations must remain undecided. Perhaps, the solitary fallen warrior A5 is a conscious pendant to the divinized Trajan, who could be recognised as well in the rider A4 as neos Alexandros; or perhaps he is instead to be understood as an allusion to the death of the emperor without an opponent. In any event, on this metaphorical level of meaning, the representations on Block A can also be explained with imperial legislation (A1), benevolence (A2), fighting strength (A3), and invincibility (A4), as well as the virtue of the virile hunt (the boar).

4.4.2 Attempt at a reconstruction of the cult statue group

Equally important as the presence of gods and heroes in the frieze, however, is also their absence for the overall interpretation of the temple building. Both Zeus/Iuppiter, as the most important god in the Greek pantheon and highest state god in Rome, and the city goddess Artemis Ephesia are missing. This absence is most unusual in such a state temple, above all due to the expressed language of the building inscription – "for Artemis Ephesia, Emperor Hadrian, and the Demos of Ephesos".

The Amazons of Blocks B and C, who flee in mirror image in the direction of the cella door or who fall on one knee precisely at the door frames, however, clearly refer to the fact that their protective goddess would grant them *asylum* in the cella.[358] In addition to Artemis Ephesia, a Zeus/Iuppiter or perhaps more likely an emperor (Trajan) assimilated to him is to be expected for the original building concept. Since 114 AD, after the first successes in the east, Trajan was the *optimus princeps*, and after the anticipated final victory over the Parthians he would have been honoured – as every contemporary would be aware – with the following title of *maximus*, and therefore completely approximated to his fictive divine adoptive father *Iuppiter optimus maximus,* as his earthly representative. Consequently Trajan, as earthly *pater patriae* and heavenly father of Artemis Ephesia, would be elevated, so to speak, to the father figure not only of the empire in general,[359] but in particular of the city of Ephesos.

Artemis Ephesia was shown as the protector not only of her city, but of the whole Roman Empire.

The group of cult statues[360] of Artemis Ephesia and (divine) emperor was probably supplemented by a protection-seeking Amazon, who embodied the Demos of the Ephesians mentioned in the building inscription as the third recipient of the temple. Precisely this scene is in fact represented on a Trajanic coin of the city of Ephesos (fig. 73).[361] It may well be the case that this coin refers to this very temple or its originally planned cult image. We cannot know whether the death of the emperor and the rededication to Hadrian – aside from the person of the emperor – caused many changes in this regard.[362] Fundamentally, such a programme with the protective divinities would have certainly been in the interests of the new ruler. The fact that there was only a modification of what the Ephesians had propounded in the Senate almost a century earlier under Tiberius, in the contest for the neocorate temple, shows that the city, undeterred, staked everything on one and the same card.

In this manner, the Trajanic temple on the Embolos probably very consciously referred to the historicising monuments[363] erected on the street already in the Hellenistic era (the Hypelaios nymphaeum) and the Augustan period (the Amazon altar at the Triodos), and revealed a sophisticated synthesis of their mythical narratives in which Artemis and the Amazons were connected with Androklos, who was then valorised as a model for later ruler images. One feels reminded of the words of Aelius Aristides about half a century later, when stating: "A small remnant of Greece, has luckily come down to our time, restored by the excellence of the present rulers".[364] But the central message of these monuments (and, of course, the contemporary literature of the Second Sophistic) was not primarily focusing on a general feeling of being *Hellene*, but much more on showing the cities as hoards of culture and the actors as glamorous intellectuals,[365] whose *patris* – here: Ephesos – was the most ancient and mother city of Asia.[366]

In sum, the effort related in planning such a sophisticated programme, one which was multivalent with regard to content as well as to the chronological period cov-

Fig. 73: Trajanic coin of the city of Ephesos with representation of Artemis Ephesia, the emperor, and an Amazon seeking protection

ered, is in sharp contrast to the size of the building and the quality of the relief friezes. The little temple on the Embolos, in the heart of the city and in the middle of additional historical as well as contemporary buildings full of allusions to the city's history, was perhaps actually a model for a neocorate temple rather than a work *eo ipso*. Perhaps it was designed to display to the emperor returning from Parthia in triumph[367] what a cleverly designed temple would have awaited him[368] had he not awarded the neocorate to Pergamon, where the *proconsul Asiae* Gaius Antius Aulus Iulius Quadratus had trumped with the Zeus Philios card,[369] but instead to Ephesos with its advocate Ti. Iulius Celsus Polemaeanus, who, as former minister of buildings, under Trajan probably co-designed the plans and the programme of the Forum Traiani.[370] There was no other choice for the Ephesians than to adapt the building and present it to the new ruler, Hadrian.[371] The new emperor awarded a total of three neocorate temples to the province of Asia, first to Kyzikos, and in 124 AD to Smyrna, with which he was closely associated also due to the presence there of the philosopher Polemos; only after the imperial visit in 129 AD were the Ephesians allowed to erect to him, as Hadrian Olympios, a gigantic provincial temple, probably in 131/132 AD, at a newly developed building location at the harbour.[372]

4.5 The honorific tombs of rhetors and sophists at the Triodos in the 2nd c. AD

The Second Sophistic, which has already been invoked in the discussion of the so-called Temple of Hadrian, extensively influenced behaviour in the public as well as private life of the urban élites in the 2nd c. AD, yet also the self-conception of the cities in their mutual rivalries. Accordingly, sophists and rhetors were often highly-paid figureheads; for example Soteros who taught in Athens was twice brought to Ephesos with an annual salary of 10,000 sestertii.[373] At least two representatives of this eminent group received publicly sponsored tombs, not coincidentally directly in front of the Library of Celsus and in an architectural connection with the agora as the traditional site of the veneration of heroes.

Fig. 74: Sarcophagus of Dionysios Rhetor, view into the tomb chamber rebuilt into a staircase in the early Byzantine period, next to the South Gate of the Agora

Fig. 75: Presumed tomb of Hypsikles, view from the south to the ascending brick vault of the tomb chamber. On the east (right) side of the vault, the partly preserved rear wall of the original wing of the South Gate with exedra, forming simultaneously the cheek of the staircase to the upper storey of the agora and to the Neronian Hall

Fig. 76: Marble arch with the epitaph of the rhetor Flavius Hypsikles from Rhodos

4.5.1 Titus Claudius Flavianus Dionysius

Around the mid–2nd c. AD, the interment of the rhetor Dionysios of Miletos, particularly esteemed by Hadrian and Antoninus Pius, took place. His sarcophagus[374] (figs. 40a. 64. 74) was found in the chamber designated as SOe, beneath the flight of stairs leading up to the so-called Neronian Hall (fig. 75), which originally served as the maintenance room for the canalisation.[375] During the construction of a staircase from the Marble Street to the South Gate along the south façade of the Neronian Hall in the 6th c., the grave chamber was destroyed, and the sarcophagus was completely pushed back to the rear wall which in part remained standing; the burial container was directly built over by the staircase, and the upper surface of its lid served as a step. During the excavations in 1977, the undamaged lead sarcophagus – in spite of the desirability of the expensive metal – was found inside the marble sarcophagus, together with the bones of the deceased.[376]

"Adopted sons" of the city as an alternative:
Not born here, but buried.

The base for the bronze tomb statue was most likely originally set up above the door of the grave chamber, on the west wall oriented towards the Library of Celsus, as the marble and the working of the base and the wall are identical. The base names Claudius Eutychus, a freedman of the orator, sophist, and imperial administrator (*procurator*), as the builder of the tomb. This statue base had already been found in 1906,[377] built into the early Byzantine stair string almost directly next to the sarcophagus, at that time no longer visible.

This situation hardly came to pass by accident, but is instead to be understood as a final testimonial on the part of the Byzantine, now-Christian city to the famous orator, honoured by Philostratos,[378] who had contributed to the great past of Ephesos as his final adoptive home. In this way, Dionysios was accorded the same respect as we have seen was the case with the burial of the sarcophagus in the Androkloneion, which probably housed the remains of Tib. Claudius Aristion.

4.5.2 Flavius Hypsikles

The tomb of Dionysios, however, was not the only burial of the 2nd c. AD in this area. J. Keil had already suspected that additional "tombs of scholars" were located opposite the Library of Celsus.[379]

We can recover such a tomb of a sophist with a degree of certainty in the immediate proximity of the tomb of Dionysios.[380] We have already spoken earlier about the southern part of the building with wings, projecting from the South Gate, with a niche oriented to the west (so-called exedra; fig. 75) that was probably originally intended for the statue of the benefactor Mithridates (figs. 39a and 40a); this served at the same time as the western border of the steps of the ascent to the Neronian Hall. In front of this, in the advanced 2nd c. AD, a brick vault was built (well recognisable in figs. 36f.), suspended to the south over a strong supporting wall (fig. 75).[381] At the southern end, the original apex of the vault lay only ca. 0.80 m above the contemporary level of the Embolos street running downhill; in the north, the clear height attained more than 2 m. The small chamber was apparently intended for only a one-time occupancy, after which it was permanently closed. This also explains the lack of a sarcophagus, since the closed tomb house allowed no view into the interior, and also no odour pollution to the exterior. The excavators of 1905 already noted in their journal: "In the vault mentioned lies a large number of crude clay vessels, yet interesting in their form, and human bones."[382]

In front of the north end of the exedra and equally to the north of the north-west corner of the brick vault, abutments were constructed upon which a marble arch marked the visible side of the new tomb chamber below the brick vault. The western visible side of this small new structure, with its north-west corner pilaster projecting to the west was faced for its entire length with ashlar blocks with slightly roughened surface. The arrangement of the blocks allows the recognition that the level of the area was considerably heightened compared to the 1st c. AD. Furthermore, a niche articulated in the form of steps can also be recognised.

The entire construction must have been filled with *opus caementicium* in its upper region, for which the brick vault served as a support and simultaneously as the grave chamber. Only in this manner can the 0.75 m wide supporting walls (fig. 75), erected out of rubble and spolia, for the relatively weak vault of square brick tiles be explained (ca. 0.30 × 0.30 × 0.055 m). The poured wall work filled the space up to the Augustan apse, which has now become completely invisible.

The oblique direction of the vault is explicable, on the one hand, due to the topography of the building plot, and on the other hand must have something to do with the original appearance of the building. The pedestrian walking through the South Gate in any event had to go around the tomb building on the west and south side; a high, towering wall block on the street corner would certainly have been an intrusive factor. The oblique vault, however, took up the existing northward slant further to the east of the steps to the Neronian Hall, and constituted a harmonious termination of the building ensemble, over which the pedestrian coming down from the Embolos had a relatively unimpeded view of the South Gate and the Celsus Library. It is therefore most likely that a sort of stepped construction was introduced over the *opus caementicium*.

A marble arch (fig. 76) with the tomb inscription of a Roman *eques* named T. Flavius Hypsikles, originally from Rhodos, was employed as a termination feature for the vaulted stepped construction (so-called corridor or ramp passage), erected immediately to the north of the tomb in the 6th c. AD and discussed above as the reason for the destruction of the Tomb of Dionysios. This was also found in 1905 in a correspondingly collapsed position, south-east of the South Gate of the agora.[383] Hypsikles was a student of the sophist Soteros who taught in Athens and Ephesos and who was a contemporary of the Ephesian Damianos.[384]

If Keil has correctly associated the name of the son T. Flavius Claudius Gorgos, recorded as the builder of the tomb, with the Senator of the same name who was sentenced to death under Septimius Severus,[385] then for the burial of Hypsikles we have a second piece of evidence for a date in the second half of the 2nd c. AD, in addition to the reference to Soteros. For the tomb, the middle era of the second half of the 2nd c. is to be preferred. Tomb building and inscription therefore belong to the same time period; furthermore, the arch with its approximate dimensions of ca. 2.70 m clear span and 4.80 m total length would be very well suited as a crowning of the north wall and as a prestigious spanning of a false gate in front of the walled-up entrance. After this, the wall sloping to the south joined up to the unworked rear side of the arch. The inscription, carved on to the side surface of the arch, in this case was oriented to the west, towards the open area in front of the Library and in the same direction as the statue base of Dionysios. A statue of the deceased or other plastic decoration could have been set up on the arch. A group of an Aphrodite and a goat, found in the so-called ramp passage in the levelling beneath the Justinianic ground level, suggests itself in particular for the sculptural ornamentation of the tomb; according to E. Atalay, this group could be supplemented at the most with a figure of Pan.[386] Aphrodite as the tomb icon of an individual who was descended from her beloved island Rhodos would in any event be an extremely obvious symbol.

The reconstruction of the building with the slanting brick vault allows the recognition of an ensemble of three honorific tombs, whose entrances, each worked out as marble archways, had a common courtyard directly next to the South Gate. To the north, adjoining the South Gate of the agora, lay the tomb of Mithridates (room SOc), to the east, that of Dionysios Rhetor (room SOe), and to the south, that of Hypsikles (figs. 64 and 75).

With the tombs of the Sophists at the South Gate of the Tetragonos Agora, the tradition of the honorific tombs on the Embolos comes to an end.[387] Whether the Parthian War or the so-called Antonine Plague after 165 AD played a role in this caesura cannot be ascertained. In any event, the cities of Asia Minor became impoverished. Under Marcus Aurelius and also later, Ephesos was assigned state financial overseers on a number of occasions.[388]

4.6 The Severan Hydreion as end point of the honorific buildings on the Embolos

The civil wars during the Severan period did not improve the situation. Whereas in many areas of the Imperium Romanum, above all in the Danubian provinces that were severely affected by the Marcomannic Wars (ca. 171–180 AD), an economic recovery termed the "Severan boom" did take place, nevertheless in Asia Minor large-scale building projects are only recorded in isolated cases.[389] Many cities suffered under heavy debts and depletion of populations. In Ephesos the further development of the city took place only sporadically and at a lesser quality. Under the Severans, for example, the so-called Acropolis hill (plan 1 no. 100) was provided with a square colonnaded structure and a dodecagonal central building, while two building inscriptions of far more than 100 m total length, found at the agora in a Late Antique reused context, point to additional, large colonnaded buildings.[390]

Only one monument from the Severan period can be identified on the Embolos; according to its building inscription, it was erected between 209 and 211 and was designated as a *Hydreion* (fig. 58).[391] In fact, the building is probably to be viewed only as a renovation of the Augustan fountain[392] in front of the Memmius Monument. The building on the Embolos,[393] which is not yet extensively published and which is modest in comparison with the massive fountain buildings of this period in other cities, for example in front of the city gates of Side and Perge on the Pamphylian coast, has a façade with the tabernacle architecture typical after the Flavian period,[394] yet which exhibits only four columns in a minimalistic design. The central area of the rear wall, between the middle columns, is emphasised by a semicircular niche. An additional water basin was located in this niche, opposite the three water basins at the façade and situated ca. 2 m higher. An imperial statue was probably set up above this basin, in similar fashion to the Nymphaeum Traiani, allowing the ruler to appear as the benefactor of the water.

The Persian and Marcomannic wars of Marcus Aurelius and Lucius Verus, the following epidemic disease and finally the age of the soldier emperors with horrific earthquakes brought a gradual end to the carefree joie de vivre of the elite in Ephesos and also of the privately sponsored building activities in the area of the Embolos for nearly a century.

This fountain marks the end of building activities in the area of the Embolos for nearly a century. Only in front of the *Hydreion* and the so-called Temple of Hadrian, provincial governors officiating under Diocletian set up statues of the Tetrarchs.[395] Larger-scale redesigning and new designing of the entire street system first occurred in the time of Theodosius I and up until the later 6th c. AD, under the altered circumstances of the Christianised imperium.[396]

The Triodos, the Octagon and the Embolos: Conclusions

1. The building history of the Embolos and its significance within the urban development of Ephesos

Until the new foundation of the city by Lysimachos, the Embolos (or Curetes Street) was part of an overland route that on the one hand linked Pygela (today Kuşadası) and other coastal sites with the Kaystros and Maiandros valleys, and on the other hand on a local level connected the Artemision and the main settlement of Ephesos, lying near to the sanctuary and laid out by Kroisos, with the village of Smyrna and the harbour Koressos. The Triodos arose at the branching off of the street near Smyrna towards Koressos (plan 2; fig. 27). This junction constituted the most important inner urban street crossing, also after the new foundation of the city after ca. 300 BC, and brought together the main streets coming from the city gates (plan 1, near no. 52). From the 7th until the late 4th c. BC, graves were set up on these roads over long stretches; these tombs are demonstrable in close succession from the area of the State Agora as far as the Tetragonos Agora and especially in the Embolos and the hillsides nearby in between them. The Hellenistic city layout indeed incorporated the Embolos into the fortified city area; due to the insufficient development of the area between the two city hills Mt. Preon and Mt. Pion (fig. 90), however, the street continued to exist as a natural terrain route in this valley furrow formed by the hills. Until the early 2nd c. BC the Embolos only served to connect the developed city in the harbour plain with the city gate on the road to Magnesia. It was only with the layout of the Gymnasium of the Neoi (plan 5) on the almost level pass in the east of the city that it attained an actual inner-city traffic function as a link between the commercial market and this gymnasium. It can only be conjectured how long the graves of the Archaic–Classical period along the trace of the road remained visible, and whether these played an influencing role, on the one hand, on the delayed development up until the Augustan urban expansion and densification, and on the other hand on the laying out of honorific tombs beginning under Octavian/Augustus.[1] But it can be assumed that the area of the Embolos was quite unsuitable for settlement purposes due to the water pouring down from the springs at the slopes of the Bülbüldağ and after rainfalls and the muddy conditions especially during winter. Similarly, a use mainly for graves corresponded with common Greek and Roman conceptions of town planning. Only with the installation of an efficient sewage water system in Augustan times or at the latest after the earthquake of 23 AD the slopes along the Embolos became appropriate areas for large and luxurious dwellings like Terrace House 2. But the ultimate aggregation of residential buildings did not happen before the paving of the street under Domitian, as is shown by the nearly palatial Terrace House 1 erected in Trajanic times and the contemporaneous reshaping of Terrace House 2.

Since the Augustan period the Embolos connected the Hellenistic city in the harbour plain with the newly inhabited areas around the Roman ruler cult centre in the upper city.

The only reliable evidence up until now that at least the lowest section of the Embolos played a significant role during the urban layout under Lysimachos is the portrait of the ruler (fig. 20) that was "buried" below the Late Antique or early Byzantine street paving in front of the Baths of Scholasticia (Varius Baths; for the findspot see plan 3, the crossing close to no. 12). At the moment, we can only speculate that the statue of the founder must have been set up in the vicinity, most likely near the Hypelaios Spring (so-called Heroon, plan 3 no. 9), which remained in function until the 5th/6th c. AD. This qualifies the negative reports about Lysimachos, probably controlled by the following Seleucid rule, in our imperial and hence later sources.

The oldest comprehensible building on the lower Embolos is the fountain (plan 3 no. 12) somewhat east of the Hypelaios Spring, which was very probably erected in honour of Ptolemaios IV and Arsinoë III, that is, at the earliest in ca. 220 BC. This structure confirms the importance of the water-abundant location for urban life, and at the same time the cult of the rulers. In the early days of Roman rule over what was now the province of Asia, with Ephesos as its most vital harbour, the supposedly older (Lysimachean?) fountain building,[2] we identify here as the Hypelaios Spring (plan 3 no. 9), was (re-)erected as a two-storeyed nymphaeum installation. The architectural decoration of the upper storey represents the foundation myth of Androklos, the alleged son of the Attic King Kodros (fig. 48), and which here appears to be assimilated to the course of life of Lysimachos. As a result of the appraisal of the information regarding the mythical city foundation, handed down by Athenaios, in the work of the early Hellenistic local historian Kreophylos, we can assume that the fountain spring already played an important role in the propaganda of rule under Lysimachos. This aspect was taken up again in the Roman Republican period, and Ephesos was therefore represented as both an Attic as well as a Lysimachean foundation. Concurrently with this, the Hellenistic dynasties of the Seleucids and Ptolemies, conquered by Rome or enemies of Rome, as well as the recently extinct Attalids were all marginalised as former rulers of the city. The gerousia, founded by Lysimachos or at least vested by him with power in urban political life, was the primary bearer of his memory. Until the late imperial period, this body remained associated with its benefactor and with the cult of Artemis Soteira, apparently endowed by him.

This specific address to the Ephesian Artemis as 'Soteira' was a decisive aspect of the initiation mysteries for the young citizens in Ortygia since the time of Lysimachos, and she was apparently honoured in this guise at the Triodos. Admittedly her altar (plan 3 no. 5) and cult are first attested via an Augustan or early imperial building and in inscriptions of the early 1st c. AD. The great esteem of the Triodos, however, certainly extends to the Hellenistic epoch and perhaps even further back. The construction of the elaborate altar at the Triodos, with the reference to the wounded Amazons set up in the Artemision, is in any event hardly accidental and is closely connected to the function of the Embolos as a site of reference for the city's history. Whether a station of the procession of the ephebes, led by the prytanis and the Curetes, towards Ortygia was set up here must remain unclear until the discovery of such a sanctuary. According to Strabon, the sacred site was located somewhere on the route between Ephesos and Pygela. At roughly the same time, an imperial cult centre for Augustus and his house was instituted in the region of the Gymnasium of the Neoi, a site which has long been misunderstood in the scholarship as the "State Agora" (plan 1 no. 18; plan 5).

We can assume that the fountain spring Hypelaios already played an important role in the propaganda of rule under Lysimachos and later on served as a landmark referring to the everlasting history of the city.

Since the Augustan period, the Embolos therefore connected the city in the harbour plain, which until that time had not grown essentially beyond the Triodos to the east, with the new ruler cult centre in the so-called upper city. In its late Augustan complete development, this cult centre consisted of a large plaza, surrounded by colonnades and halls, prominent amongst them the three-aisled *basilike stoa* in the north. The plaza contained a central temple, the prytaneion, and a cult courtyard (the so-called Rhodian peristyle) associated with it, within which the altars of Augustus and Artemis Ephesia probably stood. It was also here that the prospective young citizens assembled, paid their respects to the ruling house and the patron goddess of the city, and then proceeded over the kathodos and the sacred threshold (enbasis; plan 5 no. 14) down the Embolos to the Triodos. The mythology-laden monuments of the ktisteis and former rulers, with the Hypelaios Spring so decisive for the city foundation, lined the route. In the middle of the Hellenistic historical monuments also stood the Hexagon (plan 3 no. 11), which with Augustus and his grandchildren probably symbolised the political present and future of the city, right next to the Octagon (plan 3 no. 10), which as a tomb building of Arsinoë IV concluded the immediate Hellenistic past. At the Triodos, in turn, Artemis awaited them, for it was she in her role as Soteira who would bestow civil rights on the young citizens. These, however, took place in turn under the auspices of the omnipresent Augustus, who appeared as a provident ruler in the circular building with water feature (plan 3 no. 4), whereas (almost) his entire family looked down upon the altar from the attic of the South Gate (plan 3 no. 2).[3] The form of the gate as a typical Roman three-arched monument, even if not freestanding but set into the walls of the agora, is reminiscent of the many city gates or gate-like arches in the empire.[4] And, in fact, it functioned as a city gate inside the town, marking the border between the Hellenistic and the new Augustan quarters, now reaching far to the north beyond the old Koressian Gate. The propagandistic claims are very close to the ones formulated on the Gate of Hadrian in Athens, but much less ostentatious.

This tradition was continued by the following generations.[5] Under Titus the Flavians received a monument, the *Hydrekdocheion* of the *proconsul Asiae* Laecanius Bassus (plan 5 no. 18) in the free corner at the transition of the South Street to the Embolos, while Domitian elevated his house with the new neocorate temple (plan 1 no. 30) that looked over the Julian cult centre. At the same time, at least three new fountain installations in its immediate proximity were added to the already overabundant water supply of this city quarter: the Fountain of Domitian on the older structure of the Pollio building (plan 5 no. 16), the Apsidal Fountain directly south of it (plan 5 no. 17), and the Marnas surge tank in the South Street (plan 5 no. 19). Under the *optimus princeps* Trajan, with the Nymphaeum Traiani (plan 3 no. 18) and the Varius Baths (plan 3 no. 14) with the small temple at the street façade (plan 3 no. 15), the completion of the history was ultimately celebrated: the emperor and the city goddess appear in the (reconstructed) cult image group as permanent protectors of the people of Ephesos (fig. 73), towards which the mythological-historical past in the pronaos made its way.

The Severan Hydreion at the Memmius Monument (plan 3 no. 20) and the Tetrarchic bases, set up more than once, of the late 3rd c. AD can be seen as the logical epilogues to this tradition; these bases were set up in front of the so-called Temple of Hadrian and the Hydreion by Roman high officials. Even in the final, Late Antique – early Byzantine flowering of the city which began with Theodosius I at the end of the 4th c. AD and found its conclusion with Iustinianus in the 6th c., the Embolos was practically teeming with honorific statues and statues of Nike, the guarantor of imperial victory, secondarily brought here.[6]

This development of the Embolos into a processional street,[7] an expansion that lasted nearly a millennium and that continually had recourse to and drew on the earlier inventory, was no coincidence. The street, with its special location in the cut of the valley, constrained and focussed the lines of sight; in addition, the abundant water supply here made it into the "Broadway" of Ephesos and promoted the development into a historical mile in the sense of a "walk of fame": "... it is likely that those who commissioned further buildings to stand in this space paid close attention to what was already there, and what it said. In the metropolis of Ephesos, the desires and decisions of initial builders would be received by a wide audience of varied elites, who furthered and modified that reception with their own dedications."[8]

Analysing the map of the Embolos during the Hadrianic era provides interesting insights into the chronological pattern. The majority of buildings was constructed during the reign of Augustus, with subsequent additions and repairs occurring until the time of Nero, mostly in the lower and very upper end of the Embolos. However, the Flavian dynasty took a different approach, focusing their efforts on the area surrounding the newly established provincial Temple of the Divine Emperors (plan 1 no. 30) touching the Embolos only at its uppermost corner with the reshaping of the Pollio Monument and the neighbouring apsidal fountain (plan 5 nos. 16f. – further fountains are nos. 18f.). As to be shown in the following sub-chapter, no new intramural tombs were built in these 30 years, as if the Temple of the Divine Emperors on its high terrace should not be impurified by the shadows of death.[9]

During the Trajanic period, there was a significant resurgence in building activity, especially along the middle and northern side of the Embolos. Notable structures that were constructed during this time include the Nymphaeum Traiani, the Baths of Varius, and the Temple of Hadrian (plan 3 nos. 14f. and 18); the new Triodos was marked with its three-story gate (plan 3 no. 6; plan 4). It appears that Domitian made extensive efforts to prioritise his building programme over the previously established cult centre of Augustus (often referred to as the State Agora). However, following Domitian's downfall, the local authorities reverted to the previous policy and continued to enhance the Embolos as the main axis connecting the lower and upper quarters of the city. This involved the construction of various honorific monuments such as temples, fountains, baths, libraries, and tombs.

2. The honorific tombs on the Embolos

A new tradition, that of intramural honorific tombs,[10] began at Ephesos in the area of the Embolos with the Octagon (plan 3 no. 10), the Memmius Monument (plan 3 no. 21), and the Circular Monument on the Panayırdağ (plan 1 no. 34). Based on our current state of knowledge, we cannot determine which of the three tomb buildings is the oldest. All of them in any event belong, from an architectural and technical viewpoint, to the Augustan period.

Arsinoë IV was murdered in 41 BC. As has been outlined above, a building of this quality and at this prominent location was not possible before the Battle of Actium. The fact that it then took at least 25 years until the completion of the tomb monument is rather a question of priorities, yet also of the available finances and capacities of the architectural workshops. This may well apply to the other grave monuments as well. We can indeed date the Memmius Monument to after 34 BC, if, in fact, it was intended for the *consul suffectus* of that year. The decoration of the monument, with the figures wearing togas and Greek mantles, could have been influenced by the Zoilos Monument at Aphrodisias (or the other way round?). In that case, then, the beginning of the construction would rather be in the 20s BC, to the time in which Memmius was perhaps active in an official function in Ephesos, if he was not one of the Roman citizens killed in the Artemision during the civil wars. For the Circular Building on the Panayırdağ, due to the lack of pertinent evidence, any association with a particular individual and therefore a historical classification is superfluous. In any event, all three buildings locate close together chronologically and, due to their similarities, were perhaps erected by a single workshop. If this were the case, a relative chronology would then not apply, especially as one and the same building workshop did not require any lead time in order to employ one element of a structure – for example the filling decoration of the cassettes with vegetal decoration at the Octagon and the Circular Monument – at another building. One can state with a degree of certainty that these three tomb buildings therefore created a foundation to develop the Embolos – in addition to its other functions – as the intramural 'heroic region', and therefore to emphasise its significance as a site of civic history.

The oldest intramural tombs in Ephesos, the Octagon
and the Memmius Monument connected the great Greek history
of Ephesos with an expected superb future under Roman rule.

All three monuments must have related to foreign individuals of exceptionally high status, whose significance for the city we can nevertheless only reproduce with Arsinoë IV who fled for shelter in the Artemision. The choice of her (secondary) burial site was connected on the one hand with her origin as a Ptolemaic princess and her role as short-lived Queen of Alexandria and Cyprus, and on the other hand with the proximity of the tomb to the altar of the Amazons, which ought to document the inviolability of the right of *asylum*. This *asylum* occurred not only under the protection of Artemis Ephesia, but above all in the now new, secure, and permanently organised conditions of the *pax Augusta*.[11] The choice for the place of the Memmius Monument immediately at the corner of the Augustan cult area may underline such thoughts, especially if – as the appearance of the woollen threads (στέμματα or κληῖδες) of Artemis strongly suggest – he had been a seeker of *asylum* too.

In this respect, the Hexagon (plan 3 no. 11) was probably planned at the same time as the Octagon and the Memmius Monument; while these tomb structures can be understood both as symbols for the closure of the precarious, late Republican–Hellenistic world of states, the Hexagon marks the new beginning of the Imperium Romanum, now comprising the entire Mediterranean world and under the leadership of the Julian dynasty. In all three monuments, however, elements are incorporated that can be related to Artemis and Apollon and that express the divine protection of this new order in city and empire.

The intramural tombs eternalised the glory of heroes,
rulers, sophists, and outstanding benefactors –
and thus of the city itself.

This affinity to the Amazon altar of Artemis Soteira, who watches over her citizens in life as well as in death,[12] can also be demonstrated at the other, partly only slightly younger, tombs of Greek individuals.[13] Both the Circular Tomb on the Bülbüldağ (plan 1 no. 70) as well as the tombs (which cannot be verified with absolute certainty; see plan 3 and fig. 64) of the benefactors of the South Gate, Mazaios and Mithridates, were erected to incorporate sarcophagus burials, even if at the South Gate, secondarily to Hellenic identity, Roman citizenship via *manumissio* is evident.[14] The same holds even more true for the next generations. Inhumation burial was practised by the family in the tomb chamber under the southern end of the Neronian Hall, by C. Iulius Celsus Polemaeanus, by Tib. Claudius Aristion as well as by the Sophists T. Claudius Flavianus Dionysius and T. Flavius Hypsikles in the 2nd c. AD. Even though all of these – who in part held high and the highest functions – ostensibly placed Roman citizenship on view, they nevertheless retained the burial ritual of the Greeks; such claims for a double identity have already been described convincingly by Greg Woolf on a general level.[15] Nevertheless, for the later tombs of this group, it needs to be noted that in the 2nd c. AD cremation had also broadly fallen out of fashion even in Rome, and with the general attitude of *paideia* and the Second Sophistic with classical Athens as the ideal of a city[16], inhumation burial in sarcophagi became increasingly popular.

In contrast, the typical Roman tomb monuments of the early imperial period, which were intended for urn burials – the Memmius Monument, the Circular Monument on the Panayırdağ, and the Pollio Monument which is one or two generations later – took up their positions at the upper termination of the Embolos, near the newly erected imperial cult centre.[17] In addition to the differing burial ritual, a topographical distance also existed, one which has not yet been remarked upon in the scholarly literature. Then again, Memmius as well as Pollio refrained from mentioning in their tomb inscriptions their merits regarding the empire and the city; they represent themselves almost as private individuals. Memmius only mentions in a conspicuous manner his maternal grandfather, L. Cornelius Sulla. In this manner, their tombs are also far removed from a purely Roman perspective.

With regard to the intramural burial region on the Embolos, we can state that very different people or groups of people, based on apparently very differing motives, found their burial place here. Although individual burials dominate, family vaults also existed at the Round Monument on the Bülbüldağ and the chamber beneath the Neronian Hall. In many cases, a clear connection to generous building activities can be determined, or tomb and building structure are more or less connected. This is particularly true for the South Gate, the Neronian Hall, and the Library of Celsus. Less straightforward is the structural connection for the Pollio building and the tomb of Aristion, even if we can reconstruct the enormous building activities of both individuals from other sources. For Memmius, one could at best think of the endowment of the nymphaeum directly to the west of this tomb as a point of connection. In this case, we could here imagine a fine contrast to his grandfather, who devastated Ephesos and robbed it of its freedom, with the life-giving water supply by the grandson as a gesture of reconciliation. For the other tombs in contrast, beginning with the Octagon, the circular buildings on the Panayırdağ and the Bülbüldağ, up to the tombs of the Sophists from the 2nd c. AD, no connection to building donations can be ascertained at all, even if these – with the exception of the Octagon – also cannot be ruled out. In these cases, it was most likely the personalities and their living conditions – the princess who was not protected by the Ephesians on the one, the Sophists who who had given Ephesos the honour of their chosen place of residence on the other hand – that provided the impetus for burial within the city.

In conclusion, the conjecture may be made, even if it cannot be supported by the archaeological and historical evidence, that it can only have been the deliberate interment of Arsinoë IV that led to the grave precinct on the Embolos. Her murder in 41 BC and provisional burial will have become an issue at the latest during the sojourn of Octavian in Ephesos in the winter of 30/29 BC. The idea of erecting an honorific tomb for her near to the Triodos and amidst the monuments of her ancestors was perhaps the initial impetus, at least, however, part of a comprehensive building programme in honour of the new world ruler Octavian. In this fashion, the city paid its debt, re-established the reputation of the Artemision as a space of *asylum*, and exalted the rule of the young Roman as conqueror of internal and external wars. The roughly contemporary tomb buildings on the upper Embolos may have been planned from the beginning as equivalences in the sense of the integration of the city into the Roman dominion,[18] yet could also have equally arisen ad hoc, as a response to the deaths of high-ranking Roman personalities.

The fact that the Arsinoë monument received no inscription, and therefore was not expressly indicated as a contemporary tomb, may well be related to the intention that it should be viewed rather as a heroon, connected with the history of the city, than as a simple site of burial, similarly to the way in which the neighbouring Androkloneion or Hypelaion was reminiscent of the mythical founder (and possibly also of Lysimachos) without housing the physical remains of either of these founding figures.[19] On the other hand, contemporary people would easily have been able to recognise the hints in architecture and decoration pointing to a grave, most noticeable among those the inaccessible bench high up on the podium or the fictitious door.[20]

3. The Embolos and the water supply of the city

From the very beginning, the Embolos was closely connected with the water supply of the city. This circumstance was already evident with the prominent position of the city spring of Hypelaios near the Triodos (plan 3 no. 9), which together constitute the imagined city centre. The Ptolemaic fountain (plan 3 no. 12) in the immediate proximity was yet another structure, very probably dating to the 3rd c. BC, which provided water primarily for the garrison stationed on the Akra, but also for travellers arriving from the east and the south; this fountain would have been the first that was encountered on the developed border of the city at that time. This nymphaeum therefore rivalled the older Hypelaios Spring, and emphasised the nurturing role of the Lagid dynasty for Ephesos. The Augustan long-distance aqueducts and their associated fountains, the water feature of the *Aqua Iulia* at the lower Embolos and the Pollio nymphaeum as well as the fountain near the Memmius Monument, fed by the *Aqua Throessitica*, at the upper Embolos, marginalised the significance of the older fountain buildings in a propagandistic as well as a functional manner. This aspect was even more strongly accentuated under Domitian: in addition to the Hydrekdocheion already built under Titus (plan 5 no. 18), Domitian caused three more fountains on the South Street, at the State Agora (Fountain of Domitian on top of the Pollio building, plan 5 no. 16), and at the so-called Domitian Lane (Apsidal Fountain, this being possibly only newly adapted, plan 5 no. 17). From these structures, the best view of the new provincial temple was also possible. Aristion, already during the reign of Trajan, had erected the modernly named Street Fountain a little further along in the direction of the Magnesian Gate (plan 1 no. 15), and therefore placed this emperor in the spotlight, ahead of Domitian, for new arrivals coming in from the country. His second fountain, the Nymphaeum Traiani in the middle of the Embolos (plan 3 no. 18), was substantially more elaborately furnished.[21] In addition to the provision of drinking water at the Embolos, the Roman bathing culture was also introduced here with the adjacent Varius Baths for the public. In spite of this astounding density of fountain houses, the fact that the Severans also set up a monument with the extension of the Hydreion (plan 3 no. 20) in front of the Memmius Monument is significant. In the late 1st c. AD the Embolos had probably attained an empire-wide exemplary effect for the representation of the emperor as benefactor of water.[22] In any event – at least in Ephesos – since Lysimachos the construction of fountains allowed the respective ruler to attain the similar status of a ktistes. The fact that private individuals such as Sextilius Pollio and Claudius Aristion financed the aqueducts and/or nymphaea, acquired a great reputation as *euergetes*, and therefore could virtually receive the promise of a heroic tomb, has been understood for a long time. Apparently, however, this was not the only possibility to obtain such honours.

Supplying a city with fresh water signified a major quality of a ruler.

In a distinctive manner, during the reconstruction of the now Christian city, after one or more earthquakes, under Emperor Constantius II and his brother Constans (d. 350), and probably also at a later date, the Embolos was provided anew with a dense row of fountains, although the focal point of civic life had long since been transferred to the harbour plain around the council church dedicated to St. Mary (Theodokos) in the southern colonnade of the former Hadrianic Olympieion (plan 1, nos. 95 and 98). The façade of the Library of Celsus henceforth served as a rear wall of a fountain erected on the staircase. For these and many other fountain buildings, which were probably all fed by the repaired Domitianic Marnas aqueduct, the reliefs of the so-called Parthian Monument provided a marvellous fountain border. The Hypelaios Spring also received a new border with barrier plaques bearing Christian connotations, for which reason it is known in the literature also as the Byzantine fountain. In addition, a new fountain house (plan 3 no. 11, covering the Augustan hexagon) was laid out directly next to the abandoned Ptolemaic nymphaeum. The power of tradition operated here far beyond the actual water requirements, up until the demise of the city in the early 7th c. AD.

4. Artemis and the power of myths

More than 30 years ago, G. Rogers attempted to understand the procession of the ephebes, described in the endowment of Roman knight Vibius Salutaris of the year 104/105 AD, as a guide to the walking through of a historical city plan of Ephesos under the auspices of Artemis Ephesia.[23] Since then, our knowledge of the architectural history of the Embolos has substantially increased, so that his fundamentally convincing approach is today much more nuanced and can also be modified.

The Hellenistic refounder Lysimachos
earned a place among the heroes and heroines of the Embolos
(G. Rogers 1991).

Rogers, however, took the perspective of the early 2nd c. AD as a starting point, instead of recognising the continuous accumulation of monuments in the city, and in particular on the Embolos over the 400 years between Lysimachos and Trajan, as the factual background which first enabled such a retrospective viewpoint at all.[24] Naturally, with Salutaris the Ephesians sought appropriate versions from history for the situation in the 2nd c. AD, and thereby made use of existing monuments as historically illustrative material.[25] These buildings, however, must have been available and must have emanated meaning, whereas others, having become unimportant, had perhaps been long abandoned and replaced by new buildings or rededications, or had also become insignificant for the contemporary conception of history. Adaptions like the rebuilding of the Ptolemaic fountain – a dynasty no longer of importance or significance in the historical consideration – on the Embolos could now equally refer to Hadrian; similarly, the Domitianic rebuilding of the Attalid fountain house at the theatre also drew attention to this Flavian emperor.

The birth of Artemis in Ortygia symbolised the eternal renewal of the city from generation to generation.

Rogers is completely correct in emphasising the birth of Artemis at Ortygia as the starting point, causative for everything else, for the sacred identity and the history of the city. Against this cosmic experience, all of the other mythical and real founders of the city – the Amazons, Androklos, Lysimachos, and finally Augustus – must have felt themselves to be implements of divine will, who could only carry out their deeds with the goodwill of the goddess.[26]

The collocation of the statues mentioned in Salutaris´ donation, brought in procession to the theatre and set up near the seats of the individual groups, conveys this dominance of Artemis, with a total of nine statues. In addition to Trajan and his wife Plotina, Androklos (phyle of the Karenaioi), Euonymos (as eponymous hero of the phyle of the Euonymoi) who had discovered the marble quarry for the construction of the Artemision, Lysimachos (symbolising the phyle of the Teians, probably founded by him), and Augustus (as hero of the phyle Sebaste), that is, exclusively founding heroes (κτίστεις) are featured as historical figures in the endowment. The Demos (phyle of the Epheseis) and Mt. Pion (phyle of the Bembinaioi) stand for the remaining lines in the population. The Roman social order is juxtaposed with the Ephesian: senatus versus boule, *populus Romanus* versus gerousia, *ordo equester* versus ephebes.[27] In anticipation of the ten-years younger little temple (of Trajan/Hadrian) on the Embolos, the concept of whose accoutrements may very well have already been raised, one could formulate the conclusion as follows: under the leadership of Trajan, the divinely willed world fate (Artemis as mistress of the city and the world) was accomplished; the earlier heroes and rulers contributed to this salvation, yet nevertheless pale in comparison to Trajan, similarly to the way in which the Old Testament prophets appear pale in comparison to the Messiah in the New Testament, which arose at approximately the same time period.

It was not only the rulers, however, who built up the city and promoted its development. High-ranking Romans, *proconsules Asiae* and other senators (early on perhaps C. Memmius and later C. Iulius Celsus Polemaeanus), and the members of the *conventus civium Romanorum* who lived and operated in Ephesos (such as, e.g., C. Sextilius Pollio) or imperial freedmen (like Mazaios and Mithridates) also acted as patrons. In the Augustan and Tiberian epoch, the members of the local élites (for example the Passalas family) only by way of exception played a role. After the dissemination of Roman citizenship amongst these old Ephesian families in the Claudian–Neronian and above all the Flavian period, they increasingly emerge as main sponsors of munificence (above all, Tib. Claudius Aristion); in the early 2nd c. AD they become related by marriage with the senatorial aristocracy or then join this social class themselves (such as the Vedii). In the mid–2nd c. AD, these benefactors of urban munificence can then even be identified as ktisteis.

Many of these generous benefactors sought the proximity of the fostering and protecting mistress of the city, the omnipotent Artemis Ephesia, for their magnificent and functional buildings and then also for their tomb monuments – the sites of the Amazon altar, the Triodos, and the Processional Way. They also desired the proximity of the mythical or historical founding heroes such as Androklos or Lysimachos, with whom they were (almost) on a par. Through these spatial connections, they participated, indirectly, in the religious rituals and ceremonies connected with the divinity and the founding heroes, rites which were closely linked with social events (financial donations, free meals, games, etc.). Some of these individuals were documented, mostly in testamentary manner, as "perpetual gymnasiarchs" or "perpetual agonothetes", or, as Celsus with his long-term provision of books, took care that their names would be recorded in these civic festivals and procedures long after their own deaths. The *paideia* of the Second Sophistic encouraged these heroic attitudes, integrated the regional economic-political (building contractors) and spiritual (Sophists) élites into the glorious history of the city, and ultimately made them a part of it.

"The cosmos of antique monuments and their images
is more than their impact on the viewer: it is the order of life itself."
(variation after Hölscher 2012)

In this way, within the built-up city, the Triodos with the altar and cult statue of Artemis becomes the starting point and most distinguished site (τὸ κυριώτατον in Philostratos). Here, Androklos can find the water source and the boar, here the Amazons can seek protection, here Lysimachos can lay out the new city, and from here Augustus develops a new street system[28] in the former marine region and expands the city borders. Although the individual myths independently appeared next to each other up until the 1st c. AD, in the Trajanic period, with the Salutaris endowment and the images in the little temple on the Embolos, the entire mythology of the city and its actual history, under the auspices of Artemis and of the emperor, were syncretistically woven into a common net which was meaningful on many levels. The buildings and monuments with all their statuaries and reliefs at the Triodos and along the Embolos worked as "topographems", as witnesses of local history,[29] and thus formed the guarantee for the fortune of Ephesos, or as T. Hölscher expresses it:[30] the monuments and their "images were more than target-oriented messages from certain authors/emitters to certain recipients. They built worlds of meaningful pictures in which people could arrange their lives, and from which they could deduce their criteria of life. The cosmos of antique images is more than their impact on the viewer: it is the order of life itself."

The power of this idea persisted into Late Antiquity, also after the Christian Demeas (in the later 4th c. AD) had dragged down the demon Artemis from the altar and replaced it with the cross of Christ. An existence of the city without the powerful location of the Triodos seemed unthinkable. From here, life-giving water was drawn, here all of the heroes and rulers of the past began their actions for the building or expansion of the city, here the most important individuals of the city's history were buried and their spirits protected the living. One of these figures of identification was Arsinoë IV, and in the terms of J. Assmann her grave constituted the caesura between the glorious Helleni(sti)c past and the imperial Roman present.[31]

In search of the skull from the Octagon

1. A skull lost

Without exception, all available evidence regarding the Ephesian Octagon supports Hilke Thür's[1] suggestion that it was built as the mausoleum for the Alexandrian *puella*–Queen Arsinoë IV, youngest child of the Macedonian–Egyptian Pharaoh Ptolemaios XII. As a consequence, Ephesos has probably retained the only known Ptolemaic gravesite. Its osseous remains should therefore offer the unique opportunity to secure DNA from a Lagid family member. Yet repeated efforts have so far failed to draw sufficient samples from the postcranial skeleton.[2] Not only for this reason alone, the obvious task presented itself to investigate the whereabouts of the skull from the Octagon, which has been considered lost for decades.[3] The possibility of completing a royal Ptolemaic skeleton was reason enough to search for the bone. Since the skull has been sought repeatedly in the past,[4] we tried to understand under which conditions it vanished.

> SINCE THE OCTAGON WAS PROBABLY BUILT AS THE MAUSOLEUM FOR ARSINOË IV OF ALEXANDRIA, ITS SKULL MAY PROVIDE THE OPPORTUNITY TO SECURE PTOLEMAIC DNA.

1.1 A ghost–skull

When Josef Keil[5] (fig. 79) confirmed his suspicion concerning the funeral character of the Ephesian Octagon in 1929,[6] he wondered to whom such idiosyncratic "heroon" at this outstanding urban location might have been dedicated.[7] Very likely due to this supposition, he removed the skull from the tomb's sarcophagus to investigate the interred individual at the University of Greifswald, Germany, where he was professor at that time.[8] When he reported the outcome in 1930, Keil remained vague as to who delivered the expertise,[9] a fact that suggests a somewhat informal assessment.

One might think, however, that Keil initially asked for such an opinion in Vienna, Austria, and that Greifswald was only his second choice. At that time, Josef Weninger (fig. 77) was head of the Anthropological Institute of the University of Vienna.[10] His scientific interest in 1929 and beforehand focussed on a different field of research.[11] From 1918 onwards, his list of publications hardly contains any publication that deals with skeletal material from excavations.[12] In line with that, Weninger would have declined Keil's request which probably explains why he had to turn elsewhere. Still, Weninger may have informed Keil about Guenther Just at the University of Greifswald,[13] since the latter had just become the head of the newly founded "Abteilung für Vererbungswissenschaft" ('Department of Heredity') of its Biological Institute, and he in fact may well have been one of the "Greifswalder colleagues" to whom Keil refers.[14]

Nonetheless, Weninger dealt with the Ephesian bone at a later date. Seemingly out of nowhere, he published it in an article almost 25 years after its discovery. At that point, the skull from the Octagon vanished, making Weninger the last person who had documented access to it.[15] Accordingly, we proceeded in our enquiry from his article in order

Fig. 77: Josef Weninger (24.12.1941)

> ➢ To understand the circumstances of his dealing with the skull and, based on that,
> ➢ To develop an idea where it may have subsequently disappeared.

IN 1953, WENINGER WAS THE LAST PERSON WHO HAD DOCUMENTED ACCESS TO THE SKULL FROM THE OCTAGON.

1.2 A strange article

In 1953, Weninger published the skull from the Octagon in a somewhat peculiar article. On the one hand, he did not submit the text to an anthropological or archaeological journal, but contributed it to a Festschrift printed in the Austrian province of Carinthia[16] perhaps preferring a marginal setting for it.[17] Curiously, he saw it necessary to "justify" the examination.[18] Most interestingly though, he failed to provide any background details regarding his dealing with the Ephesian bone.

Weninger's article comes across as a straightforward narrative, as if it had simply been compiled from certain source texts. The first pages of the article are filled with the entire excavation report of the Octagon from 1930 including the footnotes,[19] in which Keil expresses his curiosity concerning the tomb's owner. Weninger proceeds with an examination protocol of the Ephesian skull consisting of altogether ninety measurements and quotients, thereby following the numbers of Martin's anthropological textbook[20] which aimed to characterise certain morphologies by means of 'objective' values in line with the concept of "physical anthropology".[21] Upon linking the skull to a second one that was found in Carnuntum, Lower Austria, in 1944 and that was allocated to him by Rudolf Egger (figs. 78f.),[22]

Tab. 4: Proponents
in the field of
Ancient Studies
in relation to the
German–national-
ist VKPW between
1924 and 1933
and to the NSDAP
(tab. 7)

Weninger attributes both to "a refined specialised type of the ancient high culture world" being the result of "domestication".[23] With such an understanding of the skull, he finally returns to Keil's report and concludes with the "confirmation of the archaeologist's [i.e. Keil's] assumption", whereby the Octagon's owner "must have been a very distinguished personality".[24]

Name, dates	Source	NSDAP registration #
Betz, Artur (1905–1985)	MittVKPW II, 1925, 3 ("Neu aufgenommen")	–
Braun, Egon (1906–1993)	MittVKPW III, 1926, 5 ("Neu aufgenommen"); MittVKPW VII, 1930, 73 ("Obmannstellvertreter")	268.669
Egger, Rudolf (1882–1969)	MittVKPW I, 1924, 5	6.125.243
Hierath, Melanie (1912–1998)	MittVKPW IX, 1932, 111 ("Aktive")	–
Keil, Josef (1878–1963)	MittVKPW I, 1924, 5f	–
Kenner, Hedwig (1910–1993)	MittVKPW VII, 1930, 73 ("Neu aufgenommen")[26]	6.282.734
Lesky, Albin (1896–1981)	MittVKPW II, 1925, 3 ("Gönner")	7.252.762
Meister, Richard (1881–1964)	MittVKPW I, 1924, 5f	–
Miltner, Franz (1901–1959)	MittVKPW I, 1924, 5 ("Obmann"); MittVKPW V, 1928, V ("Alter Herr")	6.257.215
Miltner, Helene (1904–1999)	MittVKPW VI, 1929, 8 ("Gönner")	7.886.006
Noll, Rudolf (1906–1990)	MittVKPW IV, 1927, 5 ("Neu aufgenommen")	6.127.590
Petrikovits, Harald von (1911–2010)	MittVKPW VII, 1930, 73 ("Neu aufgenommen"); MittVKPW VIII, 1931, 99 ("Obmann" after Miltner)	512.321
Praschniker, Camillo (1884–1949)	MittVKPW V, 1928	Application retracted
Reisch, Emil (1863–1933)	MittVKPW II, 1925, 3	† 1933
Saria, Balduin (1893–1974)	MittVKPW I, 1924, 7[27]	10.161.666
Schachermeyr, Fritz (1895–1987)	–	4.586.961
Schober, Arnold (1886–1959)	MittVKPW VII, 1930, 73 ("Gönner")	6.288.962
Swoboda, Erich (1896–1964)	Swoboda 1932	–
Vetters, Hermann jun. (1915–1993)	–	6.294.086

Beyond that, no more information is gained from the text so that Weninger appears reluctant to outline its framework, for which he ought to have had a reason. In particular, he does not reveal

- ➢ How the skull from the Octagon came into his hands in the first place, nor
- ➢ When and where he examined it.

Still, one may deduce that Weninger's unusual occupation with the skull

- ➢ Focuses on J. Keil as its background and
- ➢ Connects him to R. Egger as the mandating authority regarding the skeleton from Carnuntum, and in this manner
- ➢ Leads back into the pre–1945 years.

In view of that, Weninger's article on the skull from the Octagon seems to reflect certain time–dependent Austrian conditions, politically as well as academically, and it might find an explanation from such perspective. Since Camillo Praschniker, Rudolf Egger and Josef Keil were the leading figures in Ancient Studies in Vienna in the 1930s and the 1940s,[25] we commence our considerations with them.

WENINGER'S OCCUPATION WITH THE EPHESIAN SKULL FROM 1953 SEEMS TO LEAD BACK TO THE TIME BEFORE 1945.

1.3 A "triumvirate"

Praschniker,[28] Egger,[29] and Keil[30] (tab. 6) developed their careers in the interwar period of the 1920s and 1930s[31] at the 'Archäologisch–Epigraphisches Seminar' (AES)[32] of the University of Vienna (UoV) and at the Austrian Archaeological Institute (OeAI). They were students of AES professor and OeAI Director Emil Reisch,[33] whom they followed to the 'Verein Klassischer Philologen in Wien' (VKPW).[34] Tab. 4 provides an incomplete list of its participants, many of whom joined the 'National Socialist German Worker's Party' (NSDAP)[35] later on. All three were "secretaries" at the OeAI (Keil since 1904,[36] Egger and Praschniker since 1912[37]). By 1920, they were academic teachers and by 1925 professors.[38] They were members of the 'Viennese Academy of Sciences' (VAS)[39] which was renamed as the 'Austrian Academy of Sciences' (AAS) after 1945.[40] From 1935 onwards, Praschniker and Egger held the Co–Directorate of the OeAI and remained in this position also after 1938,[41] i.e. within the 'Zweigstelle Wien des Archäologischen Instituts des Deutschen Reichs' ('Viennese branch of the Archaeological Institute of the German Reich').[42] Whereas Praschniker and Keil left Austria for some time,[43] Egger always stayed in the country.[44]

A. Betz (tab. 4) addresses the era of the "triumvirate Egger, Keil, and Praschniker" in retrospect as "especially happy",[45] as does H. Kenner ("harmonious, happy").[46]

H. Vetters calls them the "triple star",[47] and F. Schachermeyr "old friends".[48] Likewise, Keil perceived "three friends [...] in almost ideal cooperation".[49] More austerely, F. Eichler described the "friendship [as] profitable".[50] Sometimes, the troika is addressed as the "Wiener Schule" ("Viennese School").[51]

Still, the trinity does not appear as homogeneous as such characterisations may suggest. In particular, the "noble men"[52] Praschniker and Egger seem to have been connected by some kind of relationship. According to Kenner, Praschniker was "in his subtle, artistic manner a counterpart and at the same time a complement to Rudolf Egger's more alpine, folk–like nature".[53] Keil even calls Egger the "personal aide" of Praschniker,[54] a statement setting him somewhat apart from the "complementary" duo. Seemingly in line with that, Praschniker followed Egger in his inclination towards NSDAP membership after Austria's 'Anschluß' ('annexation') to the 'German Reich' in 1938, whereas Keil did not join. In 1942, Praschniker and Egger had no reservations about taking "board and lodging"[55] in an NS–extermination camp which was under order of the infamous SS Hauptsturmführer Karl Chmielewski, the 'devil of Gusen' (fig. 78).[57]

> Dear Mr. Camp Leader! [...]. I therefore register my colleague, Prof. Praschniker, and myself for Friday 30 October [1942] afternoon. We would avail ourselves of your kindness for one night. [...]. With thanks in advance and Heil Hitler![58]

With the end of WW II, the reign of the "triumvirate" ended. Whereas Keil was able to resume his career as an academic bureaucrat, Egger was removed from the UoV and the OeAI, although he remained within the Academy. Praschniker died in 1949. When the 'Wiener Universitätszeitung' ('University of Vienna newspaper') reported on the memorial service for Praschniker held by the UoV, it no longer mentioned his "personal aid"[59] Egger. Instead Keil is now called "the closest colleague of the immortalised scholar".[60]

1.3.1 Camillo Praschniker (1884–1949) – an "immortalised scholar"

Camillo (Kamillo) Praschniker[61] (fig. 80; tab. 6) was Professor for Classical Archaeology at the AES of the UoV.[62] In 1932, he became a member of the VAS,[63] and in 1935 Co–Director of the OeAI along with Egger.[64] He took part in the Ephesian excavations in 1933 and 1935.[65]

Shortly after Austria's 'Anschluß' to the German Reich in March 1938, Praschniker confessed doubts regarding his Aryanism in a "questionnaire" from 08.05.1938.[66] He informed the Dean of the UoV, Viktor Christian,[67] of the "misfortune" and wrote an unsent letter to Adolf Hitler.

```
Mein Führer [...]. I have been struck by the mis-
fortune [...] to recently come to the painful real-
isation that my maternal grandmother [...] was of
Jewish descent.[68]
```

Being in this manner a "Jewish crossbreed of 2nd degree" ("jüdischer Mischling zweiten Grades"),[69] Praschniker came under pressure.[70] He "could not believe it".[71] He finally withdrew his application for NSDAP membership.[72] "In view of his scientific probation and his loyal attitude to National Socialism",[73] he was nevertheless allowed to retain his positions.

Avoiding any mention of his "Jewish grandmother",[74] he stated on record after 1945 that he had indeed applied for party membership, but that he had retracted it, having reached an "ever stronger opposition to the ideology of the NSDAP".[75] For the second time, Praschniker was classified as "tolerable".[76] He was allowed to retain his chairs at the University, the OeAI and at the AAS after a short period of segregation.[77] Concomitantly though, Praschniker had to notify previous NSDAP members or aspirants among the OeAI–staff of their (provisional) dismissal.[78] Later on, Egger said that Praschniker had "never lost his dignity, but walked uprightly his way through all the turmoil".[79] More factually, G. Wlach summarises: "His conduct during the Nazi era, as far as it can be reconstructed today from the sources, was characterised by caution, timidity and opportunism – qualities that were probably even more accentuated by the additional pressure".[80]

Praschniker is the only one of the "triumvirate" who was never addressed as 'Nestor'[81] of something according to our knowledge. Somewhat condescendingly, Egger emphasised the fascination he emitted for "housewives".[82] Praschniker died in 1949 from a kidney disorder at the age of 65 years.[83] He was buried as an "eminent personality" ("Bedeutende Persönlichkeit") in the 'Grinzinger Friedhof', Vienna, group 13, row 5, number 6.[84] Several obituaries paid tribute to his departure.[85] An issue of the annual journal of the OeAI (JOeAI) was dedicated to him in 1952.[86] In 1954, an alley was named after him in the 21st district of Vienna ('Praschnikerweg').[87] On the initiative of Hedwig Kenner (fig. 80) with, however, some curious reasoning ("difficult work [on the metopes of the Parthenon] from a swaying ladder"), Praschniker's name was inscribed in the 'Roll of Honour' of the Philosophical Faculty at the UoV in 1980,[88] where it is read until to–day.

1.3.2 Rudolf Egger (1882–1969) – "praeceptor Austriae"

Rudolf Egger[89] (figs. 78f.; tab. 6) was Professor for 'Römische Geschichte, Altertumskunde und Epigraphik' at UoV[90] since 1924[91] and a member of the VAS[92] from 1929. He was Co–Director of the OeAI together with C. Praschniker from 1935 onwards[93] with Austria Romana and the Balkans as his areas of interest.[94]

With the "annexation of the Ostmark to the Great German Reich",[95] Egger applied for membership in the NSDAP.[96] In his "questionnaire" from 07.05.1938, he stated that he had already (provisionally) entered the party as of 01.01.1938 due to his membership within the 'NS–Lehrerbund' ('NS–teachers association', NSLB).[97] Yet he received definitive NSDAP membership only in 1940.[98] In retrospect, Egger was characterised as a "politically moderately engaged historian"[99] or simply as a "naïve opportunist".[100] Pesditschek questions his National Socialist creed altogether.[101] Pfefferle – Pfefferle even doubt that Egger "deserved" being released from the UoV after 1945.[102] Upon closer inspection, however, one might draw different conclusions.

Between the World Wars, Egger was deeply rooted in various groups of the Austrian "Anschlußbewegung" ('annexation movement').[103] He was active within the VKPW (tab. 4) and belonged to the German–nationalist and anti–Semitic 'Deutsche Gemeinschaft' ('German Society').[104] In 1934, he was elected into the 'Südostdeutsche Forschungsgemeinschaft Wien' ('Southeast German Research Association Vienna'),[105] which was later "a significant factor in the National Socialist policy of ethnicity and extermination in South–Eastern Europe".[106] Quite in line with that, Egger was to become what was called an "illegal"(?) and an "energetic" party comrade.[107] The 'Deutsches Volksbildungswerk' ('German People's Education Association')[108] confirmed his National Socialist attitude.[109] His reputation was such that even the 'SS–Ahnenerbe'[110] contemplated asking his advice[111] concerning where, for example, the outstanding NSDAP members Oswald Menghin[112] and Viktor Christian[113] belonged.[114]

After 1945, Egger tried to trivialise his NSDAP membership by saying that "he had only joined the party so that the OeAI [...] could provide the "operations manager" at the excavations in Carnuntum" ("Führergrabung")[115] thus promoting an administrative reason alone. Instead, he stressed his Austrianism quite in keeping with the new dictum:

> »Looking back over my entire life«, I believe that I am »not an Austrian of mere confession, but one of action«.[116]

Still, Egger was finally dismissed from his duties at the UoV and at the OeAI.[117] He retired to the Austrian province of Carinthia.[118] He became the "Lord of the Magdalensberg"[119] where "he found the glory, he saw beckoning in Carnuntum"[120] and was allowed to expand on his crude theories.[121] Describing Egger's subsequent years, Betz[122] quotes M.T. Cicero's "otium cum dignitate" ("leisure in dignity").[123] In 1952, Egger celebrated his 70th birthday and this year marked his rehabilitation. He returned to the OeAI, now as its 'member of honour'.[124]

Egger received three commemorative publications to mark his 60th, 70th and 80th birthday in 1942,[125] 1952/54[126] and 1962/63.[127] He was named "Nestor of Austrian Ancient Studies",[128] "Nestor of research into the ancient, especially Roman history of Carinthia",[129] the "grand old man of Austrian Ancient Studies",[130] "one of the most important and successful representatives of the Wiener Schule",[131] and even "praeceptor Austriae".[132] He was honoured with rings, badges, and crosses as well as some medal.[133] In 1969, Egger died at the age of 87.[134] Several obituaries were published.[135] He is the only one of the triumvirate who was buried in a 'grave of honour' in the Viennese 'Zentralfriedhof', group 40, number 10.[136] No Viennese street is named after him.

1.3.3 Josef Keil (1878–1963) – "Nestor of Austrian Ephesos research"

Josef Keil[137] (figs. 79, 82; tab. 6) became "Institutssecretär" at the OeAI–branch of Smyrna in 1904.[138] In this position, he participated in all Ephesian campaigns until 1913,[139] i.e. Ephesos became the focus of his scientific interest.[140] It has been stated repeatedly that "Keil succeeded in resuming the excavations in Ephesos" in 1926, i.e. after World War I.[141] Yet, such merit is rather earned by the German theologian and philologist Gustav Adolf Deißmann (1866–1937; fig. 79a)[147] whose tireless efforts to raise funds for the continuation of the Ephesian project[148] at a crucial time, when the remains of Ephesos were in danger of being completely destroyed,[149] are some-

Fig. 79: a) Ephesos 1926 with the "Bohemian"[142] Franz Milter, the fund raiser G. A. Deißmann, the director of the excavations J. Keil, the Turkish Inspector General of Antiquities A. Aziz,[143] and the architect M. Theuer (from left to right).[144] b) Carnuntum 1939: H. Vetters, ?, G. Pascher,[145] R. Egger, and J. Keil (from left to right)[146]

times forgotten.[150] In other words, the interwar excavations in Ephesos including the opening of the Octagon's burial chamber would probably not have eventuated without Deißmann.[151] The enthusiasm of Deißmann for Ephesos can be sensed from an entry, which he wrote into the guestbook of the Austrian excavation house in 1926:

> Ἐν Ἐφέσῳ θύρα γάρ μοι ἀνέῳγεν μεγάλη καὶ ἐνεργής [In Ephesos, a great and powerful door has opened to me].
> With these words written in Ephesos by the Apostle of the peoples [Paulus] (1 Corinthians 16:9), I bid farewell to the Austrian House in Ephesos after six incomparable weeks. The grand door that opened to me in Ephesos led through vast sunlit slopes and through mysteriously dark ravines into the promised land of new learning. It granted me the joyful access to three millennia of Anatolian intellectual life, whose finest arts resonate within our souls. It allowed great thoughts and pious reverence to enter unimpeded. Every time I passed through this door, only kindness and trust of friends flowed towards me.[152]

From 1925, Keil is listed as Professor at the UoV.[153] However, he did not feel sufficiently valued at the institution.[154] Accordingly, he went to Greifswald, Germany, in 1927,[155] where he was considered "the epitome of a graduate of the 'Vienna School of Ancient Studies'".[156] The German–nationalist VKPW dedicated an issue of its 'Mitteilungen' ('Notifications') to him[157] and bade him an emotional farewell:

> In the feeling, however, that Keil in Greifswald as well as in Vienna would be committed to the highest service, the noble service for his own people, the celebration found an atmospheric conclusion in the singing of the Deutschlandlied.[158]

Accordingly, Keil mostly lectured in Greifswald during the time of the interwar excavations in Ephesos[159] and, in particular, when the Octagon's burial chamber was opened and the skull removed in 1929.[160]

In 1936, Keil returned as Professor for 'Griechische Geschichte, Epigraphik und Altertumskunde' to the UoV,[161] a call that was opposed by his predecessor on the chair, Adolf Wilhelm.[162] One year later, he became a member of the VAS.[163] After Austria's annexation by the Third Reich in 1938, Keil never applied for membership in the NSDAP.[164] Accordingly, he was hardly affected by the 'denazification' after 1945.[165] He kept his position at the University and remained within the Academy now as its Secretary General after Ernst Späth (1938–1945).[166] Keil finally succeeded Praschniker as Director of the OeAI in 1949,[167] and with that appointment he finally reached the height of his career, already 71 years of age. At his initiative, the Ephesian excavations recommenced in 1954[168] after an interruption of almost twenty years.

In 1950, Keil retired from the University,[169] in 1956 from the OeAI,[170] and in 1959 from the AAS.[171] An issue of the annual journal of the OeAI (JOeAI) was dedicated to him on the occasion of his 80th birthday.[172] Keil was called the "Nestor of Austrian Ephesos–research".[173] He received a medal (1953), prize (1962), and insignia of honour.[174] In 1963, Keil died at the age of 85.[175] A number of obituaries was published after his death.[176] A commemoration was held on 16.04.1964 by the AAS and the Philosophical Faculty of the UoV[177] where "words of remembrance" were spoken by Fritz Schachermeyr (fig. 83),[178] Fritz Eichler,[179] Richard Meister,[180] and Artur Betz.[181] He was buried as an "eminent personality" in the 'Neustifter Friedhof', Vienna, group E, row 2, number 13.[182] No Viennese street is named after him.

> DURING THE 1930S AND 1940S, THE "TRIUMVIRATE" EGGER, PRASCHNIKER AND KEIL ILLUMINATED ANCIENT STUDIES IN VIENNA.

1.4 Josef Weninger (1886–1959)

Josef Weninger (fig. 77; tab. 6) was an Austrian anthropologist.[183] In 1927, he became the first head of the newly founded Anthropological Institute at the UoV[184] which quickly grew under his chairmanship into the second largest of its kind within German–speaking countries between the two World Wars.[185] In the following years up to 1938, Weninger had no relation to topics of Greco–Roman archaeology[186] or to Ephesos.[187] His field of research was "physical anthropology" in the living.[188] In 1937, he was elected a member of the VAS.[189]

Besides heading the Anthropological Institute of the UoV, Weninger had his "name registered on the roster of judicial experts on human genetics" in 1932.[190] He became a forensic expert in paternity suits.[191] Weninger's expert activities experienced an "unimagined upswing".[192] He provided evidence for around 600 administrative proceedings until 1938.[193] However, his last DFG–application for support regarding a basic research project, also important for his judicial expert opinions, was rejected in 1937 probably due to his marriage.[194]

In 1928, Weninger had married the Jewish Margarete née Taubert (1886–1987, fig. 84),[195] a liaison that became a severe problem with the annexation of Austria to the 'Third Reich' in March 1938.[196] Being of "German Blood" ("Deutschblütig")[197] yet residing in a miscegenation ("Mischehe")[198] with a "fully Jewish" person ("Volljüdin"),[199] Weninger was considered to be "Jewish kin" ("Jüdisch versippt").[200] Nevertheless, he refused to divorce his wife.[201] Already on 03.05.1938, he was suspended.[202] He resigned from his chair at the Anthropological Institute,[203] and he lost his membership at the Academy.[204] After futile attempts to emigrate to Great Britain or the U.S.A. in 1938/39,[205] Weninger was allowed to work due to interventions from colleagues.[206] A set of preserved letters illustrate the events.

In 1940, NSDAP member Viktor Christian[207] was Dean of the Philosophical Faculty at the UoV.[208] He contacted the 'Reichsstatthalter in Niederdonau' Hugo Jury[209] on behalf of the 'causa Weninger'.[210] Jury, for his part, wrote to the 'Reichsminister für Wissenschaft, Erziehung und Volksbildung' Bernhard Rust[211] to Berlin in order to receive permission. On 05.03.1941, Rust approved[212] and Jury forwarded the answer on to Christian. In his letter from 22.03.1941,[213] Jury stated that he had "invited him [i.e. Weninger] to take over the processing of the palaeoanthropological material for the Museum of the Reichsgau Niederdonau and to prepare it for scientific publication".[214] Accordingly, it is stated in the 'memorial book' of the AAS: "In 1941, he [Weninger] was conscripted to work at the museum of the Reichsgau Niederdonau in Vienna, where he worked until March 1945".[215]

These statements indicate that Weninger had to work for the 'Museum of the Reichsgau Niederdonau' (MRGND) from 1941 onwards. At the same time, Weninger "followed an inclination he had been quietly harbouring for years by pursuing interesting constitutional–biological studies at the Institute for Forensic Medicine" in Vienna[216] which was therefore his place of work at that time.

> BEING OF 'JEWISH KIN', WENINGER'S ACADEMIC CAREER WAS ENDED IN 1938 AND REPLACED BY HIS COMMISSION TO THE 'MUSEUM OF THE REICHSGAU NIEDERDONAU' FROM 1941 ONWARDS.

1.5 1944: Keil's skull and Egger's skeleton

Keil's removal of the skull from the Octagon to Greifswald in 1929 had yielded an undocumented sex and age estimation which concluded that the Octagon's owner was a young female "of about 20 years".[217] Nevertheless, Keil wanted a confirmation, as he had already stated in 1930.[218] Accordingly, he may have revisited the issue when a possibility opened up under the specific conditions of German–annexed 'Ostmark'.

After the "Führergrabung" of 1939,[219] OeAI Co–Director Egger had finally received the scientific responsibility over the Roman site of Carnuntum, located on the soil of the 'Reichsgau Niederdonau'.[220] In this position, Egger made use of the newly gained anthropological resources within his sphere.[221] In 1944, he "informed" Weninger that "a well–preserved complete skeleton" had been found in Carnuntum "providing him with the opportunity to recover it",[222] or rather: he ordered him to do so. Since Ephesos was beyond the scope of Egger[223] and Keil was involved in the Carnuntum site at the time (fig. 79b),[224] it is a reasonable assumption that the latter seized the opportunity to have the skull from the Octagon comprehensibly examined. And if Weninger had been in a position to deny Keil's request in 1929, fifteen years later this was no longer the case. He was now obliged to comply. Indeed, the skull may well have been in Keil's hands in 1944, since it is hardly conceivable that he had abandoned it in Greifswald in 1929, as was later believed.[225] Such reasoning may explain

- ➤ Why Weninger examined the skull from the Octagon although it was beyond his interest (because he had to);
- ➤ How he came into possession of the skull (because Keil handed it over to him);
- ➤ Why he later published the skull along with mentioning the one from Carnuntum (because the latter had been the incentive for his examination of the former).

These circumstances suggest that Keil ordered Weninger to "prepare [the Ephesian skull] for scientific publication" in 1944 when the latter had to work for the MRGND. Considering Weninger's oeuvre before 1938 and his obligations after 1945, such a time period and his subaltern position during this specific phase of his life appear to be the most likely reasons for his dealing with the Ephesian bone. The question arises where the skull went subsequently.

> SUPPOSEDLY, WENINGER DEALT WITH THE SKULL FROM THE OCTAGON TOGETHER WITH A SKELETON FROM CARNUNTUM BETWEEN MAY 1944 AND MARCH 1945 WHEN WORKING FOR THE 'MUSEUM OF THE REICHSGAU NIEDERDONAU'.

1.6 1945: The turnaround

Weninger's fate, however, was soon about to change.[226] With the end of World War II, the MRGND was discontinued and replaced by the 'Niederösterreichisches Landesmuseum' (NOeLM),[227] Egger vanished from the OeAI–stage.[228] As one of the "banished professors recalled",[229] Weninger was reinstated at the UoV and at the Academy[230] thus resuming his academic career.[231] He had to reorganise the Anthropological Institute which turned into an all–consuming duty hardly leaving time for anything else.[232]

In conformity with that, Weninger got rid of Egger's assignment by delegating the bones of the Carnuntum sarcophagus to Helga Maria Pacher (1922–1971),[233] his "scientific assistant" at the Anthropological Institute.[234] After finishing her thesis in 1946,[235] Pacher published the "attempt at an anthropological reading" in 1949, a work reminiscent of Weninger's text in its focus on measurement and morphology.[236] Likewise, Weninger did not pursue further his "constitutional–biological studies", he had performed at the Institute for Forensic Medicine in Vienna before 1945.[237]

Assuming that Weninger had examined it in 1944/45, he probably also put the skull from the Octagon aside upon his return to the University in 1945. Regarding its subsequent fate, he either left the bone behind, or he took it with him to the Anthropological Institute.

> IN 1945, WENINGER RETURNED TO HIS ACADEMIC POSITIONS AND CEASED WORKING ON PREVIOUS ASSIGNMENTS AND SUPPOSEDLY ALSO THE SKULL FROM THE OCTAGON.

1.7 1953: Keil's skull and Egger's Festschrift

In 1942, the NSDAP member Gotbert Moro (1902–1987, fig. 81)[238] had already amended the first Festschrift for party comrade Rudolf Egger that had been partly sponsored by the "Gaupropagandaleitung" of the NSDAP in Carinthia.[239] Around 1950, he proposed a second one, this time for Egger's 70th birthday. A large number of colleagues followed the call.[240] Three volumes were filled with a total of 95 articles,[241] one of which was Weninger's text on the skull from Ephesos.[242] Obviously, Weninger did not want to ignore Egger's anniversary. This impression is confirmed by a 1952 edition of the newly founded journal 'Pro Austria Romana' (PAR) also dedicated to Egger. It contains a 'Tabula Gratulatoria' within which Weninger figures as a congratulator along with 78 others.[243]

At that time, Weninger was already severely ill.[244] Such condition may explain the 'pieced together' aspect of his article on the skull from the Octagon.[245] In order to quickly produce a text for Egger's Festschrift, Weninger filled the pages with Keil's excavation report from 1930 concerning the Octagon, added his material from 1944/45, and augmented the text with some considerations on the "noble" character of the skull based on its morphological traits.[246] Furthermore, Weninger presented four pictures of the Octagon's "calvaria".[247] Yet he did not show just images of the skull, but specific aspects according to certain "norms" (fig. 85),[248] again in line with Martin's textbook,[249] which he also followed in his descriptions.[250] Hence, Weninger applied the concept of standardised imaging which was used by the "Wiener Schule".[251] In other words, such pictures were taken from an anthropological point of view.[252]

Still, the question remains why Weninger failed to mention the pre–1945 circumstances of his occupation with the Ephesian bone. In this regard, one might reflect on the atmosphere within the Austrian academic community in the early 1950s.

1.8 Party comrades

After 1945, the reconfiguration of the Austrian academic community was successfully obstructed, amongst others, by a network whose members had come into positions from the 1920s and afterwards (tab. 8).[253] Firstly, the return of scientists who had been driven out of the country since that time was largely thwarted by its members in light of the obvious recognition that it would have endangered their chairs.[254] Secondly, attempts to shed the spotlight on individuals with an NSDAP background and hinder them from further employment within the academic institutions failed.[255]

From the 119 Academy members of 1945 altogether 66 or 53.8% had been NSDAP members or –applicants.[256] Due to the efforts of the Academy Vice–President Richard Meister[257] and Secretary General Josef Keil,[258] the situation would remain largely unaltered thereafter. In particular, Meister recognised the benefit of delaying cases of incriminated individuals in order to ride out the frenzy following the end of WW II. He succeeded in quashing the proposal of Alfons Dopsch (1868–1953)[259] "to remove all members from the Academy who had been NSDAP party members".[260] Secondly, Meister invented the condition of a "membership set dormant" obviously counting on a change of situation over time.[261] Most of such "dormant" members were finally "reactivated".[262] Accordingly, Meister's strategy resulted in the "shameful fact [that] not a single 'real member' ['wirkliches Mitglied'] of the Academy permanently lost its membership after 1945".[263] Instead, the Academy became "the refuge of professors who had been members of the NSDAP" and a "backstop" for them.[264]

R. Egger provides a good example of Meister's successful tactics. Having been a member of the NSDAP, his Academy membership was "set dormant" in 1945[265] and "reactivated" in 1947.[266] Yet, Egger did not just return to the Academy. With the further "backlash" after 1955[267] and under the reign of AAS–President and VKPW–companion Meister (fig. 82),[268] it became possible to honour an individual "of national socialist mindset"[269] such as Egger with the newly established 'Wilhelm–Hartel–Preis' "for outstanding achievements in the field of Humanities",[270] one of Austria's highest scientific awards.[271] With that and his honorary membership at the OeAI,[272] Egger had finally entered the sphere of "symbolic rehabilitation".[273] Yet he was only the first of altogether four laureates from 1957 till 1963, three of whom were former NSDAP members and the fourth an applicant.[274] Later on, also the former NSDAP members H. Vetters[275] (1975) and R. Noll[276] (1982) would receive such an accolade (figs. 80f.).[277]

The situation at the University of Vienna was not different.[278] 92 or three-quarters of its 124 professors had been NSDAP members or applicants.[279] In 1945, it was stated (tab. 5):

> No truly democratically-minded student will be able to understand that such energetic party comrades like the Germanist [Josef] Nadler,[280] the art historian [Hans] Sedlmayr,[281] the historian [Otto] Brunner,[282] the mathematician [Anton] Huber,[283] the botanist [Karl] Höfler,[284] the palaeontologist [Kurt] Ehrenberg,[285] the philologist Mewaldt,[286] the archaeologist [Rudolf] Egger[287] have still not been definitively removed from the Faculty [tab. 8].[288]

Accordingly, Pfefferle – Pfefferle call the "university elite [...] just as politically and morally corrupted as other professional groups".[289] G. Heiß goes one step further when saying that university structures in general generate a high degree of "collaborative capacity".[290] In line with that, many archaeologists and ancient historians had queued up for admission into the NSDAP in 1938.[291] Rudolf Egger (figs. 78f.),[292] Hedwig von Kenner (fig. 80)[293] and Hermann Vetters (fig. 80),[294] Franz (fig. 83) and Helene Miltner,[295] Rudolf Noll (fig. 81),[296] Camillo Praschniker (fig. 80),[297] and Arnold Schober[298] had applied for NSDAP membership (tab. 7).[299] Yet, the NS–history of Kenner and Vetters even goes back to the years 1933/34, that is, to the time of the failed fascist 'July–coup' ('Juliputsch') in Austria of 25.07.1934.[300] In her "questionnaire" from 09.08.1938, "Hedwig Henriette Josefine von Kenner" stated that she had applied already "in April or May 1933".[301] Vetters is found as "SA–Sturmmann" ("stormman") equalling the lowest rank of the 'Sturmabteilung' (SA) at the "Ortsgruppe Strozzigrund" ("local branch Strozzigrund", 8th Viennese district)[302] as of 01.12.1933 or 01.12.1934 in documents of the Viennese 'Stadt– und Landesarchiv'.[303] In other words, individuals such as Hedwig von Kenner,[304] Hermann Vetters, Egon Braun,[305] Gertrud Pascher, and Harald (von) Petrikovits (fig. 81)[306] cannot be understood as 'opportunists', i.e. as individuals who quickly and unhesitatingly adapt to a given situation out of considerations of usefulness, as many others in Austria's 1938. Rather, they had aligned themselves with the NS–ideology from the very beginning. Against this setting, it is easily understood why Otto Walter (1882–1965, OeAI Co Director 1951–1953)[307] wrote in 1946:

Fig. 80: Triptych with the NSDAP members H. Vetters (1960) and H. von Kenner (1943) next to her teacher and failed NSDAP applicant C. Praschniker (supposedly in the 1940s) (from left to right)

Fig. 81: Triptych with the NSDAP members H. v. Petrikovits (1934), G. Moro (year?) and R. Noll (year?) (from left to right)

> It is such a pity that so few people now have the courage to confess their former attitude and possibly admit that they were wrong and draw the consequences [...]. In general, one might get insane regarding humanity – in particular, if one had thought too highly of it.[308]

Clearly, the year 1945 did not introduce a lasting caesura for eminent players with German–nationalistic, anti–Semitic or NSDAP–roots.[309] There was a continuity regarding certain academic personnel who crossed such a threshold.[310] Both the Academy and the UoV were affected by the detriment.[311] For example, the NSDAP members H. Kenner[312] and H. Vetters[313] remained and were finally to become the indirect successors of the NSDAP applicant/member C. Praschniker (fig. 80) and R. Egger (figs. 78f.), respectively; R. Noll (fig. 81) became head of the 'Collection of Greek and Roman Antiquities' of the 'Kunsthistorisches Museum', Vienna.[314] J. Keil was succeeded by F. Schachermeyr at his chair at the UoV (fig. 83),[315] and by F. Knoll at the AAS;[316] F. Miltner followed him as head of the Ephesian excavations (fig. 83).[317] R. Meister became President of the AAS and, as W. Czermak later on,[318] Principal of the UoV.[319] The list could be extended. However, such individuals not only were allowed to retain or return to their positions, they were also able to shape the years to come and, in particular, subsequent scholarly generations. The Austrian economist Adolf Kozlik wrote in 1965:

> At Austrian universities, repeating, satisfied, approving and collecting students grow up to be appreciated and promoted; the others are weeded out, repotted or transplanted abroad. The result is the self–satisfied, superficial, conservative, arrogant Austrian academic, the Herr Doktor Karl.[320]

What followed were the "leaden years"[321] and "the decline of the UoV into academic insignificance".[322] Accordingly, the Austrian–American sociologist Paul Felix Lazarsfeld[323] stated in 1957:

> As to the Austrian situation at large, I find it as depressing as before. No brains, no initiative, no collaboration. Someone should make a study to find out how a country can be intellectually so dead, and at the same time have such wonderful musical festivals [...]. I should add, however, that a paranoic element of mutual distrust is characteristic of today's personal relations among the Austrians themselves.[324]

Weninger published his article in such paretic "distrustful" times. Accordingly, it is easily understandable why he felt inclined to carefully refer to the pre–1945 years within the text.[325] Nonetheless, the question arises whether such caution was in particular necessary with regard to J. Keil. Keil was supposedly the sole reason for Weninger's occupation with the skull from the Octagon and still active at the OeAI and the AAS in 1952/53.

> WHEN HE WROTE HIS ARTICLE IN THE EARLY 1950S, J. WENINGER HAD TO TAKE INTO ACCOUNT THE RESURGENCE OF A CERTAIN CLIENTELE WITHIN AUSTRIA'S ACADEMIC COMMUNITY.

1.9 A "politically not engaged historian"

U. Wolf plainly considers Josef Keil (figs. 79, 82) as a "politically not engaged historian",[326] an opinion M. Pesditschek not only reiterates,[327] but also augments by saying that he was "a thoroughly staunch opponent of National Socialism".[328] "Unlike R. Egger, he was evidently not an opportunist, and much more than the latter a historical mind".[329] The fact that J. Keil did not forward his archives to an institution in time,[330] a negligence quite remarkable for a "historian" though supposedly not without a reason, may have contributed to such an assessment.

Keil's career developed within the atmosphere of the Viennese AES, OeAI, and VKPW in the 1920s.[331] He demonstrated his "großdeutsche Gesinnung" ("Great German nationalistic sentiments") already in 1906:

> One yearns for a state of being like our German brethren have, where every individual's work brings glory and honour to the entire nation, and everyone can contribute joyfully and with the prospect of success to the ever-increasing prestige of their homeland. How long have we Austrians been denied this joy, and will it ever return?[332]

Interestingly, he did not sign the "Vow of allegiance of professors at the German Universities and High Schools to Adolf Hitler and the National Socialistic State" of November 1933 when he was residing in Germany.[333] His DFG–application of 1939 for support regarding Ephesos was rejected.[334] Still, Arthur Marchet,[335] NS–"Dozentenbundsführer",[336] Dean and subsequent Pro–Principal at the UoV,[337] stated already in spring 1938 that Keil "had always been nationally and anti–Semitically minded, so that there are no political reservations against him".[338] Moreover, he was judged "by the Gaupersonalamt as a national man who had already spoken out in favour of the NSDAP before the 'Umbruch' ('turmoil')" of 1938.[339] In retrospect, it was stated that Keil "was not a [NSDAP] member, [though having had] always saluted with a raised arm and Heil Hitler".[340]

Given such a clearing of his person, Keil had no reason to apply for NSDAP membership;[341] he could pursue his career anyway. G. Heiss points out that "in order to continue working at the University, however, it was not necessary to become a Party member let alone a Party official [...]. The Party was not concerned about non–members teaching provided that they could be considered as good German nationalists and conservatives, and that they had not been politically active for the Ständestaat".[342] Keil was by no means the only one of such reliable "non–members". To the group belonged, for example, Friedrich Kainz (1897–1977),[343] Ernst Späth (1886–1946),[344] Hugo Hassinger (1877–1952),[345] Wilhelm Czermak (1889–1953),[346] and others.[347] Yet, Heiss' recognition sheds an interesting light on the 25% of professors at the University of Vienna who remained on their chairs after 1938 without having applied for NSDAP membership.[348]

Accordingly, J. Keil became AES "Director" in 1942.[349] He was even considered worthy for the position of Vice–Dean of the Philosophical Faculty after 1943[350] next to eminent NSDAP members and University–bureaucrats such as Viktor Christian,[351]

Arthur Marchet,[352] Fritz Knoll,[353] and Eduard Pernkopf[354] (tab. 8). In 1943, Pro–Principal and Senator A. Marchet ("AM") thanked Keil:

```
I would also like to […] thank you for all the
help you have given the university and me in every
respect and ask you to continue to stand by me in
this way in the future […]. Heil Hitler![355]
```

Considering all of this, the perception of J. Keil as a "a thoroughly staunch opponent of National Socialism",[356] or merely as a "politically not engaged historian"[357] seems to fall somewhat short.[358] He is perhaps best seen as the representative of a specific academic community which developed within the German–nationalistic, anti–Semitic, and anti–democratic atmosphere of the Austrian interwar period (tab. 8).[359] Nevertheless, Keil had a certain reluctance to expose himself formally.[360] His conduct rather seems to have been dictated by a bureaucratic "sense of duty"[361] the best description of which, yet with some disturbing undertones, is delivered by Egon Braun[362]:

> *A considerable administrative talent, which was able to adapt to various tasks, enabled Keil to perform several official functions with precision.*[363]

In such a functionary mentality fit for all circumstances Keil met Richard Meister, who harboured a similar "administrative talent" that was recognised by the NS administration.[364]

JOSEF KEIL CALLED "A CONSIDERABLE ADMINISTRATIVE TALENT" HIS OWN, MAKING HIM CAPABLE "ADAPT[ING] TO VARIOUS TASKS" REGARDLESS OF THE CIRCUMSTANCES.

1.10 A "universal scholar, humanist, and wise man"[365]

The "master of adaption"[366] Richard Meister (1881–1964, fig. 82)[367] was a functionary within the academic community who held various positions throughout all the changes of regime from the 1930s onwards.[368] He was Dean of the Philosophical Faculty in 1930 and a member of the VAS since 1931.[369] He was connected to Praschniker[370], Egger,[371] and Keil within the VKPW and rooted in the 'Annexation Movement' of interwar–Austria.[372] He was a member of the 'Österreichisch–deutsche Arbeitsgemeinschaft' ('Austrian–German working society'),[373] of the 'Österreichisch–deutscher Volksbund' ('Austrian–German peoples' federation'),[374] and perhaps of the 'Deutscher Klub' ('German Club'),[375] "the gathering place of the Austrian National Socialists who had become illegal".[376]

Moreover, Meister was active within the covert anti–Semitic 'Bärenhöhle' ('bear's den') together with a set of university bureaucrats who prevented Jewish and left–wing scientists from achieving a career at the UoV (tab. 8).[377] In addition, he sought to remove Jewish teachers from the university by proposing them for retirement.[378] In other words, Meister was one of the outstanding representatives of anti–Jewish personnel policy at the university level during the Austrian interwar period, which doubtlessly recommended him after 1938. Already at that time, he had "best connections to the ministry [of education]",[379] where Otto Skrbensky[380] played a major role.[381]

"Since Meister had protected Nazis being persecuted by the Ständestaat, he had many advocates after the Anschluss" in 1938.[382] Pro–Principal Arthur Marchet[383] described him in 1940 as "undoubtedly nationally and anti–Semitically minded".[384] Meister had "joyfully and honestly welcomed the return of the Ostmark to the Reich".[385] He was an "extremely active" and "shining example in his generosity" when it came to "collections and donations" for the Nationalsozialistische Volkswohlfahrt (NSV).[386] After a short period of insecurity, Meister remained at the University.[387] In 1944, one of his speeches held at the UoV was deemed worthy of publication in the infamous 'Völkischer Beobachter'.[388] Nevertheless, Meister had not applied for NSDAP membership.

Because of such caution, Meister not only prevailed after 1945 but achieved the pinnacle of his career.[389] He became Vice–Principal (1945), Senator (1947/48, 1948/49, 1951/52), and Principal (1949/50) at the UoV, Vice–President (1945–1951) and finally President (1951–1963) of the Academy.[390] K. Taschwer describes him as the "decisive key person at the University responsible for the double failure of denazification and remigration after 1945".[391] In other words, he was one of the masterminds who ensured the maintenance of a network consisting of former NS–professors within Austria's academic institutions (tab. 8).[392] Yet, the efforts of the "black–brown eminence" did not go unnoticed at the time.

> The members of the 'Austrian Academy of Sciences' […] are in their majority still the old protection-children of the fascist era […]. The fact that they were not purged in 1945 and thereafter was above all the dubious merit of […] Austria's black-brown eminence behind the scenes: Richard Meister.[393]

> Meister's affiliation to the clique [Oswald] Menghin,[394] [Othenio] Abel,[395] [Robert] Lach[396] and their ilk clearly betrays the line he has always represented […]. Nobody dares to approach Meister and his protégés![397]

Meister was highly honoured.[398] In 1961, a Festschrift was published for him by the 'Österreichischer Bundesverlag für Unterricht, Wissenschaft und Kunst' although no editor was named.[399] Its preface was written by Heinrich Drimmel,[400] Minister of Education from 1954 till 1964,[401] who had been a student of Meister and who came under his considerable influence.[402] In 1963, Meister finally retired as AAS–President, already aged 82 years.[403] He died the following year. The obituary for Meister, written by NSDAP applicant Friedrich Kainz,[404] appears as a remarkable piece of euphemistic prose.[405] Meister was buried as an "eminent person" at the 'Hietzinger Friedhof', Vienna, group 70 row 15 grave 11. Eight years after his death, an alley was named after him in the Viennese 21st district ('Meistergasse').[406] In 2012, his grave was emptied.[407]

1.11 A Secretary General and his master[408]

Richard Meister and Josef Keil were another pair of long–term "friends" (fig. 82).[409] They knew each other from the VKPW (tab. 4), from the University, and the VAS. Both received the 'Goldene Treudienst=Ehrenzeichen' in 1942.[410] Such appreciation was one of the mass awards of the NS regime, yet one had to apply for it.[416] Like Keil,[417] Meister became responsible for the "study support for members of the Wehrmacht".[418] Neither one had applied for NSDAP membership, but instead both had supported the party financially,[419] "a key point in the [NS–] assessment of political reliability".[420] Formally unencumbered, such attention would significantly determine their reputation after 1945.

1.11.1 Two conventions

Immediately after the collapse of the Third Reich, Richard Meister and Josef Keil, the two reliable "nationally and anti–Semitically minded"[421] non–members from before 1945, re–entered the academic stage together. At the UoV, the "important"[422] bureaucrat Meister was elected Pro–Principal[423] and former Vice–Dean Josef Keil became Senator.[424]

Fig. 82: One–sided, commemorative bronze medals of the two "nationally and anti–Semitically minded"[411] friends[412] J. Keil (left)[413] and R. Meister (right)[414] as commissioned by Academy–members from the famous medallist Arnold Hartig (ÆT.S. = (anno) aetatis suae = in the year of his age)[415]

A comparable setup occurred at the Academy.[425] On 30.10.1945, twenty–one of its members met and elected Pro–Principal Meister as Vice–President of the Academy and Senator Keil as its Secretary General.[426] The electors included individuals such as Hugo Hassinger,[427] Wilhelm Havers,[428] Hermann Junker,[429] Josef Keil,[430] E. Kruppa,[431] Richard Meister,[432] Camillo Praschniker,[433] Robert Reininger,[434] and Ernst Späth (tab. 9).[435] Furthermore, the congregation was a geriatric event due to its participants belonging to a specific generation which originated in the late 19th c. Accordingly, its exclusively male participants had mostly reached the 7th and 8th decade of their lives, resulting in an overall average age of 68.6 years (tab. 9). The perseverance at the Academy after 1945 may also find an explanation from this viewpoint.

1.11.2 Viennese Monday

R. Meister had supported the election of his "friend"[436] and VKPW companion J. Keil (tab. 4; fig. 82) as Secretary General at the Academy convention on the 30.10.1945.[437] In this regard, the latter's deed may be viewed as remarkable. The arrested archive Director of the University of Vienna, NSDAP–applicant Fritz (von) Reinöhl,[438] stated on record in 1945 that Keil had "ordered the burning of the files of incriminated Nazi professors".[439] The eradication may find an explanation when we consider the fact that Keil was nominated as a substitute for Wilhelm Havers[440] on a special commission at the Philosophical Faculty in September 1945 responsible for 'denazification'.[441] It appears that Keil acted from the very beginning in favour of a certain clientele recognizing the necessity to get rid of "incriminating" evidence although the commission was actually supposed to do precisely the opposite.

In keeping with this, Meister and Keil proceeded further. The journal 'Wiener Montag'[442] addressed their joint activities at the UoV (tab. 5):

> The leaders of this [Philosophical] Faculty, Dean [Wilhelm] Czermak,[443] Vice-Dean [Ernst] Späth,[444] Pro-Principal [Richard] Meister and Senator [Josef] Keil, try to keep a number of heavily incriminated [NSDAP] party comrades as members of the Faculty.[445]

Accordingly, the relegation of "Meister and Keil, [Johannes] Mewaldt [NSDAP member][446] and [Hans] Sedlmayer" [NSDAP member][447] was demanded (tab. 5), i.e. of

> [...] the whole coterie of national and national-socialist professors, where one never knows where nationalism ends and Nazism begins. We demand the removal of all these men in the name of many thousands of living Austrians, but also in the name of the many dead who died and were ruined by National Socialism.[448]

Title	Date and page
Rückkehr von Naziprofessoren an die Wiener Universität?	12.11.1945, 3f
Universität – Brutstätte des Nationalsozialismus	26.11.1945, 3
Protektoren der Naziprofessoren	03.12.1945, 4
Ist Professor Dr. Nadler Nationalsozialist oder nicht?	03.12.1945, 5
Unhaltbare Zustände an der philosophischen Fakultät der Universität Wien	10.12.1945, 3f
Die Wiener Universität, Keimzelle des Nationalsozialismus	10.12.1945, 3
Der Fall Nadler	17.12.1945, 3
Die Einstellung des Universitätsbetriebes	24.12.1945, 4
Die Naziseuche an unseren Hochschulen	07.01.1946, 3f
Hellenische Weltanschauung des Johannes Mewaldt	07.01.1946, 4
Und die Technik? Sonderbares Wirken der Sonderkommission – Naziprofessoren kehren zurück	07.01.1946, 4
Die Zustände an unseren Hochschulen	14.01.1946, 3f
Naziprofessoren an der medizinischen Fakultät	21.01.1946, 4
Professor Dr. Amreich in Haft	21.01.1946, 1
Wiederaufbau an der Universität. Gespräch mit dem Rektor Prof. Dr. Adamovich	21.01.1946, 3f
Die Naziprofessoren an der medizinischen Fakultät	21.01.1946, 4
Nazisäuberungen und Wiederaufbau an der Universität	28.01.1946, 3f
Der Wiederaufbau der Universität	04.02.1946, 3
Der Wiederaufbau der Universität	11.02.1946, 3
Rückberufung der Professoren und Dozenten an die Wiener Universität	18.02.1946, 3f

Tab. 5: In a total of twenty articles, within the three months between 12.11.1945 and 25.02.1946, the weekly journal 'Wiener Montag' extensively addressed the problems of 'denazification'/ remigration at the University of Vienna

Whereas indeed nobody "dared to approach" Meister,[449] his protégé Keil was relieved from his duties on 27.03.1946.[450] Nevertheless, the decision was revoked within days by means of a mere telephone call from Otto Skrbensky (1887–1952),[451] who "played an extremely influential, even decisive role in the denazification of Austrian universities from spring 1945 onwards" at a ministerial level.[452] Obviously, somebody had quickly intervened on behalf of Keil. Since Meister was a close personal friend of Skrbensky,[453] it is a reasonable assumption that this somebody was him who did not want to lose his willing Secretary General whom he had only recently deployed.[454]

1.11.3 The reintegration

After this episode, Keil experienced no further inconveniences. Together with Meister, he administrated henceforth what was later labelled the "reintegration of former National Socialists within the academic milieu".[455] In 1947, "Vice–President [Richard] Meister [...] Secretary General [Josef] Keil interceded on behalf of the former National Socialists with Federal President Renner".[456] In particular, Keil intervened in support of the former NSDAP members Kurt Leuchs,[457] Friedrich Wild,[458] Walter Ruth,[459] as well as H. Kenner,[460] F. Miltner,[461] C. Praschniker,[462] and R. Egger.[463] The intensity with which such clearing efforts were pursued can be sensed from a set of letters[464] on behalf of the priest and Egyptologist Hermann Junker (member of the 'German Club', the 'bear's den', and of the NSDAP)[465] written by his 'bear's den' companions Richard Meister[466] and Wilhelm Czermak[467] as well as Josef Keil.[468] Moreover, Keil suggested refraining from deleting 'minderbelastete' ('less incriminated') individuals altogether even before the general amnesty.[469] He used himself here for a group which included,[470] for example, former NSDAP members such as Josef Nadler,[471] Heinrich von Srbik,[472] Hans Sedlmayr,[473] and Fritz Knoll.[474] At the same time, Keil recognised the benefit of reframing the VAS as AAS,[475] calling it "almost a necessity"[476] and the "sign of the completed reorganisation of the Academy".[477]

1.11.4 A succession

Against such a backdrop, it comes as no surprise how Keil handled his own succession at the University. In 1950, Keil retired from the University Institute, although he remained 'Honorary Professor'.[478] He suggested one out of the three former NSDAP members Franz Miltner,[479] Fritz Schachermeyr (fig. 83),[480] and Hermann Bengtson[481] as his successor, and thus "exclusively [...] severely incriminated and apparently still practising National Socialists or in any case racists".[482] Quite in line with his previous conduct, Keil did not consider recommending a non–incriminated person even for a secondary place. Schachermeyr received the call,[483] and he became a member of the AAS.[484] Subsequently, OeAI (Co–)Director Keil[485] placed his "close friend"[486] Miltner,[487] a "convinced racist before and after 1945 [with] no doubt whatsoever",[488] in charge of the resumed Austrian excavations in Ephesos.[489] Miltner, the "perfect leader of excavations",[490] began what Keil could not refrain from calling an "excessive pace of excavation" later on.[491]

Fig. 83: The NSDAP members F. Miltner (left, supposedly in the 1950s) and F. Schachermeyr (right, 1984)

With that, Keil ended his Ephesian time. He had participated in altogether sixteen Austrian excavation campaigns between 1904 and 1935.[492] In the end, he confessed his emotional relationship to Ephesos and Türkiye calling it his "love" and his "second home", respectively:

> *I am happy that after 19 years of absence, I could see our old excavation house again, which I first entered 49 years ago* [i.e., in 1904]*, in the best condition. I spent two days there, which belong to the most beautiful ones of my life. Not only was I able to stay at our workplace and revisit old places of the archaeological site, but also the warmth of the reception by the museum directors and representatives of the Ephesos Society in Selçuk deeply moved me, and I can only thank them from the bottom of my heart. I hope that our Austrian Archaeological Institute will be able to resume the excavations, for the advancement of science and for the country that I love like a second home.*[493]

> *The* [Ephesus] *project, to which a large part of my life's work and, I may say, my love is devoted.*[494]

Because of a "heart seizure" and on the subsequent "advice of doctors",[495] Keil retired as Secretary General from the AAS in 1957.[496] The situation at that time was such that an individual such as the former NS University Principal[497] Fritz Knoll, member of the 'German Club'[498] and of the NSDAP, could succeed him in that position.[499]

As is evident from the above, J. Weninger should not have had any illusions in the early 1950s regarding what kind of clientele had returned or persisted. In particular, he had every reason to fear J. Keil, who doubtlessly posed a threat due to his powerful position at the Academy. It is, therefore, more than comprehensible that he omitted Keil's role concerning his engagement with the skull from the Octagon in the article of 1953 resulting in a somewhat incomplete text.[500]

PROBABLY ACKNOWLEDGING KEIL'S BACKGROUND AND HIS SPECIFIC ROLE IN THE EARLY 1950S, WENINGER AVOIDED REFERRING TO THE PRE–1945 YEARS WITH REGARD TO THE SKULL FROM THE OCTAGON.

1.12 Conclusions

Trying to understand the circumstances of Weninger's publication of the skull from the Octagon, we concluded that it reached his hands in 1944. He probably examined the Ephesian bone during his exile together with a skeleton that was found in Carnuntum in 1944, because of assignments he received from Josef Keil and Rudolf Egger (fig. 79b; tab. 6), respectively. Shortly afterwards, in 1945, Weninger returned to his chair at the University of Vienna and put the osseous material aside. Accordingly, the skull either remained at the 'Museum of the Reichsgau Niederdonau', or

Tab. 6: Time line regarding C. Praschniker, R. Egger, J. Keil, and J. Weninger

Year	Text	Literature
1926	Restart of the Austrian excavations in Ephesos after WW I with Keil and Miltner	Keil 1926, 248f
1927	Vocation of Keil to the University of Greifswald	Wlach 1998, 112
1927	Appointment of Weninger as professor at the newly founded Anthropological University Institute in Vienna	Ehgartner 1959, 3
1929	Keil removes the skull from the Octagon's burial chamber and takes it to Greifswald	Keil 1930a, 45
1935	Egger and Praschniker start their Co–Directorate of the OeAI	Wlach 1998, 107
1936	Return of Keil to the University of Vienna	Wlach 1998, 112
1938/39	Weninger resignes/is excluded from the Viennese Anthropological Institute/VAS and tries to emigrate	Ehgartner 1959, 3 Weindling 2009, 112 n. 94
1941	Weninger is conscripted to the 'Museum of the Reichsgau Niederdonau'	Ehgartner 1959, 3
1942	Moro's Festschrift I for Egger	Moro 1942
1942/43	Keil becomes AES Director and Vice–Dean at the University of Vienna	University Vienna, Archives; Handbuch Reichsgau Wien 1944, 392
1944	Weninger has to work on osseous material from Carnuntum and supposedly also the skull from the Octagon	Weninger 1953, 166; Pacher 1949, 6
1945	Weninger is reinstated as Professor and puts the osseous material from 1944 aside	Ehgartner 1959, 4; Ehgartner 1956, 186
1945	Egger has to leave the OeAI and the University of Vienna	Wlach 2010, 369
1945	Keil becomes Secretary General in the Academy	Wlach 1998, 112
1949	Death of Praschniker	Eichler 1950
1952/54	Moro's Festschrift II for Egger with Weninger's article on the skull from the Octagon	Moro 1952–54, Weninger 1953
1954	Restart of the Austrian excavations in Ephesos after WW II with Miltner in charge	Miltner 1955, 23; Keil 1959, 655
1959	Death of Weninger	Ehgartner 1959
1959	Death of Miltner	Keil 1959
1962/63	Moro's Festschrift III for Egger; Death of Keil (1963)	Betz – Moro 1962–63; Schachermeyr 1965
1969	Death of Egger	Vetters 1970

Weninger took it with him to the Viennese Anthropological Institute. Eight years later, Weninger wanted to join the line of congratulants in celebration of Egger's 70th birthday. To that end, he published the skull in the second Festschrift for R. Egger, although he avoided referring to the pre–1945 background of his occupation. After that, the Ephesian bone vanished.

In conclusion, the fate of the skull as well as its publication by Weninger indeed seem to be closely linked to conditions originating in Austria's interwar times, culminating in its Third Reich period from 1938 till 1945 and also extending an influence long afterwards. Ultimately, when Thür proposed her hypothesis regarding the Octagon and Arsinoë IV in 1990,[501] all living memory of the respective events from before 1945 had faded away having been taken into their graves by the deceased proponents, so that no obvious clue of the Ephesian bone's whereabouts remained.

> THE SKULL FROM THE OCTAGON WAS UNFORTUNATE ENOUGH TO HAVE PLAYED A ROLE DURING A DESPICABLE TIME THAT WAS BEST APPROACHED CAUTIOUSLY.

1.13 Epilogue

It is hardly possible to imagine how Josef Weninger (fig. 77) and his wife Margarete (fig. 84) may have felt in the early 1950s, when they again found themselves within an academic community that was not much different from the one they had tried to escape in 1938/39. Josef Weninger's position at the Anthropological Institute after 1945 may have been inviolable enough to keep problems at bay. With his death, however, the situation developed detrimentally for Margarete Weninger. As if in a malicious comedy, former NSDAP member Emil Breitinger (fig. 84)[502] succeeded J. Weninger as head of the Anthropological Institute in 1957.[503] The Jewess Margarete Weninger became excommunicated again having had to live in a "symbolic Ghetto":[504]

> Breitinger's appointment [...] *marked the beginning of a period for Margarete Weninger* [...] *that is today referred to as 'the dark century' of the Institute's history"*.[505] *"The title of professor and her growing scientific reputation could not prevent her from remaining isolated at the Anthropological Institute after the death of her husband in 1959 and from being hindered in her work. Margarete Weninger became the victim of her colleagues in the field who had meanwhile returned to their posts* [although] *incriminated by National Socialism.*[506]

In 1953, the very year he published the skull from the Octagon, Josef Weninger retired from the Anthropological Society in Vienna due to "urgent advice of the doctor",[507] and in 1957 he retired from the University.[508] In 1959, he died at the age of 73.[509] Twenty–eight years later, in 1987, Margarete Weninger followed her husband into the grave, at the age of 91 years.[510] The couple is buried together at the 'Gersthofer Friedhof', Vienna.[511]

As Josef Weninger was described as a "conciliatory" character enabling him "to overlook many an unpleasant memory from the immediate past",[512] Margarete Weninger was said never to have har-

boured thoughts of retaliation[513] instead giving in to the inevitable. As a Jew and as a qualified woman in a male academic community,[514] she was "subjected to reprisals even before the National Socialists came to power in Austria".[515] She had lived under precarious, life–threatening conditions; her mother, dressmaker Irma Gisela (Jenny) Taubert, had been deported and murdered in 1942.[516] She suffered the consequences of the resurgence of former NSDAP members in post–war Austria's academic society and again became an outcast for many years. It hardly comes as a surprise that until now Margarete Weninger has received little attention in Austria:[517]

> It is one of the tragic failures of the Republic of Austria that those persecuted under National Socialism are often left on their own, with little or only half–hearted support, and have to deal with this past on behalf of the dull sycophants in the gallery of fellow travellers and repressors. The great scientist and persecuted Jew Margarete Weninger has never received any appreciation in this state.[518]

At the funeral of Margarete Weninger in 1987, "there was no wreath from the Alma Mater Rudolphina",[519] i.e. from the University of Vienna. No bust or relief commemorates her in the 'Arkadenhof' of the University of Vienna.[520]

Tab. 7: List of mentioned NSDAP members and applicants[533]

Name, dates; age at 1938	NSDAP registration #	Bundesarchiv Berlin, Germany (BArch)
Abel, Othenio (1875–1946); 63	6.196.288	R 9361–IX/11581
Bauer, Wilhelm (1877–1953); 61	8.468.169	R 9361–IX/1720861
Bengtson, Hermann (1909–1989); 29	2.750.176	R 9361–IX/2380856
Braun, Egon (1906–1993); 32	268.669[521]	No extant membership card
Breitinger, Emil (1904–2004); 34	4.590.084	R 9361–IX/4361458
Brunner, Otto (1898–1982); 40	9.140.316	R 9361–IX/4800877
Chmielewski, Karl (1903–1991); 35	1.508.254	R 9361–IX/5450792; R 9361–VIII/5081743
Christian, Viktor (1885–1963); 53	6.127.801	R 9361–IX/5461269
Egger, Rudolf (1882–1969); 56	6.125.243	9361–IX/7370498 and 7591627
Ehrenberg, Kurt (1896–1979); 42	9.025.892	R 9361–IX/7440205; R 9361–VIII/7681545 (Two membership cards)
Entz, Gustav (1884–1957); 54	?	Failed applicant[522]
Hirsch, Hans (1878–1940); 60	?	"Erfassungsantrag" from 07.03.1939 according to R 9361–II/416625; No extant membership card
Höfler, Karl (1893–1973); 45	6.297.168	R 9361–VIII/11441502
Huber, Anton (1897–1975); 41	3.657.531	R 9361–IX/17080798; R 9361–VIII/12600618 (Two membership cards)
Junker, Hermann (1877–1962); 61	3.391.277	R 9361–IX/18730645; R 9361–VIII/14290969
Kainz, Friedrich (1897–1977); 41	9.029.167	Applications from 25.05.1938, 20.06.1941 (R 9361–II/486037)[523] and postponement from 24.09.1940/25.02.1941 because of his sister having berated A. Hitler
Kenner, Hedwig (von) (1910–1993); 28	6.282.734	R 9361–IX/19801393
Knoll, Fritz (1883–1981); 55	6.235.774	R 9361–IX/21341063
Kralik, Dietrich (1884–1959); 54	6.106.526[524]	No extant membership card
Kruppa, Erwin (1885–1967); 53	8.459.512	R 9361–IX/23670649
Lach, Robert (1874–1958); 64	1.529.471	R 9361–V/26525; No extant membership card
Lesky, Albin (1896–1981); 42	7.252.762	R 9361–IX/25620182
Lesky, Erna (1911–1986); 27	7.252.714	R 9361–IX/25620186
Leuchs, Kurt (1881–1949); 57	1.811.429 (290.246)	R 9361–II/634141; No extant membership card
Marchet, Arthur (1892–1980); 46	1.210.876[525]	Addressed as "Party comrade" in: R 9361–VI/1914;[526] No extant membership card

Name, dates; age at 1938	NSDAP registration #	Bundesarchiv Berlin, Germany (BArch)
Menghin, Oswald (1888–1973); 50	8.123.303[527]	"Rückstellungsbeschluss" from 08.09.1939 (R 9361–II/703240); No extant membership card
Mewaldt, Johannes (1880–1964); 58	8.448.925[528]	No extant membership card
Miltner, Franz (1901–1959); 37	6.257.215	R 9361–IX/28730929
Miltner, Helene (1904–1999); 34	7.886.006	R 9361–IX/28730940
Moro, Gotbert (1902–1987); 36	7.789.765	R 9361–IX/29170885
Moro, Oswin (1895–1941); 43	7.515.477	R 9361–IX/29170898
Nadler, Josef (1884–1963); 54	6.196.904	R 9361–IX/30011237
Noll, Rudolf (1906–1990); 32	6.127.590	R 9361–IX/30800597
Oettinger, Karl (1906–1979); 32	?	According to R 4901/23633 admittance on the 01.03.1938;[529] No extant membership card
Pascher, Gertrud (1911–2002); 27	189.306[530]	No extant membership card
Pernkopf, Eduard (1888–1955); 50	1.616.421	R 9361–III/568960; No extant membership
Petrikovits, Harald (von) (1911–2010); 27	512.321	R 9361–IX/32161538 and 32161539
Pfalz, Anton (1885–1958); 53	6.301.505	R 9361–VIII/15291359
Pötzl, Otto (1877–1962); 61	9.909.922	R 9361–VIII/16000039
Praschniker, Camillo (1884–1949); 54	–	Application withdrawn
Reinöhl, Fritz (von) (1889–1969); 49	6.203.699	R 9361–VII/2073985; Applicant
Ruth, Walter (1905–1956); 33	6.220.687	R 9361–VIII/18020631
Saria, Balduin (1893–1974); 45	10.161.666	R 9361–IX/36390566 and 18310530
Schachermeyr, Fritz (1895–1987); 43	4.586.961	R 9361–IX/36531065
Schober, Arnold (1886–1959); 52	6.288.962	R 9361–VIII/20561660
Sedlmayr, Hans (1896–1984); 42	6.198.125 (302.489)[531]	R 9361–VIII/22490633
Srbik, Heinrich (von) (1878–1951); 60	6.104.788[532]	No extant membership card
Uebersberger, Hans (1877–1962); 61	1.343.337	R 9361–IX/45371460; R 9361–VIII/23551579; Two membership cards
Vetters, Hermann jun. (1915–1993); 23	6.294.086	R 9361–IX/45851100
Vetters, Hermann sen. (1880–1941); 58	6.264.883	R 9361–IX/45851099
Wild, Friedrich (1888–1966); 50	6.128.172	R 9361–IX/48630988
Wilke, Fritz (1879–1957); 59	6.293.472	R 9361–II/1205041

Name, dates	'Bear's den'	'German Club'/ 'German Community'	NSDAP	University/Academy bureaucracy	Academy member-ship
Abel, Othenio (1875–1946)	X	X	X	Prof.; Phil. Dean 1927/28; Principal 1932/33	X
Bauer, Wilhelm (1877–1953)	X	X	X	Prof.	X
Christian, Viktor (1885–1963)	X	X	X	Prof.; Phil. Dean 1938/39 & 1942/43; Pro-Principal 1943/45; Principal 1944/45	X
Czermak, Wilhelm (1889–1953)	X	X	–	Prof.; Phil. Dean 1945/46, Principal 1952/53	X
Ehrenberg, Kurt (1896–1979)	–	–	X	Prof.	–
Entz, Gustav (1884–1957)	–	X	Appl.	Prof.; Evang. Dean 1925/26, 1931/32, 1938/39–1948/49, 1952/53	–
Geyer, Rudolf (1861–1929)	X	X	–	Doz.; Phil. Dean 1945/46; Principal 1952/53	X
Hassinger, Hugo (1877–1952)	–	X	–	Prof.	X
Havers, Wilhelm (1879–1961)	–	–	–	Prof.	X
Hirsch, Hans (1878–1940)	–	X	Appl.	Prof.; Phil. Dean 1936/37	X
Huber, Anton (1897–1975)	–	–	X	Prof.	X
Junker, Hermann (1877–1962)	X	X	X	Prof.; Phil. Dean 1922/23	X
Kainz, Friedrich (1897–1977)	–	–	Appl.	Prof.	X
Knoll, Fritz (1883–1981)	–	X	X	Prof.; Principal 1938/43; AAS–Secretary General 1959/64	X
Kraelitz, Friedrich (1876–1932)	X	–	–	Prof.; † 1932	X
Kralik, Dietrich (1884–1959)	X	X	X	Prof.; Phil. Dean 1934/35	X
Kruppa, Erwin (1885–1967)	–	–	X	Prof.; Principal tech. college 1953/54; AAS–Vice-President 1957/60	X
Lach, Robert (1874–1958)	X	–	X	Prof.	X
Leitmeier, Hans (1885–1967)	X	–	–	Prof.; Phil. Dean 1949/50	X
Leuchs, Kurt (1881–1949)	–	–	X	Prof.	X
Marchet, Arthur (1892–1980)	–	–	X	Prof.; Phil. Dean 1943/44 – 1944/45, Pro-Principal 1940/41–1942/43	–
Meister, Richard (1881–1964)	X	X(?)	–	Prof.; Phil. Dean 1930/31; Principal 1949/50; Academy (Vice-) President 1945/63	X
Menghin, Oswald (1888–1973)	X	X	X	Prof.; Phil. Dean 1928/29; Principal 1935/36	X
Mewaldt, Johannes (1880–1964)	–	–	X	Prof.	X
Much, Rudolf (1862–1936)	X	X	–	Prof.; † 1936	X
Nadler, Josef (1884–1963)	–	X	X	Prof.	X
Patsch, Carl (1865–1945)	X	–	–	Prof.; Phil. Dean 1926/27	X
Pernkopf, Eduard (1888–1955)	–	X	X	Prof.; Med. Dean 1938/39, 1942/43, Principal 1943/45	X
Pfalz, Anton (1885–1958)	X	–	X	Prof.	X
Redlich, Oswald (1858–1944)	–	X	–	Prof.; Principal 1911/12; VAS–President 1919/38	X
Reininger, Robert (1869–1955)	X	X	–	Prof.	X
Späth, Ernst (1886–1946)	–	–	–	Prof.; Principal 1937/38; Academy–Secretary General 1938/45, Academy–President 1945/46	X
Srbik, Heinrich (von) (1878–1951)	X	X	X	Prof.; Phil. Dean 1932/33; Academy–President 1938/45	X
Turba, Gustav (1864–1935)	X	–	–	Prof.; † 1935	–
Uebersberger, Hans (1877–1962)	X	X	X	Prof.; Phil. Dean 1924/25; Principal 1930/31	X
Wilke, Fritz (1879–1957)	–	X	X	Prof.; Evang. Dean 1926/27, 1932/33, 1936/37	–

left Page:

Tab. 8: Selected members of the Viennese academic community originating in the 19th c., cross-referenced according to memberships (X) within the 'bear's den', the 'German Club'/'German Community' and the NSDAP plus University and Academy (Appl. = applicant)

#	Name, dates; age at 1945	Source	Comment
1	Benndorf, Hans (1870–1953); 75	https://www.biographien.ac.at/oebl_B/Benndorf_Hans_1870_1953.xml	NS opponent
2	Böhm, Leopold Karl (1886–1958); 59	https://www.geschichtewiki.wien.gv.at/Leopold_Karl_B%C3%B6hm	No documented involvement
3	Ficker, Heinrich (von) (1881–1957); 64	Pfefferle – Pfefferle 2014, 288	NSFK
4	Flamm, Ludwig (1885–1964); 60	https://www.geschichtewiki.wien.gv.at/Ludwig_Flamm	No documented involvement
5	Graff, Kasimir (1878–1950); 67	https://www.geschichtewiki.wien.gv.at/Kasimir_Romuald_Graff	No documented involvement
6	Hassinger, Hugo (1877–1952); 68	Pfefferle – Pfefferle 2014, 290	Reliable "non-member"
7	Havers, Wilhelm (1879–1961); 66	Pfefferle – Pfefferle 2014, 290	NSLB etc.
8	Junker, Hermann (1877–1962); 68	Budka – Jurman 2013	GC, 'bear's den'; NSDAP member
9	Keil, Josef (1878–1963); 67	Pfefferle – Pfefferle 2014, 293	Reliable "non-member", NSV etc.
10	Kretschmer, Paul (1866–1956); 79	https://geschichte.univie.ac.at/en/persons/paul-kretschmer-prof-dr	Feichtinger 2015, 171
11	Kruppa, Erwin (1885–1967); 60	https://austria-forum.org/af/AustriaWiki/Erwin_Kruppa	NSDAP member; AAS Vice-President 1957/60
12	Mayer, Hans (1879–1955); 66	Pfefferle – Pfefferle 2014, 335	NSV etc.
13	Meister, Richard (1881–1964); 64	Feichtinger 2015; Pfefferle – Pfefferle 2014, 298	Reliable "non-member"
14	Meyer, Stefan (1872–1949); 73	https://www.oeaw.ac.at/gedenkbuch/personen/i-p/stefan-meyer; Matis 2013, 56f.	Jewish (Alm 95, 1945, 95)
15	Praschniker, Camillo (1884–1949); 61	Wlach 2019a; Pfefferle – Pfefferle 2014, 301	Failed NSDAP applicant
16	Prey, Adalbert (1873–1949); 72	https://www.biographien.ac.at/oebl/oebl_P/Prey_Adalbert_1873_1949.xml	No documented involvement
17	Radermacher, Ludwig (1867–1952); 78	https://www.deutsche-biographie.de/gnd116322608.html#ndbcontent	No documented involvement
18	Reininger, Robert (1869–1955); 76	https://geschichte.univie.ac.at/de/personen/robert-reininger	GC, 'bear's den'; Feichtinger 2015, 171
19	Späth, Ernst (1886–1946); 59	Pfefferle – Pfefferle 2014, 304	Principal 1937/38; Secretary General 1938/45, AAS-President 1945/46
20	Wilhelm, Adolf (1864–1950); 81	Fellner – Corradini 2006, 454	No documented involvement
21	Zingerle, Josef (1868–1947); 77	Wlach 1998, 122f.	No documented involvement

Tab. 9: The 21 participants at the Academy convention on 30.10.1945 responsible for the election of R. Meister as Academy Vice-President and of J. Keil as Secretary General (Protocol of the extraordinary general meeting on the 30.10.1945; AAS-Archives, A 0997)

2. A skull regained

When analysing his article from 1953, we concluded that Josef Weninger examined the skull from the Octagon between May 1944 and March 1945 when compelled to work for the 'Museum of the Reichsgau Niederdonau' (fig. 85). Upon his return to the University of Vienna in 1945, he either left the bone behind or he took it with him to the Anthropological Institute. Accordingly, the bone should have reached either the sphere of the 'Niederösterreichisches Landesmuseum' (NOeLM) or the Collections of the University of Vienna (CVU).[534]

Having arrived at such a theory regarding the location of the skull, we put it to the test. Whereas the NOeLM turned out to be a dead end,[535] the CVU have indeed preserved a bone suspected to be the one in question. When confronted with our request in September 2022, Claudia Feigl, coordinator of the Viennese University Collections, referred us to Katharina Matiasek, curator of the collections in the De-

Fig. 85: Illustrations of the Ephesian skull in Weninger's article from 1953

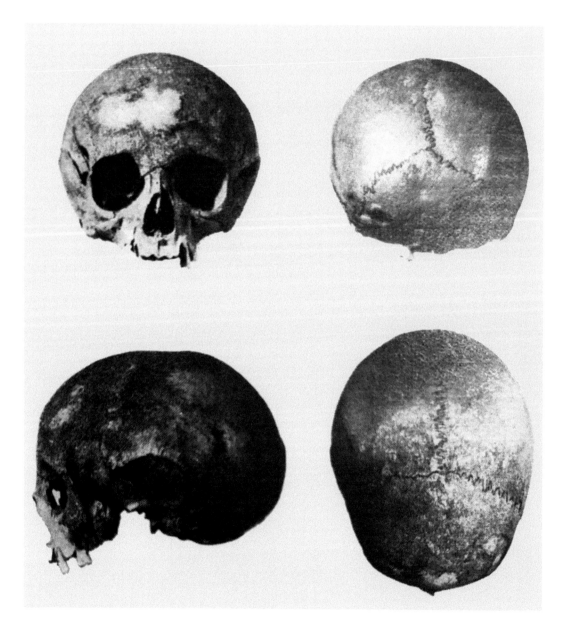

partment of Evolutionary Anthropology, who indeed remembered a skull with the inscription "Ephesus Heroengrab".[536] Yet it should take almost three months, before we could make terms for a meeting and were allowed to view the skull.

In the Collections of the University of Vienna, there is a skull being inscribed as originating from Ephesos.

2.1 "Ephesos Grave of a hero"

In December 2022, a skull was presented to us by H. Wilfing and K. Matiasek. According to Matiasek, it reached the Collections with a part of the estate of Emil Breitinger (fig. 84), the successor of Weninger as head of the Anthropological Institute in 1957,[537] and the inventory provides no further information. As Matiasek had reported, its os occipitale appeared inked with "Ephesos Heroengrab" ("Ephesos hero's grave", fig. 86), thereby recalling the title of Weninger's article from 1953 in which he refers to the Octagon just like that: "Ephesisches Heroengrab" ("Ephesian hero's grave").[538] In so doing, Weninger had obviously followed Josef Keil who had repeatedly labelled the monument a "heroon".[539] Accordingly, such an inscription of the skull unequivocally links the relic of the CVU to J. Keil and J. Weninger. Since the writing on the bone appears quite unspecific (fig. 86), it can hardly be compared to other specimens of handwriting. Accordingly, it must remain unclear when, by whom, and for what purpose the skull was inscribed as long as bones with a comparable writing of known background are missing.

Most interestingly, Matiasek showed us a worn slip of paper that she had retrieved from inside the skull through the foramen magnum. Its obverse carried a letterhead belonging to a correspondence of the administration of the 'Reichsgau Niederdonau' from 1940 aiming to promote the 'Museum of the Reichsgau Niederdonau' to the mayors of the province ("An [d]en Herrn Bürgermeister in").[540] The reverse of the paper was used as a notepad and supported the seemingly characteristic handwriting: "Schädel aus Ephesus" ("skull from Ephesus", fig. 87).[541]

Following the skull's history, such lettering should have either derived from the pen of Josef Keil,[542] Josef Weninger[543] or that of Emil Breitinger. Accordingly, we compared the script on the paper with handwriting specimens of those three (fig. 88), and the results indicated that it was written by Josef Weninger himself (fig. 89). We concluded that Weninger identified the skull with the docket from an outdated correspondence when he took it with him to the Anthropological Institute in 1945. Hence, the annotated slip provides an additional argument for his contact with the skull from the Octagon in 1944/45.

The bone had undergone a conservation treatment by being varnished so that it appeared well–preserved. Regarding this, Matiasek informed us that E. Breitinger was

Fig. 86: The
inscription
"Ephesos Heroen-
grab" at the os
occipitale of the
Viennese skull

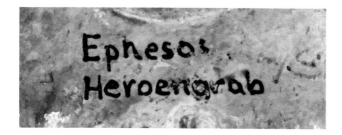

known for such a procedure. We assumed that the Viennese skull may have been
in use as a demonstration object for the "skull measurements" ("Totenschädelver-
messungen") between the late 1950s and the 1970s that Breitinger required of his
students during certain lessons.[544]

In accordance with its similarities to Weninger's images of the skull from the Octagon (fig. 85), the Viennese bone showed a missing mandible,[545] the missing cheek-

Fig. 87: Obverse
and reverse of the
worn paper sheet
that was inserted
into the Viennese
skull most likely
by J. Weninger in
1945

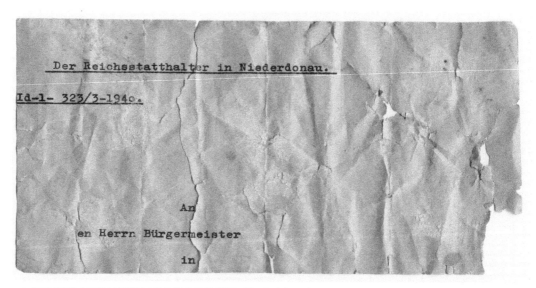

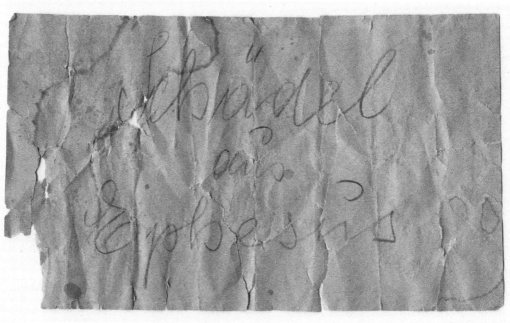

bones,[546] an open synchondrosis spheno–occipitalis,[547] the highly individual, map–like white area at the os frontale (fig. 85) plus the two teeth of the second quadrant as illustrated by Weninger.[548] With these observations, no doubts remained. The CVU have preserved the very bone that Weninger had published in 1953.[549] As a result, the skull from the Octagon is again available after being considered lost for decades, thereby making the royal Ptolemaic skeleton from Ephesos largely complete again.

In conclusion, the CVU harbours a skull that was deemed important enough to be labelled twice in the past:

➢ The older description was written by J. Weninger on a docket from the years after 1940, which he probably himself inserted into the cavum cranii, and which denotes the bone simply as "skull from Ephesus" and, thus, its origin (fig. 87);

➢ The younger writing on the occipital bone from an unknown context specifies this origin of the skull as being from a certain "hero's grave" in Ephesos (fig. 86).

As fairly unequivocal as these two pieces of information may appear, those never provoked the attention of the anthropological keepers since after 2004, i.e. for twenty years. Otherwise, it would have been understood that

➢ The skull obviously comes from an archaeological context, which would have suggested a query at the OeAI considering its longstanding research history of Ephesos;

➢ There is a missing skull from Ephesos frequently mentioned in literature;

➢ A skull from Ephesos was published by the anthropologist J. Weninger, and that

➢ The term hero's grave' was used synonymously for the Ephesian Octagon by J. Keil as well as by J. Weninger.

Accordingly, the respective association was out of reach. In other words, the Ephesian skull had always remained within the realm of Viennese anthropology since 1944, i.e. for about eighty years, and it would have remained unnoticed, if we had not conducted our enquiry.

THE UNIVERSITY OF VIENNA COLLECTIONS HAVE PRESERVED THE VERY SKULL THAT WAS PUBLISHED BY J. WENINGER IN 1953, BUT THAT HE HAD PROBABLY EXAMINED ALREADY IN 1944/45.

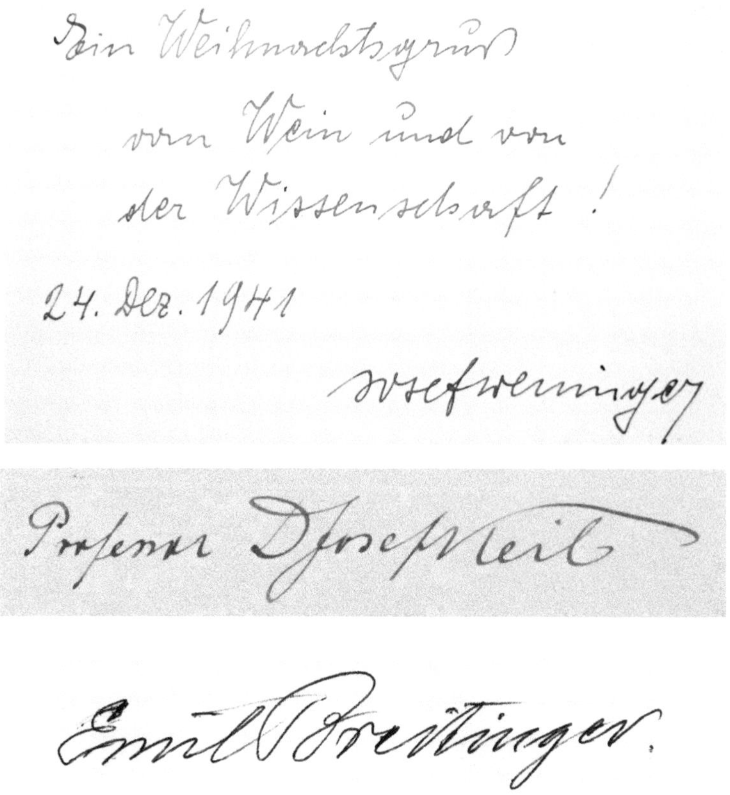

Fig. 88: Specimens of Weninger's (1941), Keil's (1927) and Breitinger's (1969) handwriting

Fig. 88: Specimens of Weninger's (1941), Keil's (1927) and Breitinger's (1969) handwriting

2.2 The end of a skull's journey

With the recognition of the final destination of the Ephesian skull's peregrination, we concluded on the following scenario:

> ➢ In 1929, J. Keil removed the bone from the Octagon's sarcophagus and brought it to the University of Greifswald where he was professor at that time, in order to receive information regarding the tomb's owner;
> ➢ At the latest in 1936, he transported the skull with him to Vienna and kept it in his department;
> ➢ In 1944, Keil consigned it to J. Weninger for a second anthropological opinion;
> ➢ In 1945, Weninger characterised the relic as "skull from Ephesus" (fig. 87) when removing it to the Anthropological Institute of the University of Vienna;
> ➢ In 1953, Weninger returned to his examination protocol of 1944/45 on the occasion of Egger's second Festschrift and published the Ephesian skull (fig. 85). For whatever reason, the bone did not find its way back to J. Keil after that;
> ➢ In 1957, Weninger retired and left the skull behind at the Anthropological Institute, so that it passed on to his successor E. Breitinger;
> ➢ In 1975, Breitinger acquired emeritus status. The Ephesian bone remained with him, which may explain why E. Reuer, S. Fabrizii–Reuer, H. Thür,[550] and F. Krinzinger[551] hunted for it in vain from the 1990s onwards;

Fig. 89: Comparison of Weningers handwriting (left; fig. 88) with the one from the Viennese paper slip (right; fig. 87) presenting the same layout of the letters 'u' (with the typical cursive wedge above) and 'h' (with the typical curved vertical stroke)

- ➢ At an unspecified time after Breitinger's death in 2004, a part of his estate, including the Ephesian bone, ended up at the CVU, where it stayed in disregard;
- ➢ In September 2022, we enquired after it and, very much to our surprise, were confronted with a skull that was unequivocally labelled as being from an Ephesian "hero's grave", the synonym of the Octagon (fig. 86).

Accordingly, the skull from the Ephesian Octagon was never lost but simply retained by its anthropological keepers, i.e. first by J. Weninger and then by E. Breitinger. The reason for that may have been their appreciation of the bone as coming from "exceptional circumstances of the finding",[552] i.e. their perception of the skull as one belonging to an outstanding personality "from the time around Christ's birth".[553] From such a perspective, Weninger "justified" his examination of the skull.[554] Probably because of this, the bone was inscribed with "Ephesos Heroengrab".

> AS IT TURNED OUT, THE SKULL FROM THE OCTAGON WAS NEVER LOST, BUT SIMPLY RETAINED AND FINALLY IGNORED.

Concluding remarks

Dating back to the early Augustan period, one of the oldest known octagonal monuments once towered in the heart of the Greco-Roman metropolis of Ephesos. Its basement houses a vault containing a local, unornamented sarcophagus. Inside, the skeleton of a single individual was found, without any accompanying grave goods.

In addition to its exceptional design, one of the intriguing aspects of this grave is found in its reluctance to reveal the identity of the intended recipient. No inscription or any other evidence point to a specific person, and even the open characterisation of the building as a burial site was avoided. Only certain architectural traits such as the false door and the inaccessible benches located at the *cella*-like core provide clues to its funerary function. Instead, several of its features suggest a wholly different understanding of the memorial.

In 1990, Hilke Thür proposed a connection between the Ephesian Octagon and Arsinoë IV of Alexandria, a historical figure who was assassinated on the holy Artemisian territory in the immediate vicinity of the city in 41 BC. The sacrilegious act was instigated by Kleopatra VII and reflects the dynastic struggles of the declining Ptolemaic rule over Egypt. Thür's proposal, however, has remained controversial and subject to ongoing discussion. Against this background, the available evidence concerning the Octagon is reviewed. Although each area investigated appears insufficient *per se* to establish a clear-cut connection between Arsinoë IV and the tomb, the sum of the evidence forms a coherent picture that hardly allows any other conclusion.

Firstly, a young female individual who died in her second decade of life, likely not older than 16 years, was interred within the Octagon. This finding is consistent with the biographical details of Arsinoë IV as recorded in ancient sources that suggest that she was born after 60 BC. In line with that, we propose that Arsinoë IV was born during Pharaoh Ptolemaios XII's exile in the Ephesian Artemision in 57/55 BC, which would make her the youngest child of her father. Furthermore, this background may also shed light on why Ptolemaios XII chose to name her Arsinoë, a name of great significance in Ephesos.

Indeed, several traits of the Octagon suggest a connection to the Ephesian Artemision. The monument takes the form of a typically structured temple-like *monopteros*, whose octagonal layout with its roots in sacred geometry, appears exceptional for the time. Furthermore, στέμματα, i.e. woollen, astragal-like cords ending in tassels, were integrated into the grave's ornamentation, a motif that would have evoked associations with the κληῖδες, the identical attribute of the Ephesian Artemis. In addition, the mausoleum was not erected just anywhere in the city, but in a location of utmost importance for the cult of Artemis Ephesia, further underscoring the proposed context.

Yet, the construction of the tomb did not immediately follow Arsinoë's sudden death in 41 BC. Instead, its construction began approximately fifteen years later, a fact consistent with the historical context. When the "inimitable lovers" Kleopatra VII and Marcus Antonius (Plut. Ant. 28. 71) became the "society of partners in death" in 30 BC (Plut. Ant. 71), the exhausting period of the Roman Civil Wars ended, having demonstrated in Egypt the result, if "drunken violence" (Strab. geogr. XVII 11), greed (Ios. ant. Iud. XV 4. Ios. c. Ap. II 5) and gluttony (Plin. nat. IX 119f.) supersede "human and divine law" (App. Rom. V 9). Even the Ephesian Artemision, Asia's foremost *asylum*, had been repeatedly violated during the previous period of disorder, threatening the glory and the economic basis of the city. In particular, the blasphemous killing of Arsinoë IV who was briefly the Lagid Queen of Alexandria and Cyprus, must have constituted a widely known scandal that could not be addressed as long as Ephesos was under the control of Kleopatra VII and Marcus Antonius.

After an unspectacular primary burial of Arsinoë IV, a memorial to these events became only possible after the suicides of Kleopatra VII and Marcus Antonius. It is suggested that the authorities of the Artemision took Arsinoë IV as an example, as she was born and killed on its holy ground. An architectural symbol was commissioned in order to announce the renewed sacrosanctity of the temenos as an aspect of the Augustan restoration. However, addressing the mere possibility of an insecure Artemisian *asylum* was a delicate issue. Therefore, a somewhat vague monument was created at a specific urban location, featuring a layout and an ornamentation that referred to its sacred context, into which the physical remains of Arsinoë IV were secondarily transferred.

The grave was built in the very centre of the rapidly expanding metropolis of Asia, at the time when Octavian/Augustus became the sole ruler of the Roman Empire. It is located between two fountain houses of historical significance and in close proximity to the large Artemis altar at the sacred Triodos. To the west stood the Hypelaios fountain house, commemorating the founders of Ephesos, the mythical Athenian prince Androklos and the Hellenistic King Lysimachos. The latter was the first husband of the later Queen Arsinoë II Philadelphe, from whom Ephesos was briefly named 'Arsinoëia', as it was commonly believed in Augustan times. To the east of the Octagon, another fountain house, dedicated to Ptolemaios IV and Arsinoë III, demonstrated the former Lagid rule over the city (ca. 246–188 BC). Thus,

Arsinoë IV was laid to rest between two monuments with strong ties to her homonymous ancestors.

With the interpretation of the Octagon as the heroon for a Greco-Egyptian heroine, the mausoleum furthermore sheds light on a specific topographical setting at an outstanding location within Ephesos, the Embolos. This area carried a special significance in the 'lived history' and 'lived religion' of Ephesos for approximately one and a half millennia, from the earliest period of the Greek colonisation until the Byzantine period. Very likely, the Octagon was the starting point for the consolidation of the lower Embolos area into a 'walk of fame' of the "first and greatest metropolis of Asia". For two more centuries, numerous nymphaea praising Roman emperors, and tombs commemorating noble and generous individuals, Roman proconsuls, local benefactors, and Sophists were built along this street.

In conclusion, all available evidence supports the interpretation of the Octagon as Arsinoë's mausoleum. Only by recognizing the monument as a royal sepulchre with a Hellenistic Greco-Egyptian background can its "peculiar" traits find a logical explanation. Accordingly, we suggest that Ephesos has preserved the only known Ptolemaic burial place, thereby illustrating a specific historic episode well-known from ancient sources.

In light of our findings, and, in particular, with our discovery of Arsinoë's skull, it may be appropriate to consider the anastylosis of the Octagon, for which a large amount of data has already been collected. The rebuilding of the Ephesian 'Arsinoëion' would not only further complete the architectural ensemble of an extraordinary location as it appeared during the 'Golden Period' of the city. Most importantly, it would also offer a final resting place for the orphaned and now nearly complete skeleton of young Arsinoë IV who experienced a tragic fate more than 2,000 years ago. Subjected to a short and violent life as a figurehead within a game of thrones, she became a girl–Queen and Caesar's trophy, only to be murdered on sacred ground before reaching adulthood. After reposing within the Ephesian temple mausoleum for two millennia, her rest was disturbed in 1929. The skull was removed from the grave, then retained and finally ignored; the postcranial skeleton was subjugated to repeated examinations. Accordingly, we suggest the return of the largely complete skeleton to its original setting, so that Arsinoë IV may be reburied in honour in the sarcophagus of the Octagon, thereby ending a century of uncertainty and restoring her peace in perpetuity.

Fig. 90: Aerial view overlooking excavated Ephesos from the west, with the central 'Curetes Street' running in the saddle between Mt. Preon (Bülbüldağ; point of view) in the foreground and the double-peaked Panayırdağ (Tracheia on the left and Mt. Pion on the right), thereby connecting the Triodos at the southeast corner of the Tetragonos Agora on the left and the Upper Agora on the right

Acknowledgements

Our work owes a great debt to the authors who have published their research over the past three decades. Without their contributions, our project would not have been possible. Furthermore, we would like to express our gratitude to those who generously responded to our requests and provided us with invaluable support.

Secil Tezer Altay (DAI Istanbul); Bernard Andreae; Maria Aurenhammer; Isabella Benda (Austrian Academy of Sciences, Vienna); Franco Benucci (Università di Padova); Wilma Buchinger (Austrian National Library, Vienna); Francesca Cappellini (Alinari Archives, Firenze); Jan Cemper-Kiesslich (University Salzburg); Joseph Coplin (Antiquarium Fine Arts Gallery, New York); Ulrike Denk (University Archives, Vienna); Vera Dittrich (Graveyard Hietzing, Vienna); Martina Düntzer (DAI Berlin); Igor Eberhard (University Vienna); Stefan Eminger (Archives Lower Austria, St. Pölten); Ralf Engel (Federal Archives, Berlin); Linda Erker (University Vienna); Susanne Fabrizii-Reuer; Claudia Feigl (University Vienna); Serge Février; Andreas Fingernagel (Austrian National Library, Vienna); Robert Fleischer; Niki Gail (Austrian Academy of Sciences, Vienna); Verena Gassner (University Vienna); Katja Geisenhainer (University Vienna); Andre Gingrich; Franz Glaser; Franz Graf-Stuhlhofer; Kurt Gschwantler; Markus Hafner (University Graz); Katharina Hasitzka-Knibbe (Austrian Academy of Sciences, Vienna); Heinrich Hemme (University of Applied Sciences, Aachen); Günther Hölbl; Matthias Hoernes (University Vienna); Sarah Homan-Cormack; Victoria Immervoll (University Vienna); Othmar Jaeggi (Université de Lausanne); Werner Jobst; Andrea Jördens (University Heidelberg); Jana Johr (Austrian Academy of Sciences, Vienna); Jennifer Karl (Austrian State Archives, Vienna); Doris Karlik (Antiquariat Klabund, Vienna); Guntram Koch (University Marburg); Thomas Koppe (University Greifswald); Barbara Kowalewska (Anthropological Society, Vienna); Eveline Krummen; Susanne Kühberger (Austrian State Archives, Vienna); Agnes Kunze (Winckelmann Society, Stendal); Michaela Laichmann (Archives City of Vienna); Nina Liebich-Koller (Austrian Social Democratic Party, Vienna); Gerald Ließ (Municipality Klagenfurt); Stefan Mach (Austrian State Archives, Vienna); Sophia Mairinger; Thomas Maisel (University Archives, Vienna); Brigitte Manzer (Graveyard Grinzing, Vienna); Ruth Marsh (The Telegraph, London); Katarina Matiasek (University Vienna); Herbert Matis; Claudia Montuschi (Biblioteca Apostolocia Vaticana); Jana Mornhinweg (Federal Archives, Berlin); Friedrich Ortner (Upper Austrian State Library, Linz/Donau); Lina Pietsch (University Hamburg); Georg Plattner (Kunsthistorisches Museum, Vienna); Eduard Pollhamer (Office of the Federal Government of Lower Austria); Walter Prochaska; Bernhard Prokisch (Office of the Federal Government of Upper Austria); Ursula Quatember (University Graz); Daniele U. Risser (University

Vienna); Samuel Sales (Bodleian Libraries); Demetrius Savvides; Bettina Schwarz (Austrian Academy of Sciences, Vienna); Stefan Sienell (Austrian Academy of Sciences, Vienna); Clara Spielvogel (ÖGB-Verlag, Vienna); Hans Taeuber; Klaus Taschwer; Maria Teschler-Nicola (Natural History Museum, Vienna); Hilke Thür; Barbara Thuswaldner; Elisabet Tsigarida (Ephorate of Antiquities of Pella); Herbert Verreth (Katholieke Universiteit Leuven);Teresa Vondrak (University Graz); Gerhard Weber (University Vienna); Sandra B. Weiss (Wiesenthal Institute for Holocaust Studies, Archives Vienna); Elfriede Wiener (Federal Office for the Protection of Monuments, Vienna); Harald Wilfing (University Vienna); Karin Wiltschke-Schrotta (Natural History Museum, Vienna); Franz Martin Wimmer; Ingemar Winkler; Gudrun Wlach; Traute Wohlers-Scharf; Stephen Wordsworth (The Council for At-Risk Academics, London); Hans-Peter Zimmer (Austrian National Library, Vienna).

However, the interpretations presented in this work are solely those of the authors, and we take full responsibility for any errors or inaccuracies.

We would also like to express our sincere appreciation to Ertem Bey and his Merkez Kıraathanesi in Attnang-Puchheim, Austria. Over the years, we have spent many hours at this establishment, enjoying countless cups of coffee while pondering the intricacies of the Octagon.

Notes

The Alexandrian Queen Arsinoë IV

1 OGIS II 741; Diod. I 44: Πτολεμαῖος ὁ νέος Διόνυσος; Eus. chron., ed. Schoene – Petermann 1876, 131: *Ptlomaeus, qui novus Dionisus appellabatur*. 167. 171. – Huß 2001, 674f.

2 Strab. geogr. XVII 1, 11; Clem. Al. strom. XXI; Cic. fam. VIII 4. – Bennett 2013, s.v. Ptolemy XII; Schäfer 2006, 19–21; Huß 2001, 703–706; Hölbl 1994, 195–205; Strack 1897, 207–211.

3 Porph. FGrHist 260 F2, 14, and Eus. chron., ed. Schoene – Petermann 1876, 167, address Kleopatra Tryphaina as the fourth daughter of Ptolemaios XII. – Thür 2015, 269: "Arsinoë IV was one of the six children of Ptolemaios XII". – Herklotz 2009, 141; Huß 2001, 692 n. 88; Hölbl 1994, 195; Green 1985, 137; Jones 1971, 28.

4 Huß 2001, 855; Van Oppen de Ruiter 2007, 535.

5 Strab. geogr. XVII 1, 11; Eus. chron., ed. Schoene – Petermann 1876, 167: *Ptlomaeus Roma rediens* [...] *vita eam* [i.e., Berenike IV] *expellebat*. – Bennett 2013, s.v. Berenike IV.

6 Strab. geogr. XVII 1, 10f.; Clem. Al. strom. XXI. – Bennett 2013, s.v. Cleopatra VII; Strack 1897, 210f. n. 46.

7 App. Rom. V 9; Bell. alex. 4; Cass. Dio XLII 43; Oros. hist. VI 16; Liv. per. 112; Eus. chron., ed. Schoene – Petermann 1876, 167. – Bennett 2013, s.v. Ptolemy XIII; Volkmann 1927b, 1756: "der älteste Sohn des Ptolemaios XII. Auletes" ("The oldest son of Ptolemaios XII Auletes"); Strack 1897, 210f n. 46.

8 On the death year of Ptolemaios XIV and his age then, see in particular Ios. ant. Iud. XV 89 ("fifteen years of age") and Eus. chron., ed. Schoene – Petermann 1876, 167–169: *Post interitum Ptlomaei, junior frater Kleopatrae cum sorore sua throni consors fuit, Ptlomaeus nuncupatus, Caesaris consensu (voluntate): atque (adeo) quintus annus Kleopatrae, primusque Ptlomaei scriptus est (scribebatur); et iisdem adhuc duo alii accedunt anni usque ad ejus necem Hoc e vivis sublato, Kleopatrae insidiis, quarto sui (hujus) anno, Kleopatrae autem octavo* ("After Ptolemaios' [XIII] death [in 47 BC], Kleopatra's younger brother, who was also called Ptolemaios [XIV], became joint ruler with his sister, as proposed by Caesar. The next year [46 BC] was called the 5th year of Kleopatra and the 1st year of Ptolemaios [XIV], and so it continued for the following two years [i.e., 45 44 BC], until he died. He was plotted against and killed by Kleopatra, in his 4th year [i.e., in 44 BC], which was Kleopatra's 8th year"). – Heinen 1966, 143 n. 4 ("44/43 BC [...] born in 59/58 BC").

9 Ios. ant. Iud. XV 89; Eus. chron., ed. Schoene – Petermann 1876, 167. – Volkmann 1927c, 1759: "jüngerer Sohn des Ptolemaios XII. Auletes" ("younger son of Ptolemaios XII Auletes"). – Bennett 2013, s.v. Ptolemy XIV; Strack 1897, 210f. n. 46.

10 Bennett 2013, s.v. Cleopatra V; Burstein 2004, 75: "sister wife Cleopatra V Tryphaina". 95; Huß 2001, 674f. 705 n. 2; Bennett 1997, 60f.; Hölbl 1994, 195f.; Green 1990, 650. 901 n. 21; Strack 1897, 65. 210 n. 43.

11 Strab. geogr. XVII 1, 11: τριῶν δ᾽ αὐτῶι θυγατέρων οὐσῶν, ὧν μία γνησία ἡ πρεσβυτάτη ("He [Ptolemaios XII] had three daughters, of whom one, the eldest [i.e. Berenike IV], was legitimate"). Pape 1906, s.v. γνήσιος (conceived in wedlock, legitimate). – Huß 2001, 705 n. 2; Bennett 1997, 60–64; Hölbl 1994, 204; Strack 1897, 67.

12 Accordingly, Grant 1977, 48. 100. 105. 157. 172, stated that Arsinoë IV was a half–sister of Kleopatra VII. Strabon's statement is doubted by Bennett 1997, 63, although "Strabo spent much time in Egypt and wrote within living memory of the Ptolemaic regime". Accordingly, Bennett 1997, 60. 63, suggests Kleopatra VI as the mother of all five children. – Thür 2015, 269.

13 BM 886: http://attalus.org/egypt/psherenptah.html (accessed on 21.04.2022). – Huß 2001, 705 n. 2 ("Harim"); Bennett 1997, 61; Strack 1897, 67.

14 Bennett 1997, 61. Different: Huß 2001, 705 n. 2.

15 OGIS 185: βασιλέως Πτολεμαίου θεοῦ Φιλοπάτορος Φιλαδέλφου καὶ τῆς βασιλίσσης καὶ τῶν τέκνων τὸ προσκύνημα παρὰ τῆι Ἴσιδι τῆι κυρίᾳ ἔγραψεν Λυσίμαχος πάρεδρος ("On behalf of King Ptolemaios the god Philopator Philadelphos and the queen and their children, Lysimachos the assessor recorded his obeisance to the Lady Isis"), http://www.attalus.org/docs/ogis/s185.html (accessed on 21.04.2023). – Bennett 1997, 60 n. 105. Pape 1906, s.v. τέκνον (the generated, the fathered, child, son, daughter).

16 Herklotz 2009, 142.

17 OGIS II 741: ὑπὲρ βασιλέως Πτολεμαίου, θεοῦ Νέου Διονύσου, καὶ τῶν τέκνων αὐτοῦ, θεῶν Νέων Φιλαδέλφων ("For [the sake of] King Ptolemaios, new Dionysos, and his children, the new sibling–loving Gods"). – Schäfer 2006, 18; Hölbl 1994, 204; Heinen 1966, 179.

18 Strab. geogr. XVII 1, 11; Eus. chron., ed. Schoene – Petermann 1876, 167: *Defunctus est (defungebatur) novus Dionisius, quattuor liberos relinquent, duos Ptolemaeos, et Kleopatram ac Arsinoem* (τελευτῶν ὁ νέος Διόνυσος ἐπὶ παιδὶ τέτρασι, Πτολεμαίοις δυσὶ, καὶ Κλεοπάτρᾳ καὶ Ἀρσινόῃ). Petschenig – Stowasser 1930, s.v. *liberi*

(born free). Pape 1906, s.v. παῖς (with respect to the age: boy, young human).

19 Plut. Ant. 86.

20 App. civ. II 84.

21 Ios. ant. Iud. XV 89.

22 Hölbl 1994, 204; Strack 1897, 210f. n. 46.

23 Strab. geogr. XVII 1, 11: δύο νήπιοι. Pape 1906, s. v. νήπιέη (nonage = not of age).

24 App. Rom. civ. V 8: παῖς.

25 App. Rom. civ. II 83: Τούς τε βασιλεύοντας αὐτῆς, εἰ καὶ παῖδές εἰσι.

26 See pp. 17f. and nn. 72. 77–80. 224.

27 According to our knowledge, the only discussion regarding some issues of the Ephesian Octagon and Arsinoë IV is provided by Bennett 2013, s.v. Arsinoe IV.

28 Caes. civ. 108: *ex duobus filiis maior et ex duabus filiabus ea, quae aetate antecedebat.* Bell. alex. 33. Eus. chron., ed. Schoene – Petermann 1876, 167: *suis natu maioribus Ptolemaeo et Kleopatrae* (τοῖς προγενεστέροις αὐτοῦ παιδὶ).

29 Strab. geogr. XVII 1, 11; Caes. civ. III 107; Bell. alex. 33; Eus. chron., ed. Schoene – Petermann 1876, 167: *fratremque suum majorem Ptlomaeum.* – Gehrke 2005, 113; Huß 2001, 705; Hölbl 1994, 204; Heinen 1966, 142–144.

30 App. civ. II 84.

31 Caes. civ. III 103; Eus. chron., ed. Schoene – Petermann 1876, 167. – Huß 2001, 707. 709. 713; Hölbl 1994, 205f.

32 Strab. geogr. XVII 1, 11: καὶ ἀπῆρε μετὰ τῆς ἀδελφῆς εἰς τὴν Συρίαν. Caes. civ. III 103; App. Rom. II 84; Liv. per. 111, 3; Eus. chron., ed. Schoene – Petermann 1876, 167; Malalas IX 217. – According to Plut. Caes. 48, Pothinos had driven Kleopatra VII out of the country. – Hölbl 1994, 206f.; Green 1990, 664; Green 1985, 154; Heinen 1966, 62f.; Strack 1897, 210f n. 46.

33 App. civ. II 84. – Pape 1906, s.v. Δαίμον (God, but also: fate, doom, destiny).

34 Hölbl 1994, 206.

35 App. civ. II 84; Liv. per. 112; Plut. Pomp. 80.

36 Liv. per. 112; Plut. Pom. 80.

37 Lucan. X 141: *candida Sidonio perlucent pectora filo* ("the white breasts shimmered through the Sidonian fabric"). Plut. Caes. 48f.; Suet. Iul. 52: *Dilexit et reginas* [...] *sed maxime Cleopatram* ("He loved Queens [...] but above all Kleopatra"). – However, a statement of Suet. Iul. 52 prevents from overrating Caesar's relationship to Kleopatra VII. The author repeats a saying, whereas Caesar was "every woman's man and every man's woman" (*omnium mulierum virum et omnium virorum mulierem*). – Hölbl 1994, 208.

38 Cass. Dio XLII 34: καὶ τότε τῇ τῆς ὥρας ἀκμῇ πολὺ διέπρεπε.

39 Eus. chron., ed. Schoene – Petermann 1876, 167: *Julio Caesare auxilium ferente Kleopatrae.* Cass. Dio XLII 36, labels Kleopatra VII as γυνή being twenty–one years of age in 48 BC.

40 Liv. per. 112; Cass. Dio XLII 35. – Huß 2001, 713f.; Hölbl 1994, 209.

41 Plut. Pomp. 79; Strab. geogr. XVII 1, 11; Bell. alex. 33; Suet. Iul. 35, 1. – Huß 2001, 705; Hölbl 1994, 204; Heinen 1966, 142–144. – Previously, C. Iulius Caesar seems to have pondered the idea to turn Egypt into a Roman province: Huß 2001, 680.

42 Cass. Dio XLII 35; Bell. alex. 33. – Schäfer 2006, 61; Huß 2001, 714; Green 1990, 666; Green 1985, 155; Heinen 1966, 142.

43 Huß 2001, 684f. 714; Hölbl 1994, 210; Heinen 1966, 91. – As to the reasons of Caesar's doing, see Suet. Iul. 35.

44 Caes. civ. III 112; Bell. alex. 4, 33; Strab. geogr. XVII 1, 11; Eus. chron., ed. Schoene – Petermann 1876, 167. – Such a relationship is also implied by Eus. chron., ed. Schoene – Petermann 1876, 167: *natu majoribus Ptolemaeo et Kleopatrae.*

45 In line with that, Kleopatra is called "the elder of the two daughters" (Bell. alex. 33: *maiorique ex duabus filiis;* Strab. geogr. XVII 1, 11: πρεσβυτάτην δὲ Κλεοπάτραν). – Bennett 2013, s.v. Arsinoe IV n. 4.

46 Mahaffy 1899, 243.

47 Brome Weigall 1914, 104.

48 Green 1990, 650. – See to that Bennett 2013, s.v. Arsinoe IV n. 4: "probably by misplaced association with Cleopatra VII, who certainly was "barely adolescent" in 58/7".

49 Gehrke 2005, 115: "eine blutjunge Prinzessin".

50 Schäfer 2006, 75: "Herrschaft des jungen Mädchens".

51 Tyldesley 2008, 104.

52 Cass. Dio XLII 36.

53 Mittag 2003, 192f. 201; Huß 2001, 714–720; Hölbl 1994, 211; Green 1985, 156; Buchheim 1960, 23. – Strack 1897, 70, states the possibility that Arsinoë IV and her brother Ptolemaios XIII had a co–regency for a short time.

54 Cassius Dio repeatedly refers to the Egyptian aversion to be "under female rule". In Cass. Dio XLII 36, he mentions the Alexandrian dislike "to be ruled by a woman (ὑπὸ γυναικὸς ἄρχεσθαι). In XLII 42, the author states the irritation "to be ruled by the eunuch and the woman" (οὗ εὐνούχου καὶ τῆς γυναικὸς ἀρχῇ). And in Cass. Dio XLII 44, he mentions Caesar's fear, because he had delivered the Alexandrians "to a woman's rule" (γυναικὶ ἄρχειν). – Heinen 1966, 119.

55 Cass. Dio XLII 36; Lucan X 356.

56 Cass. Dio XLII 39. – Bennett 2013, s.v. Arsinoe IV n. 7; Heinen 1966, 109.

57 Caes. civ. 112: *vacuam possessionem regni.* Lucan. X 522; Strab. geogr. XVII 1, 11. – Gemoll 1965, s.v. Λᾶγος (the first of the Ptolemaic lineage).

58 Huß 2001, 716; Hölbl 1994, 210; Heinen 1966, 107.

59 Huß 2001, 707; Hölbl 1994, 206.

60 Cass. Dio XLII 39: Ὁ οὖν Καῖσαρ φοβηθεὶς μὴ καὶ ὁ Ποθεινὸς τὸν Πτολεμαῖον ἐκκλέψῃ ("Caesar feared that Pothinos Pothinos might steal Ptolemaios").

61 Cass. Dio XLII 39. – Heinen 109f. n. 7.

62 Huß 2001, 716.

63 Cass. Dio XLII 39: καὶ ταύτην ἐκεῖνοι βασιλίδα. – Such record is confirmed by Cassius Dio XLIII 19, and App. civ. V 9, addressing Arsinoë IV likewise as Queen. – Liddell – Scott 1889, s.v. βασιλίς = βασίλεια (Queen, Princess). – Huß 2001, 716; Hölbl 1994, 211; Heinen 1966, 113.

64 Cass. Dio XLII 39. – Caesar states that Arsinoë IV herself aspired to the vacated throne: Caes. civ. 112: *Interim filia minor Ptolomaei regis vacuam possessionem regni sperans* [...] *sese ex regia traiecit* ("Meanwhile, the younger daughter of King Ptolemaios, hoping for the vacated throne, removed herself from the palace"). – Hölbl 1994, 210; Heinen 1966, 108 n. 5. 109.

65 Bell. civ. III 104: *praefectum regium, singulari hominem audacia*. – Achillas was amongst those who killed Cn. Pompeius Magnus (bell. civ. III 104). Huß 2001, 711; Heinen 1966, 40f.

66 Bell. alex. 4. – Huß 2001, 717; Hölbl 1994, 211.

67 Hölbl 1994, 211; Heinen 1966, 107 n. 2. 116.

68 Bell. alex. 33: *minorem, Arsinoen, cuius nomine diu regnasse impotenter Ganymeden docuimus*.

69 Bell. alex. 4: *praeoccupat Arsinoe per Ganymeden eunuchum, nutricium suum*. – Hölbl 1994, 211.

70 Bell. alex. 23: *dominatione crudelissima Ganymedis*.

71 Bell. alex. 23: *fiduciario regno*. – Heinen 1966, 117–120.

72 Hölbl 1994, 211; Heinen 1966, 107 n. 2. – Mahaffy 1899, 243, addresses Ptolemaios XIII in 48 BC likewise: "The younger boy was only of account in supplying a nominal husband for Cleopatra".

73 App. Rom. civ. II 83.

74 Bell. alex. 23: *paratam enim omnem multitudinem esse, confectam taedio puellae* ("everybody [is] wearied and tired because of the girl"). – Petschenig – Stowasser 1930, s.v. *puella* (girl, young woman) in contrast to *femina*. – Bennett 2013, s.v. Arsinoe IV n. 4: "[*puella*] could be a Latin translation of Παρθένος, i.e. a young unmarried woman".

75 Schol. to Lucan. X 521: *Arsinoe: soror Ptolemaei fuit; hanc Ganymedes quidam spado puellae acceptissimus in castra Achillae perduxit, cuius iussu Achillas occisus est et exercitui praeponitur Ganymedes* ("Arsinoe was the sister of Ptolemaios [XIII] The eunuch Ganymedes brought the most accepted girl to the camp of Achillas. At his [Ganymedes] command, Achillas was killed, and Ganymedes was appointed to lead the army").

76 Bell. alex. 4; Lucan. X 520; Cass. Dio XLII 39. – Petschenig – Stowasser 1930, s.v. *nutricius* (tutor, housemaster); Schäfer 2006, 69f.

77 App. civ. II 84 (παῖς). Caes. civ. III 103. 108. 112 (*puer*). Cass. Dio XLII 37 (παῖς). XLII 43 (παιδάριον). XLII 44 (παιδίον). Lucan. X 54. – Petschenig – Stowasser 1930, s.v. *puer* (child, boy, young man). – Pape 1906, s.v. παιδάριον and παιδίον (diminutive of παῖς: childling, little boy). s.v. παῖς (with respect to the age: boy, young human).

78 Cass. Dio XLII 42; App. civ. II 84; Caes. civ. III 108, 112; Plut. Pomp. 77. – Huß 2001, 707; Hölbl 1994, 206.

79 Strab. geogr. XVII 1, 11: ἀδελφὸν αὐτῆι νέον παντελῶς ὄντα.

80 App. civ. II 84: Ὁ δὲ ἦν μὲν περὶ τρισκαίδεκα ἔτη μάλιστα γεγονώς ("He [Ptolemaios XIII] was around thirteen years old").

81 Heinen 1966, 107 n. 2; Bevan 1927, 361. 362; Strack 1897, 210f n. 46.

82 Huß 2001, 707 n. 22; Amundsen – Diers 1969, 127–129. – See also Cens. XIV 2: *itaque primo gradu usque annum quintum decimum pueros dictos, quod sint puri, id est inpubes* ("In the first stage until the age of fifteen years, they are called boys [*pueros dictos*] because they are still pure [*purī*], i.e. not mature"). Instead of *impubes*, *inpubes* is used here. Petschenig – Stowasser 1930, s.v. *pubes* (nubile, mature). s.v. *impubes* (not mature, not adult, not nubile). s.v. *purus* (clear, pure, untainted).

83 Bennett 2013, s.v. Arsinoe IV n. 4, states that Arsinoë IV was "most likely rather older than 12 at the time", because she was [...] an actor, not a cipher [in 48 BC]. On the other hand, one can reasonably argue that in fact she [= Arsinoë IV] was only and always Ganymede's puppet".

84 Huß 2001, 721, contributes an interesting assumption regarding Arsinoë and Cyprus after 47 BC: [Betreffend Zypern] "scheint Caesar das Versprechen, das er Arsinoe IV. und ihrem Bruder gegeben hatte, unter den veränderten Umständen nicht zurückgenommen zu haben" ([Regarding Cyprus,] "Caesar does not seem to have taken back the promise he had made to Arsinoë and her brother under the changed circumstances"). – Hölbl 1994, 212; Heinen 1966, 145.

85 Bell. Alex. 33: *minorem, Arsinoen* [...] *deducere ex regno statuit*.

86 App. Rom. II 101; Vell. II 56; Oros. hist. VI 16. – Huß 2001, 721 n. 161; Hölbl 1994, 212f.; Heinen 1966, 143.

87 Cass. Dio XLIII 19: ἔν τε δεσμοῖς. – See also Schol. to Lucan. X 521: *Arsinoe: soror Ptolemaei fuit;* [...] *Hunc postea Caesar victis Aegyptiis in triumpho duxit, ut meminit Livius in libro quarto civilis belli* ("Arsinoe was the sister of Ptolemaios [XIII]. Later, after having defeated the Egyptians, Caesar led her in triumph as Livius mentions in the 4th book on the civil war").

88 Flor. epit. II 13. – Harders 2010, 61; Künzl 1988, 74–80; Petschenig – Stowasser 1930, s.v. *ferculum* (litter, ferculum).

89 Künzl 1988, 79.

90 Cass. Dio XLIII 19.

91 Cass. Dio XLIII 19. – However, Caesar presented Iuba II of Numidia, likewise a child then: App. civ. II 101.

92 Cass. Dio XLIII 19: πάμπολυν οἶκτον.

93 Cass. Dio XLIII 19: τὰ οἰκεῖα πάθη. – Harders 2010, 60f.; Schäfer 2006, 95; Huß 2001, 723 n. 16; Pape 1906, s.v. πάθη (misery, calamity). – Cassius Dio refers to such reaction on Arsinoë IV again: Cass. Dio XLIII 20. See also Cass. Dio XLIII 24 (τῶν οἰκείων κακῶν). App. civ. II 101, provides a similar phrase when the crowd at the triumph were likewise reminded of their "do-

mestic evils" (τοῖς οἰκείος κακοῖς), this time, however, caused by an image of Lucius Scipio.

94 Cass. Dio XLII 42.

95 Cass. Dio XLIII 19: καὶ ἡ Ἀρσινόη γυνή τε οὖσα καὶ βασιλὶς ποτε νομισθεῖσα ἔν τε δεσμοῖς.

96 Pape 1906, s.v. γυνή (As for the meaning of γυνή, this word denotes a woman in contrast to a man without regard to age and regardless of whether she is married or not).

97 Petschenig – Stowasser 1930, s.v. *pompa* (parade, procession).

98 Green 1990, 669; Green 1985, 157.

99 Cass. Dio XLIII 19: διὰ τοὺς ἀδελφοὺς. – Pape 1906, s.v. ἀδελφός (brother, sibling). – Harders 2010, 62; Huß 2001, 723; Hölbl 1994, 212; Heinen 1966, 142f.

100 Hölbl 1994, 212.

101 App. civ. IV 61. V 9.

102 This Serapion may have been the one who was in Rome with Ptolemaios XII as well as Caesar's envoy to Achillas in 48 BC (bell. civ. III 109; Cass. Dio XLII 36). – Huß 2001, 714f. 728. 731; Hölbl 1994, 215f.; Heinen 1966, 7 n. 1. 91 n. 2. 100–104. 145 n. 1; Buchheim 1960, 26f. 92.

103 See Cassius Dio XLII 46, referring to the not settled state of Egypt after the 'Alexandrian War'.

104 Mann 2018, 454; Pfrommer 2002, 29. 33. – See also Burstein 2004, 75: "The women of the last Ptolemies were as formidable as the men, so it is not surprising that Cleopatra's most important rivals were her sisters, Berenike IV and Arsinoe IV".

105 Plut. Ant. 25. 27. – Hölbl 1994, 208.

106 Cass. Dio XLII 34: περικαλλεστάτη γυναικῶν ἐγένετο. – Pape 1906, s.v. περικαλλής (most beautiful), a term maybe drawn from Hom. Il. V 389. Plutarch Ant. 25. – On the other hand, Plutarch Ant. 27 says that her beauty was not beyond comparison.

107 Plut. Ant. 25: τοῦτο δὴ τὸ Ὁμηρικόν, "ἐλθεῖν εἰς Κιλικίαν εὖ ἐντύνασαν ἓ αὐτήν" taken from Hom. Il. XIV 162: ἐλθεῖν εἰς Ἴδην εὖ ἐντύνασαν ἓ αὐτήν.

108 Plut. Ant. 25. Hom. Il. XIV 163f.

109 Hor. carm. I 37. – Pfeiffer 2010, 61f.; Kitchell 2015, 125–151. – On the term "monstrum" see also Cic. Catil. II 1 and Cic. Phil. XIII 49.

110 Stat. silv. III 113.

111 Kunsthistorisches Museum, Münzkabinett, RÖ 4426 (https://www.khm.at/objektdb/detail/1034722/, accessed on 21.04.2023).

112 Prop. III 11, 39: *scilicet incesti meretrix regina Canopi* ("Obviously, the whore–Queen of incestuous Canopus"). The term *regina meretrix* is also found in Plin. nat. IX 199. – Lewis – Short 1879, s.v. *meretrix* (prostitute, harlot, courtesan). – On that, see also the famous statement from the late antique Aur. Vict. vir. ill. 86: *Haec tantae libidinis fuit, ut saepe prostiterit, tantae pulchritudinis, ut multi noctem illius morte emerint* ("She had so much lust that she often offered herself, and so much beauty that many earned death from a night with her"). However, Kleopatra's reputation was such in late antiquity that Ammianus Marcellinus ascribed the erection of the Pharos Tower to her: Amm. XXII 16.

113 Pape 1906, s.v. πλεονεξία (greed, avarice). – See also Cass. Dio LI 15: Κλεοπάτρα δὲ ἄπληστος μὲν Ἀφροδίτης ἄπληστος δὲ χρημάτων γενομένη ("Kleopatra, insatiable for pleasure, insatiable for wealth").

114 Pape 1906, s.v. παρανομία (acting against laws, customs, and traditions).

115 Ios. ant. Iud. XV 89; Ios. c. Ap. II 5.

116 https://dewiki.de/Lexikon/Fulvia (accessed on 21.04.2023).

117 Plut. Ant. 10. 20.

118 Scott 1933.

119 Cic. Phil. XIII 18. – As to Fulvia's "greed" see also App. civ. IV 29, where it is described that she caused her neighbour Caesetius Rufus to be slain during the proscriptions of the second triumvirate, since he refused to sell his mansion located near to hers. Having successfully pushed him out of the way, she pinned his head to the front of her house. Val. Max. V 4.

120 App. civ. V 19. – According to App. civ. V 59, Fulvia started the 'Perusinian War' in 41/40 BC out of jealousy because of Kleopatra VII.

121 Cass. Dio XLVII 8 describes how Fulvia maltreated the dead body of M. T. Cicero by spitting on his cut–off head, opening the mouth, pulling out the tongue and piercing it with her hair pins.

122 Plut. Ant. 10.

123 Cass. Dio XLVIII 10.

124 Plut. Ant. 10: ἀλλ᾽ ἄρχοντος ἄρχειν καὶ στρατηγοῦντος στρατηγεῖν βουλόμενον.

125 Plut. Ant. 10.

126 Φιλοπάτωρ. – Huß 2001, 703; Hölbl 1994, 205; Heinen 1996, 177f.

127 Cass. Dio XLII 37. – Hölbl 1994, 208f.; Heinen 1966, 159, understands the internal Ptolemaic conflict as the one between Kleopatra VII and Pothinos, the tutor of Ptolemaios XIII. According to Plut. Caes. 48, Pothinos was responsible for the outbreak of the 'Alexandrian War'.

128 Plut. Ant. 86.

129 Lucan. X 65.

130 Huß 2001, 726.

131 Strab. geogr. XIV 6, 6: Κλεοπάτραι καὶ τῆι ἀδελφῆι αὐτῆς Ἀρσινόηι. – Green 1990, 669; Green 1985, 158; Bicknell 1977, 331f.

132 Bicknell 1977, 332.

133 Huß 2001, 727. – Also, Grant 1977, 146. 148, assumes that Serapion intended, perhaps with the support of Cassius, to return Arsinoë IV to Alexandria and to replace Kleopatra VII with her.

134 Ios. ant. Iud. XV 89: ᾧ τὴν βασιλείαν ᾔδει γενησομένην.

135 Bicknell 1977, 332.

136 App. Rom. V 1; Plut. Ant. 25. – Buchheim 1960, 9f.

137 Bicknell 1977, 337. – A possible reasoning regarding Antonius' choice between Kleopatra VII and Arsinoë IV is provided by Buchheim 1960, 23.

138 Plut. Ant. 25f.; App. Rom. V 1; Cass. Dio XLVIII 24; Athen. deipn. IV 147. – Green 1985, 159; Buchheim 1960, 22–25; Strack 1897, 210f n. 46.

139 Bicknell 1977, 334 n. 24.

140 Bell. alex. 66; Strab. geogr. XIV 5 passim. – According to Strack 1897, 211, the meeting took place at the beginning of 41 BC.

141 Martial XI 20: *Caesaris Augusti lascivos, livide, versus sex lege, qui tristis verba Latina legis: "Quod futuit Glaphyran Antonius, hanc mihi poenam Fulvia constituit, se quoque uti futuam. Fulviam ego ut futuam? Quod si me Manius oret pedicem? faciam? Non puto, si sapiam. 'Aut futue, aut pugnemus' ait. Quid quod mihi vita carior est ipsa mentula? Signa canant!* ("Spiteful reader, who read Latin words with a frown, read these six verses of Augustus Caesar: "Because Antony fucks Glaphyra, Fulvia fixed this punishment for me, that I should fuck her too. That I should fuck Fulvia? What if Manius begged me to bugger him? Would I do it? Not if I had any sense. 'Either fuck me or we fight', she says. What about my prick being dearer to me than life itself? Let the charge sound!", translation according to Nigel Kay: http://www.u.arizona.edu/~afutrell/404b/web%20rdgs/martial.html, accessed on 21.04.2022). Scott 1933, 21. 25. – However, also Marcus Antonius had no problems in addressing Octavian roughly (Suet. Aug. 68): *M. Antonius adoptionem avunculi stupro meritum* ("M. Antonius [taunted Octavian] with having earned adoption by his uncle [C. Iulius Caesar] through fornication").

142 Pape 1906, s.v. ἑταίρα (consort, concubine, i.e. an inamorata in a not derogatory sense).

143 Cass. Dio IL 32; App. civ. V 7. – Schäfer 2006, 122f.; Buchheim 1960, 56. 107 n. 80.

144 Plut. Ant. 26. – Huß 2001, 730.

145 Plut. Ant. 25. – Hölbl 1994, 206.

146 Cass. Dio XLII 34.

147 Plut. Ant. 26. – Huß 2001, 730. – On the similarities of Caesar's and Antonius's encounters with Kleopatra VII, see Sannicandro 2014, 51f. 58, both representing the archetypus of the heros who falls prey to passion *(admisit Venerem curis*, Lucan. X 75), neglects his duties and becomes indolent.

148 App. Rom. V 8: παῖδα ἔτι οὖσαν.

149 App. Rom. V 8; Plut. Ant. 3; Cass. Dio XXXIX 55–57. – Huß 2001, 691–694; Buchheim 1960, 60.

150 Plut. Ant. 25.

151 Bicknell 1977, 334.

152 App. Rom. V 8; Cass. Dio XLVIII 24. – Marcus Antonius was forty–four years old then.

153 App. Rom. V 1.

154 App. Rom. V 9; Ios. ant. Iud. XV 89.

155 Cass. Dio XLVIII 24.

156 Cass. Dio XLVIII 39: Διόνυσον ἑαυτὸν νέον αὐτός τε ἐκάλει. Plut. Ant. 60.

157 Diod. I 44; Eus. chron., ed. Schoene – Petermann 1876, 131: *Ptlomaeus, qui novus Dionisus appellabatur*. 167. 171.

158 Hölbl 1994, 266f.

159 Plut. Ant. 24: Διόνυσον αὐτὸν ἀνακαλουμένων Χαριδότην καὶ Μειλίχιον. – Pape 1906, s.v. Χαριδότης (source of joy). s.v. Μειλίχιος (protector). – For Μειλίχιος as an epitheton for Zeus, see Berti 2017, 245–262.

160 Plut. Ant. 24: Ὠμηστὴς καὶ Ἀγριώνιος. – Pape 1906, s.v. Ὠμηστὴς (eater of raw meat). s.v. Ἀγριώνιος (somebody living in the wilderness), both being epitheta of Dionysos.

161 Vell 82: *cum ante novum se Liberum Patrem appellari iussisset*. – Likewise, Kleopatra VII staged herself as Isis in public (Plut. Ant. 54).

162 Plut. Ant. 25: ῥᾷον ἤλπιζεν ὑπάξεσθαι.

163 Suet. Aug. 69: *Quid te mutavit? Quod reginam ineo? Uxor mea est [...] An refert, ubi et in qua arrigas?* ("What has changed You? Is it because I enter the Queen? She is my wife [...] Does it matter where or in what you spike?". – Lakoff 2006, 58f.; Green 1985, 159: "Is it because I get into the Queen?". Scott 1933, 40.

164 App. civ. IV 61: Σεραπίωνα, τὸν ἐν Κύπρῳ τῇ Κλεοπάτρᾳ στρατηγοῦντα. – Anastasiades 2009, 267; Huß 2001, 728. 731; Hölbl 1994, 215f.; Grant 1977, 146. 148.

165 App. Rom. V 9.

166 Green 1990, 671: "never forgiven for her [i.e. Arsinoë's] brief fling as titular queen in 48–47 [BC]".

167 Ios. c. Ap. II 57: *Corrumpens amatoriis rebus*.

168 Cass. Dio XLIX 34: ἔρωτι καὶ τῇ γοητείᾳ.

169 App. Rom. V 9. – Huß 2001, 730f. n. 27.

170 Lowrie 2015; Pfeiffer 2010, 59–62; Hölbl 1994, 226; Scott 1933.

171 Green 1990, 671; Green 1985, 160; Buchheim 1960, 23. – The tendentious perspective on M. Antonius as "the slave of the Egyptian woman" (Cass. Dio XLVIII 24) is contradicted by Ios. ant. Iud. XV 62f., where it is stated that Antonius refused Kleopatra's strong wish to have Herodes killed, instead demanding that she not interfere in such affairs.

172 App. civ. II 83: δυνατὴν ναυσὶ καὶ σίτῳ καὶ χρήμασι ("rich in ships, grain and gold"). Cic. leg. agr. II 43 *(opulentissimi regni)*. – See also the second hymn of Isidoros naming the Νεῖλον χρυσορρόαν ("the gold carrying Nile"). Jördens 2013, 281f. – Later on, this phrase was repeated by Athen. deipn. V 36, explaining it as the riches coming from the fertilising floods as well as from the gold of its sands. Pape 1906, s.v. χρυσορρόας (gold carrying). Huß 2001, 710; Hölbl 1994, 208. – Already under Ptolemaios XII, there was a constant and giant flow of "gold" towards Roman politicians (Huß 2001, 680–683. 687. 692). Also, the annexion of the "rich island" Cyprus in 58 BC seems to have been motivated by such considerations (Huß 2001, 684; Hölbl 1994, 210).

173 Bicknell 1977, 339; Buchheim 1960, 25.

174 Cass. Dio LI 5. – Huß 2001, 720. 726f; Hölbl 1994, 209.

175 Schol. to Lucan. X 521: *puellae acceptissimus*. – Buchheim, 1960, 23.

176 Buchheim 1960, 23. – Also, Green 1990, 671: "but this was done at least as much out of political calculation [...] Antony's decision to eliminate her needs no other explanation". – See the same considerations regarding C. Iulius Caesar and Kleopatra VII in Heinen 1966, 144f. Huß 2001, 720, assuming the same reasoning of C. Iulius Caesar.

177 Buchheim 1960, 24.

178 App. civ. V 9. – Also, Cass. Dio XLVIII 24, places Arsinoë's death after the meeting at Tarsos.

179 Pape 1906, s.v. ἱκεσία, ἱκέτης (plea for protection, supplicant).

180 App. Rom. V 9; Ios. ant. Iud. XV 89. – Knäpper 2018, 261f.; Chaniotis 2007, 233f.; Rigsby 1996, 386. – On the error of Appianos see below.

181 Pape 1906, s.v. παρθένος (virgin, girl, young female). – Bennett 2013, s.v. Arsinoe IV n. 4, states: "Although this could be a Latin translation of παρθένος, i.e. a young unmarried woman, it is more likely to indicate that she was still young enough to be considered a child, which in ordinary Greek usage would make her not older than 14/15" years.

182 Van Oppen de Ruiter 2007, 186f. n. 9. 253.

183 Plat. Kratylos 406b.

184 Lapps – Page – House 1919, II 447: Ἀρσινόη [...] ἡ Πτολεμαῖς παρθένος.

185 Knäpper 2018, 67.

186 Müller 2007; Naiden 2006. – Agatharchides of Knidos (2nd c. BC) addresses Arsinoë III as virgo (FGrHist: https://www.dfhg–project.org/DFHG/index.php?volume=Volumen%20tertium, accessed on 21.04.2022). Heberdey 1912c, 156, lists an architrave with the possible reading Ἀρσιν?]όη Παρθ[that was found at the Ephesian theatre.

187 Schäfer 2006, 131f.

188 App. Rom. V 9: ὑποδεξάμενόν ποτε τὴν Ἀρσινόην ὡς βασιλίδα ἀχθῆναι μὲν ἐκέλευσεν. – Schäfer 2006, 131f.; Bremmer 2004, 9f.; LiDonnici 1999; Smith 1996.

189 Diog. L. Xenoph. II 51. Plin. nat. XXXV 93.

190 Bicknell 1977, 338.

191 Bennett 2013, s.v. Arsinoe IV n. 13; Bicknell 1977, 333; Anastassiades 2009, 267.

192 Ios. ant. Iud. XV 89: τὴν δ ἀδελφὴν Ἀρσινόην ἱκετεύουσαν ἐν Ἐφέσῳ πρὸς τῷ τῆς Ἀρτέμιδος ἀποκτείνασα δι Ἀντωνίου; Ios. c. Ap. II 57.

193 Cass. Dio XLVIII 24: καὶ τοὺς ἀδελφοὺς αὐτῆς ἀπὸ τοῦ ἐν Ἐφέσῳ Ἀρτεμισίου ἀποσπάσας ἀπέκτεινε ("to drag her siblings from the temple of Artemis at Ephesos and put them to death"). – Obviously, such statement of Cassius Dio is wrong, since Kleopatra VII had no remaining siblings left at that time beyond Arsinoë IV.

194 App. Rom. V 9. – Fischer 2014a, 189 n. 86; Hölbl 1994, 212; Mahaffy 1899, 247.

195 Strab. geogr. XIV 1, 40.

196 App. Rom. V 9: Καὶ τὸν ἐν Ἐφέσῳ δὲ τῆς Ἀρτέμιδος ἱερέα, ὃν Μεγάβυζον ἡγοῦνται, ὑποδεξάμενόν ποτε τὴν Ἀρσινόην ὡς βασιλίδα ἀχθῆναι μὲν ἐκέλευσεν. – See, on the other hand, Bicknell 1977, 336 n. 39.

197 See n. 163.

198 On the resulting clientele relationship of Arsinoë IV to C. Iulius Caesar and C. Octavianus, see Scherrer, see also p. 91.

199 Bell. alex. 33.

200 Cass. Dio XLIII 19. – Hölbl 1994, 212.

201 App. Rom. V 9: πέμψας ὁ Ἀντώνιος ἀνεῖλε ("Antonius sent to have [Arsinoë] killed"). Still Schultz states "it is still unclear [...] by whom Kleopatra's sister was killed" ("Mehr als 2000 Jahre nach dem Tod der ptolemäischen Königstochter ist indes immer noch unklar, wie und durch wen Kleopatras Schwester getötet wurde"), https://www.hna.de/lokales/goettingen/goettingen-ort28741/goettinger-professor-erforscht-praehistorische-krankheiten-morde-kleopatra-mumie-91670032.html, accessed on 21.07.2022. – Marcus Antonius repeatedly sojourned in Ephesos (Plut. Ant. 24. 56. 58), also in 41 BC, the year of Arsinoë's murder (Fischer 2012, 147; Jones 1999, 93); Hörmann 1951, 281; Strack 1897, 188. 210f. n. 46).

202 ἔτους δεκάτου τῆς Γαίου Ἰουλίου Καίσαρος νίκης. – Leschhorn 1993, 221.

203 Grimm 2006, 176–183.

204 App. Rom. V 9. – See also Ios. ant. Iud. XV 89, regarding Kleopatra's παρανομία.

205 Ios. ant. Iud. XV 89: οὔθ ἱεροῦ τινος οὕτως ἀσύλου δόξαντος.

206 Ios. c. Ap. II 57: *occidit in templo*.

207 Green 1990, 667; Buchheim 1960, 24.

208 Bennett 2013, s.v. Arsinoe IV n. 4, comes quite close to such reasoning after having recognized her being a *puella* in 48 BC.

209 See the discussion in Bennett 2013, s.v. Arsinoe IV n. 4: "this has become the standard estimate". – Thür 1990, 52 n. 38, referred to such an opinion taking it from Grant 1977, 15: "Grant nimmt ohne nähere Diskussion an, daß sie [Arsinoë IV] zwischen 68 und 65 v. Chr. geboren wurde" ("Grant assumes without further discussion that she [Arsinoë IV] was born between 68 and 65 B.C.").

210 Anevlavi et al. 2020, 34 n. 47; https://www.instone-brewer.com/TyndaleSites/Egypt/ptolemies/arsinoe_iv.htm (accessed on 21.04.2022); Heinen 1966, 107 n. 2.

211 https://dewiki.de/Lexikon/Max_L._Strack (accessed on 21.04.2022).

212 Strack 1897, 211 n. 46: "Arsinoe entflieht bald nach der ersten Schlacht des Alexandrinischen Krieges um die Mitte September 48 aus der Königsburg von Caesar, wird Königin beim Landheer und weiss diese Rolle vollständig zu spielen, Dio XLII 39 [...] Danach ist ihre Geburt nicht nach 65 anzusetzen. Im Jahre 69 ist die ältere Schwester Kleopatra geboren, folglich fällt die Geburt zwischen 68–65".

213 Strack 1897, 210f. n. 46. – Such reasoning is support-ed by Bennett 2013, s.v. Arsinoe IV n. 4.

214 Bennett 1997, 60. 62, applies the same reasoning to Berenike IV in 58 BC. According to him, she was about 20 years of age in 58 BC, i.e., "old enough to act as re-gent".

215 App. civ. II 84.

216 Ios. ant. Iud. XV 89.

217 Insofar, Anevlavi et al. 2020, 34 n. 37, is wrong: "Only one firm fact can be gleaned from the sources, name-ly, that she was younger than Cleopatra, therefore subsequently was born after 69 B.C.".

218 Caes. civ. III 112; Bell. alex. 4, 33; Strab. geogr. XVII 1, 11; Eus. chron., ed. Schoene – Petermann 1876, 167.

219 Heinen 1966, 107 n. 2.

220 App. civ. II 83.

221 Bell. alex. 23; Schol. to Lucan X 521.

222 Bell. alex. 4. Lucan. X 520.

223 Strack 1897, 210f. n. 46. – Also, Bennett 2013, s.v. Ar-sinoe IV n. 4, initially "overlooked" such "item of liter-ary evidence in favour of a younger age" of Arsinoë IV.

224 Strack 1897, 210f. n. 46: "Ptolemäus XIV ist nach Ap-pianos, bell. civ. II 84 im Jahre 48 etwa 13 Jahre alt, also um 61 geboren. Die Nachricht wird im wesentli-chen bestätigt durch Caesar (bell. civ. III 103), der ihn 'puer' nennt und durch die Thatsache, dass er noch Vormünder hat".

225 Cass. Dio XLII 42: γυναικὸς ἀρχῇ.

226 Cass. Dio XLIII 19.

227 Duncan 1833, 292: "that the people, weary of subjec-tion to a woman" from Bell. alex. 23: *paratam enim omnem multitudinem esse, confectam taedio puellae.*

228 McDevitte –Bohn 1872, 394: "that the people, weary of subjection to a woman". – See also Corpus Scriptorum Latinorum: http://www.forumromanum.org/litera-ture/caesar/alexe.html (accessed on 21.04.2022).

229 Bennett 2013, s.v. Arsinoe IV n. 4, refers to such mistranslation though without naming its sources. – Pseudo–Caesar's passage was correctly translated by Way 1955, 45: "The whole population, they said, being tired and wearied of the girl".

230 https://dewiki.de/Lexikon/Walther_Judeich (accessed on 21.04.2022).

231 Mahaffy 1899, 243.

232 https://dewiki.de/Lexikon/Auguste_Bouch%C3%A9–Le-clercq (accessed on 21.04.2022).

233 https://dewiki.de/Lexikon/Ulrich_Wilcken (accessed on 21.04.2022).

234 https://dewiki.de/Lexikon/Felix_Staehelin (accessed on 21.04.2022).

235 https://dewiki.de/Lexikon/Hans_Volkmann_(Althis-toriker) (accessed on 21.04.2022).

236 Judeich 1885, 29. 70. 77 n. 1. 82.

237 Bouché–Leclercq 1904, 179 n. 1: "Enfin, Arsinoé, ca-dette d Cléopátre, mais plus ágée que ses fréres, est née entre 68 et 65" ("Finally, Arsinoe, younger than Kleopatra, but older than her brothers, was born be-tween 68 and 65") referencing Strack.

238 Wilcken 1895, 1288: "Arsinoë, jüngste Tochter des Ptolemaios XIII. Neos Dionysos, genannt Auletes, jüngere Schwester der letzten Kleopatra" ("Arsinoë, youngest daughter of Ptolemaios XIII Neos Dionysos, called Auletes, younger sister of the last Kleopatra").

239 Stähelin 1921, 753: "Arsinoë, Kleopatra's jüngste Schwester" ("Arsinoë, Kleopatra's youngest sister").

240 Volkmann 1927a, 1754: "Arsinoë IV, jüngste Tochter" des Ptolemaios XII ("Arsinoë IV, youngest daughter" of Ptolemaios XII).

241 Thür 1990, 52 n. 18, apparently mistook the superla-tive "youngest" within such literature: "Stähelin [...], Wilcken [...] und Volkmann [...] sehen in Arsinoe das jüngste Kind Ptolemaios XII" ("Stähelin [...], Wilcken [...] and Volkmann [...] see in Arsinoe the youngest child of Ptolemy XII"). As Bennett 2013, n. 4, pointed out, none of the authors, U. Wilcken, F. Stähelin and H. Volk-mann, holds such an opinion. – See also Thür 1995c, 180: "Flavius Josephus, Appianos and Dio Cassius [state that] the youngest sister of Cleopatra, named Arsinoë IV". 182: "the youngest child of Ptolemy XII". – See also, Thür 2015, 270 ("Ptolemaios XIV, the young-est of Arsinoe and her siblings"), and Thür 1999a, 424 (Arsinoë IV, "the youngest daughter of Ptolemaios XII" and the "youngest sister of Kleopatra VII").

242 Bevan 1927, 365.

243 See also Encyclopedia Britannica s.v. Arsinoe IV ("63").

244 Bevan 1927, 361. 362.

245 Bevan 1927, 366.

246 https://dewiki.de/Lexikon/Heinz_Heinen (accessed on 21.04. 2022).

247 Heinen 1966, 107 n. 2: "M. L. Strack [...] zufolge wusste Arsinoe, als sie Königin beim Heer geworden war, „diese Rolle vollständig zu spielen [...] Danach ist ihre Geburt nicht nach 65 anzusetzen". Die tatsäch-liche Führung der Armee und des Krieges übernahm jedoch Ganymedes, der nutricius der Arsinoe [...]. Wenn auch das Jahr 65 als untere Grenze nicht ganz unwahrscheinlich ist, wäre ein späteres Geburtsjahr keineswegs ausgeschlossen, vor allem wenn man an die ähnliche Rolle des 61 geborenen Ptolemaios XIII denkt".

248 Anevlavi et al. 2020, 34 n. 47; Huß 2001, 716, n. 109. – Bennett 2013, s.v. Arsinoe IV n. 4, mentions Heinen.

249 Habicht 2021, 163 ("Born between 68 and 65 BC"); Schiff 2010, 58 (seventeen years old in 48 BC); Tyldes-ley 2008, 27 ("born sometime between 68 and 65"); Burstein 2004, XIX, 75 ("60s B.C.E."); Bennett 1997, 60. 66 ("c. 67"), correcting himself in Bennett 2013, s.v. Arsinoe IV n. 4, to "c. 63–61" BC, because of Arsinoë being a puella in 48 BC. Green 1990, 650 ("Arsinoe and Cleopatra VII [...] were barely adolescent [in 58 BC] while the boys, Ptolemy XIII and Ptolemy XIV, were still infants"); Grant 1977, 15 ("between 68 and 65 BC"). 100 (c. 68). 125 ("a young girl"); Jones 1971, 317

("68–65 Arsinoe IV born"); Ludwig 1937, 28 (thirteen in 48 BC); Bevan 1889, 365 (fifteen in 48 BC).

250 Bennett 2013, s.v. Arsinoe IV n. 4, assumes that Ptolemaios XIV was born after Arsinoë IV, since the latter is mentioned first in Cass. Dio XLII 35 "implying that she was the older of the two".

251 There is also the remote possibility that Arsinoë IV was a twin of Ptolemaios XIV (Bennett 2013, s.v. Arsinoe IV n. 4). One might think, however, that such twin siblings would have been addressed in the antique sources, as this state is referred to regarding Alexandros Helios and Kleopatra Selene (Cass. Dio IL 32).

252 Strab. geogr. XVII 1, 11; Cass. Dio XXXIX 12. – Huß 2001, 686; Hölbl 1994, 200. – Eus. chron., ed. Schoene – Petermann 1876, 167, states a joint rule of Kleopatra Tryphaina and Berenike IV.

253 Cass. Dio XXXIX 16, 3: ὁ Πτολεμαῖος […] ἐς Ἔφεσον ἐλθὼν παρὰ τῇ θεῷ διῃτᾶτο ("Ptolemaios [withdrew] to Ephesos where he stayed next to the goddess"). – Huß 2001, 688. 690f.

254 Huß 2001, 691. 695.

255 Strab. geogr. XVII 1, 11.

256 Huß 2001, 674f. 686. 692; Hölbl 1994, 195f. 201.

257 Huß 2001, 692; Hölbl 1994, 201.

258 Bennett 2013, s.v. Arsinoe IV n. 4: Thür's [age] estimate places her [= Arsinoë's] birth as probably during the period of her father's exile".

259 Cic. Att. IV 10: *Puteolis magnus est rumor Ptolomaeum esse in regno*. Cass. Dio XXXIX 58. – Huß 2001, 694f.

260 Strab. geogr. XVII 1, 11.

261 App. Rom. II 84; Strab. geogr. XVII 1, 11.

262 Bell. alex. 23.

263 Cass. Dio XLIII 19; Flor. epit. II 13.

264 Strab. geogr. XIV 6, 6.

265 Huß 2001, 727; Hölbl 1994, 215.

266 Ios. ant. Iud. XV 89; Ios. c. Ap. II 57; App. Rom. V 9; Cass. Dio XLVIII 24.

267 See p. 91.

268 App. civ. II 83; Cic. leg. agr. II 43.

269 Appianos calls the 'Alexandrian War' the last of the Roman Civil Wars (App. civ. I 6. II 90. V 1). Unfortunately, his book on Egyptian history is lost, within which Appianos described the events concerning the 'Ptolemaic War' in detail (App. civ. II 90). – See on that Photios, s.v. Appianos: https://www.tertullian.org/fathers/photius_03bibliotheca.htm (accessed on 21.04.2022). Luce 1964.

270 See pp. 74–79. – Anastasiades 2009; Hölbl 1994, 37f.

271 Φιλάδελφοι.

272 Huß 2001, 726f.

273 Ios. bell. Iud. I XVIII, 4: *Etenim Cleopatra, ubi tanta cognationem suam saevitia per secuta est, ut neque propinquus sanguine superesset*. Transl. Whiston 1841, 637.

274 Ios. c. Ap. II 59. – Plut. Ant. 76, describes how M. Antonius felt betrayed by Kleopatra VII at the battle of Alexandria, when he was deserted by his troops supposedly instigated by her (Cass. Dio LI 10).

275 Cass. Dio LI 12.

276 Plut Ant. 25. – Schäfer 2006, 243f.

277 Prop. III 11, 39.

278 Bennett 2013, s.v. Cleopatra VII; Huß 2001, 747.

279 Plut. Ant. 82; Suet. Aug. 17.

280 Burstein 2004, 33.

281 Cass. Dio LI 11; Suet. Aug. 17.

282 Cass. Dio LI 13. – Hölbl 1994, 224.

283 Plut. Ant. 78; App. civ. II 101f.

284   Plut Ant. 84; Cass. Dio LI 11.

285 Cass. Dio LI 13.

286 Porph. Hor. c. I 37: *Nam et Titus Livius refert, illam* [Cleopatram] *cum de industria ab Augusto in captivitate indulgentius tractaretur idemtidem dicere solitam fuisse:* οὐ θριαμβεύσομαι. *Id est non triumphabor ab alio*. – Meyer 1874, 45.

287 Cass. Dio LI 13; Plut. Ant. 85f.

288 Aurnhammer 2019, 82.

289 Hor. carm. I 37: *non humilis mulier*. Petschenig – Stowasser 1930, s.v. *humilis* (ordinary, weak, pusillanimous).

290 According to Plut. Ant. 86, Octavian could not refrain from "admiring her lofty spirit" (ἐθαύμασε τὴν εὐγένειαν αὐτῆς). Pape 1906, s.v. εὐγένεια (nobleness, lofty spirit, high–mindedness).

291 Plut. Ant. 86; Cass. Dio LI 21. – Tronson 1999, 171.

292 Plut. Ant. 86; Cass. Dio LI 21; App. civ. II 102. – Harders 2010, 63; Hölbl 1994, 225.

293 Petschenig – Stowasser 1930, s.v. *turba* (turmoil, crowd, crush).

294 App. civ. II 101: Ἰόβα παῖς.

295 Cass. Dio IL 32: πρεσβυτέρους μὲν Ἀλέξανδρον καὶ Κλεοπάτραν καὶ δίδυμοι ("the older ones Alexandros and Kleopatra, twins"). – Bennett 2013, s.v. Alexander Helios. s.v. Cleopatra Selene.

296 Huß 2001, 749; Hölbl 1994, 226.

297 The actual last known one of the royal Ptolemaic blood line was Ptolemaios of Mauretania, a son of Kleopatra Selene and Iuba II (Cass. Dio LIX 25; Plut. Ant. 36; Suet. Cal. 26. 35). – Huß 2001, 733; Hölbl 1994, 216. 226f.

298 Eus. chron., ed. Schoene – Petermann 1876, 167. 171: *Ptlomaeus, qui novus Dionisus vocatus est* […] *cuius imperii numerantur anni XXIX. Hujus filia Kleopatra, ultma (fuit) Lagidarum generis; cujus imperii numerantur anni XXII* […] *Hujus aetate Gajus Julius Caesar (Kaisr) monarchiam exercuit in Romanos. Post quem Caesar (Kaisr) Sebastus Hoktavius, qui et Augustus, Kleopatram interfecit, imperiumque Ptlomaeorum evertit (sustulit), qui regnaverunt annos CCXCV* (Πτολεμαῖος ὁ ἐπικληθεὶς νέος Διόνυσος […] οὗ τῆς ἀρχῆς ἔτη κθ´ λογίζονται [κ = 20, θ´ = 9]. Τούτου θυγάτηρ Κλεοπάτρα ὑστάτη τῆς Λαγιδῶν γενεᾶς, ἧς ἔτη ἀριθμεῖται τῆς ἀρχῆς δύο καὶ εἴκοσιν […] Κατὰ ταύτην Γάϊος Ἰούλιος Καῖσαρ πρῶτος ἐμονάρχησε Ῥωμαίων. μεθ᾽ ὃν Καῖσαρ Σεβαστὸς Οχταούιος, ὁ καὶ Αὔγουστος, Κλεοπάτραν ἑλών, καθεῖλε τὴν τῶν Πτολεμαίων ἀρχήν, οἱ ἐβασίλευσαν ἔτη σϟέ [σ = 200, ϟ = 90, έ = 5].

An octagonal mausoleum in Ephesos

1 Heberdey 1905, 70f. – The year of the Octagon's detection is sometimes given differently: Gesellschaft der Freunde von Ephesos 2020, 2 fig. 2: "Das Oktogon an der Kuretenstraße nach der Freilegung 1906" ("The Octagon on the 'Curetes Street' after its excavation in 1906"); Thür 2011, 74 ("1903"); H. Thür, in: Scherrer 2000, 124 fig. 2: "The Octagon as uncovered in 1906".

2 At that time, i.e. before 1918: "k. k. Oesterreichisches Archaeologisches Institut" ("Imperial and Royal Austrian Archaeological Institute").

3 Keil 1957, 3; Keil 1955, 3.

4 Until now, altogether six Ephesos guides have been published, five of which by J. Keil, and the recent one by P. Scherrer: Scherrer 2000 (English version); Scherrer 1995 (German version); Keil 1964; Keil 1957; Keil 1955; Keil 1930b; Keil 1915. – Keil 1915 was inoffically translated into the English language in order to support the fund–raising efforts of G. A. Deißmann (fig. 79a) in the U.S.A. in 1925/26: Gerber 2008, 43.

5 Keil 1926, 261: "In den Budrumia, d. h. dem großen Ruinenfelde zwischen [Celsus] Bibliothek und Stadionhügel einerseits, Theater und Hafen andererseits" ("In the Bodrumia, that is, the large field of ruins between the [Celsus] Library and the Stadionhill on one side, and the theatre and the harbour on the other side"). – Wohlers–Scharf 1995, 89. 109. 143; Reisch 1930, 302f.; Benndorf 1906, 6. – However, rather 'bodrumia' from the Turkish word 'bodrum' = ruin, vault, basement, souterrain.

6 Benndorf 1898, 61f. fig. 17.

7 EED from 30.09.1904 onwards. – Waldner 2020; H. Thür, in: Scherrer 2000, 114f.

8 The "street to the east of the [Celsus] Library" was later labelled 'Curetes Street' by F. Miltner: Miltner 1955, 26: "wo diese als Kuretenstraße, wie ich diesen Abschnitt benennen möchte, nach Südosten in Richtung auf das Magnesische Tor umbiegt" ("where the road, which I would like to name Curetes Street for this section, turns southeast towards the Magnesian Gate"). – Waldner 2020, 13 n. 1; Quatember 2005, 271; U. Outschar, in: Scherrer 2000, 130–133; Keil 1944/1953; Keil 1930b, 80–83; Keil 1915, 66–69.

9 H. Thür, in: Scherrer 2000, 126f. – See pp. 131–138.

10 EED from 03.10. – 05.10.1904. – On the excavation history of the Octagon: Thuswaldner 2015, 51–60; Alzinger 1962, 123–126.

11 See the EED from 06.10. – 08.10.1929: "Finden sich weitere neue Stücke der Architektur des polygonalen Gebäudes (eines Oktogons)" ("additional new pieces of the architecture of the polygonal building (of an octagon) are found"). – Heberdey 1912a, 166. 178 ("Oktogon"); Heberdey 1907, 63–65. 71 ("Oktogon"); Heberdey 1905, 70 ("Octogon").

12 https://dewiki.de/Lexikon/Rudolf_Heberdey, accessed on 21.04.2023; Wohlers–Scharf 1995, 153f.

– Heberdey (1864–1936) participated at the Ephesian excavations from 1896 until 1911, and in 1913: Alzinger 1962, 253.

13 Schörner 2007, 240–242; H. Thür, in: Scherrer 2000, 124f.; Alzinger 1974, 40–42; Keil 1930b, 86–88; Keil 1915, 71.

14 A field railway on the 'Curetes Street' was available to R. Heberdey (Waldner 2020, 24 n. 51; Wohlers–Scharf 1995, 107) as well as to F. Miltner in the 1950s (Waldner 2020, 25).

15 EED from 10.10. – 12.10.1904: "An dem Octogon ist außer dem schon erwähnten Fundament und der Stufe auch noch ein unterer Teil einer kanelierten Säule sowie eine bankartige Stufe in situ" ("On the octagon, apart from the aforementioned foundation and the step, there is also a lower part of a grooved column and a bench–like step in situ"). – Thuswaldner 2015, 155.

16 Thuswaldner 2015, 136–138. – The excavators repeatedly refer, completely convinced, to such a finial of the monument (Heberdey 1905, 70; W. Wilberg, in: Alzinger 1974, 41; Keil 1915, 71; Keil 1930b, 87). Yet, a sphere is not mentioned in the Ephesian excavation diary (EED) of 1904. The upper half of a sphere with no trace of a "surmounting Nike" was detected within 'Terrace House 2' in 1983: Thuswaldner 2017, 134; Thuswaldner 2015, 54 fig. 44. 136–138 fig. 147; Plattner 2010, 76f. (diameter = 0.92 m); Plattner 2009, 101; H. Thür, in: Scherrer 2000, 124; Alzinger 1962, 124. – A graffiti of the Octagon's polygonal roof that was found in a room of the 'Terrace House 2' about 15 m to the south, however, does not depict a finial sphere: Rathmayr 2016, 250 GR 372 Taf. 125. Considering the finials of the funeral monument at Faverolles (Fevrier 1993, 97) and of the *horologium* at Athens (Kienast 2014, 63), a Corinthian capital would be an alternative. See p. 52.

17 Heberdey 1905, 70f.: "Auf hohem viereckigen Sockel, von unten unzugänglich, [steht] ein tempelartiger Bau ohne Innenraum, nur daß diesmal die Cella als Octogon ausgestaltet ist, das eine Peristasis von acht den Ecken des Octogons entsprechend angeordneten ionischen Säulen umgibt. Das Gebälk zeigt mancherlei Besonderheiten, als Dach ist eine achteckige Stufenpyramide gesichert, deren oberen Abschluß eine Kolossalkugel bildete. Gerne wird man sie von einer Nikefigur überragt denken und in dem Ganzen ein prächtiges Siegesdenkmal erblicken." – Accordingly, Thür 1990, 50, is incorrect in stating that the Octagon was seen "as heroon or grave of honour from the very beginning" ("Das Oktogon wurde seit seiner Freilegung als Heroon oder Ehrengrab gedeutet"); Thür 2015, 271; Thür 1995c, 180. – See Wilberg's description of the Octagon, in: Alzinger 1974, 40–42.

18 Heberdey 1905, 70f. – Thuswaldner 2015, 138; Wohlers–Scharf 1995, 208.

19   EED from 03.10. – 05.10.1904: "Besonders häufig treten jetzt Statuenfunde auf [...]. Bemerkenswert ist: Torso einer Nike" ("Statue finds are particularly frequent now [...]. Remarkable: Torso of a Nike").

20   EED from 06.10. – 08.10.1904: "Östlich des Brunnens [plan 3] finden sich neue Stücke der Architektur des polygonalen Gebäudes (eines Oktogons) und zwar Kasettendecke, Architrav und Fries in solcher Lage, wie sie nur durch Zusammensturz des unmittelbar nahe befindlichen Gebäudes fallen können. In der Tat erscheint östlich vom Brunnen das mit aufrecht stehenden großen Platten verkleidete Gußwerkfundament des Gebäudes und ganz hoch, nur etwa ½ m unter Tag eine Stufe des Stylobats in situ" ("To the east of the fountain [plan 3], new pieces of the architecture of the polygonal building (an octagon) are found, namely the coffered ceiling, architrave and frieze in such a position as they can only have fallen through the collapse of the immediately nearby building. In fact, to the east of the fountain, the foundation of the building, covered with upright large slabs, appears, and very high, only about ½ m below ground level, a step of the stylobate in situ"). – Alzinger 1962, 124.

21   The Octagon shares such a fate with the front of the 'Library of Celsus' (U. Outschar, in: Scherrer 2000, 130–133; fig. 66; plans 1 and 3), whose similarly collapsed façade was detected the year before (Wilberg 1944/1953, 1. 42; Heberdey 1905, 61–70; Heberdey 1904, 53–56).

22   EED from 03.10. – 05.11.1904.

23   W. Wilberg (1872–1956) accompanied R. Heberdey and J. Keil to the excavation campaign in Ephesos in 1904 (Heberdey 1905, 61). – Vignau-Wilberg – Vignau-Wilberg 2022; Thür 2009, 11; Wohlers–Scharf 1995, 184f.; https://dewiki.de/Lexikon/Wilhelm_Wilberg, accessed on 21.04.2023. – Wilberg participated at the Austrian excavations from 1899 until 1911, and in 1913: Alzinger 1962, 253.

24   Wilberg's description of his reconstruction was read and is cited by W. Alzinger, but is now lost: W. Wilberg, in: Alzinger 1974, 40–42 n. 131. – Thuswaldner 2017, 133; Thuswaldner 2015, 54 fig. 43. 56 fig. 48. 57 fig. 49. 62. 124 fig. 132; Quatember et al. 2013, 222: "W. Wilberg could already provide a credible reconstruction plan of the building [...]. In fact, our current reconstruction model does not differ very much from Wilberg's plan". – Thuswaldner et al. 2009, 4; Strocka 2011, 308 fig. 22. 310; Thür 2009, 11; Thür 1995c, 178; Thür 1990, 44. – Wilberg's cross section of the Octagon from 1904 was completed with the burial chamber by M. Theuer in 1929 (fig. 12b): Thuswaldner 2015, 53f. 57 fig. 49; Alzinger 1974, fig. 27; Keil 1930b, 86 fig. 49; Keil 1930a, 43f. fig. 20.

25   Heberdey 1904, 53–56.

26   Heberdey 1905, 71: "Ausgeschlossen ist schon jetzt die naheliegende Combination mit den sicherlich von einem ähnlichen Baue stammenden, vor der [Celsus] Bibliothek gefundenen Reliefs [...], da die Sockelverkleidung, glatte Marmorplatten, teils in situ, teils im Schutte liegend, fast vollständig erhalten ist" ("The obvious combination with the reliefs found in front of the [Celsus] library, which certainly originated from a similar structure, is already ruled out, as the pedestal covering, smooth marble plates, partly in situ and partly lying in the debris, is almost completely preserved"). "Although recognising Heberdey's statement, Alzinger 1962, 125, stated: "Man meinte also, jenes Monument gefunden zu haben, an dem die großen Reliefplatten der Bibliothek ursprünglich aufgestellt waren" ("So, it was believed that the monument was found, on which the large relief plates of the library were originally placed"). Interestingly, Wohlers–Scharf 1995, 208, says: "J. Keil meinte [im Oktogon] jenes Monument gefunden zu haben, dass die Partherplatten ursprünglich schmückten" ("J. Keil believed to have found the monument [i.e. the Octagon] that was originally adorned by the Parthian reliefs"). Wohlers–Scharf 1995, 215 n. 21, references this statement with "J. Keil (1955) 113f.". Unfortunately, there is no Keil 1955 in her referenced literature. Maybe, the paging refers to Keil 1964, 113f., where he described the Octagon and mentions its garland reliefs (figs. 19a-b).

27   Plattner 2018, 215f. 219–224. 227–232; Oberleitner et al. 1978, 37. – See, on the other hand, H. Thür, in: Scherrer 2000, 124: "A pair of columns and the adjacent entablature from the octagonal upper structure is re-erected in the Ephesus Museum Selçuk".

28   Those would become part of the Viennese 'Ephesos Museum' that opened in 1978 (Plattner 2018, 223. 228. 232 fig. 13; Oberleitner et al. 1978, 36f.). – Thür 1995c, 178; Wohlers–Scharf 1995, 82f. 97–103.

29   Dedication of Benndorf 1906: "Seiner Majestät dem Groszsultan Abdul Hamid II dem Beschützer und Förderer Österreichischer Forschungen in Ephesos". – On the corresponding 'Irade' (= decree), see Thuswaldner 2015, 52; Wohlers–Scharf 1995, 87. 101; Oberleitner et al. 1978, 36 fig. 20.

30   EED from 10.10.–15.10.1904: "Von Einzelfunden eine interessante Säule mit 2mal überfallenden Blattkelchen (mit Fuß) erwähnt [...] Der Brunnen wird weiter freigelegt, wobei sich eine 2. der oben erwähnten Säulen findet" ("Of single finds, an interesting column with 2 leaf calyxes (with foot) is mentioned [...] The fountain is further uncovered, where a 2nd of the above mentioned columns is found"). – Thür 2015, 273; Bennett 2013, s.v. Arsinoe IV n. 15 ("papyrus columns"); Thür 2009, 17; Oberleitner et al. 1978, 115 Inv. I 842f.

31   H. Thür, in: Scherrer 2000, 126f.

32   Keil 1923, 100. 155. 161; Heberdey 1912c, 182; Heberdey 1907, 61–64 fig. 8f.

33   https://dewiki.de/Lexikon/Josef_Keil, accessed on 21.04.2023. Wohlers–Scharf 1995, 155–157.

34 Keil 1955, 3: "Die Direktion des OeAI ,betraute' im Jahr 1915 J. Keil als ,damaligen Vertreter des Instituts am Arbeitsplatz in Smyrna', der ,die Stätte von Ephesos seit Jahren vor Augen hat und an ihrer Erschließung verdienstvoll mitgewirkt hat', mit der Abfassung eines Ephesosführers [...] eine abschließende Gesamtübersicht über das vom altösterreichischen Kaiserstaat [...] Geleistete" ("The directorate of the OeAI entrusted J. Keil in 1915, as the then representative of the institute at the workplace in Smyrna' who 'had been familiar with the site of Ephesos for years and had made valuable contributions to its exploration' with the task of writing a guidebook on Ephesos, which [...] would provide a comprehensive overview of the accomplishments of the former Austrian imperial state"). – Reisch 1913, 80f. 86. – Regarding Keil's participation at the Ephesian excavations, see Alzinger 1962, 253f.

35 Keil 1915, 71: "Über die Zweckbestimmung und die Entstehungszeit des Gebäudes gibt keine Bauinschrift Aufschluß". – Alzinger 1962, 126.

36 Heberdey 1905, 70f. – Quatember et al. 2013, 222: "a trophy–monument".

37 On 01.10.1929, Keil wrote into the EED: "Ich habe seit der Ausgrabung dieses Gebäudes die Ansicht vertreten, daß es sich [bei dem Oktogon] um ein Heroon handelt. Heberdey und Wilberg haben mir das nie geglaubt" ("Since the excavation of this building, I have been of the opinion that it [i.e. the Octagon] is a heroon. Heberdey and Wilberg never believed me"); Reisch 1930, 305; Thuswaldner 2015, 57.

38 Keil 1930a, 41: "Ich habe schon seit langem die Meinung vertreten, daß wir in diesem eigenartigen Gebäude [...] ein Heroon, und zwar das Grabhaus einer vornehmen Persönlichkeit zu sehen hätten" ("I have long held the opinion that in this peculiar building [...] we would have to see a heroon, specifically the tomb of a distinguished personality")

39 Thuswaldner 2015, 53; Keil 1930a, 41–45.

40 Curiously, the access year of the Octagon's burial vault is repeatedly given as "1926": Schultz 2022 (see n. 176: "1926"); Habicht 2021, 164 ("1926"); Waldner 2020, 89 ("1926"); Anevlavi et al. 2020, 33 ("discovered in 1926"); Thuswaldner 2017, 133 ("1929"); Thuswaldner 2015, 53 ("1929"). 57 ("1929"). 216 ("1926"); Bennett 2013, s.v. Arsinoe IV n. 4 ("1926"); Quatember et al. 2013, 222 ("1929"); Thür 2011, 74 ("1926"); Spanu 2010, 59 ("1926"); Thuswaldner 2009, 262 ("1926"); Waldner 2009, 293 n. 99 ("1926"); Kanz et al. 2009 ("1926"); Bordsen 2009; Schörner 2007, 54 ("1929"). 241 ("1926"); Schäfer 2006, 132 ("1926"); Thür 1995c, 180 ("1926"); Thür 1990, 50 ("1926"); Alzinger 1974, 40 n. 131 ("1926"); Alzinger 1972, 75 ("1929"). – Such an error seems to have been taken from Keil himself: Keil 1964, 113: "Der Zweck des Bauwerkes ist 1926 ermittelt worden" ("The purpose of the structure was identified in 1926"); Keil 1957, 105 ("1926"); Keil 1955, 93 ("1926"). – Obviously, a glitch occurred between the

number of the OeAI–annual ("26") and the excavation year it describes ("1929"), since the EED clearly places the opening of the burial chamber in 1929.

41 Keil 1930a, 38f.

42 Thuswaldner 2015, 44 fig. 30.

43 EED from 01.10.1929: "In 1m Tiefe erscheinen größere hochgestellte Steine, die sich als Wölbungssteine manifestieren. Mit großer Mühe wird einer durchschlagen, worauf sich ein Loch in eine große tiefe Kammer auftut. So besteht Hoffnung, daß das Rätsel des Baues morgen gelöst wird" ("At a depth of one metre, larger raised stones appear, manifesting themselves as arching stones. With great difficulty, one is smashed through, whereupon a hole opens up into a large deep chamber. So, there is hope that the riddle of the construction will be solved tomorrow"). – Waldner 2020, 89 n. 491; Thuswaldner 2015, 44 fig. 30. 53 fig. 41; Keil 1930a, 41.

44 Keil 1930a, 41f.: "Durch die so entstandene Lücke uns durchzwängend, gelangten wir [sic!] in eine aus gerauhten Marmorquadern ziemlich sorgfältig hergestellte und mit einem mannshohen Tonnendach aus solchen Quadern überwölbte Kammer, deren schwere, mit Feuchtigkeit vollkommen gesättigte Luft zuerst das Atmen behinderte. Nahe der Nordostwand, die zwei Nischen zum Aufstellen von Lampen und Grabbeigaben aufwies, stand ein sorgfältig gearbeiteter, aber vollkommen schmuckloser Marmorsarkophag". EED from 03.10.1929; Keil 1930a, 41f. – Accordingly, J. Keil entered the burial chamber probably together with M. Theuer, the architect of this excavation season: Thuswaldner 2015, 53. 57. 233. – Max Theuer (1878–1949): https://dewiki.de/Lexikon/Max_Theuer, accessed on 21.04.2023.

45 Keil 1930a, 42; EED from 03.10.1929. – A page of the EED (02.10. – 03.10.1929) is presented by Thuswaldner 2015, 53 fig. 42.

46 Keil 1930a, 44: Der "im Bauplane vorgesehene von der Südseite in die Kammer führende Gang". – EED on 03.10.1929.

47 EED from 03.10.1929: "Es wird die Frage sein, ob sich durch Öffnung der Tür von innen oder außen noch ein Anhaltspunkt für die Datierung gewinnen läßt" ("The question will be whether the opening of the door from the inside or the outside will still give a clue to the dating"). – Accordingly, Keil found both doors of the dromos closed.

48 One might speculate that Keil feared to damage something inside the dromos by toppling over the door.

49 EED on 08.10.1929.

50 EED on 09.10.1929.

51 Keil 1930a, 43f.: "Ein Marmorsarkophag, dessen Deckel nach Entfernung der Verklammerung zur Seite geschoben war und schief auf dem Kasten lagerte [...]. Die an einigen Stellen aus ihrer natürlichen Lage gebrachten Knochen, zwischen denen auch nicht die geringste Beigabe vorhanden war". – See the

EED from 03.10.1929: "steht nahe der Nordseite ein sauber gearbeiteter glatter Sarkophagkasten ohne jeden Schmuck, auf dem etwas verschoben, der oben geraute ebenso schmucklose Giebeldeckel liegt. Die Verschiebung und die entfernten Klammern, die Deckel und Kasten verbanden, lassen erkennen, dass der Sarkophag bereits einmal geöffnet worden ist [...]. Die Lage des Skeletts war gestört, der Kopf lag verkehrt und auch die übrigen Knochen waren nur teilweise an der ungefähr richtigen Stelle" ("Near the north side is a neatly crafted smooth sarcophagus box without any ornamentation, on which the gable lid, roughened at the top and equally unadorned, lies somewhat displaced. The displacement and the removed clamps that connected the lid and the box indicate that the sarcophagus has already been opened once [...]. The position of the skeleton was disturbed, the head was upside down and also the other bones were only partially in the approximately correct position"). – See Anevlavi et al. 2020, 33: "flat lid".

52 Keil 1930a, 43f.: "daß einmal Grabräuber in die Kammer eingedrungen waren, den Sarkophag aufgesprengt und nach wertvollen Beigaben durchsucht hatten" ("that grave robbers had once entered the chamber, burst open the sarcophagus and searched for valuable grave goods"). – EED from 03.10.1929.

53 Keil 1930a, 44: "Die Grabräuber waren aber nicht wie wir durch das Deckengewölbe, sondern durch den im Bauplane vorgesehenen von der Südseite in die Kammer führenden Gang gekommen, der am inneren Ende durch eine roh belassene, am äußeren Ende durch eine schön verzierte schwere Marmorplatte verschlossen war".

54 EED from 03.10.1929, see above n. 47. EED ... from 08.10.1929: "Am Oktogon wird versucht, den (hinteren) Kammereingang, falls ein solcher vorhanden, festzustellen" ("At the octagon, an attempt is made to determine the (rear) chamber entrance, if one exists"). EED from 09.10.1929: "Die Tür zur Grabkammer wird gefunden und freigemacht" ("The door to the burial chamber is found and unblocked"). EED from 10.10.1929: "Oktogon: Tür aufgenommen, dann Türverschlußstein geöffnet" ("Octagon: door documented, then door lock stone opened"); Keil 1930a, 44. – Therefore, Waldner 2020, 89, is incorrect in stating: "wurde 1982 und 1983 an der Rückseite des Oktogons – also im Süden des Monuments – flächig bis auf die Unterkante der Türplatte zur Grabkammer gegraben. Dabei wurde dieser südliche Zugang erstmals geöffnet" ("In 1982 and 1983, excavations were carried out at the rear of the octagon – that is, in the south of the monument – down to the lower edge of the door slab to the burial chamber. In the process, this southern access was opened for the first time"). – See the enigmatic sentence of Thuswaldner 2015, 54: "Im Jahr 1982 wurde [...] die äußere Verschlussplatte des Dromos, die schon Theuer auch von außen doku-

mentiert hatte, nach dem Eindringen der Grabräuber erstmals wieder geöffnet" ("In 1982 [...] the outer closure plate of the dromos, which Theuer had already documented also from the outside, was opened again for the first time after the invasion of the tomb raiders"). – Kader 1995, 215; Thür 1990, 50; Alzinger 1974, 42.

55 Keil 1930a, 44. – Such an idea never seems to have been questioned: Thür 2015, 272; Thuswaldner 2015, 53f.; Bennett 2013, s.v. Arsinoe IV n. 15; Schörner 2007, 99. 241; Wohlers–Scharf 1995, 208; Alzinger 1962, 126; Miltner 1958, 29.

56 Miltner 1959b, 340f.

57 EED from 06.10. – 08.10.1904.

58 EED from 03.10.1929; Keil 1930a, 44. – Schörner 2007, 99 n. 813.

59 Keil 1930a, 43: "Der Kasten war überraschenderweise bis etwa 0.1 m unter dem Rande mit Wasser gefüllt".

60 Keil wrote into his EED from 03.10.1929: "Der Kasten des Sarkophags ist fast bis zum Rande mit Wasser gefüllt. Da auch die Außenwand des Sarkophags und einzelne Steine leichte Sinterspuren zeigen, ist die Wasserfüllung des Sarkophags offenbar so zu erklären, daß von der südlich an dem Oktogon vorbeiführenden spätantiken oder byzantinischen Wasserleitung einmal Wasser in die Kammer bis über die Höhe des Sarkophags eingedrungen ist. Sei es nun, daß der Überstandhe nicht oder das Wasser unabhängig davon später anders geleitet war, jedenfalls muß es aus der Kammer verhältnismäßig rasch wieder verschwunden sein, durch Sinterablagerung aber einen luftdichten Abschluß erzeugt haben, der die Verdunstung des Wassers im Sarkophag verhinderte. In der Tat war die Luft bei meinem Einstiege noch mit Feuchtigkeit gesättigt" ("The box of the sarcophagus is filled with water almost to the rim. Since the outer wall of the sarcophagus and individual stones also show slight traces of sintering, the water filling of the sarcophagus can obviously be explained by the fact that water from the late antique or Byzantine water conduit running south past the sarcophagus once penetrated the chamber to above the height of the sarcophagus. It may be that the supernatant was not there or that the water was later conducted in a different way, in any case, it must have disappeared from the chamber relatively quickly, but by depositing sinter, it created an airtight seal, which prevented the water in the sarcophagus from evaporating. In fact, the air was still saturated with moisture when I entered").

61 See pp. 106f. with n. 84.

62 Keil 1936–37,174: "Anfang November, als katastrophale Regengüsse einsetzten" ("at the beginning of November, when catastrophic rains set in"). – Thür 2009, 9: the Curetes Street as "brook bed". – One might contemplate the idea that the Octagon was

built on a high socle because of the regular flooding of the area in pre–Augustan times.

63 H. Thür, in: Scherrer 2000, 134. 136; see here pp. 121–126.

64 U. Outschar, in: Scherrer 2000, 130–133; Keil 1944/1953. – See here pp. 175–177.

65 See here pp. 111–118.

66 See the description of such flooding at Alzinger 1962, 128: "Am Samstag, dem 14. Oktober 1905, fiel nämlich Regen, und zwar schließlich so stark, daß Schaden angerichtet wurde. Als am folgenden Tag die Ausgräber zu den Grabungsplätzen gingen, um an Ort und Stelle festzustellen, ob etwas zerstört worden sei, fanden sie den Platz vor der Bibliothek fast meterhoch mit Schutt bedeckt" ("On Saturday, October 14, 1905, it rained, and eventually it rained so heavily that damage was done. When the excavators went to the excavation sites the next day to determine on the spot if anything had been destroyed, they found the area in front of the library covered with debris nearly a metre high").

67 EED from 03.10.1929.

68 EED from 03.10.1929: "Wir haben dann das Wasser ausgeschöpft" ("We then scooped out the water").

69 Prochaska – Grillo 2012, 587.

70 Keil 1930a, 43f. EED from 03.10.1929.

71 Lucan. VIII 695, calls the vault of Alexander's tomb *antrum*. Petschenig – Stowasser 1930, s.v. *antrum* (cave, grotto).

72 Plattner 2009, 105.

73 EED from 01.10.1929 and 03.10.1929; Keil 1930a, 41. – Thuswaldner 2015, 53 fig. 41. 79 fig. 77.

74 EED from 03.10.1929; Keil 1930a, 41–44. – Thuswaldner 2015, 109 fig. 112.

75 EED from 08.10.1929; Keil 1930a, 44. – Waldner 2020, 91 fig. 18.

76 EED from 09.10.1929; Keil 1930a, 44.

77 EED from 10.10.1929; Keil 1930a, 44. – Thuswaldner 2015, 90 fig. 86, and Waldner 2020, 91 fig. 18.

78 EED from 12.10.1929; Keil 1930a, 44.

79 Keil 1930a, 45.

80 One might assume, therefore, that the mandible is still located in the anthropological collections of the University of Greifswald.

81 EED from 01.10.1929.

82 EED from 03.10.1929: "Das Rätsel ist gelöst, das Oktogon ist ein Heroon". – Keil 1944/1953, 81 n. 3; Thuswaldner 2015, 53. – Keil also called the 'Library of Celsus' a heroon: Keil 1944/1953, 81: "Bibliothek und Heroon" ("library and heroon"). 83.

83 EED from 03.10.1929: "Damit Oktogon erledigt". – Thuswaldner 2015, 54.

84 Thuswaldner 2015, 57. – As Strocka 2011, 310, points out, the Octagon was "never really published" ("ist trotz häufiger Erwähnung bis heute nicht wirklich publiziert"). Wohlers–Scharf 1995, 95. 106–118, does not mention the Octagon when describing the excavations years 1904 and 1929, and addresses the monu-

85 ment at the beginning of the third Austrian excavation period in 1954 (fig. 5).

85 Thür 1995c, 180.

86 Wohlers–Scharf 1995, 184.

87 Thür 2015, 272f.; Thür 2009, 12–20; Thür 1999a, 424; Thür 1997c, 17; Thür 1995c, 178–181; Thür 1995a, 80. 91; Karwiese et al. 1994, 26; Langmann 1991–92, 12: "Der Frage der bislang unbekannten Grabinhaberin wurde nachgegangen. Die Untersuchung, ob die ptolemäische Prinzessin Arsinoe IV, eine Schwester Kleopatras VII, die im Jahr 41 v. Chr. in Ephesos eines gewaltsamen Todes starb, mit der im Oktogon bestatteten Person identisch sein könne, konnte mit einiger Wahrscheinlichkeit positiv beantwortet werden" ("The question of the hitherto unknown grave owner was investigated. The investigation, whether the Ptolemaic princess Arsinoe IV, a sister of Kleopatra VII, who died a violent death in Ephesos in 41 BC could be identical with the person buried in the Octagon, could be answered positively with some probability").

88 Thür 2015, 271–273.

89 Thür 2011, 76: "Der ephesische Grabbau, seine Datierung und seine topographische Situation passen nun m. E. hervorragend zu einem durch antike Autoren überlieferten historischen Ereignis, in dem einer jungen Frau aus dem Königshaus der Ptolemaier eine wesentliche Rolle zukommt: Im Jahr 41 v. Chr. wurde Arsinoe IV., die jüngste Schwester Kleopatras VII. im Asyl des Artemisions in Ephesos ermordet [...]. Die historischen Fakten und der archäologische Befund fügen sich nahezu perfekt zusammen" ("The Ephesian funerary monument, its dating, and its topographical situation now, in my opinion, fit perfectly with a historical event recorded by ancient authors, in which a young woman from the Ptolemaic royal family plays a significant role. In the year 41 BC, Arsinoe IV, the youngest sister of Kleopatra VII, was murdered in the sanctuary of Artemis in Ephesos [...]. The historical facts and the archaeological evidence fit together almost perfectly").

90 Thür took such a specific age estimation from her conversations with E. Reuer. – See also, H. Thür, in: Scherrer 2000, 124: "The skeleton of a young woman, fifteen or sixteen years old".

91 Also, Bennett 2013, s.v. Arsinoe IV n. 15, refers to "the Egyptian elements of the tomb" probably understanding "the papyrus columns [...] well–known in Alexandria, and [...] the octagonal form of the mausoleum" as such. – See for these candelabra p. 33 with n. 30.

92 On the other hand, Thür 1990, 54: "Die Greifen sind jedoch in der Grabsymbolik im hellenistischen Griechenland und Kleinasien so häufig, daß ihnen kein besonderer Aussagewert beizumessen ist" ("The griffins, however, are so common in funerary symbolism in Hellenistic Greece and Asia Minor that no special significance is to be attached to them").

93   Thür 2015, 273 n. 11; Thür 2009, 17. – In fact, it seems unlikely that the "palm–leaf–style columns" belong to the architectonic context of the Octagon. – See p. 110 with n. 3 and fig. 35.

94   On the other hand, Thür 1990, 54: "Die stufenförmige Pyramide des Daches ist [...] jedoch wieder als geläu-fige Bauform für Grabbauten einzustufen und damit ohne besonderen Bezugswert zu Ägypten" ("The stepped pyramid of the roof, however, is [...] again to be classified as a common construction form for tomb buildings and thus without any particular refer-ence value to Egypt").

95   Thür 2011, 76.

96   Thür 2011, 76: "Als wahrscheinliches materielles Re-likt eines Mitglieds der ptolemaischen Herrscherfa-milie ist das Skelett aus dem Oktogon einzigartig und von höchstem Interesse für Anthropologen und His-toriker" ("As a probable material relic of a member of the Ptolemaic ruling family, the skeleton from the Octagon is unique and of great interest to anthropol-ogists and historians").

97   Spanu 2010, 60f.: "Questa identificazione non ha tro-vato un consenso unanime tra gli studiosi, ma è da ritenersi la più convincente. Certamente, si possono muovere delle riserve su alcuni criteri adottati dalla Thür, non ultimo quello relativo alla scelta della pian-ta ottagonale del mausoleo. Secondo la Thür, infatti, essa sarebbe stato un diretto richiamo all'aspetto del Faro di Alessandria, quasi una evidenza dell'apparte-nenza alla dinastia tolemaica della sepolta. Tale teo-ria appare estremamente fragile: la pianta ottago-nale risulta essere un elemento troppo generico per costituire un richiamo immediato al Faro (in questo senso sono noti esempi molto più rispondenti al suo aspetto), mentre invece appare più opportuno con-siderarla come una delle sperimentazioni eclettiche dell'architettura di età tardo–ellenistica" ("This identi-fication has not found unanimous consensus among scholars, but it is considered the most convincing. Certainly, some reservations can be made about cer-tain criteria adopted by Thür, not least the choice of the octagonal layout of the mausoleum. According to Thür, this layout would have been a direct reference to the appearance of the Lighthouse of Alexandria, almost evidence of the buried person's belonging to the Ptolemaic dynasty. This theory appears extreme-ly fragile: the octagonal layout is too generic to con-stitute an immediate reference to the Lighthouse (in this sense, there are known examples that are much more similar to its appearance). Instead, it seems more appropriate to consider it as one of the eclectic experiments of the late Hellenistic architecture").

98   Plattner 2018, 223; Thuswaldner 2017, 137; Heinz 2016, 46. 175. 192f.; Rathmayr 2016, 725 ("presum-ably"); Thuswaldner 2015, 64: "Das Alter der im Jahr 41 v. Chr. in Ephesos ermordeten ägyptischen Prin-zessin passt zu dem des im Inneren des Sarkophags aufgefundenen Skeletts" ("The age of the Egyptian princess murdered in Ephesos in 41 BC matches that of the skeleton found inside the sarcophagus"); Kimmel–Clauzet 2014, 5: "maybe of Ptolemy Arsi-noe IV"; Kienast 2014, 160: "Alle verfügbaren Infor-mationen sprechen dafür, dass das Oktogon von Ephesos als Grabbau für Arsinoe IV errichtet wurde [...]. So das überzeugende Resümee von H. Thür [...] ein Vorschlag [...], dem m. E. nichts entgegen zu set-zen ist" ("All available information indicates that the Octagon of Ephesos was built as a tomb for Arsinoe IV [...] According to the convincing summary by H. Thür [...] a proposal [...] that, in my opinion, cannot be opposed"); Bennett 2013, s.v. Arsinoe IV n. 4 ("The circumstantial case for the Octagon tomb being Ar-sinoe's is quite reasonable, though certainly not con-clusive"). n. 15 ("This identification seems quite plau-sible, though it is certainly not conclusively proved"); Ercoles 2013, 397: "Tra i monumenti funerarî, invece, l'esempio più antico è il cosiddetto Ottagono di Efe-so, costruito nella seconda metà del I sec. a.C. per ospitare le spoglie della regina di Cipro Arsinoe IV, deceduta nel 41 a.C." ("Among funerary monuments, however, the oldest example is the so–called Octagon of Ephesos, built in the second half of the 1ˢᵗ c. BC to house the remains of the Cypriot queen Arsinoe IV, who died in 41 BC"); Quatember et al. 2013, 217 ("possibly the grave of the Ptolemaic princess Arsinoe IV"); Prochaska – Grillo 2012, 587 ("supposed to be the tomb of Arsinoe IV"). Strocka 2011, 310: "Und wenn das Oktogon, wofür viel spricht, zu Ehren Arsinoes IV., einer ehemaligen Königin, errichtet wurde" ("and if the octagon, as there is much to suggest, was erected in honour of Arsinoe IV, a former queen"); Barbantani 2010, 31f.: "identified it [i.e the Ephesian Octagon] with the sepulchre of Arsinoe IV"; Plattner 2009, 105; Schäfer 2006, 132 n. 21; Huß 2001, 731 n. 28; Tyldes-ley 2008, 27; H. Thür, in: Scherrer 2000, 124: "the youngest sister of Cleopatra VII was probably buried here [i.e. inside the Octagon]"; Wohlers–Scharf 1995, 184. 208: "Nach dem neuesten Forschungsstand war das Oktogon die letzte Ruhestätte der Ptolemäerin Arsinoe IV" ("According to the latest research, the octagon was the final resting place of the Ptolemaic Arsinoe IV"); Knibbe – Thür 1995, 92; Rumscheid 1994, 160. 164; Knibbe – Langmann 1993, 54 ("perhaps the heroon for the Ptolemaic princess Arsinoe IV"). – Also, G. Hölbl supports Thür's proposal (personal commu-nication with the author).

99   Anevlavi et al. 2020, 34: "The question of whether Arsi-noe IV is in fact the tomb occupant of the Octagon and is the person buried in the sarcophagus cannot yet be viewed as definitely ascertained"; Steskal 2013, 248: "It is still debated if the Octagon actually functioned as the tomb of Arsinoe IV"; Jones 2011, 47f. n. 22: "con-siderable doubts remain"; Oesterreichisches Archae-ologisches Institut 2010, 55: "das weibliche Skelett

aus dem Oktogon (sog. Arsinoe)" ("the female skeleton from the octagon (so–called Arsinoe)"); Schörner 2007, 100: "doch muss diese Benennung auf Basis der bisher bekannten Fakten hypothetisch bleiben" ("this designation must remain hypothetical on the basis of the facts known so far"). 117: "Der Anlaß für die Bestattung einer jungen Frau im Oktogon von Ephesos ist nicht bekannt" ("The occasion for the burial of a young woman in the Octagon of Ephesos is not known"). 120 n. 1006. 201 n. 1727: "Da es keinen handfesten Hinweis auf eine Identifikation der jungen Frau gibt, ist es müßig zu überlegen, ob die gewollte Nichterkennbarkeit damit begründet werden könnte, daß es sich um eine nicht aus Ephesos stammende Frau handeln könnte, wie es H. Thür mit Arsinoe IV. vorgeschlagen hat" ("Since there is no tangible indication of an identification of the young woman, it is idle to consider whether the deliberate non–identification could be justified by the fact that it could be a woman not from Ephesos, as H. Thür suggested with Arsinoe IV."); Grüßinger 2001, 60 ("entirely hypothetical assumption"); Berns 1996, 45 n. 229; Kader 1995, 215: "spricht die Gestaltung des Oktogons m. E. gegen eine Grabinhaberin aus den Königshäusern" ("the design of the octagon argues against a tomb owner from the royal houses").

100 EED from 03.10.1929; see above n. 51.

101 Keil 1930a, 44: "eine ganz vornehme Persönlichkeit" ("quite a distinguished personality"). – Thür 2011, 74f.: "Die für einen Grabbau ungewöhnliche Lage im Zentrum der Stadt erfordert eine Person, der entweder aufgrund aristokratischer Herkunft oder aber durch besondere Verdienste um die Stadt das Privileg einer innerstädtischen Bestattung zuteil wurde. Für eine junge weibliche Person ist eine dynastische Herkunft der wahrscheinlichere Grund für das Grab im Stadtzentrum" ("The unusual location of the tomb in the city centre suggests that the individual was either of aristocratic origin or had exceptional merits towards the city, granting them the privilege of an intra–urban burial. For a young female individual, a dynastic background is the more probable reason for the tomb's placement in the city centre").

102 EED from 03.10.1929.

103 Keil 1930a, 44: "wurde die Grabkammer, der wir vorher noch den Schädel der bestatteten Person entnommen hatten, wieder sorgfältig geschlossen" ("The burial chamber, from which we had previously removed the skull of the interred individual, was carefully closed again"). – Keil does not mention the removal of the Octagon's skull within the EED, a fact that underscores the cursory character of the writings in this documentation.

104 Keil 1930a, 45. – Although one might suppose so, it is not known whether the mandible reached Greifswald.

105 Keil 1930a, 45: "eine junge Frau als der Inhaberin des Heroons" ("a young woman as the owner of the Heroon"). – Miltner 1958, 29.

106 The terminus for a calvaria plus mandibula, i.e. for a complete skull, would be 'cranium'. – See Thür 1995c, 181f.: "the cranium belonging to this skeleton"; Schörner 2007, 99 ("cranium").

107 Heine–Geldern 1955, 620: "J. Weninger […] described a young noblewoman's skull from Ephesus"; Richmond 1954, 96: "J. Weninger on the skull from an Augustan Heroon at Ephesus"; Weninger 1953, 158; https://dewiki.de/Lexikon/Josef_Weninger, accessed on 21.04.2023. – Bennett 2013, s.v. Arsinoe IV n. 3, erroneously stated that "the skull was photographed and measured in detail in the 1920s".

108 Weninger 1953.

109 Keil 1930a, 41. 44f.; Weninger 1953, 158: "Ein Schädel aus einem Ephesischen Heroengrab".

110 Keil 1930b, 87.

111 Weninger 1953, 158: "aus der Zeit um Christi Geburt". – Such phrase was taken over by Alzinger 1962, 126. 227 (regarding the 'Prytaneion'; see also, Steskal 2010, 78 n. 372, and Miltner 1956–58, 33), and by Kanz et al. 2009: "other young and powerful women who died just before Christ's birth in Ephesus". However, since the birth of Christ is usually placed in the decade between 4 BC and 6 AD, the statements appear somewhat curious (https://www.uni-erfurt.de/forschung/aktuelles/forschungsblog–wortmelder/nachgefragt–wann–wurde–eigentlich–jesus–wirklich–geboren–herr–prof–brodersen, accessed on 21.04.2023).

112 See p. 39.

113 Weninger 1953, 160. 165. – Guo et al. 2018, 810; Fins et al. 2017.

114 Weninger 1953, 161. – Hisham et al. 2018; Alhazmi et al. 2017.

115 Weninger 1953, 161. – Interestingly, Weninger's article is repeatedly ignored: Schörner 2007, 241; Thür 1995c; Rumscheid 1994, 160; Thür 1990; A. Bammer, in Oberleitner et al. 1978, 95; Alzinger 1974, 42; Alzinger 1962, 124–127; Wotschitzky 1954.

116 Weninger 1953, 161: "Das [i.e. die morphologischen Details] weist auf eine ruhige, durch nichts gestörte Entwicklung dieses Schädels hin" ("This [i.e. the morphological details] indicates a calm, undisturbed development of this skull").

117 H. Thür according to Bordsen 2009: "It disappeared in Germany during World War II". – See pp. 214f.

118 Alzinger 1972, 75.

119 BBC (23.03.2009) Cleopatra: Portrait of a killer: https://www.youtube.com/watch?v=YFWRe2TqyPk, accessed on 21.04.2023. German version: https://www.youtube.com/watch?v=XGARimnjZvE (accessed on 21.04.2023).

120 BBC news (16.03.2009) Cleopatra's mother 'was African' (http://news.bbc.co.uk/2/hi/also_in_the_news/7945333.stm, accessed on 21.04.2023); Beard M. (16.03.2009) The skeleton of Cleopatra's sister? Steady on. (https://web.archive.org/web/20090317185101/http:/timesonline.typepad.com/dons_life/2009/03/

the–skeleton–of.html, accessed on 21.04.2023), and many more contributions.

121 See the excavation reports of J. Keil (four reports covering the years 1930–1935; no excavation in 1932, 1934, and between 1936 and 1953), F. Miltner (five reports covering the years 1954–1958; no excavation in 1959), F. Eichler (nine reports covering the years 1960–1968), and H. Vetters (twelve reports covering the years 1969–1981; no excavation in 1974).

122 Oberleitner et al. 1978.

123 Personal communication with K. Gschwantler.

124 Keil 1930a, 41–45.

125 Waldner 2020, 26; Waldner 2009, 293; H. Thür, in: Scherrer 2000, 114.

126 EED from 20.09.1982: "Das seinerzeit von Keil im Scheitel geöffnete Oktogon wieder geöffnet" ("The octagon opened at the apex by Keil was reopened"). – Deep down within the socle, the opening of the vault itself was covered by a stone slab in order to inhibit the fall of earth and rubble into the chamber.

127 EED from 01.10.1929; Keil 1930a, 41. – Keil had to break a substantial hole into the stone masonry of the Octagon's pedestal from above, until he reached the vault structure (Thuswaldner 2015, 53 fig. 41. 79 fig. 77).

128 H. Thür according to Bordsen 2009: "The site of the Octagon has a grave chamber. It was opened in 1926, but the opening was very small, and no one entered it until later on".

129 Keil 1930a, 41–45.

130 The visit went unheeded in the excavation report of the OeAI (Vetters 1983, 119). – Also, the EED from 1982 does not mention the re–entry of the Octagon's burial chamber (20.09. – 22.09.1982).

131 Keil 1930a, 43.

132 On this, see Keil's EED from 12.10.1929: "Die äußere Tür in die Grabkammer wurde geschlossen, dann nach Beendigung der Aufnahmen alles wieder zugeschüttet" ("The outer door into the burial chamber was closed, then after the documentation was finished everything was filled in again").

133 EED from 21.09.1982: "Antreffen der bekrönten Oberseite der angelehnten Türplatte zur Grabkammer des Oktogon" ("Detecting the crowned top of the leaning door plate to the burial chamber of the octagon"). EED from 22.09.1982: "Oktogon: Erreichen des Fußprofiles, Öffnen der Türplatte (eingezapft), Tür 110×75×20, dahinter Dromos (260×190×86), Türplatte zur Grabkammer (mit Steckklammern verdübelt) umgestürzt (was in den letzten Tagen geschehen sein muß!)" ("Octagon: reaching the foot profile, opening the door plate (tapped in), door 110×75×20, behind it dromos (260×190×86), door plate to the burial chamber (dowelled with pegs) overturned (which must have happened in the last days!").

134 EED from 22.09.1982.

135 EED from 09.10. – 10.10.1929. – Thuswaldner 2015, 154: "Nachdem die Hanghäuser, welche unmittelbar im Süden an das Oktogon anschließen, aufgegeben und dem Verfall preisgegeben worden waren, deckte der abrutschende Schutt über die Jahrhunderte auch die Ruine des Oktogons mehr und mehr zu" ("After the terrace houses immediately adjoining the octagon to the south had been abandoned and left to dilapidate over the centuries the sliding rubble covered more and more of the ruins of the octagon"). Such an observation may explain why the Octagon is better preserved at its southern side (figs. 4, 10b).

136 EED from 03.10.1929.

137 See pp. 39f.

138 Karwiese et al. 1994, 26: "nach der Öffnung des Sarkophages [in 1929] von den Ausgräbern offenbar in die Wandnischen der Grabkammer gelegt worden" ("apparently been placed in the wall niches of the burial chamber by the excavators [in 1929] after the opening of the sarcophagus").

139 EED from 03.10.1929: "Wir haben […] den Schlamm und Sand am Boden genau durchsucht, ohne den geringsten Fund zu machen (in dem verschlossen gefundenen Sarkophag des Celsus war auch nichts)" ("We searched […] the mud and sand on the ground carefully without making the slightest finding (there was also nothing in the sealed sarcophagus of Celsus)"). – Thür 1995c, 181; Thür 1995b, 92 n. 364; Karwiese et al. 1994, 26.

140 Waldner 2020, 91 fig. 18; Thuswaldner 2015, 60 fig. 52.

141 EED fom 20.09. – 22.09.1982; Vetters 1983.

142 EED from 10.10.1929: Oktogon: "Tür aufgenommen, dann Türverschlußstein geöffnet. Dahinter Gang, der durch Λ spitz gestellte Quaderplatten gebildet wird. Dann der innere Verschlußstein" ("Octagon: door taken up, then door closure stone opened. Behind it, aisle formed by Λ pointed ashlar slabs. Then the inner closing stone"). – Thuswaldner 2015, 75f.

143 At an unknown time later on, the lid was put on top of the chest (fig. 6) probably in order to inhibit a refilling of the sarcophagus.

144 Thür 2015, 272 n. 8; Kanz et al. 2009: "most of the postcranial skeleton was discovered". – Thür 1995c, 181: "The skeleton was almost complete with the exception of the missing neck vertebrae and the cranium". – Thür 1995b, 92 n. 364; Karwiese et al. 1994, 26: "In der seit Jahren erstmals wieder zugänglichen Grabkammer des Oktogons wurde das mit Ausnahme des nach Greifswald gebrachten Schädels nahezu vollständige Skelett der Grabinhaberin, das nach der Öffnung des Sarkophages von den Ausgräbern offenbar in die Wandnischen der Grabkammer gelegt worden war, aufgefunden" ("In the burial chamber of the octagon, accessible again for the first time in years, the skeleton of the tomb owner, almost complete with the exception of the skull brought to

Greifswald, was found, which had apparently been placed in the wall niches of the burial chamber by the excavators after the opening of the sarcophagus"). – See, on the other hand, H. Thür, in Bordsen 2009: "In 1985, the back side of the chamber became accessible, and I re-found the skeleton – the bones were in two niches. The body was removed and examined".

145 Egon Reuer was a student of J. Weninger: Reuer 1976, 225.

146 1995b, 92 n. 364.

147 Thür 1995c, 182 ("correspond perfectly"); Thür 1995b, 92 n. 364; Karwiese et al. 1994, 26: "Die anthropologische Untersuchung durch E. und S. Reuer bestätigte das Greifswalder Ergebnis: Die bestattete weibliche Person starb im Alter von 15 bis 16 Jahren. Dieses Ergebnis paßt vorzüglich zu den überlieferten Lebensdaten Arsinoe's IV" ("The anthropological examination by E. and S. Reuer confirmed the Greifswald result: the buried female died at the age of 15 to 16. This result fits excellently with the transmitted dates of Arsinoe IV's life").

148 Weninger 1953, 161.

149 Personal communication with S. Fabrizii–Reuer.

150 Thür 1995b, 92 n. 364.

151 Regrettably, the manuscript is lost. Personal communication with S. Fabrizii–Reuer and H. Thür.

152 Personal communication with S. Fabrizii–Reuer. – Thuswaldner 2015, 59: "den H. Thür im Jahr 1993 als letzten verbliebenen Rest der Bestatteten noch im Sarkophag vorfand" ("which H. Thür found in 1993 in the sarcophagus as the last remaining part of the buried person"). Thür 1995c, 181f., states that "the anthropologists discovered a tooth" within the sarcophagus. Thür 1995b, 92 n. 364; Karwiese et al. 1994, 26.

153 Thür 1995c, 182: "After the initial excavations years ago, the cranium belonging to this skeleton was probably added to the collection at the University of Greifswald. Unfortunately, the collection's inventory list identifying this cranium has since been lost".

154 Karwiese et al. 1996, 22: "wurde eine sehr genaue und detailreiche dreidimensionale Aufnahme des Oktogons durchgeführt, die eine steingenaue Erfassung der Grabkammer mit einschloß".

155 Thuswaldner 2017, 134 ("170 components"); Thuswaldner 2015, 157; Quatember et al. 2013, 223 ("170 elements"); Prochaska – Grillo 2012, 587; Thür 2011, 76: "Eine zunächst projektierte reale Anastylose vor Ort in Ephesos ist aus mehreren Gründen nicht durchführbar" ("An initially planned physical anastylosis on–site in Ephesos is not feasible for several reasons"); Thuswaldner et al. 2009; Thuswaldner 2009; Österreichisches Archäologisches Institut 2008, 22: "176 analysierte Bauteile" ("176 analysed components"); Koder 2008, 411f.; Koder – Krinzinger 2007, 407; Schörner 2007, 54; Krinzinger 2006, 333; Alzinger 1972, 75.

156 Thuswaldner 2015, 60 fig. 52: "Mit den durch die Verfasserin im Sommer 2005 am Türsturz des Eingangs in die Grabkammer aufgefundenen Knochen" ("With the bones found by the author in summer 2005 at the lintel of the entrance to the burial chamber"). Waldner 2009, 293 n. 100. – Curiously, the annual OeAI–report of 2007 states that these bones were newly "discovered" at that time, although they had been in plain sight since 1982. Koder 2008, 422. Misunderstood in Waldner 2020, 91 fig. 18c: "Knochendeponie in der Nische der Grabkammer" ("bone landfill in the niche of the burial chamber"); Kanz et al. 2009 ("in 2007 [...] found in a niche of the antechamber").

157 Thuswaldner 2015, 59; Kanz et al. 2009; Koder 2008, 422.

158 Kanz et al. 2009, fig. 13.

159 A set of findings drawn from the dromos in 1982 was not retrieved any more (Waldner 2020, 26 n. 66. 89 n. 492). – Weninger 1953, 165, documents a right mandibular first molar.

160 Kanz et al. 2009; Madrigal 2009, 245.

161 Wittschieber et al. 2014.

162 Altinsoy – Gurses 2022.

163 Tisè et al. 2011.

164 Instead, two television programmes illustrating "a tale of rivalry, lust, incest, murder and power" were edited: BBC (23.03.2009) Cleopatra: Portrait of a killer: https://www.bbc.co.uk/pressoffice/pressreleases/stories/2009/03_march/15/cleopatra.shtml (accessed on 21.04.2023); https://www.youtube.com/watch?v=YFWRe2TqyPk, and the German version: arte (2010) Kleopatra – Porträt einer Mörderin: https://programm.ard.de/TV/arte/kleopatra---portraet-einer-moerderin/eid_287245721506081 (both accessed on 21.04.2023), https://www.youtube.com/watch?v=X-GARimnjZvE, accessed on 27.03.2022. – Thür 2011, 74: "Eine mediale Verarbeitung des Befundes [...] wirkungsvoll und spannend" ("A media processing [...] effective and captivating"); Kleopatras Schwester: Ein Mordfall. Die Presse from 20.03.2009. Cleopatra meets CSI, oder: Hat Liz Taylor zu Unrecht eine hellhäutige Königin gespielt? In: Frankfurter Allgemeine Zeitung from 21.03.2009. David Chater on the BBC–feature 'Cleopatra, Portrait of a Killer´, in: The Times from 21.03.2009; Thür 2011, 74. – Interestingly, K. Grossschmidt and F. Kanz were removed from the Ephesian excavations at that time, although they had been in charge of the "anthropological examinations" at the site since 2001. See the annual reports of the OeAI: Österreichisches Archäologisches Institut 2009 (Grossschmidt and Kanz are no longer mentioned); Österreichisches Archäologisches Institut 2008, 28 (only Grossschmidt is mentioned). Both are referred to in: Koder 2008, 422; Österreichisches Archäologisches Institut 2007, 422; Krinzinger 2006, 423; Krinzinger 2005, 357; Österreichisches Archäologisches Institut 2004, 376; Österreichisches Archäologisches

Institut 2003, 310. 322; Österreichisches Archäologisches Institut 2002, 380.

165 Kanz et al. 2009. Arte (2010) Kleopatra – Porträt einer Mörderin: https://programm.ard.de/TV/arte/kleopatra---portraet-einer-moerderin/eid_287245721506081, accessed on 21.04.2023.

166 Krämer et al. 2014a.

167 Krämer et al. 2014b; Ekizoglu et al. 2016.

168 Schmeling et al. 2004, 6.

169 On the unfinished dental differentiation, see Weninger 1953, 160. 165.

170 Thür 1995b, 92 n. 364.

171 Weninger 1953, 161.

172 Kanz et al. 2009; Koder 2008, 422.

173 Kanz et al. 2009; Madrigal 2009, 245.

174 Cass. Dio XLIII 19; Schol. to Lukan X 521.

175 Rudolf et al. 2020, 48–51.

176 Kanz et al. 2009. – Koder 2008, 422: "Die zarten Knochen und die kaum ausgeprägten Muskelansatzstellen deuten zudem darauf hin, dass dieses Mädchen keine schwere körperliche Arbeit verrichten musste" ("The delicate bones and the barely pronounced muscle attachments also indicate that this girl did not have to do any heavy physical work").

177 Personal communication with S. Fabrizii-Reuer. –See https://www.hna.de/lokales/goettingen/goettingen-ort28741/goettinger-professor-erforscht-praehistorische-krankheiten-morde-kleopatra-mumie-91670032.html (accessed on 21.07.2022): "Danach kann Schultz die bislang am häufigsten vermutete Todesursache nahezu ausschließen: 'Ich habe selbst den kleinsten Knochen untersucht – nirgendwo fanden sich Spuren einer Gewalteinwirkung'" ("Schultz nearly rules out the most commonly suspected cause of death: 'I myself have examined even the smallest bone – nowhere were there traces of violence'").

178 App. Rom. V 9.

179 Barry 2008, 223f. – Different: Bennett 2013, s.v. Arsinoe IV n. 15: "the lack of signs of violence, while not critical, is not what one would expect". – See the contribution that M. Schultz recently delivered into the public media (cited in n. 177). – On M. Schultz and the Octagon, see Österreichisches Archäologisches Institut 2010, 55, and tab. 3.

180 Pollanen – Chiasson 1996.

181 See p. 215.

182 Krinzinger 2005, 357.

183 Koder – Krinzinger 2007, 423; Krinzinger 2005, 358: "Im Rahmen der Erforschung des Skeletts der Grabinhaberin des Oktogons wurde eine Knochenprobe von dem Skelett entnommen, mit dem Ziel, sie einer DNA-Analyse zu unterziehen und neben einer absichernden Geschlechtsbestimmung mögliche verwandtschaftliche Beziehungen abzuklären" ("As part of the research into the skeleton of the octagon's female tomb owner, a bone sample was taken from the skeleton with the aim of subjecting it to a DNA analy-

sis and, in addition to a secure sex determination, to clarify possible family relationships").

184 Koder – Krinzinger 2007, 423.

185 Österreichisches Archäologisches Institut 2010, 55: "das weibliche Skelett aus dem Oktogon (sog. Arsinoe) [wurde] neuerlich untersucht" ("the female skeleton from the octagon (so-called Arsinoe) was re-examined").

186 Österreichisches Archäologisches Institut 2014, 27; Thür 1990, 56.

187 Österreichisches Archäologisches Institut 2016, 40.

188 Kanz et al. 2009. – See, on the other hand, Schultz (as cited in n. 177) who surmised an increased bone resorption at the skeleton that might suggest some kind of intoxication. However, the differential diagnosis of such finding is much broader and includes pathologies.

189 Kanz et al. 2009. – On the other hand, Thür 2011, 76: "Seine Ergebnisse [i.e. of Kanz et al. 2009], die ausführlich in den Film [i.e. the BBC-feature] eingeflossen sind, unterstützen die Theorie des Oktogons als Grabbau der Arsinoe IV" ("His results [i.e. of Kanz et al. 2009], which have been extensively incorporated into the film [i.e. the BBC-feature], support the theory of the Octagon as the funerary monument of Arsinoe IV").

190 Thür 2011, 74: "Ein im Zentrum von Ephesos freigelegtes Grabmonument ist [...] für lange Zeit nur wenig beachtet worden. Erst durch seine Gleichsetzung mit dem Grabmal der ptolemaischen Prinzessin Arsinoe IV. [...] hat das Interesse der Forschung und dem Bau und dem darin gefundenen Skelett der bestatteten Person deutlich zugenommen" ("A tomb monument excavated in the centre of Ephesos received little attention for a long time. It was only through its identification as the burial monument of the Ptolemaic Princess Arsinoe IV that the research interest in the structure and the skeleton found within it significantly increased").– As in 2009, public media became involved: Daily Mail from 27.02.2013: https://www.dailymail.co.uk/sciencetech/article-2285449/Have-bones-Cleopatras-murdered-sister-Archaeologists-discovery-says-hope-positive-ID.html (accessed on 21.04.2023); NBC News: https://www.nbcnews.com/news/all/expert-insists-bones-cleopatras-murdered-sister-have-been-found-flna1c8563753 (accessed on 21.04.2023), and more. – See https://rogueclassicism.com/2009/03/15/cleopatra-arsinoe-and-the-implications/, accessed on 21.04.2023.

191 After all, a certain developmental state of an osseous and dental age marker only indicates a time span within which it may occur.

192 Thuswaldner 2017, 137: "Zum Zeitpunkt ihres Todes war sie [i.e. Arsinoë IV] etwa 16–18 Jahre alt" ("At the time of her death she [i.e. Arsinoë IV] was about 16–18 years old"). Thür 2015, 272: "17.5 years". Spanu 2010, 60: "una fianculla di poco meno vent'anni" ("a young

girl of barely twenty years"). 60: "nel 41 a.C. la giovane Arsinoe (doveva avere poco più di 17 anni) fu uccisa proprio a Efeso" ("In 41 BC, the young Arsinoe (who was just over 17 years old) was killed in Ephesos"); Thür 1995c, 182: "Arsinoë therefore could not have been more than seventeen years old in 41 BCE". Thür 1990, 52: "Die Untersuchung des Skelettes der im Oktogon bestatteten Person ergab eine etwa zwanzigjährige junge Frau. Arsinoe muß zum Zeitpunkt ihrer Ermordung in Ephesos 16 bis 18 Jahre alt gewesen sein" ("The examination of the skeleton of the person buried in the octagon revealed a young woman of about twenty years. Arsinoe must have been 16 to 18 years old at the time of her murder in Ephesos").

193 Keil 1930a, 41. – Bennett 2013, s.v. Arsinoe IV n. 15 ("prominent aristocrat"); Alzinger 1974, 43.

194 Grüßinger 2001, 60.

195 Kader 1995, 214f.

196 Weninger 1953, 161.

197 Kanz et al. 2009. Thuswaldner 2015, 60: "Neben der Alterseinschätzung untersuchte Kanz auch die Entwicklung des Knochenapparates und weist auch hier, in Überreinstimmung mit den Ergebnissen Weningers, auf ein auffallend ungestörtes Wachstum hin" ("In addition to the age estimation, Kanz also examined the development of the bone apparatus and here too, in agreement with Weninger's results, points to a strikingly undisturbed growth"). – Still, one might assume that Arsinoë's health risks were considerable in view of the "incestuous" (Prop. III 11, 39. Paus. I 7, 1) relationships of the members of the royal Ptolemaic dynasty for centuries.

198 Anevlavi et al. 2020, 34.

199 Anevlavi et al. 2020, 34f. ("second half of the 1st c. B.C."); Waldner 2020, 91f. n. 496f.; Thuswaldner 2017, 133 n. 2. 136f. ("third quarter of the first c. BC"); Thür 2015, 271f. ("50–20 BC"; "built in the last quarter of the 1st c. BC"; "between the beginning of the Augustan period and the later Hellenistic period"; "This makes it uncertain whether the people of Ephesos planned and began building Arsinoe's tomb immediately after her death, perhaps under orders from her killer, or whether it was built during the Augustan period"); Rathmayr 2016, 107 n. 689 ("late Hellenistic"); Thuswaldner 2015, 61–63; 212–225 ("third quarter of the 1st c. BC"); Quatember et al. 2013, 222 ("to the 1st c. B.C."); Strocka 2011, 310 n. 59 ("I would not go below the twenties [of the 1st c. BC]"); Steskal 2010, 99. 192 ("frühkaiserzeitliche Bauten"); Waldner 2009, 298; Thuswaldner 2009, 294. 298f.; Plattner 2009, 101 n. 4. 105: "eine neue Datierung des Oktogons nunmehr in das ausgehende 1. Jh. v. Chr., in (früh)augusteische Zeit" ("a new dating of the octagon to the end of the 1st c. BC, to the (early) Augustan period"); Schörner 2007, 54 n. 441; Alzinger 1974, 42f. 85. 93. 127f. 140; Thür 1995c, 180; Knibbe – Thür 1995, 92; Alzinger 1972, 76; Alzinger – Bammer 1971, 12.

200 W. Wilberg, in: Alzinger 1974, 42. – Thuswaldner 2015, 62, misunderstands Alzinger's conclusion (Alzinger 1974, 43: "in die frühaugusteische Zeit oder in die Jahre unmittelbar davor") as Wilberg's opinion (see p. 33 with nn. 23f.).

201 Keil 1915, 71. – Weigand 1924/25, 169.

202 Keil 1930b.

203 Keil 1930a.

204 Keil 1930a, 44; Keil 1915, 71: "in das I. Jahrhundert vor Christus" ("into the first c. BC").

205 Keil 1930b, 87: "wird man das Oktogon in frührömische Zeit setzen" ("One will set the octagon in early Roman times"). Likewise, Keil 1964, 115 ("in frührömische Zeit"), Keil 1957, 106, and Keil 1955, 94. – Probably drawing from that, Brinckmann 1939, 22f., addresses the Octagon as "early Roman burial building" ("frührömischer Grabbau"), Weninger 1953, 158, as an "Ephesian hero's tomb from around the time of Christ's birth", and Richmond 1954, 96, as an "Augustan Heroön at Ephesus" when referring to Weninger's article.

206 Keil 1930b, 86f.; Keil 1930a, 44f.: "Nur wenn es gelingen sollte, auf irgendeine Weise die in dem Heroon bestattete Person zu ermitteln, wird auch die Zeitbestimmung möglich sein. Ganz so aussichtslos, wie es zunächst erscheinen möchte, ist eine solche Ermittlung des Inhabers nicht. Denn wenn es einerseits eine ganz vornehme Persönlichkeit gewesen sein muß, die ganz allein in dem stattlichen Heroon beigesetzt wurde, so lehrt das Kopfskelett, daß diese Person in dem jugendlichen Alter von etwa 20 Jahren verstorben ist. Und sollte sich der Eindruck, den meine Greifswalder Kollegen bei der Untersuchung des Schädels gewonnen haben, bestätigen, so wäre ein weiterer Anhaltspunkt gewonnen; denn wir hätten dann mit einer jungen Frau als der Inhaberin des Heroon zu rechnen".

207 See also, Miltner 1958, 30.

208 Benndorf 1906, 253 (App. Rom. V 9). 260 (Ios. ant. Iud. XV 89. Cass. Dio XLVIII 24).

209 Keil 1930b, 94.

210 Weninger 1953, 168.

211 Keil 1964, 114; Keil 1957, 105; Keil 1955, 94; Keil 1930b, 87: "In der Kammer fanden sich in schmucklosem Marmorsarkophag […] die Gebeine einer jugendlichen Person, allem Anschein nach eines Mädchens oder einer jungen Frau" ("In the chamber, in an unadorned marble sarcophagus […] the bones of a young person were found, apparently a girl or a young woman").

212 https://dewiki.de/Lexikon/Wilhelm_Alzinger, accessed on 21.04.2023.

213 Alzinger 1974, 42 ("Augustan times"). 43 ("early Augustan period or to the years immediately preceding it"). 85 ("most likely at the beginning of the Augustan period, hardly much earlier"). 93. 127 ("early Augustan period or the years immediately preceding it"). 128 ("early Augustan time"). 140 ("around a decade after

50 BC"). Alzinger 1972, 76: "am Beginn der "goldenen" Jahrhunderte von Ephesos, in den ersten Regierungsjahren des Kaisers Augustus, vielleicht sogar ein wenig früher, etwa zwischen 40 und 20 v. Chr. entstanden" ("at the beginning of the "golden" centuries of Ephesos, in the first years of the reign of Emperor Augustus, perhaps even a little earlier, around 40 to 20 BC").

214 Thür 1989, 109: "aus augusteischer Zeit". – Thür 2015, 272: "early Augustan period to the late Hellenistic period"; Thür 2001, 74: "Anhand der Datierung der Architekturdekoration kam die Mehrzahl der Forscher zu einem Baudatum in späthellenistisch–frühaugusteischer Zeit (50–20 v. Chr.)" ("Based on the dating of the architectural decoration, the majority of researchers arrived at a construction date during the Late Hellenistic to Early Augustan period (50–20 BC)").

215 See pp. 20–22.

216 Thür 2015, 272, suggests that "the tomb was planned and begun immediately after Arsinoe's death, perhaps on the orders of the murderer or by the Ephesians, or that the tomb was built during the reign of Augustus". Thür 1997c, 17: "Das Oktogon [...], wahrscheinlich als Grabbau der ptolemaischen Prinzessin Arsinoe IV. im Jahr 41 v. Chr. errichtet" ("The Octagon [...], probably built as a tomb for the Ptolemaic princess Arsinoe IV in 41 BC"). Thür 1995a, 91: "das mit einiger Wahrscheinlichkeit 41 v. Chr. erbaute Oktogon" ("the octagon, built with some probability in 41 BC").

217 Thür 2009, 16, 19: "Diese Arbeiten können sehr wohl erst 15–20 Jahre nach dem Tod der Grabinhaberin durchgeführt worden sein. Das Todesdatum bildet einen terminus postquem, nicht aber zwangsläufig einen terminus ad quem für alle Bauarbeiten" ("These works may very well have been carried out 15–20 years after the death of the grave owner. The date of death forms a terminus postquem, but not necessarily a terminus ad quem for all construction work"); H. Thür, in: Scherrer 2000, 124: "[The Octagon] is dated almost unanimously into the period 50–20 BC"; Rumscheid 1994, 164.

218 Thür 1995c, 182: "It is probable that Mark Antony intended to conceal Arsinoë's assassination by an honourable burial as far away from her native city as possible"; Thür 1990, 56.

219 Thür 2009, 18–20, questions the validity of the results, but still states: "ergibt der Grabungsbefund an der Südseite des Oktogons keine Evidenz gegen die vorgeschlagene Interpretation des Oktogons als dynastische Grabstätte der Arsinoe IV" ("the excavation findings on the south side of the octagon do not provide any evidence against the proposed interpretation of the octagon as the dynastic burial place of Arsinoe IV"). – Cormack 2004, 222.

220 Keil emptied the space on the southern side of the Octagon (fig. 10b) until, at least, the top level of the stylobate in order to open the backdoor of the dromos (EED

from 09.10. – 10.10.1929; Keil 1930a, 44), after which he refilled it again (EED from 12.12.1929; Keil 1930a, 44). Just this material was removed in 1982 (EED from 21.09. – 22.09.1982). See p. 46 and nn. 205. 213.

221 Waldner 2020, 89; Anevlavi et al. 2020, 34: "at the earliest to the last quarter of the 1st c. B.C., and therefore represent a terminus antequem[?]"; Steskal 2013, 248: "According to the newest studies, it was built at the end of the 1st c. BC"; Waldner 2009, 298; Plattner 2009, 105: "Nach der vorgestellten Analyse der Ornamentik und der technischen Beobachtungen ergibt sich daher der Schluss, dass das Oktogon erst in augusteischer Zeit errichtet wurde [...] in die beiden letzten Jahrzehnte des 1. Jhs. v. Chr. [...] in das ausgehende 1. Jh. v. Chr., in (früh) augusteische Zeit" ("According to the presented analysis of the ornamentation and the technical observations, it can therefore be concluded that the octagon was only erected in Augustan times [...] into the last two decades of the 1st c. BC [...] to the end of the 1st c. BC, in (early) Augustan era"); Österreichisches Archäologisches Institut 2000, 373: "konnten die Bauhorizonte ergraben werden, welche eine Datierung in frühaugusteische Zeit wahrscheinlich machen" ("It was possible to excavate the building horizons for the Octagon, which make a dating to the Early Augustan period probable"). – An erratic statement regarding the dating of the Ephesian mausoleum was delivered in 1978. Plattner 2009. 101 n. 4; A. Bammer, in Oberleitner et al. 1978, 96: "Das Oktogon entstand vermutlich in der 2. Hälfte des 1. Jh. n. Chr. [...] das Oktogon gehört aufgrund seiner experimentierfreudigen, undogmatischen Formen sicher nicht in die augusteische Epoche [...]. Mit der Datierung des Oktogons möchte man daher möglichst weit in die Kaiserzeit gehen" ("The Octagon was probably built in the second half of the 1st c. AD [...] due to its experimental and non–dogmatic forms, the octagon certainly does not belong to the Augustan period [...]. Therefore, when dating the Octagon, one would ideally go as far into the imperial era as possible").

222 Ios. c. Ap. II 5. Plin. nat. IX 119.

223 Gesellschaft der Freunde von Ephesos 2020, 3: "Die Bestattung einer jungen Frau in der Grabkammer und die oktogonale Form führten bisher zu einer Interpretation des sog. Oktogons als dynastische Grabstätte für die 41 v. Chr. in Ephesos ermordete Arsinoe IV. Die Auswertung der Funde aus dem südlichen Fundamentbereich und der Bauornamentik erbrachte jedoch eine eindeutige Datierung des Bauwerks in das letzte Viertel des 1. Jhs. v. Chr. Demnach dürfte das Gebäude erst rund 20 Jahre nach dem Tod Arsinoes fertig gestellt worden sein, womit alternative Szenarien auch für die Widmung des Oktogons denkbar werden" ("The burial of a young woman in the burial chamber and the octagonal shape have so far led to an interpretation of the so–called Octagon as a dynas-

tic tomb for Arsinoe IV, who was murdered in Ephesos in 41 BC. However, the analysis of the findings from the southern foundation area and the architectural ornamentation has provided a clear dating of the structure to the last quarter of the 1st c. BC. Therefore, it is likely that the building was completed only about 20 years after Arsinoe's death, opening up the possibility of alternative scenarios for the dedication of the Octagon").

224 Anevlavi et al. 2020, 34; Plattner 2009, 105; Huß 2001, 731 n. 28.

225 Huß 2001, 731 n. 28; Thür 1990, 56.

226 Bennett 2013, s.v. Arsinoe IV n. 15.

227 Huß 2001, 741.

228 Huß 2001, 731 n. 28.

229 Huß 2001, 731 n. 28: "Man wird hier eher an einen Auftraggeber zu denken haben, der in der Zeit nach 30 [BC] tätig geworden ist. Ein Mann wie Megabyzos?" ("One will have to think here rather of a principal who became active in the period after 30 [BC]. A man like Megabyzos?").

230 Bennett 2013, s.v. Arsinoe IV n. 15: "indeed one might argue that the mausoleum is more likely to have been built by Cleopatra's successful opponents than by herself or her partner, or by the city at the time of their rule".

231 Anevlavi et al. 2020, 34 n. 45: "The author [Plattner] maintains an identification of the individual buried in the Octagon as Arsinoe IV due to a different interpretation of the historical circumstances". – Plattner 2009, 105: "so ist es doch tatsächlich schwer, zur annähernd selben Zeit eine ebenso wichtige, ebenso junge und zudem weibliche Person zu fnden, der ein solch prominentes Grab zugestanden worden wäre […] ebenso gut ließe sich aber annehmen, dass der Auftrag erst nach dem Tod des Marcus Antonius und der Kleopatra unter Augustus selbst erteilt wurde" ("it is indeed difficult to find an equally important, equally young and, moreover, female person at approximately the same time who would have been granted such a prominent grave […] However, it could just as well be assumed that the order was only given after the death of Marcus Antonius and Kleopatra under Augustus himself").

232 See above n. 231.

233 Plattner 2009, 105: "ein dezidiertes Anliegen des Augustus, Frieden und Ordnung wiederherzustellen […]. Ein plakativer Akt in diesem Sinne könnte eine feierliche Umbettung der [..] ermordeten Arsinoe IV. in ein neu errichtetes Grab an prominenter Stelle in Ephesos gewesen sein" ("a decided concern of Augustus to restore peace and order […] A striking act in this sense could have been a ceremonial reburial of the […] murdered Arsinoe IV in a newly erected tomb at a prominent location in Ephesos"). – Vell. II 126, 3: *pax Augusta*; 126, 4: *Restitutae urbes Asiae*. Cass. Dio LI 20. – On a reburial, also Thür 2009, 19.

234 Prochaska – Grillo 2012, 587 fig. 3.

235 Kerschner – Prochaska 2011, 141 fig. 48.

236 Prochaska – Grillo 2012, 587.

237 Prochaska – Grillo 2012, 587. – The marble of the sarcophagus is a very massive one, a fact probably suggesting it for such a production, since the breaking risk of a worked piece was low (information kindly provided by W. Prochaska).

238 Anevlavi et al. 2020, 33. Anevlavi et al. 2020, 35, put the Octagon's sarcophagus next to later ones such as the one of Ti. Iulius Celsus Polemaeanus (see p. 177), T. Claudius Flavianus Dionysius Rhetor (see pp. 196f. and fig. 74), and Tib. Claudius Aristion (Thür 1997a,b,c). – Thür 2015, 272.

239 Anevlavi et al. 2020, 33; Oesterreichisches Archaeologisches Institut 2016, 33. – Keil detected signs of the masons on stone blocks within the dromos that should, therefore, come from the Ab–u Hayat quarry: Keil 1930b, 44; ED from 10.10.1929: "Mehrere der Seitenquaderplatten und der Deckquader des Ganges haben roh eingemeiselte Steinmetzinschriften und zwar X zweimal, Y und Z je einmal; aus den Buchstabenformen kann eine Datierung nicht gegeben werden" ("Several of the side ashlar slabs and the top ashlar of the aisle have raw chiselled stone inscriptions, namely X twice, Y and Z once each; a dating cannot be provided from the letter forms").

240 Anevlavi et al. 2020, 55; Thuswaldner 2015, 66f.; Prochaska – Grillo 2012, 590.

241 Alternatively, one might attribute the sarcophagus to the primary burial of Arsinoë IV that was secondarily relocated into the Octagon. – Anevlavi et al. 2020, 35: "Undecorated sarcophagi, with in part carefully polished upper surfaces, are not uncommon" at the time.

242 Huß 2001, 731 n. 28.

243 Anevlavi et al. 2020, 34.

244 Plattner 2009, 105; Huß 2001, 731 n. 28.

245 Hesych. s.v. ἱκέτην (πρόσφυγα = refugee).

246 Ios. ant. Iud. XV 89. App. Rom. V 9.

247 Fleischer 2002, 199, 207.

248 Whereas Flavius Iosephus (1st c. AD) and Appianos (2nd c. AD) explictly name Arsinoë IV as being murdered, Cass. Dio XLVIII 24 (2nd/3rd c. AD), states that Marcus Antonius killed Kleopatra's brothers or siblings (καὶ τοὺς ἀδελφοὺς αὐτῆς ἀπὸ τοῦ ἐν Ἐφέσῳ Ἀρτεμισίου ἀποσπάσας ἀπέκτεινε). However, Kleopatra VII had no sibling left in 41 BC. See pp. 48f. with n. 248.

249 Knäpper 2018, 32; Robinson 1973, 356.

250 Trampedach 2005; Pape 1906, s.v. ἱεροσύλία (actually: temple–plunder).

251 Berti 2017, 54f.; Pape 1906, s.v. μίασμα (maculation, pollution).

252 Ios. c. Ap. II 5. – Berti 2017, 14. 44.

253 Cass. Dio LI 20: Ἐφέσῳ …] γὰρ τότε αἱ πόλεις ἔν τε τῇ Ἀσίᾳ ("[Ephesos] was the chief place in Asia at that time"). Hence, the Ephesians were the first who were allowed to defend their sanctuary before the Roman

Senate in 22 AD (Tac. ann. III 61). – Fischer 2014a, 172–174; Fischer 2010; Fleischer 2002, 185.

254 Pape 1906, s.v. τέμενος (a separated piece of land, especially a temple precinct of a god).

255 Fischer 2014a.

256 Fleischer 2002, 186; Portefaix 1993, 197; Kukula 1906, 261f.

257 Rigsby 1996, 386.

258 App. Mithr. 61. Oros. hist. V 2.

259 Rigsby 1996, 389.

260 Freber 1993, 57–59.

261 Knäpper 2018, 259.

262 Caes. civ. III 105. – Fischer 2012, 146.

263 ἀνθρωπίνου βίου σωτῆρα: Fischer 2012, 146; Kirbihler – Zabrana 2014, 124.

264 Lehner 2004, 37 n. 126.

265 Leschhorn 1993, 221–224.

266 Fischer 2012, 146; Dobesch 1996, 58.

267 In R. Gest. div. Aug. IV 24, Augustus directly referred to the ἱεροσύλία of Marcus Antonius. Cass. Dio LI 17. – On theft in sanctuaries as blasphemous acts, see Robinson 1973.

268 Strab. geogr. XIV 1, 23.

269 App. Rom. V 4.

270 Fleischer 2002, 186. – For a financial reform and a re-establishment of the legal status of the Artemision by the constitution of Vedius Pollio in around 30/29 BC, see Scherrer 1990 and Kirbihler 2017, 144–149.

271 Huß 2001, 731 n. 28; Bennett 2013, s.v. Arsinoe IV n. 15.

272 Thür 2015, 274.

273 Keil 1930a, 41. – Thür 2015, 272; Bennett 2013, s.v. Arsinoe IV n. 15; Anevlavi et al. 2020, 33f.; Prochaska – Grillo 2012, 587; Plattner 2009, 105; Von Geisau 1967.

274 Waldner 2020, *171–173*; Keil 1944/1953, 81 n. 3. – See for the topography the chapter on the Embolos, esp. pp. 205–209.

275 For the subject of location in detail see pp. 143ff. 205ff.

276 Thür 2009, 15–18; Scherrer – Trinkl 2006, 55–57.

277 Strab. geogr. XIV 1, 20.

278 Tac. ann. III 61.

279 Benndorf 1906, 73–79; Scherrer 2008b, 321–323. 348; Thür 1989, 26. – See here pp. 111f.

280 Thür 2009, 15; Knibbe – Langmann 1993, 7f.

281 https://dewiki.de/Lexikon/Dieter_Knibbe, accessed on 21.04.2023.

282 Thür 2009, 17; Knibbe 1991.

283 Jobst 1985, fig. 2. – Personal communication with W. Jobst.

284 Lauter 1966, 118f.; Oberleitner et al. 1978, 54 Kat. 6; Bol 1998, 181f.; Weißl 2002, XII.

285 Plattern 2018, 224; Thür 2009, 17; Heberdey 1902, 64f.

286 Muss et al. 2001, 148. – Such reasoning was only set aside when components for the altar next to the Arte-

mision were urgently needed by Anton Bammer later on (Muss et al. 2001, 96; Fleischer 2002, 207).

287 Knibbe 1991, 9. 14f.

288 Fleischer 1973, 23f. Nr. E Taf. 42b.

289 Quatember 2017; Scherrer 2008a, 47–50; Fleischer 2002, 187–189. – See here pp. 179–195.

290 Fleischer 1973, 23 E 76 Taf. 42a; Miltner 1959a, 257–263.

291 Keil 1930a, 41. – Anevlavi et al. 2020, 33f.: "a prominent site within the city walls [that] suggests that only outstanding individuals should be considered as the occupant of the tomb"; Thür 2015, 271: "It is located in a part of the city reserved only for dynastic descendants or those who have rendered special services to the city"; Prochaska – Grillo 2012, 587: "situated in a prominent position of the city"; Thür 2011, 74: "Der Bau verkörpert den Architekturtyp von Herrschergrabmalen, wie sie durch das Mausoleum in Halikarnassos, das Ptolemaion in Limyra und auch den Grabbau von Belevi bei Ephesos überliefert sind" ("The structure embodies the architectural type of royal mausoleums, as evidenced by the Mausoleum at Halicarnassos, the Ptolemaion at Limyra, and the funerary monument of Belevi near Ephesos").

292 Thür 2009, 17. See pp. 122–126.

293 Heberdey 1905, 70.

294 H. Thür, in: Scherrer 2000, 124; Thür 1990, 45–49; W. Wilberg, in: Alzinger 1974, 40–42; Keil 1964, 113.

295 For example: Nero's Domus Aurea (Bruun 2007); the octagonal vestibule of the Piazza d'Oro and the Teatro Marittimo of Hadrian's Villa in Tivoli (Cipriani et al. 2017, 435 fig. 5f.; Fiska 2012, 49–51); many rooms within thermae (Brödner 1983); an octagonal monument in Aphrodisias from the 1st or 2nd c. AD (Quatember 2019, 69); a huge octagon in Pergamon that supposedly dates into the 2nd c. AD (Altay 2021); Imperial mausolea (Johnson 2009) including the lost 'church mausoleum' of Constantine I in Constantinople (Freze 2015, 279); the great Chrysotriklinos in Constantinople (Freze 2015, 282; Featherstone 2005), and finally countless churches and baptisteria including Constantine's Domus Aurea in Antioch on the Orontes (Eus. vit. Const L) and the Baptisterium at the Basilica San Giovanni in Laterano in Rome (Thayer 2012). – See the octagonal buildings in Ephesos (Büyükkolanci 1982), and in Pécs (Visy 2023). – Savvides 2020, Appendix 1.

296 Thuswaldner 2015, 186, with references to "Ayurvedic medicine", "Babylonian culture", "Christendom", and "Islam"; Barbantani 2010, 33.

297 Ercoles 2013, 397: "Anche la peculiare forma ottagonale [of the 'Stesichoreion'] non trova alcun parallelo nell'architettura greca prima dell'età ellenistica: il più antico esempio di ottagono, tutt'oggi superstite, è la Torre dei Venti di Atene, databile intorno al 100 a.C." ("The peculiar octagonal shape [of the 'Stesichoreion'] finds no parallel in Greek architecture prior to the Hellenistic period: the oldest surviving example of an

octagon is the Tower of the Winds in Athens, dating back to around 100 BC").

298 Different: Thür 1995c, 182: "As far as I know, the octagonal shape had never been used before [the Ephesian Octagon] as a funerary building"; Thür 1990, 54: "Die für einen Grabbau neue achteckige Form" ("The octagonal shape, new for a tomb").

299 Interestingly, Ercoles 2013, 394, states: "Anche se la tomba descritta dalle fonti antiche, di foggia ottagonale, non può che essere ellenistica [...], nulla esclude che essa sia un rifacimento successivo del tumulo originario, d'età arcaica" ("Although the tomb described by ancient sources, with its octagonal shape, can only be Hellenistic in style, it is possible that it is a later reconstruction of the original mound, which would date back to the Archaic period"). 397; Barbantani 2010, 30. – On the location of this grave, see Ercoles 2013, 398f., and Barbantani 2010, 30f.

300 Poll. IX 100: καὶ μὴν καὶ στησίχορος ἐκαλεῖτό τις παρὰ τοῖς ἀστραγαλίζουσιν ἀριθμός, ὃς ἐδήλου τὰ ὀκτώ· τὸν γὰρ ἐν Ἱμέρᾳ τοῦ ποιητοῦ τάφον ἐξ ὀκτὼ πάντων συντιθέντα, πεποιηκέναι τὴν, πάντ' ὀκτὼ, φασὶ παροιμίαν ("Stesichoros was called a number among the astragal players, which showed the 8. They say that the tomb of the poet in Himera, which was composed of 8 of everything, is the origin of the proverb 'all eight' [πάντ' ὀκτὼ]", translation kindly provided by E. Krummen). – Ercoles 2013, 89 Ta39 (Greek text), and Ercoles 2013, 174 Ta39 (Italian translation).

301 Suet. Paed. 1.20 – 1.22: Ercoles 2013, 88 Ta38(a) with the Greek text, and the Italian translation, Ercoles 2013, 173 Ta38(b): "'Stesicoro', quella che vale 8, poiché la tomba del poeta ad Imera, in Sicilia, constava di otto angoli" ("'Stesichoros', the one worth 8, because the poet's tomb at Imera, in Sicily, consisted of eight corners"). – Taretto 2017, 171; Barbantani 2010, 29–33. Such 'Stesichoreion' is also mentioned by Arsenius (Leutsch – Schneidewin 1839, 601 (Cent. XIII)), Eustathios (Hom. ad Il. XXIII 88), Suidas (Σ 1095), and Michael Apostolios (Cent. XV 67. Kienast 2014, 160 n. 604). – Tibaldini 2021, 87; Barbantani 2010, 29f.

302 Cic. Verr. II 2, 86. – Suidas, s.v. Stesichoros (Σ 1095): ἐκλήθη δὲ Στησίχορος, ὅτι πρῶτος κιθαρῳδίᾳ χορὸν ἔστησεν ἐπεί τοι πρότερον Τισίας ἐκαλεῖτο: Ercoles 2010, 120f. (Greek text), and the Italian translation, Ercoles 2010, 195f. Tb2: "Ebbe il nome di 'Stesicoro' perché per primo ordinò un coro con il canto accompagnato dalla cetra; in precedenza il suo nome era Tisia" ("He was named Stesichoros, because he was the first to set [ἔστησεν; see Pape 1906, s.v. ἴστημι] a chorus [χορός; see Pape 1906, s.v. χορός = the dance associated with song] to the music of the cithara, but his previous name was Tisias"). – Barbantani 2010, 23f.

303 According to Photios I, ὀκτὼ κίονας καὶ ὀκτὼ βαθμοὺς καὶ ὀκτὼ γωνίας: Ercoles 2013, 90 Ta40 (Greek text), and Ercoles 2013, 174 Ta40 with the Italian translation: "Tutto otto: alcuni affermano che Stesicoro fu sepolto con sfarzo a Catania, nei pressi delle porte chiamate in suo onore 'Stesicoree': il monumento funebre aveva otto colonne, otto gradini e otto angoli" ("All eight: some claim that Stesichoros was buried with pomp in Catania, near the gates called 'Stesichorean' in his honour: the funeral monument had eight columns, eight steps and eight corners"). – Taretto 2017, 171f.; Kienast 2014, 160 n. 604. – Pape 1906, s.v. κίων (pillar, column); s.v. βαθμος (step, threshold, footstep); s.v. γωνία (corner, edge, angle). – On a possible Pythagorean relationship of Stesichoros´ octagonal mauseoleum to his poetry, see Kimmel–Clauzet 2014, 5f., Ercoles 2013, 403–406, and Barbantani 2010, 34–39. On further associations regarding the octagonal shape of this grave, see Ercoles 2013, 399f., and Barbantani 2010, 33–39. – On the shape of the 'Stesichoreion' maybe as a cuspidal testudinatum monumentum, see Barbantani 2010, 29–31.

304 Translation kindly provided by E. Krummen.

305 Barbantani 2010, 29.

306 Ercoles 2013, 402–406. – Considering its non–octagonal shape, it is not clear, why Von Christ – Schmid – Stählin 1912, 211 n. 2, state: "[Dem ,Stesichoreion'] ähnlich ist das etruskische sogenannte Grabmal der Horatier bei Albano" ("Similar [to the 'Stesichoreion'] is the Etruscan so–called Tomb of the Horatii near Albano"). – See Ercoles 2013, 397 n. 626: "Un altro celebre sepolcro ottagonale è la semileggendaria tomba degli Orazi presso Albano" ("Another famous octagonal tomb is the semi–legendary Tomb of the Horatii near Albano").

307 Ercoles 2013, 88–92, summarises the sources for that (Suet. Paed. 1, 20–22; Poll. IX 100; Eust. Hom. ad Il. XXIII 88; Eust. Hom. ad Od. I 107); Ercoles 2013, 400f.; Barbantani 2010, 33. – Pape 1906, s.v. ἀστράγαλος describing, amongst other, the bones that were used for games; s.v. ἀστραγαλίζω (to play the game with bones); s.v. ἀστραγαλίσις (the bone game), etc.

308 Barbantani 2010, 20.

309 Alzinger 1974, 42: "Das Grundkonzept des Bauwerkes [i.e. the Ephesian mausoleum], die oktogonale Form des Aufbaues, hat sein Vorbild im Turm der Winde in Athen" ("The basic concept of the structure [of the Ephesian tomb], the octagonal shape of the design, takes its inspiration from the Tower of the Winds at Athens").

310 Vitr. I 6, 4: maxime quidem Andronicus Cyrrestes, qui etiam exemplum conlocavit Athenis turrim marmoream octagonon. Varro rust. III 5, 17: ut Athenis in horologio, quod fecit Cyrrestes. – Kienast 2014; Thiersch 1909, 80.

311 Thür 1990, 54: "Der oktogonale Grundriß kann unmöglich mit der Windrose erklärt werden" ("The octagonal groundplan cannot possibly be explained by the wind rose"). – Concerning the wind rose and the Pharos Tower, see Thiersch 1909, 80.

312 Varro rust. III 5, 17. – Lewis – Short 1879, s.v. horologium (sundial, waterclock). – See also, Vitr. IX 1, 1; IX 7,

3; IX 7, 7, and more. An approximation to the Greek word: Liddell – Scott 1940, s.v. ὡρολόγιον.

313 Thiersch 1909.

314 https://dewiki.de/Lexikon/Hermann_Thiersch, accessed on 21.04.2023.

315 Thiersch 1909, 26: "eine hellenistische Grundrißform"; Studniczka 1904, 58.

316 Thiersch 1909, 80.

317 Thür 1990, 55; Thiersch 1909, 26–31; Trethewey 2018, 35.

318 Thiersch 1909, 2. 27; El Fakharani 1974.

319 Von Hesberg 1992, 138f. fig. 83.

320 Thuswaldner 2015, 217; Thiersch 1909, 186–188.

321 Andrews 2018, 37.

322 Maligorne 2006; Joly – Février 2003, 216: "L'ensemble a été daté par G. Sauron des alentours de 20 av. J.–C., en particulier pour ses fortes analogies stylistiques avec le décor de la porte augustéenne de Langres" ("The entire complex was dated by G. Sauron to around 20 BC, particularly due to its strong stylistic similarities with the decoration of the Augustan gate of Langres").

323 Joly – Février 2003, 214–216; Février 1993. – Von Hesberg 1992, 121–159, lists such structures as "mehrstöckige Aediculabauten" ("multi–story aedicula structures"), and places the Memmius Monument and the Ephesian Octagon into this category (Von Hesberg 1992, 131. 138).

324 Février 1993, 96: "En raison de cette destruction très poussée, on ne peut dire s'il existait une chambre funéraire contenant une urne cinéraire, ou s'il s'agissait d'un cénotaphe" ("Due to this extensive destruction, it is uncertain whether there was a burial chamber containing a cinerary urn or if it was a cenotaph").

325 Joly – Février 2003, 216; Février 1993, 96.

326 Joly – Février 2003, 216; Février 1993, 96.

327 Joly – Février 2003, 216; Février 1993, 96f.: "Au–dessus d'un soubassement, de 7,70 m de côté à la base, formé de plusieurs gradins, s'élevait un socle cubique [...]. Le deuxième niveau, octogonal, à arcatures aveugles [...]. Au–dessus [of the third level], un stylobate supportait une colonnade concentrique, formée de huit colonnes entièrement rudentées et d'une colonne axiale [...]. Enfin, une toiture, à huit pans concaves, couverte d'écaillés imbriquées, portait un grand chapiteau corinthien" ("Above a base, measuring 7.70 metres on each side at the bottom, consisting of several steps, there rose a cubic pedestal [...]. The second level, octagonal in shape, featured blind arches [...]. Above the base [of the third level], a stylobate supported a concentric colonnade, comprising eight columns with fluted decorations and a central axial column [...]. Finally, a roof with eight concave sides, covered with overlapping tiles, supported a large Corinthian capital").

328 Kienast 2014, 63.

329 Février 1993, 97: "Le troisième niveau s'apparente à une tholos à huit colonnes. Il présentait à sa base une frise de couronnes de chêne" ("The third level resembles a *tholos* with eight columns. It featured at its base a frieze of oak wreaths").

330 Heberdey 1905, 70. – Thür 2015, 271, writes the sentence: "Perhaps Arsinoe entertained herself [in the Artemision] with the game of astragalus". Perhaps Thür was thinking of the famous Hellenistic 'Girl playing with knucklebones' when she stated that: https://smb.museum–digital.de/object/13033?navlang=en, accessed on 21.04.2023.

331 Heberdey 1905, 69. – Also, W. Wilberg adressed the Octagon as "octagonal small temple" ("achteckiger kleiner Tempel"): W. Wilberg, in: Alzinger 1974, 40; Quatember et al. 2013, 222: "an eight–sided temple"; Thür 2009, 17: "tempelartiger Aufbau" ("temple–like structure"); Berns 1996, 45: "Die Architektur des Oktogons wandelte den Typus des Rundtempels durch die achteckig gebrochene Form ab" ("The architecture of the octagon modified the type of the round temple by the octagonal form"); Alzinger 1962, 124: "Tempelartiger Aufbau" ("temple–like structure").

332 Thuswaldner 2017, 135; Thuswaldner 2015, 92; W. Wilberg, in: Alzinger 1974, 42; Alzinger 1962, 124.

333 Keil 1930a, 41–45.

334 Thuswaldner 2015, 136. 159: "14 Stufen" ("fourteen steps" plus one); Thür 1990, 49: "16 Stufen" ("sixteen steps"); A. Bammer, in Oberleitner et al. 1978, 95: "16 Stufen" ("16 steps"); Theuer's reconstruction, in: Alzinger 1962, 125 (15 steps); Wilberg's reconstruction (15 steps; fig. 12).

335 Max Theuer (1878–1949): https://dewiki.de/Lexikon/Max_Theuer, accessed on 21.04.2023. – Thuswaldner 2015, 57; Wohlers–Scharf 1995, 182f; Thür 1990, 51 fig. 8; Alzinger 1974, II 17 fig. 27.

336 Keil 1930a, 44f.

337 Von Hesberg 1992, 138. – Thür 2015, 273: "this unconventional tomb structure".

338 Cormack 2004, 222.

339 Anevlavi et al. 2020, 33.

340 Kader 1995, 214f.: "Völlig überrascht wird man angesichts des Standortes des Oktogons aber von der Grabkammer in seinem Sockel, die einen Sarkophag enthielt [...]. Auf den ersten Blick ist dem Oktogon seine Funktion als Grabbau nicht anzusehen, denn sein Aufbau gehört [...] eher in den Bereich konventioneller Denkmals–Architekturen [...] Zwischen der für seinen Baukörper gewählten Form und der tatsächlichen Funktion scheint ein unüberwindbarer Konflikt zu bestehen. Es stellt sich also die Frage, was den Bauherrn dazu veranlaßte, den Grabbau derart zu präsentieren, daß er im Kontext der Memorialbauten an der Kuretenstraße als Grab nicht mehr in Erscheinung trat".

341 Thür 1995c, 182; Thür 1990, 54.

342 Thür 2015, 272f. – See pp. 38f.

343 Thür 2015, 274; Thür 1995c, 182; Thür 1990, 54. – Anevlavi et al. 2020, 34 n. 44, wrongly address the "upper storey" of the Pharos as polygonal part.

344 Thür 1990, 54. 56: "Von den Bauformen [kann] die oktogonale Form mit Ägypten oder vielmehr Alexandria verbunden werden [...]. Mein Vorschlag, in der Grabherrin des Oktogons Arsinoe IV. zu sehen, fände eine wichtige Stütze, wenn man den oktogonalen Aufbau des Heroons als ein Zitat des charakteristischen achteckigen Mittelteils des Pharos deutete [...]. Die für einen Grabbau neue achteckige Form symbolisierte das Wahrzeichen Alexandrias und stellte damit zwangsläufig die Verbindung zu der ptolemaischen Prinzessin her [...]. Am Grabbau in Ephesos ist deshalb die Verwendung der oktogonalen Form als Symbol für die Herkunft und Person des Grabinhabers zu deuten". – See Thür 2015, 273; Thür 1995c, 182: "an architectural reference to the middle part of the Pharos [...]. This shape is a symbol of the lineage and identity of the person buried in the grave". – Kienast 2014, 160, supports Thür in her reasoning: "Die Verwendung der charakteristischen oktogonalen Form wäre dann eher als ein Symbol für die Herkunft und die Person der Grabinhaberin zu verstehen und hätte folglich ihren Bezug am Pharos von Alexandria, dem Wahrzeichen ihrer Heimatstadt" ("The use of the distinctive octagonal shape would then be understood as a symbol of the origin and identity of the tomb's owner, and therefore, it would refer to the Pharos of Alexandria, the landmark of her hometown"); Rumscheid 1994, 164, states: "Die oktogonale Form [...] ist auf hellenistische Bauten wie den Pharos in Alexandria und, falls er vor dem ephesischen Bau entstanden ist, den Turm der Winde in Athen zurückzuführen" ("The octagonal form [...] leads back to Hellenistic buildings such as the Pharos in Alexandria and, if it predates the Ephesian building, the Tower of the Winds in Athens"); Thiersch 1909, 80: "Das Achteck des Pharos [...] war höchstwahrscheinlich die große Windrose des alexandrinischen Hafens, der gigantische Vorläufer des Windeturms von Athen" ("The Pharos octagon was most likely the large compass rose of the Alexandrian harbour, the gigantic predecessor of the wind tower of Athens").

345 Thür 1990, 56.

346 Hom. Od. IV 351f.

347 Ant. Sid. AntGr 9.58: τὰ ἑπτὰ θεάματα τῆς οἰκουμένης. Pape 1906, s.v. θεάμα (sight, spectacle). – Thiersch 1909, 20 n. 1. – See the curious describtions of the Pharos (#2) and of the Ephesian Artemision (#7) from a medieval perspective by Beda Venerabilis (7th/8th c. AD), De Septem Mundi Miraculis Manu Hominum Factis: https://oll.libertyfund.org/title/giles-the-complete-works-of-venerable-bede-vol-4-historical-tracts-english-and-latin?html=true#lf0990-04_head_500, accessed on 21.04.2023.

348 Suet. Claud. 20.

349 Pasch – Kieburg 2019, 74–77.

350 Iuv. XII 76.

351 Val. Fl. VII 85.

352 Suet. Tib. 74.

353 Plin. nat. XXXVI 18: quales iam compluribus locis flagrant, sicut Ostiae ac Ravennae.

354 Petschenig – Stowasser 1930, s.v. Pharos with the adjective pharius (Egyptian).

355 Gemoll 1965, s.v. Φάρος with the adjective φάριος.

356 Lucan. IV 257; VIII 184; VIII 277; VIII 499.

357 Mart. III 66.

358 Mart. IV 11.

359 Mart. VI 80.

360 Mart. VII 30.

361 Mart. V 69.

362 Stat. Theb. IV 709.

363 Lucan. II 733; VIII 712.

364 Lucan. IV 724.

365 Lucan. III 260.

366 Iuv. VI 83.

367 Auson. Mos. 315. – Pfrommer 2002.

368 Auson. Mos. 330.

369 Handler 1971, 59f.; Mlynarczyk 2001, 332–337.

370 Apul. met. XI 2: nunc veneraris delubris Ephesi.

371 Apul. met. II 28.

372 Stat. Theb. I 254. – Bøgh 2013, 239 n. 33.

373 Carmen de bello Actiaco IV 4. – Dubit 2018, 18.

374 Lucan. VI 308; VIII 463.

375 Lucan. IX 1022.

376 Lucan. VII 704.

377 Lucan. X 86; Strab. geogr. XVII 1, 11.

378 Lucan. X 90–95: Non urbes prima tenebo femina Niliacas: nullo discrimine sexus reginam scit ferre Pharos. – Kleopatra's statement is repeatedly contradicted by Cassius Dio, whereby the Alexandrians deemed it "a shame to be ruled by a woman" (Cass. Dio XLII 36; XLII 42; XLII 44).

379 Flor. epit. II 13: in ferculis Nilus, Arsinoe et ad simulacrum ignium ardens Pharos ("on moving platforms the Nile, Arsinoe, and the Pharos similarly burning flames").

380 Interestingly, the Octagon appears inscribed with ΠΩΜΠΑ at the second step of the western stylobate (with a ligature of ΜΠ): Thuswaldner 2015, 148 fig. 157.

381 Schäfer 2006, 73f.; Hölbl 1994, 211.

382 Thiersch 1909, 76–83.

383 Spanu 2010, 60f.: "Tale teoria appare estremamente fragile" ("This theory appears extremely fragile").

384 Lucan. VIII 464.

385 Strab. geogr. XVII 1, 6; Plin. nat. XXXVI 18.

386 Thiersch 1909, 5. 88 Pl. IV. VIII; Handler 1971, 73. – See the similar sequence at the funeral monument of Faverolles (see p. 52 and fig. 11b).

387 Pape 1906, s.v. μονόπτερος (one-winged; an edifice with one row of columns); Thuswaldner 2017, 134.

388 Thuswaldner 2017, 134; Thuswaldner 2015, 135–138.

389 Flor. epit. II 13.

390 Thür 1995c, 182; Thür 1990, 54. 56.

391 Thuswaldner 2017, 137. 187; Plattner 2009, 101: "die oktogonale Form des Obergeschosses evoziert alexandrinische Vorbilder" ("the octagonal form of the upper floor evokes Alexandrian models"); Rumscheid 1994, 164; Thiersch 1909, 80.

392 Thuswaldner 2015, 63f.; H. Thür, in: Bordsen 2009: "This academic questioning is normal. It happens. It's a kind of jealousy".

393 Berns 1996, 45 n. 229: "Der oktogonalen Form wird man kaum einen so präzisen Sinn zuweisen können, wie es H. Thür, ÖJH 60, 1990, 54 ff. versucht hat".

394 Kader 1995, 214: "So sagt die Wahl der Form allein über den konkreten Zweck oder Anlaß dieser Architekturen nichts mehr aus" ("Thus the choice of form alone no longer says anything about the concrete purpose or occasion of these structures").

395 Kader 1995, 215: "spricht die Gestaltung des Oktogons m. E. gegen eine Grabinhaberin aus den Königshäusern". – On the other hand, Thür 2015, 273, states, "the building form [...] is of the dynastic tomb type" setting it next to the mausolea of Belevi and Halicarnassos. 273: "this unconventional tomb structure"; Thür 2009, 13: "Dynastischer Grabbau" ("dynastic grave"). 18–20. – Thür 2009, 13–20, reacted to the rejection of her proposal by Berns and Kader.

396 Huß 2001, 731 n. 28.

397 Personal communication with R. Fleischer.

398 Anevlavi et al. 2020, 34 n. 44.

399 See n. 383.

400 Schörner 2007, 120 n. 1006: "scheint der Wunsch, in der Toten eine Ptolemaierprinzessin zu sehen, diesem Gedanken zugrunde gelegt zu haben".

401 Thuswaldner 2015, 185.

402 Savvides 2021; Jones 2000, 25–30. 38f.

403 Cic. tusc. I 4: *In summo apud illos honore geometria fuit, itaque nihil mathematicis inlustrius; at nos metiendi ratiocinandique utilitate huius artis terminavimus modum.* – Petschenig – Stowasser 1930, s.v. *ratiocinor* (calculate, conclude, educe). – Petschenig – Stowasser 1930, s.v. *ratio* (e.g., reason, consideration). s.v. *cano* (e.g., sing, vocalise, state). s.v. *ratiocinatio* (conclusion, inference). – Compare Petschenig – Stowasser 1930, s.v. *vaticinor* (prophesise, warn), and Lewis – Short 1879, s.v. *sermocinor* (converse, discourse).

404 Frontin. aqu. 16: *Inertia sed fama celebrata opera Graecorum.* Petschenig – Stowasser 1930, s.v. iners (flagging, pointless, idle).

405 Vitr. VII praef., 14: *collecta in ea re ab Graecis volumina plura edita, ab nostris oppido quam pauca* ("On this matter much has been published by the Greeks, by us little"). – Jones 2000, 38f.

406 Vitr. I 1, 4: *Geometria autem plura praesidia praestate architecturae, et primum ea euthygrammi et circini tradit usum* ("Geometry provides much support to the architect; first of all, it teaches the use of the straight edge and compass"). – Petschenig – Stowasser 1930,

s.v. *circinus* (compass). Interestingly, Virtruvius uses here εὐθύγραμμος (instead of *regula*), a word that is found in Eukleides' Elements repeatedly; Liddell – Scott 1940, s.v. εὐθύγραμμος (rectilinear figure).

407 Vitr. I 1, 3: *eruditus geometria.* – Petschenig – Stowasser 1930, s.v. *erudio, eruditus* (knowledgeable); Jones 2000, 87–108. – See also, Vitr. I 1, 3f.: *peritus graphidos*; Petschenig – Stowasser 1930, s.v. *peritus* (experienced). – *Graphis = stylus*.

408 Vitr. I 2, 3. – Pape 1906, s.v. εὐρυθμία (proportion, the right ratio). – Pape 1906, s.v. ἁρμονία (the right relationship of all parts to the whole).

409 Vitr. I 2, 4. – Liddell – Scott 1940, s.v. μετρέω (to measure); s.v. συμμετρέω (to measure or calculate by comparison); s.v. συμμετρία (commensurability, in comparison with, due proportion); s.v. ἀσυμμετρία (incommensurability, disproportion).

410 Vitr. I 2, 2: *circini regulaeque modice.*

411 Ross 2016, 18. – Kienast 2014, 107: "Die [geometrische] Figur des Oktogons ist nicht nur reizvoll, sie lässt sich auch mit elementaren geometrischen Grundkenntnissen konstruieren [...]. Beide Lösungen sind sowohl auf dem Papier als auch auf der Baustelle problemlos zu bewerkstelligen – im einen Fall mit Lineal und Zirkel, im anderen mit Richtschnüren und Schnurzirkel" ("The [geometrical] shape of the octagon is not only appealing, but it can also be constructed using elementary geometrical principles [...]. Both solutions can be easily accomplished both on paper and on the construction site – in one case with a ruler and compass, and in the other case with string lines and a string compass"). In contrast: Thuswaldner 2015, 184f.

412 τετράγωνος, Eukl. elem. I 46.

413 κύκλος, Eukl. elem. VI 32.

414 Vitr. I 2, 2. – Pape 1906, s.v. ἰχνογραφία (groundplan); Pape 1906, s.v. ἴχνος (footprint, track). Pape 1906, s.v. γραφω (draw, write, incise).

415 Vitr. I 2, 2. – Pape 1906, s.v. ὀρθογραφία (drawing of a standing building from the front; elevation); Pape 1906, s.v. ὀρθος (upright).

416 Thuswaldner 2015, 158. 162.

417 Kienast 2014, 107f.

418 Thuswaldner 2015, 184f. fig. 182, focusses in her construction of an octagon on the left scheme calling it "significally more complicated" ("deutlich komplizierter"). Accordingly, she considers a "purely geometric–constructive explanation as not very satisfactory". However, a regular octagon is as easily constructed as a regular hexagon (fig. 14b).

419 Kienast 2014, 107f.: "Beide Konstruktionen ergeben das angestrebte regelmäßige Achteck, unterscheiden sich aber durch die sie prägenden Achsen – im ersten Fall gehen die Achsen durch die Eckpunkte [des Achtecks], im zweiten durch die Seitenhalbierenden [des Achtecks]" ("Both constructions yield the desired regular octagon, but differ in the axes that shape them – in the first case, the axes pass through the

vertices [of the octagon], in the second case, through the midpoints of the sides [of the octagon]").

420 γωνίαι, Eukl. elem. XI ὄρος ζ´.

421 διάστημα, Eukl. elem. I αἴτημα γ´.

422 περιφερεία, Eukl. elem. XI 1.

423 σημεῖα, Eukl. elem. XI 1.

424 ἄξονες, Eukl. elem. XII 11.

425 Passoja 2018, 7 fig.

426 The same result is gained by connecting the eight points on the sides of the basic square to its next but one neighbours.

427 Kienast 2014, 107 n. 318: "Grundfigur verschränkter Quadrate" ("basic figure of interlocked squares"). 111f.

428 Interestingly, Kienast 2014, 107f., does not realise that the groundplan of the *horologium's* octagon is based on the principle r/s.

429 See Plat. Men. 82c. – Roldán 2012, 541: "This [i.e. an ad quadratum sequence] consists in dividing each side of the square in the middle. Connecting these points results in another square that is inscribed and rotated 45°; this new square has an area that is half of that of the first square [fig. 16a]. If the procedure is repeated with the second square, a third horizontal square is produced, and its sides measure half of those of the first square. Its area is half of that of the second and one fourth of the first, and so on". – On this geometrical motif, see Kienast 2014, 109. 111f., and the ceiling construction of the Roman tomb in Mylasa from the 2nd c. AD: https://arachne.dainst.org/entity/1975910, accessed on 21.04.2023.

430 Thuswaldner 2015, 158f.

431 Thuswaldner 2015, 158 n. 409; Alzinger 1974, 41 n. 132.

432 Kienast 2014, 107.

433 Eukl. elem. I ὄρος ς´: γραμμαί.

434 Also, the "unusually wide intercolumnations" are the result of that (Thuswaldner 2015, 185; Cormack 2004, 222; Kader 1995, 214). – In comparison, neither the Pharos octagon nor the *horologium* appear as monuments subjugated to an *overall* geometry, but rather as single octagons. At the middle tier of the Pharos as seen from Thiersch's reconstruction, the polygons do not seem to relate geometrically to the square of the stand space (Thiersch 1909, Taf. VII). Although H. J. Kienast laboriously tried to assign a geometrical pattern to the *horologium*, it does not add up completely and includes some strange aspects, facts that he realised himself (Kienast 2014, 109. 111. 113. 118 fig. 161). Accordingly, Kienast 2014, 111, states: "Der Ausgangspunkt für den Entwurf [des *horologium*] war allem Anschein nach die Figur des Achtecks, das durch drei Anbauten erweitert wurde" ("The starting point for the design [of the *horologium*] was apparently the figure of the octagon, which was expanded by three additions").

435 H. Thür, in: Scherrer 2000, 98f.; Alzinger 1974, 37–40 fig. 24; Niemann – Heberdey 1906, 113–167 figs. 83, 85.

436 At the Round Monument, the circle of the building cylinder equals the inradius of r2 (ri = r/2) that is concentrically inscribed into the reference square and tilted by 45° (figs. 14c, 16a). The six main axes of the dodecagon result from the application of r/2 from the vertices of the reference square to both adjoining sides in combination with the diagonals of the reference square (fig. 14c).

437 Fleischer 2002, 208–210; U. Outschar, in: Scherrer 2000, 96f.; Outschar 1990, 76. 85; "die engen Verbindungen zum Oktogon (die zumindest für das Obergeschoß auf eine gemeinsame Bauhütte schließen lassen)" ("the close connections to the octagon (which suggest at least for the upper floor a shared construction shed)"); Alzinger 1974, 16–20. 43f. – Although the floor plan of the Memmius Monument suggests such approach, the acquis of A. Bammer (Alzinger – Bammer 1971, 46 fig. 34) is not sufficient to forward a proposal. In other words, Bammer's 3D–collage of the monument has to be dismantled and the site investigated anew.

438 Octagon (figs. 15b, 16b): Alzinger 1974, II 19 fig. 30. Round Monument on the Panayırdağ (fig. 16a): H. Thür, in: Scherrer 2000, 98f.; Alzinger 1974, 37–40 fig. 24; Niemann – Heberdey 1906, 113–167 fig. 83. Memmius Monument (fig. 16a): Mallios 2010; Outschar 1990, fig. 1f.; Alzinger – Bammer 1971. – In fact, fig. 16a as found at the Memmius Monument is the perfect illustration to prove Plato's 'doubling the square' considering the eight resulting, congruent isosceles triangles. See p. 61 with n. 453.

439 Artmann 1990, fig. 18. – On its graphical pattern, Passoja 2018, 7 fig. and fig. 16c.

440 Savvides 2021; Misailidou–Despotidou – Athanasiou 2013, fig. 18, could be used thanks to the kind permission of D. Savvides.

441 The famous Badminton Sarcophagus in the Metropolitan Museum New York shows carvings focussing on a hexagonal structure, some of which are likewise overlaid with a pattern of tight concentric circles: Bartman 1993, 61 fig. 4.

442 Savvides 2021.

443 Fitzpatrick 2007; Allmann 1877; Gracilis 1564.

444 Eukl. elem. I 47. – See Cens. XIV 12, who calls a square number *numerus quadratus* that, thus, describes a square area.

445 Eukl. elem. I 47: τρίγωνον ὀρθογώνιον.

446 Vitr. IX praef. 6f.; Aristot. metaph X 1053a: καὶ ἡ διάμετρος δυσὶ μετρεῖται καὶ ἡ πλευρά ("the diagonal [of a square] and its side are measured by two magnitudes").

447 All values are drawn from a unit square with s = 1. – At that point, one might add that x/y = √2 always refers to the Pythagoraean relationship in a right isosceles

triangle with x = hypotenuse and y = catheti: $2y^2 = x^2$ → $\sqrt{2}y = x$ → $\sqrt{2} = x/y$.

448 Eukl. elem. X 9: ἀσύμμετρος. – See also, Aristot. metaph. I 983a (ἀσύμμετρος), and Plat. Hipp. mai. 303ß (ἄρρητος = that what cannot be expressed or told). – Pape 1906, s.v. ῥητός (said, defined, determined); s.v. ἀσύμμετρος (not fitting together, incommensurable); Kindi 1994, 5-10.

449 E.g., Eukl. elem. X 21: ἄλογός. – Pape 1906, s.v. ἄλογός (beyond calculation, not expressible, not part of a ratio); Kindi 1994, 6-10.

450 The diagonal of a unit square (with s = 1) equals $\sqrt{2}$.

451 Eukl. elem. X 117: Προκείσθω ἡμῖν δεῖξαι, ὅτι ἐπὶ τῶν τετραγώνων σχημάτων ἀσύμμετρός ἐστιν ἡ διάμετρος τῇ πλευρᾷ μήκει ("[...] The diagonal of a square is incommensurable in length with its side").

452 Thuswaldner 2015, 185.

453 Plat. Men. 82b–85c; Vitr. IX praef.; Theon Smyrn. I 1.

454 The fact that the side length of the inner square encompassing the pseudo–*cella* and, thus, representing the very core of the structure equals the one of the regular octagon inscribed into the reference square (s_8), reminds one of an interesting statement whereby "the Romans constructed their altars from octagonal shapes that surrounded it" (Passoja 2018, 5). Unfortunately, the author did not provide a source for this statement, and did not answer our request. One might add another remarkable aspect of proportionality within the Octagon's ground plan: the three differing areas of the Octagon's grid (fig. 15c), i.e. $(\Delta_{s-r})^2$, $s_8\Delta_{s-r}$ and s_8^2, are likewise related by the factor $\sqrt{2}$, i.e. $\sqrt{2}(\Delta_{s-r})^2 = s_8\Delta_{s-r}$ and $\sqrt{2}s_8\Delta_{s-r} = s_8^2$.

455 Vitr. I 2, 3: *Eurythmia est venusta species commodusque in compositionibus membrorum aspectus. haec efficitur cum membra operis convenientis sunt altitudinis ad latitudinem* ("Eurythmia is the graceful and adequate appearance in the composition of the parts. It is achieved when the parts of the work [*membra operis*, actually 'appendages'] match each other [*convenientis sunt*], [e.g.] height and width"). – Pape 1906, s.v. ῥυθμός (proportion, symmetry, euphony).

456 This value is taken at the level of the stylobate: W. Wilberg, in: Alzinger 1974, 40.

457 Thuswaldner 2017, 133 ("15m"); Thür 2015, 271 ("13.5m"); Thuswaldner 2015, 162 ("14.3m"). 166 ("14.3m"); Quatember et al. 2013, 222 ("13m"); Thuswaldner 2007, 4 ("13m"); Von Hesberg 1998, 153 ("almost 15m"); Thür 1990, 49 ("13.5m"); Miltner 1958, 29 ("18m"); Wilberg's reconstruction (fig. 12, ca. 15m).

458 Thuswaldner 2015, 166: "Schließlich bilden auch die Gesamthöhe [ab Fußprofil] von 1.430 cm und die Gesamtbreite in Höhe der Orthostaten von 887 cm zueinander den goldenen Schnitt" ("Finally, the total height [from base profile] of 1,430 cm and the total width at the height of the orthostats of 887 cm form the golden cut to each other").

459 Thuswaldner 2015, 163f. – Interestingly, Thuswaldner uses here the (modern) Latin version "proportio divina", which does not occur in the various translations of the Greek source text since Pacioli 1509b.

460 Thuswaldner 2015, 164 n. 425: "Erstmals erwähnt wird der goldene Schnitt bereits bei Euklid im zweiten Buch der Elemente [...] Euklid, II 11" ("The golden section is first mentioned by Eukleides in the second book of Elements [...] Euklid, II 11"). – From a terminological point of view, the 'Golden' cut (= section) separates a straight line, so that the resulting two segments are related by the 'Golden' proportion.

461 Pacioli 1509b.

462 Ohm 1835, 194.

463 Pape 1906, s.v. στοιχεῖον (component, element, but in geometry also: point, line, area).

464 The manuscript of the pre–Theon text is housed in the Bibliotheca Apostolica Vaticana in Rome (Vat. Gr. 190: https://digi.vatlib.it/view/MSS_Vat.gr.190.pt.1, accessed on 21.04.2023). Heiberg – Menge 1883–1885, translates and expands on the Vatican–Euclid. – See Fitzpatrick 2008.

465 The second manuscript is kept at the Bodleian Library in Oxford (MS. D'Orville 301; https://digital.bodleian.ox.ac.uk/objects/d4a23501–0b98–4aff–acd6–fe06fe9b62e3/, accessed on 21.04.2023), and is considered the Theonine edition of Eukleides. – Theon of Alexandria (4th c. AD) himself seems to mention his edition of Eukleides' Elements in the commentaries on the *Canones manuales* of Klaudios Ptolemaios (ὡς ἐδείχθη ἐν τῷ τρίτῳ τοῦ ἕκτου τῶν στοιχείων ὅτι). Heath 1908, 46; Halma 1821, 201, with the Greek text and a French translation: "car il a été démontré dans la troisième proposion du sixième livre des Eléments" ("as it has been demonstrated in the third proposition of the sixth book of the Elements").

466 Vat. Gr. 190, 100. Bodleian Library MS. D'Orville 301, 114.

467 Eukl. elem. I β´; Eukl. elem. I δ´; Eukl. elem. II β´: II 10: εὐθεῖα γραμμή.

468 Eukl. elem. VI 30. – Accordingly, what was called the 'Golden' proportion φ later on, was from Eukleides' point of view a certain geometrically gained proportional relationship of two straight lines.

469 Lorenz 1781, 86 (definition 3); Gracilis 1564, 51 (definition 3).

470 On Eukleides' definition of λόγος and ἀνάλογος, see Eukl. elem. V ὅρος γ´, and Eukl. elem. V oros ς´, respectively.

471 Pape 1906, s.v. μέσος (in the middle, in between).

472 See a list of Eukleides editions in Wardhaugh – Beeley – Nasifoglu 2020, and at: https://www.omnia.ie/?navigation_function=3&europeana_query=Eukleid%C3%A9s, accessed on 21.04.2023.

473 E.g., Fitzpatrick 2008, 156.

474 Lorenz 1781, 108: "nach stetiger Proportion".

475 Heiberg 1884 II, 171: "*rationem extremam ac mediam*".

476 Warius 1763, 169: "In de uyterste en middelste reden te deelen" ("to divide in the outermost and middle ratio"). See also, Van Schooten 1617, 78: "Een rechte linie na de wterste en middel reden, te deelen" ("To divide a straight line into its extreme and mean ratio").

477 Tacquet 1762, 146: *extrema ac media ratione*.

478 Ozanam 1699, 184: *in extremam* und *mediam rationem*.

479 Clavius 1627, 91: *extrema ac media ratione*.

480 J. Kepler, ed. Frisch 1871, 140.

481 Gracilis 1558, 59.

482 Scheubelius 1550, 309: *per extremam ac mediam rationem*.

483 Hervagium 1546, 164: *extrema ac media ratione*.

484 Feltrio 1599, 93.

485 Dou 1618, 178: "proportioniert zertheilen".

486 Holtzman 1562, 182: "proportzlich zertailen".

487 Ratdolt 1482, 102: *proportionem habentem medium duoque extrema* (propositio 29). – Ratdolt's translation of AKML seems to describe the cut straight line with two endpoints and the sectional point in–between, which may have been taken as *extrema et media ratio* later on; this, however, does not make much sense.

488 Pacioli 1509a, 55 (Propositio 29).

489 Pacioli 1509b.

490 Thuswaldner 2015, 164: "die eher komplizierte Konstruktion des goldenen Schnittes" ("the rather complex construction of the golden cut").

491 Thuswaldner 2015, 164 fig. 172.

492 Eukl. elem. VI ὅρος β΄. VI 30. – Fitzpatrick 2008, 156. 188f.; Lorenz 1781, 31f. 108; Gracilis 1564, 21. 59.

493 Eukl. elem. XIII 5. – Fitzpatrick 2008, 510f.; Lorenz 1781, 326f.; Gracilis 1564, 115.

494 Pape 1906, s.v. ἄκρος (topmost, but also excellent, sublime, exclusive, and noble).

495 Thür 2015, 271; Thür 1990, 49.

496 All values in a unit square with s = 1.

497 Lorenz 1781, 32; Gracilis 1564, 59. – See also, Eukl. elem. VI 30.

498 Eukl. elem. VI ὅρος β΄.

499 Vitr. I 2, 2. – Petschenig – Stowasser 1930, s.v. *regula* (ledge, slat).

500 Vitr. I 2, 3–4.

501 Thuswaldner 2015, 160–166.

502 Thuswaldner 2015, 185.

503 Ramzy 2015, 151; Reynolds 2008, 57; Kappraff 2002, 125–127 fig. 6; Kappraff 2000, 47 fig. 4; Williams 1994; Brunés 1967.

504 Plat. symp. VIII: ἀεὶ ὁ θεὸς γεωμετρεῖ. – Pape 1906, s.v. γεωμετρέω (to measure land).

505 Pape 1906, s.v. σφονδύλος (vertebra; spindle whorl, i.e. the flywheel at the whorl). – Curiously, Plato's association appears as a quite accurate description of the ecliptic plane ("the eight spindle whorls within each other") on the one hand, and of the earth's movement, in particular, if one considers the earth's rotational axis as the spindle shaft (tilted by ca. π/3 to the ecliptic plane), and the globe as the flywheel mass.

506 Plat. rep. X 617b: [...] φωνὴν μίαν ἱεῖσαν, ἕνα τόνον ἐκ πασῶν δὲ ὀκτὼ οὐσῶν μίαν ἁρμονίαν ξυμφωνεῖν. See also, Plat. rep. X 616d: ὀκτὼ γὰρ εἶναι τοὺς ξύμπαντας σφονδύλους ("There are eight spindle whorls altogether").

507 Theon Smyrn. I 1. III 16.

508 Pape 1906, s.v. τέλειος (perfect, absolute, in full).

509 Theon Smyrn. I 32.

510 Τέλειος ἀριθμός ἐστιν ὁ τοῖς ἑαυτοῦ μέρεσιν ἴσος ὤν ("A perfect number is that which is equal to its own parts", i.e. it equals the sum of its divisors, Eucl. elem. VII ὅρος κβ΄). Accordingly, the first two "perfect" Euklidean integers are 6 (= 1+2+3) and 28 (= 1+2+4+7+14). – See also, Theon Smyrn. I 32.

511 Theon Smyrn. II 2. II 12. III 15. – Barbantani 2010, 34.

512 Vitr. I 1, 3; I 1, 8f.; I 1, 13.

513 See p. 52.

514 Van der Waerden 1966, 381–390.

515 Theon Smyrn. II 48: περιέχουσα τὰ πάντα σφαῖρα ὀγδόη, ὅθεν ἡ παροιμία "πάντα ὀκτώ" φησι. Συν ὀκτὼ δὴ σφαίρησι κυλίνδετο ὁ κύκλω ἐνάτην περιγαίην, ‹Ἐρατοσθένης φησίν. Transl. Waterfield 1988, 103f.

516 Τιμόθεος φησι καὶ παροιμίαν εἶναι τὴν 'πάντα ὀκτώ' δια τὸ τοῦ κόσμου τὰς πάσας ὀκτὼ σφαίρας περὶ γην κυκλεῖσθαι, καθά φησι καὶ Ἐρατοσθένης ("Timothy also tells us that there is the proverb "All is eight", since the spheres of the world that revolve around the earth are eight in number, as Eratosthenes also says: These eight spheres also harmonise with each other as they make their revolutions, the ninth around the earth". Transl. according to Broderson 2021, 195). – See also, Theon Smyrn. III 15.

517 Cic. rep. VI 18.

518 Hor. carm. 12; Sen. nat. VII 17; Suet. Iul. 88; Cass. Dio XLV 7.

519 Iaml. theol. arith.: περὶ ὀκτάδος.

520 Hdt. II 43.

521 Zenob. cent. V, 78: πάντα ὀκτώ: Εὔανδρος ἔφη ὀκτὼ τοὺς πάντων εἶναι κρατούντας θεούς: Πῦρ, Ὕδωρ, Γῆν, Οὐρανόν, Σελήνην, Ἥλιον, Μίθρας, Νύκτα. ‹Ἄλλοι δέ φασιν ἐν Ὀλυμπία τὰ πάντα εἶναι ἀγωνίσματα ὀκτώ, Στάδιον, [Δόλιχον,] Δίαυλον, ‹Ὁπλίτην, Πυγμήν, Παγκράτιον καὶ τὰ λοιπά αφ› ὧν εἰρήσθαι πάντα ὀκτώ: Leutsch – Schneidewin 1839, 151.

522 Theon Smyrn. II 47: ἡ ὀγδοάς.

523 Cens. XVIII 4–5.

524 Cens. XVIII 6: *ob hoc in Graecia multae religiones hoc intervallo temporis summa caerimonia coluntur, Delphis quoque ludi, qui vocantur Pythia, post annum octavum olim conficiebantur.*

525 Cens. XVIII 4: *octaetêris facta, quae tunc enneaetêris vocitata, quia primus eius annus nono quoque anno redibat* ("an octaeteris, which was then called Enneaeteris again, because its initial year always returned in the ninth year").

526 Hom. Od. XIX 178f. Transl. Butler 1999.

527 Costanza 2021, 8f.; Ercoles 2010, 90 Ta40 (Photios I, Suidas, and M. Apostolios, and the Italian translation, Ercoles 2010, 174 Ta40.

528 Obbink – Gonis 2009, 71–74. – Το πάντα ὀκτώ in relation to the Stesichoros' grave, see p. 52.

529 "Die Zahl Acht nennen die Pythagoräer die Zahl der Gerechtigkeit und der Fülle, und zwar, weil sie zuerst unter allen in gleiche gerade Zahlen geteilt werden kann, nämlich in vier; auch bei der wiederholten Teilung (zweimal Zwei) findet dasselbe Verhältnis statt. Wegen dieser Gleichheit der Teilung erhielt sie den Namen der Gerechtigkeit": http://www.philos-website.de/index_g.htm?autoren/agrippa_von_nettesheim_g.htm~main2 (accessed on 21.04.2023). However, the number four was considered as the number of justice: Röd 2009, 73.

530 Bachofen 1880, 113: "Die Universalität des πάντα ὀκτώ bleibt bestehn und verkündet die Wahrheit des Wortes, dass Alles auf Erden nur im Zusammenhang, Nichts in Isolirtheit auftritt und begreiflich wird".

531 Heinz 2016, 175; Huß 2001, 731 n. 28.

532 W. Wilberg, in: Alzinger 1974, 40.

533 Vitr. III 2, 7: *Dipteros autem octastylos* […] *uti est* […] *Ephesi Dianae ionica a Ctesiphon constituta*. Vitruvius wrongly addresses Χερσίφρων ὁ Κνώσιος as "Ctesiphon". – Vitr. VII praef., 12 and X 2, 11; Plin. nat. XXXV 21; Strab. geogr. XIV 1, 22.

534 Plin. nat. XXXVI 56. Remarkably, such relationship also applies to the columns of the Octagon: lower column diameter (d) = 46,5 cm, column height without base and without capital (h) = 377 cm, i.e. 8d = 372 cm (Thuswaldner 2015, 161f.).

535 Huß 2001, 731 n. 28.

536 Kader 1995, 214f.

537 Kader 1995, 214f.

538 In keeping with that, one of the Octagon's coffers shows, somewhat hidden, a cornucopia (Thuswaldner 2015, 205), a Ptolemaic symbol (Pfrommer 2002, 39f. with an effigy).

539 Pape 1906, s.v. βουκράνιον from βούς (cow, ox, bull) and κρανίον (head).

540 Pape 1906, s.v. ταινία (band, bandage, ribbon).

541 Grüßinger 2001, 57–61.

542 Bammer 1968–71, 29: "Das Stemma, eine aus Wollfäden zu Knoten gebundene Schnur, deren Enden in drei Teilen ausläuft" ("The stemma, a cord made of wool threads tied into knots, with its ends branching out into three parts"). Pape 1906, s.v. στέμμα (band; woollen threads wound around olive branches indicating certain entities belonging to a sacred context). Thuswaldner 2015, 210: "geknotete Wollbinden" ("Knotted woollen bandages"). Grüßinger 2001, 20 n. 66. – Following Alzinger 1974, Thür 1990, 49, addresses the στέμμα as 'infula', which actually names something else. Alzinger 1974, 41 n. 133: "astragalartig geknotete infulae […] astragalierte infulae" ("as-

tragalus–like knotted infulae […] astragalus–like infulae"); Thuswaldner 2015, 124. 210: "perlschnurartige Gehänge […] geknotete Wollbinden" ("astragal–like hangings […] knotted woollen bandages"). Remarkably, Schörner 2007, 201, Kader 1995, 214, and Rumscheid 1994, 163f., ignore the στέμματα of the Octagon's frieze altogether. – Petschenig – Stowasser 1930, s.v. *infula* (woollen bandage, head band, broad white fabric with crimson stripes etc.); Petschenig – Stowasser 1930, s.v. *vitta* with a similar meaning. – On typology and usage of the στέμμα, see Schreiber 2012, 233 fig. 1a (type 11 according to Krug 1968). 234 fig. 1c (type 11 according to Krug 1968).

543 Pape 1906, s.v. θύσανος (tassel); Hom. Il. XIV 181: ζώνη ἑκατὸν θυσάνοις (Hera's "belt with a hundred tassels").

544 McCredie et al. 1992, 56–63.

545 Napp 1933, 4f.; Bohn 1885, II Pl. XXX. – Further examples at Bammer 1968–71, 29.

546 Waldner 2020; Seiterle 1999, 255 Pl. 45/2. – Alzinger 1974, 44, points out the similarities of the garlands of the Memmius Monument and the Octagon (fig. 19c).

547 Outschar 1990, 76. 85; "die engen Verbindungen zum Oktogon (die zumindest für das Obergeschoß auf eine gemeinsame Bauhütte schließen lassen)" ("the close connections to the Octagon (which suggest at least for the upper floor a shared masons' workshop)"). – Fleischer 2002, 208–210; U. Outschar, in: Scherrer 2000, 96f.; Alzinger – Bammer 1971, 71 ("Girlandentambour"). 81 (referencing Alzinger 1974 ("1972"), 41f., where, however, the Octagon is described); Thür 1990, 50; Alzinger 1974, 16–20. 43f.; see pp. 156–160.

548 Knäpper 2018, 45; Thuswaldner 2015, 210.

549 Seiterle 1999, 251–255.

550 Thuswaldner 2015, 210; Fleischer 2002, 209.

551 Grüßinger 2001, 20 n. 66.

552 Agelidis 2014, 79, 87; Fleischer 2002, 214f.

553 Schreiber 2012, 236 fig. 6: "die für den Kult typischen Wollbinden, die allerdings seltener von Personen getragen werden und häufig den Kultort oder auch das Opfertier schmücken" ("the woolen bandages typical of the cult, which are, however, seldom worn by people and often decorate the place of worship or also the sacrificed animal").

554 Papagianni 2016, 62–74.

555 Fleischer 2002, 214.

556 Fleischer 2002, 192–194.

557 Hesych. s.v. κληΐδες (καὶ παρὰ Ἐφεσίοις τῆς θεοῦ τὰ στέμματα): https://el.wikisource.org/wiki/%CE%93%CE%BB%CF%8E%CF%83%CF%83%CE%B1%CE%B9/%CE%9A, accessed on 21.04.2023.

558 Pape 1906, s.v. κλείς (key, lock, bolt, clavicle, thwart, strait, pass).

559 Hom. Il. XXII 324. – This killing at a specific anatomical site appears to be represented at the famous Ludovisi Gaul who is about to drive his sword home into the left supraclavicular fossa from above, just behind the

medio–anterior convexity of the clavicle, and towards the heart.

560 Hom. Od. XXI 47–50.

561 Illustrated in Alzinger 1974, fig. 29.

562 Thuswaldner 2015, 125 fig. 134. 209–211 fig. 211. – Still, Alzinger 1974, 44, states: "Beim Oktogon liegen die Infulae, vermutlich aus Platzmangel, über den Binden" ("At the octagon, the infulae are placed above the taeniae, presumably due to a lack of space").

563 In order to facilitate the comparison, the images of Thür were artificially converted into black and white photographs.

564 Apoll. Rhod. I 358. 395; Hom. Od. II 419.

565 See Kallimachos' hymn to Apollon (εἰς Ἀπόλλωνα) from the 3rd c. BC: https://www.hellenicgods.org/kalli-machushymntoapollo, accessed on 21.04.2023.

566 Smith 1875, s.v. navis. Different: Pape 1906, s.v. κλείς (because the rowing benches connect the ship›s walls).

567 Hor. carm. III 24, and Ov. trist. III 12: trochus. – Petschenig – Stowasser 1930, s.v. trochus (hoop). Pape 1906, s.v. τροχός (wheel or in general everything of circular shape).

568 Prop. III 14. – Petschenig – Stowasser 1930, s.v. clavis (key).

569 Accordingly, we do not agree with Thür 2011, 76: "der ephesische Grabbau kann für die Rekonstruktion der bislang unbekannten alexandrinischen Gräber der Ptolemaier und damit von Kleopatra ein wertvolles Bindeglied sein" ("the Ephesian funerary monument can serve as a valuable link in the reconstruction of the hitherto unknown Alexandrian tombs of the Ptolemies, including the one of Kleopatra").

570 Bennett 2013, s.v. Arsinoe IV n. 15; Thür 1990, 52.

571 https://dewiki.de/Lexikon/Volker_Michael_Strocka, accessed on 21.04.2023.

572 Strocka 2011, 307–310 figs. 21. 23. – Thuswaldner 2015, 117 fig. 124. 120 fig. 127.

573 https://dewiki.de/Lexikon/Friedmund_Hueber, accessed on 21.04.2023. – On F. Hueber: Bammer 2010, 45; Thür 1999c, 164f. n. 12.

574 Alzinger 1974, 41 n. 132: "die Achteckwinkel [wurden] nicht genau konstruiert" ("the octagon angles [were] not constructed accurately"); Thuswaldner 2015, 117: "dass deren Bearbeitung an den Kanten niemals einen exakten Fugenschluss [...] zulassen" ("that their processing at the edges never allows for a perfect joint closure"). 158: "dass [bei] der Errichtung keine besondere Sorgfalt in die Maßgenauigkeit gelegt wurde" ("that no special care was taken in ensuring dimensional accuracy during the construction"). 160: "dass auch im Grundriss nur wenig Sorgfalt in die maßgetreue Umsetzung des Entwurfes gelegt wurde. Aufgrund der geringen Präzision in der Ausführung" ("that even in the floor plan, little care was taken in the accurate implementation of the design. Due to the low precision in the execution"). 165: "Das nachlässige Vorgehen bei der baulichen Umsetzung [...] unpräzise Bauausführung" ("The careless approach in the construction implementation [...] The imprecise construction execution"), etc.

575 Strocka 2011, 310: "Als ich Dich, lieber Friedmund [Hueber], um nähere Angaben bat [...] gabst Du bereitwillig Auskunft [...]. »Die Platte [...] ist an ihrem rechten Ende schräg nach hinten geschnitten, so dass sie das rechte Ende einer Seite eines achteckigen Prismas darstellt« [...]. Wenn die Platte «das rechte Ende einer Seite eines achteckigen Prismas darstellt«, kommt einem sofort (und Dir wahrscheinlich schon, als Du das schriebst) das Oktogon in den Sinn, das ja unmittelbar östlich des sogenannten Heroons [= der ‚Brunnen'] am Unteren Embolos liegt".

576 Thuswaldner 2017, 134; Thuswaldner 2015, 67. 92. 117f. 120–122. 124. 165. 207f. 213.

577 Thuswaldner 2015, 139: "Eindeutig kann der Block dennoch nicht dem Bau zugeschrieben werden, da die Verbauung des Blocks im Straßenpflaster der Kuretenstraße erst zu einem Zeitpunkt möglich gewesen sein kann, als das Oktogon bereits eingestürzt war. Gemäß Strocka erfolgte die Verbauung des Friesblocks noch in der Spätantike, als die Kuretenstraße noch einen zentralen Bereich der Stadt darstellte. Nachdem aber ein großer Teil der Bauteile im Zuge der Freilegung auf der Kuretenstraße im Bereich des Oktogons vorgefunden wurde, musste das Gebäude in spätantiker Zeit nach wie vor aufrecht stehen" ("Nevertheless, the block cannot be unequivocally attributed to the construction, since the block could only have been built into the pavement of the Curetes Street at a time when the Octagon had already collapsed. According to Strocka, the frieze block was laid in late antiquity, when the Curetes Street was still a central area of the city. However, since a large part of the building components was found in the course of the excavation upon the Curetes Street in the area of the Octagon, the building must still have been standing upright in late antiquity"). – Strocka 2011, 309: "»jedenfalls spätantik am Unteren Embolos verbaut« [...] Zweitverwendung als Bodenbelag" ("»in any case, used in late antiquity at the Lower Embolos« [...] secondary use as pavement").

578 Information kindly provided by W. Prochaska. – Thuswaldner 2015, 67; Prochaska – Grillo 2012, 587.

579 Thür 1995c, 178–181; Thür 1990.

580 Keil 1964, 115; Keil 1957, 106; Keil 1955, 94; Keil 1930b, 87.

581 Keil 1930a, 41.

582 Thiersch 1909, 26.

583 Weninger 1953, 168; Keil 1930a, 41. 44.

584 Weninger 1953, 161; Keil 1930a, 45.

585 Weninger 1953, 166. 168.

586 Keil 1964, 114; Keil 1957, 105; Keil 1955, 94; Keil 1930b, 87.

587 Weninger 1953, 161.

588 Keil 1964, 114; Keil 1957, 105f.; Keil 1955, 94; Keil 1930a, 41; Keil 1930b, 87.

589 Miltner 1958, 29.

590 Keil 1964, 113–115; Keil 1957, 105–107; Keil 1955, 92–94.

591 Strack 1897, 210f. n. 46. – H. Heinen published his distrust in Strack's reasoning only in 1966 (Heinen 1966, 107 n. 2), i.e. after Keil's death in 1963.

592 Weninger 1953.

593 Thür 1990.

594 Anevlavi et al. 2020, 34.

595 Thür 2011, 74.

596 Strack 1897, 210f. n. 46.

597 Thür 1990, 56.

598 David Chater on the BBC–feature 'Cleopatra, Portrait of a Killer', in: The Times from 21.03.2009: "The historian Neil Oliver, with his usual unwavering certainty, tells us that the skeleton of a young female found at Ephesus is that of Princess Arsinoe, the younger sister of Cleopatra, who was dragged out of the temple of Artemis and murdered by Mark Antony on Cleopatra's orders. The evidence? Well, the bones were found in the tomb of someone important from the same period, who may have been beautiful. There was no evidence of disease, so – who knows? – perhaps she was murdered. The tomb, moreover, had an octagonal shape, reminiscent of the Great Pharos Lighthouse at Alexandria. It all sounds like a triumph of conjecture over certainty and the programme is not helped by hammy dramatisations".

599 Thuswaldner 2015, 212.

600 Gesellschaft der Freunde von Ephesos 2020, 3.

601 H. Thür, in: Scherrer 2000, 124: "[The date of the Octagon], together with the age of the young woman, supports the interpretation of the building as the burial monument of Arsinoë IV".

602 Thür 2011, 76: "Der ephesische Grabbau, seine Datierung und seine topographische Situation passen nun m. E. hervorragend zu einem durch antike Autoren überlieferten historischen Ereignis, in dem einer jungen Frau aus dem Königshaus der Ptolemaier eine wesentliche Rolle zukommt" ("The Ephesian funerary monument, its dating, and its topographical situation now, in my opinion, fit perfectly with a historical event recorded by ancient authors, in which a young woman from the Ptolemaic royal family plays a significant role").

603 Thür 2011, 76 (see above n. 96); Bennett 2013, s.v. Arsinoe IV n. 15.

604 Thür 2011, 76.

Arsinoë(s) in Ephesos – the historical background

1 Paus. I 6, 2; Curtius Rufus, Alex. IX 8, 22; Suda, s.v. Lagos (= Aelianus, Frg. 285). – For a thorough discussion see Collins 1997; further: Carney – Ogden 2010, 127–129; Huß 2001, 90.

2 See for an overview: Huß 2001, 265–335; Hölbl 1994, 26–45.

3 On Lysimachos: Paus. I 9, 5–7. – In general on the city foundations of this period and the intentions behind them: Cohen 1995, 63–72 (on Ephesos esp. 70f. and 177–180).

4 We do not follow (and shall not further discuss) the opinion of Mohr 2007, gathered from his interpretation of the written sources, esp. Strabon, that Lysimachos built his city on the same ground as already Kroisos had done; his argumentation is not convincing in any point.

5 According to Diod. XX 107, 4 the sympathies of the Ephesians apparently continued to lie with Demetrios Poliorketes.

6 IK 15, 1449. On this Bengtson 1937, 210–214; to the events of 302/301, cf. also Calapà 2009, 344.

7 Arr. exped. Alex. I 18, 2. – On Alexander and Ephesos cf. now Calapà 2009, 338–341.

8 Cf. e.g. the Ephesian bestowal of citizenship in 300 on the Rhodian Nikagoras, IK 15, 1453, or the support by the Ephesians of the exiles from Priene friendly to Demetrios, IK 16, 2001. The prevailing opinion that Demetrios possessed Ephesos continuously from 302 or 301 until 295, cf. on this Knibbe 1970, 254f., or Calapà 2009, 343f., needs to be more closely examined in the future with the aid of the coinage and citizenship decrees.

9 Bengtson 1937, 215–220.

10 Knibbe 1970, 254f.; Calapà 2009, 344f.

11 Plut. Demetrios 35, 5; Polyainos V 19; Frontin. strat. III 3, 7. – Similarly, already Benndorf 1906, 89.

12 Karwiese 1970, 303–306 and 321f.; his later theory (Karwiese 1995, 65f.) that the contemporary usage of both city names should be evidence that Ephesos near the Artemision, in addition to the new city of Arsinoeia, continued to exist as its own polis, was justly rejected by Calapà 2009, 345f.

13 IK 15, 1453 (Nikagoras) and 1454 (for Leukippos of Olynthos). – On the division into phylai and chiliasties, cf. Engelmann 1996. – Only the Kolophonians, who were the only ones, who had fought against Lysimachos (Paus. VII 3, 4f.), were not organised in a phyle or chiliastys of their own, but distributed to other unities.

14 Knibbe 1970, 256.

15 IK 14, 1441; Maier 1959, 241f. no. 72, thinks that Athenis was most likely a wealthy metoecus who financially supported the construction of the fortifica-

16 IK 14, 1440; cf. on this Keil 1913, esp. 243.

17 Cf. on this pp. 79f.

18 Inscriptions from Ephesos: IK 14, 1381; IK 15, 1855. Honorary inscription of the Ionian League for Hippostratos of Miletos, 389/388 BC, found in Smyrna: IK 24, 577. In addition, further examples from Chios (SEG 35, 1985, 926) and Miletos: Syll. I³ 368 Z24 = Hermann – Rehm 1997, 157f. no. 10. – Coins: Head 1911, 574; Karwiese 1970, 303f. and 321f.

19 Polyainus VIII 57.

20 Polyb. XXI 46, 4; Liv. XXXVIII 39. – On Kolophon see Cohen 1995, 183–187.

21 Strab. XII 4, 7 [565]; XIV 1, 37 [646]. – Cf. on this Lichtenberger – Nieswandt – Salzmann 2008, 395 with n. 48.

22 Burstein 1982, 198f. with n. 6; equally Dimitriev 2007, 145 n. 41; cf. also Lichtenberger – Nieswandt – Salzmann 2008, 395 with n. 49.

23 Strab. XIV 1, 20; s. on this p. 84.

24 IK 14, 1381; cf. on this also the long decree IK 11a, 4, from the year 297/96, regulating property relations and mortgages after a war, but which can also very well refer to the necessary sale of land during the relocation of the city.

25 Keil 1943, 101f. no. 1; cf. on this now Scherrer 2021, esp. 64.

26 Cf. on this also Knibbe 1998, 93; Knibbe 1995, 145. – see also above p. 78.

27 Scherrer 2007, 345f.

28 Langmann 1993, 284. – In this respect it appeared possible that, as Knibbe 1995, 145, emphasised, for this reason the Artemision was burned, deliberately and with the knowledge of the priesthood, already half a century earlier in order to be able to rebuild it after this "accident" at a higher level and with contemporary splendour; cf. already on this also Karwiese 1991, who deems as probable the lightning strike, given in certain ancient sources – all evidence collected in Karwiese 1991 –, as the cause of the fire.

29 Cf. Calapà 2009, 352–356, who in general emphasises the strategic value of Ephesos. Daubner 2011, 42–44, underscores the importance to the Seleucids of the harbour as the end point of a route coming from Syria; while Winter 2011, esp. 73, underscores its value as a large harbour for the Ptolemaic fleet on the connecting route Alexandria – Athens.

30 Cf. on the ruling couple now in particular Müller 2009.

31 On the history of Ephesos in the Hellenistic period cf. e.g. Knibbe 1998, 94–97; Calapà 2009.

32 IK 12, 199; Kotsidu 2000, 477 no. 358; Pfeffer 2008, § 31; Calapà 2009, 352 n. 91; Calapà 2010.

33 Meadows 2013, 1. 7–10, esp. 8; reinforcing this, also Bricault 2014, 9f. – This dating was already proposed at Knibbe – İplikçioğlu 1981/82, 92 no. 11, although without argumentational support.

34 Fassa 2015, 8 n. 33: "Ephesos is the oldest example for these inscriptions."

35 Bricault 2014.

36 IK 12, 199 = SEG 33, 1983, 942 = SEG 39, 1989, 1232 = SEG 43, 1993, 749; Bulletin épigraphique 2011, 511; Knibbe – İplikçioğlu 1981/82, 92 no. 11; Knibbe – Engelmann – İplikçioğlu 1989, 235f. no. 1; Knibbe – Engelmann – İplikçioğlu 1993, 150; Calapà 2010, 200; Reading here according to Meadows 2013, 3.

37 SEG 1983, 39, 1989, 1234; Knibbe – Engelmann – İplikçioğlu 1989, 237f. no. 4; Calapà 2010, 201. Reading according to Meadows 2013, 5.

38 Meadows 2013, 4–9 (on the phrourarchs esp. 5 with n. 14; on the remaining double-dedications esp. 6f.). – On the Ptolemaic phrourarchs attested in Ephesos, cf. Hölbl 2004, 49, on their role in general, Chaniotis 2003, 441.

39 Bricault 2014, 8 fig. 3. The break between the two joined-together parts of Fragment 2 is located precisely at the height of the lower border of Fragment 1; the stone was therefore broken cruciform into four parts, of which only the part at the lower right is missing.

40 Calapà 2010, 200; Meadows 2013, 5.

41 On the site of the excavation work in 1977, cf. Vetters 1978, 270. At that time the rooms were still assigned to Residential Unit 6, for which reason the inscription is absent in Taeuber 2016.

42 Taeuber 2016, 255f. IST 13 pl. 136, repeats the original reading of Knibbe – İplikçioğlu 1981/82, 134f. no. 142, but gives the following very worthwhile information: preservation: "zwei aneinander passende Fragmente einer dicken Platte aus weißem Marmor, rechts gebrochen"["two fragments which fit together of a thick plaque of white marble, broken at the right"; findspot: "Schuttaushub nördlich R 38 und R 38a" ["rubble spoil north of R 38 and R 38a"] (EED 10.09.1980); measurements: "H 47.5 cm, W 22.5 cm, D 10 cm, H of letters 1.5–2 cm; storage: EM, Inv.-no. 4058; Depot-no. 2048."

43 Cf. Rathmayr 2016, Pl. 1.

44 See pp. 139f.

45 Inscriptiones Cretae III 4.18 (p. 115f.): βασιλεῖ Πτολεμαίωι Φιλοπάτορι | καὶ βασιλίσσηι Ἀρσινόηι | τὸ ὕδρευμα καὶ τὸ Νυμφαῖον | Λεύκιος Γαΐου Ῥωμαῖος φρουράρχων. – It is perhaps no coincidence that such water constructions were erected in "occupied" areas outside the core areas of Alexandria and Egypt.

46 Knibbe – Engelmann – İplikçioğlu 1989, 237f. no. 4, have the definite article τὸ in their reading, which is based on personal inspection. When Meadows 2013, 5, denies the letter O on the basis of a photograph of a squeeze in which he could not recognise any remains of the letter, then this is a weak argument. Nevertheless, his supplementation of the following remains of a letter to N instead of B appears to be a better reading.

47 Most recently Kirbihler 2016, 360 with n. 9, who justifiably deplores the lack of a research synthesis for the Lagidai in Ephesos.

48 Subsequently she immediately was venerated as a deity in all parts of the Ptolemaic kingdom – above all as New Isis and Aphrodite, and therefore patroness of seafaring in the harbour cities, and would thus have been addressed as goddess (θεά) instead of queen (Βασιλίσση) in the inscription. For a probable honouring as Aphrodite in the so-called rock crevice temple, cf. p. 95.

49 See above pp. 80f. with n. 29–32.

50 Frontin. strat. III 9, 10.

51 Buraselis 1982, 203–206, esp. 203: "Ephesos was Seleucid up until 246."

52 Most recently Iossif – Lorber 2021, 218f., who discuss some Ephesian tetradrachms minted with the head of Ptolemy III.

53 Meadows 2013, 1. 7–10; Bricault 2014, 9f.

54 On the loyalty of the Ephesians to Antiochos III up to 188 BC, cf. Liv. XXXVII 45, 1, on this Knibbe 1970, 259.

55 IK 14, 1082 and 1101; on this, now, Scherrer 2021, 72.

56 Knibbe 1970, 259; Knibbe 1998, 97 and 99; Calapà 2009, 357f. – This famous freedom inscription from Rome (ILS 34) is dated variously between 167 BC and Sulla: *Populus Ephesiu[s populum Romanum] / salutis ergo, quod o[ptinuit maiorum] / suorum leibertatem ....* Thereby it cannot be clarified if this freedom of the city was restored already under the Attalids, after 133 BC in the course of the establishment of the province, or first (considerably) later after the Mithraditic War and the "Ephesian Vespers" of 88 BC.

57 For the Attalid building programme see pp. 97. 101. 140.

58 Laubenberger – Prochaska 2011, 43–49 (quote p. 46). – A second, smaller than life-size portrait head, found in Ephesos without more precise information on the find-spot (at that time, work was primarily carried out at the Curetes Street), is found in the Selcuk Müzesi, Inv. 8/38/72, and is still unpublished (a manuscript by M. Aurenhammer has been completed for quite some time). Cf. on the heads also Ladstätter 2016, 253 with n. 133.

59 Probably an inscription Ἀρσι[νόη? —] on an architrave (IK 12, 343; found fragmented and secondarily built into a Late Antique wall above the Hellenistic nymphaion in front of the theatre) originally was somehow connected to the portrait in the façade of the stage building.

60 Laubenberger – Prohaska 2011, 46: "The head overall is strongly reminiscent both of female (Aphrodite, Artemis) as well as male (Apollon, Dionysos) divine images, yet, in the style of the Ptolemaic portraits with few personal characteristics, it is nevertheless clearly portrait-like."

61 Knibbe – Langmann 1993, 14f.; Knibbe 1995, 144f.

62 See above p. 76.

63 e.g. IK 15, 1449; cf. on this now Rogers 2012, 40f. 71–74; Bauer 2014, 84f., nevertheless indicates that this is an unusual case. Compare the text of Strab. XIV 1, 21 (above p. 75).

64 Cautiously deliberative in this issue, Calapà 2009, 349 with n. 75.

65 Summarizing on this now Bauer 2014, 78–219.

66 Strab.: XIV 1, 4. On the text see p. 126.

67 Summarizing on this Scherrer 2021; see also pp. 97f.

68 Extensively on this Scherrer 2021, 69f.

69 IK 12, 442.

70 Knibbe – Engelmann – İplikçioğlu 1993, 113–122; on the authorship of the oldest letter by Caesar cf. Bauer 2014, 103–116.

71 On *Soteira* and the mysteries accompanying the taking up of new citizens in Ortygia, which he traces back to Lysimachos, cf. extensively Rogers 2012, esp. 75–88. How, precisely, this (Artemis) Soteira is related to Artemis Ephesia and how old her cult actually is, unfortunately lies beyond the scope of our knowledge. For an important altar of Artemis (Soteira) in the city centre see pp. 122–126.

72 IK 11, 26 esp. lines 4 and 18; see also p. 119 with n. 34. – Cf. Rogers 1991, esp. 62–68; Rogers 2012, esp. 39–49. 71–79 and 83–88.

73 IK 11a, 27–37; on the seating order esp. Kolb 1995; on the interpretation of the endowment, extensively Rogers 1991.

74 Ryan 2022, 15f., stresses the role of the ephebes as the bearers of the city's future, and combines the statues carried by them with monuments along the processional route as symbols of the city's fortune.

75 Extensively on this, see Rogers 1991, 84.

76 See on this pp. 139 and 211.

77 On this, see pp. 21f. 48.

78 On the cultic honours for Arsinoë II in the Ptolemaic kingdom, cf. Grabowski 2014, 26–32; Pfeiffer 2008, esp. § 30–32; Hölbl 2004, 37f. and 94–98; Hauben 1983.

79 See pp. 23–26.

80 See pp. 23. 145. 151.

81 Dobesch 1996, 58; see also above p. 49.

82 On Caesar and Ephesos, comprehensively, see now Kirbihler 2016, 365–381.

83 Vell. II 126; Cass. Dio LI 20. – On Augustus as ktistes in Ephesian inscriptions cf. IK 12, 252, an honour by the young citizens in their gymnasium (=later so-called State Agora) from the early Augustan period. – On the chronology of the cultic veneration of Augustus in Ephesos, see now Kirbihler 2016, 382–402.

84 Scherrer 1990; on the person of Vedius Pollio cf. Kirbihler 2007; on the dating of his mission esp. Kirbihler 2017, 144–149.

The architectural development of Hellenistic Ephesos and the expansion of the city under Augustus

1 On the name of the hill, cf. Engelmann 1991, 282; ancient references at Strab. XIV 1, 4 (on this see below, p. 126) and Antoninus Liberalis 11. 1. On extensive geo-archaeological surface surveys see Groh 2006, 48–50 (here Fig. 21 and 25). The assertion by Ladstätter, 2016, 251 (the exact opposite on p. 238), that the micro-climate and the traffic situation would have made a settlement here insalubrious, is applicable at best after the transition from Late Antiquity to the Byzantine period.

2 Herakl. DK 22 B 12: ποταμοῖς τοῖς αὐτοῖς ἐμβαίνομέν τε καὶ οὐκ ἐμβαίνομεν.

3 On the rising water level and the coastal displacement, as well as harbour possibilities in the historical period, cf. Stock et al. 2014; Stock et al. 2016; Brückner et al. 2017.

4 On the historical settlement geography, cf. Scherrer 2007.

5 Bammer – Muss 1996, 55. – On the original location of the Artemision at the coast, and its displacement and the ground alluvion, cf. Brückner – Kraft – Kayan 2008.

6 The most recent summary of research at Ladstätter 2016, 253–256.

7 IK 16, 2061 II lines 14–16 (ca. 102–114 AD); IK 17/1, 3066 (around 105 or 109 AD).

8 IK 11, 20; intensively dealt with by Friesen 2022.

9 On the expansion of the sanctuary at Samothrake and the stay there of Arsinoë II before her marriage to Ptolemaios II, cf. Müller 2009, esp. 60.

10 IK 15, 1503 (found

11 Friesen 2022, 127 and 131.

12 On the 3rd c. BC inscriptions, see now Bricault 2014, 10. On the cult of Isis and Sarapis at Ephesos, already Keil 1947; Keil 1954; Walters 1995. A new discovery of an inscription at Knibbe – Engelmann – İplikçioğlu 1993, 133 no. 28 ("probably still Hellenistic").

13 Taxes and other dues are mentioned for Alexander and Lysimachos; see the historical section above, p. 76.

14 Strab. XIV 1, 26. – For the localisation of the laguna Selinousia in the former bay between the Artemision and the Tracheia with the Koressos harbour see Scherrer 2007, 345f.

15 Serv. Aen. I 720; Athenaios XIII 31. An honorary decree for a certain Damoteles (2nd c. BC), found on the south side of the Roman harbour by the pier, refers to a sanctuary in the context of the club house of the Rhodian (?) merchants in Ephesos; cf. Knibbe – Engelmann – İplikçioğlu 1993, 125f. no. 17 (with a summary of all Aphrodite inscriptions found at Ephesos so far); for the sanctuary cf. also Calapà 2009, 347 with n. 60;

on the cult of Aphrodite Daitis at Ephesos (3rd c. AD) Keil 1914, on this IK 14, 1202.

16 Ladstätter 2016, 257–260, with discussion of the earlier literature.

17 Gassner 2007.

18 Ladstätter 2016, 259. – A cultic worship of Arsinoë II in Ephesos could scientifically be based only on the – meanwhile outdated – assumption of a Ptolemaic dominion over Ephesos under Ptolemaios II and Arsinoë II in the years around 276 BC; on this, see above, pp. 80–84.

19 Strab. XIV 1, 24. On the state of research into this jetty, Ladstätter 2016, 262f.

20 On this, cf. now Ladstätter 2016, 255f.

21 Extensively on this Ladstätter 2016, 261f. with fig. 18.

22 On the precise argument for the location see pp. 128f.

23 Liv. XXXVI 43, 8; XXXVII 10, 12; XXXVII 11, 3.

24 Vetters 1983, esp. 114; S. Karwiese, in: Scherrer 2000, 188; Scherrer 2001, 63f.; Ladstätter 2016, 250f. fig. 13.

25 Paus. I 9, 7 (on this see above, p. 76).

26 IK 14, 1381.

27 See p. 79.

28 Aristot. pol. VII 12, 1331 a 24f. 32–35 and b 1–2; cf. also already Xen. kyr. I 2, 3, and Plat. nom. 778c; on the discussion about this for Ephesos, already Alzinger 1970, 1603; Alzinger 1999, 389f. – for the subject in general see Segev 2019 and Hinsch 2015.

29 Consequently, the decades' long discussion of whether the West Agora, already functioning before 281, and the Commercial Agora (later Tetragonos Agora) could be identical, takes care of itself. In addition, it ensures that the West Agora must lie to the west of the Tetragonos Agora due to its name. In spite of this, voices are continually raised that do not want to accept this; cf. on this the following pages with the discussion about the so-called State Agora.

30 IK 17/1, 3009; on the interpretation of the two-aisled basilica as this *auditorium* cf. Scherrer – Trinkl 2006, 36–38. The older interpretation of the auditorium as a space for the speeches of the Sophists (cf. Engelmann 1993a; Hueber 1997b, 83–85; recently taken up again by Burrell 2009, 87) is to be rejected due to the obvious connotation of the Latin term with "magistrate" (*auditor*).

31 Hofbauer et al. 2017, 433 and 438. According to the few roughly datable remains, also the koilon does not appear to be older; cf. Hofbauer et al. 2017, 441f.; Styhler-Aydin 2022, 41 and 68–70.

32 The Augustan or slightly later alteration works seem to have been limited to the koilon, while the Doric proscenium architecture, earlier identified as Augustan, arose first in the Flavian, probably more precisely Domitianic period: Hofbauer et al. 2017, 442f. and 449; for Roman building activities in the time before Domitian see Styhler-Aydin 2022, 71–77.

33 IK 11, 27–36, on this, Kolb 1995 and above p. 89.

34 Particularly emphatic proponents of this thesis, for example: Alzinger 1974, esp. 146 and 149; Alzinger 1999; Hueber 1997a, 253f. 257; in spite of the already published, distinct evidence for a gymnasium, in addition Groh 2006, 66, 113 and passim, and trusting his unfounded assertions, Calapà 2009, 346; Ladstätter 2016 assembled the finds from the early 3ʳᵈ c. BC (coin hoard and West Slope pottery), yet concluded from the lack of architectual finds, "Shortly before the middle of the century – in about 260 BC – not only can an obvious quantitative increase in finds be recognised, but, far more, the diversity of types, including stamped amphorae, lamps, various lustre wares, points to a permanent settlement activity, without nevertheless being able to deduce a concrete function for the find-spot."

35 Engelmann 1993, 288f.; Thür 2007a; Scherrer 2021, 70–77.

36 On the buildings for the imperial cult: Scherrer 1990, 98–101; Thür 2007b.

37 Thür 2007b, esp. 79–81.

38 S. Karwiese, in: Scherrer 2000, 168; Scherrer 2001, 72f.

39 On the dating of the first building Steskal 2010, 77–99; the famous Curetes inscriptions begin, however, distinctly later, perhaps directly under Tiberius, cf. Scherrer 2015, 795–797.

40 Steskal 2010, 77f. with n. 370.

41 Bier 2011, 81–85.

42 The diametrical opinions on the function were already formulated at Fasolo 1962, 17 ("the large place, modernly named State Agora, unlikely to have been the old city centre, based on its building history and location far removed from the harbour") and Hueber 1997a, 257 ("State Agora in a central location in a well populated, relatively flat location").

43 Cf. on the corresponding agones for youths in the Hellenistic period, and other evidence: Scherrer 2021, esp. 72f.

44 For the more recent research on this cf. e.g. Marksteiner 1999, esp. 415f.; Groh 2006, 61-65; Sokolicek 2016, 97; Ladstätter 2016, 240.

45 Cf. the map entry at Wheler 1682, book III fig. 6. – On the tower, already Benndorf 1899, esp. 21–25; extensively, Seiterle 1970, 65–72.

46 Keil 1912, 186–188.

47 IK 11, 3, esp. lines 3–5; cf. also Maier 1959, 238ff. no. 71: … ἐξαιρούμεθα παρὰ θάλασσαν ὁδὸν πόδα / [ε]ἴκοσι ἀποτέμνοντες ἀπὸ τῆς γῆς, πλάτος πόδα εἴκοσι εἰς τὸ τεῖχος διὰ / τῆς γῆς Κλειτ[ο]φῶ[ν]τος. – Transl. according to Wankel IK 11, 3, and Seiterle 1970, n. 6.

48 IK 11, 27 lines 50. 424. 564.

49 On the course of the wall, see preliminarily Scherrer 2001, 62f.; polemically against this, Groh 2006, 62–64.

50 The map of Ladstätter 2016, fig. 2 (here fig. 29) gives a very different course of the wall along mount Panayırdağ, which will be discussed in the coming paragraphs.

51 Scherrer 2001, 63, at that time designated as "Upper and Lower Castle"; agreeing with the akra on the peak of the Tracheia, Ladstätter 2016, 253 with fig. 2 no. 18, yet she nevertheless assumes another course of the city wall, further down at the foot of the slope, whereby the akra would then be in an isolated location within the city area, which is strategically a questionable state of affairs. See also pp. 107f.

52 On the inscription, see above, pp. 23–26.

53 The lower part of this enclosure is taken as a part of the main wall by Ladstätter 2016, fig. 2 (here fig. 29), while the upper part is negated.

54 On this cf. Baier 2016, esp. 33 (dated to about the mid-2ⁿᵈ c. BC) and 53–56 (features of a residence). See now the monograph of Baier 2023 (published when this manuscript already was in preparation for print). – The building, which was continually expanded and restructured up until Late Antiquity, probably served in the imperial period as a banqueting house, according to the numerous inscriptions of societies on the marble wall revetments.

55 This akra is mentioned in the dedicatory inscription found in Terrace House 2 and extensively dealt with above pp. 80–84.

56 Plin. n. h. V 115.

57 IK 11, 27, lines 212. 425. 566; IK 13, 730 line 9.

58 Scherrer 2006a, 69–72; Scherrer – Trinkl 2006, 13f. – Ladstätter 2016, 243, would like to explain the Hellenistic gate by the north gate of the agora as a passage for a diateichisma, since the course of the Hellenistic city wall as reconstructed by her does not lead here (see above, n. 50f.).

59 Cf. p. 108 with n. 91.

60 Engelmann 1997.

61 Scherrer 2006a, 69; Scherrer 2007, 333; cautiously in agreement, Ladstätter 2016, 243f.

62 Scherrer 2006a, 69.

63 IK 12, 422A; the inscription at the so-called Hadrian's Gate, where the Marble Street ends, makes sense then primarily when the name of the Hellenistic country road was transferred to the so-called Marble Street immediately after the expansion of the agora to the east as the consequently necessary relocation of the traffic axis. Based on the preserved remains of the name Τιβέ[ριος] the grammateus Tib. Claudius Lucceianus, in office in 114/115 AD, could be intended; if this is so, the dating of the gate structure would in any event fall in the Trajanic period; cf. Thür 1989, esp. 69–73 and 133f.; H. Thür, in: Scherrer 2000, 130; Scherrer 2001, 76; Scherrer 2008, 47.

64 Similarly, already, Thür 1995, 65 n. 18.

65 Cf. e.g Rumscheid 1998, 43–45. Also here, as at the Koressian Gate in Ephesos, due to the overall topography the location of the wall projecting from the gate

on the wrong side (shield-bearing side for the attackers) must have been accepted.

66 Wood 1877, 111–120; Seiterle 1982, esp. 145; Sokolicek 2010 and 2020, 110f., assumes an older gate directly beneath or close to the existing gate structure.

67 Seiterle 1998.

68 Scherrer 2006a, 65–68.

69 Sokolicek 2009, esp. 341, presupposes an erection of the gate in the late 2nd or early 1st c. BC above the older city wall. Similarily Sokolicek 2010, 377: "The frequency of the early Hellenistic finds in the area of the fortification wall, above all however in the filling of the foundation pit in section 1/09, allows the conclusion that, with the oldest wall in the region of the Magnesian Gate we are dealing with the early Hellenistic city gate erected under Lysimachos, upon which – at a later date – the Magnesian Gate was built. The early Hellenistic find material is limited to the area of the city wall, while find material from the region of the gate originates from later periods." Sokolicek 2010, 378: "There was an early Hellenistic gate building of unknown architecture, for which all strata are lacking. The destruction and removal of this older gate building could have occurred around the middle of the 2nd c. BC, because the gate needed to be enlarged. The ground plan that is visible today can in any event not be early Hellenistic, because it is built over the older city wall."

70 Lohner-Urban 2023, esp. 61f.

71 As a connection to the Augustan city gate, originally erected in isolation, at Side (cf. Lohner-Urban – Scherrer 2016; Lohner-Urban 2017) a new land wall was erected about a century later; this, equally, was not defensive and displayed a purely representative character (on this, cf. Grebien 2018); on Perge, where the city wall was only erected in individual sections, cf. Martini 2016. – In general, on the expanded function and semantics of city gates in the Roman imperial period, see now Fröhlich 2022, esp. 46 and 281–292.

72 A typical feature of Augustan and later imperial city gates, see Fröhlich 2022, 287.

73 Authors view precisely this so-called sawtooth section as characteristic for the Hellenistic walls. In general on this idea, e.g. Rumscheid 1998, 41.

74 Rumscheid 1998, 195–211.

75 Benndorf 1906, 91.

76 McNicoll 1986, 308: "The result was a circuit which often bore little or no relationship to the area actually occupied."

77 Scherrer 2005, 112f. fig. 2.

78 For the earth deposits over the former city gate below the north gate of the Augustan agora, a great deal of building debris (broken mud bricks) from demolished houses was used; cf. on this Scherrer – Trinkl 2006, 34; on the broad absence of Hellenistic architectural remains in the area of the intersection with the Embolos

to the east of the Marble Street, cf. now Waldner 2020, 167–170.

79 On a "street paving" of the period after 200 BC and a fountain set up at a roughly contemporary time under Terrace House 1, cf. Ladstätter 2003, esp. 42 and 73. On terracing and artisanal usage of the area under Terrace House 2 at the earliest after the middle of the 2nd c. BC, cf., summarising, Ladstätter 2002, esp. 33; Ladstätter 2010; Ladstätter – Lang-Auinger 2001.

80 Cf. on this also Ladstätter 2016, 251f.

81 On the designation cf. already Keil 1935, 88–90.

82 The Hellenistic architectural remains after the later 3rd/2nd c. BC at the north-east corner of the Marble Street and the Curetes Street appear to be oriented neither according to the (later) course of the Curetes Street nor according to the grid system. On the basis of these building remains, Waldner 2020, 167–170, undertook a series of highly theoretical considerations that have little validity due to the small-scale approach of the investigations and the existence of the orientation only at the northern side of the street at its lowest end. In any event, the south edge of the course of the street was already identical in this area with the course of the street in the imperial period, at least since the construction of the so–called Heroon of Androklos (on this, see below) in the mid–1st c. BC.

83 IK 17/1, 3008 line 19; cf. also Waldner 2020, 166.

84 *Embolos*: IK 15, 2000; IK 16, 2017 line 4; *Embolitai*: IK 17/1, 3059.

85 cf. Thür 1995, 84.

86 Scherrer 2001, 80–86; a different plan by Groh 2006, 56–61, who disregards without discussion a number of known, yet not corresponding streets; or, in places that stratigraphically display demonstrably no streets or divergent streets (cf. e.g. Waldner 2020, 168), he employs these for his grid.

87 Keil 1912, 184f., who however still thought of a Late Antique origin, already wrote that the mortared wall work of this section at most profited from a re-use of Hellenistic building stones. – Nevertheless, this existing building stock was frequently invoked for the early Hellenistic period, recently – due to the use of the corresponding building blocks in Roman and Byzantine buildings at Koressos – by Ladstätter 2016, 240f. With the solution proposed now, the thesis of a diateichisma, to which the Hellenistic gate underneath the north gate of the agora would have served as a passageway, is now superfluous (cf. Ladstätter 2016, 243). The Augustan stretch of wall over the two peaks of the Panayırdağ was then also incorporated into the Byzantine city wall.

88 Already seen by Keil 1912, 185, who added these parts to the byzantine constructions. See also Ladstädter 2016, 240f.

89 IK 13, 730 Z9.– on this, cf. Engelmann 1997, 133.

90 One would like to assume that the stadium, completed under Domitian, with a very much enlarged seat-

ing area, partly leant directly against the city wall. This would explain the sharp bend with which the Byzantine wall – which was led around the stadium outside – connects to the Augustan city wall.

91 IK 17/1, 3013: The agoranomos Aurelius Metrodorus caused the *Plateia in Koressos* – probably in the Severan period – to be paved.

92 Repeated references in the endowment inscription of Salutaris from the year 104/105 AD: IK 11a, 27 line 212. 425. 566.

93 Attempts to localise this have frequently been undertaken in the region of the Byzantine city wall, that is, to the north of the stadium, thus already by Wood 1877, 138f. – Against this, already Knibbe – Langmann 1993, 18–20. – On the various attempts at localisation in the area between the theatre and the Vedius Gymnasium cf. Karwiese 1985, 219; Scherrer 2001, 63. 67; Knibbe 2002, 215f.; Scherrer 2007, 333.

The protector of Ephesos – Artemis and her sacred Triodos

1 The name appears repeatedly in the endowment inscription of Salutaris from the year 104/105 AD, cf. IK 11, lines 50. [211]. 424. 564; slightly differently, Paus. VII 2, 9: ἐπὶ πύλας τὰς Μαγνήτιδας.

2 Feissel 1999.

3 The find-spot is sometimes erroneously connected to the Octagon: A. Bernhard-Walcher, in: Oberleitner et al. 1978, 115 cat.-no. 163f.; Thür 2009, 17. But the EED (10th–12th and 13th–15th of Oct. 1904) reports the street in front of the fountain in the west of the Octagon (cf. Androklos monument or Hypelaios) and the street near the so-called Gate of Hadrian as the find-spots (see for that also above p. 33 with n. 30 and p. 39 with nn. 91 and 93. The last positioning in the street paving, obviously in front of the Hypelaios fountain, ought anyway to date to the 5th/6th c. – One would like to speculate, most likely, that the candelabras were relocated to the front of the Byzantine fountain basin (see for that p. 132 fig. 47) from a tomb close by, perhaps that of Tib. Claudius Aristion. This would match with a presumable dating of the candelabras to the 2nd c. AD. Borchardt 1897, 47–49, already provides good comparative examples from the New Kingdom and early imperial Egypt.

4 Scherrer – Trinkl 2006, 18 und 61.

5 See pp. 101f. 108 and fig. 31.

6 On the tombs, see pp. 144f. 201 and plan 2.

7 Knibbe 1991, 6.

8 Strab. XIV 1, 20; cf. also Tac. ann. III 61; Paus. VII 5, 10.

9 On this, comprehensively, Rogers 2012.

10 For the attempts at localising Ortygia, cf. Keil 1922–24, 113–119. Keil's allocation failed because he identified the river Kenchrios with the Değirmen çay, that is, the river that we may assume today had the name Marnas in antiquity. The older attempt, already by Benndorf 1906, 76–78 with additional arguments, to locate it in today's Arvalya valley west of the Bülbüldağ – followed until today by most scholars (cf. e.g. Knibbe 1991, 6) – suffers from the fact that here there is absolutely no water course worth mentioning, but only a small brook.

11 On this street, found during the foundation excavations under the library, cf. Vetters 1973, 181 (where it is falsely dated to the Archaic period); Scherrer 2001, 81; Scherrer – Trinkl 2006, 55–57.

12 Scherrer 2005, esp. 120 (on the dating of the relocation of the street).

13 See p. 102 n. 63 and p. 172 n. 238.

14 The lower three lines were already published in SE 439*2 (Ionia: Ephesos), but this has not been recognised up until now; text and translation here follow Knibbe – Engelmann – İplikçioğlu 1993, 123f. no. 13. Intended here is either Herakleides or his brother Alexandros Passalas, the latter serving as *prytanis* in the years 4 and 14 AD; the fact that the inscription does not mention this makes the brother Herakleides more likely as sponsor of the work. Their father Apollonios Passalas was *prytanis* already in 19 BC (IK 11, 9) and participated earlier in the construction of the imperial cult centre at the so-called State Agora (cf. IK 13, 902: erection of a statue of Augustus in a temenos). – To which building the ashlar block originally belonged has not yet been questioned, and would be clarified at best by close analysis on the spot. One might suppose that the most likely original position of this inscription was in front of the eastern protruding wing of the South Gate.

15 Knibbe – Langmann 1993, 55 with n. 166, falsely transfer the name 'Triodos' to the agora's South Gate itself, although Knibbe 1991, 6 with n. 7, had clearly expressed himself in a more nuanced manner: "The forking lay in the Archaic period roughly in the place where later the South Gate of the agora stood; …". Knibbe – Langmann 1993, 55, date the inscription in the first publication to the time immediately after the completion of the South Gate: "The 0.036 – 0.024 m letter heights are typical for the turn of the eras…" and: "Already the first winter after the completion of the Gate … will have shown that it was necessary to erect a barrier in the Gate's passages, that hindered water from flowing unchecked into the agora…".

16 For this, cf. Scherrer – Trinkl 2006, 35. Still before the discovery of the Triodos inscription, Hueber 1984, 17, spoke in favour of a Neronian date for the renovation, yet neither of the two Passalas brothers could have lived that long.

17 See pp. 168f.

18 On the Sophist and the Ephesian evidence regarding him: Fischer 2014, 36f., who however erroneously comprehends the funerary inscription as an honour to the living figure by the city.

19 On the excavation findings Jobst 1983, esp. 162–164 and 211f. with n. 7f. – On the sarcophagus and an inscription on a base for Dionysios IK 17/1, 3047; on the entire find and its context cf. Scherrer – Trinkl 2006, 44f.

20 Philostr. soph. I 63 (p. 526) - see Stefec 2016. Transl. following Fischer 2014, 136 n. 48.

21 Engelmann 1995, 86f.

22 The term was already used by Arist. pol. 1331 b1 to mark the most prestigious place in the city.

23 IK 17/1, 3059 lines 11–13. See for this inscription also p. 121.

24 On this, cf. also Knibbe – Langmann 1993, 54.

25 IK 14, 1300 (from a Late Antique wall opposite the Octagon), lines 7f.: Ἔμβολον ... τὸ κάλλιστον ἄστεος.

26 South Gate: IK 12, 567. On divinities on gates in Ephesos, cf. Weißl 1998, 239–242 (agora and other buildings in the city) and 252 (Nemesis reliefs at the Magnesian Gate).

27 The joint representation of Artemis and Hekate has been occasionally encountered since the 3rd c. BC, but the relatively infrequent monuments are mostly found in the 1st/2nd c. AD, cf. Sarian 1992, 1006 no. 238–245.

28 On this, cf. Weißl 1998, 170, also with reference to a Triodos inscription from Delos, ID 1417 Delos (IG XI): Ἀρτεμίσιον τὸ ἐ/πὶ τῆς τριόδου / καὶ ἀπὸ τοῦ Ἀρτε/ - - -. For Hekate protecting city gates, e.g. in Miletos, see now Fröhlich 2022, 90.

29 Knibbe – Engelmann – İplikçioğlu 1993, 130–132 no. 25; it remains unclear which oracle was visited, Knibbe – Engelmann – İplikçioğlu 1993, 131, surmise that it should have been either Klaros or Didyma. – The carrier of the inscription was a marble orthostat, reused in Late Antiquity as a paving slab of the Marble Street directly in front of Hadrian's Gate, yet which originally could have belonged, most likely, to the wall revetment of the altar building at the Triodos, to be discussed further below.

30 On this, Merkelbach 1991.

31 Knibbe 1991, 15.

32 IK 14, 1265.

33 Engelmann 1993, 287f.

34 IK 11, 26 esp. Z 4 and 18; although indeed the name of the goddess near Soteira is lacking due to a lacuna in the inscription, nevertheless from the context Artemis can almost imperatively be assumed.

35 On this cf. Rogers 2012, esp. 217. The gerousia had played an important role in the mysteries on the birthday of Artemis since the time of Lysimachos.

36 Hom. Aph. 16–20; for the Greek text and English translation see Olson 2012; see also Petrovic 2010, 214f., who expressed her surprise about the phrase "city of righteous men", but exactly here we find the tertium comparationis between the Anatolian city-goddess, the potnia Aswiya (Pylos Fr. 1202; cf. Morris 2001, 135–38; Morris 2008, esp. 57) and Greek Artemis, so that the historical goddess could be named Artemis Ephesia.

37 On this, Rogers 2012 passim.

38 Susini 1955, 341–343 no. 1 fig. 1 (3–2. c. BC); on this cf. Wallensten 2011, 27. – The epithet was also carried by Hekate, for example in Lagina, which additionally strengthens the similarity of both deities. Cf. Laumonier 1958, 420 with n. 7; on Hekate Soteira in prophecy and magic: Johnston 1990.

39 Krinzinger 2021, 158. Gassner 1997, 58, already considered a connection with the processions to Ortygia.

40 Gassner 1997, 56–59 with cat.-no. 153–161 and pl. 81.

41 For the argumentation, extensively, Scherrer – Trinkl 2006, 20–22. – In spite of this, Ladstätter 2016, 247 and 249 fig. 11, referring to the original excavation report of Jobst 1983, 178–183, took up again the long obsolete (early) Hellenistic dating.

42 See above p. 116 and n. 23 for the Greek text.

43 Knibbe 1991, 5–7.

44 Jobst 1983, esp. 225–229; Jobst 2005.

45 Nevertheless, he attempted (Knibbe 1991, 9f.) a strange compromise with a later recontextualisation of the altar to a "cenotaph of L. Verus and (Parthian) victory altar", without addressing the religio-political difficulties of such a new meaning. Decidedly against a Parthian monument at this location, Oberleitner 2009, 412–415; recently, extensively on the location of the Parthian monument, Thür 2020a.

46 Jobst 1983, 215–236, esp. 229; Jobst 2005, esp. 175.

47 Hueber 1984, 23 n. 9. – Hueber 1997a, 262–264 and 269 with pl. 43 (equally Hueber 1997b, 84f.), instead of an altar structure, following H. Engelmann 1993a, proposed an interpretation as an auditorium (mentioned in IK 17/1, 3009), as place of legal trials of the Roman provincial administration; this is, however, probably to be identified in the Neronian Hall with a tribunal in its northern area, on this cf. Scherrer – Trinkl 2006, 36–38.

48 Jobst 2005, 175.

49 Hueber 1997b, 90. – We are most grateful to F. Hueber for his friendly verbal information to P. Scherrer regarding the form of the clamp holes employed, during one of our numerous conversations about and on the "Lower Embolos".

50 See now Thür 2005, 155f. (with further bibliographic data). – Rejecting Thür's interpretation of the altar, Burrell 2009, 83-86, who with Jobst assumes a construction of the altar after the so-called Hadrian's Gate and, with Engelmann and Hueber, furthermore assumes a function as an auditorium.

51 Thür 2005, 360f. figs. 4f.

52 Thür 2005 (cf. esp. p. 357 and 362), did not include the meander blocks in her reconstruction due to their

findspot elsewhere, yet did indicate that there would be enough room for them.

53 First Bammer 1967, 10–22; Bammer 1966/67, Beibl. 22–43; a selection, in addition: Bammer 1984, 130–139; Muss 1984; Muss – Bammer – Büyükkolancı 2001, esp. 45–54. 96–99; Bammer 2008; Muss 2018; Bammer – Muss 2021, 125.

54 The entire older discussion in the literature assembled at Thür 2005, 156f. – cf. e.g. in particular: Lauter 1966, 119; Ridgway 1974, 15f.; Ridgway 1976, 82; Bol 1998, 42 and 181f.; summarising: Weißl 2002.

55 Alzinger 1980, 826; Scherrer 1990, 92–98. – Bammer employed the converse argumentation, namely, that the *Ara Pacis* is dependent on the late Classical altar of the Artemision.

56 On this, see p. 119 with nn. 32f. Engelmann 1993, 87, states that additional, similar column drums in close proximity to the altar are present in Late Antique structures.

57 Knibbe – Engelmann 1984, 142f. Inv. 4369. The dating is approximately determined due to the mentioning of Vedia Papiane.

58 IK 14, 1351 (the commentary speaks about vandalism, but the elaborated inscription reports much more an action supported or even carried out by the city's officials). On this, already Knibbe 1991, 12; cf. also Thür 1989, 19 and 129–131, who nevertheless preferred to see this as a reference to a statue on Hadrian's Gate.

59 Transl. by M. Hafner (Univ. of Graz).

60 Thür 2005, 360f. figs. 4f.

61 Plin. n. h. XXXIV 53: *venere autem in certamen laudatissimiquamquam diversis aetatibus geniti, quoniam fecerant Amazonas, quae cum in templo Dianae Ephesiae dicarentur, placuit eligi probatissimam ipsorum artificum qui praesentes erant iudicio, cum apparuit, eam esse quamomnes secundam a sua quisque iudicassent; haec est Polycliti, proxuma ab ea Phidiae, tertia Cresilae, quarta Cydonis, quinta Phradmonis.*
Plin. n.h. XXXIV 75: *Cresilas (fecit) el Amazonem volneratam.* Cf. on this also Luk. imag. 4: (τῶν Φειδίου ἔργων τί μάλιστα ἐπήνεσας; … τὴν Ἀμαζόνα τὴν ἐπερειδομένην τῷ δορατίῳ. – Luk., imag. 6: ἔτι καὶ στόματος ἁρμογὴν ὁ αὐτός (Φειδίας) καὶ τὸν αὐχένα, παρὰ τῆς Ἀμαζόνος λαβών (παρέξει).

62 The traditional number of five Amazons was questioned by Weber 2008, since only three types exist in Roman copies; this, however, could be related to the fact that only three were also set up as copies in Athens, whence they were disseminated into the Roman world.

63 On the traditional names of the Amazons cf. Fischer 2010, esp. 19–22.

64 IK 17/2, 5115: † δέρκε[ο πῶς] κόσμησε τόσοις χρυσαυγέσιν ἔργοις [τόσῳ χρυσαυγέι μόχθῳ] καὶ Σ[τέφανο]ς Πτελέην καὶ Πτελέη Στέφανον †. For Ptelee see also IK 12, 286, a statue of Antoninus (Pius?) by the artist Dorotheos.

65 Kall. Dian. 237–247. Translation (Fischer 2020, 18 n. 10): "The Amazons, who clamour for war, have once erected a wooden cult image to you at the foot of an oak trunk in Ephesos lying on the coast, Hippo has completed the sanctuary."

66 Hyg. fab. 223 and 225; 2nd c. AD.

67 Cf. for this also Herakleid. Lemb. 66.

68 Plin. n. h. V 115.

69 How Haimon, the ancestor of the Thessalians (Hesych. s.v. Haimonia) slid into Plinius' list remains a mystery. Thus, this name has sometimes be altered by editors to *Samornion* is a reference to Samos, where Androklos may have stayed a while before founding Ephesos. One might assume that Plinius confused the hill called Hermaion, in the very West of the city (plan 2; cf. Benndorf 1898, 19–21), with Haimonion. – The name Tracheia may well have slid into Plinius´ text, if he had used Strabon as his source.

70 Strab. XIV 1, 4. – Additional later authors with similar statements, above all Stephanos of Byzantium, collected at Fischer 2010, 22.

71 Cf. Fleischer 2002, esp. 187. 194. 197; Fischer 2010, 19f.

72 Bammer – Muss 2021, 124: "In these free-standing images, nonetheless, the danger that the Amazons can bring is not (any longer) represented, but instead their vulnerability and their need for protection in the asylum of the temples, that is granted to them after the battles with the Greek heroes." – In general on the meaning of the Amazons seeking supplication in Ephesos: Fleischer 2002; Hölscher 2000.

73 Comprehensively on this, see Quatember 2017 (on the friezes esp. 110–125). – See also pp. 183–195.

74 On the interpretation of the friezes in the so-called Temple of Hadrian see below, pp. 182–194.

75 See above, pp. 50f.

The Embolos – a walk of fame

1 Athenaios VIII 62 (p. 361c–e); translation mainly following Olson 2020. – On the broadly disseminated ancient foundation myths with fish and/or death of a boar, cf. Scherrer 2014; cf. also now for the foundation myth of Virunum, Zimmerman 2021, who transfers its creation to the period of the 2nd Sophistic. The narrative material was also frequently used for the foundations of mediaeval monasteries, e.g. the Bavarian Kremsmünster in 777 in today's Upper Austria, pointing to the non-historical son of Duke Tassilo III named Gunther, who was killed by a boar while hunting, as the occasion for the founding.

2 FGrH 417. See also on Kreophylos of Ephesos: Jacoby 1922, col. 1710.

3 See for the different locations: Scherrer 2007, 347.

4   Ladstätter 2016, 237 and 256; on this, see pp. 92–96.

5   Hdt. 1, 26,

6   Fröhlich 2022, 299.

7   Ladstätter 2016, 261, however, assumes that the term λίμην only indicated civil harbours, whereas military harbours – as Strab. XIV 1, 24, for Ephesos – always were indicated by the term νηορία. Such a distinction, however, cannot be assumed as doctrinaire in the literature. But this distinction is probably not of great importance as we do not know for certain if there were two harbours in the city of Lysimachos at all, one for commerce and one for war ships, or only one harbour, which served for all needs.

8   Strab. XIV 1, 4.

9   The different editors and their comments do not agree whether it said (at the end of the text): νῦν (the recent city) or ποτε (the former city, see manuscript F), which was changed to τότε in the edition of Meineke 1895.

10   Strab. XIV 1, 21 (for the Greek text see above, p. 75).

11   After 100 years of research, we now are certain about the fact that Koressos is only the harbour and the settlement nearby, but the mountain name was Tracheia; see Engelmann 1991, 286–291.

12   On the localisation, Scherrer – Trinkl 2006, 60f., with previous literature.

13   Miller 2019, esp. 19–44.

14   See above, pp. 86–88. – Engelmann 1991, 278–280 attempted to explain the reference to the gymnasium as marginalia that had slipped into the text; at the time of the publication of his article the gymnasium of the gerousia was still not an issue. Strabo must have inserted the reference himself, however, because during his time this gymnasium was already built and probably connected to the new *Aqua Iulia*, financed by Augustus himself. On the privileges of the gerousia at this period, see above, pp. 88 and 119.

15   On this, see pp. 139f. with n. 49.

16   See pp. 82f. and 139f.

17   Such wells, chronologically prior to the early imperial residences, have recently been published: Waldner 2020, 109–128 (well at the north-west corner of the Terrace House 2, room WT 2, directly behind the Hypelaios); Thür 2014, 197 and 201f. (Terrace House 2, dwelling unit 6, courtyard:); Rathmayr 2016, 144 (Terrace House 2, dwelling unit 7); Lang-Auinger 1996, 176 (Terrace House 1, Atrium).

18   On the Triodos, see pp. 111–117.

19   Curtius 1872, 35f.

20   Russo 1999, 34f. figs. 12–19, for the rebuilding of the heroon, according to the barrier plaques, states, "Ma la datazione non anteriore alla metà circa del VI sec. …". Thür 1999a, 117, pointed to the 5th c. AD.

21   Cf. also H. Thür, in: Scherrer 2000, 128.

22   Thür 1995, esp. 63; there, also p. 80f. for the research history. The older dating proposals, up until the inves-

tigation by H. Thür, preferred a time range from the Augustan period to the mid-1st c. AD.

23   For an extensive description of the building, see Thür 1995, 82–88; with the additions proposed by Strocka 2011, 304f., the structure would be even slightly taller.

24   Thür 1995, 85. Thür also at first published the opinion that the water duct leading under the building was part of the original layout, but – as she informed us orally – the Hellenistic water supply must have looked very different. Her new publication (in preparation) will discuss that problem extensively, see for now Thür 2020b, 405.

25   Cf. Kader 1995, 216f.

26   Thür 1995, 88f.

27   Thür 1995, 91–97 (quotation on p. 97).

28   Berns 2003, 193 (2nd half of 2nd c. BC); cf. Thür 2009, 20.

29   The detailed investigation of the stratigraphically relevant pottery by Waldner 2020, 57, resulted in "isolated fragments of Pergamene appliqué ware, that appears in Ephesos first after the end of the 2nd c. B.C." To this fits the observation on p. 59 (similarly also on p. 62): "Noteworthy … is the almost complete absence of vessels of Eastern Sigillata A (ESA), which in Ephesos is represented at the earliest after the last quarter of the 2nd c. BC." – Her relativisation of the dating on p. 88f., with a frequently repeated assumption of a repositioning at least once or even many times of the very small pieces of the finds, however, is not comprehensible, leading her to an overall evaluation of the foundation levelling and an "erection of the heroon in the 2nd quarter up until the middle of the 1st c. BC." (p. 89). The small pieces of the finds, however, were probably due not to frequent repositioning, but rather due to conscious choice or smashing, since the foundation indeed needed to consist of a dense packing. Large, bulky pottery fragments would have been highly counterproductive.

30   Thür 1995, 97–99. – For the Temple of Hadrian, cf. Quatember 2017, for frieze block A esp. 116f. and pp.180–186.

31   Thür 1995, 89 and 99 with fig. 26, interprets the biga as a battle chariot and a recourse to the colonial period. Cf. already, however, the heroic chariot ride of the deceased ruler in the late 5th c. BC at the Heroon of Trysa (where horses and chariot nevertheless remain in a horizontal position) at Landskron 2016, 203–206 pl. 163–166 (with numerous comparative examples).

32   Thür 1995, 102, was on the way to this addition, but did not take the final step of naming the building as the city fountain, probably because the interpretation as an Androkloneion distorted her view. Differently, H. Thür, in: Scherrer 1995, 128 [= Scherrer 2000, 128]; similarly, Thür 2009, 16. For criticism of the attribution of the frieze as a representation of the myth of Androklos (absence of a boar), cf. Strocka 2011, 307.

33   All of the archaeological, numismatic, and epigraphic evidence for Ephesos at Rathmayr 2010. Notewor-

thy thereby is the frequent presence of Androklos in bath-gymnasia, which indeed always constituted a historical background with pedagogical claims.

34 Paus. VII 2, 8–9. – On this, cf. also the extensive commentary of Thür 1995, 63–65, and Fischer 2010, 22–26 (with numerous additional literary, numismatic, and epigraphic evidence).

35 For the translation of this special section about the route "in direction to the Olympieion" see Scherrer 1999.

36 Strab. XIV 1, 3.

37 Pausanias as a sophist: Von Wilamowitz-Moellendorf 1928, 156; more elaborate now Plattner 2022, esp. 201–210.

38 Paus. VII 2, 7. – On this, see also above, pp. 124–126, and pp. 183–194.

39 The localisation is intensely discussed in the scholarship and is dependent, on the one hand, on how one interprets Pausanias' phrase, on the route "to the Olympieion" or "past the Olympieion", and, on the other hand, whether one wants to recognise the large, Hadrianic, neocorate temple in the harbour plain as the Olympieion or not; on this, cf. Scherrer 1999. The older, already outdated interpretation that, in addition to the huge Hadrianic temple there was an additional (very much older) temple to Zeus Olympios, is taken up again by Burrell 2003, 46–49.

40 Thür 1995, 77–79 and 102f. The tumulus lay most likely on the long strip of land of the Tracheia projecting into the sea; by Thür 1995, 78, it is connected with the so-called acropolis hill (plan 1 no. 100) opposite the stadium.

41 Pherekydes is not precisely datable; he probably wrote in the later 5th and early 4th c. BC. His construction of the sons of Kodros as founders of numerous cities of Asia Minor is nevertheless purely fictional and subordinated to the Athenian foreign policy of this period. Androklos was probably originally called Androkles and was most likely Messenian; in any event he came with his people from the Peloponnese, which is supported by diverse names of phylai, chyliasties, and personal names in Ephesos, and sanctuaries for Zeus Mainalos, Zeus Patroos, and Apollon Patroos. – For an overview, cf. already Toepffer 1894.

42 Thür 1995, 103. – Not without interest for the dating is the epigram, investigated by Fischer 2010, of Antipatros (2nd c. BC) on Androklos with a description of the most beautiful buildings, probably written around 130 BC.

43 Thür 1995, 71–74; Rathmayr 2010, 22 - 24 (IK 12, 501, base of a statue of Androklos; IK 13, 644, donations of oil on "Androklos' Day"; IK 17/2, 4371, "Androkloneion"). – In addition, an architrave with the beginning of an inscription ANΔPO... comes from Terrace House 1 (IK 15, 1943); this architrave was perhaps walled in over the door to the plaza on the street side. For the building evidence also Thür 1997a,

19–21. – Did the sacred olive tree perhaps once stand in the middle of this small plaza, in the shade of which the celebrations could favourably take place?

44 For the stratigraphically appraisable pottery, cf. Outschar 1997.

45 On the results and a dating in the later 3rd c. BC: Thür 1999, 423; see also Thür 2020b, 402f. – Strocka 2005, 347f. figs. 25f., dates the lions' head discovered, similar to Belevi, in the first half of the 3rd c. BC.

46 On the stratigraphic situation and the finds, cf. Waldner 2020, 31–39.

47 Meadows 2013, 9.

48 See above, pp. 80–84.

49 On this, Ladstätter 2016, 252. One could only collect water in cisterns or at best fetch it from the gorges which were very difficult to access. On the geological situation Rantitsch – Prochaska 2011, 250f.

50 See above p. 101 with n. 54. – The ensemble is also briefly discussed by Ladstätter 2016, 262f.

51 Suggestions for the dating are given by Wilberg 1923a, esp. 262 (2nd c. BC.), and Alzinger 1974, 70f. and 146 (2nd/1st c. BC, in any case "older than the Octagon"); Thür 2020b, 401–403 (3rd c. BC, because of the supposed connection with a Lysimachian aqueduct).

52 Cf. below, p. 174.

53 Atalay – Türkoğlu 1972/75, esp. 123f. with n. 1 (circumstances of the discovery without very precise localisation; the "thin layer of cement" mentioned here on the head is somewhat enigmatic, perhaps this is instead rather a layer of sinter), and 129–142 (on the significance).

54 Lichtenberger – Nieswandt – Salzmann 2008, 399 no. 11 (with additional bibliography); Kovacs 2018, 155 n. 143 (with additional bibliography): "Even though the identification with the Diadochoi [scil. Lysimachos] ... as before is contested and for now cannot be confirmed, the dating of the head in the 1st quarter of the 3rd c. BC is not to be doubted ...".

55 H. = 0.42 m (including a preserved portion of the neck).

56 On the rebuilding works in the 5th/6th c. AD, often not precisely datable in detail, cf. Thür 1991; Waldner 2020.

57 In agreement also Lichtenberger – Nieswandt – Salzmann 2008, 394 n. 40.

58 See above, pp. 86–88.

59 Strocka 2011, 303f., thought on the upper area of the ground floor wall. In contrast, H. Thür wrote in a personal communication (E-Mail of 7. Sept. 2022) to the authors: "Strocka was correct that the weapon reliefs belong to the fountain; yet they could not – as he proposes – belong to the uppermost level of the Doric ground floor storey, since there the architectural elements are 80 cm tall. They fit very well, however, as parapet plaques at the east and west side of the Ionic upper storey."

60 Strocka 2011, 298–307.

61 Fundamentally: Polito 1998; cf. also Grüßinger 2001, esp. 147f.

62 Cf. also Strocka 2011, 307. The actual affiliation has to be examined in the context of an architectonic reconstruction.

63 See above, p. 141 with n. 53.

64 Cf. above, p. 179; on the portrait, Aurenhammer 1997.

65 For a possible localisation, cf. Thür 1997c and below, pp. 178f. – See also Schörner 2007, 252f. Kat. A 25.

66 Thuk. hist. II 43, 2; on Aristion IK 17/1, 3217 (cf. Thür 1997, 150).

67 Hegesander at Athenaios I 18a about Kassandros, who at the age of 35 was still not yet successful at this; on this, Seyer 2007, 142.

68 Paus. Damasc. FHG IV 470 fr. 4 (= FGrHist III C, 854, F 10).

69 On the assimilation of Androklos, and other youthful mythical city founders, to Alexander cf. also Rathmayr 2010, 42.

70 Von Graeve 1970, esp. 124–138 with pl. 36–38. According to V. v. Graeve (p. 136–138) the type was first created for the representation of Alexander as a mounted hunter based on Oriental prototypes. Cf. on this, Seyer 2007, esp. 99f. and 117f., as well as his discussion (p. 104 and 140) of the hunting frescoes in the tomb at Vergina, which is attributed to Philippos II or Philippos III Arrhidaios; esp. also the lion hunt anecdote in Curtius Rufus VIII 1, 18, whereby Alexander was forbidden in future to hunt lions alone and on foot (extensively interpreted at Seyer 2007, 106f.), while the battle against the lion on foot is still impressively represented on the hunting mosaic from Pella (Alexander and Lysimachos doing battle against the lion?; cf. Seyer 2007, 106f.).

71 Cf. on the significance of the lion hunt for Lysimachos as a successor of Alexander, and his coinage: Seyer 2007, 126–133.

72 See extensively above, pp. 50f., and pp. 151f.

73 A good overview of the state of research at that time at Scherrer – Trinkl 2006, 149–164. Empty burial pits were, e.g., found underneath the Terrace Houses, below the foundations of the circular building with water feature which can be described as the south-east corner of the Tetragonos Agora, and most recently on the street to the Prytaneion (so-called Clivus Sacer) directly to the north of the State Agora (on this, Ladstätter – Steskal. – Yazıcı 2018, 16). – It would be interesting to know if also the third street leading from Pygela from the west to the Triodos (the so-called Ortygia Street) also featured such burials, but here relevant excavations are lacking.

74 For the problematic interpretation of "emptied graves" on a general level see Brent 2020. The destruction of tombs and removal of skeletons inside the city boundaries in Roman cities by officials was regulated in the charter like the one for the colonia Genetiva Iulia Urso in Spain (lex Ursonensis § 73). Similar regulations may have existed in Greek cities in the East of the Roman Empire as well, cf. Schörner 2007, 14–16 and 18.

75 See for a discussion on this topic pp. 201f.

76 Schörner 2007, 209–288, lists only 29 secured graves with archaeological records from early Archaic to Roman Imperial times, and the same number for additional epigraphic or literary terstimonials.

77 Plut. Aratos 53, 2f. – Cf. Schörner 2007, 14f. and 75.

78 For the actual honorific or heroic tombs of particularly deserving individuals sanctioned in Greek cities see Schörner 2007, esp. 20–34; for Hellenistic and Roman (till the early 3rd c. AD) poleis in Asia minor, frequently in connection with the agora, but also near the bouleuterion, the theatre or gymnasia-baths-complexes see also Cormack 2004, 37–49, for the locations esp. p. 44f.; cf. also Strocka 2009, 252f.

79 See on this pp. 23–26.

80 Serv. Aen. XI 206. – This law was even valid for vestals who were accused of unchastidy and sentenced to death; see for that Bätz 2012, 165–286; Fröhlich 2022, 302–307.

81 For the epigram of a certain Damagetes see p. 22.

82 Essential preparatory work for the connection between hero cult and water in Ephesos has already been carried out by Thür 1995c; Thür 1997b; Thür 2020b.

83 For the financing of the agora and the buildings at the State Agora primarily by imperial freedmen and the local conventus civium Romanorum cf. Scherrer 2007a.

84 IK 15, 1522.

85 For the transformation of the Gymnasium of the Neoi into an imperial cult centre cf. Thür 2007a.

86 On the stratigraphic dating: Scherrer – Trinkl 2006, 32; on the terrace wall, cf. p. 121 with n. 41.

87 The relatively soft mortar consisting of almost pure, smeary lime in the opus caementicium core is the same that was also used in other areas of the Augustan agora (Scherrer – Trinkl 2006, 34). Miltner 1956–58, 50, describes the same mortar for the circular building on the Bülbüldağ (see pp. 162f.).

88 The original impression of the location of the structure was altered after the earthquake of 23 AD with the subsequent construction of the so-called Neronian Hall along the Marble Street that extended ca. 3 m further to the east compared to the original agora site. Due to its extending into the urban space, precisely at the starting point of the new Augustan city grid towards the west and the north, Scherrer – Trinkl 2006, 35 interpreted the building as a symbolic groma; in agreement, Thür 2009, 17; against this, Groh 2006, 76 n. 92, who wants to recognise a different street grid. Hueber 1984, 9, thought that the circular building was completely dismantled with the erection of the Neronian Hall, but then it would be inexplicable how almost its entire architectural inventory should have remained preserved for 600 years.

89 In the older literature, the circular building was viewed as Hellenistic, cf. Jobst 1983, esp. 184–190. 197f. (He-

roon); Hueber 1984, 9; Hueber 1997a, 267; Hueber 1997b, 71–73 figs. 88–90 (water clock); H. Thür, in: Scherrer 2000, 136–138 with fig. 137/1.

90 The claimed Lysimachean (cf. Wiplinger 2006a) or at least Hellenistic aqueduct, thereby a precursor of the late Augustan *Aqua Throessitica*, at Wiplinger 2006, 23–25 (cf. on this also Ladstätter 2016, 251 with figs. 14f) is devoid of any argumentation for such an early date. The culvert beaten into the city wall for the *Aqua Throessitica*, from its building style (cf. at Ladstätter 2016, 251 fig. 14, the method of the joints, the employment of thin stone plaques instead of massive ashlar blocks at the lower corner of all places, etc.) clearly reveals a late origin; also a Hellenistic date for the aqueduct bridges, not closely investigated and apparently built from ashlars without mortar (Ladstätter 2016, 252 fig. 15) is not substantiated.

91 IK 12, 401. – Since Augustus is named alone as the building's patron, a date for the *Aqua Iulia* before 4 AD appears fairly certain, since the second Augustan long-distance aqueduct, the *Aqua Throessitica* (cf. IK 12, 402), co-financed by C. Sextilius Pollio, expressly names Tiberius as co-regent (on this, see p. 163). – Whether the water conduit ran down over the Embolos or coursed along the Marble Street needs first to be confirmed. It is quite possible that the spring house – perhaps Augustan from the building technique – above the mountain village of Şirince constitutes the origin of this aqueduct; on this, see Forchheimer 1923, 238–243; Wiplinger 2006, 25f.; Ersoy 2006, 44 with fig. 7.

92 A close parallel – also in time – is provided by the construction of an aqueduct in Nicopolis in Syria (ca. 21–30 AD); CIL III 6703: *[Ti(berius) Caesa]r Imp(erator) divi Aug(usti) f(ilius) Augustus divi Iuli n(epos) / [pontif(ex)] maxim(us) co(n)s(ul) IIII tr(ibunicia) potest(ate) / [aquam] Augustam Nicopoli[m] adducendam curavit / [cur(ante) Cn(aeo)] Saturnino leg(ato) Cae[s]aris Augusti.*

93 On this discussion and a probable supply of the gymnasium of the gerousia – at that time assumed in front of the theatre, now to the west of the agora – by the *Aqua Iulia* cf. already Scherrer 2006b, 45–47. Naturally, also the supply of the commercial agora with the necessary fresh water would have to have been considered.

94 At that time, good construction progress must have been made on the *Aqua Throessitica* (6 km in length), even when it was first opened later. – The *Aqua Iulia* had a length of 8 km, if it was fed by the spring near Şirince, and it eventually had a channel to the Artemision that was diverted in the Byzantine period to the Ayasoluk with the Church of St John; on this, cf. Wiplinger 2006, 22–26.

95 Cf. Longfellow 2011, 61–76, esp. 74; Rathmayr 2014, 324.

96 Thür 1996, 15, for the pottery from the affiliated building levels, states a date in the late 1st c. BC; according

to Waldner 2020, 108, the find material belongs to the second half of the 1st c. BC.

97 Thür 1996, 14f. figs.7–9; Thür 1999, 424.

98 Cf. on this also Berns 2003, 44f. and 194; Waldner 2020, 106–108.

99 Eichler 1966, 593f., saw that both of the plaques fitted together back to back, and wavered between an identification as a base or as an altar. Alzinger 1974, 21, concluded that they belonged to a statue base.

100 Eichler 1966, 594; A. Bernhard-Walcher, in: Oberleitner et al. 1978, 111 cat.-no. 152.

101 Eichler 1966, 595–597, does not mention the female figure in a mantle.

102 Eichler 1966, 595.

103 IK 12, 253: Αὐτοκράτορι Καίσαρι θεοῦ υἱῶι καὶ Γαίωι Καίσαρι καὶ Λευκίωι Καίσαρι καὶ Μάρκωι Ἀγρίππαι Μάρκου υἱῶι / [---] τῶν τέκνων. – Especially the close similarities in decorative details to the Agora South Gate are mentioned by: Eichler 1966, 593f.; Alzinger 1974, 20f.; Krinzinger 2021, 159f.

104 Waldner 2020, 106, supposes a completion first "at the beginning of the 1st c. AD" based on the ceramic evidence; but this ought to be too late, due to the forms of the architectural ornament.

105 Cf. recently Waldner 2020, 109: "Whether the Hexagon arose originally based on the polygonal building form, as it were complementarily to or in competition with the Octagon adjacent to the west, or whether it itself provided the impetus for the polygonal ground plan of the neighbouring monument, cannot be ascertained with certainty, since the dating of the Hexagon within the second half of the 1st c. BC cannot be further narrowed down. A contemporary construction of both buildings can also not be ruled out. The question of the original commissioner or sponsor of the Hexagon can equally not be definitively answered" ("Ob das Hexagon ursprünglich in Anlehnung an die polygonale Bauform und gewissermaßen komplementar oder in Konkurrenz zu dem westlich anschließenden Oktogon entstand oder seinerseits impulsgebend für den polygonalen Grundriss des benachbarten Monuments war, ist nicht mit letzter Sicherheit zu ermitteln, da die Datierung des Hexagons innerhalb der zweiten Hälfte des 1. Jahrhunderts v. Chr. nicht klar eingegrenzt werden kann. Auch eine gleichzeitige Errichtung beider Bauten ist nicht auszuschließen. Ebenso wenig lässt sich die Frage nach dem ursprünglichen Auftraggeber oder Stifter des Hexagons beantworten").

106 It is almost impossible to evaluate the time management, from planning to completion, of the numerous Augustan buildings in Ephesos and the capacity of the available building workshops. In any event, according to a few stratigraphic pieces of evidence on the rear side, the Octagon was probably first completed towards the end of the 1st c. BC, as was the South Gate

of the Agora, although here work was certainly carried out under greater pressure.

107 Also, Krinzinger 2021, 160, and Spanu 2020, 385, stressed this issue.

108 Still in 10/9 BC their own honorific inscriptions were set up for Livia and both Iuliae on the Magdalensberg in Noricum by the Norican *civitates* (a fourth inscription for Augustus is uncertain); cf. Šašel 1967, 70–74.

109 Serapeum Stele Paris, LV 335; vgl. auch Plut. Caesar 49, 10; Cass. Dio IL 41, 1.

110 A daughter and two sons of Kleopatra by Marcus Antonius were brought to Rome and brought up by Octavia, the sister of Octavian and widow of Marcus Antonius.

111 Cicero already compared Octavian, probably at the latter's wishes, with Alexander: see Cic. phil. III 14, V 28, V 44, V 48, 1XIII 25. – In the summer of 30 BC, Octavian visited the grave of Alexander in Alexandria and touched his corpse, whereby Alexander's magical powers should be transferred to him (Sueton. Aug. 18, 1; supplemental, Cass. Dio LI 16, 5; on this Kienast 1969, 450–452). Fundamentally on Alexander as role model for Augustus: Kienast 1969; cf. also Kienast 1982, esp. 28. 64. 213. 282. 285. 377.

112 Von Hesberg 2003, 52–57.

113 Cf. the roughly contemporary claims by Aphrodisias in Caria, which were invented or at least strongly supported by C. Iulius Zoilos, a freedman of Octavian/Augustus, to be a sister-city of Rome, because the city's patron goddess Aphrodite was indeed the mother of Aeneas. – On the close relationship between Octavian and Zoilos, cf. Reynolds 1982, esp. 96–99, document 10; Smith 1993, 4–13.

114 There could have been, nevertheless, a Latin version of the inscription set up at other locations, similarly as at the South Gate of the agora.

115 Vitr. VII 1, 4. – On the early examples from Pompeii cf. Blake 1930, 109 and pl. 26 no. 4 (Casa del Centenario, with a simple honeycomb pattern as surface decoration). – In Pergamon (Oecus in the Peristyle House II, to the west of the Lower Agora) an example of honeycomb decoration can be found already in the Julio-Claudian period, presumably after the earthquake of 17 AD; cf. Scheibelreiter-Gail 2011, 341–344.

116 Woytek 422f. no. 470v pl. 94; Sestertius (cos VI) 112/114, RIC 631. 632, Strack 438.

117 On the villa and the mosaic: Ehmig 2005; Hornung 2008/2011. – The role of the hexagon and the mosaic as the architects' measure for the whole building is represented perhaps in somewhat exaggerated fashion, given all the existing irregularities in the mosaic; see Krumme 2021.

118 Brown 1939, 286f. emphasizes the otherwise not verifiable appearance of the motif also in a number of roof constructions of the sanctuaries at Baalbek, and derives the motif from the Bel cult in Palmyra; he sees a "planetarium" with 6 planets circling around the main planet. On this, cf. also Hajjar 1977, esp. 280f.

119 Schütz 1991, 55f.

120 Arist. phys. III. c. 1.

121 Varro rust. III 16, 5. Translation following Hales 2001, 1.

122 Hales 2001, esp. 1f. (on the history of the problem).

123 The background was probably his own secluded life on his manor in the Sabine hills after the proscription by Marcus Antonius and the pardon by Octavian in 43 BC until his death in 27 BC.

124 On the life of Varro cf. Lehmann 2018.

125 Karwiese 1995, 152–164. 168–184. 197–207.

126 IK 16, 2109; in general, on the priestesses named *Melissa* cf. Fritz 1931, esp. 526. In addition, around 100 AD the female name Melissa is attested in the Ephesian upper classes, apparently a priestesses' name referring to service at the temple: IK 12, 508.

127 On the end of the function of the *Megabyzos* in the Augustan period, Bremmer 2006, § 1 (text with n. 23–29), who indicates that Strab. XIV 1, 23, mentions the *Megabyzos* already in the past.

128 The *Neopoiai*, later *Neopoioi*, were already mentioned in inscriptions in 302, that is in the first phase of rulership of Lysimachos over Ephesos (IK 15, 1449) and appear up until the late imperial period (e.g. IK 14, 1044). On the office, cf. Dignas 2002, 192f.

129 Karwiese 1995, 14.

130 Paus. VIII 13, 1: "In the territory of Orchomenos, on the left of the road from Anchisiai, there is on the slope of the mountain the sanctuary of Artemis Hymnia. The Mantineans, too, share it . . . a priestess also and a priest. It is the custom for these to live their whole lives in purity, not only sexual but in all respects, and they neither wash nor spend their lives as do ordinary people, nor do they enter the home of a private man. I know that the "entertainers" of the Ephesian Artemis live in a similar fashion, but for a year only, the Ephesians calling them Essenes. They also hold an annual festival in honor of Artemis Hymnia." – Cf. Bremmer 2006, § 4 (part of text with n. 77–89).

131 Gruben 1997, 393–402 and 413.

132 Kirbihler 2016, esp. 204f. 218f. 348–350.

133 Schütz 1990, 446–448; Schütz 1991, 62f.

134 Cass. Dio IL 8, 1; comp. Hekster – Rich 2006, 154.

135 Prop. II 31, describing the inner room of the temple: "And between his mother and sister, the Pythian god himself strums as he sings" (Translation: D. R. Slavitt 2002).

136 Sueton. Aug. 5: *Natus est Augustus M. Tullio Cicerone C. Antonio conss. XIIII. Kal. Octob., paulo ante solis exortum, regione Palati, ad Capita Bubula, ubi nunc sacrarium habet, aliquanto postquam excessit constitutum.*

137 Columella rust. 5.

138 King 2010, esp. 457f.

139 Tac ann. III 61. – Translation by A.-J. Church – W. J. Brodribb – S. Bryant.

140 On this see pp. 179–195.

141 On Pergamon: Raeck 1993; Schowalter 1998, esp. 240f.; on the meaning of the reliefs in the pronaos

142 and a theoretical conception of the lost cult image in the so-called Temple of Hadrian in Ephesos according to coin images, see pp. 193–195.

142 On the type, cf. Von Hesberg 1992, esp. 124–138.

143 The fundamental publication of Alzinger – Bammer 1971 supersedes in many ways; cf. also Alzinger 1974, esp. 16–20; for the total reconstruction Outschar 1990.

144 Alzinger 1974, 65.

145 IK II 403.

146 On the identification cf. Broughton 1952, 410; Wiseman, ClQ 17, 1967, 164ff.; Alzinger 1974, 18f.; with caution Outschar 1990, 84f. n. 100; Halfmann 2001, 27; in contrast, Tuchelt 1979, 110ff.; sceptically, Kirbihler 2016, 99f. with n. 259.

147 See above pp. 146–148.

148 Until now, only an immigrant from Delos (?) during the Tibero-Claudian period is known; cf. Kirbihler 2016, 311 and 349f.

149 Alzinger 1974; Mallio 2010, no. 3, who argues for a date of the togati "at the turn of the 1st c. AD".

150 Mallios 2010, no. 3.

151 On the allegorical frieze of the Zoilos tomb (ca. 20 BC) in Aphrodisias, with virtues (Andreia, Time, and Aion are preserved) and civic personifications (demos and polis of Aphrodisias as well as Rome), Smith 1993, esp. 14–23.

152 See for that pp. 68–70.

153 Outschar 1990, 84f.: 3rd or 4th quarter of the 1st c. BC, but most likely after 34 BC and before the South Gate (3 BC); U. Outschar, in: Scherrer 2000, 98, argued for the 3rd quarter of the 1st c. BC, whereby only the time between 34 and ca. 25 BC came into question. Alzinger 1974, 125, emphasises for example the coinciding form of the cymation with the Temple of Augustus at Antiochia ad Pisidiam, and recognises a prototype for the heart cymation in the socle of the Ara Pacis.

154 This also makes speculation about a construction around the middle of the 1st c. BC as recently by Spanu 2010, 56 (repeated by Lafli – Buora in 2023, esp. 64), obsolete. An attribution of the monument to the father C. Memmius, who is only mentioned in the inscription in the filiation, as the initiator of a monument for his deceased son, lacks any plausibilitiy.

155 On this, extensively, Outschar 1990, 57–65.

156 On this, see pp. 160–162.

157 Alzinger 1974, 18; Outschar 1990, 85 n. 100. – Strocka 2009, 253, expressed doubts, as a grave chamber is lacking. Roman senators at this time, however, hardly were buried in sarcophagi and tomb chambers, but in urns, which could be located in a small wall niche and then walled in within these.

158 Proposed recently again by Lafli – Buora 2023, 63. For the difficulties of such a reading see already Spanu 2010, 64.

159 Similarly, already Outschar 1990, 84f. n. 100. – On the Pollio building, see pp. 163–168.

160 As postulated by Spanu 2010, 64.

161 Alzinger 1974, 149, sees on the one hand a mixture of "typically Greek structure" and "Roman façade appearance", yet emphasises on the other hand (p. 19) the triumphal-arch character of the monument and sees the elevation as "specifically Roman" (p. 150); he would like to see the architect as "in origin connected with the west" (p. 138). – Focussing on the Italian architectural features: Torelli 1988; Torelli 1997; 162–167; Spanu 2010, 57–59.

162 Bammer 1972–75; Bammer 2007, 57f.; Lafli – Buora 2023. – Rejecting this, for example, Halfmann 2001, 27 n. 85.

163 Appian hist. XII 61–63.

164 Cic. Flacc. 75. – See Schörner 2007, 78f. and 278 Kat. B 21.

165 Schörner 2007, 79f. and 280f. B 23.

166 Schörner 2007, 79f. and 281–283 B 24.

167 See pp. 168f.

168 On the political dominance of the *conventus civium Romanorum* and the Italians (partially probably vested with the lower *ius Italicum* than citizenship) in Ephesos in the Augustan period cf. Scherrer 2007a and Kirbihler 2016, passim, esp. 223–228.

169 Schowalter 2022, 141: "The tower [cf.: of Memmius] … was the focal point for people coming from any direction."

170 Bammer 1968–71, esp. 29 Fig. 1. 2a-b. 4; Alzinger 1974, 43 Fig. 34; see also pp. 67–70 with nn. 546f.

171 See pp. 60 and 67 n. 547.

172 See p. 49.

173 Niemann – Heberdey 1906; Alzinger 1974, 37–40; Rumscheid 1994, 165–169.

174 Niemann – Heberdey 1906, 143f. 165.

175 Keil 1964, 115f. – On P. Servilius Isauricus, now extensively Kirbihler 2011; Kirbihler 2016, 362f.

176 Alzinger 1974, 101.

177 Alzinger 1974, e.g. 71f. 100f. 140; in accordance also Rumscheid 1994, 169.

178 Gerkan 1921, 92 n. 2; it seems that nothing changed since then: Bozza 2020, 62, still counts the Memmius Monument, the Octagon and the round Monument on the Panayırdağ as the oldest ones in Asia Minor where *opus caementicium* was used. – Unfortunately, the precise composition or consistency of the mortar used at the Round Monument on the Panayırdağ is not documented.

179 Already Alzinger 1974, 94, compared the "brittle acanthus leaves" of the Round Monument with other Augustan buildings in Asia Minor. G. Niemann (Niemann – Heberdey 1906, 157) was already struck by a number of "Roman" elements on the building, but he did not draw the appropriate conclusions for the dating.

180 See above p. 158.

181 A. Bammer, in: Oberleitner et al. 1978, 99f.

182 The form of the acanthus leaves with their completely closed eyes in any event clearly speaks against a post-Augustan date.

183 On this see also Thür 1997b, 73.

184 On this, see above pp. 146–149.

185 Cf. Von Hesberg 1992, 138 and fig. 79.

186 Berns 2003, 199–202 cat.-no. 11A8, calls the monument a *tumulus*, but to obtain certainty about the exact outer form new investigations were needed.

187 Excavation report: Miltner, 1956, 49–53; further, on the building: Miltner 1958, 30; Alzinger 1974, 57f.; H. Thür, in Scherrer 2000, 154.

188 Miltner 1956, 50; Alzinger 1974, 58 (dating after 10 AD).

189 Cf. Alzinger 1974, 142, who sees conformities with the approximately contemporary Pollio building and who places the tomb in the circle of the western architectural schools (identified by him as Group A).

190 A fine and early example of the mind-set "Becoming Roman – Staying Greek", cf. Woolf 1994.

191 On the leading personalities of the Augustan and Tiberian periods in Ephesos cf. Kirbihler 2016, 403–427, on the Passalas esp. p. 427–431; the so-called Great Donor List from the period after the earthquake in 23 AD shows additional candidates, on this now extensively Kirbihler 2016, 436–449.

192 On C. Sextilius Pollio see Kirbihler 2016, 431–435, all epigraphical designations of his name compiled at p. 432.

193 On the aqueduct, consisting of a bundle of parallel laid clay pipes cf. Wiplinger 2006, 23–25, who nevertheless – without sound arguments – assumes an already (early) Hellenistic existence (how, e.g., should the aqueduct have previously functioned without the *pons* erected by Sextilius Pollio?); see also above n. 90 and 94. The building inscriptions of the aqueduct (IK 12, 402) and its bridge (IK 17/1, 3092) name Augustus and Tiberius as rulers; cf. on this Scherrer 2006b, 46f.; on Augustus as builder of this water conduit Horster 2001, esp. 194. 197. 205.

194 The building complex has never been more closely examined; its building elements that are recognisable today ought to belong broadly to the 2nd/3rd c. Already probably in the Augustan period, however, the complex replaced the Hellenistic Gymnasium of the Neoi (see p. 97), which had to be transferred to the east due to the new imperial cult centre and the prytaneion also erected here (cf. pp. 97f.).

195 On this now Kirbihler 2016, 436–449, on the donations by Sextilius Pollio and his family, totalling 8,000 denarii, esp. p. 438 and 449.

196 IK 12, 404; AE 1993, 1479.

197 IK 12, 405–407. Alzinger 1974, 28, wanted to connect the statue bases (IK 12, 407) found in the Varius Bath at the lower Embolos, with the Basilike Stoa.

198 IK 13, 717A.

199 Alzinger 1974, 66 and 138f.; cf. also Thür 1997b, 70–72.

200 Thür 1997b, 70f.; also, Strocka 1989, 79 n. 15, already conjectured a connection with a fountain.

201 Thür 2020b, 410.

202 See pp. 173f.

203 Alzinger 1974, 138f. and 143.

204 Bammer 1978–80, esp. 73–78.

205 Cf. Plattner – Schmidt-Colinet 2005, 249f.

206 Probably, as Thür 2023, 17f., has argued, this new aqueduct was bult by Tib. Claudius Aristion.

207 For these two public fountains see also below pp. 167. 200. 204. In any case it would have been logical to build the water-bearing channel along the South Street and from there send partitions into the baths east of the State Agora and into the fountains along the Domitian Lane.

208 Fleischer 1972.

209 Cf. e.g. Andreae, 1977; Andreae 1999, 162–177.

210 Thür 2007a, 85.

211 The entire history of research at Maschek 2008, 293–299.

212 Aurenhammer 1990, 174, refers to correspondences with the Claudian group from Baiae. Already Andreae 1977, 9, himself saw a dating ceiling up to the Augustan period. Andreae 1999, 161 and 177, saw the group as standing at "the transition from late Hellenistic to Roman art" and emphasised (p. 162 and 171) the stylistic relationship with the reliefs on the Memmius Monument. Summarising, Maschek 2008, 298, who proceeds from differing production dates of individual statues in the 2nd and 1st c. BC.

213 Cf. on this Andreae 1999, who, in his summary and discussion of Polyphemos–Odysseus monuments in the post-Classical period mainly lists Etrusco-Italic find spots; for the often-postulated Greco-Hellenistic prototypes for Ephesos, Sperlonga, Baiae and the Domus Aurea, he provides no evidence. However, in discussing the works by Athanodoros, Hagesandros, and Polydoros of Rhodos, Pollitt 1986, 126, says, "on balance it seems most reasonable to view the Sperlonga sculptures [and the Laokoon] as neither purely Hellenistic nor purely Roman but rather as exemplars of a mixed tradition which has been called 'the magnificent afterlife of the Hellenistic baroque'."

214 For this it would be important above all, for all of the fountains on the western side of the State Agora, also for the *hydrekdocheion* of Laecanius Bassus (78/79 AD) located much further to the south, to determine their affiliation to a specific aqueduct by excavation or analysis of the micronutrients in the water.

215 IK II 449.

216 See for this list pp. 163f. with n. 195.

217 Thür 2020b, 406–409. – see also pp. 165 and 200.

218 Indifferent to the problem of this close architectural connection, Schowalter 2022, 142: "... either the builders of the water basins saw their work as a complement to the Memmius Monument, or they showed very little regard for it ...".

219 Balty 1991, esp. 14f.

220 Cf. already Hueber 1997b, 74: [the South Gate] "is three-axled and its function as an entrance is accordingly formed like a funnel." And further (p. 76): "that it was built into an existing colonnade in the form of a funnel, was never free-standing, and can only be viewed as a portal design of the entrance to a market building." For the overall planning and integration, cf. Scherrer – Trinkl 2006, 29. – Burrell 2009, 74, refers again to the old triumphal arch theory and does not know the projecting wing structures; her work was, however, written without being aware of the fundamental excavation publication (Scherrer – Trinkl 2006). The revival of the old opinion that it was a free-standing triumphal or honorific gate (similarly also Krinzinger 2021, 158f.) is completely obsolete due to the now secure excavation evidence. Even if a function in the sense of an honorary monument was intended, the protruding wings would not have been unorthodox, as Spanu 2020, 383–385, emphasises; a good parallel is provided by the contemporary free-standing city gate of Ariminum with heavy round towers framing the three-arched-gate. But, of course, the Ephesian gate is a rare mixture of Hellenistic and Roman architectural features (Spanu 2020, 384f.).

221 On the complex building evidence Scherrer – Trinkl 2006, 30–34.

222 At the latest during the construction of the library, the eastern wing no longer existed; it could have been destroyed already during the earthquake of 23 AD. The connection of the gate pilaster is nevertheless still preserved today on the exterior wall of the South Gate.

223 On this, Scherrer – Trinkl 2006, 30–34. – Thür 1997a, 73f., and Spanu 2020, 383f., agreed with this interpretation of the chambers, while Strocka 2009, 253, as well as Krinzinger 2021, 158f., expressed doubt about the building evidence and accordingly its usage.

224 Cf. Lang 1984, 23f; Rose 1997, 172–174 no. 112. – On the role of the two, and other *liberti* of the imperial house in Ephesos, cf. Kirbihler 2016, 418–427.

225 IK 13, 851. – The style of writing of the name diverges slightly from the building inscription of the South Gate (IK 17/1, 3006); in this, Burrell 2009, 72 n. 14, recognised an indication that the attribution of the inscription to the tomb of Mithridates at the South Gate was "less likely", yet at the same time admitted that the misspelling *(Imb)erator* for Agrippa in the building inscription IK 17/1, 3006 overturned this argument again.

226 Cf. p. 97 with n. 30. On the following, cf. Scherrer – Trinkl 2006, 42.

227 Cf. Karwiese 1997a, 284 and 303f. with Profile 10 and figs. 29f. (Sondage 3/81).

228 IK 17/1, 3003.

229 IK 11, 20 line 19; on the family, especially Tib. Claudius Metrodorus and another brother Tib. Claudius Phei-

sinus, the first *archiereus* at the Domitianic imperial temple in 89/90 AD (IK 12, 232. 233. 238) cf. Halfmann 2001, 37; Kirbihler 2003, 465; Burrell 2009, 75–77; cf. also Kirbihler 2016, 254 and 438 (a priestess Claudia in the so-called Donors' List, perhaps our Metrodora?). In the Neronian period, the family apparently came to Ephesos from Teos, and Metrodora seems to have held a high office later in Chios.

230 Longfellow 2011; Rathmayr 2014.

231 On the first Ephesian neokoros, Friesen 1973; the argumentation of Burrell 2004, 59–66, who revisits the earlier theory of a neokoros under Nero, and sees its renewal under Domitian, is unconventional.

232 On the probable timeframe in which the first neokoros was awarded, 82–84 AD, cf. Friesen 1993, 29–49; Dräger 1993, 122–136; Halfmann 2001, 40.

233 On the state of research on the temple and altar cf. Pohl 2002, 19 and 173; Maschek 2008, 283–285.

234 For the situation of the new temple in the urban topography and optical effects caused by the narrowed Domitian Lane, see Schowalter 2022.

235 Landskron 2020.

236 IK 12, 449. To this end, the restoration of a building by Tigellius in IK 12, II 446; to its full extent the degree was first correctly interpreted by Dräger 1993, 151–164.

237 Cf. p. 107 with n. 83.

238 Comprehensively Thür 1989, with dating of the gate structure to 116/117, right at the time of the change of regime from Trajan to Hadrian. – Unrewarding for the question of the ruling emperor, whether Trajan or Hadrian, is the fragmentary building inscription IK 12, 329; Thür 1989, 69f. no. 1. – The inscription applied to the gate on the occasion of the paving of the plateia makes reference, with great probability, to the grammateus of the people for the year 114/115, Tib. Claudius Lucceianus. For the dating, cf. Strocka 2017, 402–407.

239 The building inscription IK 17/1, 3005, at the agora West Gate belongs at the earliest to the year 83 (Domitian as Germanicus); it appears to presuppose the disappearance of the street running here outside the agora first to the south and then to the east. The entire traffic, therefore, probably up until the construction of the new road behind the Triodos altar, must have been directed obliquely across the agora from the West Gate to the South Gate. On this, cf. Scherrer – Trinkl 2006, 28.

240 Scherrer 2008.

241 On this, cf. Quatember 2008; Strocka 2017, 405 and 414.

242 Since the water supply of Aristion crosses the Curetes Street near the Nymphaeum Traiani and runs below Terrace House 2 to the west, it is probable that the so-called Serapeion, under construction at the same time, is that sanctuary that Aristion connected to the

water supply, following the remains of an inscription (IK 17/2, 4105).

243 Plin. ep. VI 31, 3; for the person of Ariston, extensively Scherrer 1997, 115–139; on Iulia Lydia Laterane cf. Kirbihler 2009, 62f.

244 Wörrle 1973, 475 with n. 28.

245 Kirbihler 2003, 292–299 (daughter), Scherrer 2006b, 55 with n. 53 (rather, granddaughter); Kirbihler 2009, 62; on the testimonia and the family of Varius, cf. now also Quatember 2017, 28–46.

246 For this, it is necessary to envision the employment of a building workshop at a number of these buildings, erected in short succession and partially overlapping in time, and sponsored by a variety of clients. Thür 1985, 184f., already confirmed that the capitals with reed decoration from the Library of Celsus, from the so-called Hadrian's Gate and that of the so-called Street Fountain (cf. for the building Quatember 2008, for the dating esp. 227f. and 255), erected approximately contemporaneously or perhaps immediately before the Nymphaeum Traiani, certainly originated from one and the same workshop.

247 On this, cf. Quatember 2017, 132f.

248 IK 12, 415–417 and 419.

249 On the Harbour Gymnasium recently, Thür 2020a; Thür 2021. On the appellation, Karwiese 1997b.

250 On the statues: Strocka 1989; Aurenhammer 1990, 23f. no. 1, 139f. no. 117; on the fountain building recently Plattner – Schmidt-Colinet 2005, 246–248; Rathmayr 2014, 311f.

251 On the dating and the inscriptions: Scherrer 2006b, 48–53. The Marnas aqueduct was restored and perhaps extended or connected to additional springs under Antoninus Pius (IK 15, 1530). The Değirmendere aqueduct recently described by Wiplinger 2006, 30–35, is probably to be identified with the multi-phase Marnas aquaeduct. Inscriptions mention an *old Marnas spring* (Knibbe 1993, 145 no. 71) and the *new Marnas* (IK 15, 1530, under Antoninus Pius) – but in no way is it to be identified with the *Aqua Iulia*, as Özis et al. 2005, 213 claim; on this see also Scherrer 2006b, 51 and 53.

252 Longfellow 2011, 61–76, esp. 74: "The first known monumental fountain dedicated to an Emperor honored him with a display that was truly imperial in nature."

253 See pp. 165–167.

254 Yegül 1994, 105; Schowalter 2022, 148–150.

255 On this esp. Rathmayr 2014, 311–314; Scherrer 2008, esp. 42f.

256 IK 12, 417; Wilberg 1923a; Alzinger 1974, 70f. und 146; cf. also M. Büyükkolancı – D. Tüzün, in: Scherrer 2000, 164; Scherrer 2006b, 50. – Thür 2020b, 402, dates the extension into the 2nd c. AD.

257 Halfmann 1979, 133 no. 37.

258 On the contemporary mode of endowing libraries and using them as one's own heroon see Portale 2011, 119–123.

259 IK 17/2, 5101.

260 IK 17/2, 5113 lines 3f. – on the building, cf. fundamentally Keil 1944/1953; in addition: Hueber 1997b, 77–83 (with older bibliography); Hoepfner 2002, 123–126.

261 Halfmann 1979, 111f. no. 16.

262 On the inscriptions for the Ephesian Mouseion: Keil 1905; Laffi 2006; Thür 2021, 224f. (history of research).

263 On the so-called Hadrian's Gate, see p. 112 n. 13 fig. 49.

264 On this cf. Scherrer 2005, esp. 131–137; a counter proposal to locate the Mouseion in the Harbour Gymnasium: Thür 2021.

265 Cf. esp. Strocka 1988.

266 On this extensively Strocka 2009; Portale 2011, 127–132.

267 For the statues of father and son, cf. Strocka 2013.

268 IK 17/2, 5108 – 5111. Whether Ennoia (IK 17/2, 5110) was therefore an original virtue of Celsus can no longer be determined; against this: Strocka ca. 2009, 247. – In addition, in the upper storey a statue of Celsus was replaced by one of a certain Stephanos, probably the person responsible for the last renovation of this city quarter in the Justinianic period, IK 17/2, 5115; on this, cf. p. 125 with n. 64

269 Portale 2011, 134–144.

270 IK 17/2, 5101–5114.

271 IK 17/2, 5113.

272 In spite of the anastylosis and the prominence of the building, a comprehensive publication of the most recent research has unfortunately still not occurred; Wilberg – Theuer – Eichler – Keil 1944/1953 remains fundamental for the building.

273 Strocka 2009, 248f. (with older bibliography in n. 15).

274 J. Keil, in: Wilberg – Theuer – Eichler – Keil, 1944/1953, 46.

275 Strocka 2009. 248; Portale 2011, 127f.

276 Cic. Att. II 1. 4. For this, see Nagy 1998, esp. 196f. – see also Portale 2011, 122, stressing the importance of the physical presence of the body of the deceased.

277 On the aqueduct, Wiplinger 2006a, 26–30; Wiplinger 2006b, 19–38.

278 On the precise dating, Strocka 2017, 415f.

279 The name of the bath building is mentioned in honorific inscriptions (IK 13, 672 and IK 17/1, 3080 line 14) for the sophist Flavius Damianus (Severan period). The fragmentary building inscription for the latrines: IK 2, 455; the term *paidiskeion* used here, which has many meanings, led Miltner to the interpretation as a house of pleasure, a completely false designation for the adjacent residential building that is still very much favoured by tour guides. – On the inscriptions from the Varius Baths with new findings, see now Quatember 2017, 28–46 and 125–129; on the building that is still not extensively published, and which is primarily preserved in a Late Antique renovation phase, cf. Büyükkolancı – H. Thür – B. Tuluk, in: Scherrer 2000, 122.

280 On this, see pp. 179–195.

281 Building inscription: IK 12, 424; on the building, comprehensively Quatember 2017; cf. also Strocka 2017, 407–418.

282 Fundamentally Quatember 2011; on the statue programme and the precise dating, Strocka 2017, 407–418.

283 IK 12, 425; IK 13, 638; cf. Scherrer 1997, 138: … πολλοῖς καὶ μεγάλοις ἔργοις κοσμήσαντα τὴν πόλιν or τὴν πατρίδα ἡμῶν.

284 Thür 1997c; Cormack 2004, 42. 153. 223.

285 Quatember 2017; for the reconstruction, Quatember – Thuswaldner – Kalasek (2013).

286 IK 12, 429: [Ἀρτέμιδι Ἐφεσίᾳ καὶ Αὐτοκράτορι Καίσα]ρι Τραιανῶι Ἁδριανῶι Σεβαστῶ[ι] καὶ τῶι νεωκόρωι Ἐφεσί[ων δήμ]ωι Πόπλιος Κυιντίλιος Ποπλίου υἱὸς Γαλερία/[Οὐάλης Οὐάριος — σὺν — τῇ γυναι]κὶ καὶ Οὐ[α]ρίλλῃ θυγα[τ]ρὶ τὸν ναὸν ἐκ θεμελίων σὺν παντὶ τῶι κόσμωι καὶ τὸ ἐν αὐτ[ῷ ἄγαλμα ἐκ] τῶν ἰδίων ἀνέθηκεν, ἐπὶ ἀνθυπάτου Σερβαίου Ἰννόκεντος, γραμματεύοντος τοῦ δήμου τὸ β´/Ποπλίου Οὐηδίο[υ Ἀν]τωνείνου ἀσιάρχου, ὑποσχομένου δὲ ἐπὶ Τί(του) Κλαυδίου Λουκκ[ειανοῦ γραμματέω]ς τοῦ δήμου. For the fundamental dating to 117/118 according to the *proconsul*, see Wörrle 1973, who nevertheless at p. 471 n. 7 and p. 474 concedes that it is possible that his period of office was also a year later, whereby the completion of the building could have occurred in the first half of 119. The more precise chronological limitation of the vowing arises from the varying tenures of office of the civic officials (beginning with 23 September as the first day of the new year of the Asian calendar) and the imperial provincial administration, since the proconsuls presumably took up their office in June, when the sea was calm. For the accession to office of the *proconsules Asiae* on 1 July, cf. Dräger 1993, 140. For the beginning date of the civic officials in Asia as 23 September, cf. Kirbihler 2003, 202. – In the older scholarship, a superseded dating in the period of the 2nd Ephesian neocorate for Hadrian around 136 AD is still found, cf. Engelmann 1972, on this Wörrle 1973, esp. 471.

287 Quatember 2017, esp. p. 110–112. See already Bol 1998, 132 n. 783; Scherrer 2008, 48–50.

288 Iannantuono 2021 attempted – depending heavily on the approach of Roger 1991 – to present the temple and above all the frieze as a historicising monument with the connections between Hadrian, Artemis Ephesia and the Demos of Ephesos; her analysis, however, fails due to the false identification of many figures and her indecision whether the programme was designed for Trajan or for Hadrian.

289 Quatember 2017, 269–273, offers extensive descriptions and analyses employing exemplary integration of the older literature.

290 Miltner 1959, 271f. (after the year 393 n. Chr.) Fleischer 1967, 57–60 (3rd or beginning of the 4th quarter of the 4th c. AD); this dating was vehemently defended by Fleischer 2002, 187f.

291 Brenk 1968. – An extensive discussion of the entire history of research on the frieze with several additional dating approaches and detailed argumentation at Quatember 2017, 107–110.

292 IK 12, 305 (lines 1–3) and 306; cf. now on this, Quatember 2017, 84f. and 248–250.

293 Thus, already Saporiti 1964, 275; against this, e.g. Fleischer 1967, 37; Quatember 2017, 117.

294 Quatember 2017, esp. 116, who appears to think about an intentional shortening in the course of the Late Antique reconstruction of the south-west corner after an earthquake; it could also have been simply a realigned or rectified break.

295 Zanker 1970, 513f.: "… it shows in the best-preserved scene the defeat of the Dacians, the prototype was apparently an Alexander battle…" – Cf. also Leander Touati 1987, 21 and passim, pl. 3.

296 Cf. e.g.: Woytek 2010, 228 no. 79a pl. 12 = RIC 418 = Strack 1931, p. 89 pl. IV 330: sestertius from the 3rd consulate (100 AD): Trajan in cuirass and with billowing mantle and no helmet rides to the right with lance. Additional types (au and aes): Woytek 290-293 no. 202f. pl. 38f., p. 296f. no. 208f pl. 42: "Trajan in military costume (yet without helmet) with billowing mantle springs to the right, raises his spear against the Dacians."
On this, Strack 1931, p. 119f. and no. 81 as well as pl. I 80 and app. IV 48 = RIC 208f., 104/111; RIC 534–545, sestertii, asses and dupondii 106/111 = Strack 1931, no. 361 (Dacian falls in front of the horse) and pl. V 360 (Dacian beneath the horse). – Zanker 1970, 514 n. 48: "The pictorial scheme appears to have played a significant role in Trajanic pictorial propaganda; it is encountered on one of the metopes in Adamklissi (Florescu, Monumentul de la Adamklissi Tropaeum Traini [1960] 444 fig. 206, Metope XXVIII) and on many coins. It probably ultimately goes back to Alexander." The fact that here the horse is not galloping, as one regularly must read (Fleischer 1967, 26: "rider springing to the right…."; recently Quatember 2017, 269 no. 713R A4: "…man on a horse galloping away to the right."), can be seen from the fact that the rear legs of the horse stand firmly on the ground next to each other, in order to bear the entire weight of the horse and rider that will in any minute descend rapidly onto the enemy.

297 Fleischer 2002, esp. 193 and 198f.

298 Fleischer 1967, 26: "Part of the mantle is held by the angled left hand and falls down in two points." Cf. also Quatember 2017, 269 no. 713R A1.

299 Franceschini 2021, esp. 54: "To understand the meaning of the mantle figure, we also require the help of literary sources, which clearly refer to an Athenian context, in which the himation denotes the affiliation to the male polis acting in the Athenian public space. … wearing the himation turns even the Thracian Or-

pheus into an Hellene, showing that mantle figures refer not only to the Athenian polis as a socio-cultural background, but moreover to a broadly perceived Greek koine."

300 On this, see the recent discussions of the subject by Langner 2012 and Franceschini 2018; 2021.

301 Cf. above, pp. 127–138 with the corresponding passages in Athenaios VIII 62 p. 361; Strab. XIV 1, 3 [p. 632]; 1, 4 [p. 634]; 1, 21 [p. 640]; Paus. VII 2, 6.

302 In this way already Saporiti 1964, 270f., and more recently Rathmayr 2010, 34f., identify the figure of the warrior.

303 For the identification of Hypelaios already Fleischer 1967, 36.

304 On the meaning of these Amazon statues, cf. Fleischer 2002, esp. 193 and 198f.

305 Fleischer 2002, 198: "After the exertion of the battle, the wounded Amazon Sciarra also rests, and supports herself against a pillar."

306 On this see p. 143.

307 On this see, for example, Schmidt-Colinet 1996.

308 All of the coin images that show Androklos as slayer of the boar are younger than our frieze and date to the Hadrianic up to the Gallienic period. Here there are depictions of the hunt on foot as well as on horseback, and images of Androklos with the already killed boar. Extensively on this see Rathmayr 2010, 25–27.

309 Coin images with the speared boar alone: BMC, Greek Coins, Ionia, nos. 280. 290. 297. 322f.

310 On this, Rathmayr 2010, 33 n. 85. – In addition, there is a cassette slab (probably from the harbour wharf) with a boar and the inscription ΚΤΙΣΤΑ; for this Thür 1995, 68 fig. 5; Rathmayr 2010, 37 fig. 20.

311 Cf. e.g. a statue of a benefactor from the time of Antoninus Pius, from the Vedius Gymnasium, at Rathmayr 2010, 28–31.

312 On this, see pp. 133f. and fig. 48.

313 For this already Thür 1995, 98f.

314 Iannantuono 2021, 249, saw in the warriors Androklos "surrounded by his companions in the colonisation of Asia Minor (A3), indigenous enemies (A5), …"

315 For conquered figures without an opponent, since Hellenistic art, cf. Hölscher 1985.

316 Saporiti 1964, 270.

317 Fleischer, 1967, 36; equally Iannantuono 2021, 249.

318 On this see pp. 88f.

319 Philostr. Apollonios VIII 7, 25 (p. 313); text following Boter 2022; translation following Fischer 2014b, 125.

320 Fleischer 1967, 28.

321 Fleischer 1967, 39.

322 For the Ephesian Amazon sagas, already in overview Fleischer 1967, 39–41; Steskal 1997, esp. 16–22, Fleischer 2002, 187 and 190.

323 Cf. e.g. the summaries and in part own interpretations at Steskal 1997, 40–43; Quatember 2017, 105–125.

324 Saporiti 1964, 271–273; Brenk 1968, 239 with n. 9.

325 Fleischer 1967, 38f.; Fleischer 2002, 190f.

326 At first, Fleischer 1967, 38.

327 Fleischer 1967, 41; Fleischer 2002, 190f.; Saporiti 1964, 271f., recognised in turn B6 as Theseus.

328 Fleischer 2002, 190. The description and identification of most figures on this block, as well as the interpretation of those represented, at Fleischer 1967, esp. 29–31 and 39–42, have since been generally accepted in the literature, but see Quatember 2011, 117f., esp. for the panther.

329 Cf. also Fleischer 2002, 187; particularly important is the clear presence of these myths in the 2nd c. AD at Plut. qu. Gr. 56, and Paus. VII 2, 7. cf. however also Eust. in Dion. Per. 828; Etym. Magn. s.v. Ἔφεσος.

330 Tac. ann. III 6l.

331 Quatember 2017, 119.

332 Fleischer 1967, 32–34; Quatember 2017, 120–122 and 272f.

333 Cf. on this most recently Fleischer 2002, 187f.

334 Fleischer 1967, esp. 45f.; on this now also extensively Quatember 2017, esp. 110–113.

335 Stewart 1993, 243–252.

336 Steskal 1997, 52: "One almost gains the impression that the frontal representational image in the relief is closer to statuary sculpture than to the frieze-like continuous representation."

337 Fleischer 1967, 49. – Quatember 2017, 122, would like to recognise P. Servilius Isauricus here.

338 We would like to thank Sarah Cormack for her remark, when reading and translating the text, that a Roman stola here is more likely than the Greek peplos, commonly assumed until now.

339 Fleischer 1967, 49, on typological grounds justifiably rejects an identification with Kybele (on the so–called Rock Sanctuary of Meter at Koressos, the Androklos settlement, see recently Kerschner – Kowalleck – Steskal 2008, 116f.), who in Ephesos, like Aphrodite, enjoyed great veneration (cf. on this, Oster 1990, 1667).

340 Fleischer 1967, 49.

341 Fleischer argued for Dionysos: Fleischer 1967, 49; equally, Fleischer 2002, 189.

342 Fleischer 1967, 50. – Quatember 2017, 120, thought that she recognised hooves on the animal, but the almost horizontal, slight incision on the only recognisable rear leg of the animal is set much too high up to be a place where a delicate hoof could begin. A deer or a fawn would also have a completely different head. Quatember's interpretation as Apollon with the attributes of Artemis (similarly also Iannantuono 2021, 252) is convincing neither iconographically nor in terms of content.

343 Cf. Quatember 2017, 100f. and 104; Iannantuono 2021, 248. – Strocka 2017, 440f., wanted to interpret the bust in contrast as Victoria Augusta.

344 On this, cf. p. 188 and pp. 192f. with n. 353.

345 For this cf. also Rathmayr 2010, esp. 26–32.

346 Fleischer 1967, 50.

347 Fleischer 1967, 49.

348 Fleischer 1967, 46.

349 Miltner 1959, 270–273; then more elaborately, Miltner 1960, 95–97. – More recently, a series of Ephesian local heroes has been proposed for the identification of figure D9, on this see Quatember 2017, 121.

350 Fundamentally agreeing with the Trajanic hairstyles of a number of figures on Block D, Iannantuono 2021, 262f. and 265, yet who nonetheless identifies figure D9 as the temple benefactor Quintilius Vales – and the neighbouring goddesses as his wife and daughter, without explaining how the Ephesian citizen family members would have attained divine honours during their lifetime.

351 The interpretation of Rathmayr (2010, 35 n. 101–102; followed by Iannantuono 2021, 249), that with the figure of Androklos a reference to Hadrian as founder of the city was intended, could have occurred at the most in a secondary reinterpretation.

352 See pp. 111–117 (Triodos) and p. 138 (Androkloneion).

353 Curtius Rufus VIII 10, 1 (Alexander in the footsteps of Dionysos in India); Strab. XV 1, 41 (elephants as the privilege of rulers); on this, Ziegler 2003, 120 ("since that time, elephants could belong to the firm repertoire of a recourse to Alexander").

354 Cf. the scene at the Persian Gulf and Trajan's alleged self-comparison with Alexander (Cass. Dio LXVIII 30, 1), after Trajan had visited the death chamber of Alexander in Babylon (Cass. Dio LXVIII 29, 1).

355 Extensively on this, Strocka 2017, 438–449.

356 Cf. above n. 322. – Paus. VII 2, 7f., relates that when Androklos came, the Amazons already lived around the sanctuary [of Artemis] and had nothing to fear from the Ionians, but instead exchanged oaths with them.

357 In this sense Lang-Auinger 2010 argued that the broad-room temple is to be understood as an allusion to Trajan's military merit; against this, Quatember 2017, 137.

358 Thus, already Saporiti 1964, 273.

359 Cf. also Trajan as cosmocrator in IG 5, 386.

360 Strocka 2017, 440f., lists alternative proposals for the original occupant(s) of the temple, coming down in favour of Victory.

361 Karwiese 2016, 142 (12B+11B) and 5.2 p 76f.

362 For the final cult image, Rathmayr 2010, 35, conjectures a statue of Hadrian in the type of Androklos the hunter, which however would have hardly corresponded to the emperor. In the many subtle references in the architectural decoration, as well as the so-called tendril female above the door lintel of the cella, Outschar 1990 already recognised allusions to a heroon, yet nevertheless followed the late dating of Engelmann 1972 to the 130s and extrapolated an Androklos-Antinoos heroon.

363 A similar basic tendency as an overall interpretation also at Iannantuono 2021, 264f.

364 Ael. Arist. or. 23, 51.

365 See for that Borg 2004.

366 Jones 2004, esp. 20: "When we pass out of the world of literature into the actual world in which these people moved, the home-city, the patris, is a central, perhaps the central, focus of loyalty and cultural memory. … The search for antiquity is also expressed, for example, in the competition for first place, prôteia, which underlay Aristides' speech to the three cities, for this competition is really about priority of a different kind, priority in time. Hence the pride not only of the three leading cities of Ephesos, Smyrna and Pergamon, but also of Sardes, the capital of Pausanias' Lydia. This rejoiced in the title of 'autochthonous' or 'protochthonous,' later adding 'most ancient (presbistê), mother city of Asia and all Lydia'; this last epithet implies both antiquity and the reverence due to age, 'most august'."

367 Strocka 2017, esp. 438–449, justifies the construction of the building at precisely this location not only with the expected return of the victorious emperor in 117, but also interprets the Terrace House 1 opposite as a residence for Trajan, for which there is no evidence. Trajan, if he in fact ever trod on Ephesian soil, can only have resided in the residence of the proconsul Asiae; anything else would have been unthinkable in terms of security policy, in spite of the romantic notions of the adventus of the emperor at Plinius paneg. 22f or in the reliefs of the Column of Trajan (on this, Strocka 2017, 434–438).

368 Fleischer 2002, 192: "We find ourselves in the environment of the employment of myths, encountered in the Greek east particularly in the 2nd c. AD and designed to increase pride in the homeland, myths whose connections with the Second Sophistic and the Panhellenion of Hadrian have been intensively investigated in recent scholarship."

369 For the Temple of Trajan in Pergamon, we can probably assume that construction began under the proconsulate of Quadratus in ca. 108/109 AD (cf. Halfmann 1979, 112–114 no. 17); cf., summarising, Schowalter 1998. For Quadratus and his family see now Kirbihler 2023.

370 For this, cf. Strocka 2017, 401.

371 Already Rogers 1991, 143, wrote concerning the dedication of the temple to Hadrian: "… the idea of a new founder during the second century AD only had, or could be given, meaning within the historical context of previous Greek founders at Ephesos."

372 Burrell 2004, 66–70, following an older, already obsolete theory (based on coins falsely ascribed to Ephesos) (on this, cf. Scherrer 1999), wrongly separates the neocorate temple from a presumed, older Olympieion. The Ephesian Olympic Games were first the contests of the Domitianic, then of the Hadrianic neocorate temple; cf. Lehner 2004, esp. 182–184.

373 Cf. Fischer 2014b, 134f.

374 IK 15, 426.

375 On the significance of the burial place highlighted by Philostratos, see pp. 115f. – Extensively on the ev-

idence: Jobst 1983, 162ff.; on the overall situation of the tomb, Scherrer – Trinkl 2006, 44. See also Schörner 2007, 254f. Kat. A 27.

376 Atalay 1978–80, 57.

377 IK 17/1, 3047: [ἡ βουλὴ καὶ] ὁ δῆμος / [Τ(ίτον) Κλ(αύδιον)] Φ[λαουιαν]ὸν Διονύσιον / [τὸν] ῥήτορα καὶ σοφιστὴν / [δ]ὶς ἐπίτροπον τοῦ Σεβαστοῦ / Κλ(αύδιος) Εὔτυχος τὸν ἑαυτοῦ πάτρωνα. – *The boule and the demos, for T. Claudius Flavianus Dionysius, the orator and sophist, the twice procurator of the emperor. Claudius Eutyches for his patron.*

378 See above, pp. 115f.

379 Keil 1953, 6 n. 13.

380 Extensive discussion of the complex evidence at Scherrer – Trinkl 2006, 45–48.

381 Jobst 1983, 209f., based on stratigraphic and topographic observations as well as finds of lamps, dates the building to after the mid-2nd c. AD.

382 EED 27.10.–1.11.1905, cited according to Jobst 1983, 161.

383 IK 13, 673; Keil 1953, 16f., already thought about a tomb building in the immediate vicinity of the find spot, yet was confused by the reuse in the Byzantine corridor.

384 Cf. the honours for Soteros by ten of his students, including Hypsikles, IK 15, 1548. The entire group was dismissed by Philostratos (soph. II 23) as amateurs worthy of little respect. – cf. Fischer 2014b, 134f.

385 Keil 1953, 17.

386 Atalay 1978–80, 58–64.

387 On the almost complete falling off of honorific tombs in the cities in the later 2nd c., cf. Strocka 2009, 255.

388 IK 13, 696 und IK 17/1, 3049f. For the function, the inscriptions use the terms ἐπίσκοπος and λογιστής or *curator rei publicae*). – In general, on the role of the episkopos since the late Hellenistic period in Ephesos: Kirbihler 2005, esp. 161–168.

389 On this, cf. Gliwitzky 2010.

390 IK 17/1, 3001 und 3002.

391 IK 12, 435f.

392 Thür 2020b, 406–409; On this, cf. pp. 167f.

393 Keil 1964, 122; H. Thür, in: Scherrer 2000, 100.

394 On the development of the tabernacle façades of fountain buildings from older theatre façades, cf. Quatember 2011, 90–99.

395 IK 12, 305 (Temple of Hadrian; mentioned are Diocletian as Augustus, and Constantius Chlorus and Galerius as Caesars; the statue of Maximian as Augustus was replaced under Theodosius I by that of his father Theodosius, cf. IK 12, 306), IK 12, 308f. (Hydreion; during the double rule before 293 AD, in addition to Diocletian the second base must have named Maximian). – Nevertheless, statues of the Tetrarchs are numerous at Ephesos: other find spots are, e.g., the theatre (IK 12, 307), the macellum (so-called Tomb of Luke, IK 12, 309A) and the West Gate of the agora (IK 12, 311A).

396 Cf. Thür 1999; Thür 1999a; Thür 2009; Waldner 2020.

The Triodos, the Octagon and the Embolos: Conclusions

1 Supporting such a culture of memory, cf. e.g. Thür 1999, 425; Cormack 2004, 42. – Against this, e.g. Strocka 2009, 253.

2 Besides the hypothetical connection with a statue of Lysimachos, the many reused ashlar blocks used for the not visible inner parts of the late Hellenistic fountain house indicate an older building structure.

3 In addition to the persons mentioned in the building inscription – Augustus and Livia, Agrippa and Iulia maior – these are above all the grandchildren and heirs to the throne, as the preserved plinth for the statue of L. Caesar, IK 17/1, 3007, substantiates. – For the magnificence of these monuments as honorary arches for the imperial family see Eck 2005, 156.

4 Woodhull 2004, 88: "By the early empire, it [= the arched gate] became a quintessentially Roman design and had spread to towns across the empire as a marker of a city's Romanization. To build one was to make claims about a city's or patron's romanitas." – Compare on that now Fröhlich 2022, 341. 345f. 349–354.

5 This is why Yegül 1994, 103, called the Embolos a "remarkable layering of urban history".

6 Rouché 2002.

7 Summarising the discussions about the imperial-era processions: Quatember 2017, 133–135. – For the Late Antique processions cf. esp. Rouché 2009.

8 Burrell 2009, 70–72.

9 Compare Schowalter 2022, esp. 148–150.

10 For a catalogue and comprehensive discussion see Cormack 2004, 41–49 and 222–226.

11 Although the term *pax Romana* is first encountered in written form at Sen. dial. I 4, 14, nevertheless the *ara Pacis Augustae* as well as the entire statements of the *res gestae divi Augusti* allow the *pax Augusta* to be inferred as a contemporary concept.

12 The overseeing of the rites of passage at births, entry into adult life, and death are the etiological responsibilities of the city goddess in her all-encompassing function as mistress over life and death of the community.

13 The importance of a location of the tombs along the processional way and at the Triodos, thus in close proximity of the deceased to the tutelary god(dess), is also stressed by Portale 2011, esp. 115–119.

14 Swain 1996, 17–131; Jones 2004; see on that recently Hafner 2021, 26f.: "… during the movement of the Second Sophistic 'Greekness' and Greek heritage were greater than at any other time, and … Greek identity came before any loyalty to Rome".

15 Woolf 1994.

16 Jones 2004; Hafner 2020.

17 Strocka 2009, 253, classifies these buildings as mere cenotaphs, since the necessary tomb chamber for sarcophagi is lacking in them.

18 In this sense one could already understand Rogers 1991, 88–90.

19 On the characteristics of intramural tombs in general see Cormack 2004, 46–48.

20 Cormack 2004, 40f. and 222.

21 This probably very conscious deployment of a variety of high financial resources is apparent in the function; whereas the Street Fountain actually served the water supply, the Nymphaeum on the Embolos was primarily a magnificent building, with the actual possibility for retrieving water remaining secondary; cf. Quatember 2011, 101f.

22 Cf. Longfellow 2011, esp. 67–76; Rathmayr 2014, 324.

23 Rogers 1991.

24 Rogers wrote in 1991, 137: "For his efforts, the Hellenistic refounder earned a place among the heroes and heroines of the Embolos, half way between the Romans of the upper City and the Ionians of Koressos on the map of foundation." – It was naturally precisely the opposite: the honorary mile was founded by Lysimachos, and those who came later grouped themselves around him.

25 Rogers 1991, 140: "… the Ephesians' remaking of the past in AD 104 was only part of a long drawn-out social process, during which the city as a whole gradually asserted a particular civic Identity …"

26 Rogers 1991, 144–149.

27 Rogers 1991, 84f.

28 Scherrer 2001, 81–85; see also Scherrer – Trinkl 2006, 35.

29 The term "topographem" was introduced by Plattner 2022, 25–28, to describe the function of historical buildings in the sense of memorials.

30 Hölscher 2012, 39: "Die Bildwerke waren mehr als zielgerichtete Botschaften von bestimmten Autoren/ Sendern an bestimmte Empfänger. Sie bildeten Welten von sinnvollen Bildern, in denen die Menschen ihr Leben einrichten und von denen sie ihre Maßstäbe des Lebens ableiten konnten. Der Kosmos der antiken Bildwerke ist mehr als ihre Wirkung auf den Betrachter: Er ist die Ordnung des Lebens selbst."

31 With Assmann 2018, 157–158, one can describe the entirety of the buildings as signs of "work of cultural memory" or circulation sites of "cultural meaning" in the sense of a construction of a continuation of a Greece of the past. On this, cf. also Assmann, 2018, 140: cultural meaning is "the supply of common values, experiences, expectations, and interpretations that constitutes the symbolic world of meaning or the worldview of a society." and p. 143: "Cultural meaning does not circulate and reproduce itself by itself. It must be circulated and staged."

In search of the skull from the Octagon

1 Wohlers–Scharf 1995, 184.

2 A recent reference to Oesterreichisches Archäologisches Institut 2016, 40, is found in the public media from 17.07.2022 with a somewhat curious idea: https://www.hna.de/lokales/goettingen/ goettingen-ort28741/goettinger-professor-erforscht-praehistorische-krankheiten-morde-kleopatra-mumie-91670032.html (accessed 21.07.2022). – Oesterreichisches Archäologisches Institut 2014, 27; Oesterreichisches Archäologisches Institut 2010, 55; Kanz et al. 2009; Koder – Krinzinger 2007, 423; Krinzinger 2005, 358.

3 Habicht 2021, 164: "since WW II the skull is unfortunately lost"; Anevlavi et al. 2020, 34 n. 49: "the excavators, who still had the original skull at their disposal […]. Unfortunately, since then, the skull has been lost". – Thuswaldner 2015, 59; Kanz et al. 2009; Thür 2009, 17: "der heute verschollene, aber publizierte Schädel der Bestatteten" ("the now lost but published skull of the buried woman").

4 Thuswaldner 2015, 59f.: "Einen Versuch, den Schädel wieder zu finden, unternahm H. Thür mit E. und S. Reuer. Zu dem zunächst in Greifswald vermuteten Schädel sollte der Abgleich mit einem zugehörigen Zahn führen, den H. Thür im Jahr 1993 als letzten verbliebenen Rest der Bestatteten noch im Sarkophag vorfand. Auf eine Suche in Greifswald konnte verzichtet werden, da Weningers Publikation aus dem Jahr 1953 Untersuchungen zugrunde lagen, die nach den durch die Greifswalder Wissenschaftler vorgenommenen Analysen in Wien durchgeführt wurden. Die Suche in Wien blieb jedoch erfolglos" ("An attempt to find the skull was made by H. Thür with E. and S. Reuer. The skull, which was initially assumed to be in Greifswald, was to be matched with a tooth that H. Thür had found in the sarcophagus in 1993 as the last remaining part of the buried body. A search in Greifswald could be dispensed with, because Weninger's publication from 1953 was based on examinations carried out in Vienna after the analyses carried out by the Greifswald scientists. The search in Vienna, however, remained unsuccessful"). – Krinzinger 2005, 359: "Die Suche nach dem Schädel des Skeletts in den Skelettsammlungen des Anthropologischen Instituts in Wien und im Naturhistorischen Museum verlief bisher leider ergebnislos" ("The search for the skull within the skeletal collections of the Anthropological Institute in Vienna and in the Natural History Museum has unfortunately been fruitless so far"). – Thür 1995c, 182: "After the initial excavations years ago, the cranium belonging to this skeleton was probably added to the collection at the University of Greifswald".

5 Wlach 1998, 111f.; https://dewiki.de/Lexikon/Josef_ Keil (accessed on 21.04.2022).

6 Keil 1930a, 41.

7 Keil 1930a, 41. 44f.
8 Wlach 1998, 112. – Keil wrote the seven excavation reports from 1929 onwards in Greifswald: Keil 1929a, 67f.; Keil 1929b, 51f.; Keil 1930a, 65f.; Keil 1932, 71f.; Keil 1933, 43f.; Keil 1935b, 151f.; Keil 1936–37, 213f.
9 Thuswaldner 2015, 59; Keil 1930a, 45.
10 Ehgartner 1959, 3; https://dewiki.de/Lexikon/Josef_Weninger (accessed on 21.04.2022).
11 Teschler–Nicola 2005a,b; Hayek 1960, 433–436; Ehgartner 1959, 3.
12 Ehgartner 1959, 5. – The publication list Weninger wrote when trying to travel abroad in 1938/39, names three titles: Grabfunde der jüngsten Bronzezeit von Skotniki bei Krakau (1915); Pfahlbauten (1922); Die Funde aus den praehistorischen Pfahlbauten im Mondsee (1927): University of Oxford, Bodleian Libraries, Shelfmark M.S. S.P.S.L 360/1–2.
13 Klee 2005, 293f.; https://ns–zeit.uni–greifswald.de/projekt/personen/just–guenther/ (accessed on 21.04.2022); https://dewiki.de/Lexikon/G%C3%BCnther_Just (accessed on 21.04.2022).
14 Keil 1930a, 45.
15 Kanz et al. 2009: "In 1953, the skull showed up for the last time, or at least photographs of it".
16 Weninger 1953.
17 Such a setting may have contributed to the fact that the article is sometimes ignored: Schörner 2007, 241; Thür 1995c; Rumscheid 1994, 160; Thür 1990; Oberleitner et al. 1978, 95; Alzinger 1974, 42.
18 Weninger 1953, 158: "Wenn man es unternimmt, einen einzelnen Schädel anthropologisch zu bearbeiten und zu deuten, so müssen die Fundumstände eine solche Darstellung ganz besonders empfehlen und rechtfertigen" ("If one undertakes the anthropological processing and interpretation of a single skull, the circumstances of the finding must particularly recommend and justify such a presentation").
19 Keil 1930a, 41–45 = Weninger 1953, 158–160.
20 Weninger 1953, 161 n. 6; Martin 1914, 519–538.
21 Feichtinger – Geiger 2022b, 217–222; Feichtinger et al. 2022, 104–107; Wolf 2008, 124f.
22 Wlach 1998, 108–110; https://dewiki.de/Lexikon/Rudolf_Egger_(Historiker) (accessed on 21.04.2022). – Egger was in charge of Carnuntum only until 1945.
23 Pacher 1949, 6; Weninger 1953, 168.
24 Weninger 1953, 168: "Der anthropologische Bericht bestätigt die Annahme des Archäologen, daß es eine ganz vornehme Persönlichkeit gewesen sein muß, die ganz allein in dem stattlichen Heroon beigesetzt wurde". – Keil 1930a, 44f.; Miltner 1958, 29f.
25 Wlach 2019b, 346: "Geprägt waren Archäologie und Alte Geschichte in den dreißiger und vierziger Jahren von drei Personen: Camillo Praschniker, dem Ordinarius für Klassische Archäologie, Rudolf Egger, dem Ordinarius für Römische Geschichte und Epigraphik, und Josef Keil, dem Ordinarius für Griechische Geschichte" ("Archaeology and ancient history were shaped in the 1930s and 1940s by three persons: Camillo Praschniker, professor of Classical Archaeology, Rudolf Egger, professor of Roman history and epigraphy, and Josef Keil, professor of Greek history"). – Pesditschek 2010, 287.
26 See also, Kenner in her "Der Reichsstatthalter. Der Reichskommissar – Fragebogen" from 09.05.1938 (Austrian Staatsarchiv, Vienna).
27 See also, Wlach 2020a.
28 https://dewiki.de/Lexikon/Camillo_Praschniker(accessed on 21.04.2022).
29 https://dewiki.de/Lexikon/Rudolf_Egger_(Historiker) (accessed on 21.04.2022).
30 https://dewiki.de/Lexikon/Josef_Keil (accessed on 21.04.2022).
31 On the general atmosphere of such a time, see Heiss 1999, 267f.
32 On the 'Archaeologisch–Epigraphisches Seminar' of the UoV, see Schörner 2021a,c; Schörner 2016, 347f.; Marchhart 2020, 162; Keil 1951, 297f.
33 https://dewiki.de/Lexikon/Emil_Reisch (accessed on 21.04.2022); Schörner 2016, 347. 352f.; Fellner – Corradini 2006, 341f.; Wlach 1998, 104f.; Schachermeyr 1965, 242. – Reisch also promoted F. Miltner: Krierer 2001, 217f.
34 Ulf 1985, 47. – Reisch was also a member of the German–nationalist 'Deutscher Klub': Mattes et al. 2022, 600; Huber et al. 2020, 51 n. 332.
35 https://dewiki.de/Lexikon/Liste_von_NSDAP–Parteimitgliedsnummern (accessed on 21.04.2022) with an incomplete list.
36 Pesditschek 2010, 308.
37 Piccottini 1970b, 87; Eichler 1950, 196; Reisch 1913, 79.
38 Übersicht der akademischen Behörden, Professoren, Privatdozenten, Lehrer, Beamten usw. an der Universität für das Studienjahr 1924/25: https://www.digital.wienbibliothek.at/periodical/pageview/2927609 (accessed on 21.04.2022).
39 Pfefferle – Pfefferle 2014, 138. 301.
40 BGBl Nr. 569, 630 (09.05.1947). – Mattes – Uhl 2022, 455; Keil 1948.
41 Wlach 1998, 107. 109.
42 Wlach 2020b, 420.
43 Wlach 1998, 106; Reisch 1930, 266.
44 Wlach 1998, 108f.
45 Betz 1970, 580: "eine besonders glückliche Zeit". Betz 1968, 108. Betz used the image of the 'triumvirate' already in his article for the Wiener Zeitung from 12.10.1958, Nr. 237, 6: Hofrat Professor Keil – 80 Jahre. – On Praschniker/Egger and Praschniker/Keil, see Wlach 2019a, 361.
46 Kenner cited according to Wlach 2010, 346: "Damit begannen für unser Institut harmonische, glückliche Zeiten" ("This was the beginning of harmonious, happy times for our Institute"). – See also, Wlach 2019b, 346. 357; Gutsmiedl – Schümann 2013, 249; Borchhardt 1994.

47 Vetters 1970, 368: "Ein international anerkanntes Dreigestirn von Forschern, die drei Freunde: Rudolf Egger, als Althistoriker der römischen Zeit, der Historiker und Epigraphiker Josef Keil und der feinsinnige Archäologe Camillo Praschniker" ("An internationally recognised triple star of researchers, the three friends: Rudolf Egger, as an ancient historian of the Roman period, the historian and epigraphist Josef Keil and the subtle archaeologist Camillo Praschniker").

48 Pfefferle – Pfefferle 2014, 158; Schachermeyr 1965, 244.

49 Keil 1951, 297f.: "Wir waren drei Freunde […] in geradezu idealer Zusammenarbeit". – Keil 1941, 259.

50 Eichler 1950, 197: die "in ertragreicher Freundschaft verbundenen Direktoren" (the "directors united in profitable friendship").

51 Pesditschek 2010, 289; Werner 1970, 227f.; Lesky 1953, 169.

52 Vetters 1970, 373: Egger, "ein edler Mensch". – Keil 1951, 301: Praschnikers "schlichte Bescheidenheit eines edlen Menschen". – Moro 1950, 2: Praschniker, ein "unvergeßlich gütiger und vornehmer Mensch" (an "unforgettably kind and distinguished person").

53 Kenner cited according to Wlach 2010, 346: "Praschniker war von seiner Studienzeit her mit Rudolf Egger […] befreundet und in seiner feinsinnigen, künstlerischen Art ein Gegenpol und gleichzeitig eine Ergänzung zu dem mehr alpinen, volksnahen Wesen von Rudolf Egger. Seit 1936 war ein dritter Freund, Josef Keil, […] der dritte Vorstand unseres Institutes" ("Praschniker had been friends with Rudolf Egger […] since his student days and was in his subtle, artistic manner a counterpart and at the same time a complement to the more alpine, folk–like nature of Rudolf Egger. Since 1936 a third friend, Josef Keil, […] was the third director of our institute"). – One hopes that Kenner is not referring here to the topic "alpine race" according to Günther 1930, 113–130.

54 Keil 1951, 298: "Egger war der persönliche Helfer von Praschniker".

55 Egger cited according to Wlach 2020b, 433: "Kost und Quartier".

56 Unhaltbare Zustände an der philosophischen Fakultät der Universität Wien, Wiener Montag from 10.12.1945, 3.

57 Klee 2005, 91. "Als wenn es täglich Brot für ihn wäre". Walter Chmielewski über seinen Vater Karl, der als KZ–Kommandant der „Teufel von Gusen" genannt wurde, Wiener Zeitung from 09.02.2016: https://www.wienerzeitung.at/nachrichten/kultur/mehr–kultur/800128–Als–wenn–es–taeglich–Brot–fuer–ihn–waere.html (accessed on 21.04.2022).

58 Egger cited according to Wlach 2020b, 433: "Sehr geehrter Herr Lagerführer! […] Ich melde daher meinen Kollegen, Prof. Praschniker, und mich für Freitag 30. Oktober nachmittag an. Wir würden Ihre Güte für eine Nacht in Anspruch nehmen. […] Mit Dank im Voraus und Heil Hitler!".

59 Keil 1951, 298.

60 Gedenkfeier für Prof. C. Praschniker. Wiener Universitätszeitung from 15.12.1949, 5: "Samstag, den 10.12.1949, fand vormittags im vollbesetzten Senatssaal der Universität die Gedenkfeier für den verstorbenen ordentlichen Professor der Archäologie der Universität Wien, Camillo Praschniker, statt. Die Ansprachen des Rektors, Prof. Dr. Richard Meister, des Generalsekretärs der österreichischen Akademie der Wissenschaften und engsten Mitarbeiters des verewigten Gelehrten, Prof. Dr. Josef Keil, der Pd. Dr. Hedwig Kenner und einer Studentin gaben ein umfassendes Bild der Persönlichkeit und des Lebenswerkes des berühmten österreichischen Archäologen" ("Saturday, 10.12.1949, the memorial service for the late professor of archaeology at the University of Vienna, Camillo Praschniker, took place in the morning in the fully occupied Senate Hall of the University. The speeches of the Principal, Prof. Dr. Richard Meister, the Secretary General of the Austrian Academy of Sciences and closest colleague of the immortalised scholar, Prof. Dr. Josef Keil, Pd. Dr. Hedwig Kenner and a student gave a comprehensive picture of the personality and life's work of the famous Austrian archaeologist"). MAGW 80, 1950, 372 ("commemoration" on the 10.12.1949 with a eulogy of J. Keil). – Wlach 2019a, 374.

61 Wlach 2019a; Pfefferle – Pfefferle 2014, 166f. 301; Wlach 2012; Fellner – Corradini 2006, 326f.; Wlach 1998, 106f.; Kenner 1988; https://dewiki.de/Lexikon/Camillo_Praschniker (accessed on 21.04.2022).

62 Übersicht der akademischen Behörden, Professoren, Privatdozenten, Lehrer, Beamten usw. an der Universität für das Studienjahr 1924/25: https://www.digital.wienbibliothek.at/periodical/pageview/2928228 (accessed on 21.04.2022).

63 Pfefferle – Pfefferle 2014, 138. 301.

64 Wlach 1998, 106f.; Wlach 2012, 80; Pesditschek 2010, 291.

65 Keil 1935b, 104; Keil 1936–37, 173.

66 Praschniker's "Der Reichsstatthalter. Der Reichskommissar – Fragebogen" from 08.05.1938 (Austrian Staatsarchiv, Vienna): "Ich vermute, dass eine meiner Urgrossmütter mütterlicherseits jüdischer Abstammung ist" ("I suspect that one of my maternal great–grandmothers is of Jewish descent"). Accordingly, there is a discrepancy in Praschniker's statements (grandmother vs. great–grandmother). – Wlach 2019a, 316 (Anna Henriette Breitenfeld). 365–368; Pfefferle – Pfefferle 2014, 157f. – There is no documentation on Anna Henriette Breitenfeld within the archives of the Viennese Wiesenthal Institute for Holocaust Studies (information kindly provided by S. B. Weiss). – On the self–presentation within such "questionnaires", see Heiß 1993, 144f.; https://dewiki.de/Lexikon/Viktor_Christian (accessed on 21.04.2022).

67 Gingrich 2021; Pfefferle – Pfefferle 2014, 166–168; Leitner 2010; Klee 2005, 92.

68 Praschniker cited according to Wlach 2019a, 366f. 375–378: "Mein Führer, [...] Mich hat das Unglück getroffen, dass ich [...] vor Kurzem zur schmerzlichen Erkenntnis kommen musste, dass meine Großmutter mütterlicherseits [...] jüdischer Abstammung war". – Pfefferle – Pfefferle 2014, 158. 166f.

69 NSDAP – Gauleitung Wien from 21.03.1943 (Bundesarchiv Berlin, Germany). Wlach 2019a, 368.

70 Praschniker cited according to Wlach 2019a, 363: "dass die ständige Nervenanspannung usw. nicht nur meine leibliche, sondern auch meine geistige Konstitution anzugreifen beginnen" ("that the constant nervous tension etc. are beginning to attack not only my physical but also my mental constitution"). 365–369. – Wlach 2012, 86.

71 In his letter to Adolf Hitler, Praschniker wrote: "Meine nationale Haltung ist auch während der Systemzeit immer eindeutig ausgesprochen und als solche anerkannt gewesen. Meine Einstellung zur NSDAP habe ich durch Beiträge und dadurch bekundet, dass ich Studierende, deren nationalsozialistische Einstellung bekannt war und die deshalb Schwierigkeiten bei ihrem Studium zu erwarten hatten, förderte" ("My national stance has always been clearly expressed and recognised as such, even during the system period. I expressed my attitude towards the NSDAP through contributions and by supporting students whose National Socialist attitude was known and who therefore had to expect difficulties in their studies"), cited according to Wlach 2019a, 366.

72 NSDAP, Gaugericht Wien from 29.05.1942 (Bundesarchiv Berlin, Germany). Wlach 2019a, 369 n. 319; Raggam – Blesch 2014, 81; Pfefferle – Pfefferle 2014, 166.

73 Cited according to Pfefferle – Pfefferle 2014, 167: "im Hinblick auf seine wissenschaftliche Bewährung und seine loyale Einstellung zum Nationalsozialismus". Gauleitung Wien from 20.06.1941: "Der Obgenannte war schon während der Verbotszeit national eingestellt und gehörte dem deutschen Schulverein Südmark als Mitglied an [...]. Dr. Parschniker [sic!] ist in politischer und charakterlicher Hinsicht einwandfrei" ("The above-mentioned was already nationally minded during the prohibition period and belonged to the German school association Südmark as a member [...]. Dr. Parschniker [sic!] is impeccable in political and character terms"). – Wlach 2019a, 368; Wlach 2012, 75 n. 7; Pfefferle – Pfefferle 2014, 157f.; https://dewiki.de/Lexikon/Deutscher_Schulverein (accessed on 21.04.2022).

74 Pfefferle – Pfefferle 2014, 219.

75 Wlach 2019a, 369 n. 320; Pfefferle – Pfefferle 2014, 167; Wlach 2012, 88.

76 Klos – Feichtinger 2022, 191 ("tragbar"); Pfefferle – Pfefferle 2014, 157f.

77 Klos – Feichtinger 2022, 191; Pfefferle – Pfefferle 2014, 158; Alm 98, 1948, 32.

78 Wlach 2019a, 372.

79 Egger 1950, 28: "In den schweren Entscheidungen, an denen unsere Generation so reich ist, hat Praschniker nie die Würde verloren, sondern ist aufrecht seinen Weg durch alle Wirrnisse gegangen" ("In the difficult decisions that our generation is so rich in, Praschniker never lost his dignity, but walked uprightly his way through all the turmoil").

80 Wlach 2019a, 375: "Sein Verhalten während der NS–Zeit, soweit es heute aus den Quellen rekonstruiert werden kann, war von Vorsicht, Ängstlichkeit und Opportunismus bestimmt – Eigenschaften, die durch den zusätzlichen Druck der NS–Zeit wohl noch stärker hervortraten".

81 https://dewiki.de/Lexikon/Nestor_(Mythologie) (accessed on 21.04.2022).

82 Egger 1950, 26: "Nicht wenige geplagte Hausfrauen haben das Unmögliche möglich gemacht, um die Stunde von 11 bis 12 Uhr bei P. [Praschniker] nicht zu versäumen" ("Quite a few harried housewives have done the impossible so as not to miss the 11 am to 12 am hour with P. [Praschniker]").

83 Pfefferle – Pfefferle 2014, 168; Egger 1950, 24.

84 https://austria–forum.org/af/AustriaWiki/Grinzinger_Friedhof (accessed on 21.04.2022).

85 Wlach 2019a, 314f. n. 5. – E.g., Keil 1951, Eichler 1950, Walter 1950, and Egger 1950. Professor Dr. Camillo Praschniker gestorben. Der Lebensgang des berühmten Archäologen: Josef Keil ("J. K.") in der Wiener Zeitung from 05.10.1949, 3: "Damit hat die Wiener Universität einen ihrer besten Lehrer, Österreich einen Gelehrten von hohem Ansehen und erfolgreichen Erwecker und treuen Hüter seiner Vergangenheit, die klassische Archäologie einen ihrer bahnbrechenden Vertreter verloren" ("With this, the University of Vienna has lost one of its best teachers, Austria a scholar of high repute and successful reviver and faithful guardian of its past, classical archaeology one of its pioneering representatives").

86 Oesterreichisches Archaeologisches Institut 1952 ("Camillo Praschniker in memoriam").

87 Czeike 1992–1997 IV, 592; https://www.geschichtewiki.wien.gv.at/Praschnikerweg?uselayout=mobile (accessed on 21.04.2022).

88 "Ehrung beantragt von Prof. Hedwig Kenner in Würdigung seines wissenschaftlichen Gesamtwerkes, wobei sie die Arbeit an den »am Parthenon verbliebenen Metopen [...] in lebensgefährlich schwieriger Arbeit von einer schwankenden Leiter aus [...]« besonders hervorhob. Der Akademische Senat beschloss am 30. Oktober 1980, den Namen Camillo Praschniker in die marmorne Fakultäts–Ehrentafel der Philosophischen Fakultät einzumeisseln und zu vergolden" ("Honour requested by Prof. Hedwig Kenner in appreciation of his entire scientific work, whereby she particularly emphasised the work on the »metopes remaining on the Parthenon [...] in perilously difficult work from

a swaying ladder [...]«. On 30 October 1980, the Academic Senate decided to engrave and gild the name of Camillo Praschniker on the marble faculty honour plaque of the Faculty of Arts"): https://geschichte.univie.ac.at/en/print/35374 (accessed on 21.04.2022).

89 Pfefferle – Pfefferle 2014, 287; Pesditschek 2010, 290–307; Hammerschmid 2009, 95–97; Fellner – Corradini 2006, 107f.; Wlach 1998, 108–110; https://dewiki.de/Lexikon/Rudolf_Egger_(Historiker) (accessed on 21.04.2022).

90 Wlach 1998, 109; Pfefferle – Pfefferle 2014, 287; Pesditschek 2010, 291; Wlach 1998, 109; Vetters 1970, 366; Betz 1970, 577; Reisch 1930, 266.

91 Übersicht der akademischen Behörden, Professoren, Privatdozenten, Lehrer, Beamten usw. an der Universität für das Studienjahr 1924/25: https://www.digital.wienbibliothek.at/periodical/pageview/2927609 (accessed on 21.04.2022).

92 Pfefferle – Pfefferle 2014, 137.

93 Wlach 1998, 109; Pesditschek 2010, 291; Betz 1970, 580.

94 Wlach 2010, 351f.; Betz 1970, 580; Vetters 1970, 373–382; Werner 1970, 227; Keil 1941, 261.

95 Egger 1940, 516: "seit dem Anschlusse der Ostmark an das Großdeutsche Reich".

96 Pesditschek 2010, 292.

97 Egger's "Der Reichsstatthalter. Der Reichskommissar – Fragebogen" from 07.05.1938 (Austrian Staatsarchiv, Vienna): "Überführung in PO [Politische Organisation] in Durchführung" ("Transfer to PO [Political Organisation] in progress"). – Wlach 2020b, 438 n. 69; Pesditschek 2010, 292. 300–302; Hammerschmid 2009, 96; Müller – Ortmeyer 2017, 11: "Der Nationalsozialistische Lehrerbund (NSLB) war eine verbrecherische Organisation, die nach dem 8. Mai 1945 von den Alliierten mit gutem Grund verboten wurde. Der organisatorisch und inhaltlich an die NSDAP angeschlossene NS–Lehrerbund wirkte als Arm des Staates in Schule und Erziehungsinstitutionen" ("The National Socialist Teachers' Association (NSLB) was a criminal organisation that was banned by the Allies after 8 May 1945, with good reason. The NS–Lehrerbund, which was affiliated to the NSDAP in terms of organisation and content, acted as an arm of the state in schools and educational institutions"). – https://dewiki.de/Lexikon/Nationalsozialistischer_Lehrerbund (accessed on 21.04.2022).

98 Wlach 1998, 109; Pfefferle – Pfefferle 2014, 157; Pesditschek 2010, 292; Wlach 2010, 349; Hammerschmid 2009, 96.

99 Wolf 1996, 93; Pesditschek 2010, 289.

100 Pfefferle – Pfefferle 2014, 157: "Im offenen, fast naiv anmutenden Opportunismus"; Pesditschek 2010, 302. 306. 314.

101 Pesditschek 2010, 304–307.

102 Pfefferle – Pfefferle 2014, 102 n. 348.

103 Rosar 1971, 29–65; https://www.geschichtewiki.wien.gv.at/Anschlussbewegung (accessed on 21.04.2022).

104 Mattes et al. 2022, 588. 600; Huber et al. 2020, 39; Huber 2020b, 17. 32. 36; Staudinger 1989, 260f.

105 Feichtinger et al. 2022, 94–104; Fürst 2012, 179f.; Svatek 2010, 3; Fahlbusch 2001, 491; https://dewiki.de/Lexikon/S%C3%BCdostdeutsche_Forschungsgemeinschaft (accessed on 21.04.2022).

106 Cited according to Feichtinger et al. 2022, 96; Heiss 1999, 270.

107 Unhaltbare Zustände an der philosophischen Fakultät der Universität Wien, Wiener Montag from 10.12.1945, 3.

108 https://dewiki.de/Lexikon/Kraft_durch_Freude (accessed on 21.04.2022).

109 Pesditschek 2010, 294.

110 https://dewiki.de/Lexikon/Forschungsgemeinschaft_Deutsches_Ahnenerbe (accessed on 21.04.2022).

111 https://www.karawankengrenze.at/ferenc/index.php?r=documentshow&id=148 (accessed on 21.04.2022); Pesditschek 2010, 292f.

112 Pfefferle – Pfefferle 2014, 299; https://dewiki.de/Lexikon/Oswald_Menghin (accessed on 21.04.2022).

113 Pfefferle – Pfefferle 2014, 285; https://dewiki.de/Lexikon/Viktor_Christian (accessed on 21.04.2022).

114 Mader 2021, 381. 386.

115 Pfefferle/Pfefferle 2014, 157: "damit das »Österreichische Archaeologische Institut«, dessen Direktor er war, auch den »Betriebsführer« bei den Ausgrabungen in Carnuntum stellen könne". – Wlach 2020b, 424–432; Pesditschek 2010, 302; Hammerschmid 2009, 96; Kandler 1998, 53–57; Rudolf 1995; Egger 1940.

116 Egger cited according to Pfefferle – Pfefferle 2014, 119 n. 382: "»Überschaue ich mein ganzes Leben«, so glaube ich »kein Österreicher bloss des Bekenntnisses, sondern einer der Tat zu sein«".

117 Pfefferle – Pfefferle 2014, 102. 113. 115f. 157; Pesditschek 2010, 300–303; Hammerschmid 2009, 97.

118 Pfefferle – Pfefferle 2014, 116. 158; Pesditschek 2010, 303; Wlach 2010, 369.

119 Werner 1970, 225 ("Herr des Magdalensberges"). 229.

120 Pfefferle – Pfefferle 2014, 159: "Den Ruhm, den er in Carnuntum winken sah, fand er auf dem Magdalensberg".

121 Ebner 2009, 60; De Bernardo-Stempel – Hainzmann 2020, 125. 135f. 167f. 198. 290. 336f. etc. – In particular, it was Egger's essential concern to draw a continuity between German–speaking Carinthia and its Celtic–Roman past and thereby to erase its Slavic history (Pesditschek 2010, 290 n. 12. 295, on Egger's anti–Slovenian resentment). To this end, he converted a Late Antique residential house from the 5th c. AD on the Ulrichsberg (Egger: "The holy mountain") into a Noreia-sanctuary from the 1st c. AD (Harl 1989). Likewise, Egger turned Roman thermae and an Augustan temple on top of the Magdalensberg into the "Seat of the tribes of Noricum" (Dolenz 2014). These at least partially intentional misinterpretations are still indelible reading material in Carinthian history books today.

122 Betz 1968, 109.

123 Cic. Sest. XLV 98. Cic. fam. I 9, 21.

124 Pesditschek 2010, 303; Vetters 1970, 371; PAR 2, 1952, 33.

125 Moro 1942; PAR 2, 1952, 33. – Vetters 1970, 371, and Werner 1970, 229, do not mention Egger's first Festschrift from 1942.

126 Moro 1954; Moro 1953; Moro 1952.

127 Betz 1968, 109; Betz – Moro 1963; Betz – Moro 1962.

128 Betz 1968, 108: "Der Nestor der österreichischen Altertumsforscher Rudolf Egger".

129 Piccottini 1970b, 86: "Nestor der Erforschung der antiken, vor allem römerzeitlichen Geschichte Kärntens".

130 Betz 1969, 127.

131 Lesky 1953, 169: "steht er in der Tradition jener Wiener Schule, zu deren bedeutendsten und erfolgreichsten Vertretern ihn die Geschichte der Altertumswissenschaft zählt und zählen wird" ("he stands in the tradition of the Viennese School, to whose most important and successful representatives the history of classical studies he is counted and will be counted").

132 Betz 1952, 18. 21; Petschenig – Stowasser 1930, s.v. *praeceptor* (teacher).

133 Taschwer 2018a, 29; Pesditschek 2010, 292. 304; Piccottini 1970b, 87; Betz 1968, 110.

134 Wlach 1998, 109.

135 Werner 1970; Piccottini 1970; Piccottini 1970b; Saria 1969; Vetters 1970.

136 Pesditschek 2010, 304; Czeike 1992–1997 II, 129. http://www.viennatouristguide.at/Friedhoefe/Ehrengraeber_Wien/ListeA_Z/liste_E.htm (accessed on 21.04.2022).

137 Pfefferle – Pfefferle 2014, 293; Pesditschek 2010, 307–315; Hammerschmid 2009, 97–99; Fellner – Corradini 2006, 216; Wlach 1998, 111f.; Wohlers–Scharf 1995, 155–157; Lesky 1948.

138 Taeuber 2021, 313; Pesditschek 2010, 308; Kandler – Wlach 1998, 22; Wohlers–Scharf 1995, 85f.; Schachermeyr 1965, 242; Braun 1964, 522; Heberdey 1905, 61. – On the OeAI–secretaries of that time, see Schörner 2015, 577. – In other words, Keil participated at the Austrian Ephesian campaign for the first time in 1904, the very year, the Octagon was detected: Alzinger 1962, 253.

139 Schachermeyr 1965, 242; Heberdey 1912b, 88; Heberdey 1912a, 157; Keil 1912; Heberdey 1907, 63; Heberdey 1905, 61.

140 Schachermeyr 1965, 249. 252–261; Pfefferle – Pfefferle 2014, 293. – Keil participated at all Austrian excavation campaigns from 1904 until 1935: Alzinger 1962, 253.

141 E.g., Pesditschek 2010, 309; Wlach 1998, 112; Schachermeyr 1965, 243f.; Braun 1964, 522. – Keil 1936–37; Keil 1935b; Keil 1933; Keil 1932; Keil 1930a; Keil 1929a; Keil 1929b; Keil 1926. – See also, https://gepris–historisch.dfg.de/person/5105955? (accessed on 21.04.2022). – This idea seems to go back to C. Pra-

schniker who wrote in 1938: "Die Wiederaufnahme der Aufdeckung von Altephesus nach dem Kriege wurde seiner [i.e. Keil's] Initiative verdankt" ("The resumption of the excavation of ancient Ephesus after the war was thanks to his [i.e., Keil's] initiative"), cited according to Taeuber 2021, 319 fig. 13.5.

142 Gerber 2008, 41.

143 Keil 1930a, 249. – As "representative of the Turkish Ministry of Education", Aziz was present at the Austrian excavations from 1926 until 1930: Alzinger 1962, 253.

144 Wohlers–Scharf 1995, 182–184.

145 Kandler 1998, 54 fig. 34.

146 In order to provide another perspective on these early images, we artificially colorised those with one of the usual software available (https://www.img2go.com/de/bild–faerben, accessed on 21.04.2023).

147 https://de.wikipedia.org/wiki/Adolf_Dei%C3%9Fmann (accessed on 21.04.2022).

148 Taeuber 2021, 316; Gerber 2010, 134–160. 164–166. 168–170. 173–177; Zabehlicky 1998, 43; Wohlers–Scharf 1995, 106f. 112f. fig. 55: "A. Deißmann, Initiator, Protektor und Organisator der finanziellen Mittel der Grabungen in der Zwischenkriegszeit" ("A. Deißmann, the initiator, protector, and organizer of the financial resources for the excavations during the interwar period"). 115. 118. 127; Alzinger 1962, 165f. 186. 196. – Accordingly, Keil called Deißmann the "reviver" of the post–war Ephesos project in a letter from 05.10.1936: Gerber 2010, 153. 177; Miltner 1958, 133. – See also Keil's excavation reports: Keil 1930a, 5f.; Keil 1929b, 6; Keil 1929a, 67f.; Keil 1926, 300.

149 See a letter of Deißmann from 21.02.1927, cited according to Gerber 2010, 150: "It is a pity to say that the inhabitants of the Turkish village Selchouk (formerly called Ayasoluk) have plundered and are still plundering these venerable ruins in a horrible measure when they are erecting their houses and stables, most of them being 'Muhadschirs' (Turkish immigrants and refugees) who have no houses when they arrive". See also, Grund 1911, 206, who describes Ajasoluk as "a small impoverished village, whose houses are built from fragments of ancient Byzantine and Turkish buildings" ("ein kleines ärmliches Dorf, dessen Häuser aus Baustücken antiker, byzantinischer und türkischer Bauten errichtet sind"). – A. Gerber at https://rune.une.edu.au/web/handle/1959.11/27522 (accessed on 21.04.2023): "These bulletins [i.e. the Protestant Weekly Letters] gave him [i.e. Deißmann] internationally influential connections through which he was able – virtually single–handedly – to organise the necessary funds to revive the archaeological excavation of ancient Ephesus in 1926. Since archaeological work had ceased there in 1913, this 1,600 ha site had become badly neglected, with much of it in imminent danger of permanent loss due to annual flooding and persistent looting". – Regarding the con-

stant danger of the Ephesian residuals becoming destroyed, take note of Wood 1877, 238, who found a limekiln in the Artemision, of Benndorf 1906, 5, and of Auinger 2009, 32 n. 34, mentioning a tobacco field at the site of the 'Curetes Street'. – On the desperate situation of that time regarding priceless artefacts in general, see a description of Deißmann from 1927 relating to the Topkapı Sarayı in Istanbul, cited according to Gerber 2010, 163: "Es war unschwer zu erkennen, daß es sich hier um Teile der legendenumrankten Serai–Bibliothek handeln müsse. Infolge ihrer seither ungünstigen Lagerung waren diese Reliquien durch Feuchtigkeit und andere Zerstörungsursachen zum Teil in einem sehr bedenklichen Zustand" ("It was not difficult to recognize that these must be parts of the legendary Serai Library. Due to their unfavourable storage conditions since then, these relics were in a very precarious state, partially damaged by moisture and other causes of destruction").

150 Gerber 2010, 39, writes: "Yet his [i.e. Deißmann's] unique and long protracted rescuing role for the once–foremost city in Asia has today been almost completely forgotten; and even among archaeologists and historians few would associate his name with archaeology, fewer still with the salvaging of Ephesus' extraordinary story". Accordingly, Gerber 2010, 155f., points out that Deißmann is not recognised any more within a photograph from the 1920s, not even by modern day researchers in Ephesos. However, the role of Deißmann was repeatedly highlighted in the past: Miltner 1958, 133; Keil 1930b, V. – Deißmann participated at the Austrian excavations from 1926 until 1929: Alzinger 1962, 253.

151 At that time (i.e. 1930), Keil seems to have faced "trouble" from Adolf Wilhelm (1864–1950), who was 'Professor für griechische Altertumskunde und Epigraphik' at the University of Vienna and as such predecessor on this chair of Keil: "Von Wilhelm kommt nichts, und wenn's kommt, gibt's Ärger die Fülle" ("Nothing comes from Wilhelm, and when it does, there's trouble aplenty"), cited according to Wohlers–Scharf 1995, 121 fig. 58. – On the personal animosities between A. Wilhelm and J. Keil, see Taeuber 2021, 320; Pesditschek 2009, 247f.

152 "Ἐν Ἐφέσῳ θύρα γάρ μοι ἀνέῳγεν μεγάλη καὶ ἐνεργής. Mit diesen in Ephesos geschriebenen Worten des Völkerapostels [Paulus] (1. Kor. 16,9) nehme ich nach sechs unvergleichlichen Wochen Abschied vom Österreicher Haus in Ephesos. Die Große Tür, die sich mir in Ephesos aufgetan hat, führte über weite sonnenbeglänzte Halden und durch geheimnisdunkle Schluchten in das gelobte Land neuen Lernens; eröffnete mir den beglückenden Zutritt zu drei Jahrtausenden anatolischen Geisteslebens, dessen beste Künste in unseren Seelen nachzittern; gestattete großen Gedanken und frommer Ehrfurcht ungehemmten Eingang. Aus dieser

Tür flutete mir, so oft ich sie durchschritt, von den Freunden nichts als Güte und Vertrauen entgegen. Ephesos, 17. Oktober 1926 bis 26. November. G. Adolf Deißmann, Berlin". – The original quote of 1 Corinthians 16:8–9 is as follows: ἐπιμενῶ δὲ ἐν Ἐφέσῳ ἕως τῆς πεντηκοστῆς· θύρα γάρ μοι ἀνέῳγεν μεγάλη καὶ ἐνεργής, καὶ ἀντικείμενοι πολλοί ("But I will tarry in Ephesus until Pentecost. For a great and effective door has opened to me, and there are many adversaries"; translation according to the New King James Version).

153 Übersicht der akademischen Behörden, Professoren, Privatdozenten, Lehrer, Beamten usw. an der Universität für das Studienjahr 1924/25: https://www.digital.wienbibliothek.at/periodical/pageview/2927609 (accessed on 21.04.2022).

154 See a letter from J. Keil to T. Wiegand from 12.05.1927, cited according to Gerber 2010, 160f.: "Ich bin schließlich mit dem Gefühle geringsten Wertes weggegangen [...]. 25 Jahre habe ich dann fast Oesterreich in Krieg und Frieden gedient! Ergebnis: 400 Mark monatlich [...]. Zu dumm, daß ich mich innerlich doch etwas kränke" ("I finally walked away with the feeling of the lowest value [...]. I served Austria for almost 25 years in war and peace! Result: 400 marks per month [...]. It's a shame that deep down inside I still feel somewhat hurt").

155 Taeuber 2021, 313. 316; Pesditschek 2010, 309; Wlach 1998, 112; Schachermeyr 1965, 244; Berve 1965, 164; Reisch 1930, 266.

156 Taeuber 2021, 324: "Josef Keil stellte, wie schon die Greifswalder Berufungskommission festhielt, das Musterbeispiel eines Absolventen der ‚Wiener Schule der Altertumswissenschaft' dar, der in Klassischer Philologie [...] ebenso zuhause war wie als Universitätsprofessor in der Alten Geschichte und als Ausgräber einer der bedeutendsten antiken Stätten in der Klassischen Archäologie, am meisten jedoch in seiner eigentlichen Leidenschaft, der Griechischen Epigraphik" ("Josef Keil represented, as noted by the Greifswald appointment committee, the epitome of a graduate of the ‚Vienna School of Ancient Studies', who was equally at home in Classical Philology [...], as a university professor in Ancient History and as an excavator of one of the most important ancient sites in Classical Archaeology, but most importantly in his true passion, Greek Epigraphy").

157 MittVKPW IV, 1927: "ΠΡΟΠΕΜΠΤΙΚΟΝ. Josef Keil, dem Forscher, Lehrer und Freund anlässlich seiner Berufung zum Ordinarius nach Greifswald". – Pape 1906, s.v. προπεμπτικός (for accompaniment).

158 MittVKPW IV, 1927, 6: "In dem Gefühle aber, daß Keil in Greifswald ebenso wie in Wien dem höchsten Dienste obliegen werde, dem hehren Dienste für das eigene Volk, fand die Feier in der Absingung des Deutschlandliedes einen stimmungsvollen Abschluß". – The German National atmosphere of that time can

be sensed from an entry of H. Hörmann (1894–1985; Wohlers–Scharf 1995, 172f.) into the guestbook of the Austrian excavation house from 13.10.1928: "Wie St. Stefans Dome zu Passau und Wien Ihre stolzen Silhuetten in der Flut eines Deutschen Stromes spiegeln, wie trotz künstlicher Schranken beide Städte seit den Tagen des Nibelungenlieds durch gemeinsames Schicksal verbunden sind, so haben sich auf dem altehrwürdigen Boden von Ephesos Söhne beider Nachbarstämme brüderlich zusammengefunden. Zum Dienste an der Menschheit, nachzuspüren ihren heiligste Schätzen. Hans Hörmann. 13. Oktober 1928" ("As St. Stephen's Cathedrals in Passau and Vienna proudly reflect their silhouettes in the flood of one German river, and despite artificial barriers, both cities have been connected by a shared destiny since the days of the Nibelungenlied, so have the sons of both neighbouring tribes found fraternal unity on the venerable grounds of Ephesos. They have come together to serve humanity and seek out its most sacred treasures"; highlighting in original), cited according to Wohlers–Scharf 1995, 122 fig. 59.

159 Gerber 2010, 161.

160 Keil 1930a, 41–45.

161 Taeuber 2021, 320; Pesditschek 2010, 309; Wlach 1998, 112; Schachermeyr 1965, 244.

162 Pesditschek 2012a, 180f.; Pesditschek 2010, 309: der "mit ihm mittlerweile verfeindete Adolf Wilhelm" (the "now hostile to him, Adolf Wilhelm"); Pesditschek 2009, 246–251, outlines the ramifications of this vocation, where R. Egger, F. Schachermeyr, F. Miltner, and others played their roles. In particular, the behaviour of R. Egger appears remarkable. – In an unusually overt obituary on A. Wilhelm, Keil 1952 described him as follows: 311: "sein an sich schwächlicher Körper" ("his inherently weak body"). 312: "ein stark entwickelter Ehrgeiz" ("a strong developed ambition"). 316: "er hatte durch sein ganzes langes Leben niemals ein Heim oder auch nur ein gemütliches Zuhause" ("Throughout his entire long life, he never had a home or even a cozy place to call his own"); "er hatte niemals einen wirklichen intimen Freund zu Seite gehabt" ("He had never had a true intimate friend by his side"); "immer ein Einsamer geblieben und man wird sein Leben, abgesehen von vielleicht von der Athener Zeit, kaum ein glückliches nennen können" ("He has always remained a loner, and apart from perhaps his time in Athens, one can hardly call his life a happy one"); "das leidenschaftliche Bestreben […] allen anderen zuvorzukommen, beherrschten ihn und seine Arbeit unerbittlich" ("The passionate endeavor […] to surpass everyone else consumed him and his work relentlessly"); "So konnte er im Leben niemals zur Ruhe und zum Frieden kommen" ("As a result, he could never find peace and tranquility in his life").

163 Taeuber 2021, 319 fig. 13.5; Schachermeyr 1965, 245.

164 Wlach 2010, 349f. – See his "Fragebogen" from 07.09.1938 and the "Personalblatt" from 07.05.1945 (both contained within his personal file of the University Archives, Vienna).

165 Pfefferle – Pfefferle 2014, 94.

166 Feichtinger 2022, 432; Pfefferle – Pfefferle 2014, 136; Pesditschek 2010, 312; Matis 1997, 62; Schachermeyr 1965, 245; https://dewiki.de/Lexikon/Ernst_Sp%C3%A4th (accessed on 21.04.2022).

167 Taeuber 2021, 322; Wlach 1998, 112; Schachermeyr 1965, 248.

168 Pesditschek 2010, 312; Schachermeyr 1965, 248; Berve 1965, 165; Eichler 1963, 1. 4; Miltner 1955; Alm 104, 1954, 217f. 284.

169 Pfefferle – Pfefferle 2014, 293.

170 Letter from F. Eichler (20.02.1957) to the deanship of the Philosophical Faculty of the Viennese University (University Vienna, Archives).

171 Wlach 1998, 112.

172 Oesterreichisches Archaeologisches Institut 1956–58: "Josepho Keil. Octogenario. De Instituto Archaeologico Austriaco. Optimo Merito. A.D. III. ID. Oct. A. MCMLVIII".

173 Stiglitz – Knibbe 1998, 68.

174 https://www.geschichtewiki.wien.gv.at/Josef_Keil (accessed on 21.04.2022); https://de–academic.com/dic.nsf/dewiki/2481921#.C3.96sterreichisches_Ehrenzeichen_f.C3.BCr_Wissenschaft_und_Kunst_.281935.E2.80.931938_und_seit_1955.29 (accessed on 21.04.2022); Pesditschek 2010, 312.

175 Pesditschek 2010, 313.

176 Berve 1965; Schachermeyr 1965; Braun 1964; Eichler 1963. – Typically, the mentioned obituaries hardly refer to involvements in the NS regime: Budka – Jurman 2013, 307.

177 Alm 114, 1964, 412.

178 Pesditschek 2007; https://dewiki.de/Lexikon/Fritz_Schachermeyr (accessed on 21.04.2022).

179 Wlach 1998, 115f.; Kunze 1972.

180 Feichtinger 2015; https://dewiki.de/Lexikon/Richard_Meister (accessed on 21.04.2022).

181 On the commemoration from 16.04.1964 (University Vienna, Archives); https://homepage.univie.ac.at/sonja.reisner/ULG–Projekt/betz.pdf (accessed on 21.04.2022).

182 Taeuber 2021, 324; https://de.wikipedia.org/wiki/Neustifter_Friedhof (accessed on 21.04.2022).

183 Fischer 1961; Gedda 1959; Ehgartner 1959; Ehgartner 1956; https://dewiki.de/Lexikon/Josef_Weninger (accessed on 21.04.2022).

184 Geisenhainer 2021a, 86. 104; Geisenhainer 2021c, 141f.; Pusman 2008, 152; Ehgartner 1959, 3; Gedda 1959, 511.

185 Teschler–Nicola 2005a, 117; Ehgartner 1959, 5.

186 Ehgartner 1959, 5f.

187 Weninger is not mentioned within the eight excavation reports from the interwar period: Keil 1936–37;

Keil 1935b; Keil 1933; Keil 1932; Keil 1930a; Keil 1929a; Keil 1929b; Keil 1926.

188 Seidler 1989, 81: "Weninger begründete in den 1930er Jahren die Wiener morphologische Schule" mit starker Ausrichtung auf die Rassenkunde" ("Weninger founded the ‚Viennese morphological school' in the 1930s with a strong focus on racial studies"). Gedda 1959, 511f.; Ehgartner 1959, 2f.

189 Feichtinger et al. 2022, 42.

190 Teschler–Nicola 2005a, 116; Teschler–Nicola 2004, 16f.

191 Milanich 2019, 155f.; Wolf 2008, 49f.; Teschler–Nicola 2004, 18; MAGW 81, 1951, 4; Weninger 1938, 204.

192 Teschler–Nicola 2018, 188; Wolf 2008, 49f.; Pusman 2008, 81f. 155; Teschler–Nicola 2005a, 115; Teschler–Nicola 2004, 18; MAGW 81, 1951, 4.

193 Weninger 1938, 204.

194 Teschler–Nicola 2018, 186; Berner 2010, 22; https://gepris–historisch.dfg.de/person/5113464? (accessed on 21.04.2022).

195 Geisenhainer 2021a, 115f.; Geisenhainer 2021b, 931; Fuchs 2002b, 809–812; Hauser 1988; Reuer 1976; https://dewiki.de/Lexikon/Margarete_Weninger (accessed on 21.04.2022).

196 Klos – Corradini – Mazohl 2022, 73; Feichtinger – Geiger 2022b, 246; Geisenhainer 2021b, 938. 941. 959; Leitner 2010, 6f.; Pusman 2008, 290; Matis 1997, 45.

197 When trying to emigrate to Great Britain in 1938/39, J. Weninger provided a "curriculum vitae", wherein he wrote: "Ich wurde am 15. Mai 1886 in der Stadt Salzburg (Österreich, jetzt Deutschland) geboren. Meine Eltern stammen aus Bauern– und Handwerkerfamilien aus Oberösterreich. Ich bin römisch–katholisch und rein arischer Abstammung" ("I was born on 15 May 1886 in the city of Salzburg (Austria, now Germany). My parents come from farming and artisan families from Upper Austria. I am Roman Catholic and of pure Aryan descent"): University of Oxford, Bodleian Libraries: Shelfmark M.S. S.P.S.L 360/1–2.

198 Fritz 2018; Seidler 1989, 88: "Privilegierte Mischehe" ("privileged miscegenation").

199 Fuchs 2002b, 810.

200 § 1 Z 1 Gesetz zum Schutze des deutschen Blutes und der deutschen Ehre (15.09.1935). Feichtinger – Geiger 2022a, 158.

201 Geisenhainer 2021b, 935; Gingrich 2021, 386; Pusman 2008, 208.

202 The Daily Telegraph and Morning Post from May 4, 1938: "Three professors dismissed [...]. Three well–known university professors have been suspended from their duties to–day. One is Prof. Viktor Hess of Innsbruck, a Nobel prize–winner [...]. Another suspension is that of the Vienna professor of anthropology, Josef Weininger. The third case is that of Prof. Hans Benndorf". Victor Franz Hess (1883–1964) was married to Jewish Maria Bertha née Warner–Breisky, both emigrated to the U.S.A. in November 1938: https://www.oeaw.ac.at/gedenkbuch/personen/a–h/victor–hess#:~:text=Victor%20Hess%20emigrierte%20gemeinsam%20mit,Konsulent%20der%20U.S.%20Radium%20Corporation (accessed on 21.04.2022). – See also, Matis 2013, 59–61.

203 Feichtinger et al. 2022, 104; Mader 2021, 391; Geisenhainer 2021b, 933. 938. 941. 959; Gingrich 2021, 386; Taschwer 2016a, 239; Leitner 2010, 7; Berner 2010, 19. 28; Pusman 2008, 207f.; Seidler 1989, 81; Hauser 1988, 277; Winkler 1986, 2: "Damit begannen für Josef und Margarete Weninger sieben Jahre der Verfolgung" ("This marked the beginning of seven years of persecution for Josef and Margarete Weninger"). – See also, Bundesarchiv Berlin. Germany, R 73/15621: https://invenio.bundesarchiv.de/invenio/main.xhtml (accessed on 21.04.2022).

204 Feichtinger – Geiger 2022b, 219; Feichtinger et al. 2022, 35. 42; Gingrich 2021, 386; Suppan 2013, 15f.; Matis 2013, 58; Leitner 2010, 6; Matis 1997, 30f. 45; Hayek 1960, 430; https://www.oeaw.ac.at/gedenkbuch/personen/q–z/josef–weninger (accessed on 21.04.2022).

205 University of Oxford, Bodleian Libraries: Shelfmark M.S. S.P.S.L 360/1–2. – Weindling 2009, 112 n. 94; https://www.oeaw.ac.at/gedenkbuch/personen/q–z/josef–weninger. Against such a backdrop, Seidler's statements delivered without any sort of proof appear incomprehensible (Seidler 1989, 83, 88).

206 Geisenhainer 2021a, 932f. 941; Pusman 2008, 208; Matis 1997, 45; Seidler 1989, 84. 88.

207 Rupnow 2010, 85; Fellner – Corradini 2006, 79; https://dewiki.de/Suche?q=Viktor+Christian (accessed on 21.04.2022).

208 Gingrich 2021, 377. – Regarding Weninger's relation to Christian, see Leitner 2010, 3. 5. 8. 21, and Geisenhainer 2021b, 932–941.

209 Klee 2005, 293; https://dewiki.de/Lexikon/Hugo_Jury (accessed on 21.04.2022).

210 Leitner 2010, 8, and Geisenhainer 2021b, 935, mention a letter of Christian to Rust.

211 https://dewiki.de/Lexikon/Bernhard_Rust (accessed on 21.04.2022).

212 Klee 2005, 516. "Der Reichsminister für Wissenschaft, Erziehung und Volksbildung" Bernhard Rust am 05.03.1941 an den "Herrn Reichsstatthalter in Niederdonau" Hugo Jury (Archiv der Universität Wien).

213 "Der Reichsstatthalter in Niederdonau" Hugo Jury am 22.03.1941 an den "Herrn Prof. Dr. V. Christian, Dekan der philosoph. Fakultät an der Universität Wien" (Archiv der Universität Wien).

214 Ehgartner, 1959, 3. – Weninger published two texts between 1941 and 1945 according to Ehgartner 1959, 6: Pittioni – Weninger 1944; Weninger 1941. – Yet, Weninger was not the only one who was assigned to such an institution. In 1938, he had already been preceded by the prehistorian Richard Pittioni: Fellner – Corradini 2006, 319; Czeike 1992–1997 IV, 558f.; Friesinger 1985, 181; https://dewiki.de/Lexikon/Richard_Pittioni

(accessed on 21.04.2022). Thus sharing a similar fate, Weninger's greetings to Pittioni from 1941 are found in the estate of the latter (figs. 77, 88). Furthermore, Pittioni edited the Festschrift commemorating the 70th anniversary of Weninger later on (Pittioni 1956).

215 https://www.oeaw.ac.at/gedenkbuch/personen/q–z/ josef–weninger (accessed on 21.04.2022): "1941 wurde er am Museum des Reichsgaues Niederdonau in Wien arbeitsverpflichtet, wo er bis März 1945 tätig war". Ehgartner 1959, 3.

216 Ehgartner 1959, 3: "Nebenbei ging Weninger einer seit Jahren im stillen gehegten Neigung nach, indem er am Institut für gerichtliche Medizin interessante konstitutions–biologische Studien betrieb".

217 Keil 1930a, 45.

218 Keil 1930a, 45: "Und sollte sich der Eindruck, den meine Greifswalder Kollegen bei der Untersuchung des Schädels gewonnen haben, bestätigen" ("And should the impression gained by my colleagues in Greifswald from the examination of the skull be confirmed").

219 Wlach 2020b, 424–432; Kandler 1998, 53–57.

220 Wlach 2020b, 420. 431; Kandler 1998, 55; Wlach 1998, 108; Rudolf 1995, 218.

221 Pittioni – Weninger 1944.

222 Weninger 1953, 166: "Im Jahr 1944 teilte mir Rudolf Egger mit, daß er in einem Sarkophag in Carnuntum ein gut erhaltenes, vollständiges Skelett gefunden habe. Er gab mir die Möglichkeit das Skelett zu bergen". Pacher 1949, 6.

223 Vetters 1970, 373–382. – There is not a single publication of Egger dealing with an Ephesian issue according to our knowledge.

224 Wlach 2020b, 431. 427.

225 Thuswaldner 2015, 59; Thür 1995c, 182: "After the initial excavations years ago, the cranium belonging to this skeleton was probably added to the collection at the University of Greifswald. Unfortunately, the collection's inventory list identifying this cranium has since been lost".

226 https://www.oeaw.ac.at/gedenkbuch/personen/q–z/ josef–weninger (accessed on 21.04.2022).

227 Niederösterreichisches Landesmuseum: https://www. geschichtewiki.wien.gv.at/Nieder%C3%B6sterreichisches_Landesmuseum (accessed on 21.04.2022).

228 Wlach 2020b, 424. 432; Wlach 1998, 109. – Vetters 1970 and Werner 1970 completely ignore Egger's conduct between 1938 und 1945: Vetters 1970, 368f. 373: "ein edler Mensch" ("a noble man"); Werner 1970, 226: "eine humane Persönlichkeit" ("a humane individual").

229 Verbannte Professoren zurückberufen, Wiener Kurier 37, 08.10.1945, 2; Pusman 2008, 256.

230 Matis – Suppan 2022, 130; Feichtinger – Geiger 2022b, 218; Geisenhainer 2021b, 960; Mader 2021, 391; Matis 1997, 45. 63; Alm 95, 1945, 95.

231 Feichtinger – Geiger 2022a, 147; Geisenhainer 2021b, 960; Seidler 1989, 90; Hauser 1988, 277; Ehgartner 1959, 4. – Weninger's sister–in–law, Heidi Jacobs née

Taubert, wrote on 06.11.1946: "My brother in law, Prof. Josef Weninger has been reinstated at the University and feels quite happy" (University of Oxford, Bodleian Libraries: Shelfmark M.S. S.P.S.L 360/1–2).

232 Ehgartner 1959, 4; Ehgartner 1956, 186: "Nun galt es die verlegten Sammlungen wieder zurückzubringen, das Institut wieder neuzuordnen und aufzubauen und die wissenschaftliche Forschung dort fortzusetzen, wo sie für ihn zwangsweise abgebrochen worden war. Eine unendlich mühsame Arbeit, bei der es zahllose Schwierigkeiten zu überwinden gab" ("Now it was the time to bring back the misplaced collections, to reorganise and rebuild the Institute and to continue scientific research where it had been forcibly interrupted for him. An infinitely arduous task, with countless difficulties to overcome").

233 Weninger 1953, 166.

234 Feichtinger – Geiger 2022b, 220; Fuchs 2002a, 544: "1944/45 Laborantin am Anthropologischen Institut; 1949/50 zweite Assistentin am Anthropologischen Institut [von Prof Josef Weninger]" ("1944/45 laboratory assistant at the Anthropological Institute; 1949/50 second assistant at the Anthropological Institute [of Prof. Josef Weninger]". Hanusch 1953, 5.

235 Pacher 1946.

236 Pacher 1949.

237 Ehgartner 1959, 3f.

238 Fellner – Corradini 2006, 288f.; Moro 1942. – Gotbert Moro (1902–1987) was an Austrian historian and, amongst other things, Director of the "Landesmuseum für Kärnten": https://dewiki.de/Lexikon/Gotbert_ Moro (accessed on 21.04.2022). His speech to the "German Youth" from 21.03.1938 is preserved: "Deutsche Jugend! Eine gewaltig große, eine wundersam herrliche Zeit ist angebrochen! Der deutsche Frühling zieht durch die Lande" etc. etc. ("German Youth! A tremendously great, a wondrously glorious time has dawned! The German Spring is sweeping through the land" etc. etc.), http://wwwu.uni–klu.ac.at/elechner/schulmuseum/schulchroniken/gklagenfurt1937.PDF (accessed on 21.04.2022). – Baum 2003, 106. – Also, G. Moro's brother, Oswin Moro (1895–1941), was a member of the NSDAP: https://dewiki.de/Lexikon/Oswin_Moro (accessed on 21.04.2022).

239 Moro 1942 with contributions amongst others from J. Keil, C. Praschniker, F. Miltner, E. Swoboda, A. Betz, and B. Saria.

240 Amongst the authors are: A. Betz, F. Eichler, J. Keil, H. Kenner, A. Lesky, F. Miltner, R. Noll, R. Pittioni, A. Schober, and H. Vetters.

241 Vetters 1970, 371; Moro 1954; Moro 1953; Moro 1952. – Interestingly, Wotschitzky does not mention Weninger's article on the Ephesian skull in his review of the "quite copious festive gift": Wotschitzky 1954.

242 Weninger 1953.

243 PAR 2, 1952, 16f. (including A. Alföldi, W. Alzinger, A. Betz, E. Braun, F. Eichler, J. Keil, H. Kenner, F. Miltner,

R. Noll, G. Pascher, R. Pittioni, B. Saria, A. Schober, E. Swoboda, H. Thaller, and H. Vetters, just to name a few).

244 MAGW 82, 1953, 121. – J. Weninger died four years later, on 28.03.1959 (Alm 110, 1961, 94). A memorial was held on the 10.06.1959, whereby Richard Meister gave a speech (Alm 110, 1961, 503).

245 Weninger 1953.

246 Weninger 1953, 168.

247 Weninger 1953, 160.

248 Within this context, the term "norm" (i.e. standard) derives from anthropological cranioscopy indicating that a skull should be viewed from six sides ("according to the standard/norm/rule"): from above ("norma verticalis"), from below ("norma basilaris"), from the front ("norma frontalis"), from behind ("norma occipitalis"), and from the sides ("norma lateralis dextra et sinistra"). Weninger illustrates 4 out of the six norms and describes five.

249 Morris–Reich 2013; Martin 1914, 486f.

250 Weninger 1953, 161. – Weninger pursued such an anthropological presentation of a skull also in one of his last publications: Weninger 1959. – See also, Pacher 1949, 57 Taf. I.

251 When trying to emigrate to Great Britain in 1938/39, J. Weninger provided a "curriculum vitae", wherein he wrote: "Durch die Forschungsarbeiten in den Kriegsgefangenenlagern und durch meine wissenschaftliche Tätigkeit am Institute [für Anthropologie] habe ich eine morphologisch–anthropologische Forschungsrichtung ausgebaut, die in der deutschen Anthropologie und Rassenkunde als die ‚Wiener Schule' Geltung erlangt hat" ("Through the research work in the prisoner–of–war camps and through my scientific work at the Institute [for Anthropology], I have developed a morphological–anthropological line of research that has gained recognition in German anthropology and racial studies as the 'Viennese School'"): University of Oxford, Bodleian Libraries: Shelfmark M.S. S.P.S.L 360/1–2; Pusman 2008, 154; Teschler–Nicola 2005a, 115; Ehgartner 1959, 3; Gedda 1959, 511; Weninger 1938, 202.

252 Kanz et al. 2009.

253 Taschwer 2020; Taschwer 2015a, 147–150; Heiss 1999, 269f.

254 Taschwer 2018b, 10; Taschwer 2015b, 56; Taschwer 2015a, 251; Stifter 2014, 365–372; Benetka 1998, 214–217.

255 Stifter 2014, 346–365; Erker 2017, 183f.; Benetka 1998, 214–217.

256 Klos – Schlögl – Andorfer 2022, 384f.; Feichtinger – Uhl 2018, 236; Feichtinger – Hecht 2013b, 177. – See here the self–image of the Academy members from 22.06.1945: "Die Akademie geht aus dem abgelaufenen Zeitraum seit 1938 mit gutem Gewissen hervor. Sie hat dem Druck dieser Jahre nur verschwindend wenige, unbedeutende und ihr auferlegte Konzessionen gemacht" ("The Academy emerges from

the elapsed period since 1938 with a clear conscience. It has made only a few, insignificant and imposed concessions to the pressures of these years"), cited according to Feichtinger – Hecht 2013b, 172 (Protokoll der Gesamtsitzung der Akademie der Wissenschaften from 22.06.1945).

257 https://dewiki.de/Lexikon/Richard_Meister (accessed on 21.04.2022).

258 https://dewiki.de/Lexikon/Josef_Keil (accessed on 21.04.2022).

259 Fellner – Corradini 2006, 97.

260 Klos – Feichtinger 2022, 168; Stifter 2014, 343f.; Feichtinger – Hecht 2013b, 171–174. – Die Naziseuche an unseren Hochschulen, Wiener Montag from 07.01.1946, 3: "Professor Meister war es, der dieser Forderung des Hofrates Dopsch in ziemlich scharfer Form entgegentrat" ("It was Professor Meister who countered this demand of Hofrat Dopsch in a rather sharp manner").

261 Klos – Feichtinger 2022, 175. 193; Pfefferle – Pfefferle 2014, 136f.; Alm 97, 1947, 90f.: "Es wurden daher gemäß dem Verbotsgesetz diejenigen wirklichen Mitglieder und korrespondierenden Mitglieder im Inlande, von denen festgestellt werden konnte, daß sie entweder Illegale oder Mitglieder der SS oder SA gewesen waren, aus der Reihe der Mitglieder der Akademie [sic!] ausgeschieden und in analoger Anwendung des Erlasses vom 2. August 1945 die Mitgliedschaft aller wirklichen Mitglieder sowie der Ehrenmitglieder und korrespondierenden Mitglieder im Inlande, die Angehörige der Partei gewesen waren, als ruhend erklärt" ("Therefore, in accordance with the Prohibition Act, those real members and corresponding members of whom it could be established that they had been either illegals or members of the SS or SA were expelled from the ranks of the Academy, and, in analogous application of the decree of 2 August 1945, the membership of all real members as well as of the honorary members and corresponding members who had been members of the Party was declared suspended").

262 Klos – Feichtinger 2022, 181f.; Feichtinger 2022, 434; Feichtinger – Uhl 2018, 236.

263 Taschwer 2015b, 55: "eine beschämende Tatsache, dass an der Österreichischen Akademie der Wissenschaften kein einziges "wirkliches Mitglied" der Akademie nach 1945 dauerhaft seine Mitgliedschaft verlor und einige pensionierte Ex–Nazis – wie Fritz Knoll, Uni–Rektor von 1938 bis 1943 – an der ÖAW sogar noch eine zweite Karriere machten" ("the shameful fact that at the AAS not one of its 'real members' permanently lost its membership after 1945 and some retired ex–Nazis – such as Fritz Knoll, Principal of the University from 1938 to 1943 – even made a second career at the AAS").

264 Budka – Jurman 2013, 308 ("rescue society"); Klos – Feichtinger 2022, 195; Taschwer 2018b, 10; Erker 2017, 181.

265 Klos – Feichtinger 2022, 175.

266 Matis – Suppan 2022, 131 n. 413; Pfefferle – Pfefferle 2014, 113. 287; Pesditschek 2010, 303; Alm 101, 1951, 59f.; Alm 100, 1950, 59; Alm 98, 1948, 29.

267 Erker 2017, 183.

268 Pfefferle – Pfefferle 2014, 298.

269 Pesditschek 2010, 294.

270 Matis – Suppan 2022, 147; Feichtinger – Geiger 2022c, 288; Pesditschek 2010, 304.

271 Feichtinger – Geiger 2022d, 416; Matis – Suppan 2022, 147.

272 Pesditschek 2010, 303; Vetters 1970, 371; PAR 2, 1952, 33.

273 Taschwer 2018a, 29; Erker 2017, 184.

274 1957: Rudolf Egger (Wlach 2010, 349). 1959: Albin Lesky (Seebacher 2020, 108). 1961: Friedrich Kainz (applicant; Gelbmann 2005, 1). 1963: Fritz Schachermeyr (Pesditschek 2007, 55 n. 98). – However, there only seems to be a 'Leskygasse' in Vienna: Autengruber et al. 2013, 300f.; Erker 2017, 184f.

275 https://dewiki.de/Lexikon/Hermann_Vetters_ (Arch%C3%A4ologe) (accessed on 21.04.2022). Wlach 2019a, 372 n. 334; Wohlers–Scharf 1995, 163f.

276 https://dewiki.de/Lexikon/Rudolf_Noll (accessed on 21.04.2022).

277 https://de–academic.com/dic.nsf/dewiki/2630020 (accessed on 21.04.2022).

278 Taschwer 2018b, 778f.; Erker 2017, 177f.; Stifter 2014, 331; Fleck 1996, 74f.

279 Pfefferle – Pfefferle 2014, 264f.

280 Pfefferle – Pfefferle 2014, 300; https://dewiki.de/Lexikon/Josef_Nadler (accessed on 21.04.2022).

281 Pfefferle – Pfefferle 2014, 303; https://dewiki.de/Lexikon/Hans_Sedlmayr (accessed on 21.04.2022).

282 Pfefferle – Pfefferle 2014, 284; https://dewiki.de/Lexikon/Otto_Brunner_(Historiker) (accessed on 21.04.2022).

283 Pfefferle – Pfefferle 2014, 291.

284 Pfefferle – Pfefferle 2014, 291; https://dewiki.de/Lexikon/Karl_H%C3%B6fler (accessed on 21.04.2022).

285 Pfefferle – Pfefferle 2014, 287; https://dewiki.de/Lexikon/Kurt_Ehrenberg (accessed on 21.04.2022).

286 Pfefferle – Pfefferle 2014, 299; https://dewiki.de/Lexikon/Johannes_Mewaldt (accessed on 21.04.2022).

287 Pfefferle – Pfefferle 2014, 287; https://dewiki.de/Lexikon/Rudolf_Egger_(Historiker) (accessed on 21.04.2022).

288 Unhaltbare Zustände an der philosophischen Fakultät der Universität Wien, Wiener Montag from 10.12.1945, 3: "Kein wirklich demokratisch gesinnter Student wird verstehen können, daß so tatkräftige Parteigenossen, wie der Germanist [Josef] Nadler, der Kunsthistoriker [Hans] Sedlmayr, der Historiker [Otto] Brunner, der Mathematiker [Anton] Huber, der Botaniker [Karl] Höfler, der Paläontologe [Kurt] Ehrenberg, der Philolog [Johannes] Mewaldt, der Archäolog [Rudolf] Egger immer noch nicht endgültig aus der Fakultät

entfernt worden sind". – On the NSDAP members mentioned, see tab. 7.

289 Pfefferle – Pfefferle 2014, 9f.: "dass diese universitäre Elite ebenso politisch und moralisch korrumpiert war wie andere Berufsgruppen" ("that this university elite was just as politically and morally corrupted as other professional groups").

290 Heiß 1993, 146.

291 Wlach 2010, 349. – In a decision of a Viennese "Einspruchskommission" from 04.12.1946, it is stated: "Dieses Eintrittsdatum und diese Nummer sind ein voller Beweis, dass der Einspruchswerber wegen seiner Verdienste um die Partei in der Verbotszeit von der NSDAP als verlässlicher Nationalsozialist anerkannt wurde. Denn mit dem Eintrittsdatum 1.5.1938 und einer Mitgliedsnummer unter 6,600.000 wurden nur solche Personen in die Partei aufgenommen, die vor dem 13.3.1938 Leistungen für dieselbe erbracht haben" ("This date of entry and this number are full proof that the objector was recognised by the NSDAP as a reliable National Socialist because of his services to the party during the prohibition period. For with the entry date of 1.5.1938 and a membership number below 6,600,000, only those persons were admitted to the Party who, before 13.3.1938, had rendered services to the same"), cited according to Schedlmayer 2010, 26.

292 https://dewiki.de/Lexikon/Rudolf_Egger_(Historiker) (accessed on 21.04.2022).

293 Apart from the VKPW, Kenner was also a member of the anti–Semitic 'Deutscher Schulverein Südmark' (Staudinger 1989, 268–270), and of the Aryan and anti–Semitic 'Deutsche Studentenschaft' (https://geschichte.univie.ac.at/de/glossar/deutsche-studentenschaft-dst, accessed on 21.04.2022): Kenner's "Der Reichsstatthalter. Der Reichskommissar – Fragebogen" from 09.05.1938 (Austrian Staatsarchiv, Vienna). Such a background makes Kenner's NS–affinity much more logical. Still, Gutsmiedl–Schümann 2013 is capable of ignoring Kenner's NSDAP involvement and its career consequences (https://geschichte.univie.ac.at/de/personen/hedwig–kenner, accessed on 21.04.2022) calling her a "researcher of human kindness and humanistic spirit", an embellishment Schörner rightly points out (Schörner 2020, 130). – Interestingly, the father of H. Kenner, the academic painter Anton Josef Ritter von Kenner (1871–1951, Szemethy 2015), manufactured a drawn reconstruction of the Parthenon's cult statue based on instructions of C. Praschniker (Praschniker 1952, 7 n. 2, Taf.).

294 https://dewiki.de/Lexikon/Hermann_Vetters_ (Arch%C3%A4ologe) (accessed on 21.04.2022). Also, his father, Hermann Vetters sen., was a NSDAP member, https://dewiki.de/Lexikon/Hermann_Vetters_(Geologe) (accessed on 21.04.2022). – Danner 2015, 42–44. 49. 70–71. – See the 'Vettersgasse' in Autengruber et al. 2014, 127; Mertz 2020, 365.

295 https://dewiki.de/Lexikon/Franz_Miltner (accessed on 21.04.2022). Pesditschek 2012a, 182; Wohlers–Scharf 1995, 157–159. – Helene Miltner née Zurunić, Gräfin von Balogh: Krierer 2001, 217; https://www.vol.at/50–jahre–gluecklich–vereint/5680526, accessed on 21.04.2022.

296 https://dewiki.de/Lexikon/Rudolf_Noll (accessed on 21.04.2022).

297 https://dewiki.de/Lexikon/Camillo_Praschniker (accessed on 21.04.2022).

298 Mindler 2011; Fellner – Corradini 2006, 370; https://dewiki.de/Lexikon/Arnold_Schober (accessed on 21.04.2022); Eichler 1961.

299 A set of mainly NSDAP members and –applicants such as C. Praschniker, R. Egger, H. von Kenner, H. Vetters, R. Noll, and maybe G. Pascher (Wlach 2020b, 438 n. 60) had met each other at the so–called 'Führergrabung' in Carnuntum: Wlach 2020b, 424–432; Wlach 2019a, 355f.; Wlach 2012, 82–84; Kandler 1998, 53–57; Rudolf 1995, 216.

300 https://www.geschichtewiki.wien.gv.at/Juliputsch (accessed on 21.04.2022).

301 Kenner's "Der Reichsstatthalter. Der Reichskommissar – Fragebogen" from 09.05.1938 (Austrian Staatsarchiv, Vienna). – Schörner 2020, 126–128; Duma 2020, 92; Wlach 2019b, 369; Schörner 2016, 353.

302 Reichsgau Wien (1942) Die NSDAP–Gauleitung Wien, 278: https://www.findbuch.at/files/content/adressbuecher/1942_dr_om_ksk/17__Wien_NSDAP_und_staatliche_Verwaltung.pdf (accessed on 21.04.2022).

303 Wlach 2019b, 349. https://www.geschichtewiki.wien.gv.at/Hermann_Vetters_(Arch%C3%A4ologe) (accessed 21.04.2022). Information kindly provided by M. Laichmann from the Viennese 'Stadt– und Landesarchiv'.

304 https://dewiki.de/Lexikon/Hedwig_Kenner (accessed on 21.04.2022).

305 Wlach 2020b, 423.

306 Joachim 2013, 5: "Petrikovits beteiligte sich in Wien wie in Kärnten an diesem Putschversuch" [i.e. am ‚Juliputsch' 1934] ("Petrikovits participated in this attempted coup [i.e. the 'July Coup' of 1934] both in Vienna and in Carinthia"); Rüger 2010; https://dewiki.de/Lexikon/Harald_von_Petrikovits (accessed on 21.04.2022).

307 Fellner – Corradini 2006, 438; Wlach 1998, 113f.; Wohlers–Scharf 1995, 106; Kenner 1965. – Walter and Keil held the Co–Directorate of the OeAI from 1949 onwards. https://dewiki.de/Lexikon/Otto_Walter_(Arch%C3%A4ologe) (accessed on 21.04.2022).

308 Cited according to Kankeleit 2016, 19: "Es ist so schade, dass so wenig Menschen jetzt den Mut haben, ihre frühere Einstellung zu bekennen und ev. zuzugeben, dass sie sich geirrt haben, und die Konsequenzen ziehen [...]. Überhaupt könnte man an der Menschheit irre werden – besonders wenn man sie früher zu hoch eingeschätzt hat".

309 On the continuity from before 1938 and after 1945: Erker 2021a; Erker 2021b, 280; Erker 2017.

310 Feichtinger – Geiger 2022b.

311 Erker 2017, 187; Pfefferle – Pfefferle 2014, 265.

312 Borchhardt 1994, 284; Schörner 2021b; Schörner 2020; Duma 2020, 90–93; Schörner 2016, 353; Gutsmiedl–Schümann 2013, 250; PAR 1, 1951, 43. – Kenner seems to have changed her name from Hedwig von Kenner to Hedwig Kenner after 1945. Insofar, Gutsmiedl–Schümann 2013, 248, is wrong. Still, she was buried as Hedwig von Kenner in 1993: http://www.friedhof–ansichten.de/archives/9720 (accessed on 21.04.2022).

313 Wlach 1998, 117f.

314 https://dewiki.de/Lexikon/Rudolf_Noll (accessed on 21.04.2022).

315 https://dewiki.de/Lexikon/Fritz_Schachermeyr (accessed on 21.04.2022).

316 https://dewiki.de/Lexikon/Fritz_Knoll (accessed on 21.04.2022).

317 https://dewiki.de/Lexikon/Franz_Miltner (accessed on 21.04.2022).

318 https://dewiki.de/Lexikon/Wilhelm_Czermak_(%C3%84gyptologe) (accessed on 21.04.2022). Pfefferle – Pfefferle 2014, 159–161. 285.

319 https://dewiki.de/Lexikon/Richard_Meister (accessed on 21.04.2022).

320 "An österreichischen Universitäten wachsen wiedergebende, befriedigte, zustimmende und sammelnde Studenten auf, die geschätzt und gefördert werden, die anderen werden ausgejätet, umgepfropft oder ins Ausland verpflanzt. Das Ergebnis ist der selbstzufriedene, oberflächliche, konservative, überhebliche österreichische Akademiker, der Herr Doktor Karl", cited according to König 2012, 46. On the Austrian figure 'Herr Karl', archetypically staged by H. Qualtinger, see: https://www.youtube.com/watch?v=hZip_JrKqcY (accessed on 21.04.2022).

321 Erker 2017, 178: "die bleiernen Jahre".

322 Taschwer 2015b, 56; Taschwer 2015a, 263f.; Heiss 1999, 274.

323 https://dewiki.de/Lexikon/Paul_Felix_Lazarsfeld (accessed on 21.04.2022).

324 Cited according to Heiss 1999, 274, and Fleck 1996, 92.

325 Weninger 1953.

326 Pesditschek 2010, 289. 313f.; Wolf 1996, 95.

327 Pesditschek 2010, 316.

328 Pesditschek 2010, 314: "ein durchaus standhafter Gegner des Nationalsozialismus". – This opinion is adopted by Taeuber 2021, 320: "Dem Nationalsozialisismus stand Keil jedoch reserviert bzw. ablehnend gegenüber" ("However, Keil had a reserved or rejecting stance towards National Socialism"). 324: "Auch in einer sehr schwierigen Zeit [...] verfolgte er seine Ziele ungeachtet aller Widerstände und Hindernisse ohne sich dabei jedoch charakterlich zu verbiegen" ("Even in a very difficult time [...], he pursued his goals re-

gardless of all resistance and obstacles, without compromising his character").

329 Pesditschek 2010, 314: "Er war offenbar anders als Egger kein Opportunist, und viel mehr als dieser ein historischer Kopf". – Interestingly, Pesditschek 2010 ignores the archive studies of Hammerschmid 2009.

330 Accordingly, his estate is largely lost. Personal communication with B. Schwarz from the AAS.

331 His teacher, AES–professor and OeAI Director Emil Reisch (Wlach 1998, 104f.; https://dewiki.de/Lexikon/Emil_Reisch, accessed on 21.04.2022) was active within the VKPW and was also a member of the German–nationalist 'Deutscher Klub'. Mattes et al. 2022, 600; Huber et al. 2020, 51 n. 332. – See a description of Keil in his OeAI personal file: "Als echter Sohn des Sudetenlandes ist Keil ein kernfester Deutscher" ("As a true son of the Sudetenland, Keil is a steadfast German"), cited according Taeuber 2021, 316.

332 J. Keil in a letter to O. Benndorf from 18.06.1906: "Man sehnt sich nach einem Zustande, wie ihn unsere deutschen Brüder haben, wo jede Arbeit des einzelnen zugleich der Größe und dem Ansehen des gesamten Volkes Ruhm und Ehre bringt und jeder freudig und mit Aussicht auf Erfolg mitwirken kann an des Vaterlandes stets sich mehrendem Ansehen. Wie lange ist uns Österreichern diese Freude schon versagt und wird sie jemals wiederkommen?", cited according to Taeuber 2021, 320 n. 15.

333 Bekenntnis der Professoren an den deutschen Universitäten und Hochschulen zu Adolf Hitler und dem nationalsozialistischen Staat: https://archive.org/details/bekenntnisderpro00natiuoft/page/n1/mode/2up?view=theater (accessed on 21.04.2022).

334 https://gepris–historisch.dfg.de/person/5105955? (accessed on 21.04.2022).

335 https://geschichte.univie.ac.at/de/personen/arthur–marchet–prof–dr–– (accessed on 21.04.2022).

336 https://dewiki.de/Lexikon/Nationalsozialistischer_Deutscher_Dozentenbund (accessed on 21.04.2022).

337 Handbuch Reichsgau Wien 1941, 930. Pfefferle – Pfefferle 2014, 154.

338 Hammerschmid 2009, 98: "Er wurde durch Marchet telefonisch beurteilt, in dessen Abschrift stand, dass der Hochschulprofessor 1936 'auf Grund eines normalen Vorschlages' nach Wien kam, er hatte sich bei Grabungen in Ephesos ausgezeichnet und sei 'immer national und antisemitisch eingestellt, sodaß gegen ihn keinerlei politische Bedenken vorliegen'" ("He was assessed by Marchet by telephone, whose transcript stated that the university professor had come to Vienna in 1936 'on the basis of a normal suggestion', that he had distinguished himself in excavations in Ephesos and that he was "always nationally and anti–Semitically minded, so that there are no political reservations against him at all").

339 Hammerschmid 2009, 98: "Im Mai 1939 wurde Keil vom Gaupersonalamt als nationaler Mann bezeich-

net, der sich schon vor dem Umbruch für die NSDAP ausgesprochen hatte".

340 Unhaltbare Zustände an der philosophischen Fakultät der Universität Wien, Wiener Montag from 10.12.1945, 3: "Pg. [Party comrade] Mewaldt hat gleich seinem Kollegen Senator Keil, der nicht Pg. war, bis zum Umbruch stets mit stramm erhobenem Arm und Heil Hitler gegrüßt".

341 On his memberships, e.g. at the 'Reichsluftschutzbund' and the 'Nationalsozialistische Volkswohlfahrt', see Pesditschek 2010, 310.

342 Heiss 1999, 269; Heiß 1993, 141. 151.

343 Pfefferle – Pfefferle 2014, 310; Gelbmann 2005. – Member of the 'Deutscher Klub': Weisz 2009, 74f.; https://dewiki.de/Lexikon/Friedrich_Kainz (accessed on 21.04.2022).

344 Pfefferle – Pfefferle 2014, 304; https://dewiki.de/Lexikon/Ernst_Sp%C3%A4th (accessed on 21.04.2022).

345 Pfefferle – Pfefferle 2014, 290; https://dewiki.de/Lexikon/Hugo_Hassinger (accessed on 21.04.2022). – On his memberships, see BArch 4901/13265 (e.g., Deutscher Schulverein Südmark). – On the 'Hassingergasse', see Autengruber et al. 2014, 104f.

346 Pfefferle – Pfefferle 2014, 285; Erker 2021a, 56; Erker 2021b, 280; https://dewiki.de/Lexikon/Wilhelm_Czermak_(%C3%84gyptologe) (accessed on 21.04.2022).

347 Mattes et al. 2022, 580f.

348 Pfefferle – Pfefferle 2014, 264f.; Heiß 1993, 151: "Es ist also davon auszugehen, daß unter den Österreichischen Professoren einige (unterschiedlich intensiv und lange) Befürworter und Anhänger des Nationalsozialismus waren, ohne je formal Parteimitglieder gewesen zu sein" ("It can therefore be assumed that among the Austrian professors some were (with varying intensity and for varying lengths of time) supporters and followers of National Socialism without ever having been formal party members").

349 Der Reichsminister für Wissenschaft, Erziehung und Volksbildung from 13.08.1942: "[…] bestelle ich Sie hiermit zum Direktor des Archäologisch–spigraphischen [sic!] Seminars der Universität Wien" (University Vienna, Archives). Wlach 2020b, 421; Hammerschmid 2009, 99.

350 Handbuch Reichsgau Wien 1944, 392; Rektorat der Universität Wien 1943b, 26; ibid. 1944a, 26; ibid. 1944b, 16; Pfefferle – Pfefferle 2014, 110; Pesditschek 2010, 310.

351 V. Christian was Dean, Vice–Principal, and Principal at the University of Vienna before 1945: https://geschichte.univie.ac.at/de/personen/viktor–christian–o–univ–prof–dr–phil (accessed on 21.04.2022); Pfefferle – Pfefferle 2014, 285; https://dewiki.de/Lexikon/Viktor_Christian (accessed on 21.04.2022).

352 A. Marchet was Senator, Pro–Principal, and Dean at the University of Vienna before 1945: https://geschichte.univie.ac.at/de/personen/arthur–marchet–prof–dr––

(accessed on 21.04.2022); Pfefferle – Pfefferle 2014, 297.

353 F. Knoll was Senator and Principal at the University of Vienna before 1945: https://geschichte.univie.ac.at/de/personen/fritz–friedrich–knoll–o–univ–prof–dr–phil (accessed on 21.04.2022); Pfefferle – Pfefferle 2014, 294; Taschwer 2013; https://dewiki.de/Lexikon/Fritz_Knoll (accessed on 21.04.2022).

354 E. Pernkopf was Principal and Dean at the University of Vienna before 1945: https://geschichte.univie.ac.at/de/personen/eduard–pernkopf–o–univ–prof–dr–med (accessed on 21.04.2022); Pfefferle – Pfefferle 2014, 110. 325; Pesditschek 2010, 310; Handbuch Reichsgau Wien 1944, 391f. – Christian, Knoll, and Pernkopf were members of the 'German Club': Huber 2020a, 51. 61. 67; https://dewiki.de/Lexikon/Eduard_Pernkopf (accessed on 21.04.2022).

355 Letter to J. Keil by Arthur Marchet from 12.10.1943 (University of Vienna, Archives): "Ich danke Ihnen bei dieser Gelegenheit aber auch für alle die Hilfe, die Sie der Universität und mir in jeder Beziehung zuteil werden lassen und bitte Sie auch in Zukunft so zur Seite zu stehen". Hammerschmid 2009, 98.

356 Pesditschek 2010, 314.

357 Wolf 1996, 95.

358 Pesditschek 2010, 314.

359 Feichtinger – Hecht 2013a, 162: "Der Althistoriker Keil fungierte von 1945 bis 1959 als Generalsekretär und Sekretär der phil.–hist. Klasse [...]. Ebenso wie [Ernst] Späth und Meister zählten auch [Adalbert] Prey und Keil zu jenem Netzwerk von Akademiemitgliedern, die in der Zeit des autoritären Ständestaats ihren beruflichen Aufstieg genommen und die Zeit des Nationalsozialismus unbeschadet überstanden hatten" ("From 1945 to 1959, the ancient historian Keil served as General Secretary and Secretary of the phil.–hist. Class [...]. Like Späth and Meister, Prey and Keil belonged to the network of Academy members who had risen professionally during the authoritarian Ständestaat and survived the National Socialist era unscathed"). Benetka 1998, 215.

360 In a letter from 04.12.1931, O. Menghin, member of the 'bear's den' and NSDAP, describes J. Keil as follows: Keil "scheint aber in Professorenkreisen nicht sehr beliebt, vielleicht weil er ein etwas gerader Michel ist" ("Keil, however, doesn't seem to be very popular among professors, maybe because he is a bit of a straight guy"), cited according to Pesditschek 2009, 209.

361 Braun 1964, 524. – Taeuber 2021, 324: Keil's "vorbildliches Pflichtbewußtsein" (Keil's "exemplary sense of duty").

362 https://dewiki.de/Lexikon/Egon_Braun (accessed on 21.04.2022).

363 Braun 1964, 524: "Eine beachtliche administrative Begabung, die verschiedenartigen Aufgaben sich anzupassen verstand, befähigte Keil, mehrere amtliche Funktionen mit Präzision zu versehen". – Accordingly, Keil said in a letter from 01.06.1959 about himself that "he was accustomed to persevering in any position he was placed in for as long as he was capable" ("Gewohnt, auf jedem Posten, auf den ich gestellt wurde, solange auszuharren, als ich es vermag"), cited according to Taeuber 2021, 323 fig. 13.7. At that time, i.e. in 1959, R. Meister was President of the AAS. – Wlach 2019a, 373. 374: "Der anscheinend stets geschickt agierende Keil" ("The seemingly always skilfully acting Keil").

364 Investigation of the Gauleitung Vienna about Meister from 05.06.1940, cited according to Heiß 1993, 159 n. 58: "Er hat sich mit großem Eifer um die Geschäftsführung des philosophischen Dekanats und des Rektorats gekümmert [...]. Er besitzt eine erstaunliche Gesetzeskenntnis und ist sehr geschickt in der Abfassung von Memoranden, von Vorschlägen, Prüfungsordnungen, etc. vorgegangen. Er hat sich hiedurch zahllose große Verdienste um seine Fakultät erworben [...]. Er erhielt daher das Fach Latein, um auf diese Art seine für die Universität wichtige Arbeitskraft zu erhalten" ("He has taken care of the management of the Philosophical Deanery and the Rectorate with great zeal [...]. He possesses an astonishing knowledge of the law and has been very skilful in the drafting of memoranda, of proposals, examination regulations, etc. He has thereby earned countless great merits for his Faculty [...]. He was therefore given the subject of Latin in order to maintain in this way his manpower, which is important for the university"). – See also, Graf–Stuhlhofer 1998, 156f.

365 Paplauskas – Ramunas 1961, 98. 103.

366 Feichtinger 2015, 173: "Der Meister der Anpassung".

367 Feichtinger 2015, Taschwer 2015a, 240–246; Fellner – Corradini 2006, 277f.; https://dewiki.de/Lexikon/Richard_Meister (accessed on 21.04.2022).

368 Duma 2020, 66; Feichtinger 2015, 173: "Richard Meister. A serving university professor in four political regimes"; Benetka 1998, 189 n. 4: "Politische Regime kamen und gingen – Meister blieb" ("Political regimes came and went – Meister remained").

369 https://geschichte.univie.ac.at/de/personen/richard–meister–o–univ–prof–dr–phil (accessed on 21.04.2022). – On Meister during the 'Ständestaat', see Mattes et al. 2022, 580, and Feichtinger 2022, 427.

370 Praschniker was active within the VKPW and within the 'Deutscher Schulverein Südmark' according to Gauleitung Wien from 20.06.1941, and from his "Der Reichsstatthalter. Der Reichskommissar – Fragebogen" from 08.05.1938 (Austrian Staatsarchiv, Vienna).

371 Egger was active within the 'Deutsche Gemeinschaft', the VKPW, the 'Südostdeutsche Forschungsgemeinschaft Wien', and the 'Deutsche Studentenschaft': https://dewiki.de/Lexikon/Deutsche_Studentenschaft (accessed on 21.04.2022).

372 https://www.geschichtewiki.wien.gv.at/Anschlussbewegung (accessed on 21.04.2022).

373 Rosar 1971, 49.

374 https://de–academic.com/dic.nsf/dewiki/1182086 (accessed on 21.04.2022); Graf–Stuhlhofer 1998, 155; Rosar 1971, 45–53.

375 Huber et al. 2020, 35; Feichtinger 2015, 173f. ("member of the German Club"); Budka – Jurman 2013, 309. – On Meister's German–nationalist engagements, see Heiß 1993, 159f n. 60f.

376 Mattes et al. 2022, 580; Feichtinger 2015, 173.

377 The 'Bärenhöhle' was a covert, anti–Semitic, German–nationalist, and anti–Socialist network at the Viennese University with 19 members (tab. 8), all of whom were also Academy members except G. Turba: Erker 2021a, 44f.; Taschwer 2018b; Taschwer 2016a,b; Feichtinger 2015, 173; Pfefferle – Pfefferle 2014, 160f.; Budka – Jurman 2013, 309. – Abel, Christian, Menghin, Much, and others had been labelled as "Hakenkreuzprofessoren" ("Swastika professors") already in 1924: Urban 2021, 233. The newspaper 'Der Tag' from 26.07.1924 calls Abel, Christian, Junker, Menghin, and Much members of a "University–German Clique" ("Mitglieder der universitätsdeutschen Clique").

378 Erker 2021a, 45f.

379 Erker 2021a, 52.

380 https://geschichte.univie.ac.at/de/personen/otto–skrbensky (Accessed on 21.04.2022).

381 Erker 2021a, 55.

382 Heiss 1999, 271; Heiß 1993, 140.

383 Pfefferle – Pfefferle 2014, 297.

384 Cited according to Feichtinger 2015, 173f.

385 Gauleitung Wien from 05.06.1940, cited according to Heiß 1993, 160 n. 64.

386 Gauleitung Wien from 20.05.1940, cited according to Heiß 1993, 160 n. 66: "Bei Sammlungen und Spenden beteiligt sich [Meister] nach Berichten der Blockwalterin der NSV [Nationalsozialistische Volkswohlfahrt] äußerst rege, er ist in seiner Gebefreudigkeit ein leuchtendes Beispiel". – On Keil and the NSV, see Pesditschek 2010, 310. https://dewiki.de/Lexikon/Nationalsozialistische_Volkswohlfahrt (accessed on 21.04.2022).

387 On Meister's initial problems and the redeployment, see Heiß 1993, 140.

388 Erziehung und Universität. Eine Immatrikulationsrede von Univ.–Professor Dr. Richard Meister, in: Völkischer Beobachter 166 from 14.06.1944, 4. https://dewiki.de/Lexikon/V%C3%B6lkischer_Beobachter (accessed on 21.04.2022).

389 Graf–Stuhlhofer 1998, 156.

390 https://geschichte.univie.ac.at/de/personen/richard–meister–o–univ–prof–dr–phil (accessed on 21.04.2022); Pfefferle – Pfefferle 2014, 298. Feichtinger – Uhl 2018, 250; Feichtinger 2015, 176.

391 Taschwer 2015b, 56; Budka – Jurman 2013, 309.

392 Benetka 1998, 191. 197–204. 217.

393 Der neue Vorwärts. Wochenblatt für fortschrittliche Sozialisten in Österreich from 15.07.1951, cited according to Feichtinger – Hecht 2013c, 194.

394 https://dewiki.de/Lexikon/Oswald_Menghin (accessed on 21.04.2022).

395 Taschwer 2014. Taschwer 2012. https://dewiki.de/Lexikon/Othenio_Abel (accessed on 21.04.2022).

396 https://dewiki.de/Lexikon/Robert_Lach (accessed on 21.04.2022). See the 'Robert–Lach–Gasse' in Autengruber et al. 2014, 91f.

397 The musicologist R. Ficker in 1946, cited according to Taschwer 2016a, 146: "Meisters Zugehörigkeit zur Clique Menghin, Abel, Lach und Konsorten verrät deutlich die Linie, die er seit jeher vertreten hat [...]. An Meister und seine Schützlinge traut sich niemand heran!". Clearly, Ficker refers here to the 'bear's den', of which Meister, Menghin, Abel, Lach "and their ilk" were participants (tab. 8). https://dewiki.de/Lexikon/Rudolf_von_Ficker (accessed on 21.04.2022).

398 https://www.geschichtewiki.wien.gv.at/Richard_Meister (accessed on 21.04.2022); Kainz 1965, 270f. – In 1964, the AAS finally decided to honour him with the medal "Bene merito": Alm 114, 1964, 137; Hahn 1985, 28 #81, Taf. 10 #81 plus button–badge: Hahn 1985, 54 #188.

399 Oesterreichischer Bundesverlag für Unterricht, Wissenschaft und Kunst 1961.

400 Oesterreichischer Bundesverlag für Unterricht, Wissenschaft und Kunst 1961, 4f.: "der Strahlungsbereich der Persönlichkeit Richard Meister" ("the radiation range of the personality Richard Meister"). https://dewiki.de/Lexikon/Heinrich_Drimmel (accessed on 21.04.2022).

401 Interestingly, Drimmel played a significant role at the restart of the Ephesian excavations after WW II. A direct contact of him to Keil is documented by Wohlers–Scharf 1995, 127–129 fig. 61. – See also a letter of F. Miltner to H. Drimmel from 09.11.1957: Wohlers–Scharf 1995, 159–161 fig. 77. – Miltner 1958, 133.

402 Feichtinger – Geiger 2022c, 305 n. 149; Erker 2021, 59; Feichtinger 2015, 176.

403 Feichtinger 2022, 439.

404 Pfefferle – Pfefferle 2014, 310; https://dewiki.de/Lexikon/Friedrich_Kainz (accessed on 21.04.2022).

405 Kainz 1965.

406 https://www.geschichtewiki.wien.gv.at/Meistergasse?uselayout=mobile (accessed on 21.04.2022).

407 https://de.wikipedia.org/wiki/Hietzinger_Friedhof (accessed on 21.04.2022). Information kindly provided by the administration of the Hietzinger Friedhof. – In Austria, most resting places at cemeteries are rented for a certain period of time, usually for ten years. If the dues are not paid after that again, for example because the family line has ended or interest has been lost, a grave is emptied and the place rented anew.

408 Feichtinger 2015, 173: "Der Meister [...] und seine Helfer".

409 Schachermeyr 1965, 242.

410 Meister: Feichtinger 2015, 174. – Keil: Pesditschek 2010, 310.

411 Meister: cited according to Feichtinger 2015, 173f. – Keil: cited according to Hammerschmid 2009, 98.

412 Schachermeyr 1965, 242.

413 Regarding Keil from 1958: 80th birthday – "ÆT.S.80": Hahn 1985, 28 #80, Taf. 10; Pesditschek – Feldmann 2012; Hartig 1964, 75.

414 Regarding Meister from 1951: 70th birthday – "ÆT.s.LXX": Hahn 1985, 27 #77, Taf. 9; Hartig 1964, 59. 76. – There is a second and similar Hartig medal with the inscription: "Richardus Meister olim praeses societas Universitatis": https://geschichte.univie.ac.at/de/personen/richard–meister–o–univ–prof–dr–phil (accessed on 21.04.2022).

415 The tradition of Hartig medals goes back to the 1920s. Such medals were dedicated to, e.g., Wilhelm Bauer (1937, Hahn 1985, 26 #73, Taf. 9), Alfons Dopsch (1938, Hahn 1985, 26 #74, Taf. 9), Heinrich (von) Ficker (1951, Hahn 1985, 27 #78, Taf. 9), Hans Hirsch (1938, Hahn 1985, 27 #75, Taf. 9. Fellner – Corradini 2006, 187. See, 'Hans–Hirsch–Park' in Autengruber et al. 2014, 29f.), Oswald Redlich (1928, Hahn 1985, 25 #66, Taf. 7), and Heinrich (von) Srbik (1930; https://scopeq.cc.univie.ac.at/Query/detail.aspx?ID=3809, accessed on 21.04.2022). The 'committee' of the Academy taking care of the Josef Keil medal was headed by R. Meister (archive information kindly provided by S. Sienell).

416 Budka – Jurmann 2013, 307.

417 Handbuch Reichsgau Wien 1944, 392; Rektorat der Universität Wien 1943a, 28; ibid. 1943b, 26; ibid. 1944a, 26; ibid. 1944b, 16.

418 Rektorat der Universität Wien 1944b, 16; Feichtinger 2015, 173f.

419 On Keil, see Hammerschmid 2009, 116. – On Meister, see Heiß 1993, 160 n. 66.

420 Heiß 1993, 140.

421 Keil: Hammerschmid 2009, 98. – Meister: Feichtinger 2015, 173f.

422 Heiß 1993, 159 n. 58.

423 Feichtinger 2015, 175f. – The protocol of the votes from 25.04.1945 is preserved in the Archives of the UoV (Report of J. Keil in Akademischer Senat GZ 10 ex 1944/45 from 25.04.1945, courtesy of U. Denk). Amongst the electors were counted, e.g., the NSDAP members/–applicants F. Kainz (Pfefferle – Pfefferle 2014, 310), O. Pötzl (Pfefferle – Pfefferle 2014, 327), F. Wilke (Pfefferle – Pfefferle 2014, 346), G. Entz (Pfefferle – Pfefferle 2014, 345), W. Havers (Pfefferle – Pfefferle 2014, 290), H. Leitmeier (https://dewiki.de/Lexikon/Hans_Leitmeier, accessed on 21.04.2022), H. Mayer (Pfefferle – Pfefferle 2014, 335; BArch R 9361–V/28436), and E. Späth (Pfefferle – Pfefferle 2014, 304). Taschwer 2015a, 240.

424 Pfefferle – Pfefferle 2014, 20 n. 26. Pesditschek 2010, 312. https://geschichte.univie.ac.at/de/personen/josef–keil (accessed on 21.04.2022).

425 Protokoll der außerordentlichen Gesamtsitzung am 30. Oktober 1945 (AAS, Archives, A 0997; archive information kindly provided by S. Sienell). Feichtinger 2022, 433.

426 Alm 97, 1947, 9 ("Wahlsitzung der Gesamtakademie"). 90; Matis – Suppan 2022, 129.

427 Pfefferle – Pfefferle 2014, 290; https://dewiki.de/Lexikon/Hugo_Hassinger (accessed on 21.04.2022).

428 Pfefferle – Pfefferle 2014, 290; https://dewiki.de/Lexikon/Wilhelm_Havers (accessed on 21.04.2022). – On his NSV membership see BArch R 4901/13265.

429 Pfefferle – Pfefferle 2014, 160f.; https://dewiki.de/Lexikon/Hermann_Junker (accessed on 21.04.2022). – See Meister's invitation letter to Junker from 25.10.1945 on http://www.afrikanistik.at/pdf/pubmat/aoeaw_brief-meister_19451025.pdf (accessed on 21.04.2022).

430 https://dewiki.de/Lexikon/Josef_Keil (accessed on 21.04.2022).

431 Feichtinger et al. 2013, 187.

432 https://dewiki.de/Lexikon/Richard_Meister (accessed on 21.04.2022).

433 https://dewiki.de/Lexikon/Camillo_Praschniker (accessed on 21.04.2022).

434 https://geschichte.univie.ac.at/de/personen/robert–reininger (accessed on 21.04.2022). Heiß 1993, 141.

435 Pfefferle – Pfefferle 2014, 304; https://dewiki.de/Lexikon/Ernst_Sp%C3%A4th (accessed on 21.04.2022).

436 Schachermeyr 1965, 242.

437 Taschwer 2018b, 778f.; Stifter 2014, 343 n. 1463; Pfefferle/Pfefferle 2014, 110; Pesditschek 2010, 312.

438 Denk 2019, 417; Maisel 2013, 26; Just 2010, 107f. 144, Hutterer – Just 2007, 315; Fellner – Corradini 2006, 341; Huter 1969.

439 Die Naziseuche an unseren Hochschulen, Wiener Montag from 07.01.1946, 3; Taschwer 2015a, 72 n. 417; Stifter 2014, 343 n. 1463.

440 Pfefferle – Pfefferle 2014, 290.

441 Pfefferle – Pfefferle 2014, 77.

442 https://www.geschichtewiki.wien.gv.at/Wiener_Montag (accessed on 21.04.2022).

443 Pfefferle – Pfefferle 2014, 285; https://dewiki.de/Lexikon/Wilhelm_Czermak_(%C3%84gyptologe) (accessed on 21.04.2022).

444 Pfefferle – Pfefferle 2014, 304.

445 Unhaltbare Zustände an der philosophischen Fakultät der Universität Wien, Wiener Montag from 10.12.1945, 3: "Von den Führern dieser Fakultät Dekan [Wilhelm] Czermak, Prodekan [Ernst] Späth, Prorektor [Richard] Meister und Senator [Josef] Keil wird versucht, eine Reihe schwer belasteter Parteigenossen als Mitglieder der Fakultät zu halten". See also: Die Universität, Keimzelle des Nationalsozialismus, Wiener Montag from 10.12.1945, 3. Die Rückkehr von Naziprofessoren an die Wiener Universität, Wiener Montag from

12.11.1945, 4. – Meister and Czermak were addressed as "protectors of Nazi professors" ("Protektoren der Naziprofessoren"), Wiener Montag from 03.12.1945, 4; Taschwer 2015a, 244f.; Stifter 2014, 343; Benetka 1998, 197.

446 Pfefferle – Pfefferle 2014, 299.

447 Pfefferle – Pfefferle 2014, 303; Rückkehr von Naziprofessoren an die Wiener Universität, Wiener Montag from 12.11.1945, 3f.

448 Der Fall Nadler, Wiener Montag from 17.12.1945, 3: "Meister und Keil, Mewaldt und Sedlmayer, der ganze Klüngel nationaler und nationalsozialistischer Professoren, bei denen man nie weiß, wo der Nationalismus aufhört und der Nazismus anfängt. Wir fordern die Entfernung all dieser Männer im Namen vieler Tausender lebender Österreicher, aber auch im Namen der vielen Toten, die an dem Nationalsozialismus gestorben und verdorben sind". See also: Die Wiener Universität, Keimzelle des Nationalsozialismus, Wiener Montag from 10.12.1945, 3. Universität – Brutstätte des Nationalsozialismus, Wiener Montag from 26.11.1945, 3, etc. (tab. 5).

449 The musicologist R. Ficker in 1946, cited according to Taschwer 2016a, 146.

450 Pfefferle – Pfefferle 2014, 110; Pesditschek 2010, 312.

451 Pfefferle – Pfefferle 2014, 110; Pesditschek 2010, 312; Hammerschmid 2009, 99; Benetka 1998, 196. 204 n. 56.

452 https://geschichte.univie.ac.at/de/personen/otto–skrbensky (accessed on 21.04.2022); Taschwer 2015b, 56: "Otto Skrbensky war der bis 1952 verantwortliche Sektionschef im Unterrichtsministerium. Skrbensky war bereits im Austrofaschismus für die politischen Säuberungen an den Hochschulen zuständig gewesen und spielte nicht nur eine Schlüsselrolle bei der kulanten Entnazifizierung, sondern auch bei der noch sehr viel halbherzigeren Remigration" ("Otto Skrbensky was the responsible section head in the Ministry of Education until 1952. Skrbensky had already been responsible for the political cleansing of the universities during Austrofascism. He not only played a key role in the accommodating denazification, but also in the even much more half–hearted remigration"). Taschwer 2015a, 241f.; Feichtinger – Hecht 2013c, 193.

453 Ash 2015, 138.

454 Taschwer 2018b, 778f.; Stifter 2014, 343 n. 1463; Pfefferle – Pfefferle 2014, 110; Pesditschek 2010, 312.

455 Stifter 2014, 346–365; Klos – Feichtinger 2022, 186; Erker 2017, 175; Feichtinger 2015, 175; Pfefferle – Pfefferle 2014, 136; Feichtinger – Hecht 2013c, 191.

456 Feichtinger – Uhl 2022, 258: "Für die ehemaligen Nationalsozialisten setzten sich Vizepräsident Meister und Generalsekretär Keil bei Bundespräsident Renner ein, als sie am 21. Jänner 1947 mit der Einladung zu einer Ansprache bei der Festsitzung in der Präsidentschaftskanzlei vorstellig wurden".

457 Pfefferle – Pfefferle 2014, 163–165. 296; Fellner – Corradi 2006, 207; https://dewiki.de/Lexikon/Kurt_Leuchs (accessed on 21.04.2022). See the 'Leuchsweg' in Autengruber et al. 2014, 107f.; Mertz 2020, 365.

458 Pfefferle – Pfefferle 2014, 306.

459 Feichtinger – Geiger 2022a, 155f.; Feichtinger – Hecht 2013c, 191f.; Wild 1956.

460 https://dewiki.de/Lexikon/Hedwig_Kenner (accessed on 21.04.2022).

461 Wlach 2019b, 370; Krierer 2001, 223.

462 Wlach 2019a, 371, https://dewiki.de/Lexikon/Camillo_Praschniker (accessed on 21.04.2022).

463 Pesditschek 2010, 303 n. 88; Wlach 2019a, 373; Wlach 1998, 109; https://dewiki.de/Lexikon/Rudolf_Egger_(Historiker) (accessed on 21.04.2022).

464 See Keil's letters to the ministry of education from 01.02.1949 and from 22.12.1949 (http://www.afrikanistik.at/pubmat.htm, accessed on 21.04.2022), Meister's invitation to Junker from 25.10.1945 (http://www.afrikanistik.at/pdf/pubmat/aoeaw_brief–meister_19451025.pdf, accessed on 21.04.2022), and a letter from W. Czermak to "Rector magnificus" R. Meister from 27.11.1949 (http://www.afrikanistik.at/pdf/pubmat/auw_brief–czermak_19491127.pdf, accessed on 21.04.2022).

465 Huber 2020a, 60; Schneider 2012, 146. 175–178.

466 Pfefferle – Pfefferle 2014, 298.

467 Pfefferle – Pfefferle 2014, 159–161. 285.

468 Budka – Jurman 2013, 304. 310f.

469 Bundesverfassungsgesetz vom 21.04.1948, über die vorzeitige Beendigung der im Nationalsozialistengesetz vorgesehenen Sühnefolgen für minderbelastete Personen, BGBl 99/1948. Feichtinger et al. 2013, 185f.; Feichtinger – Hecht 2013b, 185.

470 Feichtinger – Hecht 2013b, 183.

471 Füllenbach 2017; Pfefferle – Pfefferle 2014, 300; https://dewiki.de/Lexikon/Josef_Nadler (accessed on 21.04.2022).

472 Pesditschek 2013; Pfefferle – Pfefferle 2014, 304; Fellner – Corradini 2006, 385f.; https://dewiki.de/Lexikon/Heinrich_Srbik (accessed on 21.04.2022).

473 Pfefferle – Pfefferle 2014, 303; https://dewiki.de/Lexikon/Hans_Sedlmayr (accessed on 21.04.2022).

474 Pfefferle – Pfefferle 2014, 294; https://dewiki.de/Lexikon/Fritz_Knoll (accessed on 21.04.2022).

475 BGBl Nr. 569, 630 (09.05.1947).

476 Feichtinger – Geiger 2022c, 277.

477 Mattes – Uhl 2022, 455 n. 82.

478 Dekanat of the Philosophical Faculty from 20.12.1949 (University Vienna, Archives). – Interestingly, only ⅔ of the commission voted for Keil (25 yes, 9 no, 3 abstentions), i.e. the proposal had to face considerable opposition. Pfefferle – Pfefferle 2014, 110; Pesditschek 2010, 312; Wlach 1998, 112.

479 Marchhart 2020, 162. 166; Pesditschek 2012a, 182: "Mit größter Wahrscheinlichkeit trat er [i.e. Miltner] bereits am 1. Oktober 1937 – also noch illegal – in die

NSDAP ein" ("Most likely, he [i.e. Miltner] joined the NSDAP already on October 1, 1937, so still illegal"); Wlach 1998, 126–128; Wolf 1996, 89; Ulf 1985; Keil 1961; Keil 1959; Alm 101, 1951, 37; Alm 100, 1950, 66; Alm 99, 1949, 37.

480 Pesditschek 2007, 54f.; Wolf 1996, 89; Czeike 1992–1997 V, 56; https://dewiki.de/Lexikon/Fritz_Schachermeyr (accessed on 21.04.2022).

481 Rebenich 2009, 57 n. 82; Wolf 1996, 93; https://dewiki.de/Lexikon/Hermann_Bengtson (accessed on 21.04.2022).

482 Pesditschek 2010, 314: "schwerst belastete und offenbar auch noch weiterhin praktizierende Nationalsozialisten oder jedenfalls Rassisten". Not accepting Keil's involvement, Pesditschek 2010, 314, has to explain somewhat laboriously his still "surprising and unsettling" intention with the long–term friendship to F. Miltner.

483 Budka – Jurman 2013, 303f. ("complete rehabilitation"); Pesditschek 2007, 61f.

484 Alm 107, 1957, 65; Alm 106, 1956, 68; Alm 105, 1955, 68; Feichtinger – Hecht 2013c, 195f.

485 Pesditschek 2010, 312; Keil 1961, 363; Keil 1959, 655.

486 Keil 1961, 361. – The closeness of the two can be sensed from a letter that J. Keil wrote to F. Miltner on 18.07.1930 ("Lieber Franzl!"): Wohlers–Scharf 1995, 120f. fig. 58. – On this special relationship, see Taeuber 2021, 322: "Das Verhältnis der beiden Männer [i.e. of Keil and Miltner] zueinander war so gut, daß es Keil auch über ideologische Differenzen [...] hinwegsehen ließ" ("The relationship between the two men [i.e. of Keil and Miltner] was so good that it allowed Keil to overlook ideological differences between them").

487 Miltner was the successor of Keil as 'scientific secretary' at the OeAI in 1927 (Reisch 1930, 266); both took part at the restarted excavations in Ephesos from 1926 till 1931 (Keil 1933, 5; Keil 1932, 5; Keil 1930a, 5; Keil 1929b, 6; Keil 1929a, 6; Keil 1926, 249). – Curiously, former NSDAP member Miltner received the 'Theodor Körner Preis' from the left political side in 1958 (Rathkolb – Mulley 2013, 70; Pesditschek 2012a, 191; Krierer 2001, 224), an accolade that is hardly mentioned any more. Miltner died in 1959 from a brain haemorrhage (Völkl 1959, 189: "Death tore the restless worker away"), at 58 years of age (Eichler 1959, 1). As Praschniker, he is buried as an "eminent personality" in the 'Grinzinger Friedhof', Vienna (https://austria–forum.org/af/AustriaWiki/Grinzinger_Friedhof (accessed on 21.04.2022). After 1971, an alley was named after him in the 11th district of Vienna ('Miltnerweg'; Czeike 1992–1997 IV, 270).

488 Pesditschek 2012a, 191: "jedenfalls völlig außer Zweifel, dass Miltner vor und nach 1945 überzeugter Rassist gewesen ist" ("There is no doubt whatsoever that Miltner was a convinced racist both before and after 1945"). –C. Praschniker mentions Miltner's "occasionally peculiar character" ("Miltners Persönlichkeit, die

mitunter befremdet"), cited according to Pesditschek 2012a, 181.

489 Braun 1964, 523; Miltner 1955. – However, Miltner had been familiar with Ephesos for a long time, he was fluent in the Turkish language and his reputation within the Turkish administration was quite high (Krierer 2001, 218; Stiglitz – Knibbe 1998, 68f.; Keil 1961, 362f.). He was present at the Austrian excavations from 1926 until 1931, and from 1955 until 1959: Alzinger 1962, 253f.

490 R. Egger, cited according to Pesditschek 2012a, 181: "wobei dieser [i.e. F. Miltner] schon damals [i.e. 1933] im von Rudolf Egger verfaßten Kommissionsbericht als »perfekter Leiter von Ausgrabungen bezeichnet« wurde" ("whereby this person [i.e. F. Miltner] was already [i.e. in 1933] referred to as a "perfect leader of excavations" in the commission report written by Rudolf Egger at that time").

491 Keil 1961, 371f.: "Die Übersteigerung des Grabungstempos". Maybe, Keil refers here to O. Benndorf who had warned already in 1893: "Es ist nicht wünschenswert, daß die große Arbeit in kurzer Zeit forciert werde. In raschen, überhasteten Grabungen gehen oft die wichtigsten Beobachtungen [...] verloren" ("It is not desirable for the significant work to be rushed in a short period of time. In quick and hasty excavations, the most important observations are often lost"), cited according to Wohlers–Scharf 1995, 73. – On the lack of documentation regarding Miltner's excavations, Auinger 2009, 31: "F. Miltner trieb seine Grabungen zügig voran, weshalb detaillierte Beobachtungen nicht möglich waren und der Befund nicht genau dokumentiert wurde" [...]. Das Verschüttungsmaterial auf der Straße wurde ohne detaillierte Beobachtung und Dokumentation der Stratigraphie weggeräumt ("F. Miltner proceeded swiftly with his excavations, which is why detailed observations were not possible, and the findings were not accurately documented [...]. The debris on the street was cleared without detailed observation and documentation of the stratigraphy"). – Miltner 1958, 133: "Da es gelungen ist, die Grabung in angemessenem Umfang zu motorisieren, sodaß Österreich heute die größte und modernste Ausgrabung in Anatolien betreibt, war es möglich, raumgreifend den Stadtteil zwischen [Celsus] Bibliothek und Odeion freizulegen" ("Since it has been successful to motorize the excavation to an appropriate extent, allowing Austria to operate the largest and most modern excavation in Anatolia today, it was possible to extensively uncover the district between the [Celsus] Library and the Odeion"). – On Miltner's technical efforts and the resulting criticism, see Quatember 2005, 276f. E.g., A. v. Gerkan stated: "Offenbar haben sie alle in Ephesos eine starke Vorliebe für technische Einrichtungen, denn auch für die Grabung selbst verwenden sie motorisiertes Gerät. Auch dieses erfordert technisches Personal,

Techniker oder gar Ingenieure. Aus diesen Kreisen stammt ein jetzt kursierender Ausspruch, sie grüben so schnell, dass die Archäologen nicht nachkommen könnten. Hoffentlich ist das übertrieben, aber es zeigt doch, wohin der Ehrgeiz geht und das Ziel" ("Apparently, they all have a strong preference for technical facilities in Ephesos, as they even use motorised equipment for the excavation itself. This also requires technical personnel, technicians, or even engineers. From these circles comes a statement that is currently circulating: they are digging so fast that the archaeologists can't keep up. Hopefully, this is an exaggeration, but it does show where the ambition is heading and what the goal is"), cited according to Quatember 2005, 278 n. 60.

492 1904–1908, 1911–1913, 1926–1931, 1933, and 1935: Alzinger 1962, 253.

493 Keil's entry into the diary of the Austrian excavation house from 19.04.1953, cited according to Alzinger 1962, 212: "Ich bin glücklich, daß ich nach 19jähriger Abwesenheit unser altes Ausgrabungshaus, das ich vor 49 Jahren [i.e. in 1904] das erste Mal betreten habe, in bestem Zustande wiedersehen und zwei Tage in ihm verleben konnte, die zu den schönsten meines Lebens gehören. Nicht nur, daß ich an unserer Arbeitsstätte weilen und alte Plätze des Ruinenfeldes wieder besuchen konnte – auch die Herzlichkeit des Empfanges durch die Direktoren der Museen sowie die Vertreter der Ephesos–Society in Selcuk haben mich auf das tiefste gerührt, und ich kann ihnen nur von ganzem Herzen danken. Ich hoffe, daß es unserem Österreichischen Archäologischen Institut möglich sein wird, die Ausgrabungen wieder aufzunehmen, zur Förderung der Wissenschaft und des Landes, das ich liebe, wie eine zweite Heimat".

494 From a letter to Heinrich Drimmel, Minister of Education, from 25.04.1956, cited according to Wohlers–Scharf 1995, 128: "Dem [Ephesos] Unternehmen, dem ein großer Teil meiner Lebensarbeit und meiner – ich darf es so sagen – meiner Liebe gehört".

495 Taeuber 2021, 322f. fig. 13.7: "Herzanfall [...] der Rat der Ärzte".

496 See, Keil's letter of resignation at Taeuber 2021, 323 fig. 13.7.

497 Rektorat der Universität Wien 1939, 19; Pfefferle – Pfefferle 2014, 294.

498 Huber 2020a, 61; https://dewiki.de/Lexikon/Fritz_Knoll (accessed on 21.04.2022).

499 Taschwer 2013, 54.

500 Weninger 1953.

501 Thür 1995c, 178–181; Thür 1990.

502 Massin 1999, 40: "der Dozent der Anthropologie Emil Breitinger [...] als SS–Oberscharführer, Schulungsleiter im RuSHA–SS" (Rasse– und Siedlungshauptamt der SS), 60 n. 87. In other words, Breitinger was one of the many "anthropologists, human geneticists and racial hygienists" who were members of the NSDAP, SS or SA: Massin 1999, 37. https://dewiki.de/Lexikon/Emil_Breitinger (accessed on 21.04.2022).

503 Rektorat der Universität Wien 1959, 34, 71.

504 Seidler 1987, 180.

505 Winkler 1986, 2f.: "Mit der Bestellung Breitingers [...] begann für Margarete Weninger [...] eine Zeit, die heute als 'das dunkle Jahrhundert' der Institutsgeschichte bezeichnet wird". Seidler 1987, 180.

506 Fuchs 2002b, 811: "Der Professorentitel und ihre wachsende wissenschaftliche Reputation konnten nicht verhindern, daß sie nach dem Tod ihres Mannes 1959 am Anthropologischen Institut isoliert blieb und in ihrer Arbeit behindert wurde. Margarete Weninger wurde das Opfer [...] ihrer mittlerweile auf die Posten zurückgekehrten, nationalsozialistisch belasteten Fachkollegen". Winkler 1986, 3. – Hauser 2005b, 107, misrepresented the situation when she wrote: "He [Breitinger] had got to know and come to appreciate him [J. Weninger] and his wife Margarete Weninger many years before" ("Ihn [J. Weninger] und seine Frau Margarete Weninger hatte er [E. Breitinger] schon viele Jahre vorher kennen und schätzen gelernt").

507 MAGW 82, 1953, 121.

508 https://www.geschichtewiki.wien.gv.at/Josef_Weninger (accessed on 21.04.2022).

509 Hayek 1960; Ehgartner 1959; Gedda 1959; Breitinger 1959; Pittioni 1956; Ehgartner 1956.

510 Fuchs 2002b; Hauser 1988; Seidler 1987; Winkler 1986.

511 https://austria–forum.org/af/AustriaWiki/Gersthofer_Friedhof (accessed on 21.04.2022).

512 Ehgartner 1959, 4: "Die Achtung, die er als Mensch besaß sowie die konziliante Art, über manche unangenehme Erinnerung aus der unmittelbaren Vergangenheit hinwegzusehen, machten ihn zu einem gern gehörten Berater und Befürworter" ("The respect he possessed as a human being, as well as the conciliatory way enabling him to overlook many an unpleasant memory from the immediate past, made him a much–loved advisor and advocate").

513 Hauser 1988, 277; Seidler 1987, 179f.

514 Winkler 1986, 1.

515 Taschwer 2018b, 772; Stifter 2014, 292f.; Winkler 1986, 2.

516 Geisenhainer 2021a, 116 n. 226; Gingrich 2021, 386; Winkler 1986, 2. – There is no documentation on Jenny Taubert in the archives of the Viennese Wiesenthal Institute for Holocaust Studies (information kindly provided by S. B. Weiss). The sister of Margarete Weninger, Heidi Taubert, emigrated to the UK and was "married to a British subject and has thus become herself British," now named Haidée Jacobs: University of Oxford, Bodleian Libraries: Shelfmark M.S. S.P.S.L 360/1–2.

517 Winkler 1986, 4: "Die große Wissenschaftlerin und verfolgte Jüdin Margarete Weninger hat in diesem Staat nie eine Würdigung erhalten" ("The great scientist

and persecuted Jew Margarete Weninger has never received any appreciation in this state"). Probably, Winkler refers here also to the fact that M. Weninger was not deemed worthy to become a member of the AAS, unlike the NSDAP members Erna Lesky (Seebacher 2020, 108) and H. Kenner (Duma 2020, 65, 90). An issue of the MAGW 107, 1977, was dedicated to M. Weninger as a Festschrift in honour of her 80th birthday.

518 Seidler 1987, 179: "Es zählt zu den tragischen Versäumnissen der Republik Österreich, daß Verfolgte des Nationalsozialismus oft auf sich selbst gestellt, kaum oder nur halbherzig unterstützt, diese Vergangenheit stellvertretend für die stumpfen Claqueure auf der Galerie der Mitläufer und Verdränger zu bewältigen haben. Die große Wissenschafterin und verfolgte Jüdin Margarete Weninger hat in diesem Staat nie eine Würdigung erhalten".

519 Seidler 1987, 179: "bei ihrem Begräbnis gab es auch keinen Kranz der Alma Mater Rudolphina".

520 Instead, the memorials of Robert Reininger (1967), Ernst Späth (1961), and Rudolf Much (1952) are found there: https://monuments.univie.ac.at/index.php?-title=Arkadenhof_der_Universit%C3%A4t_Wien (accessed on 21.04.2022).

521 Wlach 2020b, 437 n. 56.

522 Schwarz 2021, 9.

523 Gelbmann 2005.

524 https://www.duhoctrungquoc.vn/wiki/de/Dietrich_Kralik (accessed on 21.04.2022). Fellner – Corradini 2006, 235f.

525 Pfefferle – Pfefferle 2014, 297.

526 https://provenienzforschung.gv.at/beiratsbes-chluesse/Leitmeier_Hans_2021–11–05.pdf (accessed on 21.04.2022): "NSDAP–member since 1932". Pfefferle – Pfefferle 2014, 154.

527 Schumann – Freitag 2014, 35 n. 149; Urban 2021, 269.

528 Pfefferle – Pfefferle 2014, 299.

529 Schedlmayer 2010, 59 n. 335.

530 Wlach 2020b, 437 n. 60.

531 https://www.stadt-salzburg.at/ns–projekt/ns–stras-sennamen/univ–prof–dr–hans–sedlmayr/ (accessed on 21.04.2022).

532 Pesditschek 2012b, 298.

533 The list is not complete, since NSDAP membership files in Berlin only cover around 80% of its original stock: Huber 2012, 14.

534 https://bibliothek.univie.ac.at/sammlungen/ (accessed on 31.08.2022).

535 We would like to thank E. Pollhammer responsible for the Museum Carnuntinum and his team for their search efforts.

536 K. Matiasek on 14.09.2022: "Ich habe aber in deutlicher Erinnerung, dass dort [i.e. in der Anthropologischen Sammlung der Universität Wien] ein menschlicher Schädel mit der Aufschrift 'Ephesos Heroengrab' verwahrt wird. Inzwischen habe ich die Publikation von Kanz und Grossschmidt gesehen, und werde den Schädel an der Anthropologischen Sammlung mit dieser und dem von ihnen mitgeschickten Bild [i.e. the image from Weninger 1953, 160] abgleichen" ("However, I clearly remember that a human skull with the inscription 'Ephesos hero's Grave' is kept there [i.e. in the anthropological collection of the University of Vienna]. In the meantime, I have seen the publication by Kanz and Grossschmidt, and I will compare the skull at the Anthropological Collection with this and the image [i.e. the image from Weninger 1953, 160] you sent me").

537 https://dewiki.de/Lexikon/Emil_Breitinger (accessed on 21.04.2022).

538 Weninger 1953, 158: "Ein Schädel aus einem Ephesischen Heroengrab" ("A skull from an Ephesian hero's tomb").

539 Keil 1944/1953, 81 n. 3; Keil 1930a, 41. 44f.

540 "To the Mayor of". According to information kindly provided by S. Eminger (Archives of Lower Austria), the reference number IId–1–323/3–1940 (an 'Id'–reference does not exist) belongs to a file that describes the sending of advertising posters to the mayors of the province in order to promote the 'Museum des Reichsgaues Niederdonau'.

541 G. Weber, head of the Anthropological Institute of the UoV, permitted the reproduction of pictures achieved by K. Matiasek (figs. 86f.). Apart from these images, we were not allowed to present photographs of the Ephesian skull.

542 https://dewiki.de/Lexikon/Josef_Keil (accessed on 21.04.2022).

543 https://dewiki.de/Lexikon/Josef_Weninger (accessed on 21.04.2022).

544 Resetarits 2022, 101f. Rektorat der Universität Wien 1959, 80: "Kraniologisch–Osteologisches Praktikum (Art– und Rassenmerkmale am Skelett)". Rektorat der Universität Wien 1958, 76: "Anthropologisches Praktikum I (Kraniologie)".

545 Weninger 1953, 160.

546 Weninger 1953, 161.

547 Weninger 1953, 161.

548 Weninger 1953, 165.

549 Weninger 1953.

550 Thuswaldner 2015, 59f.

551 Krinzinger 2005, 359: "Die Suche nach dem Schädel des Skeletts in den Skelettsammlungen des Anthropologischen Instituts in Wien und im Naturhistorischen Museum verlief bisher leider ergebnislos" ("The search for the skull within the skeletal collections of the Anthropological Institute in Vienna and in the Natural History Museum has unfortunately been fruitless so far").

552 Weninger 1953, 168.

553 Weninger 1953, 158.

554 Weninger 1953, 158. 160.

Plans

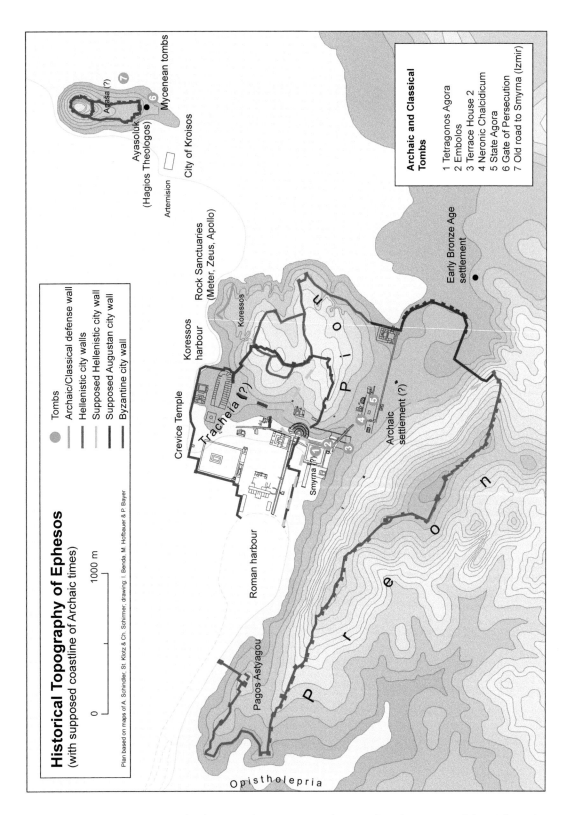

Plan 2: Historical topography of Ephesos with new proposals regarding the course of the Hellenistic and Augustan city walls

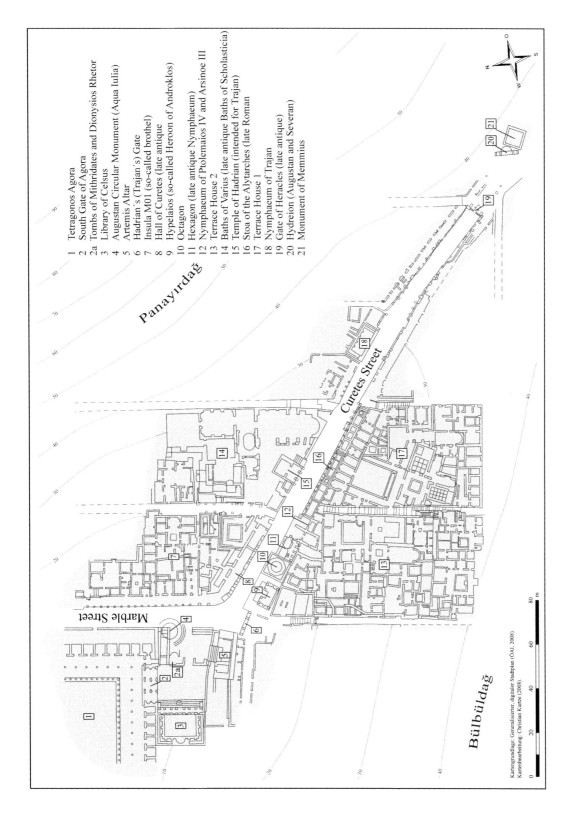

Plan 3: Buildings along the Embolos (Curetes Street)

1 Tetragonos Agora
2 South Gate of Agora
2a Tombs of Mithridates and Dionysios Rhetor
3 Library of Celsus
4 Augustan Circular Monument (Aqua Iulia)
5 Artemis Altar
6 Hadrian´s (Trajan´s) Gate
7 Insula M01 (so-called brothel)
8 Hall of Curetes (late antique
9 Hypelaios (so-called Heroon of Androklos)
10 Octagon
11 Hexagon (late antique Nymphaeum)
12 Nymphaeum of Ptolemaios IV and Arsinoe III
13 Terrace House 2
14 Baths of Varius (late antique Baths of Scholasticia)
15 Temple of Hadrian (intended for Trajan)
16 Stoa of the Alytarches (late Roman
17 Terrace House 1
18 Nymphaeum of Trajan
19 Gate of Heracles (late antique)
20 Hydreion (Augustan and Severan)
21 Monument of Memmius

Panayırdağ

Marble Street

Curetes Street

Bülbüldağ

Kartengrundlage: Generalisierter, digitaler Stadtplan (ÖAI, 2008).
Kartenbearbeitung: Christian Kurtze (2008).

0   20   40   60   80 m

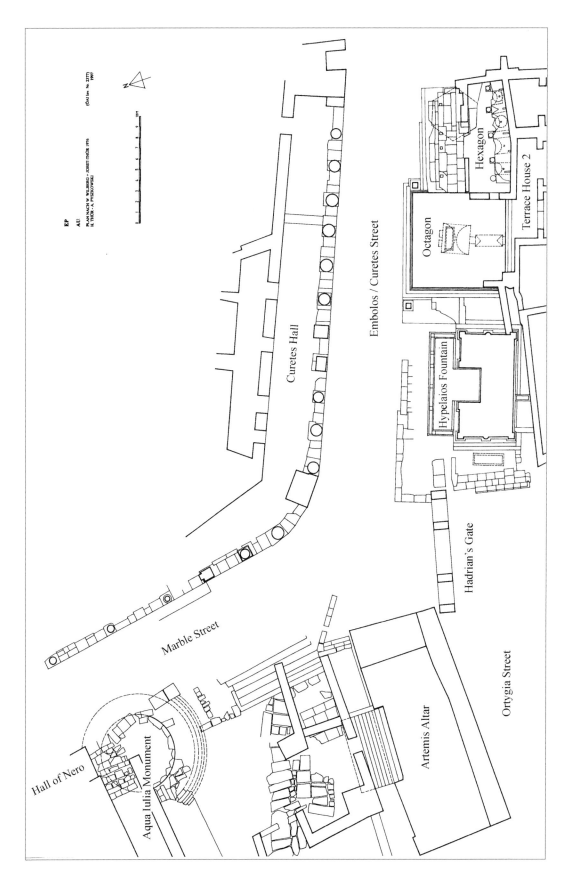

Plan 4: The Triodos in the Roman imperial period

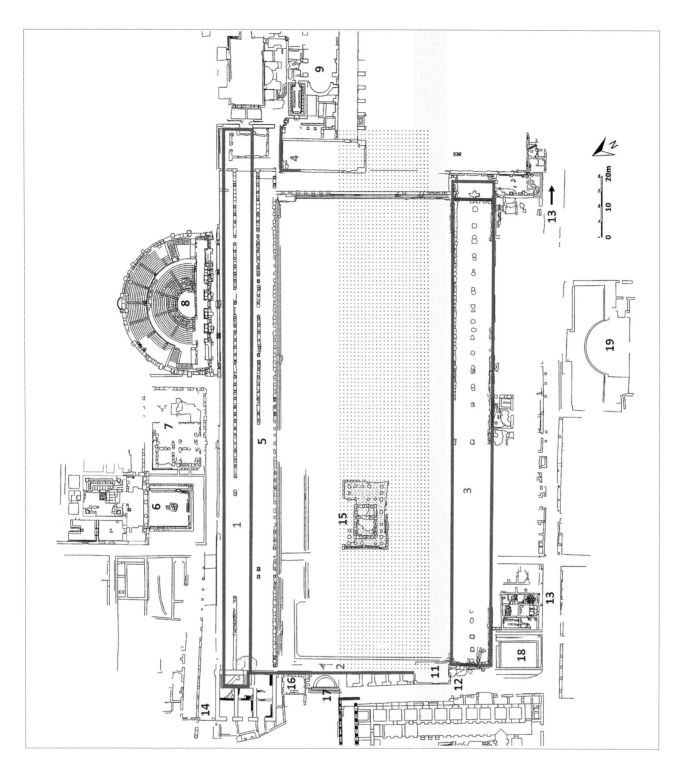

Plan 5: Historical architectural development in the area of the so-called State Agora; parts of the Hellenistic gymnasium (nos. 1–4 and 10) are marked with coloured lines: 1) Hellenistic North-Stoa with small Chalcidicum in the West (marked red; between 220 and 180 BC); 2) Hellenistic western border wall of gymnasium (built simultaneously with North-Stoa); 3) Hellenistic Southstoa (appr. 1st half of 2nd c. BC; secondarily closed entrance in the West marked in blue); 4) so-called North-East-Building (Roman Republican or Augustan); 5) Basilike Stoa (11 AD) with Neronian Chalcidicum in the West; 6) Prytaneion (1st phase beginning at the end of 1st c. BC); 7) so-called Rhodian Peristyle (early Augustan); 8) Bouleuterion (at the earliest end of 1st c. AD); 9) Baths of Roman Imperial times, partly situated over Hellenistic and Augustan Gymnasium of the Neoi); 10) Main Gate and Gateway to the Gymnasium and later State Agora (marked green; Roman Republican or Augustan); 11) so-called Pedestal building A, probably built over former entrance to the gymnasium (approx. 1st half of 1st c. AD); 12) Domitian Lane; 13) South Street; 14) Tomb of Pollio; 15) Apsidal Fountain; 16) Hydrekdocheion of Laecanius Bassus; 17) Kathodos with Enbasis; 18) Surge tank and fountain house of the Marnas aqueduct; 19) Late or post-Augustan Temple

List of abbreviations

AAS	Austrian Academy of Sciences / Oesterreichische Akademie der Wissenschaften
AD	Anno Domini
AES	Archaeologisch-Epigraphisches Seminar
ÆT.S.	(anno) aetatis suae
AGW	Anthropologische Gesellschaft in Wien
AKML	ἄκρος καὶ μέσος λόγος
BArch	Deutsches Bundesarchiv
BC	Before Christ
c.	Century
Cat	Catalogue
CVU	Sammlungen an der Universitaet Wien
D	Depth
Δ	Difference
DAI	German Archaeological Institute / Deutsches Archaeologisches Institut
DFG	Deutsche Forschungsgemeinschaft
Dm	Diameter
EED	Ephesian excavation diary
et al.	et alii (and others)
GC	German Club
H.	height
KHM	Kunsthistorisches Museum, Vienna
L	Left / Length
MRGND	Museum des Reichgaues Nieder-donau
Mt.	Mount
NOe	Niederoesterreich(isch)
NOeLM	Niederoesterreichisches Landes-museum
NS	Nationalsozialistisch
NSDAP	Nationalsozialistische Deutsche Arbeiterpartei
NSFK	Nationalsozialistisches Fliegerkorps
NSLB	Nationalsozialistischer Lehrerbund
NSV	Nationalsozialistische Volkswohlfahrt
OOe	Oberoesterreich(isch)
Oe	Oesterreich(isch)
OeAI	Austrian Archaeological Institute / Oesterreichisches Archaeologisches Institut
P.	Page
PO	Politische Organisation
Post.	Posterior
R	Right
SA	Sturmabteilung
SS	Schutzstaffel
UoV	University of Vienna
VAS	Viennese Academy of Sciences / Wiener Akademie der Wissen-schaften
VKPW	Verein klassischer Philologen Wien
W.	Width
WW I	World War I

List of journals

AA	Archaeologischer Anzeiger des Deutschen Archaeologischen Instituts
Acta Inst. Sueciae Rom	Acta Instituti Romani Regni Sueciae
AJA	American Journal of Archaeology
Alm	Almanach der Oesterreichische Akademie der Wissenschaften
Ann. Naturhist. Mus. Wien	Annalen des Naturhistorischen Museums in Wien
AntK	Antike Kunst
AnthropolAnz	Anthropologischer Anzeiger
AnzAW	Anzeiger fuer die Altertumswissenschaft (Innsbruck)
AnzWien	Anzeiger der Oesterreichischen Akademie der Wissenschaften in Wien, Philos. Hist. Klasse
ArchA	Archaeologia Austriaca
Arch Hist Exact Sci	Archive for History of Exact Sciences
AW	Antike Welt
BEFAR	Bibliothèque des Ecoles Françaises d'Athènes et de Rome
Beibl.	Beiblatt of the
BerMatOeAI	Berichte und Materialien des Oesterreichischen Archaeologischen Instituts
BJB	Bonner Jahrbuecher
BJHS	British Journal for the History of Science
BMC	British Museum, Catalogue of Coins
CIL	Corpus inscriptionum Latinarum
Coll Anthropol	Journal of the Croatian Anthropological Society
DenkschrWien	Denkschriften der philosophisch-historischen Klasse der Oesterreichischen Akademie der Wissenschaften
EPRO	Etudes Preliminaires aux Religions Orientales dans L'Empire Romain
FiE	Forschungen in Ephesos
Forensic Sci Int	Forensic Science International
Forensic Sci Med Pathol	Forensic Science, Medicine and Pathology
GrRomByzSt	Greek, Roman, and Byzantine Studies
Hum Biol	American Journal of Human Biology
IG	Inscriptiones Graecae
IK	Inschriften griechischer Staedte Kleinasiens
Int J Legal Med	International Journal of Legal Medicine
Inv.	Inventory
IstMitt	Istanbuler Mitteilungen des Deutschen Archaeologischen Instituts
JbayAW	Jahrbuch der Bayerischen Akademie der Wissenschaften
JdI	Jahrbuch des Deutschen Archaeologischen Instituts

JOeAI	Jahreshefte des Oesterreichischen Archaeologischen Instituts
JRA	Journal of Roman Archaeology
JRS	Journal of Roman Studies
LCL	Loeb Classical Library
MAGW	Mitteilungen der Anthropologischen Gesellschaft in Wien
MemAmAcRome	Memoirs of the American Academy in Rome
Mem. Descr. Carta Geol. d'It.	Memorie Descrittive Della Carta Geologica d'Italia
MIOeG	Mitteilungen des Instituts fuer Oesterreichische Geschichtsforschung
MittVKPW	Mitteilungen des Vereines klassischer Philologen in Wien
Nexus Netw J	Nexus Network Journal
OeZG	Oesterreichische Zeitschrift fuer Geschichtswissenschaften
OZP	Oesterreichische Zeitschrift fuer Politikwissenschaft
OeZKD	Oesterreichische Zeitschrift fuer Kunst und Denkmalpflege
PAR	Pro Austria Romana
RE	Realencyclopaedie der classischen Altertumswissenschaft
RIC	Roman Imperial Coinage
SEG	Supplementum epigraphicum Graecum
SoSchrOeAI	Sonderschriften des Oesterreichischen Archaeologischen Institutes in Wien
ZPE	Zeitschrift fuer Papyrologie und Epigraphik

Bibliography

Agelidis S. (2014) Vom Palladion zur Nikephoros. Der Kult der Athena im Kontext der Herrschaftslegitimation im spätklassischen und hellenistischen Pergamon, IstMitt 64, 75–128

Alhazmi A. – Vargas E. – Palomo J. M. et al. (2017) Timing and rate of spheno-occipital synchondrosis closure and its relationship to puberty, PLoS ONE 12,8, e0183305

Allmann G. J. (1877) Greek Geometry from Thales to Euclid, Hermathena 3,5, 160–207

Altay S. T. (2021) A late recompense. The rediscovered monumental octagon at Pergamon, Adalya 24, 215–228

Altinsoy H. B. – Gurses M. S. (2022) Applicability of proximal humeral epiphysis ossification for forensic age estimation according to the Vieth method. A 3.0 T MRI study, Rechtsmedizin 32, 26–35

Alzinger W. (1970) RE Suppl XII 1588–1704 s.v. Ephesos B. Archäologischer Teil

Alzinger W. (1962) Die Stadt des siebenten Weltwunders. Die Wiederentdeckung von Ephesos (Wien)

Alzinger W. (1972) Die Ruinen von Ephesos (Vienna)

Alzinger W. (1974) Augusteische Architektur in Ephesos, SoSchrOeAI 16 (Vienna)

Alzinger W. (1980) Ephesos vom Beginn der römischen Herrschaft in Kleinasien bis zum Ende der Principatszeit: Archäologischer Teil, in: ANRW II 7, 2 (Berlin) 811–831

Alzinger W. (1999) Das Zentrum der lysimachischen Stadt, in: Friesinger H. – Krinzinger F. (eds.), 100 Jahre österreichische Forschungen in Ephesos. Akten des Symposiums Wien 1995, DenkschrWien 260 = Archäologische Forschungen 1 (Vienna) 389–392

Alzinger W. – Bammer A. (1971) Das Monument des C. Memmius, FiE VII (Vienna)

Ambrosi G. M. (2012) Pre-Euclidian geometry and Aeginetan coin design. Some further remarks, Arch Hist Exact Sci 66, 557–583

Amundsen D. W. – Diers C. J. (1969) The age of menarche in classical Greece and Rome, Hum Biol 41,1, 125–132

Anastassiades A. (2009) Two Ptolemaic queens and Cyprus. Iconographic issues, Cahiers du Centre d'Etudes Chypriotes 39,1, 259–270

Andreae B. (1977) Vorschlag für eine Rekonstruktion der Polyphemgruppe von Ephesos, in: Höckmann U. – Krug A. (eds.), Festschrift Frank Brommer (Mainz) 1–11

Andreae B. (1999) Odysseus. Mythos und Erinnerung (Mainz)

Andrews T. (2018) Greek Tholoi of the Classical and Hellenistic Periods. An Examination (Ontario)

Anevlavi V. – Bielefeld D. – Ladstätter S. et al. (2020) Marble for the Dead. The Quarry of Ab-u Hayat, Ephesos, and its Products, JOeAI 89, 11–60

Antike Welt (2019) Auferstehung der Antike. Archäologische Stätten digital rekonstruiert. Sonderheft Antike Welt (Darmstadt)

Artmann B. (1990) Mathematical motifs on Greek coins, The Mathematical Intelligencer 12,4, 43–50

Ash G. A. (2015) Die Universität Wien in den politischen Umbrüchen des 19. und 20. Jahrhunderts, in: Ash G. A. – Ehmer J. (eds.), Universität - Politik - Gesellschaft (Vienna) 29–172

Assmann J. (2018) Das kulturelle Gedächtnis. Schrift, Erinnerung und politische Identität in frühen Hochkulturen, 8. Aufl. (München)

Atalay E. (1978–80) Neue Funde aus Ephesos, JOeAI 52 Beibl., 53–64

Atalay E. – Türkoğlu S. (1972–75) Ein frühhellenistischer Porträtkopf des Lysimachos in Ephesos, JOeAI 50 Beibl., 123–150

Auinger J. (2009) Zum Umgang mit Statuen hoher Würdenträger in spätantiker und nachantiker Zeit entlang der Kuretenstrasse in Ephesos, in: Ladstätter S. (ed.), Neue Forschungen zur Kuretenstraße von Ephesos. DenkschrWien 382 (Vienna) 29–52

Aurenhammer M. (1990) Die Skulpturen von Ephesos. Bildwerke aus Stein. Idealplastik I, FiE X 1 (Vienna)

Aurenhammer M. (1997) Das Porträt eines Kaiserpriesters, in: Thür H. (ed.), „… und verschönerte die Stadt …" – KAI ΚΟΣΜΕΣΑΝΤΑ ΤΗΝ ΠΟΛΙΝ. Ein ephesischer Priester den Kaiserkultes in seinem Umfeld, SoSchrOeAI 27 (Vienna) 41–53

Aurnhammer A. (2019) „Make Death Proud to Take Us": Der Tod der Kleopatra in Literatur und Kunst den Frühen Neuzeit, in: Brink C. – Falkenhayner N. – von den Hoff R. (eds.) Helden müssen sterben. Von Sinn und Fragwürdigkeit des heroischen Todes (Baden-Baden) 81–101

Autengruber P. – Nemec B. – Rathkolb O. – Wenninger F. (2013) Straßennamen Wiens seit 1860 als „Politische Erinnerungsorte" (Vienna)

Autengruber P. – Nemec B. – Rathkolb O. – Wenninger F. (2014) Umstrittene Wiener Straßennamen. Ein kritisches Lesebuch (Vienna)

Bachofen J. J. (1880) Antiquarische Briefe vornehmlich zur Kenntniss der ältesten Verwandtschaftsbegriffe 1/XI (Berlin–Boston) 101–113

Baier C. (2016) Eine hellenistische Palastanlage oberhalb des Theaters von Ephesos und ihre Entwicklung bis in die Spätantike (Thesis Brandenburg University of Technology, Cottbus – Senftenberg)

Baier C. (2023) Die Palastanlage oberhalb des Theaters von Ephesos, FiE XVII 1 (Vienna)

Balty J. C. (1991) Porträt und Gesellschaft in der römischen Welt, Trierer Winckelmannsprogramme 11 (Mainz)

Bammer A. (1966–67) Tempel und Altar der Artemis von Ephesos, JOeAI 48 Beibl., 21–44

Bammer A. (1967) Geometrie und Ornament als Antithese bei Doppelmäandern in Ephesos, in: Braun E. (ed.),

Festschrift für Fritz Eichler zum achtzigsten Geburtstag, (Vienna) 10–22

Bammer A. (1968-71) Beiträge zur ephesischen Architektur, JOeAI 49, 1-40

Bammer A. (1972–75) Die politische Symbolik des Memmiusbaues, JOeAI 50, 220–222

Bammer A. (1978–80) Elemente flavisch-trajanischer Architekturfassaden aus Ephesos, JOeAI 52, 67–90

Bammer A. (1984) Das Heiligtum der Artemis von Ephesos (Vienna)

Bammer A. (2007) Zum Monument des C. Memmius in Ephesos, in: Meyer M. (ed.), Neue Zeiten – Neue Sitten. Zu Rezeption und Integration römischen und italischen Kulturguts in Kleinasien, Wiener Forschungen zur Archäologie 12 (Vienna) 57–61

Bammer A. (2008) Der archaische und klassische Hofaltar, in: Muss U. (ed.), Die Archäologie der ephesischen Artemis. Gestalt und Ritual eines Heiligtums (Vienna) 277–284

Bammer A. (2010) Die Österreichischen Grabungen in Ephesos von 1961 bis 2008: Technologie, Wirtschaft und Politik. Anatolia Antiqua 18, 35–58

Bammer A. – Muss U. (1996), Das Artemision von Ephesos. Das Weltwunder Ioniens in archaischer und klassischer Zeit, Zaberns Bildbände zur Archäologie (Mainz/Rhein)

Bammer A. – Muss U. (2021) Amazonen in Kleinasien, in: Koller K. – Quatember U. – Trinkl E. (eds.), Stein auf Stein. Festschrift für Hilke Thür zum 80. Geburtstag, Keryx 8 (Graz) 119–128

Barbantani S. (2010) Three Burials (Ibycus, Stesichorus, Simonides). Facts and fiction about lyric poets in Magna Graecia in the epigrams of the Greek Anthology (Alessandria)

Barry W. D. (2008) Exposure, Mutilation, and Riot. Violence at the Scalae Gemoniae in Early Imperial Rome, Greece and Rome 55,2, 222–246

Bartman E. (1993) Carving the Badminton Sarcophagus, Metropolitan Museum Journal 28, 57–75

Bätz A. (2012) Sacrae virgines. Studien zum religiösen und gesellschaftlichen Status der Vestalinnen (Paderborn)

Bauer E. (2014) Gerousien in den Poleis Kleinasiens in hellenistischer Zeit und der römischen Kaiserzeit. Die Beispiele Ephesos, Pamphylien und Pisidien, Aphrodisias und Iasos, Münchner Studien zur Alten Welt 11 (Munich)

Baum W. (2003) Kunstzerstörungen und Bücherverbrennungen im wilden Kärnten, OeZG 14,1, 103–113

Benetka G. (1998) Entnazifizierung und verhinderte Rückkehr. Zur personellen Situation der akademischen Psychologie in Österreich nach 1945, OeZG 9, 188–217

Bengtson H. (1937) Die Strategie in der hellenistischen Zeit. Ein Beitrag zum antiken Staatsrecht I, Münchner Beiträge zur Papyrusforschung und antiken Rechtsgeschichte 26 (Munich)

Benndorf O. (1898) Vorläufige Berichte über die Ausgrabungen in Ephesus I, JOeAI 1 Beibl., 53–72

Benndorf O. (1899) Topographische Urkunde aus Ephesos, JOeAI 2 Beibl., 15–36

Benndorf O. (1906) Zur Ortskunde und Stadtgeschichte, FiE I (Vienna) 9–110

Bennett C. (1997) Cleopatra V Tryphaena and the genealogy of the later Ptolemies, Ancient Society 28, 39–66

Bennett C (2013) Egyptian Royal Genealogy/Ptolemaic Dynasty: https://www.instonebrewer.com/TyndaleSites/Egypt/ptolemies/genealogy.htm (accessed on 21.04.2022)

Berner M. (2010) Race and physical anthropology in interwar Austria, Focaal—Journal of Global and Historical Anthropology 58, 16–31

Berns C. (1996) ΣΗΜΑΤΑ. Untersuchungen zu den Grab- und Memorialbauten des späten Hellenismus und der frühen Kaiserzeit in Kleinasien (Cologne)

Berns C. (2003) Untersuchungen zu den Grabbauten der frühen Kaiserzeit in Kleinasien, Asia Minor Studien 51 (Bonn)

Berti I. (2017) Gerechte Götter? Vorstellungen von göttlicher Vergeltung im Mythos und Kult des archaischen und klassischen Griechenlands, Propylaeum (Heidelberg)

Berve H. (1965) Nachrufe. Josef Keil, in: Jahrbuch der Bayerischen Akademie der Wissenschaften, 163–167

Betz A. (1952) Rudolf Egger und die Austria Romana. PAR, 4, 18–21

Betz A. (1968) Rudolf Egger – 85 Jahre alt. Carinthia I, 108–110

Betz A. (1969) Rudolf Egger †, AnzAW 22, 127–128

Betz A. (1970) Rudolf Egger und die Universität Wien. Carinthia I 160,3, 576–581

Betz A. – Moro G. (1962) Römische Antike und frühes Christentum. Ausgewählte Schriften von Rudolf Egger zur Vollendung seines 80. Lebensjahres, Vol. I (Klagenfurt)

Betz A. – Moro G. (1963) Römische Antike und frühes Christentum. Ausgewählte Schriften von Rudolf Egger zur Vollendung seines 80. Lebensjahres, Vol. II (Klagenfurt)

Bevan E. R. (1927) The House of Ptolemy. A History of Hellenistic Egypt under the Ptolemaic Dynasty (Chicago)

Bicknell P. J. (1977) Caesar, Antony, Cleopatra and Cyprus, Latomus 36,2, 325–342

Bier L. (2011) The Bouleuterion at Ephesos, FiE IX 5 (Vienna)

Blake M. E. (1930) The Pavements of the Roman Buildings of the Republic and Early Empire, MemAmAcRome 8, 7–159

Bøgh B. (2013) The Graeco-Roman cult of Isis, in: Hammer O. et al. (eds.), The handbook of religions in ancient Europe (Stocksfield) 228–241

Bohn H. G. (1851) Caesar's commentaries on the Gallic and Civil Wars (Finsbury)

Bohn R. (1885) Das Heiligtum der Athena Polias Nikephoros. Altertümer von Pergamon II (Berlin)

Bol R. (1998) Amazones Volneratae. Untersuchungen zu den Ephesischen Amazonenstatuen (Mainz)

Borchardt L. (1897) Die Aegyptische Pflanzensäule (Berlin)

Borchhardt J. (1994) Hedwig Kenner †, Gnomon 66,3, 284–286

Bordsen J. (2009) Ephèse (Turquie): Bones found are probably those of Cleopatra's half-sister, http://www.archeolog-home.com/pages/content/ephese-turquie-bones-found-are-probably-those-of-cleopatra-s-half-sister.html, accessed on 21.04.2022

Borg B. E. (2004) Glamorous intellectuals: Portraits of pepaideumenoi in the second and third centuries AD, in: Borg B. E. (ed.), Paideia: Die Welt der zweiten Sophistik/ The World of the Second Sophistic (Berlin – New York) 157–178

Börker C. – Merkelbach R. (eds.) (1980) Inschriften griechischer Städte aus Kleinasien 15. Die Inschriften von Ephesos V (Cologne)

Börker C. – Merkelbach R., mit Hilfe v. Engelmann H. – Knibbe D. (eds.) (1979) Inschriften griechischer Städte aus Kleinasien 12. Die Inschriften von Ephesos II (Cologne)

Boter G. (2022) Vita Apollonii Tyanei (Berlin – Boston)

Botz G. (1980) Die österreichischen NSDAP-Mitglieder. Probleme einer quantitativen Analyse aufgrund der NSDAP-Zentralkartei im Berlin Document Center, in: Mann R. (ed.), Die Nationalsozialisten. Analysen faschistischer Bewegungen (Stuttgart) 98–136

Bouché-Leclercq A. (1904) Histoire des Lagides. Tome II. Adamant Media Corporation (Massachusetts)

Bozza S. (2020) The Adoption of roman building Techniques in Asia Minor, 30 Years Later, in: Lohner-Urban U. – Quatember U. (eds.), Zwischen Bruch und Kontinuität / Continuity and Change. Architektur in Kleinasien am Übergang vom Hellenismus zur römischen Kaiserzeit / Architecture in Asia Minor during the transitional period from Hellenism to the Roman Empire, Byzas 25, 57–72

Brandt O. (2011) Understanding the Structures of Early Christian Baptisteries, in: Hellholm D. (ed.), Ablution, Initiation, and Baptism. Late Antiquity, Early Judaism, and Early Christianity, 1587–1610 (Berlin – Boston)

Braun E. (1964) Josef Keil, Gnomon 36,5, 521–524

Breitinger E. (1959) Josef Weninger, 1886–1959, AnthropolAnz 23,2/3, 236–238

Bremmer J. N. (2004) The spelling and meaning of the name Megabyxos, ZPW 147, 9–10

Bremmer J. N. (2006) Priestly Personnel of the Ephesian Artemision. Anatolian, Persian, Greek, and Roman Aspects, in: Dignas B. – Trampedach K. (eds.), Practitioners of the Divine. Greek Priests and Religious Officials from Homer to Heliodorus (Cambridge)

Brenk B. (1968) Die Datierung der Reliefs am Hadrianstempel in Ephesos und das Problem der tetrarchischen Skulptur des Ostens, IstMitt 18, 238–258

Brent L. (2020) Sealed and Revealed: Roman Grave-opening Practices, Journal of Roman Archaeology 33, 129–146

Bricault L. (2014) Une dédicace-double d'Éphèse pour Ptolémée, Arsinoé, Sarapis et Isis, in: Bricault L. – Veymiers R. (eds.), Bibliotheca Isiaca III (Paris) 7–10

Brinckmann A. E. (1939) Handbuch der Kunstwissenschaft II.2 (Potsdam)

Brodersen K. (ed.) (2014) Philostratos. Leben der Sophisten (Wiesbaden)

Broderson K. (2021) Theon von Smyrna. Mathematik für die Platonlektüre – Griechisch Deutsch (Darmstadt)

Brödner E. (1983) Die römischen Thermen und das antike Badewesen. Eine kulturhistorische Betrachtung (Darmstadt)

Brome Weigall A. E. P. (1914) The Life and times of Cleopatra, Queen of Egypt (Edingburgh – London)

Broughton T. R. S. (1952) The magistrates of the Roman Republic, vol. 2 (New York)

Brown D. F. (1939) The hexagonal Court in Baalbek, AJA 43, 285–288

Brückner H. – Herda A. – Kerschner M. – Müllenhoff M. – Stock F. (2017) Life cycle of estuarine islands – from the formation to the landlocking of former islands in the environs of Miletos and Ephesos in western Asia Minor (Turkey), JASc Reports, 876–894

Brückner H. – Kraft J. C. – Kayan İ. (2008) Vom Meer umspült, vom Fluss begraben – zur Paläogeographie des Artemisions, in: Muss U. (ed.), Die Archäologie der ephesischen Artemis. Gestalt und Ritual eines Heiligtums (Vienna) 21–31

Brunés T. (1967) The secrets of ancient geometry, Vol. I, II (Copenhagen)

Bruun C. (2007) Nero's architects, Severus and Celer, and residence patterns in Rome, Scripta Classica Israelica 26, 73–86

Buchheim H. (1960) Die Orientpolitik des Triumvirn M. Antonius (Heidelberg)

Budka J. – Jurman C. (2013) Hermann Junker. Ein deutsch-österreichisches Forscherleben zwischen Pyramiden, Kreuz und Hakenkreuz, in: Bickel S. – Fischer-Elfert H. W. – Loprieno A. – Richter S, (eds.) Ägyptologen und Ägyptologien zwischen Kaiserreich und Gründung der beiden deutschen Staaten (Berlin) 299–331

Buraselis K. (1982) Das hellenistische Makedonien und die Ägäis. Forschungen zur Politik des Kassandros und der drei ersten Antigoniden (Antigonos Monophthalmos, Demetrios Poliorketes und Antigonos Gonatas) im Ägäischen Meer und in Westkleinasien (Munich)

Burrell B. (2003) Temples of Hadrian, not Zeus, GrRomByzSt 43,1, 31–50

Burrell B. (2004) Neokoroi. Greek Cities and Roman Emperors, Cincinnati Classical Studies. New Series 9 (Leiden – Boston)

Burrell B. (2009) Reading, hearing, and looking at Ephesos, in: Johnson W. A. – Parker H. N. (eds.), Ancient Literacies: The Culture of Reading in Greece and Rome (Oxford) 69–95

Burstein S. M. (1982) Arsinoe II Philadelphos. A Revisionist View, in: Adams W. L. – Borza E. N. (eds.), Philipp II, Alexander the Great and the Macedonian Heritage (Washington D.C.) 197–212

Burstein S. M. (2004) The reign of Cleopatra (Westport London)

Butler S. (1999) The Odyssey by Homer – rendered into English prose: www. Gutenberg.org

Büyükkolanci M. (1982) Zwei neugefundene Bauten der Johannesbasilika von Ephesos. Baptisterium und Skeuophylakion, IstMitt 32, 236–257

Calapà A. (2009) Das Stadtbild von Ephesos in hellenistischer Zeit. Kontinuität und Wandel, in: Matthaei A. – Zimmermann M. (eds.), Stadtbilder im Hellenismus (Berlin) 334–359

Calapà A. (2010) Due dediche a sovrani Tolemaici da Efeso e l'espansione Tolemaica in Ionia negli anni settanta del III sec. A.C., Studi Ellenistici 24, 197–210

Carney E. – Ogden D. (2010) Philip II and Alexander the Great: Father and Son, Lives and Afterlives (Cambridge)

Chaniotis A. (2003) The divinity of Hellenistic rulers, in: Erskine A. (ed.), A companion to the Hellenistic world (Oxford) 431–445

Chaniotis A. (2007) Die Entwicklung der griechischen Asylie. Ritualdynamik und die Grenzen des Rechtsvergleichs, in: Burckhardt L. – Seybold K. – von Ungern-Sternberg J. (eds.), Gesetzgebung in antiken Gesellschaften. Israel, Griechenland, Rom (Berlin) 233–246

Cipriani L. – Fantini F. – Bertacchi S. (2017) The Geometric Enigma of Small Baths at Hadrian's Villa. Mixtilinear Plan Design and Complex Roofing Conception, Nexus Netw J 19, 427–453

Clavius C. (1627) Euclidis Elementorum Libri XV [...] (Köln)

Cohen G. M. (1995) The Hellenistic settlements in Europe, the Islands, and Asia Minor (Berkeley – Los Angeles – Oxford)

Collins N. L. (1997) The Various Fathers of Ptolemy I, Mnemosyne 50, 436–476

Cormack S. (2004) The space of death in Roman Asia minor (Vienna)

Costanza S. (2021) Nomi antichi e moderni dei tiri di astragali. Fonti letterarie, lessicografiche e folcloriche, Incontri di Filologia Classica 20, 1–30

Curtius E. (1872) Beiträge zur Geschichte und Topographie Kleinasiens. Ephesos, Smyrna, Sardeis (Berlin)

Czeike F. (1992–97) Historisches Lexikon Wien (Vienna)

Danner P. (2015) Görings Geologen in der Ostmark. „Bodenforschung" in Österreich für den Vierjahresplan von 1936 bis 1939 – eine Archivstudie, Berichte der Geologischen Bundesanstalt 109 (Vienna)

Daubner F. (2011) Seleukidische und attalidische Gründungen in Westkleinasien – Datierung, Funktion und Status, in: Daubner F. (ed.), Militärsiedlungen und Territorialherrschaft in der Antike (Berlin - New York) 41–63

De Bernardo-Stempel P. – Hainzmann M. (2020) Fontes Epigraphici Religionum Celticarum Antiquarum I. Provincia Noricum. 1. Die Gottheiten in ihren sprachlichen und kultischen Erscheinungsformen (Vienna)

Denk U. (2019) Das Archiv der Universität Wien – Geschichte, Bestände, Aufgaben, in: Elbel P. (ed.), Österreichische Archive. Geschichte und Gegenwart (Brno) 401–426

Dignas B. (2002) Economy of the Sacred in Hellenistic and Roman Asia Minor (Oxford)

Dimitriev S. (2007) The Last Marriage and the Death of Lysimachus, GrRomByzSt 47, 135–149

Dobesch G. (1996) Caesar und Kleinasien, Tyche 11, 51–77

Dolenz H. (2014) Der Magdalensberg um die Zeitenwende. Baugeschichte der ersten Hauptstadt Österreichs, in: Dolenz D. – Knappinger J. (eds.), Magdalensberg. Kulturraum – Naturjuwel – Lebensraum (Klagenfurt) 24–60

Dou I. P. (ed.) (1618) Die sechs ersten Bücher Euclidis, deß höchgelärten weitberümbten Griechischen Philosophi und Mathematici [...] (Amsterdam)

Douglas Olson S. (2020) Athenaeus Naucratites. Deipnosophistae. Volumen III.A. Libri VIII–XV (Berlin – Boston)

Dräger M. (1993) Die Städte der Provinz Asia in der Flavierzeit. Studien zur kleinasiatischen Stadt- und Regionalgeschichte, Europäische Hochschulschriften, Series 3, Vol. 576 (Frankfurt)

Dubit R. (2018) A Song of Arms and of the Woman. Confronting Cleopatra in the Augustan Era through the Carmen de Bello Actiaco (Thesis College of William and Mary, Williamsberg)

Duma V. (2020) Frauenkarrieren in der Männerwelt. Möglichkeiten, Ausschlüsse und Vertreibung. Zu den ersten zehn weiblichen Mitgliedern der Österreichischen Akademie der Wissenschaften, AnzWien 155,1/2, 63–100

Duncan W. (1833) The Commentaries of Caesar, translated into English (London)

Ebner D. (2009) Entwicklung der archäologischen Forschung und deren museale Präsentation ab dem 20. Jahrhundert in Kärnten (Thesis University of Vienna, Vienna)

Eck W. (2005) Ehret den Kaiser. Bögen und Tore als Ehrenmonumente in der Provinz Iudaea, in: Perani M. (ed.), „The Words of a wise Man's Mouth are Gracious" (Qoh 10,12). Festschrift für Günter Stemberger on the Occasion of his 65th Birthday, Studia Judaica 32 (Berlin – New York) 153–165

Egger R. (1940) Die neuen Grabungen von Carnuntum, in: Archäologisches Institut des Deutschen Reiches, Bericht über den VI. Internationalen Kongress für Archäologie. Berlin 21. - 26. August 1939 (Berlin) 516–517

Egger R. (1950) Camillo Praschniker †, Carinthia I 140, 24–28

Ehgartner W. (1956) Josef Weninger 70 Jahre alt, AnthropolAnz 12,2, 184–186

Ehgartner W. (1959) Josef Weninger †, MAGW 88/89, 1–7

Ehmig U. (2005) Der Besitzer der Bad Kreuznacher Peristylvilla – ein Händler ostmediterraner Lebensmittel? Münstersche Beiträge z. antiken Handelsgeschichte 24,2, 175–191

Eichler F. (1950) Camillo Praschniker †, Gnomon 22,3/4, 196–198

Eichler F. (1959) Franz Miltner †, JOeAI 44 Beibl., 1f

Eichler F. (1961) Arnold Schober †. Alm 110, 1960, 372–377

Eichler F. (1963) Josef Keil †, JOeAI 46 Beibl., 1–6

Eichler F. (1966) Ein augusteisches Denkmal in Ephesos, Wiener Studien 79, 592–597

Ekizoglu O. – Hocaoglu E. – Inci E. et al. (2016) Forensic age estimation via 3-T magnetic resonance imaging of ossification of the proximal tibial and distal femoral epiphyses. Use of a T2-weighted fast spin-echo technique, Forensic Sci Int 260, 102e1–102.e7

El Fakharani F. (1974) The "Lighthouse" of Abusir in Egypt, Harvard Studies in Classical Philology 78, 257–272

Engelmann H. (1972) Der Tempel des Hadrian in Ephesos und der Proconsul Servaeus Innocens, ZPE 9, 91–96

Engelmann H. (1991) Beiträge zur ephesischen Topographie, ZPE 89, 275–295

Engelmann H. (1993a) Celsusbibliothek und Auditorium in Ephesos, JOeAI 62, 105–109

Engelmann H. (1993b) Zum Kaiserkult in Ephesos, ZPE 97, 279–289

Engelmann H. (1995) Philostrat und Ephesos, ZPE 108, 77–87

Engelmann H. (1996) Phylen und Chiliastyen von Ephesos, ZPE 113, 94–100

Engelmann H. (1997) Der Koressos, ein ephesisches Stadtviertel, ZPE 115, 131–135

Engelmann H. – Knibbe D. – Merkelbach R. (eds.) (1980a) Inschriften griechischer Städte aus Kleinasien 13. Die Inschriften von Ephesos III (Cologne)

Engelmann H. – Knibbe D. – Merkelbach R. (eds.) (1980b) Inschriften griechischer Städte aus Kleinasien 14. Die Inschriften von Ephesos IV (Cologne)

Engelmann H. – Nollé J. (eds.) (1984) Inschriften griechischer Städte aus Kleinasien 17, 3.4. Die Inschriften von Ephesos VIII, 1/2 (Cologne)

Ercoles M. (2013) Stesicoro: Le Testimonianze Antiche (Bologna)

Erhard Ratdolt (1482) Elementa geometrica: Preclarissimus liber elementorum Euclidis perspicacissimi […] (Venice)

Erker L. (2017) Die Rückkehr der „Ehemaligen". Berufliche Reintegration von früheren Nationalsozialsten im akademischen Milieu in Wien nach 1945 und 1955, Zeitgeschichte 44,3, 175–192

Erker L. (2021a) Die Universität Wien und die Diktatur der vielen Namen. Ein Beitrag zur Faschismusforschung, in: Moos C. (ed.), (K)ein Austrofaschismus? Studien zum Herrschaftssystem 1933–1938 (Vienna) 42–57

Erker L. (2021b) Die Universität Wien im Austrofaschismus (Göttingen)

Ersoy A. (2006) Water-related Constructions in the Sirince Rural Area in the Eastern Territory of Ephesos, in: Wiplinger G. (ed.), Cura Aquarum in Ephesus, Proceedings of the Twelfth International Congress on the History of Water Management and Hydraulic Engineering in the Mediterranean Region, Ephesus/Selçuk, Turkey, Oktober 2-10, 2004, Bulletin antieke beschaving. Annual Papers on Classical Archaeology, Suppl. 12 = SoSchrOeAI 42 (Leuven – Paris – Dudley) 41–44

Fahlbusch M. (2001) Politische Beratung in der NS-Volkstumspolitik. Südostdeutsche Forschungsgemeinschaft Wien, Annali dell'Istituto storico italo-germanico in Trento 27, 467–492

Fasolo F. (1962) L'architettura di Efeso, Bollettino del Centro di studi per la storia dell'architettura 18, 7–88

Fassa E. (2015) Sarapis, Isis, and the Ptolemies in Private Dedications. The Hyper-style and the Double Dedications, Kernos 28, 1–20

Featherstone M. J. (2005) The Chrysotriklinos seen through De Ceremoniis in: Hoffmann L. M. – Anuscha Monchizadeh A. (eds.), Zwischen Polis, Provinz und Peripherie. Beiträge zur byzantinischen Geschichte und Kultur (Wiesbaden) 833–840

Feichtinger J. (2015) Richard Meister. Ein dienstbarer Hochschulprofessor in vier politischen Regimen, in: Ash M. G. – Nieß W. – Pils R. (eds.), Geisteswissenschaften im Nationalsozialismus. Das Beispiel der Universität Wien (Vienna) 169–176

Feichtinger J. (2022) Chronologie. Die Akademie der Wissenschaften 1847–2022, in: Feichtinger J. – Mazohl B. (eds.), Die Österreichische Akademie der Wissenschaften 1847–2022. Eine neue Akademiegeschichte (Vienna) 401–455

Feichtinger J. – Geiger K. – Sienell S. (2022) Die Akademie der Wissenschaften in Wien im Nationalsozialismus und im Kontext der Akademien im „Altreich", in: Feichtinger J. – Mazohl B. (eds.), Die Österreichische Akademie der Wissenschaften 1847–2022. Eine neue Akademiegeschichte (Vienna) 11–141

Feichtinger J. – Geiger K. (2022a) 1945. Die Neuordnung der Akademie, in: Feichtinger J. – Mazohl B. (eds.), Die Österreichische Akademie der Wissenschaften 1847–2022. Eine neue Akademiegeschichte (Vienna) 143–160

Feichtinger J. – Geiger K. (2022b) Transformierte Kontinuitäten. Akademieforschung nach 1945 im Schatten des Nationalsozialismus, in: Feichtinger J. – Mazohl B. (eds.), Die Österreichische Akademie der Wissenschaften 1847–2022. Eine neue Akademiegeschichte (Vienna) 201–248

Feichtinger J. – Geiger K. (2022c) Die Selbstfindung der Akademie in der nationalen und internationalen Forschungslandschaft (1945–1970), in: Feichtinger J. – Mazohl B. (eds.), Die Österreichische Akademie der Wissenschaften 1847–2022. Eine neue Akademiegeschichte (Vienna) 275–316

Feichtinger J. – Geiger K. (2022d) Strategien und Praktiken der Selbsterneuerung. Die ÖAW zwischen 1970 und der Gegenwart, in: Feichtinger J. – Mazohl B. (eds.), Die Österreichische Akademie der Wissenschaften 1847–2022. Eine neue Akademiegeschichte (Vienna) 369–446

Feichtinger J. – Hecht D. J. (2013a) Aufgaben und Wirkungskreis des neuen Präsidiums, in: Feichtinger J. – Matis H. – Sienell S. – Uhl H. (eds.), Die Akademie der Wissenschaften in Wien 1938 bis 1945 (Vienna) 159–169

Feichtinger J. – Hecht D. J. (2013b) Die Entnazifizierung der Akademie der Wissenschaften, in: Feichtinger J. – Matis

H. – Sienell S. – Uhl H. (eds.), Die Akademie der Wissenschaften in Wien 1938 bis 1945 (Vienna) 171–187

Feichtinger J. – Hecht D. J. (2013c) 1945 und danach. Eine Zäsur und zwei Kontinuitäten, in: Feichtinger J. – Matis H. – Sienell S. – Uhl H. (eds.), Die Akademie der Wissenschaften in Wien 1938 bis 1945 (Vienna) 189–197

Feichtinger J. – Matis H. – Sienell S. – Uhl H. (eds.) (2013) Die Akademie der Wissenschaften in Wien 1938 bis 1945. Katalog zur Ausstellung (Vienna)

Feichtinger J. – Uhl H. (2018) Zwischen Gelehrtengesellschaft und Forschungsakademie. Die Österreichische Akademie der Wissenschaften 1945–1965, in: Feichtinger J. – Uhl H. (eds.), Die Akademien der Wissenschaften in Zentraleuropa im Kalten Krieg: Transformationsprozesse im Spannungsfeld von Abgrenzung und Annäherung (Vienna) 231–262

Feichtinger J. – Uhl H. (2022) Verdrängung und Erinnerung. Zur Gedächtnisgeschichte des Nationalsozialismus an der ÖAW (1945–2022), in: Feichtinger J. – Mazohl B. (eds.), Die Österreichische Akademie der Wissenschaften 1847–2022. Eine neue Akademiegeschichte (Vienna) 251–271

Feissel D. (1998) Vicaires et proconsuls d'Asie du iv´ au vi´ siècle. Notes sur l'administration du diocese asianique au Bas-Empire, in Les gouverneurs de province dans l'Antiquité Tardive, AntTard 6, 91–104

Feissel D. (1999) Straßenbeleuchtung im spätantiken Ephesos, in: Scherrer P. – Taeuber H. – Thür H. (eds.), Steine und Wege. Festschrift für Dieter Knibbe, SoSchrOeAI 32 (Vienna) 25–29

Fellner F. – Corradini D. A. (2006) Österreichische Geschichtswissenschaft im 20. Jahrhundert (Vienna – Cologne – Weimar)

Feltrio F. (1599) Degli Elementi d'Euclide libri quindici […] (Pesaro)

Février S. (1993) Le mausolée gallo-romain de Faverolles (Haute-Marne), in: Monde des morts, monde des vivants en Gaule rurale, Actes du Colloque ARCHEA/AGER (Orléans, 7–9 février 1992) Tours: Fédération pour l'édition de la Revue archéologique du Centre de la France, 93-98

Février S. (2000) La restitution architecturale du mausolée de Faverolles, in Walter H. (éd.) La sculpture d'époque romaine dans le Nord, dans l'Est des Gaules et dans les régions avoisinantes: acquis et problématiques actuelles, Actes du Colloque international de Besançon, 12–14 mars 1998, Besançon, Presses universitaires de Franche-Comté (coll. Annales littéraires), 203-213

Fins P. – Pereira M. L. – Afonso A. et al. (2017) Chronology of mineralization of the permanent mandibular second molar teeth and forensic age estimation, Forensic Sci Med Pathol 13,3, 272–277

Fischer E. (1961) Josef Weninger †, Zeitschrift für Morphologie und Anthropologie 51,2, 236–237

Fischer J. (2010) Ephesos und das Artemision im Spiegel der antiken Mythologie, Diomedes 5, 17–27

Fischer J. (2012) Herrscherverehrung im antiken Ephesos, in: Danek G. – Hellerschmid I. (eds.), Identitätsstiftende Handlungskomplexe (Vienna) 139–157

Fischer J. (2014a) Das Artemision von Ephesos. Ein antikes Pilgerziel im Spiegel der literarischen und epigraphischen Überlieferung, in: Olshausen E. – Sauer V. (eds.), Mobilität in den Kulturen der antiken Mittelmeerwelt. Stuttgarter Kolloquium zur Historischen Geographie des Altertums 11, 171–203

Fischer J. (2014b) Redner, Sophisten und Philosophen im römischen Ephesos, in: Fischer J. (ed.), Der Beitrag Kleinasiens zur Kultur- und Geistesgeschichte der griechisch-römischen Antike. Akten des Internationalen Kolloquiums Wien, 3.–5. November 2010, Archäologische Forschungen 24 (Vienna) 125–151

Fiska G. (2012) Das Teatro Marittimo in der Villa Hadriana (Thesis University of Vienna, Vienna)

Fitzpatrick R. (2008) Euclid's elements of geometry. The Greek text of J.L. Heiberg (1883–1885) from Euclidis Elementa, edidit et Latine interpretatus est I.L. Heiberg, in aedibus B.G. Teubneri, 1883–1885 edited, and provided with a modern English translation, https://farside.ph.utexas.edu/books/Euclid/Elements.pdf

Fleck C. (1996) Autochthose Provinzialisierung. Universität und Wissenschaftspolitik nachg dem Ende der nationalsozialistischen Herrschaft in Österreich, OeZG 7, 67–92

Fleischer R. (1967) Der Fries des Hadrianstempels in Ephesos, in: Braun E. (ed.), Festschrift für Fritz Eichler zum achtzigsten Geburtstag dargebracht vom Österreichischen Archäologischen Institut (Vienna) 23–71

Fleischer R. (1972) Aphroditetorso vom Pollionymphäum in Ephesos, JOeAI 2. Beiheft, 165–171

Fleischer R. (1973) Artemis von Ephesos und verwandte Kultstatuen aus Anatolien und Syrien, EPRO 35

Fleischer R. (2002) Die Amazonen und das Asyl des Artemision von Ephesos, JdI 117, 185–216

Forchheimer P. (1923) Wasserleitungen, FiE III (1923) 224–255

Franceschini M. (2018) Attische Mantelfiguren. Relevanz eines standardisierten Motivs der rotfigurigen Vasenmalerei, Zürcher Archäologische Forschungen 5 (Rahden/Westfalen)

Franceschini M. (2021) Iconographic Series in Attic Vase Painting: Technical Simplification or Semantic Strategy?, in: Reinhardt A. (ed.), Strictly Economic? Ancient Serial Production and its Premises. Panel 3.18, Archaeology and Economy in the Ancient World – Proceedings of the 19th International Congress of Classical Archaeology, Cologne/Bonn 2018 20 (Heidelberg) 45–59

Freber P. G. (1993) Der hellenistische Osten und das Illyricum unter Caesar (Stuttgart)

Freze A. (2015) Byzantine Octagon Domed Churches of the 11th Century and the Roman Imperial Architecture, Actual Problems of Theory and History of Art 5, 277–286

Friedmann I. (2011) Der Prähistoriker Richard Pittioni (1906–1985) zwischen 1938 und 1945 unter Einbeziehung der Jahre des Austrofaschismus und der beginnenden Zweiten Republik, Archaeologia Austriaca 95, 7–99

Friesen S. (1993) Twice Neokoros. Ephesus, Asia and the Cult of the Flavian Imperial Family (Leiden)

Friesen S. (2022) The Customs House Inscription from Ephesos. Exchange, Surplus, Ideology, and the Divine, in: Black A. – Thomas C. M – Thompson T. W. (eds.), Ephesos as a Religious Center under the Principate (Tübingen) 115–138

Friesinger H. (1985) In memoriam Richard Pittioni (1906-1985), MAGW 115, 181–182

Frisch C. (ed.) (1871) Joannis Kepleri astronomi Opera Omnia I (Frankfurt)

Fritz K. v. (1931) RE XV/1 524–528 s.v. Melissa

Fritz P. (2018) „Mischehen" in der NS-Zeit (Thesis University of Graz, Graz)

Fröhlich S. (2022) Stadttor und Stadteingang. Zur Alltags- und Kulturgeschichte der Stadt in der römischen Kaiserzeit, Studien zur Alten Geschichte 32 (Göttingen)

Fuchs B. (2002a) Pacher, Helga Maria, in: Keintzel B. – Korotin I. (eds.) Wissenschafterinnen in und aus Österreich: Leben – Werk – Wirken (Vienna – Cologne – Weimar) 544–545

Fuchs B. (2002b) Weninger, Margarete, in: Keintzel B. – Korotin I. (eds.) Wissenschafterinnen in und aus Österreich: Leben – Werk – Wirken (Vienna – Cologne – Weimar) 809–812

Füllenbach E. H. (2017) Josef Nadler, in: Fahlbusch M. – Haar I. – Pinwinkler A. (eds.), Handbuch der völkischen Wissenschaften. Akteure, Netzwerke, Forschungsprogramme (Berlin – Boston) 533–540

Fürst H. (2012) Von der Deutschtümelei zum Deutschnationalismus, von der Volksgeschichte zum Volkstumskampf. Kämpfende Wissenschaft im Dienst nationalsozialistischer Politik für den deutschnationalen Kultur- und Volkstumskampf in Südosteuropa (Thesis University of Vienna, Vienna)

Gabelmann H. (1979) Römische Grabbauten der frühen Kaiserzeit, Kleine Schriften zur Kenntnis der römischen Besetzungsgeschichte Südwestdeutschlands 22 (Stuttgart)

Gassner V. (1997) Das Südtor der Tetragonos Agora. Keramik und Kleinfunde, FiE XIII 1,1 (Vienna)

Gassner V. (2007) Kultkeramik aus dem sgn. Felsspalttempel in Ephesos, in: Seres 2007. IV. Uluslararsı Katılımlı Seramik, Cam, Emaye Sır ve Boya Semineri (Eskisehir) 298–386

Gassner V. (2020) In memoriam Herma Stieglitz, JOeAI 89, 7–9

Gedda L. (1959) In memoriam Dr. Josef Weninger, Acta Geneticae Medicae et Gemellologiae 8,4, 511–512

Gehrke H. J. (2005) Prinzen und Prinzessinnen bei den späten Ptolemäern, in: Alonso Troncoso V. (ed.), ΔΙΑΔΟΧΟΣ ΤΗΣ ΒΑΣΙΛΕΙΑΣ. La figura del sucesor en la realeza helenística, Gerión Anejos. Serie de Monografías. Anejo IX (Madrid) 103–117

Geiger K. – Feichtinger J. (2022) Die kaiserliche Akademie im Ersten Weltkrieg (1914–1918), in: Feichtinger J. – Mazohl B. (eds.), Die Österreichische Akademie der Wissenschaften 1847–2022. Eine neue Akademiegeschichte (Vienna) 473–519

Geisenhainer K. (2021a) „Rassenkunde" und „Rassenhygiene" an der philosophischen Fakultät 1923–1938, in: Gingrich A. – Rohrbacher P. (eds.), Völkerkunde zur NS-Zeit aus Wien (1938–1945) (Vienna) 85–128.

Geisenhainer K. (2021b) Auseinandersetzungen um die institutionelle Verortung von „Rassenkunde" und „Rassenhygiene" am Beispiel Wien 1938–1943, in: Gingrich A. – Rohrbacher P. (eds.), Völkerkunde zur NS-Zeit aus Wien (1938 – 1945) (Vienna) 927–965

Geisenhainer K. (2021c) Gescheiterte Interventionen. Otto Reche und seine Wiener Nachfolge 1936–1928, in: Gingrich A. – Rohrbacher P. (eds.), Völkerkunde zur NS-Zeit aus Wien (1938–1945) (Vienna) 129–152

Gelbmann G. (2005) Erratum und Memorandum zu meinem Buch über Friedrich Kainz, <https://geschichte.univie.ac.at/de/albin-lesky> (accessed on 21.04.2022)

Gemoll W. (1965) Griechisch-deutsches Schulwörterbuch und Handwörterbuch (Munich – Vienna)

Gerber A. (2008) Gustav Adolf Deissmann (1866–1937) and the revival of archaeological excavations at Ephesus after the First World War, JOeAI 75, 39-46

Gerber A. (2010) Deissmann the Philologist. Beihefte zur Zeitschrift für die neutestamentliche Wissenschaft und die Kunde der älteren Kirche 171 (Berlin–Boston)

Gerkan A. v. (1921) Das Theater von Priene, als Einzelanlage und in seiner Bedeutung für das Hellenistische Bühnenwesen (Munich – Leipzig)

Gesellschaft der Freunde von Ephesos (2015) 120 Jahre Österreichische Forschungen in Ephesos, <https://www.ephesos.at/clubdesk/fileservlet?id=1000082> (accessed on 21.04.2022)

Gesellschaft der Freunde von Ephesos (2020) Information über den Stand der Ausgrabungen 1/20, https://www.ephesos.at/clubdesk/fileservlet?id=1000054 (accessed on 21.04.2022)

Gingrich A. (2021) Viktor Christian und die Völkerkunde in Wien 1938–1945. Universität, Anthropologische Gesellschaft und Akademie der Wissenschaften., in: Gingrich A. – Rohrbacher P. (eds.), Völkerkunde zur NS-Zeit aus Wien (1938–1945) I (Vienna) 373–423

Gliwitzky C. (2010) Späte Blüte in Side und Perge. Die pamphylische Bauornamentik des 3. Jahrhunderts n.Chr. (Bern)

Goulet R. – Lehmann Y. (2018) Varro (Marcus Terentius), in: Goulet R. (ed.), Dictionnaire des philosophes antiques 7 (Paris) 94–133

Grabowski T. (2014) The Cult of the Ptolemies in the Aegean in the 3rd Century BC, ELECTRUM 21, 21–41

Gracilis S. (1558) Euclidis Elementorum Libri XV Graece et Latine [...] (Coloniae)

Graeve V. v. (1970) Der Alexandersarkophag und seine Werkstatt (Berlin)

Graf-Stuhlhofer F. (1998) Opportunisten, Sympathisanten und Beamte. Unterstützung des NS-Systems in der Wiener Akademie der Wissenschaften, dargestellt am Wirken Nadlers, Sriks und Meisters. Wiener Klinische Wochenschrift 110, 152–157

Grant M. (1977) Kleopatra (Bergisch Gladbach)

Grebien M. (2018) The City Walls of Side. Are they Hellenistic Fortifications?, in: Kahya T. – Özdizbay A. – Tüner Önen N. – Wilson M. (eds.), International Young Scholars Conference II. Mediterranean Anatolia 04–07 November 2015 (Antalya) 369–380

Green P. (1985) The last of the Ptolemies, Grand Street 4,3, 133–168

Green P. (1990) Alexander to Actium. The Hellenistic Age (London)

Grimm G. (2006) Kleopatra – eine königliche Hure?, in: Andreae B. – Rhein K. (eds.), Kleopatra und die Caesaren (Munich) 176–183

Groh S. (2006) Neue Forschungen zur Stadtplanung in Ephesos, JOeAI 75, 47–116

Gruben G. (1997) Naxos und Delos. Studien zur archaischen Architektur der Kykladen, JdI 112, 261–416

Grüßinger R. (2001) Dekorative Architekturfriese in Rom und Latium. Ikonologische Studien zur römischen Baudekoration der späten Republik und Kaiserzeit (Thesis Heidelberg University, Heidelberg)

Grund A. (1911) Ephesus und Milet, Lotos 59, 203–213

Guarducci M. (1942) Inscriptiones Creticae III (Rome)

Günther H. F. R (1930) Rassenkunde des deutschen Volkes (Munich)

Guo Y. C. – Chu G. – Olze A. et al. (2018) Age estimation of Chinese children based on second molar maturity, Int J Legal Med 132,3, 807–813

Gutsmiedl-Schümann D. (2013) Hedwig Kenner (1910-1993). Forscherin von menschlicher Güte und humanistischem Geist, in: Fries J. E. – Gutsmiedl-Schümann D. (eds.), Ausgräberinnen, Forscherinnen, Pionierinnen. Ausgewählte Portraits früher Archäologinnen im Kontext ihrer Zeit. Frauen – Forschung – Archäologie (Münster) 247–254

Habicht M. E. (2021) Das fremde Ägypten (Zurich)

Hafner M. (2020) Der ‚Mythos Athen‘ im literarischen Diskursfeld fiktionaler Erzählprosa der Kaiserzeit – am Beispiel von Lukian, Chariton und Heliodor, in: Cecconi P. – Tornau C. (eds.), Städte und Stadtstaaten zwischen Mythos, Literatur und Politik, BzA 383 (Berlin – Boston) 249–268

Hafner M. (2021) Beyond comparison? Literary appropriation and Its Effects on (Post-) Augustan Greco-Roman Text Production, Primerjalna književnost 44.2, 2021 (Special Issue: B. Zabel [ed.], Ancient Literary Traditions in Comparative Literature) 21–37

Hahn W. (1985) Die Medaillensammlung der Österreichischen Akademie der Wissenschaften. Ein Katalog. DenkschrWien 182 (Vienna)

Hajjar Y. (1977) La triade d'Héliopolis-Baalbek 1, Études Préliminaires Aux Religions Orientales Dans l'Empire Romain 59 (Leiden)

Hales T. C. (2001) The Honeycomb Conjecture. Discrete & Computational Geometry. 25 (1) https://link.springer.com/article/10.1007/s004540010071 doi:10.1007/s004540010071

Halfmann H. (1979) Die Senatoren aus dem östlichen Teil des Imperium Romanum bis zum Ende des 2. Jahrhunderts n. Chr., Hypomnemata 58 (Göttingen)

Halfmann H. (2001) Städtebau und Bauherren im westlichen Kleinasien. Ein Vergleich zwischen Pergamon und Ephesos, IstMitt Beiheft 43 (Tübingen)

Halma M. (1821) Θέωνος Ἀλεξανδρέως Ὑπόμνήμα εἰς τὸ πρῶτον τῆς Πτολεμαίου Μαθηματικῆς Συντάξεως. Commentaire de Théon d'Alexandrie I (Paris)

Hammerschmid S. (2009) „Die Rolle der Geschichtswissenschaft während des Dritten Reiches" am Beispiel der Universität Wien (Thesis University of Vienna, Vienna)

Handbuch Reichsgau Wien 1941, 63/64 amtlich redigierter Jahrgang. Deutscher Verlag für Jugend und Volk (Vienna)

Handbuch Reichsgau Wien 1944, 65/66 amtlich redigierter Jahrgang. Deutscher Verlag für Jugend und Volk (Vienna)

Handler S. (1971) Architecture on the Roman coins of Alexandria, AJA 75,1, 57–74

Hanusch G. (1953) Osteuropa-Dissertationen 1945-1950. Deutschland, Österreich, Schweiz. Jahrbücher für Geschichte Osteuropas NF 1,4, 1–44

Harders A. C. (2010) Hellenistische Königinnen in Rom, in: Kolb A. (ed.), Augustae. Machtbewusste Frauen am römischen Kaiserhof? Herrschaftsstrukturen und Herrschaftspraxis II. Akten der Tagung in Zürich 18.–20.9.2008 (Berlin) 55–74

Harl O. (1989) Wie heilig ist der Ulrichsberg in Kärnten?, Archaeologia Austriaca 73, 101–115

Hartig A. (1964) Aus meinem Leben. Vom Bauernjungen zum Künstler. Erlebnisse mit porträtierten Persönlichkeiten (Vienna)

Hauben H. (1983) Arsinoé II et la politique extérieure de l'Égypte, in: van't Dack E. – van Dessel P. – van Gucht W. (eds.), Egypt and the Hellenistic World. Proceedings of the International Colloquium Leuven 24–26 May 1982, Studia Hellenistica 27 (Lovanii) 99–127

Hauser G. (1988) In memoriam Frau Professor Dr. Margarete Weninger, AnthropolAnz 46,3, 277

Hauser G. (2005a) In memoriam Eugen Reuer, AnthropolAnz 63,3, 351–352

Hauser G. (2005b) In memoriam Emil Breitinger 15.10.2004 - 01.05.2004, AnthropolAnz 63,1, 107–108

Hayek H. (1960) Josef Weninger †, Alm 109, 1959, 427–436

Head B. V. (1911) Catalogue of the Greek Coins of Ionia, Historia Nummorum 2 (Oxford)

Heath T. L. (1908) The thirteen books of Euclid's Elements (London)

Heberdey R. (1902) Vorläufiger Bericht über die Ausgrabungen in Ephesus V, JOeAI 5 Beibl., 53–66

Heberdey R. (1904) Vorläufiger Bericht über die Grabungen in Ephesus 1902/03 VI, JOeAI 7 Beibl., 37–56

Heberdey R. (1905) Vorläufiger Bericht über die Grabungen in Ephesus 1904 VII, JOeAI 8 Beibl., 61–80

Heberdey R. (1907) Vorläufiger Bericht über die Grabungen in Ephesus 1905/06 VIII, JOeAI 10 Beibl., 61–78

Heberdey R. (1912a) Vorläufiger Bericht über die Grabungen in Ephesos 1907-1911 IX, JOeAI 15 Beibl., 157–182

Heberdey R. (1912b) Vorläufiger Bericht über die Grabungen in Ephesos 1913 XI, JOeAI 15 Beibl., 77–88

Heberdey R. (1912c) Inschriften, FiE II (Vienna) 95–203

Heinen H. (1966) Rom und Ägypten von 51 bis 47 v. Chr. (Thesis University of Tübingen)

Heinz W. (2016) Kleine Kulturgeschichte der Achtzahl (Berlin)

Heiß G. (1993) ... wirkliche Möglichkeiten für eine nationalsozialistische Philosophie? Die Reorganisation der Philosophie (Psychologie und Pädagogik) in Wien 1938 bis 1940, in: Fischer K. R. – Wimmer F. M. (eds.), Der geistige Anschluß. Philosohie und Politik an der Universität Wien 1938 (Vienna) 130–169

Heiß G. (1999) '... As the Universities in Austria Were More Pillars of Our Movement Than Those in the Old Provinces of the Reich'. The University of Vienna from Nazification to De-Nazification, Digestive Diseases 17, 267–278

Hekster O. – Rich J. (2006) Octavian and the Thunderbolt: The Temple of Apollo Palatinus and Roman Traditions of Temple Building, Classical Quarterly 56/1, 149–168

Herklotz F. (2009) Ptolemaios XII. – Versager oder siegreicher Pharao, in: Fitzenreiter M. (ed.), Das Ereignis. Geschichtsschreibung zwischen Vorfall und Befund, Workshop vom 03. bis 05.10.2008 in Berlin (London) 137–153

Herrmann P. – Rehm A. (1997) Inschriften von Milet I, Milet 6,1 (Berlin – New York)

Hervagium I. (1546) Euclidis megarensis Mathematici clarissimi elementorum Geometricorum libri XV […] (Basel)

Hinks R. (1928) A portrait of a Ptolemaic Queen, The Journal of Hellenic Studies 48, 239–243

Hinsch M. (2015) Aristoteles und die zwei Agorai. Die Ordnung des öffentlichen Raums in literarischen Quellen des 4. Jhs. v. Chr., <https://www.academia.edu/17403463/Aristoteles_und_die_zwei_Agorai_2015_> (accessed on 03.12.2022)

Hirschberg W. (1977) Prof. Dr. Margarete Weninger 80 Jahre! (1896-1976), MAGW 107

Hisham S. – Flavel A. – Abdullah N. et al. (2018) Quantification of spheno-occipital synchrondrosis fusion in a contemporary Malaysian population, Forenisc Sci Int 284, 78–84

Hoepfner W. (ed.) (2002) Antike Bibliotheken, Zaberns Bildbände zur Archäologie, Sonderbände der Antiken Welt (Mainz)

Hofbauer M. – Öztürk A. – Styhler G. – Leisser C. – Göçmen D. (2017) Zusammenfassung und chronologischer Überblick, in: Krinzinger F. – Ruggendorfer P. (ed.), Das Theater von Ephesos. Archäologischer Befund, Funde und Chronologie, FiE II 1 (Vienna) 433–473

Hölbl G. (1994) Geschichte des Ptolemäerreiches. Politik, Ideologie und religiöse Kultur von Alexander dem Großen bis zur römischen Eroberung (Darmstadt)

Hölscher T. (1985) Die Geschlagenen und Ausgelieferten in der Kunst des Hellenismus, AntK 28, 120–136

Hölscher T. (2000) Die Amazonen von Ephersos: ein Monument der Selbstbehauptung, in: Agathos daimōn. Mythes et cultes. Études d'iconographie en l'honneur de Lilly Kahil, Bulletin de Correspondance Hellénique Supplément 38 (Athen) 205–218

Hölscher T. (2012) Bilderwelt, Lebensordnung und die Rolle des Betrachters im antiken Griechenland, in: Dally O. – Moraw S. – Ziemssen H. (eds.), Bild – Raum – Handlung. Perspektiven der Archäologie (Berlin – Boston) 19–44

Holtzman W. (ed.) (1562) Die sechs erste Bücher Euclidis vom Anfang oder Grund der Geometrj […] (Basel)

Hörmann H. (1951) Die Johanneskirche, FiE IV 3 (Baden near Vienna)

Hornung S. (2011) Luxus auf dem Lande. Die römische Palastvilla von Bad Kreuznach 2 (Bad Kreuznach)

Horster M. (2001) Bauinschriften römischer Kaiser. Untersuchungen zu Inschriftenpraxis und Bautätigkeit in Städten des westlichen Imperium Romanum in der Zeit des Prinzipats, Historia Einzelschriften 157 (Stuttgart)

Huber A. (2012) Eliten/dis/kontinuitäten. Kollektivporträt der im Nationalsozialismus aus „politischen" Gründen vertriebenen Hochschullehrer der Universität Wien (Thesis University of Vienna, Vienna)

Huber A. (2020a) Antisemitische Schaltzentrale. Die Deutsche Gemeinschaft und Österreichs Hochschulen in der Ersten Republik, <https://www.academia.edu/42048759/Antisemitische_Schaltzentrale_Die_Deutsche_Gemeinschaft_und_%C3%96sterreichs_Hochschulen_in_der_Ersten_Republik> (accessed on 21.04.2022)

Huber A. (2020b) Kornblume und Hakenkreuz, Die Mitglieder des Deutschen Klubs 1908 bis 1939, <https://www.academia.edu/42038355/Kornblume_und_Hakenkreuz_Die_Mitglieder_des_Deutschen_Klubs_1908_bis_1939> (accessed on 21.04.2022)

Huber A. – Erker L. – Taschwer K. (2020) Der Deutsche Klub. Austro-Nazis in der Hofburg (Vienna)

Hueber F. (1984) Der Embolos, ein urbanes Zentrum von Ephesos, AW 15/4, 3–30

Hueber F. (1997a) Ephesos. Gebaute Geschichte. Antike Welt, Sonderband (Mainz)

Hueber F. (1997b) Zur städtebaulichen Entwicklung des hellenistisch-römischen Ephesos. Phylen, Embolos,

Olympieion, Horologion, Statthalterpalast, Auditorium, Parthermonument, Marienkirche, IstMitt 47, 251–269

Huß W. (2001) Ägypten in hellenistischer Zeit 332–30 v. Chr. (Munich)

Huter F. (1969) Fritz von Reinöhl, MIOeG 77, 542–543

Hutterer H. – Just T. (2007) Zur Geschichte des Reichsarchivs Wien 1938–1945, Tagungsdokumentationen zum Deutschen Archivtag 10, 313–325

Iannantuono K. (2021) Artemis, Trajan and the Demos in Parade. A Reinterpretation of the Reliefs at the so-called Temple of Hadrian at Ephesos, JOeAI 90, 245–272

Iossif P. P. – Lorber C. C. (2021) Monetary Policies, Coin Production, and Currency Supply in the Seleucid and Ptolemaic Empires, in: Fischer-Bovet Ch. – von Reden S. (eds.), Comparing the Ptolemaic and Seleucid Empires. Integration, Communication, and Resistance (Cambridge) 191–230

Jacoby F. (1922) RE XI,2 1710 s.v. Kreophylos 2

Joachim H. E. (2013) Der Archäologe, Althistoriker und Museumsmann Harald von Petrikovits. Eine biographische Skizze, BJB 212, 3–17

Jobst W. (1983) Embolosforschungen I. Archäologische Untersuchungen östlich der Celsusbibliothek in Ephesos, JOeAI 54 Beibl., 149–242

Jobst W. (1985) Zur Standortbestimmung und Rekonstruktion des Parthersiegaltares von Ephesos, JOeAI 56, 79–82

Jobst W. (2005) Parthermonument und Pergamonaltar. Hellenistische und römische Triumphalkunst in Kleinasien, in: Ganschow T. (ed.), Otium. Festschrift für Volker Michael Strocka (Remshalden) 171–179

Johnson M. L. (2009) The Roman imperial mausoleum in Late Antiquity (Cambridge)

Johnston S. I. (1990) Hekate Soteira. A Study of Hekate´s Roles in the Chaldean Oracles and Related Literature, American Classical Studies 21 (Atlanta)

Joly M. – Février S. (2003) Nouvelle Restitution du Mausolée de Faverolles, Revue Archéologique Nouvelle Série 1, 214–216

Jones C. P. (1999) Atticus in Ephesos, ZPE 124, 89–94

Jones C. P. (2004) Multiple identities in the age of the Second Sophistic, in: Borg B. E. (ed.), Paideia: Die Welt der zweiten Sophistik/ The World of the Second Sophistic (Berlin – New York) 13–21

Jones H. L. (1929) The Geography of Strabo in Eight Volumes, Vol. VI (London – Cambridge)

Jones M. W. (2000) Principles of Roman Architecture (New Haven – London)

Jones P. J. (1971) Cleopatra. A source book (Norman)

Jones W. H. S. (1918) Pausanias. Description of Greece, Vol. I, Books 1-2 (London – Cambridge)

Jones W. H. S. (1933) Pausanias. Description of Greece, Vol. III, Books, 6-8.21 (London – Cambridge)

Jördens A. (2013) Griechische Texte aus Ägypten, in: Janowski B. – Schwemer D. (eds.) Texte aus der Umwelt des Alten Testaments 7 Hymnen, Klagelieder und Gebete (Gütersloh) 272–309

Judeich W. (1885) Caesar im Orient: Kritische Übersicht der Ereignisse vom 9. August 48 bis October 47 (Leipzig)

Just T. (2010) Das Haus-, Hof- und Staatsarchiv in der NS-Zeit, Mitteilungen des Österreichischen Staatsarchivs 54, 103–147

Kader I. (1995) Heroa und Memorialbauten, in: Wörrle M. – Zanker P. (eds.) Stadtbild und Bürgerbild im Hellenismus (Munich) 199–229

Kainz F. (1965) Richard Meister †, Alm 114, 1964, 267–311

Kandler M. (1998) Unter fremdem Namen. Die Jahre 1938 –1945, in: Kandler M. – Wlach G. (eds.), 100 Jahre Österreichisches Archäologisches Institut 1898–1998 (Vienna) 49–60

Kandler M. – Wlach G. (1998) Imperiale Größe. Das k.k. österreichische archäologische Institut von der Gründung im Jahre 1898 bis zum Untergang der Monarchie, in: Kandler M. – Wlach G. (eds.) 100 Jahre Österreichisches Archäologisches Institut 1898–1998. SoSchrOeAI 31 (Vienna) 13-35

Kankeleit A. (2016) Das Deutsche Archäologische Institut in Athen während der NS-Zeit, Exantas 24,4, 12–19

Kanz F. – Grossschmidt K. – Kiesslich J. (2009) Arsinoë IV of Egypt, sister of Cleopatra identified? Osseous and molecular changes. Poster presented at the 77th Annual Meeting of the American Association of Physical Anthropologists Columbus, Ohio

Kappraff J. (2000) The arithmetic of Nicomachus of Gerasa and its applications to systems of proportion, Nexus Netw J 2, 41–55

Kappraff J. (2002) Beyond measure. A guided tour through nature, myth, and number (New Jersey – London – Singapore – Hong Kong)

Karwiese S. (1970) RE Suppl XII 297–364 s.v. Ephesos C. Numismatischer Teil. Die Münzprägung von Ephesos

Karwiese S. (1985) Koressos – Ein fast vergessener Stadtteil von Ephesos, in: Pro Arte Antiqua. Festschrift für Hedwig Kenner, SoSchrOeAI 18, 214–225

Karwiese S. (1991) Herostratos. Versuch einer Ehrenrettung, in: Erol Atalay Memorial. Ege Üniversitesi Edebiyat Fakültesi Yayınları (İzmir) 89–95

Karwiese S. (1995) Groß ist die Artemis von Ephesos. Die Geschichte einer der großen Städte der Antike (Vienna)

Karwiese S. (1997a) Das Südtor der Tetragonos Agora in Ephesos. Die archäologische Evidenz aus den Fundamentsondierungen, JOeAI 66 Beibl., 253–318

Karwiese S. (1997b) Die Hafenthermen von Ephesos. Ihr ursprünglicher Name und ihr erster(?) Gymnasiarch, in: Thür H. (ed.), „... und verschönerte die Stadt ...“ – ΚΑΙ ΚΟΣΜΕΣΑΝΤΑ ΤΗΝ ΠΟΛΙΝ. Ein ephesischer Priester des Kaiserkultes in seinem Umfeld, SoSchrOeAI 27 (Vienna) 141–146

Karwiese S. (2016) Die Münzprägung von Ephesos 5,2. Corpus und Aufbau der römerzeitlichen Stadtprägung. Statistiken, Metrologie und Kommentare, Veröffent-

lichungen des Institutes für Numismatik und Geld-
geschichte 18 (Phoibos – Vienna)

Karwiese S. et al. (1994) Ephesos, JOeAI 63, Grabungen
1993, 9–31

Karwiese S. et al. (1996) Ephesos, JOeAI 65, Grabungen
1995, 5–32

Keil J. (1905) Ärzteinschriften aus Ephesos, JOeAI 8, 128–138

Keil J. (1912) Vorläufiger Bericht über die Arbeiten in Ephesos 1912 X, JOeAI 15 Beibl., 183–212

Keil J. (1913) Ephesische Bürgerrechts- und Proxenie-
dekrete aus dem vierten und dritten Jahrhundert v.
Chr., JOeAI 16, 231–244

Keil J. (1914) Aphrodite Daitis, JOeAI 17, 145–147

Keil J. (1915) Ephesos. Ein Führer durch die Ruinenstätte
und ihre Geschichte (Vienna)

Keil J. (1922–24) Ortygia, die Geburtsstätte der ephesischen
Artemis, JOeAI 20–21, 113–119

Keil J. (1923) Inschriften, FiE III (Vienna) 91-168

Keil J. (1926) Vorläufiger Bericht über die Ausgrabungen in
Ephesos XII, JOeAI 23 Beibl., 247–300

Keil J. (1929a) Vorläufiger Bericht über die Ausgrabungen in
Ephesos XIII, JOeAI 24 Beibl., 5–68

Keil J. (1929b) Vorläufiger Bericht über die Ausgrabungen in
Ephesos XIV, JOeAI 25 Beibl., 5–52

Keil J. (1930a) Vorläufiger Bericht über die Ausgrabungen in
Ephesos XV, JOeAI 26 Beibl., 5–66

Keil J. (1930b) Ephesos. Ein Führer durch die Ruinenstätte
und ihre Geschichte (Vienna)

Keil J. (1932) Vorläufiger Bericht über die Ausgrabungen in
Ephesos XVI, JOeAI 27 Beibl., 5–72

Keil J. (1933) Vorläufiger Bericht über die Ausgrabungen in
Ephesos XVII, JOeAI 28 Beibl. 5–44

Keil J. (1935a) Das Martyrium des heiligen Timotheus in
Ephesos, JOeAI 29, 82–92

Keil J. (1935b) Vorläufiger Bericht über die Ausgrabungen in
Ephesos XVIII, JOeAI 29 Beibl., 103–152

Keil J. (1936–37) Vorläufiger Bericht über die Ausgrabungen
in Ephesos XIX, JOeAI 30, Beibl. 173–214

Keil J. (1940) Das Serapeion von Ephesos, in: Archäologisches Institut des Deutschen Reiches (ed.), Bericht
über den VI. Internationalen Kongress für Archäologie.
Berlin 21. - 26. August 1939 (Berlin) 473

Keil J. (1941) Professor Dr. Rudolf Egger zum 60. Geburts-
tage, Carinthia I 131,2, 259–261

Keil J. (1943) Drei neue Inschriften aus Ephesos, JOeAI 35
Beibl., 101–108

Keil J. (1947) Das Serapeion von Ephesos, in: In memoriam
Halil Edhem I, Türk Tarih Kurumu Yayinlarindan VII.
Ser. No. 5 (Ankara) 181–192

Keil J. (1948) Alm 97, 1947, Vorwort

Keil J. (1951) Camillo Praschniker †, Alm 100, 1950, 292–306

Keil J. (1952) Nachruf Adolf Wilhelm, Alm 101, 1951, 307–327

Keil J. (1953) Vertreter der 2. Sophistik in Ephesos, JOeAI 40,
5–26

Keil J. (1954) Denkmäler des Sarapiskultes in Ephesos, Anz-
Wien 91, 217–228

Keil J. (1955) Ephesos. Ein Führer durch die Ruinenstätte
und ihre Geschichte (Vienna)

Keil J. (1957) Ephesos. Ein Führer durch die Ruinenstätte
und ihre Geschichte (Baden near Vienna)

Keil J. (1959) Franz Miltner †, Gnomon 31,7, 654–655

Keil J. (1961) Franz Miltner †, Alm 110, 1960, 361–372

Keil J. (1964) Ephesos. Ein Führer durch die Ruinenstätte
und ihre Geschichte (Vienna)

Keil J. (ed.) (1944/1953) Die Bibliothek, FiE V 1 (Vienna)

Kenner H. (1933) Ein archaischer Beckenuntersatz aus Rhodos, MittVKPW 10, 112–116

Kenner H. (1957) F. Eichler zum 70. Geburtstag, AnzAW 10,
303–304

Kenner H. (1965) Otto Walter †, Gnomon 37,8, 846–847

Kenner H. (1988) Camillo Praschniker 1884–1949, in: Lullies
R. (ed.), Archäologenbildnisse. Porträts und Kurzbio-
graphien von klassischen Archäologen deutscher
Sprache (Mainz) 224–225

Kerschner M. – Kowalleck I. – Steskal M. (2008) Archäologische Forschungen zur Siedlungsgeschichte von Ephesos in geometrischer, archaischer und klassischer Zeit.
Grabungsbefunde und Keramikfunde aus dem Bereich
von Koressos, JOeAI Ergänzungsheft 9 (Vienna)

Kerschner M. – Prochaska W. (2011) Die Tempel und Altäre
der Artemis in Ephesos und ihre Baumaterialien, JOeAI
80, 73–154

Kienast D. (1969) Augustus und Alexander, Gymnasium 76,
430–456

Kienast D. (1982) Augustus: Prinzeps und Monarch
(Darmstadt)

Kienast H. J. (2014) Der Turm der Winde (Wiesbaden)

Kimmel-Clauzet F. (2014) Poets' Tombs and Conceptions of
Poetry in Ancient Greece. Tombs of the poets: between
text and material culture (Durham)

Kindi V. (1994) Incommensurability, incomparability, irra-
tionality, Methodology and Science 27, 41–55

King R. J. (2010) Ad capita Bubula. The Birth of Augustus
and Rome´s Imperial Centre, The Classical Quarterly,
n.s. 60,2, 450–469

Kirbihler F. (2003) Les notables d'Ephèse. Essai d'histoire
sociale (133 av. J.-C. – 262 ap. J.-C.). (Thesis University
of Tours, Tours)

Kirbihler F. (2005) L. Cusinius, épiscopos à Ephèse, JOeAI
74, 151–173

Kirbihler F. (2007) P. Vedius Rufus, père de P. Vedius Pollio,
ZPE 160, 261–271

Kirbihler F. (2009) Aspects des stratégies familiales à Éphèse
(Ier s. av. J.-C. – IIIe s. apr. J.-C.), in: Briquel-Chatonnet
F. et al. (eds.), Femmes, cultures et sociétés dans les
civilisations méditerranéennes et proche-orientales de
l'Antiquité, Topoi Suppl. 10 (Lyon) 53–66

Kirbihler F. (2011) Servilius Isauricus proconsul d´Asie. Un
gouverneur populaire, in: Barrandon N. – Kirbihler F.
(eds.), Les gouverneurs et les provinciaux sous la République romaine (Rennes) 249–272

Kirbihler F. (2016) Des grecs et des Italiens à Éphèse. Histoire d´une intégration croisée (133 A C 48 p. C.), Ausonius Éditions, Scripta Antiqua 88 (Bordeaux)

Kirbihler F. (2017) Les problèmes d'une mission publique entre République et Empire. P. Vedius Pollio en Asie, in: Cavalier L. – Ferriès M.-C. – Delrieux F. (eds.), Auguste et l'Asie Mineure (Bordeaux) 129–152

Kirbihler F. (2023) C. Antius A. Iulius Quadratus, oder wie die Familie eines Freundes des Kaisers zwischen Trajan und den Severern den Weg von Pergamon nach Ephesos fand, in: Lohner-Urban U. – Spickermann W. – Trinkl E., Itineraria, vol. II. Rund ums Mittelmeer. Festschrift für Peter Scherrer zum 65. Geburtstag, Keryx 10 (Graz) 135–142

Kitchell K. F. (2015) A defense of the "monstrous" animals of Pliny, Aelian, and others, Preternature 4,2, 125–151

Klee E. (2005) Das Personenlexikon Drittes Reich. Wer war was vor und nach 1945? (Frankfurt am Main)

Klos S. – Corradini D. A. – Mazohl B. (2022) Störfall Gender. Weibliche Mitglieder - wissenschaftliche Mitarbeiterinnen - Förderpolitik - Forschungsperspektiven, in: Feichtinger J. – Mazohl B. (eds.), Die Österreichische Akademie der Wissenschaften 1847–2022. Eine neue Akademiegeschichte (Vienna) 63–175

Klos S. – Feichtinger J. (2022) Die Praxis der Entnazifizierung an der Akademie (1945–1948), in: Feichtinger J. – Mazohl B. (eds.), Die Österreichische Akademie der Wissenschaften 1847–2022. Eine neue Akademiegeschichte (Vienna) 163–199

Klos S. – Schlögl M. – Andorfer P. (2022) ÖAW M|I|N|E: Auswertungen und Struktur der Webapplikation zu Mitgliedern, Institutionen, Netzwerken und Ereignissen der ÖAW, in: Feichtinger J. – Mazohl B. (eds.), Die Österreichische Akademie der Wissenschaften 1847–2022. Eine neue Akademiegeschichte (Vienna) 367–398

Knäpper K. (2018) Hieros Kai Asylos. Historia. Einzelschriften 250 (Stuttgart)

Knibbe D. (1970) RE Suppl XII 249–297 s.v. Ephesos A. Historischer Teil

Knibbe D. (1991) Das "Parthermonument" von Ephesos. (Parthersieg)altar der Artemis (und Kenotaph des L. Verus) an der "Triodos", BerMatOeAI 1 (Vienna) 5–18

Knibbe D. (1995) Via Sacra Ephesiaca. New Aspects of the Cult of Artemis Ephesia, in: Koester H. (ed.), Ephesos. Metropolis of Asia, Harvard Theological Studies 41 (Cambridge) 141–154

Knibbe D. (1998) Ephesus – ΕΦΕΣΟΣ. Geschichte einer bedeutenden antiken Stadt und Portrait einer modernen Großgrabung (Frankfurt et al.)

Knibbe D. (2002) Topographica Ephesiaca. Damianosstoa, Androklosgrab – Olympieion und Koressos, JOeAI 71, 207–219

Knibbe D. – Engelmann H. – İplikçioĝlu B. (1989) Neue Inschriften aus Ephesos XI, JOeAI 59, Beibl. Sp. 161–238

Knibbe D. – Engelmann H. – İplikçioĝlu B. (1989), Neue Inschriften aus Ephesos XI, JOeAI 59, 1989, Bbl. Sp. 161–238

Knibbe D. – Engelmann H. – İplikçioĝlu B. (1993) Neue Inschriften aus Ephesos XII, JOeAI 62, 113–150

Knibbe D. – Engelmann H. (1984) Neue Inschriften aus Ephesos X, Fundjahr 1983, JOeAI 55, 137–149

Knibbe D. – İplikçioĝlu B. (1981–82) Neue Inschriften aus Ephesos VIII, JOeAI 53, 87–150

Knibbe D. – Langmann G. (1993) Via Sacra Ephesiaca I, BerMatOeAI 3 (Vienna)

Knibbe D. – Thür H. (1995) Via Sacra Ephesiaca II, BerMatOeAI 6 (Vienna)

Koder J. (2008) Jahresbericht 2007, JOeAI 77, 399–443

Kolb F. (1999) Die Sitzordnung von Volksversammlung und Theaterpublikum im kaiserzeitlichen Ephesos, in: Friesinger H. – Krinzinger F. (eds.), 100 Jahre österreichische Forschungen in Ephesos. Akten des Symposiums Wien 1995, Denkschr_Wien 260 = Archäologische Forschungen 1 (Vienna) 101–105

Korotin I. – Stupnicki N. (eds.) (2018) Biografien bedeutender österreichischer Wissenschafterinnen (Vienna – Cologne – Weimar)

Kotsidu H. (2000), TIMH KAI DOXA. Ehrungen für hellenistische Herrscher im griechischen Mutterland und in Kleinasien unter besonderer Berücksichtigung der archäologischen Denkmäler (Berlin)

Kovacs M. (2022) Vom Herrscher zum Heros. Die Bildnisse Alexanders des Großen und die Imitatio Alexandri, Tübinger Archäologische Forschungen 34 (Tübingen)

Krämer J. A. – Schmidt S. – Jürgens K. U. et al. (2014a) Forensic age estimation in living individuals using 3.0T MRI of the distal femur, Int J Legal Med 128,3, 509–514

Krämer J. A. – Schmidt S. – Jürgens K. U. et al. (2014b) The use of magnetic resonance imaging to examine ossification of the proximal tibial epiphysis for forensic age estimation in living individuals, Forensic Sci Med Pathol 10,3, 306–313

Krierer K. R. (2001) »Bilder aus dem deutschen Leben. Germanische Köpfe der Antike«. Eine Skizze zu Franz Miltner, in: Blakolmer F. – Szemethy H. D. (eds.) Akten des 8. Österreichischen Archäologentaes am Institut für Klassische Archäologie der Universität Wien vom 23. bis 25. April 1999 (Vienna) 217-224

Krinzinger F. (2005) Jahresbericht 2004, JOeAI 74, 317–378

Krinzinger F. (2006) Jahresbericht 2005, JOeAI 75, 315–371

Krinzinger F. (2021) Mazaeus et Mithridates patronis. Zum Südtor der Tetragonos Agora, in: Ployer R. – Svoboda-Baas D. (eds.), Magnis Itineribus. Festschrift für Verena Gassner zum 65. Geburtstag (Vienna) 153–162

Krug A. (1968) Binden in der griechischen Kunst. Untersuchungen zur Typologie (6. – 1. Jahrh. v.Chr.) (Thesis University of Mainz)

Krumme W. (2021) Die Rekonstruktion römischer Architektenzeichnungen für die Grundrisse des Oceanus Mosaiks und der Peristyl Villa in Bad Kreuznach, <https://www.regionalgeschichte.net/bibliothek/aufsaetze/krumme-die-rekonstruktion-roemischer-architektenzeichnungen-fuer-die-grundrisse-des-oceanus-mo-

saiks-und-der-peristyl-villa-in-bad-kreuznach.html> (accessed on 27.10.2022)

Kukula R. C. (1906) Literarische Zeugnisse über den Artemistempel von Ephesos, FiE I (Vienna) 237–274

Kunze E. (1972) Fritz Eichler (12.10.1887 - 16.1.1971), Jahrbuch der Bayerischen Akademie der Wissenschaften, 234–241

Künzl E. (1988) Der römische Triumph. Siegesfeiern im antiken Rom (Munich)

Ladstätter S. (2002) Die Chronologie des Hanghauses 2, in: Krinzinger F. (ed.), Das Hanghaus 2 von Ephesos. Studien zu Baugeschichte und Chronologie, Archäologische Forschungen 7, 9–40

Ladstätter S. (2003) Keramik, in: Lang-Auinger C. (ed.), Hanghaus 1 in Ephesos. Funde und Ausstattung, FiE VIII 4 (Vienna) 22–85

Ladstätter S. (2010) Hellenistische Bebauung, in: Krinzinger F. (ed.), Hanghaus 2 in Ephesos. Die Wohneinheiten 1 und 2. Baubefund, Ausstattung, Funde, FiE VIII 8 (Vienna) 81–83; 426–428

Ladstätter S. (2016) Hafen und Stadt von Ephesos in hellenistischer Zeit, JOeAI 85, 233–272

Ladstätter S. (2019) The So-called Imperial Cult Temple for Domitian in Ephesos, in: Schowalter D. – Ladstätter S. – Friesen St. – Thomas Ch. (eds.), Religion in Ephesos Reconsidered. Archaeology of Spaces, Structures, and Objects. Supplements to Novum Testamentum 177 (Leiden) 11–40

Ladstätter S. – Lang-Auinger C. (2001) Zur Datierung und kunsthistorischen Einordnung einer Apollon Kitharodos-Statuette, in: Krinzinger F. (ed.), Studien zur hellenistischen Keramik in Ephesos, JOeAI Erg.-Heft 2, 71–81

Ladstätter S. – Steskal M. – Yazıcı R. (2018) Clivus Sacer, Wissenschaftlicher Jahresbericht des Österreichischen Archäologischen Instituts 2018 (Vienna) 15–17

Laffi U. (2006) L'iscrizione di Efeso sui privilegi di insegnanti, sofisti, medici (I. Ephesos, 4101), Studi ellenistici 19, 453–521

Lafli E. – Buora M. 2023: The memory of Sulla in Ephesus, Cercetări Arheologice 30/1, 61–68

Lakoff R. T. (2006) Vulgar Latin. Comparative Castration (and comparative theories of syntax), Style 40,1, 56–61

Landskron A. (2015) Das Heroon von Trysa: Ein Denkmal in Lykien zwischen Ost und West: Untersuchungen zu Bildschmuck, Bauform und Grabinhaber, Schriften des Kunsthistorischen Museums 13, 2 Bände (Vienna)

Landskron A. (2020) Monumentale Altäre und ihr Bildschmuck im Hellenismus und in der Kaiserzeit. Der Altar des Domitianstempels von Ephesos, in: Lohner-Urban U. – Quatember U. (eds.), Zwischen Bruch und Kontinuität. Architektur in Kleinasien am Übergang vom Hellenismus zur römischen Kaiserzeit, Internationale Tagung Graz, 26-29 April 2017, Byzas 25, 2020, 215–230

Lang G. (1984) Ein Zwischenbericht zur Anastylose des Südtores der Agora von Ephesos, AW 15,4, 23–30

Lang-Auinger C. (1996) Wasserversorgung, in: Lang-Auinger C. – Forstenpointner G. – Lang G. – Outschar U. – Vetters W. (eds.), Hanghaus 1 in Ephesos: der Baubefund, FiE VIII 3 (Vienna)

Lang-Auinger C. (2010) Der Hadrianstempel in Ephesos – ein Tempel nach mesopotamischen Vorbild?, in: Aybek S. – Öz A. K. (eds.), Yolların Kesiştiği Yer. The Land of the Crossroads. Festschrift für Recep Meriç, Metropolis Ionia 2 (Istanbul) 191–196

Lange B. (2013) Anthropologische Visualisierungen zur ,Rassendiagnose', in: Lange B. (ed.), Die Wiener Forschungen an Kriegsgefangenen 1915–1918, 153–265

Langmann G. (1967) Eine spätarchaische Nekropole unter dem Staatsmarkt zu Ephesos. Festschrift F. Eichler, JOeAI Beih 1, 103–123

Langmann G. (1993) Smyrna gefunden, in: Dobesch G. – Rehrenböck R. (eds.), Die epigraphische und altertumskundliche Erforschung Kleinasiens: Hundert Jahre Kleinasiatische Kommission der Österreichischen Akademie der Wissenschaften. Akten des Symposiums vom 23. bis 25. Oktober 1990 (1993) 283–287

Langner M. (2012) Mantle-figures and the Athenization of Late Classical Imagery, in: Schierup S. – Rasmussen B. B. (eds.), Red-figure Pottery in its Ancient Setting. Acts of the International Colloquium held at the National Museum of Denmark, Copenhagen November 5.–6. 2009 (Aarhus) 11–20

Lapps B. – Page T. B. – House D. (1919) The Loeb Classical Library. Greek Anthology Vol. II. (London – New York)

Laubenberger M. – Prochaska W. (2011) Untersuchungen zur Marmorprovenienz von zwei Porträtköpfen aus Ephesos im Kunsthistorischen Museum in Wien, in: Technologische Studien. Kunsthistorisches Museum 2011/8, 42–65

Laumonier A. (1958) Les cultes indigènes en Carie, BEFAR 188 (Paris)

Lauter H. (1966) Zur Chronologie römischer Kopien nach Originalen des 5. Jahrhunderts (Munich)

Leander Touati A.-M. (1987) The Great Trajanic Frieze, Acta Inst. Sueciae Rom ser. In 40, 45 (Stockholm)

Lehmann Y. (2018) Varro (Marcus Terentius), in: Goulet R. (ed.), Dictionnaire des philosophes antiques 7 (Paris) 94–133

Lehner M. F. (2004) Die Agonistik im Ephesos der römischen Kaiserzeit (Thesis University of Munich), <https://edoc.ub.uni-muenchen.de/3261/1/Lehner_Michael.pdf> (accessed on 30.01.2021)

Leitner I. M. (2010) „Bis an die Grenzen des Möglichen". Der Dekan Viktor Christian und seine Handlungsspielräume an der Philosophischen Fakultät 1938–1943, in: Mitchel G. A. – Nieß W. – Pils R. (eds.), Geisteswissenschaften im Nationalsozialismus (Göttingen) 49–78

Leschhorn W. (1993) Antike Ären (Stuttgart)

Lesky A. (1948) Hofrat Josef Keil zum 70. Geburtstag, Anz-AW 1, 97–98

Lesky A. (1953) Amor und Dido, in: Moro G. (ed.), Festschrift für Rudolf Egger. Beiträge zur älteren europäischen Kulturgeschichte 2 (Klagenfurt) 169–178

Leutsch E. L. – Schneidewin F. G. (1839) Corpus paroemiographorum graecorum. Zenobius, Diogenianus, Plutarchus, Gregorius Cyprius (Göttingen)

Lewis C. T. - Short C. (1879) A Latin Dictionary (Oxford)

Lichtenberger A. – Nieswandt H.-H. – Salzmann D. (2008) Ein Porträt des Lysimachos? Anmerkungen zu einem anonymen Herrscherbild auf den Münzen von Lysimacheia, Asia Minor Studien 65, 391–407, pl. 50

Liddel H. G. – Scott R. (1940) A Greek-English Lexicon (Oxford)

LiDonnici L. (1999) The Ephesian Megabyzos. Priesthood and religious diplomacy at the end of the classical period, Religion 29, 201–214

Lohner-Urban U. – Scherrer P. (2016) Hellenistische Prunktore – Ein wissenschaftlicher Irrtum? Vorläufige Grabungsergebnisse vom Osttor von Side aus der Kampagne 2012, in: Frederiksen R. – Müth S. – Schneider P. I. – Schnelle M. (eds.), Focus on Fortifications. New Research on Fortifications in the Ancient Mediterranean and the Near East, Fokus Fortifikation Studies, vol. 2 (Oxford – Philadelphia) 232–243

Lohner-Urban U. (2017) Aspects of public memory at the East Gate of Side, in: Mortensen E. – Pedersen P. – Poulsen B. – Seifert M. (eds.), Cityscapes and monuments of remembrance in western Asia Minor (Oxford) 222–225

Lohner-Urban U. (2023), Die pamphylischen Hoftore als Zeichen von urbanitas und dignitas, in: Lohner-Urban U. – Spickermann W. – Trinkl E., Itineraria, vol. II. Rund ums Mittelmeer. Festschrift für Peter Scherrer zum 65. Geburtstag, Keryx 10 (Graz) 57–64

Loidl-Baldwin V. (2021) Walter Hirschberg. Zwischen Karriere und Lehrverbot, in: Gingrich A. – Rohrbacher P. (eds.), Völkerkunde zur NS-Zeit aus Wien (1938 – 1945) (Vienna) 341–368

Longfellow B. (2011) Roman Imperialism and Civic Patronage: Form, Meaning, and Ideology in Monumental Fountain Complexes (Cambridge)

Lorenz J. F. (1781) Euklids Elemente, fünfzehn Bücher (Halle)

Lowrie M. (2015) The Egyptian Within. A Roman Figuration of Civil War, in: Vinken B. (ed.), Translatio Babylonis (Paderborn) 13–28

Ludwig E. (1937) Cleopatra. The story of a Queen (New York)

Mader B. (2021) Die personelle Struktur der Prähistorischen Kommission in der NS-Zeit, in: Gingrich A. – Rohrbacher P. (eds.), Völkerkunde zur NS-Zeit aus Wien (1938–1945) (Vienna) 382–399

Madrigal L. (2009) Program of the seventy-eight Annual Meeting of the American Association of Physical Anthropologists to be held at the Sheraton Chicago Hotel and Tower (Chicago)

Mahaffy J. P. (1899) A History of Egypt IV. The Ptolemaic Dynasty (New York)

Maier F. G. (1959) Griechische Mauerbauinschriften I, Vestigia 1 (Munich)

Maisel T. (2013) Alt-Registratur, Service- oder Forschungseinrichtung? Der Ausbau des Archivs der Universität Wien zum „Zentralarchiv" der Alma Mater Rudolphina, Mitteilungen der Österreichischen Gesellschaft für Wissenschaftsgeschichte 30, 13–33

Maligorne Y. (2006) Décor architectonique et datation de la tombe monumentale de Faverolles (Haute-Marne), Bulletin de la Société Archéologique Champenoise 99 (4), 60-73

Mallios Y. 2010: Ephesus (Antiquity), Monument of Memmius, in: Encyclopaedia of the Hellenic world, vol. 1: Asia Minor, Athens: Foundation of the Hellenic World, 181–192 <http://www.ehw.gr/l.aspx?id=8258> (accessed on 15 February 2023)

Mann C. (2018) Könige, Poleis und Athleten in hellenistischer Zeit, Klio 100,2, 447–449

Marchhart H. (2020) Franz Miltner (1901–1959). Klassischer Archäologe, Althistoriker und Epigraphiker - Ein Lebensbild, in: Modl D. – Peitler K. (eds.) Archäologie in Österreich 1938–1945 (Graz) 158–172

Marksteiner T. (1999) Bemerkungen zum hellenistischen Stadtmauerring von Ephesos, in: Friesinger H. – Krinzinger F. (eds.), 100 Jahre österreichische Forschungen in Ephesos. Akten des Symposiums Wien 1995, Denkschr_Wien 260 = Archäologische Forschungen 1 (Vienna) 413–419

Martin R. (1914) Lehrbuch der Anthropologie in systematischer Darstellung (Jena)

Martini W. (2016) Form, Funktion und Bedeutung der Stadtmauern von Perge in Pamphylien", in: Frederiksen R. – Müth S. – Schneider P. I. – Schnelle M. (eds.), FOCUS ON FORTIFICATIONS New Research on Fortifications in the Ancient Mediterranean and the Near East. Monographs of the Danish Institute at Athens, Volume 18 (Oxford) 220–231

Maschek D. (2008) Domitian und Polyphem. Kritische Anmerkungen zur hermeneutischen Methode in der antiken Kunstgeschichte am Beispiel Ephesos, JOeAI 76, 279–300

Massin B. (1999) Anthropologie und Humangenetik im Nationalsozialismus oder: Wie schreiben deutsche Wissenschaftler ihre eigene Wissenschaftsgeschichte?, in: Kaupen-Haas H. – Saller C. (eds.), Wissenschaftlicher Rassismus. Analysen einer Kontinuität in den Human- und Naturwissenschaften (Frankfurt – New York)

Matis H. (1997) Zwischen Anpassung und Widerstand. Die Akademie der Wissenschaften in den Jahren (1938–1945) (Vienna)

Matis H. (2013) Folgen des „Anschlusses", in: Feichtinger J. – Matis H. – Sienell S. – Uhl H. (eds.), Die Akademie der Wissenschaften in Wien 1938 bis 1945 (Vienna) 55–62

Matis H. – Suppan A. (2022) Sapere Aude. Die Österreichische Akademie der Wissenschaften seit 1918. Berichte, Fakten, Analysen - ein Kompendium (Vienna)

Mattes J. – Corradini D. A. – Klos S. – Mazohl B. (2022) Umbrüche und Kontinuitäten. Die Akademie in der Zwischenkriegszeit, in: Feichtinger J. – Mazohl B. (eds.), Die Österreichische Akademie der Wissenschaften 1847–2022. Eine neue Akademiegeschichte (Vienna) 521–608

Mattes J. – Uhl H. (2022) Die Akademie zieht Zwischenbilanz. Akademiejubiläen als Momente der Selbstreflexion, in: Feichtinger J. – Mazohl B. (eds.), Die Österreichische Akademie der Wissenschaften 1847–2022. Eine neue Akademiegeschichte (Vienna) 437–468

McCredie J. R. – Roux G. – Shaw S. M. – Kurtich J. (1992) The Rotunda of Arsinoe (Princeton)

McDevitte W. A. – Bohn H. G. (1872) Caesar's commentaries on the Gallic and Civil Wars (New York)

McNicoll A. (1986) Developments in Techniques of Siegecraft and Fortification in the Greek World ca. 400–100 B.C., in: Leriche P. – Tréziny H. (eds.), La fortification dans l'histoire du monde Grec. Actes du Colloque International Valbonne 1982 (Paris) 305–313

Meadows A. (2013) Two 'Double' Dedications at Ephesus and the Beginning of Ptolemaic Control of Ionia, Gephyra 10, 1–12

Meister R. (1933) Bedeutung und Umfang des Lateinischen Schrifttums im Mittelalter und in der Neuzeit. Verein Klassischer Philologen in Wien, Parerga 2 (Vienna)

Meriç R. – Merkelbach R. – Nollé J. – Şahin S. (eds.) (1981) Inschriften griechischer Städte aus Kleinasien 17, 1.2. Die Inschriften von Ephesos VII, 1.2 (Cologne)

Merkelbach R. (1991) Ein Orakel des Apollon für Artemis von Koloe, ZPE 88, 70–72

Merkelbach R. – Nollé J., mit Hilfe v. Engelmann H. – İplikçioğlu B. – Knibbe D. (eds.) (1980) Inschriften griechischer Städte aus Kleinasien 16. Die Inschriften von Ephesos VI (Cologne)

Mertz G. (2020) „Das Braun der Erde". Die Träger der Haidinger Medaille der Geologischen Bundesanstalt und der Nationalsozialismus, Jahrbuch der Geologischen Bundesanstalt 160,1-4, 359–408

Meyer G. (1874) Pomponii Porphyrionis Commentarii in Q. Horatium Flaccum. Lipsiae in aedibus B. G. Teubneri (Leipzig)

Milanich N. B. (2019) Paternity. The elusive quest for the father (Cambridge)

Miller A. v. (2019) Archaische Siedlungsbefunde in Ephesos, FiE XIII 3 (Vienna)

Miltner F. (1955) XX. Vorläufiger Bericht über die Ausgrabungen in Ephesos, JOeAI 42 Beibl., 23–60

Miltner F. (1956-58) XXI. Vorläufiger Bericht über die Ausgrabungen in Ephesos, JOeAI 43 Beibl., 1–88

Miltner F. (1958) Ephesos. Stadt der Artemis und des Johannes (Vienna)

Miltner F. (1959a) XXII. Vorläufiger Bericht über die Ausgrabungen in Ephesos, JOeAI 44 Beibl., 243–314

Miltner F. (1959b) XXIII. Vorläufiger Bericht über die Ausgrabungen in Ephesos, JOeAI 44 Beibl., 315–380

Miltner F. (1960) Eine Reliefplatte vom Tempel Hadrians in Ephesos, in: Fischer W. (ed.), Festschrift Richard Heuberger, Schlern-Schriften 206 (Innsbruck) 93–97

Mindler U. (2011) Arnold Schober und die Archäologie an der Universität Graz in der NS-Zeit, in: Schübl E. – Heppner H. (eds.), Universitäten in Zeiten des Umbruchs, 197–210 (Münster – Berlin – Vienna – Zurich)

Misailidou-Despotidou V. – Athanasiou F. (eds.) (2013) The Galerian Complex. A visual tour of the Imperial Residence in Thessaloniki. Hellenic Ministry of Culture and Sports (Thessaloniki)

Mittag P. F. (2003) Unruhen im hellenistischen Alexandria, Historia 52,2, 161–208

Mlinar J. (2019) Balduin Saria (1893-1974)."Ein deutschsprachiger Sohn der Untersteiermark", in: Hruza K. (ed.), Österreichische Historiker. Lebensläufe und Karrieren 1900–1945 III (Vienna) 379–403

Mlynarczyk J. (2001) Isis Pharia, Eros, and the sea travels across the Eastern Mediterranean, Studia Archaeologica, 332–337

Mohr M. (2007) An welcher Stelle lag die archaisch-klassische Siedlung von Ephesos?, JOeAI 76, 301–320

Moro G. (1950) Vorwort, Carinthia I 140, 1–2

Moro G. (ed.) (1942) Aus dem römischen und germanischen Kärnten. Festschrift für Rudolf Egger zum 60. Geburtstag (Klagenfurt)

Moro G. (ed.) (1952) Beiträge zur älteren Europäischen Kulturgeschichte. Festschrift für Rudolf Egger I (Klagenfurt)

Moro G. (ed.) (1953) Beiträge zur älteren Europäischen Kulturgeschichte. Festschrift für Rudolf Egger II (Klagenfurt)

Moro G. (ed.) (1954) Beiträge zur älteren Europäischen Kulturgeschichte. Festschrift für Rudolf Egger III (Klagenfurt)

Morris S. (2001) The prehistoric background of Artemis Ephesia: a solution to the enigma of her 'breasts'?" in: Muss U. (ed.), Der Kosmos der Artemis von Ephesos SoSchrÖAI 37 (Vienna) 135–151

Morris S. (2008) Zur Vorgeschichte der Artemis Ephesia, in: Muss U. (ed.), Die Archäologie der ephesischen Artemis. Gestalt und Ritual eines Heiligtums (Vienna) 57–62

Morris-Reich A. (2013) Anthropology, standardization and measurement. Rudolf Martin and anthropometric photography, BJHS 46,3, 487–516

Müller A. (1997) Dynamische Adaptierung und „Selbstbehauptung". Die Universität Wien in der NS-Zeit, Geschichte und Gesellschaft 23,4, 592–617

Müller S. (2007) Arsinoë III. als Artemis? Zur Ikonographie ptolemäischer Königinnen, AnzWien 142, 137–157

Müller S. (2009) Das hellenistische Königspaar in der medialen Repräsentation. Ptolemaios II. und Arsinoe II (Berlin)

Müller S. – Ortmeyer B. (2017) Die ideologische Ausrichtung der Lehrkräfte 1933-1945. Herrenmenschentum, Rassismus und Judenfeindschaft des Nationalsozialistischen Lehrerbundes (Weinheim – Basel)

Murer C. (2018) From the tombs into the city. Grave robbing and the reuse of funerary spolia in Late Antique Italy, Acta ad archaeologiam et artium historiam pertinentia 30,16, 115–137

Muss U. (1984) Das Wiener Amazonenrelief, Jahrbuch der Kunsthistorischen Sammlungen in Wien 80, 7–34

Muss U. (2018) Der Altar des Artemision und die Ionische Renaissance, in: Frielinghaus H. – Schattner T. G. – Wesenberg B. (eds.), Ad summum templum architecturae. Forschungen zur antiken Architektur im Spannungsfeld der Fragestellungen und Methoden (Möhnesee) 35–51

Muss U. – Bammer A. – Büyükkolanci M. (2001) Der Altar des Artemisions von Ephesos, FiE XII 2 (Vienna)

Nagy G. (1998) The Library of Pergamon as a Classical Model, in: Koester H. (ed.), Pergamon.Citadel of the Gods, Harvard Theological Studies 46 (Valley Forge) 185–232

Naiden F.S. (2006) Ancient supplication (New York)

Napp A. E. (1933) Bukranion und Guirlande (Thesis Heidelberg Universitiy, Heidelberg)

Neumann W. (1988) Gotbert Moro (1902–1987). Zum Gedächtnis und Dank, Carinthia I 178, 7–14

Niemann G. – Heberdey R. (1906) Der Rundbau auf dem Panayırdağ, FiE I (Vienna) 143–180

Obbink D. – Gonis N. (2009) The Oxyrhynchus Papyri LXXIII (London)

Oberleitner W. (2009) Das Partherdenkmal von Ephesos. Ein Siegesmonument für Lucius Verus und Marcus Aurelius, unter Mitarbeit von A. Landskron, D. Maschek, H. Müller, A. Pyskowski-Wyżykowski, S. Seren, H. Thür. 2 Bde. Schriften des Kunsthistorischen Museums 11 (Vienna)

Oberleitner W. – Gschwantler K. – Bernhard-Walcher A. – Bammer A. (1978) Funde aus Ephesos und Samothrake (Vienna – Heidelberg)

Ohm M. (1835) Die reine Elementar-Mathematik II (Berlin)

Olson S. D. (2012) The Homeric Hymn to Aphrodite and Related Texts Text, Translation and Commentary (Berlin – Boston)

Oster R. (1990) Ephesus as a Religious Center under the Principate, I. Paganism before Constantine, ANRW II 18,3 (Berlin – New York) 1661–1728

Österreichischer Bundesverlag für Unterricht, Wissenschaft und Kunst (ed.) (1961) Erkenntnis und Erziehung. Festschrift für Richard Meister (Vienna)

Österreichisches Archäologisches Institut (ed.) (1952) JOeAI 39 (Vienna)

Österreichisches Archäologisches Institut (ed.) (1956–58) JOeAI 43 (Vienna)

Österreichisches Archäologisches Institut (ed.) (2000) Jahresbericht 1999. Ephesos 371–382 (Vienna)

Österreichisches Archäologisches Institut (ed.) (2008) Wissenschaftlicher Jahresbericht 2008. Ephesos 13–29 (Vienna)

Österreichisches Archäologisches Institut (ed.) (2009) Wissenschaftlicher Jahresbericht 2009. Ephesos 11–24 (Vienna)

Österreichisches Archäologisches Institut (ed.) (2010) Wissenschaftlicher Jahresbericht 2010. Ephesos 20–57 (Vienna)

Österreichisches Archäologisches Institut (ed.) (2014) Wissenschaftlicher Jahresbericht 2014. Ephesos 5–60 (Vienna)

Österreichisches Archäologisches Institut (ed.) (2016) Wissenschaftlicher Jahresbericht 2016. Ephesos 5–48 (Vienna)

Österreichisches Archäologisches Institut (ed.) Jahresbericht 2001 (2002) JOeAI 71. Ephesos 359-382

Österreichisches Archäologisches Institut (ed.) Jahresbericht 2002 (2003) JOeAI 72. Ephesos 302-322

Österreichisches Archäologisches Institut (ed.) Jahresbericht 2003 (2004) JOeAI 73. Ephesos 349-378

Österreichisches Archäologisches Institut (ed.) Jahresbericht 2006 (2007) JOeAI 76. Ephesos 401-425

Outschar U. (1990) Zum Momument des C. Memmius, JOeAI 60, 57–85

Outschar U. (1997) Die keramischen Funde aus dem und unter dem Sarkophag westlich des „Androklos-Heroons" an der Kuretenstraße, in: Thür H. (ed.), „.... und verschönerte die Stadt ..." – ΚΑΙ ΚΟΣΜΕΣΑΝΤΑ ΤΗΝ ΠΟΛΙΝ. Ein ephesischer Priester des Kaiserkultes in seinem Umfeld, SoSchrOeAI 27 (Vienna) 27–40

Ozanam J. (1699) Neue Ubung Der Feldmeß-Kunst, So wol auff dem Papier, als auff dem Feld [...] (Bern)

Özis Ü. – Atalay A. – Becerik M. – Özdikmen K. (2005) Aqua Iulia. Die Kenchrios(Degirmendere)-Fernwasserleitung von Ephesos, in: Brandt B. – Gassner V. – Ladstätter S. (eds.), Synergasia. Festschrift für Friedrich Krinzinger, vol. 1 (Vienna) 213–219

Pacher H. M. (1946) Biometrischer Vergleich der Bevölkerungsgruppen von St. Jakob im Rosenthal (Kärnten) und Marienfeld im Banat (Rumänien) (Thesis University of Vienna, Vienna)

Pacher H. M. (1949) Ein Skelett aus Carnuntum und der Versuch seiner anthropologischen Deutung, Archaeologia Austriaca 4, 5–71

Pacioli L. (1509a) Euclidis megarensis philosophi acutissimi mathematicorumque omnium [...] (Venice)

Pacioli L. (1509b) Divina proportione [...] (Venice)

Papagianni E. (2016) Attische Sarkophage mit Eroten und Girlanden (Ruhpolding)

Pape W. (1906) Griechisch=Deutsches Handwörterbuch (Braunschweig)

Paplauskas-Ramunas A. (1961) Die pädagogische Ausstrahlung Österreichs. Richard Meister, in: Österreichischer Bundesverlag für Unterricht, Wissenschaft und Kunst (ed.), Erkenntnis und Erziehung. Festschrift für Richard Meister (Vienna) 87–104

Pasch E. – Kieburg H. (eds.) (2019) Auferstehung der Antike. Archäologische Stätten digital rekonstruiert. Sonderheft Antike Welt (Darmstadt)

Passoja D. (2018) Variations on a theme of the silver ratio, <https://www.researchgate.net/publication/323738869_Variations_on_a_Theme_of_the_Silver_Ratio> (accessed on 21.04.2022)

Pesditschek M. (2007) Die Karriere des Althistorikers Fritz Schachermeyr im Dritten Reich und in der Zweiten Republik, Mensch – Wissenschaft – Magie. Mitteilungen der Österreichischen Gesellschaft für Wissenschaftsgeschichte 25, 41–71

Pesditschek M. (2009) Barbar, Kreter, Arier. Leben und Werk des Althistorikers Fritz Schachermeyr, Band 1 (Saarbrücken)

Pesditschek M. (2010) Wien war anders – Das Fach Alte Geschichte und Altertumskunde, in: Ash M. G. – Nieß W. – Pils R. (eds.), Geisteswissenschaften im Nationalsozialismus. Das Beispiel der Universität Wien (Vienna) 287–316

Pesditschek M. (2012a) Franz Miltner (1901–1959), in: Brands G. – Maischberger M. (eds.), Lebensbilder. Klassische Archäologen und der Nationalsozialismus I (Rahden) 177–191

Pesditschek M. (2012b) Heinrich (Ritter von) Srbik (1878–1951), in: Hruza K. (ed.), Österreichische Historiker. Lebensläufe und Karrieren 1900–1945. Vol. 2 (Vienna – Cologne – Weimar) 263–328

Pesditschek M. (2013) Heinrich (von) Srbik (1878–1951) und die Akademie der Wissenschaften, in: Feichtinger J. – Matis H. – Sienell S. – Uhl H. (eds.), Die Akademie der Wissenschaften in Wien 1938 bis 1945. Katalog zur Ausstellung (Vienna) 37–46

Pesditschek M. – Feldmann A. (2012) Die Josef-Keil-Medaille 1958 von Arnold Hartig, Münstersche Numismatische Zeitung 42,1, 1–7

Petrovic I. (2010) Transforming Artemis: from the goddess of the outdoors to city goddess, in: Bremmer J. N. – Erskine A. (eds.), The gods of ancient Greece: identities and transformations (Edinburgh) 209–227

Petschenig M. – Stowasser J. M. (1930) Stowassers Lateinisch-Deutsches Schul- und Handwörterbuch (Vienna)

Petzold R. G. (ed.) (1987–90) Inschriften griechischer Städte aus Kleinasien 24, 2. Die Inschriften von Smyrna 2 (Cologne)

Pfefferle R. – Pfefferle H. (2014) Glimpflich Entnazifiziert. Die Professorenschaft der Universität Wien von 1944 in den Nachkriegsjahren (Vienna)

Pfeiffer S. (2008) Griechische Herrscherverehrung und griechischer Kult für die Herrscher, in: Herrscher- und Dynastiekulte im Ptolemäerreich. Münchner Beiträge zur Papyrusforschung und antiken Rechtsgeschichte (Munich) 31–76

Pfeiffer S. (2010) Octavianus-Augustus und Ägypten, in: Coşkun A. – Heinen H. – Pfeiffer S. (eds.), Repräsentation von Identität und Zugehörigkeit im Osten der griechisch-römischen Welt. Aspekte ihrer Repräsentation in Städten, Provinzen und Reichen (Frankfurt) 55–79

Pfrommer M. (2002) Königinnen vom Nil (Mainz am Rhein)

Piccottini G. (1970a) Rudolf Egger 1882 - 1969. Carinthia I 160, 571–574

Piccottini G. (1970b) Rudolf Egger †, Österreichische Zeitschrift für Kunst und Denkmalpflege 24, 86–87

Pittioni R. (ed.) (1956) Festschrift zum 70. Geburtstag von Professor Dr. Josef Weninger, Archaeologia Austriaca 19/20 (Vienna)

Pittioni R. – Weninger J. (1944) Zwei gotische Gräber aus Marchegg, Lkr. Gänserndorf, Niederdonau, Natur und Kultur 29 (Vienna – Leipzig)

Plattner A. (2022) Ekphrasis und Resonanz. Die Beschreibung von Gegenständen, Ritualen und Heiligtümern bei Pausanias und ihre Bedeutung in der Zweiten Sophistik (unprinted Diss. Univ. Graz)

Plattner G. A. (2009) Zur Bauornamentik des Oktogons von Ephesos, in: Ladstätter S. (ed.), Neue Forschungen zur Kuretenstraße von Ephesos. Denkschriften der philosophisch-historischen Klasse 382 (Vienna) 101–106

Plattner G. A. (2010) Spolien aus den Räumen WT 1 und WT 2 im Hanghaus 2 in Ephesos, in: Mangartz F. (Mainz) Die byzantinische Steinsäge von Ephesos. Baubefund, Rekonstruktion, Architekturteile. Monographien des Römisch-Germanischen Zentralmuseums 86 (Verlag des Römisch-Germanischen Zentralmuseums) 59–97

Plattner G. A. (2018) Ephesos in Wien. Präsentationskonzepte von antiker Skulptur und Architektur in den Dauerausstellungen des Kunsthistorischen Museums, in: Maischberger M. – Feller B. (eds.), Aussenräume und Innenräume, Berliner Schriften zur Museumsforschung 37 (Berlin) 215–233

Plattner G. A. – Schmidt-Colinet A. (2005) Beobachtungen zu drei kaiserzeitlichen Bauten in Ephesos, in: Brandt B. – Gassner V. – Ladstätter S. (eds.), Synergasia. Festschrift für Friedrich Krinzinger, Vol. I (Vienna) 243–255

Pohl D. (2002) Kaiserzeitliche Tempel in Kleinasien unter besonderer Berücksichtigung der hellenistischen Vorläufer, Asia Minor Studien 43 (Bonn)

Polito E. (1998) Fulgentibus Armis. Introduzione Allo Studio Dei Fregi D'Armi Antichi, Xenia Antiqua Monografie 4 (Rome)

Pollanen M. S. – Chiasson D. A. (1996) Fracture of the hyoid bone in strangulation. Comparison of fractured and unfractured hyoids from victims of strangulation, J Forensic Sci 41,1, 110–3

Pollitt J. J. (1986) Art in the Hellenistic Age (Cambridge)

Portale E. C. (2011) Ancora sulla Kelsiane Bibliotheke di Efeso, in Mediterraneo antico XIV/1-2, 107–148

Portefaix L. (1993) Ancient Ephesus. Processions as media of religious and secular propaganda, Scripta Instituti Donneriani Aboensis 15, 197–210

Praschniker C. (1940) Die Skulpturen des Mausoleum von Belevi, in: Archäologisches Institut des Deutschen Reiches (ed.), Bericht über den VI. Internationalen Kongress für Archäologie. Berlin 21.–26. August 1939 (Berlin) 405–406

Praschniker C. (1950) Der Meister von Virunum, ein Bildhauer aus der Römerzeit, Carinthia I 140, 3–23

Praschniker C. (1952) Das Basisrelief der Parthenos, JOeAI 39, 7–12

Prochaska W. – Grillo S. M. (2012) The marble quarries of the metropolis of Ephesos and some examples of the use for marbles in Ephesian architecture and sculpturing, in: Gutiérrez Garcia M. A. – Lapuente Mercadal P. – Rodà de Llanza I. (eds.), Interdisciplinary Studies on Ancient Stone. Proceedings of the IX Association for the Study of Marbles and Other Stones in Antiquity (ASMOSIA) Conference (Tarragona), 584–591

Pusman K. (2008) Die „Wissenschaft vom Menschen" auf Wiener Boden (1870–1959) (Vienna)

Quaß F. (1993) Die Honoratiorenschicht in den Städten des griechischen Ostens. Untersuchungen zur politischen und sozialen Entwicklung in hellenistischer und römischer Zeit (Stuttgart)

Quatember U. (2005) Zur Grabungstätigkeit Franz Miltners an der Kuretenstraße, in: Brandt B. – Gassner V. – Ladstätter S. (eds.) Synergia. Festschrift für Friedrich Krinzinger (Vienna) 271–278

Quatember U. (2008) Der Brunnen an der Straße zum Magnesischen Tor in Ephesos, JOeAI 77, 219–264

Quatember U. (2011) Das Nymphäum Traiani in Ephesos, FiE XI 2 (Vienna)

Quatember U. (2017) Der sogenannte Hadrianstempel an der Kuretenstrasse. Textband, Tafelband, Planmappe, FiE XI 3 (Vienna)

Quatember U. (2019) The Bouleuterion Court of Aphrodisias in Caria. A Case Study of the Adaptation of Urban Space in Asia Minor from the Roman Imperial Period to Late Antiquity and Beyond, IstMitt 69, 59–102

Quatember U. – Thuswaldner B. – Kalasek R. et al. (2013) The virtual and physical reconstruction of the Octagon and Hadrian's Temple in Ephesos, in: Bock H. G. et al. (eds.), Scientific Computing and Cultural Heritage 3, 217–228

Querel F. (2019) The portraits of the Ptolemies, in: Palagia O. (ed.), Handbook of Greek sculpture I (Berlin – Boston) 194–224

Raeck W. (1993) Zeus Philios in Pergamon, AA 1993, 381–387

Raggam-Blesch M. (2014) „Mischlinge" und „Geltungsjuden", in: Löw A. – Bergen D. L. – Hájková A. (eds.), Alltag im Holocaust (Munich – Oldenburg) 81–97

Ramzy N. S. (2015) The Dual Language of Geometry in Gothic Architecture. The Symbolic Message of Euclidian Geometry versus the Visual Dialogue of Fractal Geometry, Peregrinations: Journal of Art and Architecture 5,2, 135–172

Rantitsch G. – Prochaska W. (2011) Die hydrogeologische Situation des Panayırdağ als Bewertungsgrundlage für die Wasserversorgung der vorlysimachischen Siedlung, JOeAI 80, 243–254

Ratdolt E. (1482) Preclarissimus liber elementorum Euclidis perspicacissimi […] (Venice)

Rathkolb O. – Mulley K. D. (eds.) (2013) Theodor Körner Fonds zur Förderung von Wissenschaft und Kunst. Preisträger/innen 1954–2013 (Vienna)

Rathmayr E. (2010) Die Präsenz des Ktistes Androklos in Ephesos, AnzWien 145, 19–60

Rathmayr E. (2014) Kaiserverehrung in öffentlichen Brunnenanlagen, in: Fischer J. (ed.), Der Beitrag Kleinasiens zur Kultur- und Geistesgeschichte der griechisch-römischen Antike, Akten des Internationalen Kolloquiums Wien, 3.–5. November 2010, DenkschrWien 469 (Vienna) 309–332

Rathmayr E. (ed.) (2016) Hanghaus 2 in Ephesos. Die Wohneinheit 7. Baubefund, Ausstattung, Funde, FiE VIII 10 (Vienna)

Rebenich S. (2009) Hermann Bengtson und Alfred Heuß. Zur Entwicklung der Alten Geschichte in der Zwischen- und Nachkriegszeit, in: Losemann V. – Droß K. – Velte S. (eds.), Alte Geschichte zwischen Wissenschaft und Politik. Gedenkschrift Karl Christ (Wiesbaden) 181–206

Reisch E. (1913) Bericht über die Gesamtsitzung des österr. Archäologischen Institutes während der Jahre 1912 und 1913, JOeAI 16, 77–90

Reisch E. (1923) Vorwort, FiE III (Vienna) I-III

Reisch E. (1930) Bericht über die Gesamtsitzung des Österreichischen Archäologischen Institutes 1930, JOeAI 26, 263–312

Rektorat der Universität Wien (ed.) (1939) Personalstand der Universität Wien (Vienna)

Rektorat der Universität Wien (ed.) (1943a) Personal= und Vorlesungs=Verzeichnis für das Sommersemester 1943 (Vienna)

Rektorat der Universität Wien (ed.) (1943b) Personal= und Vorlesungs=Verzeichnis für das Wintersemester 1943/44 (Vienna)

Rektorat der Universität Wien (ed.) (1944a) Personal= und Vorlesungs=Verzeichnis für das Sommersemester 1944 (Vienna)

Rektorat der Universität Wien (ed.) (1944b) Personal=Verzeichnis. Studienjahr 1944/45 (Vienna)

Rektorat der Universität Wien (ed.) (1958) Vorlesungs=Verzeichnis für das Wintersemester 1958/59 (Vienna)

Rektorat der Universität Wien (ed.) (1959) Vorlesungs=Verzeichnis für das Wintersemester 1959/60 (Vienna)

Resetarits L. (2022) Krowod. Erinnerungen an meine Jugend (Vienna)

Reuer E. (1976) Frau Professor Dr. Margarete Weninger zum 80. Geburtstag, AnthropolAnz 35,2/3, 225–226

Reynolds J. (1982) Aphrodisias and Rome, JRS Monographs 1 (London)

Reynolds M. (2008) The octagon in Leonardo's drawings, Nexus Netw J 10, 51–76

Richmond I. A. (1954) Review festschrift for R. Egger, The Antiquaries Journal 34, 94–96

Ridgway B. S. (1974) A Story of Five Amazons, AJA 78, 1–17

Ridgway B. S. (1976) The Amazon´s belt. Addendum to a Story of Five Amazons, AJA 80, 82

Rigsby K. J. (1996) Asylia. Territorial Inviolability in the Hellenistic World (Berkeley – Los Angeles – London)

Robinson O. (1973) Blasphemy and sacrilege in Roman Law, Irish Jurist 8,2, 356–371

Röd W. (2009) Geschichte der Philosophie I (Munich)

Rogers G. M. (1991) The Sacred Identity of Ephesos. Foundation Myths of a Roman City (London – New York)

Rogers G. M. (2012) The Mysteries of Artemis of Ephesos. Cult, Polis and Change in the Graeco-Roman World (New Haven)

Roldán F. (2012) Method of Modulation and Sizing of Historic Architecture, Nexus Netw J 14, 539–553

Rosar W. (1971) Deutsche Gemeinschaft. Seyss-Inquart und der Anschluß (Vienna – Frankfurt – Zürich)

Rose C. B. (1997) Dynastic Commemoration and Imperial Portraiture in the Julio-Claudian Period (Cambridge)

Ross D. M. (2016) Determining the use of mathematical geometry in the ancient Greek method of design, The Mathematical Intelligencer 38,2, 17–28

Roueché C. (2002) The image of Victory. New Evidence from Ephesos, in: Deroche V. – Feissel D. – Morrisson C. – Zuckerman C. (eds.), Mélanges Gilbert Dagron, Travaux et mémoires 14 (Paris) 527–546

Roueché C. (2009) The Kuretenstraße: the imperial presence in Late Antiquity, in: Ladstätter S. (ed.), Neue Forschungen zur Kuretenstraße von Ephesos, DenkschrWien 382 (Vienna) 155–169

Rudolf E. (1995) Pompeji vor den Toren Wiens. Die ‚Führergrabung‘ von Carnuntum 1938/1940, Hephaistos 13, 187–220

Rudolf E. – Kramer J. – Winkler I. et al. (2020) Morphologies of Medial Clavicular Ossification (Münster)

Rüger C. B. (2010) Harald von Petrikovits. Ein Nachruf, BJB 208, X–XIII

Rumscheid F. (1994) Untersuchungen zur kleinasiatischen Bauornamentik. Beiträge zur Erschließung hellenistischer und kaiserzeitlicher Skulptur und Architektur (Mainz)

Rupnow D. (2010) Brüche und Kontinuitäten – Von der NS-Judenforschung zur Nachkriegsjudaistik, in: Ash M. G. – Nieß W. – Pils R. (eds.), Geisteswissenschaften im Nationalsozialismus. Das Beispiel der Universität Wien (Vienna) 79–110

Russo E. (1999) La scultura a Efeso in età paleocristiana e bizantina, in: Pillinger R. – Kresten O.– Krinzinger F. – Russo E. (eds.), Efeso paleocristiana e bizantina. Frühchristliches und byzantinisches Ephesos, Symposium Rom 1996, DenkschrWien 282 = Archäologische Forschungen 3 (Vienna) 26–53

Ryan G. (2022) Greek Cities and Roman Governors. Placing Power in Imperial Asia Minor (London – New York)

Sannicandro L. (2013) Der "dekadente" Feldherr: Caesar in Ägypten, Mnemosyne 67/1, 50-64

Saporiti N. (1964) A Frieze from the Temple of Hadrian in Ephesos, in: Sandler L. F. (ed.), Essays in memory of Karl Lehmann, Marsyas Suppl. 1 (New York) 269–278

Saria B. (1969) Rudolf Egger (1882 - 1969), Südost-Forschungen 28, 290–293

Sarian H. (1992) LIMC VI, 985–1018 s. v. Hekate

Šašel J. (1967) Huldigung norischer Stämme am Magdalensberg in Kärnten. Ein Klärungsversuch, Historia 16, 70–74

Savvides D. (2021) The conceptual design of the Octagon at Thessaloniki, Nexus Netw J 23, 395–432

Schachermeyr F. (1965) Josef Keil †, Alm 114, 1964, 241–261

Schäfer C. (2006) Kleopatra (Darmstadt)

Schalles H.-J. (2004) Review zu Halfmann H (2001) Städtebau und Bauherren im römischen Kleinasien. Ein Vergleich zwischen Pergamon und Ephesos, BJB 201, 646–650

Schedlmayer C. (2010) „Die Zeitschrift ‚Kunst dem Volk‘. Populärwissenschaftliche Kunstliteratur im Nationalsozialismus und ihre Parallelen in der akademischen Kunstgeschichtsschreibung" (Thesis University of Vienna, Vienna)

Scheibelreiter-Gail V. (2011) Die Mosaiken Westkleinasiens. Tessellate des 2. Jahrhunderts v. Chr. bis Anfang des 7. Jahrhunderts n. Chr., SoSchrOeAI 46 (Vienna)

Scherrer P. (1990) Augustus, die Mission des Vedius Pollio und die Artemis Ephesia, JOeAI 60, 87–101

Scherrer P. (1997) Das Ehrengrab des Kaiserpriesters am Embolos – Eine Personensuche, in: Thür H. (ed.), „… und verschönerte die Stadt …" – ΚΑΙ ΚΟΣΜΕΣΑΝΤΑ ΤΗΝ ΠΟΛΙΝ. Ein ephesischer Priester des Kaiserkultes in seinem Umfeld, SoSchrOeAI 27 (Vienna) 113–139

Scherrer P. (1999) Am Olympieion vorbei …? Pausanias' Wegbeschreibung in Ephesos und der hadrianische Neokorietempel, in: Scherrer P. – Taeuber H. – Thür H. (eds.), Steine und Wege. Festschrift für Dieter Knibbe, SoSchrOeAI 32 (Vienna) 137–144

Scherrer P. (2001) The historical topography of Ephesos, in: Parrish D. (ed.), Urbanism in Western Asia Minor. New Studies on Aphrodisias, Ephesos, Hierapolis, Pergamon, Perge and Xanthos, JRA Suppl. 45 (Portsmouth) 57–87

Scherrer P. (2005) Das sogenannte Serapeion in Ephesos: ein Mouseion?, in: Hoffmann A. (ed.), Ägyptische Kulte und ihre Heiligtümer im Osten des Römischen Reiches, Byzas 1 (Istanbul) 109–138

Scherrer P. (2006a) Die Fernwasserversorgung von Ephesos in der römischen Kaiserzeit. Synopse der epigraphischen Quellen, in: Wiplinger G. (ed.), Cura Aquarum in Ephesus, Proceedings of the Twelfth International Congress on the History of Water Management and Hydraulic Engineering in the Mediterranean Region, Ephesus/Selçuk, Turkey, Otober 2–10, 2004, Bulletin antieke beschaving, Annual Papers on Classical Archaeology, Suppl. 12 = SoSchrOeAI 42 (Leuven – Paris – Dudley) 45–58

Scherrer P. (2006b) Hellenistische und römische Stadt-tore in Kleinasien unter besonderer Berücksichtigung von Ephesos, in: Schattner T. G. – Valdés Fernández F. (eds.), Stadttore. Bautyp und Kunstform – Puertas de ciudades. Tipo arquitectónico y forma artística, Akten der Tagung in Toledo vom 25.–27. September 2003, Iberia Archaeologica 8 (Mainz) 63–78

Scherrer P. (2007a) Der conventus civium Romanorum und kaiserliche Freigelassene als Bauherren in Ephesos in augusteischer Zeit, in: Meyer M. (ed.), Neue Zeit-en – Neue Sitten. Zu Rezeption und Integration römi-schen und italischen Kulturguts in Kleinasien, Wiener Forschungen zur Archäologie 12 (Vienna) 63–75

Scherrer P. (2007b) Von Apaša nach Hagios Theologos. Die Siedlungsgeschichte des Raumes Ephesos von prähis-torischer bis in byzantinische Zeit unter dem Aspekt der maritimen und fluvialen Bedingungen, JOeAI 76, 321–351

Scherrer P. (2008) Die Stadt als Festplatz. Das Beispiel der ephesischen Bauprogramme rund um die Kaiserneoko-rien Domitians und Hadrians, in: Rüpke J. (ed.), Fest-rituale in der römischen Kaiserzeit, Studien und Texte zu Antike und Christentum 48 (Tübingen) 33–62

Scherrer P. (2014) Hunting the boar – The fiction of a local past in foundation myths of Hellenistic and Roman ci-ties, in: Alroth B. – Scheffer C. (eds.), Attitudes towards the past in Antiquity. Creating Identities, Proc. Of an In-ternat. Conference held at Stockholm Univ., 15–17 May 2009, Acta Universitatis Stockholmiensis, Stockholm Studies in Classical Archaelogy 14 (Stockholm) 113–119

Scherrer P. (2015) The Kouretes in Ephesos. Thoughts on their origin, duties, and engagement in cult and social life. Review article of: Guy MacLean Rogers, The Mys-teries of Artemis of Ephesos. Cult, Polis, and Change in the Graeco-Roman World, Journal of Roman Archaeol-ogy 28, 792–802

Scherrer P. (2021) Agorai und Gymnasia – Anmerkungen zur Stadtstruktur von Ephesos in hellenistischer Zeit, in: Koller K. – Quatember U. – Trinkl E. (eds.), Stein auf Stein. Festschrift für Hilke Thür zum 80. Geburtstag, Keryx 8 (Graz) 63–80

Scherrer P. (ed.) (1995) Ephesos. Der neue Führer (Vienna)

Scherrer P. (ed.) (2000) Ephesus – The New Guide (Revised edition, Istanbul)

Scherrer P. – Trinkl E. (2006) Die Tetragonos Agora in Ephe-sos. Grabungsergebnisse von archaischer bis in byzan-tinische Zeit – ein Überblick. Befunde und Funde klas-sischer Zeit, FiE XIII 2 (Vienna)

Scheubelius J. (ed.) (1550) Euklidis Megarensis, Philosophi & Mathematici excellentissimi, sex libris priores, de Geometricis principiis, Graeci & Latini [...] (Basel)

Schiff S. (2010) Cleopatra. A life (Boston)

Schmeling A. – Schulz R. – Reisinger W. et al. (2004) Studies on the time frame for ossification of the medial clavicu-lar epiphyseal cartilage in conventional radiography, Int J Legal Med 118,1, 5–8

Schmidt-Colinet A. (1996) Zur Ikonographie der hadria-nischen Tondi am Konstantinsbogen, in: Blakolmer F. (ed.), Fremde Zeiten. Festschrift für Jürgen Borchhardt Vol. 2 (Vienna) 261–273

Schneider T. (2012) Ägyptologen im Dritten Reich. Bio-graphische Notizen anhand der sogenannten „Stein-dorff-Liste", Journal of Egyptian History 5, 120–247

Schoene A. – Petermann J. H. (1876) Eusebii Chronicorum Libri duo (Berlin)

Schörner H. (2007) Sepulturae graecae intra urbem: Unter-suchungen zum Phänomen der intraurbanen Bestat-tungen bei den Griechen. Boreas – Münsteraner Bei-träge zur Archäologie, Beiheft 9 (Möhnesee)

Schörner H. (2015) Äußerer Zwang und innerer Antrieb. Die Dynamik des Faches Klassische Archäologie während der ersten Hälfte des 20. Jahrhunderts, in: Fröschl K. A. – Müller G.B. – Olechowski T. – Schmidt-Lauber B. (eds.), Reflexive Innensichten aus der Universität. Disziplinengeschichten zwischen Wissenschaft, Ge-sellschaft und Politik (Vienna) 575–585

Schörner H. (2016) Die Disziplin Klassische Archäologie an der Universität Wien in der 1. Hälfte des 20. Jahrunderts (1898-1951), in: Grabherr G. – Kainrath B. (eds.), Akten des 15. Österreichischen Archäologentages in Inns-bruck 27.02. - 01.03.2015 (Innsbruck) 347–358

Schörner H. (2020) Hedwig Kenner als Assistentin an der Archäologischen Sammlung (1936–1945) und dem Archäologisch-Epigraphischen Seminar (1948–1951) der Universität Wien, in: Modl D. – Peitler K. (eds.), Archäologie in Österreich 1938–1945 (Graz) 122–137

Schörner H. (2021a) Das Archäologisch-Epigraphische Seminar (1876 bis 1956), in: Schörner G. – Kopf J. (eds.), 1869–2019. 150 Jahre Klassische Archäologie an der Universität Wien (Vienna) 43–47

Schörner H. (2021b) Hedwig Kenner. Von der Assistentin (seit 1936) zur Professorin (1961 bis 1980), in: Schörner G. – Kopf J. (eds.), 1869–2019. 150 Jahre Klassische Archäologie an der Universität Wien, 69–72

Schörner H. (2021c) Die Disziplin Klassische Archäologie an der Universität Wien in der 1. Hälfte des 20. Jahrhun-derts (1898–1951), in: Grabherr G. – Kainrath B. (eds.), Akten des 15. Österreichischen Archäologentages in Innsbruck 27. Februar–1. März 2014 (Innsbruck) 347–358

Schowalter D. (1998) The Zeus Philios and Trajan Temple. A Context for Imperial Honors, in: Koester H. (ed.), Perga-mon, Citadel of the Gods. Archaeological Record, Liter-ary Description, and Religious Development, Harvard Theological Studies 46, 233–249

Schowalter D. (2022) Ephesos under the Flavians. The Domitiansplatz as a Marker of Local and Imperial Identity, in: Black A. – Thomas C. M. – Thompson T. W. (eds.), Ephesos as a Religious Center under the Princi-pate (Tübingen) 139–160

Schreiber T. (2012) Die funktionale Binde, in: Lichtenberger A. – Martin K. – Nieswandt H.–H. – Salzmann D. (eds.), Das Diadem der hellenistischen Herrscher - Übernahme, Transformation oder Neuschöpfung eines Herrschaftszeichens? Euros - Münstersche Beiträge zu Numismatik und Ikonographie 1 (Bonn) 233–247

Schumann D. – Freitag L. E. (2014) Ehrungen der Universität Göttingen (Ehrenbürger und -doktoren) in der NS-Zeit und der Umgang mit ihnen nach 1945

Schütz M. (1990) Zur Sonnenuhr des Augustus auf dem Marsfeld. Eine Auseinandersetzung mit E. Buchners Rekonstruktion und seiner Deutung der Ausgrabungsergebnisse, aus der Sicht eines Physikers, Gymnasium 97, 432–457

Schütz M. (1991) Der Capricorn als Sternzeichen des Augustus, Antike und Abendland 37, 55–67

Schwarz K. W. (2021) „Wie verzerrt ist nun alles!" Die Evangelisch-Theologische Fakultät in Wien in der NS-Ära (Vienna)

Scott K. (1933) The political propaganda of 44–30 B.C., Memoirs of the American Academy in Rome 11, 7–49

Seebacher F. (2020) Erna Lesky, „Herrin" der Sammlungen des Josephinums. Wissensrepräsentation und Wissensproduktion im Zentrum der Geschichte der „Wiener Medizin", in: Seidl J. – Kästner I. (eds.), Tauschen und Schenken. Wissenschaftliche Sammlungen als Resultat europäischer Zusammenarbeit (Düren) 107–130

Segev M. (2019) Aristotle's Ideal City-Planning: Politics 7.12, The Classical Quarterly 69/2, 585–596

Seidler H. (1987) Docendo Discitur in memoriam Margarete Weninger, MAGW 117, 179–182

Seidler H. (1989) Anthropologen im Widerstand? Ein kurzer Versuch zu Vergangenheit und Gegenwart, in: Zenner M. (ed.), Der Widerstand gegen den Nationalsozialismus. Eine interdisziplinäre didaktische Konzeption zu seiner Erschließung (Bochum) 67–121

Seiterle G. (1970) Die hellenistische Stadtmauer von Ephesos (Thesis University of Zurich, Zurich)

Seiterle G. (1982) Das Hauptstadttor von Ephesos, AntK 25, 145–149

Seiterle G. (1998) Magnesisches Tor, JOeAI 67, Grabungen 29

Seiterle G. (1999) Ephesische Wollbinden. Attribut der Göttin, Zeichen des Stieropfers, in: Friesinger H. – Krinzinger F. (eds.), 100 Jahre Österreichische Forschungen in Ephesos (Vienna) 251–254

Seyer M. (2007) Der Herrscher als Jäger. Untersuchungen zur königlichen Jagd im persischen und makedonischen Reich vom 6.–4. Jahrhundert v. Chr. sowie unter den Diadochen Alexanders des Großen, Wiener Forschungen zur Archäologie 11 (Vienna)

Slavitt D. R. (2002) The Elegies by Propertius, Sextus (Berkely)

Smith J. O. (1996) The High Priests of the temple of Artemis at Ephesus, in: Lane E. N. (ed.), Cybele, Attis and related cults, 323–335

Smith R. R. R. (1993) The Monument of Zoilos, Aphrodisias 1 (Zabern – Mainz)

Smith W. (1875) Dictionary of Greek and Roman Biography and Mythology (London)

Sokolicek A. (2009) Zwischen Stadt und Land: Neues zum Magnesischen Tor in Ephesos. Erste Ergebnisse, JOeAI 78, 2009, 321–347

Sokolicek A. (2010) Chronologie und Nutzung des Magnesischen Tores von Ephesos, JOeAI 79, 259–281

Sokolicek A. (2016) Betwixt and Between – The Cultural Roles of the Magnesian Gate in Greek-Roman Ephesus, in: Weissenrieder A. (ed.), Borders Terminologies, Ideologies, and Performances (Tübingen) 95–113

Spanu M. 2010: Appunti sui monumenti funerari intra moenia a Efeso. Aspetti architettonici e urbanistici. In: M. Valenti (ed.), Monumenta. I mausolei romani, tra commemorazione funebre e propaganda celebrativa. Atti del Convegno di Studi (Monte Porzio Catone, 25 ottobre 2008), Tusculana - Quaderni del Museo di Monte Porzio Catone 3, Rome: Edizione Exòrma, 53–66

Spanu M. (2020) Honorary Arches and Gates in Asia Minor up to the reign of Trajan, in: Lohner-Urban U. – Quatember U. (eds.), Zwischen Bruch und Kontinuität / Continuity and Change. Architektur in Kleinasien am Übergang vom Hellenismus zur römischen Kaiserzeit / Architecture in Asia Minor during the transitional period from Hellenism to the Roman Empire, Byzas 25, 381–397

Stähelin F. (1921) RE XI/1 Sp. 753 s.v. 20) Kleopatra VII. Philopator

Staudinger E. G. (1989) Vereine als Träger des Anschlußgedankens, Zeitschrift des Historischen Vereines für Steiermark Jahrgang 80, 257–275

Stefec R. (2016) Flavii Philostrati Vitae Sophistarum (Oxford)

Steskal M. (1997) Stadtgründungsmythen von Kleinasien und ihre Ikonographie am Beispiel von Ephesos (Thesis University of Vienna, Vienna)

Steskal M. (2010) Das Prytaneion in Ephesos, FiE IX 4 (Vienna)

Steskal M. (2013) Wandering cemeteries. Roman and Late Roman burials in the capital of the province of Asia, in: Henry O. (ed.), Le mort dans la ville. 2èmes rencontres d'Archéologie de L'IFEA. Istanbul 14–15 novembre 2011, 243–257

Stevenson G. (2022) "Do not harm the suppliant". Inviolability and Asylum at Ephesos and in the Book of Revelation, in: Black A. – Thomas C. M. – Thompson T. W. (eds.), Ephesos as a Religious Center under the Principate (Tübingen) 189–204

Stewart A. (1993) Faces of Power. Alexander's image and Hellenistic politics (Berkeley – Los Angeles)

Stifter C. H. (2014) Zwischen geistiger Erneuerung und Restauration. US-amerikanische Planungen zur Entnazifizierung und demokratischen Neuorientierung österreichischer Wissenschaft 1941–1955 (Vienna – Cologne – Weimar)

Stiglitz H. – Knibbe D. (1998) Die Entwicklung des Österreichischen Archäologischen Institutes von 1945 bis in die Gegenwart, in: Kandler M. – Wlach G. (eds.), 100 Jahre Österreichisches Archäologisches Institut 1898–1998 (Vienna) 61–77

Stock F. et al. (2014) The palaeo-geographies of Ephesos (Turkey), its harbours and the Artemision – a geoarchaeological reconstruction for the timespan 1500–300 BC, Zeitschrift für Geomorphologie 58,2, 33–66

Stock F. et al. (2016) Human impact on Holocene sediment dynamics in the Eastern Mediterranean – the example of the Roman harbour of Ephesus, Earth Surface Processes and Landforms 41, 980–996

Strack M. L. (1897) Die Dynastie der Ptolemäer (Berlin)

Strack P. L. (1931) Untersuchungen zur römischen Reichsprägung des zweiten Jahrhunderts I. Die Reichsprägung zur Zeit des Traian (Stuttgart)

Strocka V. M. (1988) Wechselwirkungen der stadtrömischen und kleinasiatischen Architektur unter Trajan und Hadrian, IstMitt 38, 291–307

Strocka V. M. (1989) Zeus, Marnas und Klaseas. Ephesische Brunnenfiguren von 93 n. Chr., in: Başgelen N. – Lugal M. (eds.), Festschrift J. İnan (Istanbul) 77–92

Strocka V. M. (2005) Griechische Löwenkopf-Wasserspeier in Ephesos, in: Brandt B. – Gassner V. – Ladstätter S. (ed.), Synergia, Festschrift für Fritz Krinzinger (2005) 337–348

Strocka V. M. (2009) Die Celsusbibliothek als Ehrengrab am Embolos, in: Ladstätter S. (ed.), Neue Forschungen zur Kuretenstraße von Ephesos. Akten des Symposiums für Hilke Thür vom 13. Dezember 2006 an der Österreichischen Akademie der Wissenschaften, Archäologische Forschungen 15 (Vienna) 247–259

Strocka V. M. (2011) Ephesische Spolien (von der Neronischen Halle, dem Heroon und dem Oktogon), in: Jäger-Klein C. – Kolbitsch A. (eds.), Fabrica et ratiocinatio in Architektur, Bauforschung und Denkmalpflege. Festschrift für Friedmund Hueber (Vienna – Graz) 291–311

Strocka V. M. (2013) Celsus oder Aquila? Zur Panzerstatue Istanbul 2453, in: Kökdemir G. (ed.), Orhan Bingöl'e 67. Yaş Armağan = Festschrift Orhan Bingöl (Ankara) 597–610

Strocka V. M. (2017) Trajan in Ephesus, JOeAI 86, 397–456

Studniczka F. (1904) Tropaeum Traiani (Leipzig)

Styhler-Aydin G. (2022) Der Zuschauerraum des Theaters von Ephesos. Baubefund und architekturhistorische Analyse, mit Beiträgen von M. Aurenhammer – Th. Köberle – J. Weber, FiE II 2 (Vienna)

Suppan A. (2013) „Anschluss" und NS-Herrschaft Österreich 1938–1945, in: Feichtinger J. – Matis H. – Sienell S. – Uhl H. (eds.), Die Akademie der Wissenschaften in Wien 1938 bis 1945 (Vienna)

Susini G. (1955) Iscrizioni greche di Megiste e della Licia nel Museo di Mitilene, Annuario della Scuola archeologica di Atene e delle missioni italiane in Oriente 30–32 (N.S. 14–16), 1952–54, 341–353

Svatek P. (2010) „Wien als Tor nach dem Südosten" – Der Beitrag Wiener Geisteswissenschaftler zur Erforschung Südosteuropas während des Nationalsozialismus, in: Hermetinger D. (ed.), Geisteswissenschaften im Nationalsozialismus. Die Universität Wien 1938–1945 (Vienna – Göttingen) 111–140

Swain S. (1996) Hellenism and Empire. Language, Classicism, and Power in the Greek World, AD 50–250 (Oxford)

Swoboda E. (1932) Octavian und Illyricum. Verein Klassischer Philologen in Wien, Parerga 1 (Vienna)

Szemethy H. D. (2015) Anton Josef Ritter von Kenner (1871–1951), in: Borchhardt J. (ed.), Der Zorn Poseidons und die Irrfahrten des Odysseus (Vienna) 194–207

Tacquet T. (1762) Elementa Euclidea Geometriae Planae, ac Solidae […] (Venice)

Taeuber H. (2016) Graffiti und Inschriften, in: Rathmayr E. (ed.), Hanghaus 2 in Ephesos. Die Wohneinheit 7. Baubefund, Ausstattung, Funde, FiE VIII 10 (Vienna) 233–257

Taeuber H. (2021) Josef Keil. Alte Geschichte im Gegenwind der Zeitgeschichte, in: Froehlich S. (ed.) Altertumswissenschaft in Greifswald. Porträts ausgewählter Gelehrter 1856 bis 1946, 313–325

Taretto E. (2017) Poets and places: sites of literary memory in the Hellenistic world (Thesis Durham University)

Taschwer K. (2012) Othenio Abel, Kämpfer gegen die „Verjudung" der Universität, Der Standard from 09.10.2012

Taschwer K. (2013) Die zwei Karrieren des Fritz Knoll. Wie ein Botaniker nach 1938 die Interessen der NSDAP wahrnahm – und das nach 1945 erfolgreich vergessen machte, in: Feichtinger J. – Matis H. – Sienell S. – Uhl H. (eds.), Die Akademie der Wissenschaften in Wien 1938 bis 1945. Katalog zur Ausstellung (Vienna) 47–55

Taschwer K. (2014) Der Inkor-Rektor. Eine kurze politische Biografie des Paläontologen Othenio Abel (1875–1946) unter besonderer Berücksichtigung seines Wirkens an der Universität Wien, <https://www.academia.edu/6918847/Der_Inkor-Rektor._Eine_kurze_politische_Biografie_des_Pal%C3%A4ontologen_Othenio_Abel_1875_1946_unter_besonderer_Ber%C3%BCcksichtigung_seines_Wirkens_an_der_Universit%C3%A4t_Wien._2014> (accessed on 21.04.2022)

Taschwer K. (2015a) Hochburg des Antisemitismus. Der Niedergang der Universität Wien im 20. Jahrhundert (Vienna)

Taschwer K. (2015b) Rezension zu Pfefferle/Pfefferle 2014, OZP – Austrian Journal of Political Science 44,1, 55–56

Taschwer K. (2015c) Die Bärenhöhle, eine geheime antisemitische Professorenclique der Zwischenkriegszeit, <https://www.academia.edu/11680945/Die_B%C3%A4renh%C3%B6hle_eine_geheime_antisemitische_Professorenclique_der_Zwischenkriegszeit_2015_> (accessed on 21.04.2022)

Taschwer K. (2016a) Geheimsache Bärenhöhle. Wie eine antisemitische Professorenclique nach 1918 an der Universität Wien jüdische Forscherinnen und Forscher vertrieb. Beiträge zur Holocaustforschung des Wiener Wiesenthal Instituts für Holocaust-Studien 3, 221–242

Taschwer K. (2016b) Die Bärenhöhle, eine geheime antisemitische Professorenclique der Zwischenkriegszeit, in: Fritz R. – Rossolinski-Liebe G. – Starek J. (ed.) Alma Mater Antisemitica. Akademisches Milieu, Juden und Antisemitismus an den Universitäten Europas zwischen 1918 und 1939 (Vienna) 221–244

Taschwer K. (2018a) Ehre, wem Ehre nicht unbedingt gebührt, in: Pinwinkler A. – Koll J. (eds.), Zuviel der Ehre? Interdisziplinäre Perspektiven auf akademische Ehrungen in Deutschland und Österreich, (Vienna – Cologne – Weimar) 307–345

Taschwer K. (2018b) Braun-schwarze Beziehungsgeflechte. Zur Bedeutung antisemitischer Netzwerke im akademischen Milieu der Zwischenkriegszeit und zu ihren Nachwirkungen nach 1938 und 1945, in: Enderle-Burcel G. – Reiter-Zatloukal I. (eds.), Antisemitismus in Österreich 1933–1938 (Vienna – Cologne – Weimar) 769–784

Taschwer K. (2020) Universität Wien Ende April 1945. Die verpasste Stunde null, Der Standard from 01.05.2020

Teschler-Nicola M. (2004) The Diagnostic Eye – On the History of Genetic and Racial Assessment in Pre-1938 Austria, Coll Anthropol 28,2 Suppl., 7–29

Teschler-Nicola M. (2005a) Aspekte der Erbbiologie und die Entwicklung des rassenkundlichen Gutachtens in Österreich bis 1938, in: Gabriel H. E. – Neugebauer W. (eds.), Vorreiter der Vernichtung. Eugenik, Rassenhygiene und Euthanasie in der österreichischen Diskussion vor 1938 (Vienna – Cologne – Weimar) 99–111

Teschler-Nicola M. (2005b) Praktische Relevanz einer Wissenschaft: Der Sachverständige Josef Weninger und die erbbiologische Grundlagenforschung der ‚Wiener Schule', in: Gabriel H. E. – Neugebauer W. (eds.), Vorreiter der Vernichtung. Eugenik, Rassenhygiene und Euthanasie in der österreichischen Diskussion vor 1938 (Vienna – Cologne – Weimar) 112–138

Teschler-Nicola M. (2018) Erbbiologie und "Volkstums"-Forschung am Wiener Anthropologischen Institut. Das „Marienfeld-Projekt" 1933/34, Banatului, S.N., Arheologie – Istorie 26, 181–188

Thayer D. T. (2012) The Lateran Baptistery. Memory, Space, and Baptism (Thesis University of Tennessee, Knoxville)

Thiersch H. (1909) Pharos. Antike, Islam und Occident (Leipzig – Berlin)

Thür H. (1985) Ephesische Bauhütten in der Zeit der Flavier und der Adoptivkaiser, in: Lebendige Altertumswissenschaft. Festschrift für Hermann Vetters (Vienna) 181–187

Thür H. (1989) Das Hadrianstor in Ephesos, FiE XI 1 (Vienna)

Thür H. (1990) Arsinoë IV, eine Schwester Kleopatras VII, Grabinhaberin des Oktogons von Ephesos? Ein Vorschlag JOeAI 60, 43–56

Thür H. (1995a) Der ephesische Ktistes Androklos und (s)ein Heroon am Embolos, JOeAI 64, 63–103

Thür H. (1995b) Die Ergebnisse der Arbeiten an der innerstädtischen Via Sacra, im Embolosbereich, in: Knibbe D. – Thür H. (eds.), Via sacra Ephesiaca II, BerMatOeAI 6 (Vienna) 84–95

Thür H. (1995c) The Processional Way in the City as a Place of Culte and Burial, in: Koester H. (ed.), Ephesos. Metropolis of Asia. An Interdisciplinary Approach to its Archaeology, Religion, and Culture, Harvard Theological Studies 41 (Valley Forge) 157–199

Thür H. (1996) Prozessionsstraße (Via Sacra) im Bereich Kuretenstraße/Heroa/Hadrianstor, JOeAI 65, Grabungen 13–15

Thür H. (1997a) Girlandensarkophag und Porträt eines Kaiserpriesters im Fund- und Primärkontext - Bestandteil eines Ehrengrabes am Embolos?, in: Thür H. (ed.), „… und verschönerte die Stadt …" – KAI KOΣMEΣANTA THN ΠOΛIN. Ein ephesischer Priester des Kaiserkultes in seinem Umfeld, SoSchrOeAI 27 (Vienna) 69–75

Thür H. (1997b) Grabungsbericht der Sondage an der Westseite des „Androklos-Heroons", in: Thür H. (ed.), „… und verschönerte die Stadt …" – KAI KOΣMEΣANTA THN ΠOΛIN. Ein ephesischer Priester des Kaiserkultes in seinem Umfeld, SoSchrOeAI 27 (Vienna) 17–26

Thür H. (1997c) Zum Standort eines Ehrengrabes des Aristion am Embolos, in: Thür H. (ed.), „… und verschönerte die Stadt …" – KAI KOΣMEΣANTA THN ΠOΛIN. Ein ephesischer Priester des Kaiserkultes in seinem Umfeld, SoSchrOeAI 27 (Vienna), 151–156

Thür H. (1999a) Der Embolos. Innovation und Tradition anhand seines Erscheinungsbildes, in: Friesinger H. – Krinzinger F. (eds.), 100 Jahre österreichische Forschungen in Ephesos. Akten des Symposiums Wien 1995, DenkschrWien 260 = Archäologische Forschungen 1 (Vienna) 421–428

Thür H. (1999b) Die spätantike Bauphase der Kuretenstraße, in: Pillinger R. – Kresten O. – Krinzinger F. – Russo E. (eds.), Efeso paleocristiana e bizantina. Frühchristliches und byzantinisches Ephesos, Symposium Rom 1996, DenkschrWien 282 = Archäologische Forschungen 3 (Vienna) 104–120

Thür H. (1999c) ‚Via Sacra Ephesiaca'. Vor der Stadt und in der Stadt, in: Scherrer P. – Taeuber H. – Thür H. (eds.), Steine und Wege. Festschrift für Dieter Knibbe, SoSchrOeAI 32 (Vienna) 163-172

Thür H. (2005) Altarstudien aus Ephesos, in: Brandt B. – Gassner V. – Ladstätter S. (ed.), Synergasia. Festschrift für Friedrich Krinzinger, Vol. I (Vienna) 355–362

Thür H. (2007a) Das Gymnasion an der oberen Agora in Ephesos, in: Christof E. – Koiner G. – Lehner M. – Pochmarski E. (eds.), ΠOTNIA ΘHPΩN. Festschrift für Gerda Schwarz zum 65. Geburtstag, Veröffentlichungen des Inst. für Archäologie d. Univ. Graz 8 (Vienna) 403–414

Thür H. (2007b) Wie römisch ist der sog. Staatsmarkt in Ephesos?, in: Meyer M. (ed.), Neue Zeiten – Neue Sitten. Zu Rezeption und Integration römischen und italischen Kulturguts in Kleinasien, Wiener Forschungen zur Archäologie 12 (Vienna) 77–90

Thür H. (2009) Zur Kuretenstraße von Ephesos. Eine Bestandsaufnahme der Ergebnisse aus der Bauforschung, in: Ladstätter S. (ed.), Neue Forschungen zur Kuretenstraße von Ephesos. DenkschrWien 382 (Vienna) 9–28

Thür H. (2011) Arsinoe IV. und ihr Grabbau in Ephesos, in: Acta Carnuntina. Mitteilungen der Gesellschaft der Freunde Carnuntums 1, 74–76

Thür H. (2014) Wasserwirtschaftliche Einrichtungen, in: Thür H. – Rathmayr E. (eds.), Hanghaus 2 in Ephesos. Die Wohneinheit 6. Baubefund, Ausstattung, Funde, FiE VIII 9 (Vienna) 197–218

Thür H. (2015) Efes'te Hellenistik Öncesi Dönemdeki Ünlü Kadınlar: VII. Kleopatra ve IV. Arsinoe (Famous Women in the Pre-Hellenistic Period in Ephesus: Cleopatra VII and Arsinoe IV), in: Darga A. M. (ed.), Anadolu'da Kadın On Bin Yıldır Eş, Anne, Tüccar, Kraliçe 268-274

Thür H. (2020a) Die Friese des ›Partherdenkmals‹ und die Hafenthermen von Ephesos, JOeAI 89, 371–408

Thür H. (2020b) Brunnenanlagen und Wasserversorgung in Ephesos in hellenistischer und frührömischer Zeit, in: Lohner-Urban U. – Quatember U. (eds.), Zwischen Bruch und Kontinuität / Continuity and Change. Architektur in Kleinasien am Übergang vom Hellenismus zur römischen Kaiserzeit / Architecture in Asia Minor during the transitional period from Hellenism to the Roman Empire, Byzas 25, 399–417

Thür H. (2021) Zum ephesischen Mouseion, Römisches Österreich 44, 223–231

Thür H. (2023) … und verschönerte die Stadt: Tiberius Claudius Aristion in Ephesos – revisited, in: Lohner-Urban U. – Spickermann W. – Trinkl E., Itineraria, vol. II. Rund ums Mittelmeer. Festschrift für Peter Scherrer zum 65. Geburtstag, Keryx 10 (Graz) 11–20

Thür H. (ed.) (1997) „… und verschönerte die Stadt …" – KAI ΚΟΣΜΕΣΑΝΤΑ ΤΗΝ ΠΟΛΙΝ. Ein ephesischer Priester des Kaiserkultes in seinem Umfeld, SoSchrOeAI 27 (Vienna)

Thuswaldner B. (2009) Zur computergestützten steingerechten Rekonstruktion des Oktogons in Ephesos, in: Ladstätter S. (ed.), Neue Forschungen zur Kuretenstraße von Ephesos. DenkschrWien 382 (Vienna) 261–281

Thuswaldner B. (2015) Das Oktogon von Ephesos. Rekonstruktion, Deutung und Präsentation (Thesis University of Vienna, Vienna)

Thuswaldner B. (2017) Das Oktogon von Ephesos. Rekonstruktion, Deutung und Präsentation, in: Koldewey-Gesellschaft (ed.), Bericht über die 49. Tagung für Ausgrabungswissenschaft und Bauforschung vom 4. bis 8. Mai 2016 in Innsbruck, 133–139

Thuswaldner B. – Flöry S. – Kalasek R. et al. (2009) Digital Anastylosis of the Octagon in Ephesos, Journal on Computers and Cultural Heritage 2,1, 1–30

Tibaldini M. (2021) Talus: etymology of a ludonym and how the names of an ancient gaming practice could be indicative of processes of cultural transmission and stratification, Sapiens ubique civis 2, 69-104

Tisè M. – Mazzarini L. – Fabrizzi G. et al. (2011) Applicability of Greulich and Pyle method for age assessment in forensic practice on an Italian sample, Int J Legal Med 125,3, 411–6

Toepffer J. (1894) RE I,2, col. 2145–2147 s. v. Androkleidai

Torelli M. 1988: Il monumento efesino di Memmius, Scienze dell'Antichità. Storia archeologia antropologia 2, 403–442

Torelli M. 1997: Il rango, il rito e l'immagine. Alle origini della rappresentazione storica romana, Saggi di archeologia 2 (Milano)

Trampedach K. (2005) Hierosylia. Gewalt in den Heiligtümern, in: Fischer G.– Moraw S. (eds.) Die andere Seite der Klassik. Gewalt im 5. und 4. Jahrhundert v. Chr. (Stuttgart) 143–165

Trethewey K. (2018) Ancient Lighthouses (Torpoint)

Tronson A. (1999) What the poet saw. Octavian's triple triumph, 29 BC, Acta Classica 42, 171–186

Tuchelt K. (1979) Frühe Denkmäler Roms in Kleinasien. Beiträge zur archäologischen Überlieferung aus der Zeit der Republik und des Augustus, Teil 1. Roma und Promagistrate, IstMitt Beih. 23 (Tübingen)

Turpin W. (2016) Ovid, Amores (Book I) (Cambridge)

Tyldesley J. A. (2008) Cleopatra. Last Queen of Egypt (London)

Ulf C. (1985) Franz Miltner, in: Bichler R. (ed.), 100 Jahre Alte Geschichte in Innsbruck. Franz Hampl zum 75. Geburtstag (Innsbruck) 47–59; 104–106

Urban O. H. (2021) Ein Prähistoriker und Unterrichtsminister in der NS-Zeit. Oswald Menghin und die „Kulturkreislehre" von Pater Wilhelm Schmidt, in: Gingrich A – Rohrbacher H. (eds.), Völkerkunde zur NS-Zeit aus Wien (1938–1945) (Vienna) 231–292

Van der Waerden B. L. (1966) Erwachende Wissenschaft. Ägyptische, Babylonische und Griechische Mathematik (Basel – Stuttgart)

Van Oppen de Ruiter B. F. (2007) The Religious Identification of Ptolemaic Queens with Aphrodite, Demeter, Hathor and Isis (Thesis University of New York)

Van Schooten F. V. (1617) De Propositien vande XV. Boucken der Elementen Euclidis […] (Leyden)

Vetters H. (1970) Rudolf Egger †, Alm 119, 1969, 363–382

Vetters H. (1973) Ephesos. Vorläufiger Grabungsbericht 1972, AnzWien 110, 175–194

Vetters H. (1974) Ephesos. Vorläufiger Grabungsbericht 1973, AnzWien 111, 211–226

Vetters H. (1978) Ephesos. Vorläufiger Grabungsbericht 1977, AnzWien 115, 263–274

Vetters H. (1983) Ephesos. Vorläufiger Grabungsbericht 1982, AnzWien 120, 111–163

Vignau-Wilberg P. – Vignau-Wilberg T. (2022) Bauzeichnung und Rekonstruktion. Der Bauforscher Wilhelm Wilberg und die Archäologie um 1900 (Regensburg)

Visy Z. (2023) Eine weitere oktogonale Grabkammer in dem frühchristlichen Friedhof von Pécs, in: Lohner-Urban U. – Spickermann W. – Trinkl E., Itineraria, vol. I. Entlang der Donau. Festschrift für Peter Scherrer zum 65. Geburtstag, Keryx 10 (Graz) 85–88

Völkl K. (1959) Nachruf für Franz Miltner, AnzAW 12, 189–191

Volkmann H. (1927a) RE XXIII/2 Sp. 1748-1755 s.v. 33) Ptolemaios XII

Volkmann H. (1927b) RE XXIII/2 Sp. 1756–59 s.v. 35) Ptolemaios XIII

Volkmann H. (1927c) RE XXIII/2 Sp. 1759–60 s.v. 36) Ptolemaios XIV. Philopator

Von Christ W. – Schmid W. – Stählin O. (1912) Geschichte der griechischen Litteratur (München)

Von Geisau H. (1967) Der Kleine Pauly 1103–1105 s.v. Heroenkult 2

Von Hesberg H. (1992) Römische Grabbauten (Darmstadt)

Von Hesberg H. (2003) Römisches Ornament als Sprache. Die sanfte Gegenwart der Macht, in: de Blois L. et al. (eds), The Representation and Perception of Roman Imperial Power. Proceedings of the Third Workshop of the International Network Impact of Empire (Roman Empire, c. 200 B.C. – A.D. 476), Rome, March 20–23, 2002 (Brill – Leiden) 48–68

Von Hesberg H. (2018) Vitruv und sein Umgang mit der Vergangenheit., in: Beyer A. (ed.), Die Präsenz der Antike in der Architektur (Berlin – Boston) 36–55

Von Wilamowitz-Moellendorff U. (1928) Erinnerungen. 1848–1914 (Leipzig)

Waldner A. (2009) Heroon und Oktogon. Zur Datierung zweier Ehrenbauten am unteren Embolos von Ephesos anhand des keramischen Fundmaterials aus den Grabungen von 1989 und 1999, in: Ladstätter S. (ed.), Neue Forschungen zur Kuretenstraße von Ephesos. DenkschrWien 382 (Vienna) 283–315

Waldner A. (2020) Die Chronologie der Kuretenstrasse. Archäologische Evidenz zur Baugeschichte des unteren Embolos in Ephesos von der lysimachischen Gründung bis in die byzantinische Zeit, FiE XI 4 (Vienna)

Wallensten J. (2011) Apollo and Artemis. Family Ties in Greek Dedicatory Language?, in: Haysom M. – Wallensten J. (eds.), Current approaches to religion in ancient Greece, Papers presented at a symposium at the Swedish Institute at Athens, 17–19 April 2008, Acta Instituti Atheniensis Regni Sueciae, Ser. in 8°, 21 (Stockholm) 23–39

Walter O. (1950) Professor Camillo Praschniker †, AnzAW 3, 1-4

Walters J. C. (1995) Egyptian Religions in Ephesos, in: Koester H. (ed.), Ephesos, Metropolis of Asia, Harvard Theological Studies 41, 281–309

Wankel H. (ed.) (1979) Die Inschriften von Ephesos Ia, Inschriften griechischer Städte aus Kleinasien 11 (Cologne)

Wardhaugh B. – Beeley P. – Nasifoglu Y. (2020) Euclid in print, 1482–1703. A catalogue of the editions of the Elements and other Euclidean works (Oxford)

Warius P. (1763) Dezes eerste, elfte entwaalfde Boeken Euclidis [...] (Amsterdam)

Waterfield R. (1988) The theology of arithmetic translated by Robin Waterfield (Grand Rapids)

Weber M. (2008) Neues zu den Amazonen von Ephesos, Thetis 15, 45–56

Weindling P. (2009) Eugenics, Race, and Welfare in Interwar Vienna, in: Holmes D. – Silverman L. (eds.), Interwar Vienna. Culture between tradition and modernity (New York) 81–113

Weißl M. (1998) Torgottheiten. Studien zum sakralen und magischen Schutz von griechischen Stadt- und Burgtoren unter Einbeziehung der benachbarten Kulturen (Thesis University of Vienna, Vienna)

Weißl M. (2002) Zum Kontext des Wiener Amazonenreliefs, Forum Archaeologiae 25/XII, <http://farch.net/> (accessed on 27.10.2022)

Weisz F. (2009) Der frühe Heintel. Leben, Werk und Lehre von 1912 bis 1949. Mit einem kurzen Überblick über sein späteres Schaffen (Thesis University of Vienna, Vienna)

Weninger J. (1938) 25 Jahre Anthropologisches Institut an der Universität Wien, MAGW 68, 191–205

Weninger J. (1941) Eine seltsame Mehrbestattung aus der frühen Bronzezeit von Schleinbach in Niederdonau. Niederdonau, Natur und Kultur 10 (Vienna – Leipzig)

Weninger J. (1953) Ein Schädel aus einem Ephesischen Heroengrab aus der Zeit um Christi Geburt, in: Moro G. (ed.), Beiträge zur älteren Europäischen Kulturgeschichte. Festschrift für Rudolf Egger II (Klagenfurt) 158–168

Weninger J. (1959) Eine menschliche Calotte (Schädeldach) mit scharfen Schnittspuren an den Knochenrändern, in: Egger R. (ed.), Die Ausgrabungen auf dem Magdalensberg 1956 und 1957, Carinthia I 149, 123–128

Werner J. (1970) Rudolf Egger. 11.4.1882–7.5.1969, in: Jahrbuch der Bayerischen Akademie der Wissenschaften, 225–230

Whiston W. (1841) The Works of Josephus (London)

Wilberg W. (1923a) Die Agora, FiE III (Vienna) 1–90

Wilberg W. (1923b) Das Brunnenhaus am Theater, FiE III (Vienna) 266–273

Wilberg W. (1944/1953) Das Gebäude, in: Keil J. (ed.) Die Bibliothek, FiE V 1 (Vienna) 1–42

Wilcken U. (1895) RE II/1 Sp. 1288 s.v. 28) Arsinoë

Wild F. (1956) Walter Ruth, Jahrbuch des Österreichischen Volksliedwerkes 5, 120

Williams K. (1994) The Sacred Cut revisited. The pavement of the Baptistery of San Giovanni, Florence, The Mathematical Intelligencer 16,2, 18–24

Winkler E. M. (1986) Ein Leben für die Wissenschaft vom Menschen. Frau Univ.-Prof. Dr. Margarete Weninger zum 90. Geburtstag, MAGW 116, 1–4

Winter E. (2011) Formen ptolemäischer Präsenz in der Ägäis zwischen schriftlicher Überlieferung und archäologischem Befund, in: Daubner F. (ed.), Militärsiedlungen und Territorialherrschaft in der Antike (Berlin – New York) 65–77

Wiplinger G. (2006a) Der lysimachische Aquädukt von Ephesos und weitere Neuentdeckungen von 2005, Schriftenreihe der Frontinus-Gesellschaft 27, 121–126

Wiplinger G. (2006b) Stand der Erforschung der Wasserversorgung in Ephesos/Türkei, Schriftenreihe der Frontinus-Gesellschaft 27, 15–48

Wiplinger G. (2006c) Wasser für Ephesos. Stand der Erforschung der Wasserversorgung, in: Wiplinger G. (ed.), Cura Aquarum in Ephesus, Proceedings of the Twelfth International Congress on the History of Water Management and Hydraulic Engineering in the Mediterranean Region, Ephesus/Selçuk, Turkey, Otober 2–10, 2004, Bulletin antieke beschaving. Annual Papers on Classical Archaeology, Suppl. 12 = SoSchrOeAI Instituts 42, Vol. I (Leuven – Paris – Dudley) 23–37

Wiseman T. P. (1967) Lucius Memmius and His Family, The Classical Quarterly n. s. 17, 164–167

Wittschieber D. – Schulz R. – Vieth V. et al. (2014) The value of sub-stages and thin slices for the assessment of the medial clavicular epiphysis. A prospective multi-center CT study, Forensic Sci Med Pathol 10,2, 163–169

Wlach G. (1998) Die Akteure. Die Direktoren und wissenschaftlichen Bediensteten des Österreichischen Archäologischen Institutes, in: Kandler M. – Wlach G. (eds.) 100 Jahre Österreichisches Archäologisches Institut 1898–1998. SoSchrOeAI 31 (Vienna) 99–132

Wlach G. (2010) Klassische Archäologie in politischen Umbruchzeiten. Wien 1938–1945, in: Ash M. G. – Nieß W. – Pils R. (eds.), Geisteswissenschaften im Nationalsozialismus. Das Beispiel der Universität Wien (Vienna) 343–370

Wlach G. (2012) Camillo Praschniker, in: Brands G. – Maischberger M. (eds.), Lebensbilder. Klassische Archäologen und der Nationalsozialismus (Rahden) 75–90

Wlach G. (2014) Arnold Schober – Leben und Werk, in: Trinkl E. (ed.), Akten des 14. Österreichischen Archäologentages am Institut für Archäologie der Universität Graz vom 19. bis 21. April 2012 (Vienna) 457–470

Wlach G. (2019a) Camillo Praschniker (1884–1949). Wiedergewinnung aus der Zerstörung, in: Hruza K. (ed.), Österreichische Historiker. Lebensläufe und Karrieren 1900 - 1945 III (Vienna) 313–378

Wlach G. (2019b) Klassische Archäologie in politischen Umbruchzeiten. Wien 1938–1945, in: Ash G. – Nieß W. – Pils R. (ed.), Geisteswissenschaften im Nationalsozialismus. Das Beispiel der Universität Wien (Vienna) 343–370

Wlach G. (2020a) Balduin Saria. Biographische Skizze eines Archäologen vor dem Hintergrund der politischen Umbrüche des 20. Jahrhunderts, in: Modl D. – Peitler K. (eds.), Archäologie in Österreich 1938–1945 (Graz) 174–189

Wlach G. (2020b) Das Österreichische Archäologische Institut unter der Direktion Praschniker/Egger von 1935 bis 1945/1949, in: Modl D. – Peitler K. (eds.), Archäologie in Österreich 1938–1945 (Graz) 420–445

Wohlers-Scharf T. (1995) Die Forschungsgeschichte von Ephesos (Frankfurt/Main Berlin Bern New York Wien)

Wolf M. A. (2008) Eugenische Vernunft. Eingriffe in die reproduktive Kultur durch die Medizin 1900–2000 (Vienna – Cologne – Weimar)

Wolf U. (1996) Litteris et patriae. Das Janusgesicht der Historie (Stuttgart)

Wood J. T. (1877) Discoveries at Ephesus (London)

Woodhull M. (2004) Matronly patrons in the early Roman Empire. The case of Salvia Postuma, in: McHardy F. – Nathalie E. (eds.), Women's Influence on Classical Civilization (London – New York) 75–91

Woolf G. (1994) Becoming Roman, Staying Greek. Culture, Identity and the Civilizing Process in the Roman East, Proceedings of the Cambridge Philological Society 40, 116–143

Wörrle M. (1973) Zur Datierung des Hadrianstempels in Ephesos, AA 1973, 470–477

Wotschitzky A. (1954) Festschrift für Rudolf Egger, AnzAW 7, 21–24

Woytek B. (2010) Die Reichsprägung des Kaiser Traianus (98–117), 2 Vol., Veröffentlichungen der Numismatischen Kommission 48 = Moneta Imperii Romani (MIR) 14 (Vienna)

Yegül F. K. (1994) The street experience of Ancient Ephesus, in: Çelik Z. – Favro D. – Ingersoll R. (eds.) Streets: Critical Perspectives on Public Space (Berkely) 95–110

Zabehlicky H. (1998) Der Kampf gegen die Auflösung. Das Österreichische Archäologische Institut in der Zwischenkriegszeit 1918–1938, in: Kandler M. – Wlach G. (eds.), 100 Jahre Österreichisches Archäologisches Institut 1898–1998 (Vienna) 37-48

Ziegler R. (2003) Caracalla, Alexander der Große und das Prestigedenken kilikischer Städte, in: Heedemann G. – Winter E. (eds.), Neue Forschungen zur Religionsgeschichte Kleinasiens, Elmar Schwertheim zum 60. Geburtstag gewidmet, Asia Minor Studien 49 (Bonn) 115–131

Zimmermann M. (2021) Der Gründungsmythos von Virunum als Zeugnis städtischen Selbstverständnisses, Acta Mvsei Porolissensis 43, 183–190

Sources of plans and figures

AAS/OeAI, Vienna	Plans 1 (Scherrer 2000); Plan 3 (Thür 2009, fig. 1); Plan 4 (Thür 1999, plan 2); Fig. 3 (A-W-OAI-N III 0358); Fig. 4 (A-W-OAI-N III 0038); Fig. 5a (A-W-OAI-N-SWA-000806); Fig. 6 (A-W-OAI-Dia-013920); Fig. 10b (ÖAW A-W-OAI-DIA-006564); Fig. 12a (ÖAW A-W-OAI-PLN-14389); Figs. 14-16, 18b,c (ÖAW A-W-OAI-PLN-23700); Fig. 20 (Ladstätter 2016, fig. 4); Fig. 21 (Scherrer 2021, fig. 1); Fig. 22 (P. Scherrer); Fig. 23 (adapted from the plan by Rathmayr 2016 pl. 1); Fig. 25 (Scherrer 2021, Fig. 2); Fig. 26 (Scherrer – Trinkl 2006, plan 7); Fig. 27 (Scherrer – Trinkl 2006, plan 18); Fig. 29 (after Ladstätter 2016, fig. 2); Fig. 30 (Scherrer – Trinkl 2006, fig. 19); Fig. 33 (Scherrer – Trinkl 2006, plan 8); Fig. 36 (Scherrer – Trinkl 2006, fig. 7); 37 (Scherrer – Trinkl 2006, fig. 11); Fig. 39 (Scherrer – Trinkl 2006, plan 14); Fig. 40 (Scherrer – Trinkl 2006, plan 15); Fig. 41 (Reconstruction: Wilberg 1923a, between pp. 78 and 79); Fig. 48 (partial reconstruction Thür 1995, 87 fig. 17); Fig. 49a (Thür 2020, 404 fig. 5); Fig. 49b (Thür 2009, fig. 6); Fig. 50 (N. Gail); Fig. 55 (Plan: H. Thür; Karwiese et al. 1997, 15 fig. 7); Fig. 56 (drawing A. Bammer, in: Eichler 1966, fig. 2); Fig. 59 (Outschar 1990, 69 fig. 13); Fig. 60 (reconstruction G. Niemann Heberdey – Niemann 1906, 146 fig. 78); Fig. 61 (Miltner 1956–58, 51 fig. 28); Fig. 63 (reconstruction Thür 1997b, fig. 28); Fig. 64 (Scherrer – Trinkl 2006, plan 17); Fig. 68 (Quatember 2017, tab. 5); Fig. 69 (Quatember 2017, pl. 3/2; Photo: Niki Gail); Fig. 72 (Quatember 2017, pl. 240/2); Fig. 79a (AT-OeAI-99-00161116); Fig. 79b (AT-OeAI-99-00191274); Fig. 82 (N. Gail); Fig. 88 (Breitinger; AAS-Archives, Anthropologische Kommission 1969); Fig. 90 (AT-OeAI-99-00257728)
Alzinger W.	Fig. 12b, 17b (Alzinger 1974, II 17 fig. 27)
Antikensammlung, Staatliche Museen zu Berlin, Germany	Fig. 2 (Media-ID 00014339); Fig. 71
Bildarchiv Photo Marburg, Germany	Fig. 19b (B 7.007; Jan Gloc, Paul Haag, 1986)
Bundesarchiv Berlin, Germany	Fig. 78a (R 9361-VIII/7591627); Fig. 78b (R 9361-VIII/5081743)
Février S.	Fig. 11b
Journals	Fig. 80 (Vetters: Carinthia I 150, 18 fig.; Kenner: Schörner 2020, 126 Abb. 4; Praschniker: Carinthia I 140, 3a fig.); Fig. 81 (Petrikovits: Joachim 2013, 7 Abb. 3; Moro: Neumann 1988, 9 fig.); Fig. 83 (Miltner: Marchhardt 2020, 158 Abb. 1); Fig. 84 (Breitinger: Hauser 2005b, 107 fig.; Weninger: Hirschberg 1977); Fig. 85 (Weninger 1953, 160 fig.)
Karwiese S.	Fig. 73 (after RPC 2, Pl. 90, no. 2055)
KhM, Vienna	Jacket (ANSA I 1633 A-M); Fig. 11a (ANSA_XIV_Z_268_201502_02); Fig. 24 (Inv.-no I 876; Laubenberger – Prochaska 2011. fig. 1); Fig. 35 (Inv.-no. I 843); Fig. 45 (Inv.-no. I 811); Fig. 57 (Inv.-no. I 845A–E)
Lorenz J. F.	Fig. 17a (Lorenz 1781, 32 fig.)

Ludwig-Boltzmann-Institut für Denkmalpflege und archäologische Bauforschung	Fig. 38 (Hueber 1984, 16 Abb. 14); Fig. 54 (Hueber 1997a, fig. 88)
Matiasek K.	Figs. 86f.
memoiresdeguerre.com	Fig. 83 (Schachermeyr: https://www.memoiresdeguerre.com/article-schachermeyr-fritz-117519821.html)
Münzner H.	Fig. 5b (TUR-Ephesos-1954-03-34; Medienarchiv T. Gade)
Rudolf E.	Figs. 7-10a, 19a; Figs. 14-16, 18b,c (adapted from ÖAW A-W-OAI-PLN-23700); Fig. 17 (adapted from Alzinger 1974, II 17 fig. 27); Fig. 18a (adapted from Savvides 2020, fig. 1a); Fig. 19a; Fig. 89 (Weninger's paper slip from the skull of Ephesos)
Savvides D.	Fig. 18a (Savvides 2020, fig. 1a)
Scherrer P.	Plan 5 (Scherrer 2021, fig. 3); Figs. 28, 32, 34, 42f., 51-53, 62, 65, 67, 70; 74-76
Scherrer P. – Hofbauer M.	Fig. 31
Scherrer P. – Hofbauer M. – Bayer P.	Plan 2
Thiersch H.	Fig. 13a (Thiersch 1909, Tafel VIII)
Thür H.	Fig. 19c; Fig. 44; Figs. 46f.; Fig. 58
University Vienna, Archives	Fig. 77 (From the estate of R. Pittioni, photo album 1938 – 1941); Figs. 88 (Weninger: From the estate of R. Pittioni, photo album 1938 – 1941; Keil: letter to the "Dekanat der philosophischen Fakultät der Universität Wien" from 31.05.1927); Fig. 89 (Weninger: From the estate of R. Pittioni, photo album 1938 – 1941)
Wikipedia	Fig. 1 (Marie-Lan Nguyen - Own work, Public Domain, https://commons.wikimedia.org/w/index.php?curid=496809); Fig. 13b (by ?, author information is lacking; Own work, Public Domain, https://commons.wikimedia.org/w/index.php?title=File:Qaitbay_citadel_Alexandria.JPG&oldid=615215484); Fig. 66 (Benh LIEU SONG, Ephesos, Celsus Library Façade. CC BY-SA 3.0)

Index